U.S. Coins

December 4-5 & 7, 2014 | Houston

Signature® Floor Sessions 1-4
(Floor, Telephone, HERITAGE Live!,® Internet, Fax, and Mail)

George R. Brown Convention Center
Hall E • 3rd Level • Rooms 370 A & B
1001 Avenida De Las Americas • Houston, TX 77010

Session 1
Thursday, December 4 • 1:00 PM CT • Lots 3001-3436

Session 2 - PREMIER
Thursday, December 4 • 6:30 PM CT • Lots 3437-3959

Session 3
Friday, December 5 • 1:00 PM CT • Lots 3960-4450

Session 4
Friday, December 5 • 6:00 PM CT • Lots 4451-5009

Signature® Internet Session 5
(HERITAGE Live!® Internet, Fax, & Mail only Session)

Session 5
Sunday, December 7 • 2:00 PM CT • Lots 7001-8628

LOT SETTLEMENT AND PICK-UP
Friday, December 5 • 10:00 AM – 1:00 PM CT
Saturday, December 6 • 9:00 AM – 12:00 PM CT

Extended Payment Terms available. Email: Credit@HA.com

Lots are sold at an approximate rate of 200 lots per hour, but it is not uncommon to sell 150 lots or 250 lots in any given hour.

This auction is subject to a 17.5% Buyer's Premium.

TX Auctioneer licenses: Paul Minshull 16591; Samuel Foose 11727; Robert Korver 13754; Scott Peterson 13256; Bob Merrill 13408; Mike Sadler 16129; Andrea Voss 16406; Jacob Walker 16413; Wayne Shoemaker 16600; Chris Dykstra 16601; Teia Baber 16624; Jennifer Marsh 17105; Shawn Schiller 17111; Mark Prendergast 17118; Fiona Elias 17126; Brian Nalley 17134; Mike Provenzale17157; Amelia Barber 17364; Nathan Schar 17365; Kathleen Guzman 16142; Alissa Ford 17104;Edward Beardsley 16632: Sarah Davies 17505: Anthony Singleton 17507: Helen Goblirsch 17508:Caroline Ervin 17509: David Boozer 17510: Marina Medina 17512: Holly Culbreath 17513: GaryFournerat 17514.

PRELIMINARY LOT VIEWING
By appointment only. Please contact Roy Porras at 214-409-1295 or RoyP@HA.com to schedule an appointment.
(All times subject to change)

Heritage Auctions, Dallas
3500 Maple Avenue • Dallas, TX 75219

Monday, November 17 – Tuesday, November 25
9:00 AM – 6:00 PM CT Excluding Weekends

LOT VIEWING
George R. Brown Convention Center
Hall E - Heritage Lot Viewing Area
1001 Avenida De las Americas • Houston, TX 77010

Wednesday, December 3 • 11:00 AM - 6:00 PM CT
Thursday, December 4 – Friday, December 5
9:00 AM – 6:00 PM CT
Saturday, December 6 • 9:00 AM – 12:00 PM CT

View lots & auction results online at HA.com/1212

BIDDING METHODS:
HERITAGE Live!® Bidding
Bid live on your computer or mobile, anywhere in the world, during the Auction using our HERITAGE Live!® program at HA.com/Live

Live Floor Bidding
Bid in person during the floor sessions.

Live Telephone Bidding (floor sessions only)
Phone bidding must be arranged on or before Wednesday, December 3, by 12:00 PM CT.
Client Service: 866-835-3243.

Internet Bidding
Internet absentee bidding ends at 10:00 PM CT the evening before each session. HA.com/1212

Fax Bidding
Fax bids must be received on or before Wednesday, December 3, by 12:00 PM CT. Fax: 214-409-1425

Mail Bidding
Mail bids must be received on or before Wednesday, December 3.

Phone: 214.528.3500 • 877-HERITAGE (437-4824)
Fax: 214.409.1425
Direct Client Service Line: 866.835.3243
Email: Bid@HA.com

This Auction is catalogued and presented by Heritage Numismatic Auctions, Inc., doing business as Heritage Auctions.

© 2014 Heritage Numismatic Auctions, Inc.

HERITAGE is a registered trademark and service mark of Heritage Capital Corporation. Registered in U.S. Patent and Trademark Office.

Steve Ivy
CEO
Co-Chairman of the Board

Jim Halperin
Co-Chairman of the Board

Greg Rohan
President

Paul Minshull
Chief Operating Officer

Todd Imhof
Executive Vice President

U.S. Coin Specialists

David Mayfield
Vice President
Numismatics

Jim Stoutjesdyk
Vice President
Numismatics

3500 Maple Avenue • Dallas, Texas 75219
Phone 214-528-3500 • 877-HERITAGE (437-4824)
HA.com/Coins

Consignment Directors: David Mayfield, Win Callender, Chris Dykstra, Mark Feld, Sam Foose, Jim Jelinski, Bob Marino, Brian Mayfield, Harry Metrano, Sarah Miller, Al Pinkall, Mike Sadler, LeeAnn Sparkman, Beau Streicher

Cataloged by: Mark Van Winkle, Chief Cataloger
Mark Borckardt, Senior Numismatist; David Stone, George Huber, Brian Koller, John Sculley, Jon Amato, Zeke Wischer, John Salyer, Jacob Lipson

Dear Bidder:

The year is never complete without our Official Auction at the Houston Money Show of the Southwest. It is once again our pleasure to welcome you to this high-note event, which offers the combined consignments from more than 140 different contributors and over 2,000 exciting floor lots – all presented in four, fast-moving Floor Sessions. The Signature Internet Session® offers an additional 1,600+ lots for your bidding pleasure.

Houston is known for its diversity as a city and as an exciting numismatic auction venue. Here are a few important highlights from the sale:

COLONIALS: A circa-1652 New England (NE) Shilling – possibly the finest known Noe 1-A – graded AU55 PCGS. Neither the renowned Roper nor the Norweb collections contained a Noe 1-A specimen.

EARLY DOLLARS: A 1797 Draped Bust Dollar in AU58 PCGS is an example of the rarely seen terminal die state, a coin that will entice variety collectors and late die state enthusiasts alike. Two other early dollars – both AU55 NGC examples of the centered Draped Bust BB-52 variety – offer a choice for bidders, with one example lightly toned, and the other imbued with colorful shades of deep, rich patina.

NOTABLE SILVER: A Condition Census 1797 16 Stars JR-1 dime certified MS62 PCGS headlines early silver type, as does a nice 1794 Flowing Hair half dollar in VF20 PCGS. An 1889-CC Morgan dollar graded MS64 PCGS is especially high-end for the assigned grade. A 1926-D quarter, certified MS67 Full Head by PCGS, represents the single finest Full Head representative of this issue at either PCGS or NGC, and the issue is in many respects the ultimate condition rarity of the series.

EXCEPTIONAL GOLD: A pair of proof gold issues will intrigue specialists. A 1908 Saint-Gaudens double eagle in PR65 Satin NGC – possibly unique, with a long and distinguished provenance -- displays a stunning "Roman Gold" proof finish. It is the only piece that has been consistently recognized in the literature as a 1908 Roman Finish proof. Not to be outdone in the eye-appeal arena, a 1915 Indian ten, graded PR66 by PCGS, is tied for the finest "sandblast" proof finish at PCGS. It is a visually remarkable gold coin. Among business strikes, an unexpected addition to the roster of rare, high-grade 1870-CC double eagles makes its first appearance at auction in nearly 30 years, graded AU50 PCGS with outstanding visual and technical merit.

We sincerely hope you can join us for this event in Houston. For those who are unable to attend in person, there are many methods to place your bids. To bid in "real time" we offer live telephone bidding or interactive online bids through Heritage Live!® Of course, we are happy to accept your bids via e-mail, fax, or regular mail before the auction.

Come see us in Houston! We wish you every success when bidding and, as always, value your participation.

Sincerely,

Greg Rohan

President

Todd Imhof

Executive Vice-President

Denomination Index

SESSION ONE

COLONIALS

3001 1652 Oak Tree Sixpence — Damaged — ANACS. VG8 Details. Noe-16, W-360, Salmon 1-A, R.5. 1.84 gm. As is usual for Noe-16, the reverse is well defined relative to the obverse. About two-thirds of the reverse has VF sharpness but the upper left reverse is featureless. The obverse shows only the letters HVSETS and traces of the lower tree branches. The surfaces are somewhat wavy, and indistinct areas are moderately pitted. An early die state without the sometimes present vertical crack between the L and D in ENGLAND. Listed on page 39 of the 2015 *Guide Book*. PCGS# 19

3002 1652 Pine Tree Shilling, Small Planchet — Plugged — NGC Details. Fine. Noe-29, W-930, Salmon 11-F, R.3. 64.8 gn. A smoothed and featureless area affects the upper right obverse quadrant, and the opposite upper left area on the reverse. A stone-gray shilling with mint clips that affect the tops of DO NEW. Listed on page 39 of the 2015 *Guide Book*. PCGS# 24

3003 (1670-75) St. Patrick Farthing VF25 NGC. Breen-212, W-11500. Ex: Eric P. Newman Collection. Breen's "Masonic" three-dot grouping appears after REX and PLEBS, but no "sea beasts" are present beneath the king. Moderately granular across dark olive fields, with sharp detail on the deep brown devices. A few thin obverse marks are noted near 12 o'clock. Listed on page 41 of the 2015 *Guide Book*. PCGS# 42

3004 (c. 1828) American Plantations 1/24 Part Real, Restrike MS62 PCGS. Newman 5-D, W-1160, R.5. The heavy die crack on the right obverse identifies the most familiar of Newman's restrike varieties. This sharply struck and unmarked representative retains its initial silvery luster in protected areas, while the open fields have toned deep gray and exhibit the granular texture invariably seen on both originals and restrikes. Listed on page 41 of the 2015 *Guide Book*. Population: 6 in 62, 7 finer (10/14). PCGS# 52

3005 (c. 1828) American Plantations 1/24 Part Real, Restrike MS63 PCGS. Newman 5-D, W-1160, R.5. Eleven strings in harp. A remarkably attractive light walnut-brown and gunmetal-gray example with boldly brought-up devices and unabraded surfaces. Struck a few degrees off-center toward 7:30. The flan has a thin radial crack, as struck, at 2 o'clock, and the reverse has an edge flaw near the T in PART. A small spot on the base of the F in FRAN, and mint-made flaws on the rider's hip, horse's tail, and a chain link are of little consequence. Listed on page 41 of the 2015 *Guide Book*. Population: 7 in 63, 0 finer (10/14). *Ex: ANA Signature (Heritage, 8/2006), lot 5.* PCGS# 52

3006 (1694) London Elephant Token, Thick Planchet XF45 NGC. Hodder 2-B, W-12040, R.2. Struck slightly off-center, but with no loss of detail on the main devices, just uneven definition of the dentils. A deep lavender-brown example with a number of tiny planchet laminations, but no distracting abrasions seen on either side of the piece. Listed on page 46 of the 2015 *Guide Book*. Census: 3 in 45, 24 finer (10/14). PCGS# 0

3007 (1694) London Elephant Token, Thick Planchet XF45 PCGS. Hodder 2-B, W-12040, R.2.
A deep brown-gray example of the most commonly seen variety among the London Elephant tokens. The rims are somewhat incomplete, but the major devices are well-delineated and only slightly worn. A few small, superficial abrasions are noted on the reverse. Listed on page 46 of the 2015 *Guide Book*. PCGS# 55

3008 (1694) London Elephant Token, Thick Planchet AU53 PCGS. Hodder 2-B, W-12040, R.2. An unabraded and only briefly circulated steel-gray and walnut-brown example. Struck on a planchet with minor striations on each side. A few specks of aqua obverse verdigris are noted between 9 and 10 o'clock. Listed on page 46 of the 2015 *Guide Book*. PCGS# 55

1722 Rosa Americana Halfpenny
Martin 2.1-B.1, D. G. REX MS62 Brown

3009 1722 Rosa Americana Halfpenny, D. G. REX MS62 Brown PCGS. M. 2.1-B.1, W-1218, R.4. The early variety with DEI GRATIA abbreviated. This sharply impressed representative is light olive-tan and deep brown with the latter shade prevalent on the obverse. Unabraded, though trivial flan flaws are noted near the R in ROSA. The reverse legends are strike doubled. Listed on page 42 of the 2015 *Guide Book*. Population: 7 in 62 Brown, 2 finer (10/14). PCGS# 101

1722 Rosa Americana Penny, MS62
Martin 2.2-C.1, W-1264

3010 1722 Rosa Americana Penny, UTILE MS62 PCGS. CAC. M. 2.2-C.1, W-1264, R.4. Although unwanted in the American colonies, the Rosa Americana pennies circulated in England (albeit for a discount). Well-struck with original and brassy olive-gold patina, medium-brown accents visit the high points and fields. An attractive example of William Wood's coinage. CAC-approved for quality and eye appeal. Listed on page 42 of the 2015 *Guide Book*. Population: 5 in 62, 5 finer (10/14). PCGS# 113

3011 1723 Rosa Americana Halfpenny, Crown AU58 NGC. M. 3.7-F.1, W-1236, R.4. Deep mahogany-brown surfaces with light rub on the highest points. Portions of the rims show roller marks from the planchet, as made. Listed on page 43 of the 2015 *Guide Book*. *Ex: Atlanta ANA Signature (Heritage, 4/2006), lot 2, which realized $1,610.* PCGS# 119

3012 1722 Hibernia Halfpenny, Type Two, Harp Right MS63 Brown PCGS. CAC. M. 3.3-C.1, W-12810, R.5. A beautiful chocolate-brown example. Free from abrasions, though the base of the king's neck has minor strike-throughs (as issued) and a small spot is concealed on the shoulder curl. A late die state with moderate crumbling on the reverse, as made. Listed on page 44 of the 2015 *Guide Book*. Population: 3 in 63 Brown, 0 finer (10/14). PCGS# 170

3013 1723 Hibernia Farthing, D:G:REX MS64 Brown PCGS. M. 1.1-Bc.1, W-12350, R.5. A golden-brown near-Gem with glimpses of red at the date and GEORGIUS. Marks are absent, and obverse edge flaws at 2 and 5 o'clock are of mint origin. Listed on page 44 of the 2015 *Guide Book*. Population: 11 in 64 Brown, 0 finer (10/14). PCGS# 173

3014 **1723 Hibernia Farthing, D:G:REX MS64 Brown PCGS. CAC. Martin 1.1-Bc.1, W-12240, R.5.** Eleven harp strings, dots before and after the date. A beautiful mahogany-brown example with strong reddish overtones. Well-centered and sharply struck, with weakness noted only on some of the dentils. Mark-free on both sides. Listed on page 44 of the 2015 *Guide Book*. PCGS# 173

3015 **1723 Hibernia Farthing, DEI GRATIA MS64 Brown PCGS. CAC. M. 2.1-Bc.4, W-12350, R.4.** 11 harp strings, stop after 1723. This is a lovely, mildly glossy, mahogany-tan example with utterly smooth, unblemished surfaces and impressive luster. A sharply struck, well-centered piece that seems very near to the Gem level of preservation. Listed on page 44 of the 2015 *Guide Book*. PCGS# 176

3016 **1773 Virginia Halfpenny, Period MS64 Brown NGC. N. 24-K, W-1570, R.1.** The iridescent olive-green fields are semiprooflike, usual for the Virginia series. Well struck and mark-free with a small spot between the EX in REX. Listed on page 45 of the 2015 *Guide Book*. PCGS# 240

3017 **1773 Virginia Halfpenny, Period MS64 Brown PCGS. CAC. N. 27-J, W-1585, R.2.** A sharply struck example of this Virginia halfpenny variety, showing much original mint luster and strong accents of lilac, rose, and sky-blue across the chocolate-brown surfaces. Faint die rust is evident, but there are no abrasions or planchet problems noted on either side of this gorgeous example. Listed on page 45 of the 2015 *Guide Book*. Population: 63 in 64 (2 in 64+) Brown, 5 finer (10/14). PCGS# 240

3018 **1773 Virginia Halfpenny, Period MS63 Red PCGS. N. 27-J, W-1585, R.2.** Peach-red illuminates the legends, curls, and shield elements. The high points are gunmetal-gray. A small spot is near the O in GEORGIVS. Housed in a green label holder. Listed on page 45 of the 2015 *Guide Book*. PCGS# 242

3019 **1773 Virginia Halfpenny, No Period, MS64 Red and Brown NGC. CAC. N. 3-F, W-1455, High R.4.** Seven harpstrings. A repunched 1 in the date identifies the Newman variety. Orange-red outlines the legends and shield, while open areas are sea-green. A pleasing near-Gem of the scarcer No Period subtype. Listed on page 45 of the 2015 *Guide Book*. PCGS# 244

3020 **1773 Virginia Halfpenny, No Period MS64 Red and Brown PCGS. CAC. N. 4-G, W-1460, R.3.** Substantial orange-red outlines the letter, curls, and shield elements. The cheek is deep brown and the open fields are medium brown. Well preserved and evenly impressed. Struck from a rusted obverse die. Listed on page 45 of the 2015 *Guide Book*. PCGS# 244

1773 Virginia Halfpenny, MS65 Red and Brown
Newman 4-G, Seven Harp Strings

3021 **1773 Virginia Halfpenny, No Period MS65 Red and Brown PCGS. N. 4-G, W-1460, R.3.** About 50/50 brown and orange on the obverse with the reverse largely orange, this is a lovely near-Gem example of this available Seven Harp Strings variety. Much luster remains on both sides, with glimmers of ice-blue near the obverse rims. Listed on page 45 of the 2015 *Guide Book*. *Ex: Richard Picker, coin envelope accompanying.* PCGS# 244

3022 **1787 Massachusetts Half Cent — Clipped Planchet — AU58 PCGS. Ryder 5-A, W-5960, R.3.** The second M in COMMON is high, characteristic of this collectible Ryder pairing. A fairly small curved clip is noted between 1 and 2 o'clock, as struck and caused by slightly overlapping punches through the planchet strip. An unmarked medium brown example with mint-made flan granularity at the centers. Listed on page 59 of the 2015 *Guide Book*. PCGS# 296

3023 **1788 Massachusetts Half Cent AU50 PCGS. Ryder 1-B, W-6010, R.2.** A golden-brown and gunmetal-gray example with moderate wear, though HALF CENT is clear. Void of marks though the obverse border has a small lamination at 5 o'clock and minor aqua verdigris near 9 o'clock. Listed on page 59 of the 2015 *Guide Book*. PCGS# 308

3024 **1788 Massachusetts Cent, Period AU53 NGC. Ryder 1-D, W-6190, R.3.** Massachusetts coppers are among the most well-made of all the state-issued copper coinages, generally produced on high-quality planchets. The present piece displays a bold strike and virtually complete detail. Medium chocolate-brown patina blankets the smooth surfaces, offering pleasing eye appeal. A few small, scattered spots of oxidation are noted, but are not overly detracting. Listed on page 59 of the 2015 *Guide Book*. Census: 13 in 53, 31 finer (10/14). PCGS# 311

3025 **1786 Connecticut Copper, Hercules Head VF35 PCGS. M. 5.3-N, W-2575, R.2.** This is a rare *Guide Book* variety, with the so-called Hercules Head, currently represented by only 20 coins in the PCGS Population Report. This example was struck off-center, with most of ONNEC off of the flan on the obverse. The piece was made from a damaged planchet, as seen clearly on the reverse along the edge at 2 o'clock, as well as on the portrait's head. The left side of the reverse shows a clashed die image of a reversed ORI from the obverse. Listed on page 61 of the 2015 *Guide Book*. Population: 1 in 35, 4 finer (10/14). PCGS# 334

3026 **1787 Connecticut Copper, Muttonhead XF45 PCGS. M. 1.2-C, W-2720, R.3.** A relatively late die state with partially lapped legends. The crudely designed Muttonhead variety is a distinct type within the challenging Connecticut series. The present medium brown example displays glimpses of luster along with moderate granularity and a minor obverse rim mark at 3 o'clock. Listed on page 61 of the 2015 *Guide Book*. Population: 6 in 45, 3 finer (10/14). PCGS# 343

1787 Connecticut Copper, AU53
Popular Muttonhead Variety
Miller 1.2-C

3027 **1787 Connecticut Copper, Muttonhead AU53 NGC. M. 1.2-C, W-2720, R.3.** Ex: The Old New England Collection. The Whitman *Colonial Encyclopedia* refers to the present die marriage as one of the most distinctive and famous issues in the Connecticut series. The mailed bust left is unusually large and bears a serene expression. The reverse is nearly as well-known, since it is the only die in the series with a topless Liberty. Relatively early in the die's life, the dies were lapped, severely weakening the legends. They are faint on the present example, as made. The medium brown surfaces are well-defined given the die state, though the centers are incompletely brought up. Nicely centered and nearly free from marks. The upper-right quadrant is somewhat granular. Listed on page 61 of the 2015 *Guide Book*. PCGS# 343

3028 **1787 ETLIB INDE Small Head Right Connecticut Copper VF35 PCGS. M. 1.1-A, W-2700, R.3.** This *Guide Book* variety is much scarcer than the usually encountered Draped Bust Left design. A medium brown and steel-blue example with a small mint-made curved clip at 5:30. Struck slightly off center toward 12 o'clock. Moderately granular with faint thin marks at the centers. Listed on page 61 of the 2015 *Guide Book*. Population: 2 in 35, 3 finer (10/14). PCGS# 346

3029 **1787 Nova Eborac Copper, Seated Left AU55 PCGS. Breen-986, W-5755, R.3.** Struck off-center on the reverse with the top of figure head and the left side peripheral legends off of the flan. A pleasingly smooth walnut-brown example with a few dark spots and mild porosity noted in the fields. Free of distracting abrasions on both sides. The usual dies that are seen for this private New York City issue. Listed on page 68 of the 2015 *Guide Book*. Population: 6 in 55, 12 finer (10/14). PCGS# 478

3030 **1787 Nova Eborac Copper, Seated Right XF40 PCGS. Breen-987, W-5760, R.4.** An unblemished olive-brown example. Sharper than the usual example, particularly on Liberty's head. Struck moderately off center toward 3 o'clock, with most of EBORAC off the flan. The date is fully present. Listed on page 68 of the 2015 *Guide Book*. PCGS# 475

3031 **1787 Nova Eborac Copper, Seated Right XF40 PCGS. Breen-987, W-5760, R.4.** This mahogany-brown example is reasonably well-centered, although the tops of EBO and the lower parts of 87 in the date are off the flan. Mild porosity is evident on each side, but noteworthy abrasions are absent. Listed on page 68 of the 2015 *Guide Book*. PCGS# 475

3032 **1787 New Jersey Copper, Outlined Shield AU53 PCGS. Maris 46-e, W-5245, R.1.** A chocolate-brown piece that retains noticeable mint gloss. The familiar variety with die sinking near the date and prominent clashes from the shield above the plow. Small marks are noted near the B in PLURIBUS and the R in CAESAREA. Listed on page 70 of the 2015 *Guide Book*. Population: 11 in 53, 21 finer (10/14). PCGS# 503

1787 New Jersey Copper, XF45
No Sprig Above Plow, Maris 46-e

3033 **1787 New Jersey Copper, No Sprig above Plow XF45 NGC. Maris 46-e, W-5250, R.1.** A late die state striking, with the diagnostic die bulge above the date and pronounced die clashing of the shield covering the central obverse. The reverse shows resulting weakness at the center (from die damage) as always seen for the variety. The obverse is struck slightly off-center north, with resultant loss of the sawtooth denticles at the top. The reverse is more accurately centered. Attractive medium-brown color with surface gloss remaining, despite a few areas of minor porosity. A short cut at RIB of PLURIBUS. Listed on page 69 of the 2015 *Guide Book*. Census: 9 in 45, 27 finer (10/14). PCGS# 506

3034 **1787 New Jersey Copper, Serpent Head VF30 PCGS. Maris 54-k, W-5295, R.3.** The distinctive horse head variety with a lengthy, curved neck. This medium brown piece has occasionally granular surfaces and a light impression on portions of NOVA and PLURIBUS. Several degrees off center toward 7 o'clock. Listed on page 70 of the 2015 *Guide Book*. PCGS# 518

1785 Vermont Copper, XF40
RR-2, VERMONTS Landscape

3035 **1785 Vermont Copper, VERMONTS XF40 PCGS. RR-2, Bressett 1-A, W-2005, R.2.** A medium brown Republic copper with clear types. Due to the absence of a raised rim, the legends show uneven wear. Marks are chiefly confined to a couple of tiny rim nicks. The few unimportant planchet flaws are usual for the series. Listed on page 72 of the 2015 *Guide Book*. PCGS# 539

1785 Vermont Landscape Copper, XF45
RR-2, W-2005, VERMONTS

3036 **1785 Vermont Copper, VERMONTS XF45 PCGS. RR-2, Bressett 1-A, W-2005, R.3.** In 1785, the Vermont House of Representatives passed legislation granting Reuben Harmon Jr., who had moved from Massachusetts in 1760, the right to produce copper coinage for the Republic. This is a later die state of the Ryder-2 variety with the VERMONTS legend. Of the six collectible Vermont Landscape varieties, RR-2 and RR-6 are assigned the same URS-11 rarity rating (500-999 pieces) in the *Whitman Encyclopedia of Colonial and Early American Coins*. However, the present RR-2 variety approaches the rarer end of that rarity rank, while RR-6 falls at the common end of that range. Colonial type collectors will be interested to know that this variety with the VERMONTS legend is considerably scarcer than the type with VERMONTENSIUM.

The pleasing reddish-brown surfaces exhibit sharply struck design elements, save for faint softness on the V in VERMONT and the 1 in the date. A few expected marks and planchet flaws appear on each side. Listed on page 72 of the 2015 *Guide Book*. PCGS# 539

3037 **1781 North American Token AU58 PCGS. CAC. Breen-1144.** Generally golden-brown in color, with areas of charcoal-gray toning seen on the harp and the lower reverse. No handling marks or planchet problems are relevant. Crisply defined for the type, and verdigris is minimal. Listed on page 73 of the 2015 *Guide Book*. Population: 4 in 58 (1 in 58+), 0 finer (10/14). *Ex: Dallas Signature (Heritage, 7/2006), lot 60.* PCGS# 589

3038 **1787 Auctori Plebis Token AU58 NGC. Breen-1147, W-8770, R.3.** A lightly abraded deep chocolate-brown example. Luster shimmers from the motifs. Although of English origin, the Auctori Plebis token resembles the Draped Bust Left Connecticut copper. Listed on page 74 of the 2015 *Guide Book*. PCGS# 601

3039 **1783 Nova Constellatio Copper, Pointed Rays, Large US, AU50 PCGS. CAC. Crosby 1-A, W-1860, R.4.** A lightly circulated golden-brown and lime-green representative. Abrasions are minimal though the obverse border has unimportant flan flaws. Listed on page 54 of the 2015 *Guide Book*. Population: 11 in 50, 12 finer (10/14). PCGS# 804

3040 1783 Nova Constellatio Copper, Pointed Rays, Large US, AU53 PCGS. Crosby 1-A, W-1860, R.4. A well centered and problem-free chocolate brown example. The strike is consistent aside from softness on the 17 in the date. Hints of olive-green luster reside in protected regions. Listed on page 54 of the 2015 *Guide Book*. PCGS# 804

3041 1783 Nova Constellatio Copper, Blunt Rays AU50 PCGS. CAC. Crosby 3-C, W-1875, R.3. Deep lavender-brown patina covers each side of this impressive example. Sharply struck except near the T in CENT. The reverse has light die cracks through the N in UNITED and the M in AMERICA. The left half of the reverse has a slightly rough surface. There are a few tiny contact marks on the cheek, but this example is otherwise relatively clean. Listed on page 54 of the 2015 *Guide Book*.
Ex: New York, NY Signature (Heritage, 7/2002), lot 5853. PCGS# 807

3042 1787 Fugio Cent, Club Rays, Rounded Ends VF35 NGC. N. 4-E, W-6685, R.3. A boldly struck example of this popular Fugio copper variety, showing club rays with rounded ends. The mildly glossy, light-brown surfaces are somewhat unevenly worn, but essentially abrasion-free. Listed on page 88 of the 2015 *Guide Book*. PCGS# 904

3043 1787 Fugio Cent, STATES UNITED, 4 Cinquefoils, Pointed Rays VF30 PCGS. N. 13-X, W-6855, R.2. This Pointed Rays variety was well-represented in the Bank of New York hoard, and examples are available to the average collector. This example is well-detailed for the grade and housed in a green label PCGS holder. The smooth mahogany-tan surfaces show clash marks from the reverse ring on the obverse, but there are no mentionable abrasions on either side of the piece. The eye appeal of this example is pleasing. Listed on page 87 of the 2015 *Guide Book*. PCGS# 883

3044 1787 Fugio Cent, UNITED STATES, Cinquefoils VF20 PCGS. CAC. N. 16-H, W-6920, R.5. A very scarce variety distinguished by a vertical reverse break at 6:30 and a low D in MIND. The chocolate-brown surfaces are attractive. Wear is even except near the upper left portion of the sundial. Listed on page 87 of the 2014 *Guide Book*. PCGS# 889

3045 1787 Fugio Cent, New Haven Restrike, Copper MS65 Brown PCGS. N. 104-FF, W-17560. The "New Haven" Fugio coppers were struck from copy dies circa-1860 at the private Scoville Mint in Waterbury, Connecticut. Ever since, they have been collected as part of the series. The present well struck and undisturbed Gem displays attractive chestnut-gold and sea-green toning. Listed on page 88 of the 2015 *Guide Book*. PCGS# 916

1794 Talbot, Allum & Lee Cent, NEW YORK
MS65 Brown, Small Ampersand, Fuld-4, W-8590

3046 1794 Talbot, Allum & Lee Cent, NEW YORK MS65 Brown PCGS. CAC. Fuld-4, W-8590, R.1. Small ampersand. A marvelous Gem example of this highly popular token cent, issued by the Talbot, Allum, & Lee company of New York City. The upper left tip of the N in NEW, on the upper reverse, is distant from the lower right tip of the second T in TALBOT. This piece is fully struck with beautifully preserved, blemish-free surfaces that exhibit lovely, deep rose-brown coloration. Listed on page 76 of the 2014 *Guide Book*. Population: 3 in 65 Brown, 1 finer (10/14). PCGS# 634

3047 1795 Talbot Allum & Lee Cent MS65 Brown NGC. CAC. Fuld-1, W-8620, R.1. Chocolate-brown dominates though faded red lingers with the legends. A boldly struck, smooth, and satiny Gem example of this famous Early American token. Listed on page 76 of the 2015 *Guide Book*. Census: 5 in 65 Brown, 0 finer (10/14). PCGS# 640

1795 Talbot, Allum & Lee Cent
Fuld-1, W-8620, MS65 Red and Brown

3048 1795 Talbot, Allum & Lee Cent MS65 Red and Brown PCGS. Fuld-1, W-8620, R.1. A pleasing example of the moderately available 1795 issue. Fire-red and dusky olive-green alternate across this satiny and alertly struck Gem. The reverse is gorgeously preserved, and the obverse has only unimportant contact with a few faint signs of carbon. Listed on page 76 of the 2015 *Guide Book*. Population: 10 in 65 Red and Brown, 0 finer (10/14).
Ex: FUN Signature (Heritage, 1/2008), lot 108; Long Beach Signature (Heritage, 2/2009), lot 110. PCGS# 641

1795 Talbot, Allum & Lee Cent, MS65
Fuld-1, Lustrous Red and Brown
Tied for Finest at PCGS or NGC

3049 1795 Talbot, Allum & Lee Cent MS65 Red and Brown PCGS. CAC. Fuld-1, W-8620, R.1. The variant with the edge lettering WE PROMISE TO PAY THE BEARER ONE CENT. An attractive example of the issue, minted in England and imported for use in early New York commerce. Red luster shines through at the margins and in the recesses surrounding the central motifs. Smooth, umber-brown patina covers the fields and the high points of the devices. Housed in a green label holder with CAC endorsement for eye appeal and quality. Listed on page 76 of the 2015 *Guide Book*. Population: 10 in 65 Red and Brown, 0 finer (10/14). PCGS# 641

3050 1783 Georgivs Triumpho Token AU55 PCGS. CAC. Baker-7, W-10100, R.3. A charming chocolate-brown Washington piece with strong portrait definition. Marks are minimal, and each side has only one subtle lilac spot. The large die break on the upper reverse is usual for the variety. Unlike many similarly-dated Washington pieces, the Georgivs Triumpho is believed contemporary to the 1780s. Listed on page 79 of the 2015 *Guide Book*. Population: 14 in 55, 9 finer (10/14). PCGS# 664

1783 Georgivs Triumpho Copper, MS62 Brown
Sole Mint State PCGS Example, Baker-7

3051 **1783 Georgivs Triumpho Token MS62 Brown PCGS. Baker-7, W-10100, R.3.** The present piece is the only example certified as Mint State by PCGS (10/14). A chocolate-brown and tan Washington piece with generally unabraded surfaces. Sharply struck for the issue. The usual late die state with a heavy break in front of the caged Britannia.

The Georgivs Triumpho is the only 1783-dated Washington piece actually struck in the 1780s. The design is intriguing in that the obverse bust is based on that of King George III on Irish 1775-1782 coppers but the reverse shows a symbolic Britannia contained by a wall with 13 vertical bars held together by a frame with the French fleurs de lis at the corners. Perhaps no portrait of George Washington was then available to the engraver. Listed on page 79 of the 2015 *Guide Book*.
Ex: Long Beach Signature (Heritage, 2/2005), lot 5046; ANA Signature (Heritage, 3/2008), lot 103. PCGS# 664

3052 **1783 Washington & Independence Cent, Draped Bust, No Button, Copper Restrike, Engrailed Edge PR66 Brown PCGS. CAC. Baker-3, W-10370, R.5.** The well-made mid-19th century W.S. Lincoln proof restrike. The deep brown surfaces exhibit powder-blue and walnut-tan undertones. Sharply struck and free from marks. Listed on page 80 of the 2015 *Guide Book*. PCGS# 685

1783 Washington & Independence Cent, Draped Bust
No Button, Copper Restrike, Engrailed Edge
Baker-3, W-10370, PR67 Brown

3053 **1783 Washington & Independence Cent, Draped Bust, No Button, Copper Restrike, Engrailed Edge PR67 Brown PCGS. Baker-3, W-10370, R.5.** A great example of this W.S. Lincoln restrike in copper with an engrailed edge. Both sides display well-mirrored fields and clean, impeccably preserved surfaces. The strike definition is superb, and the eye appeal of the coin is outstanding. Listed on page 80 of the 2015 *Guide Book*. Population: 4 in 67 Brown, 0 finer (10/14). PCGS# 685

3054 **1783 Washington & Independence Cent, Draped Bust, No Button, Silver Restrike PR62 PCGS. Baker-3A, W-10380, R.6.** The elusive silver version of the W.S. Lincoln restrike produced in the mid-19th century. This sharply detailed proof has excellent contrast between the deeply mirrored fields and lustrous devices. Both sides are brilliant with only a hint of gold and iridescent toning. Listed on page 80 of the 2015 *Guide Book*.
Ex: Houston Signature (Heritage, 12/2009), lot 20, which realized $2,070. PCGS# 688

3055 **1791 Washington Large Eagle Cent AU55 PCGS. CAC. Baker-15, W-10610, R.2.** A deep walnut-brown cent with pleasing sharpness and noticeable mint gloss. The hair above the ear shows minor wear. Smooth except for a slender vertical line on the cheek. Listed on page 81 of the 2015 *Guide Book*. PCGS# 702

3056 **1795 Washington Grate Halfpenny, Large Buttons, Lettered Edge, AU58 PCGS. Baker-29, W-10990, R.6.** The rare Lettered Edge variant of the Large Buttons Grate token, usually seen with a reeded edge. Gunmetal-blue fields and ebony-brown devices cede to mahogany-brown borders. A few curved lines on the central reverse were on the planchet prior to the strike. Listed on page 83 of the 2015 *Guide Book*. PCGS# 743

3057 **1795 Washington Liberty & Security Halfpenny, Plain Edge AU53 PCGS. Baker-31C, W-11000, High R.6.** Scarcer than the London Edge variety. A smooth medium brown example. The profile and eagle are lightly impressed. A broad line on the reverse is as made, on the planchet prior to the strike. The flan diameter is slightly small and aligned with the collar at 10 o'clock, thus the upper half of SECURITY is off the flan. Listed on page 84 of the 2015 *Guide Book*. PCGS# 752

1795 Washington Liberty & Security Halfpenny
Baker-31B, W-11010, BIRMINGHAM Edge
MS63 Brown

3058 **1795 Washington Liberty & Security Halfpenny, BIRMINGHAM Edge MS63 Brown PCGS. Baker-31B, W-11010, R.5.** Part of the Conder series of British tokens, the 1795 Washington Liberty and Security tokens have four edge variants. The BIRMINGHAM lettered edge is moderately less rare than the other three varieties. A dusky mahogany-brown example with satin luster, a typical strike, and relatively few marks. Listed on page 84 of the 2015 *Guide Book*. PCGS# 758

3059 **Undated Washington Liberty & Security Penny MS62 Brown PCGS. CAC. Baker-30, W-11050, R.2.** Olive-green, powder-blue, and lilac undertones appear when this deep brown copper is rotated beneath a light. No marks are remotely consequential. The strike shows inexactness, usual for the variety, on the lower stars and right (facing) wing. Listed on page 84 of the 2015 *Guide Book*. PCGS# 767

3060 **Undated Washington Liberty & Security Penny MS63 Brown PCGS. Baker-30, W-11050, R.2.** Lavender and lime-green encompass this satiny and smooth example. The strike shows blending on the epaulets. During the late 18th century, England must have admired Washington considerably, given the number of Conder token varieties with his image held in esteem. Listed on page 84 of the 2015 *Guide Book*. PCGS# 767

3061 **Undated Washington Liberty & Security Penny MS62 Red and Brown PCGS. Baker-30, W-11050, R.2.** The usual plain rims variant of this early and skillfully executed Washington medal. Refreshingly free from marks, and the obverse border retains the initial mint red, though the fields and motifs are chiefly olive-brown. A couple of slender lamination streaks extend from the G in GEORGE to the epaulets, and the right (facing) wing is lightly brought up. In a green label holder. Listed on page 84 of the 2015 *Guide Book*. Population: 1 in 62 Red and Brown, 18 finer (10/14). PCGS# 768

3062 **1795 Washington North Wales Halfpenny, Plain Edge, One Star at Each Side of Harp AU53 PCGS. CAC.** Baker-34, W-11150, R.3. Ex: Harry A. Orr. The North Wales halfpenny was intended to appear worn even when new, to facilitate acceptance in circulation. Thus, the harp and bust of Washington are lightly impressed. But the plentiful orange-gold luster near the harp confirms a relatively high technical grade. Otherwise, this lightly circulated and unblemished example is medium brown with olive-green undertones. Listed on page 84 of the 2015 *Guide Book*. PCGS# 770

Washington Success Medal, VF30
Baker-265A, Large Silvered Planchet

3063 **Undated Washington Success Medal, Large Size, Plain Edge, Silvered VF30 NGC.** Baker-265A, W-10905, R.5. This is the usual variety with the die crack from Washington's nose, although infrequently encountered with substantial silvering as displayed on this piece. The underlying brass is evident on the worn areas, especially on the obverse. Slight corrosion is evident on the reverse. Listed on page 84 of the 2015 *Guide Book*. PCGS# 787

HALF CENTS

3064 **1793 C-3, B-3, R.3 — Damage — PCGS Genuine. Fine Details.** Predominantly toned chestnut-brown, although the portrait has an outline of orange-red. Four small digs are clustered together near the H in HALF, and spots are noted near Liberty's eye, the 3 in the date, and the I and first S in UNITED STATES. Our EAC grade AG3. PCGS# 35009

3065 **1794 Normal Head, C-1a, B-1a, R.3, VG8 NGC.** LIBERTY, OF AMERICA, and the fraction are bold. Most of UNITED is clear. HALF CENT, STATES, and the date are faint but can be discerned. Slightly off center toward 9 o'clock; the cause of the uneven wear. A walnut-brown example, refreshingly void of verdigris or consequential marks. Our EAC grade Good 5. PCGS# 35018

1794 Half Cent, Fine 15
C-4a, Small Letters Edge

3066 **1794 Normal Head, Small Letters Edge, C-4a, B-6b, R.3, Fine 15 PCGS.** Manley Die State 4, with a prominent die bulge on the lower-left obverse and a crack from the reverse rim through the M in AMERICA. Three obverse dies and four reverse dies were used to strike the half cents of this year, but two different edge lettering styles were also employed. Of these, the Small Letters variant is the more readily available for date representation. This example shows even, honest wear, with strong detail remaining for the grade. Deep brown patina blankets the recesses, leaving the relief elements with a slightly brighter auburn hue. No environmental damage is observed. Our EAC grade VG8. PCGS# 35036

3067 **1803 C-1, B-1, R.1, AU55 NGC.** Manley Die State 2.0. The scarcest of the three major die states, which features a crack above HALF but without any branch crack below. A lightly marked deep brown half cent with substantial cartwheel sheen despite moderate wear on the cheek and curls. Our EAC grade VF35. PCGS# 35128

1804 C-8, B-7 Half Cent, MS62 Brown
Popular Spiked Chin Variety

3068 **1804 Spiked Chin, C-8, B-7, R.1, MS62 Brown PCGS. CAC.** The Spiked Chin 1804 half cent ranks among the most popular early copper varieties. This pleasing example features lovely intermingled olive-brown, steel, and golden-tan patina on both sides, with excellent cartwheel luster. Our EAC grade AU50. PCGS# 35167

1804 Half Cent, MS64 Brown
C-12, B-11, Crosslet 4

3069 **1804 Crosslet 4, No Stems, C-12, B-11, R.2, MS64 Brown NGC.** Hints of red remain in the crevices on each side of this glossy light brown near-Gem. The central devices are crisply struck, and the surfaces are free of environmental impairments. Clash marks in the field behind Liberty's head and fine die rust in the obverse fields are characteristic of this moderately available variety. Overall, this coin represents an excellent opportunity to acquire a pleasing Draped Bust type representative. Our EAC grade AU55. PCGS# 35173

3070 **1804 Plain 4, No Stems, C-13, B-10, R.1, MS62 Brown NGC.** Manley Die State 2.0 without obverse dentils. This well struck Draped Bust type coin has rich gunmetal-blue and mahogany-brown toning. A loupe indicates a tick on the central curl and small spots above the bust tip and beneath the 1 in the date. Our EAC grade AU55. PCGS# 35176

3071 **1806 Large 6, Stems, C-4, B-4, R.1 — Rotated Dies — MS61 Brown NGC.** Manley Die State 1.0. A medium-brown example with smooth surfaces except for spots on the jaw, the second T in STATES, and the 6 in the date. The dies are rotated about 30 degrees clockwise. Our EAC grade XF45. PCGS# 35200

3072 **1809/6 9 Over Inverted 9, C-5, B-5, R.1, MS62 Brown NGC.** The deep lavender-brown surfaces of this Mint State example are remarkably smooth and virtually undisturbed, although what appears to be mint-made roughness is apparent on Liberty's cheek. Traditionally referred to as an 1809 Over 6 overdate, this variety is actually the result of an inverted 9 punched into the date area and later corrected. Our EAC grade AU50. PCGS# 35233

1825 Half Cent, C-2, B-2, MS64 Brown
Boldly Struck, Glossy Example

3073 **1825 C-2, B-2, R.1, MS64 Brown PCGS. CAC.** Manley Die State 2, with fine die rust throughout much of each side and faint clash marks on the reverse. The strike is bold, with sharply delineated hair curls, complete border denticles on each side, and moderately well-defined radial lines on the stars. Shades of reddish-brown, chocolate-tan, and pale burgundy cover glossy surfaces, with subtle mint luster seen when turned in-hand. Our EAC grade AU55. PCGS# 35249

3074 **1849 Large Date, C-1, B-4, R.2, MS64 Brown PCGS.** A sharply struck Choice half cent with semiprooflike medium brown and olive surfaces. Smooth except for a graze above the F in HALF and a brief diagonal line on Liberty's cheek. Our EAC grade AU55. PCGS# 35318

3075 **1853 C-1, B-1, R.1, MS65 Brown PCGS.** Only one die variety is known, despite a healthy mintage of more than 129,000 coins. This is a boldly struck example, with sharp central devices and well-defined stars. The obverse dentils grow weak near 3 o'clock, but are otherwise strong on each side. Glossy auburn-brown patina leaves tinges of lighter brown color near the borders. A high-end example, housed in an old green label holder. Our EAC grade MS60. PCGS# 35327

3076 **1855 C-1, B-1, R.1, MS66 Brown NGC.** The only known die variety. This example is impressively preserved, with delicate, glossy surfaces that reveal small tinges of coppery-orange luster in the protected regions and deep purple and burgundy toning elsewhere. The obverse denticles grow weak on the right side, but the design elements are otherwise well brought up. Our EAC grade MS63. Census: 14 in 66 (1 in 66 ★) Brown, 0 finer (10/14). PCGS# 35333

LARGE CENTS

1793 Chain Cent, Fine Details
S-2, B-2, AMERICA

3077 **1793 Chain, AMERICA, S-2, B-2, High R.4 — Altered Surfaces — PCGS Genuine. Fine Details.** An excellent piece for the budget-minded type collector, this moderately well-circulated Chain cent shows bold relief elements on the reverse, with slightly dulled but still clear legends and portrait on the obverse. Glossy reddish-brown patina encompasses each side, featuring minor granularity that accounts for the PCGS Genuine grade. The AMERICA variety is slightly more plentiful than its earlier AMERI. counterpart, ideal for the type collector's cabinet. Our EAC grade AG3. PCGS# 35435

1793 Wreath Cent, AG3
S-11b, B-16b, Lettered Edge

3078 **1793 Wreath, Lettered Edge, S-11b, B-16b, R.4, AG3 PCGS.** Die State C/A, with the obverse clash marks faded, but still discernable. The scarcer Lettered Edge variant, two leaves after DOLLAR. A prime type coin for the budget-minded collector, this well-circulated example shows extensive, albeit even, wear. The central devices remain bold, though much of the reverse legends are obscured by wear. Smooth, chocolate-brown color blankets each side, making this piece quite appealing for the grade. Our EAC grade Good 4. PCGS# 35474

3079 **1793 Wreath, Lettered Edge, S-11c, B-16c, Low R.3, Fair 2 PCGS.** A single leaf on the edge after DOLLAR. A generally chocolate-brown Wreath cent with granular surfaces and no visible abrasions. All four date digits emerge beneath a loupe. The portrait is well outlined and the trefoil is clear. Most of the wreath is evident. Our EAC grade Poor 1. PCGS# 35477

3080 **1794 Head of 1794, S-31, B-13, R.1, Fine 15 PCGS.** The "Marred Field" variety, noted for its dull die flaws on the left obverse field. A chocolate-brown cent with glossy, unmarked surfaces. A slight rim ding is noted near the C in AMERICA. Our EAC grade VG8. PCGS# 35558

1794 Cent, VF35
S-44, B-33, Head of 1794

3081 **1794 Head of 1794, S-44, B-33, R.1, VF35 PCGS.** A late die state example, with a bold radial die crack from the reverse rim at 12:30, and two more on the obverse, one from the denticles below the 79 in the date and the other from the rim near the tip of the cap. The borders are complete and the central relief elements bold. Deep burgundy-brown patina blankets each side, with numerous light, scattered ticks visible on each side upon close examination. Our EAC grade Fine 15. PCGS# 35597

3082 **1796 Reverse of 1794, S-109, B-15, R.3 — Damage — PCGS Genuine. XF Details.** A radial crack through the T in LIBERTY and a die break below the E in UNITED confirm the Sheldon marriage. A moderately and evenly granular ebony-brown cent with moderate rim dings at 1 and 5 o'clock on the obverse and at 1, 7, and 11 o'clock on the reverse. Our EAC grade VG10. PCGS# 35798

1797 Stems Cent, XF45
S-136, B-7, Reverse of 1797

3083 **1797 Reverse of 1797, Stems, S-136, B-7, R.3, XF45 NGC.** Breen Die State III. The reverse is cracked from the rim between RI into the field, with areas of die clashing visible especially around the fraction and near the bow. Numerous small marks dot the surfaces on both sides of the coin, most of which are seen only with a glass. Otherwise, the fields and devices are glossy with a pleasing, medium-brown color. Well-centered and sharply struck on the obverse, with some bluntness of strike on the reverse. Seldom available any finer for the variety. Our EAC grade VF20. PCGS# 35939

1797 S-140, B-22 Cent, AU Sharpness
Early Die State

3084 **1797 Reverse of 1797, Stems, S-140, B-22, R.1 — Environmental Damage — NGC Details. AU.** Breen Die State I. The serifs of B and T are broken in LIBERTY, while the main reverse diagnostics of this S-140 variety are a pair of die lines — one from the fraction bar to the ribbon, the other from the left stem to the base of U in UNITED. Overall granularity is the most obvious evidence of Environmental Damage, although this large cent retains considerable appeal. The early die state and unmarked surfaces complement deep brown color with some glimpses of red. Our EAC grade Fine 15.

1799 S-189 Large Cent, VG8 Details

3085 **1799 S-189, B-3, R.2 — Corroded — ANACS. VG8 Details.** Considerable detail remains, especially on the reverse of this example. Both sides exhibit a combination of tan, olive, and steel-brown, with noticeable corrosion, surface roughness, and other imperfections. Here is an excellent opportunity to acquire a genuine 1799 large cent at a likely an affordable price. Our EAC grade AG3. PCGS# 36140

3086 **1809 S-280, B-1, R.2, VF20 PCGS.** Breen Die State V. Principally olive-brown but mahogany toning resides in reverse legends. Small marks are noted near the profile and the M in AMERICA. The only dies for the date, which is underrated relative to the 1804. Our EAC grade Fine 12. PCGS# 36466

3087 **1812 Small Date, S-290, B-2, R.1 — Altered Surfaces — PCGS Genuine. AU Details.** Cleaned and retoned, with a surface appearance that suggests this piece was whizzed or similarly treated. The result is magenta and blue with trace or light corrosion. This late die state piece has clash marks and flow lines that are especially prominent on the reverse. Our EAC grade VF20. PCGS# 36499

3088 **1816 N-2, R.1, MS64 Brown NGC. CAC.** Obverse rim die breaks and a repunched N in ONE identify the collectible Newcomb variety. The late die state with additional rim crumbling between stars 11 and 12. A beautiful medium to deep brown cent. Well preserved and attractive. Our EAC grade AU55. PCGS# 36526

3089 **1818 N-7, R.1, MS64 Red and Brown PCGS.** An intermediate die state with a die crack from star 1 toward the date. This well struck Choice cent displays considerable brick-red about the stars and legends, although open areas are gunmetal-gray. A small spot noted above the 81 in the date. In a first generation holder. Our EAC grade MS63. PCGS# 36620

3090 **1818 N-10, R.1, MS64 Red and Brown NGC.** Die State B, with bold, circumnavigating die cracks connecting all of the obverse stars. The reverse is well-balanced with red and burgundy hues, though the obverse is largely in favor of the former color. The strike is slightly soft around the borders, as is characteristic of this later die state. Recutting on the I and E in LIBERTY is diagnostic of this variety. Housed in a prior generation holder. Our EAC grade MS62. PCGS# 36629

3091 **1838 N-3, R.1, MS64 Red and Brown PCGS.** An extra tiny dot on the reverse above the center dot and an unbroken E in LIBERTY on the obverse identify this available variety. This example displays well-balanced coppery-red and auburn-brown luster, with carefully preserved, attractive surfaces. Slight striking weakness is seen on some of the obverse stars, as usual. Our EAC grade MS63. PCGS# 37187

3092 **1839 Head of 1838, Beaded Cords, N-2, R.2, MS64 Brown PCGS.** The early die state with bold die lines near STAT and RICA. This glossy golden-brown near-Gem is unabraded save for a rim tick near star 5. The grade is limited solely by minor carbon within the wreath and on the upper left obverse. Our EAC grade MS60. PCGS# 37225

3093 **1839 Booby Head, N-6, R.2, MS63 Brown PCGS.** Die cracks from the U and D in UNITED help attribute this deep chocolate-brown cent. The satiny surfaces are devoid of relevant marks or spots. Encapsulated in an old green label holder. Our EAC grade AU55. PCGS# 37240

3094 **1839 Booby Head, N-7, R.2, MS62 Brown PCGS.** A lustrous olive-green cent with traces of mint red in design crevices. The strike is bold except on the left margins. A slender mark noted on the cheek. N-7 is distinctive for its lapped reverse. The compass point indentation on the central reverse die resembles an accent mark. Our EAC grade AU55. PCGS# 37243

3095 **1851 N-15, R.4, MS65 Red and Brown PCGS.** A glowing, coppery-red example with steel-blue accents amid substantial mint luster. Bold detail covers the central devices and legends, although areas of softness at the borders result in lightly struck or merged dentils, and several stars lack their centers. There are no other distractions to mention since the surfaces are virtually mark-free, and the eye appeal is great. Our EAC grade MS63. PCGS# 406690

3096 **1851 N-43, R.5, MS66 Red and Brown PCGS.** A very scarce variety distinguished by die lines near the first and final stars, a die lump on the rim near the C in AMERICA, and a die line atop the upper serif of the E in CENT. Unknown to Newcomb, N-43 is described in the J.R. Grellman reference. Lustrous and mark-free with dusky orange-red fields and deep brown centers. Certified in a green label holder. Our EAC grade MS63. PCGS# 406785

3097 1853 N-13, R.1, MS64 Red NGC. Die State b, as usual for Mint State pieces. A small lump below the I in LIBERTY and recutting on the base of the 1 in the date easily confirms the variety. This example is luminous with coppery-red luster, and also boasts sharp central devices. The peripheral stars and denticles are softly defined, a product of the later die state. Our EAC grade MS64. PCGS# 403930

3098 1853 N-24, R.2, MS66 Brown PCGS. Die State b. Deep olive-green toning dominates although hints of rose-red are also present. Sharply struck and satiny. Nearly mark-free aside from a tick on the E in STATES. Our EAC grade MS60. Population: 14 in 66 Brown, 2 finer (4/14).
Ex: Long Beach Signature (Heritage, 9/2007), lot 117. PCGS# 406036

3099 1855 Upright 55, N-4, R.1, MS64 Red and Brown PCGS. Die State a, with the reverse uncracked. This is one of the more often seen Upright 5s varieties, ideal for type or date purposes. This piece displays well-balanced coppery-orange and pale burgundy toning, with minimal carbon. Some of the obverse stars are not fully defined, though the strike is otherwise well-executed. Our EAC grade MS63. PCGS# 46953

3100 1855 Slanted 55, Knob Ear, N-9, R.1, MS65 Brown PCGS. Grellman Die State e. The famous *Guide Book* variety with a high relief die break above Liberty's ear. The "knob" is present beneath the T in LIBERTY but has yet to extend beneath the Y. A well struck olive-brown Gem that exhibits impressive eye appeal. Our EAC grade MS60. PCGS# 403958

FLYING EAGLE CENTS

3101 1857 MS64 PCGS. The immensely popular Flying Eagle cents were only struck from 1856 to 1858, and the first year 1856 coins are a low-mintage rarity. This 1857 example would make a good choice for type purposes. It is sharply struck and lustrous with rich tan-gold color imbued with highlights of rose. A trivial nick on the upper reverse field is the only surface flaw in evidence. NGC ID# 2276, PCGS# 2016

3102 1857 MS64+ PCGS. With one of the most distinctive yet short-lived designs of all U.S. cents, the Flying Eagle cent is enormously popular with collectors. This example is well-struck with pleasing olive-tan coloration and bold luster. A few trivial nicks keep it from grading as a Gem. NGC ID# 2276, PCGS# 2016

1857 Flying Eagle Cent, MS65
Luminous Type Representative

3103 1857 MS65 PCGS. Soft, satiny luster in shades of apricot, rose, and coppery-gold encompasses carefully preserved surfaces on each side of this Gem type coin. The strike is bold throughout, with no signs of carbon spotting. A few minor die cracks are noted in the margins, not unusual for a late die state. PCGS has encapsulated just 14 numerically finer representatives (10/14). NGC ID# 2276, PCGS# 2016

3104 1858 Small Letters MS64 PCGS. Low Leaves, Open E in ONE hubbed over a Close E. A lustrous peach-gold near-Gem with pleasing preservation and impressive eye appeal. The strike is sharp except for minor blending on the edge of the tail. NGC ID# 2279, PCGS# 2020

INDIAN CENTS

1860 Indian Cent, MS66
Conditionally Elusive

3105 1860 MS66 PCGS. CAC. Rounded Bust. The Rounded Bust variant is significantly more plentiful than its Pointed Bust counterpart, though both varieties are elusive at the Premium Gem grade level. This piece shows well-struck devices and satiny bronze-gold luster. A few microscopic specks are noted upon close examination, though the unaided eye finds nothing of distraction on this well-preserved survivor. Population: 45 in 66 (2 in 66+), 9 finer (10/14). NGC ID# 227F, PCGS# 2058

1864 Indian Cent, L on Ribbon, MS64 Red
Spectacular Snow-3, FS-2302 Variety

3106 1864 L On Ribbon, Repunched Date, Snow-3, FS-2302, MS64 Red PCGS. An intensely lustrous near-Gem example of the scarcer With L on Ribbon variety of this date. Dramatic repunching of 186 is noteworthy on this Snow-3 variety, with an especially impressive spread noted on the 1. A boldly struck example with a couple of faint grayish spots and a couple of minuscule marks on the obverse. Population (for the With L variety): 46 in 64 Red, 37 finer (10/14). PCGS# 37413

3107 1869 MS64 Brown PCGS. CAC. This lovely Choice example showcases razor-sharp design elements beneath glossy burgundy-brown and coppery-orange toning, with hints of original luster in the recesses. The 1869 Indian cent is an elusive date in Mint State, and this example must have just missed a Red and Brown designation. Population: 64 in 64 Brown, 16 finer (11/14). NGC ID# 227T, PCGS# 2094

3108 1869/69 Snow-3g, FS-301, MS64 Red NGC. The 69 is repunched north. Once regarded as an overdate, the variety nonetheless remains listed in the *Guide Book.* Fully struck and lustrous with an unabraded appearance. Principally orange-gold although the central reverse displays minute gray freckles. PCGS# 37476

3109 1871 MS64 Red and Brown NGC. This elusive semikey date boasts the fourth lowest mintage of series (less than 4 million coins), trailing only the key 1877 and the two late-series San Francisco issues. In Mint State grades, however, the 1871 is second only to the 1877 in overall rarity. This Choice Red and Brown coin displays intermingled coppery-orange and auburn hues, with well-struck design elements. A few faint carbon flecks accompany the grade. NGC ID# 227V, PCGS# 2101

3110 **1871 MS65 Red and Brown PCGS.** Bold N in ONE. The well-preserved lustrous surfaces of this spectacular Gem remain mostly original red, but a few areas of light brown patina are evident on both sides. Population: 61 in 65 Red and Brown, 0 finer (11/14). NGC ID# 227V, PCGS# 2101

3111 **1873 Closed 3 MS64+ Red and Brown PCGS. CAC.** A high-end Choice specimen with well-detailed design elements and a Closed 3 in the date. The original red surfaces have mellowed to light brown and lilac in some areas, but few signs of contact are evident. PCGS has graded 38 numerically finer examples (10/14). NGC ID# 227X, PCGS# 2110

3112 **1877 XF45 NGC.** This Indian Head key date displays original brown surfaces and crisp definition over the design elements. The feathers on the headdress retain nearly all detail and LIBERTY is bold. A couple of minute ticks do nothing to affect the coin's appeal. NGC ID# 2284, PCGS# 2127

1877 Indian Cent, AU58
Important Key Date

3113 **1877 AU58 NGC. CAC.** One of the major road blocks in the completion of a date and mintmark set of Indian cents, the key-date 1877 is widely sought in all grades, but is especially difficult to find in the upper circulated range with pleasing eye appeal. This near-Mint example displays glossy auburn patina, with sharp devices and just the barest touch of rub on the high points of the motifs. The lower point of the N in ONE is weak, as is diagnostic of genuine 1877 cents. NGC ID# 2284, PCGS# 2127

3114 **1878 MS65 Red PCGS.** Full Red examples of this slightly better issue are scarce in all grades, but are particularly so at the Gem grade level. This example is sharply struck with warm sun-orange luster that blends well with subtle semiprooflike mirroring in the fields. A few tiny specks are noted near the rims, but are not obtrusive. Population: 50 in 65 Red, 15 finer (11/14). NGC ID# 2285, PCGS# 2132

3115 **1888 MS65 Red PCGS.** Lustrous, copper-red color illuminates the smooth surfaces. Unlike many of the 4,582 proofs minted, which were struck only once, this Gem shows clear signs of multiple strikes and the details displayed are expectedly sharp. Small marks are minimal and small carbon specks dot both sides. Population: 30 in 65 Red, 15 finer (11/14). NGC ID# 228G, PCGS# 2168

3116 **1899 MS66 Red NGC. Snow-23.** A beautiful apricot-gold and olive cent. Lustrous and unabraded with a few minute tan freckles on the cheek and central reverse. The date is repunched, a match for the Snow photo for variety 23, although the accompanying description is incorrect. NGC ID# 228U, PCGS# 2204

3117 **1900 MS66 Red PCGS.** The well-preserved original red surfaces of this delightful Premium Gem show a few hints of rose and a few microscopic specks of carbon, with vibrant mint luster throughout. The design elements are sharply detailed and eye appeal is outstanding. Population: 80 in 66 (8 in 66+) Red, 8 finer (10/14). NGC ID# 228V, PCGS# 2207

3118 **1909 MS66 Red PCGS.** Eagle Eye Photo Seal, card included. A magnificent olive-green and orange-gold Premium Gem, certainly as nice as some of the few examples certified finer. Patience and a strong glass are required to find even the most trivial imperfections. *Ex: Long Beach Signature (Heritage, 6/2006), lot 267.* NGC ID# 2297, PCGS# 2237

3119 **1909-S MS62 Brown PCGS. CAC.** Ex: Teich Family Collection. Cataloged as "almost full mint red" for its 1960 Stack's appearance, this coruscating key date cent is now richly patinated sea-green and tan-brown. Refreshingly free from marks. *Ex: Jim S. White Collection (Stack's, 2/1960), lot 354.* NGC ID# 2298, PCGS# 2238

3120 **1909-S MS64 Red and Brown PCGS. CAC.** The top three headdress feather tips are slightly soft, a diagnostic of genuine 1909-S Indian cents, though the remainder of the devices are sharply impressed. Faint traces of auburn color preclude a full Red designation from PCGS, though the overall appeal is remarkably vibrant. No major abrasions are observed, and close examination reveals only a few tiny specks near the obverse rims. NGC ID# 2298, PCGS# 2239

1909-S Indian Head Cent, MS64 Red
Lively Orange Surfaces

3121 **1909-S MS64 Red PCGS. CAC.** Ex: Teich Family Collection. Excellent mint luster swirls on this orange-gold cent, the final date of the series with a low mintage of 309,000 pieces. The strike, while not full, is relatively sharp in critical areas such as the headdress feather detail. A few obverse flecks do not detract from the overall eye appeal of this vibrant Red San Francisco representative. NGC ID# 2298, PCGS# 2240

PROOF INDIAN CENTS

3122 **1859 PR63 PCGS.** From an ambitious mintage of 800 pieces, this sharply detailed Select proof offers reflective fields and lightly marked red surfaces that show a few hints of lilac and light brown. The Laurel Wreath reverse is a popular one-year design. NGC ID# 2299, PCGS# 2247

1864 Copper-Nickel Cent, PR65
Elusive as a Proof

3123 **1864 Copper-Nickel PR65 PCGS. CAC.** A recorded mintage of just 370 proof copper-nickel Indian cents in 1864 contributes to the issue's scarcity in Gem condition. The present example shows soft golden-orange color, with highly reflective fields and fully struck, frosty devices. A few faint flecks are observed upon close examination, though the overall appeal is excellent. Population: 44 in 65, 10 finer (10/14). NGC ID# 229E, PCGS# 2265

3124 **1870 PR65 Brown PCGS.** A lovely Gem proof, this 1870 example displays glassy fields coated with rich olive, gold, and pale lavender-brown toning. The design elements are fully defined, with no evidence of surface contact. A few faint, grade-limiting hairlines in the fields are fully masked by the rich patina. Population: 2 in 65 Brown, 0 finer (11/14). NGC ID# 229N, PCGS# 2297

3125 **1909 PR66 Red PCGS.** The fiery proof surfaces of this Premium Gem proof final-year Indian cent exhibit attractively blended orange, gold, and pale blue-green. Population: 16 in 66 Red, 2 finer (10/14). NGC ID# 22AY, PCGS# 2416

LINCOLN CENTS

3126 **1909 VDB Die Doubled Obverse, FS-1101, MS64 Red PCGS.** The 190 in the date and the RTY in LIBERTY are obviously die doubled. Among the most desirable varieties of the single-year VDB type. Boldly struck and lustrous with rich peach-gold color and only minor carbon and contact. PCGS# 37633

3127 **1909-S VDB AU58 ANACS.** A pleasing near-Mint example of this sought-after key issue, with just a trace of wear on the sharply impressed design elements. The olive-brown surfaces are lightly abraded and the designer's initials are bold. NGC ID# 22B2, PCGS# 2426

3128 **1909-S VDB MS63 Brown PCGS.** This well-preserved key date example shows typically sharp design features and a somewhat streaky, woodgrain finish across the obverse. The reverse is smooth and satiny, and both sides of the coin are abrasion-free. NGC ID# 22B2, PCGS# 2426

3129 **1909-S VDB MS63 Brown NGC.** Medium chocolate-brown patina yields to satiny underlying luster that is revealed when rotated beneath a light. Small tinges of coppery-orange color are also seen in the crevices, and the design elements are boldly impressed. Attractive examples of this key-date Lincoln cent are always in demand, regardless of color designation. NGC ID# 22B2, PCGS# 2426

3130 **1909-S VDB MS64 Red and Brown PCGS.** Sharply struck with lovely, shimmering mint luster, this near-Gem example also exhibits a pleasing mixture of coppery-red and lime-green toning over each side. A modest degree of scattered carbon, mostly seen on the obverse, seemingly restricts the grade of this unmarked key date cent. NGC ID# 22B2, PCGS# 2427

3131 **1909-S VDB MS64 Red and Brown PCGS.** Sharply struck throughout with bold VDB, this first-year key Lincoln cent displays a mix of original red and light brown patina, with a couple of small carbon spots on the obverse. NGC ID# 22B2, PCGS# 2427

1909-S VDB Cent, MS65 Red and Brown
Vivid Multihued Patina

3132 **1909-S VDB MS65 Red and Brown PCGS.** This luminous Gem will draw much attention from series collectors for its key date status, though the true appeal of this particular coin lies in its array of blended cherry-red, amber, orange-gold, and deep violet toning. The strike is also sharp, and a few faint specks are of little significance amid the rich, eye-catching patina. PCGS has granted only 35 Red and Brown coins a numerically finer grade (10/14). NGC ID# 22B2, PCGS# 2427

1909-S VDB Cent, MS65 Red and Brown
Attractively Patinated, Significant Mint Red

3133 **1909-S VDB MS65 Red and Brown PCGS.** High-end examples of this key Lincoln cent issue are always in strong demand. The present coin displays sharply brought up motifs and carefully preserved, satiny surfaces. Radiant coppery-orange luster encompasses much of each side, though some light olive overtones in the left-hand fields preclude a full Red designation from PCGS, which has seen only 35 numerically finer Red and Brown examples (10/14). NGC ID# 22B2, PCGS# 2427

1909-S VDB Cent, MS65 Red and Brown
Premier Lincoln Key

3134 **1909-S VDB MS65 Red and Brown PCGS Secure. CAC.** This Red and Brown Gem yields dominance to the former color, with only a few wisps of pale burgundy toning intermixed throughout. The strike is sharp and the frosty surfaces deliver warm, luminous luster. A small speck near the S in TRUST appears to be the only sign of carbon, though this is almost completely missed by a casual study of the surfaces. PCGS has certified only 35 numerically finer coins in the Red and Brown color category (10/14). NGC ID# 22B2, PCGS# 2427

1909-S VDB Cent, MS65 Red
Outstanding Cornerstone Issue Example

3135 **1909-S VDB MS65 Red PCGS.** Collectors have sustained strong demand for the 1909-S VDB from the removal of designer Victor David Brenner's initials in August 1909 until today. Only 484,000 S-mint coins were stuck with initials, and the number of survivors — especially in comparable grades — fails to satisfy demand. This amazing Gem has orange-gold surfaces and glistening mint luster. The strike is sharp throughout. A small carbon speck occurs above the T in CENTS, and only a few ticks on Lincoln's cheek are worthy of mention. NGC ID# 22B2, PCGS# 2428

1909 Lincoln Cent, MS67 Red
Shimmering Reddish-Orange Glow

3136 **1909 MS67 Red PCGS.** First-year-of-issue coins were usually well-saved, making them popular candidates for type representation. The 1909 Lincoln cent is a prime example of this, but even it yields to scarcity at the lofty MS67 grade level. This is a glowing amber-orange example, with a bold strike and rich, frosty luster. The strike is crisp and close scrutiny with a loupe is needed to find any microscopic specks. Population: 73 in 67 (4 in 67+) Red, 0 finer (10/14). NGC ID# 22B3, PCGS# 2431

3137 **1910-S MS66 Red and Brown PCGS. CAC.** The well-preserved surfaces of this delightful Premium Gem remain mostly original red, but a few highlights of light brown show on both sides. The design elements are well-detailed and the surfaces are brightly lustrous. Population: 4 in 66 Red and Brown, 0 finer (11/14). NGC ID# 22B6, PCGS# 2439

3138 **1913-D MS65 Red PCGS. CAC.** The 1913-D Lincoln cent is very scarce in MS65 condition, and finer examples are rare. This sharply detailed Gem displays lustrous original red surfaces with a few microscopic specks of carbon. PCGS has graded 18 numerically finer examples (10/14). NGC ID# 22BE, PCGS# 2464

3139 **1914-D AU58 PCGS. CAC.** The sharply detailed design elements of this attractive near-Mint specimen show just a trace of wear on the high points and the original red surfaces have mellowed to olive-brown, but only the most insignificant abrasions are evident. The 1914-D is a key issue, sought-after in all grades. NGC ID# 22BH, PCGS# 2471

1914-D Cent, MS62 Red and Brown
Seldom Seen in This Grade

3140 **1914-D MS62 Red and Brown PCGS. CAC.** The satiny surfaces of this key Lincoln cent exhibit a blend of orange mint color and iridescent toning ranging from light tan to deeper violet on each side. A sharp strike is evident at the centers and along the borders. The 1914-D is in great demand regardless of grade, and is actually more challenging in Mint State than the more widely sought 1909-S VDB. NGC ID# 22BH, PCGS# 2472

3141 **1915-S MS64 Red and Brown PCGS. CAC.** The well-preserved surfaces of this attractive Choice example display a mix of original red and light brown patina, with bright luster underneath. The design elements are sharply detailed throughout. PCGS has graded 19 numerically finer examples (11/14). NGC ID# 22BM, PCGS# 2484

3142 **1916-S MS65 Red and Brown NGC. CAC.** The wide color palette on this attractive coin spans gold, orange, red, and lavender, with generous luster and a good strike, although a couple of minor flecks appear on each side. NGC ID# 22BR, PCGS# 2493

3143 **1919 MS67 Red PCGS.** Lustrous orange color and virtually pristine surfaces are among the attributes this Superb Gem cent possesses. Only a few minuscule hints of carbon are present. Population: 68 in 67 (2 in 67+) Red, 16 finer (10/14). NGC ID# 22BY, PCGS# 2515

3144 **1919-S MS65 Red and Brown PCGS. CAC.** The 1919-S Lincoln is a notable series rarity. This Gem Red and Brown example has delightful golden coloration and is sharply struck save for slight weakness limited to the upper left part of O in ONE. Population: 32 in 65 Red and Brown, 0 finer (11/14).
Ex: Palm Beach Signature (Heritage, 11/2004), lot 5505; Central States Signature (Heritage, 5/2005), lot 5566; FUN Signature (Heritage, 1/2007), lot 1785. NGC ID# 22C2, PCGS# 2520

3145 **1922-D MS65 Red PCGS.** While not quite as popular as its No D counterpart, the 1922-D Lincoln cent is a scarce issue in Gem full Red condition, and is rarely seen finer. This example displays a bold strike, with satiny orange and cherry-gold luster. A few faint flecks on the obverse are not distracting. PCGS has encapsulated just 10 numerically finer full Red examples (10/14). NGC ID# 22C8, PCGS# 2539

3146 **1922 No D, Strong Reverse, FS-401, VF30 PCGS. CAC.** A pleasing chocolate-brown representative of the rare Strong Reverse no mintmark 1922 cent. Marks are trivial aside from a faded diagonal field line near the top of the right wheat ear. PCGS# 37676

1922 No D Cent, AU50
Strong Reverse

3147 **1922 No D, Strong Reverse, FS-401, AU50 PCGS. CAC.** The Strong Reverse, also known as Die Pair Two, is the single true 1922 No D variety, always in strong demand from collectors. This pleasing piece has the usual weak obverse showing few details, but with a full reverse. Only a trace of actual wear is evident on either side, with attractive medium brown surfaces. PCGS# 37676

1922 No D Cent, AU53
FS-401, Strong Reverse

3148 **1922 No D, Strong Reverse, FS-401, AU53 PCGS.** Die Pair 2, with the second 2 in the date bold. The Philadelphia Mint did not strike cents in 1922, though a small number of "plain" Lincolns were produced after the mintmark was polished off a Denver working die. This *Guide Book* variety is widely popular, and is seldom available in high grades. The present AU example shows even chocolate-brown patina, with a few deep reddish tints in the recesses. An attractive, fully original example. PCGS# 37676

3149 **1923-S MS64 Red and Brown PCGS. CAC.** Even amber-red toning blankets both sides of this Choice example, with limited signs of carbon. The strike is slightly soft on the finer obverse details, as is typical of this San Francisco issue. PCGS has encapsulated only 18 numerically finer pieces within the color designation (10/14). NGC ID# 22CB, PCGS# 2547

3150 **1923-S MS64 Red and Brown PCGS. CAC.** A slightly better date in Mint State, especially with any degree of remaining mint red. This glossy, Choice example displays intermingled shades of apricot-red, auburn, burgundy, and olive, with a few tiny threads of deep blue running throughout each side. The strike is above-average for the issue, and the surfaces are devoid of major abrasions or carbon. PCGS has certified just 18 numerically finer Red and Brown examples (11/14). NGC ID# 22CB, PCGS# 2547

3151 **1926-S MS64 Red and Brown PCGS.** Pale coppery-red and soft olive-brown hues blend over the glossy surfaces of this Choice example. A few small carbon flecks on the obverse and a couple tiny abrasions near the E in ONE limit the grade on this piece, but are not obtrusive to the unaided eye. The 1926-S Lincoln is a slightly better date in the upper Mint State grades. PCGS has certified only 15 Red and Brown examples numerically finer than this one (11/14). NGC ID# 22CL, PCGS# 2574

3152 **1926-S MS64 Red and Brown PCGS.** A precisely struck Choice representative of this low mintage and conditionally challenging branch mint issue. Blushes of peach-gold remain although medium brown is predominant. A subtle spot above the 6 in the date. Encased in a green label holder. NGC ID# 22CL, PCGS# 2574

3153 **1931-S MS66 Red PCGS. CAC.** A delightful Premium Gem example, with sharply detailed design elements and lustrous original red surfaces that show only minor signs of contact and a few microscopic specks of carbon. Population: 97 in 66 Red, 0 finer (10/14). NGC ID# 22D4, PCGS# 2620

1936-S Cent, MS67 Red
Tied for Finest at PCGS and NGC

3154 **1936-S MS67 Red PCGS.** Glowing, lustrous fields display olive, red, and lilac accents amid overall flame-orange coloration throughout this meticulously struck San Francisco cent. A few microscopic flecks do not disturb the visual appeal. Neither PCGS nor NGC have certified a numerically finer example of the issue. Population: 52 in 67 Red, 0 finer (10/14). NGC ID# 22DG, PCGS# 2656

3155 **1936-S MS67 Red PCGS.** Well-struck with flashy mint luster and pleasing red-orange coloration. An impressive Superb Gem example of this San Francisco issue from an original mintage of 29 million coins, only a tiny percentage of which have achieved this lofty ranking at both of the major grading services combined. Population: 52 in 67 Red, 0 finer (10/14). NGC ID# 22DG, PCGS# 2656

3156 **1936-S MS67 Red PCGS.** A remarkably preserved example of this Depression-era cent issue from the San Francisco Mint. Well-struck with fine satiny mint luster and blemish-free surfaces. Population: 52 in 67 Red, 0 finer (10/14). NGC ID# 22DG, PCGS# 2656

3157 **1947 MS67 Red NGC. CAC.** An important opportunity for the competitive Registry Set collector, this radiant Superb Gem is tied with just 21 others as the finest certified at NGC (11/14). Satiny luster showcases eye-catching coppery-orange luster and beautifully preserved surfaces. A truly exceptional Lincoln. NGC ID# 22EN, PCGS# 2752

3158 **1948 MS67 Red NGC.** A Registry-grade example, this Superb Gem radiates satiny, coppery-orange luster. Some faint, horizontal die polishing marks are present on the reverse, though the striking sharpness remains pleasing. A few microscopic flecks are noted in the left obverse field, but are not discernable to the unaided eye. Census: 57 in 67 Red, 0 finer (10/14). NGC ID# 22ES, PCGS# 2761

3159 **1948 MS67 Red NGC.** Rich cherry-red toning and splendid mint frost are displayed across both sides of this impressive Superb Gem example. Housed in an early-generation NGC holder. The beautifully radiant surfaces are impeccably preserved. A potential Registry Set candidate. Census: 57 in 67 Red, 0 finer (10/14). NGC ID# 22ES, PCGS# 2761

3160 **1954 MS67 Red NGC.** Another Registry-quality Lincoln, this rose-red Superb Gem is tied with just eight others as the finest certified at NGC (11/14). The strike is sharp and the surfaces are seemingly devoid of carbon. Faint, parallel die striations are observed in the fields, a product of poor-quality die polishing. NGC ID# 22FC, PCGS# 2815

3161 **1955 Doubled Die Obverse, FS-101 — Cleaning — PCGS Genuine. AU Details.** One of the most profound Mint blunders in 20th century numismatics, the die doubling on this *Guide Book* variety can be easily seen with naked eye. This example displays a myriad of colors, including olive, amber, russet, and deep orange. The central motifs are well-defined. PCGS# 37910

3162 **1955 Doubled Die Obverse, FS-101 — Scratches — NGC Details. AU.** The most dramatic doubled die error in the Lincoln series. The doubled letters in IN GOD WE TRUST exhibit nearly complete separation, and both hubbings are equally prominent. Toned deep olive-brown with light high-point wear. A pinscratch extends from the L in PLURIBUS to the base of the E in CENT. PCGS# 37910

3163 **1955 Doubled Die Obverse, FS-101, AU58 NGC.** A satiny deep brown example of the desirable doubled die error. Friction on the cheekbone and the top of the ear indicate a brief stint in circulation. Nearly unabraded except for a cluster of thin marks on the reverse rim near 2:30. PCGS# 37910

3164 **1955 Doubled Die Obverse, FS-101, AU58 NGC.** Plum-red, olive, and gold undertones emerge from the partly lustrous deep brown surfaces. Marks are minimal, and carbon is confined to a spot between the RU in TRUST. The best known die variety in the Lincoln series. PCGS# 37910

1955 Cent, MS64 Brown
FS-101, Doubled Die Obverse

3165 **1955 Doubled Die Obverse, FS-101, MS64 Brown NGC.** This *Guide Book* variety ranks as one of the most profound mint blunders of the 20th century, as the obverse die doubling can be easily seen with the naked eye. This Choice example displays luminous burgundy and auburn-red patina, with glossy luster revealed when tilted beneath a light. Visually superior to most examples of this issue that are offered at auction. PCGS# 37910

1955 Cent, Glossy MS64 Brown
Doubled Die Obverse

3166 **1955 Doubled Die Obverse, FS-101, MS64 Brown PCGS. CAC.** The doubling is evident even to the unaided eye. This *Guide Book* variety is seldom seen in Mint State, and is rare above the Choice grade level, regardless of color designation. This example shows deeply glossy auburn-brown patina, with small tinges of coppery-red in the protected regions. The strike is well-executed, and the eye appeal is exceptional. PCGS# 37910

1955 Doubled Die Obverse Cent
A Pleasing MS64 Brown

3167 **1955 Doubled Die Obverse, FS-101, MS64 Brown PCGS. CAC.** Uniform light brown patination runs over both sides of this near-Gem. The date and all obverse lettering are dramatically doubled. The design elements are generally softly struck, a typical characteristic of this issue. No significant contact marks or spots are evident. A very pleasing Brown example. PCGS has seen only eight numerically finer pieces in this color designation (10/14). PCGS# 37910

1955 Doubled Die Obverse Cent
MS63 Red and Brown

3168 **1955 Doubled Die Obverse, FS-101, MS63 Red and Brown NGC.** The legends display mint orange-gold throughout, though the borders and high points are olive-brown. This unabraded and satiny representative is free from abrasions or spots, and will charm the advanced Lincoln cent collector. The 1955 FS-101 was the first widely recognized doubled die variety since the spread between letters can be seen by the unaided eye. PCGS# 37911

1955 FS-101 Cent, MS64 Red and Brown
Famous Doubled Die Obverse

3169 **1955 Doubled Die Obverse, FS-101, MS64 Red and Brown PCGS.** Variety collecting is an active and important part of today's numismatic environment. However, when the 1955 Doubled Die cent was discovered in 1956, the scene was different, and few collectors were interested in such things. This variety was the first to gain wide-spread popularity, due primarily to its high visibility. The 1955 Doubled Die cent continues to enjoy widespread demand today. This pleasing Choice Mint State piece exhibits satiny luster with attractively blended orange and bluish-brown color. PCGS# 37911

3170 **1959 MS67 Red PCGS.** Rose-red and coppery-orange hues blend into the nearly undisturbed surfaces of this well-defined Superb Gem. A few faint freckles are noticed upon close examination, though these are undetectable to the unaided eye. PCGS has encapsulated only 13 pieces in MS67 Red, and none finer (11/14). NGC ID# 22FS, PCGS# 2854

3171 **1972 Doubled Die Obverse, FS-101, MS66 Red PCGS. CAC.** A dramatic *Guide Book* variety, widely sought by Lincoln cent and error collectors alike. This Premium Gem example displays vibrant coppery-red luster and well-struck design elements. A few faint toning flecks are not discernable to the unaided eye. Population: 2 in 66 Red, 0 finer (10/14). PCGS# 38013

3172 **1983 Doubled Die Reverse, FS-801, MS67 Red PCGS.** The Lincoln Memorial and all reverse legends are strongly die doubled north. The most spectacular of several doubled die varieties known for the issue. A mark-free orange-red Superb Gem, perfect aside from inconsequential minute obverse tan flecks. PCGS# 38063

PROOF LINCOLN CENTS

3173 **1910 PR65 Red and Brown NGC.** A delightful Gem, with lustrous original red surfaces that have mellowed to light brown and lilac in some areas. The design elements are sharply detailed and no mentionable distractions are evident. Census: 43 in 65 Red and Brown, 8 finer (11/14). NGC ID# 22KT, PCGS# 3307

1914 Lincoln Cent, PR66 Brown
Significant Red-Brown Patina

3174 **1914 PR66 Brown PCGS.** Proof cent production declined to just 1,365 coins in 1914, down from 2,983 pieces the year before, and high-grade survivors are seldom seen. This Premium Gem example shows a rich blend of deep burgundy, auburn, and orange-brown patina over delicately preserved matte surfaces. The strike is full throughout, as is an attractive characteristic of the matte proof Lincolns. Population: 22 in 66 (2 in 66+) Brown, 2 finer (10/14). NGC ID# 22KX, PCGS# 3318

3175 **1915 PR65 Red and Brown PCGS.** Due to ever decreasing interest in the matte finish of the new proof coins, sales of proof cents continued to gradually decline in 1915, and high-grade survivors exhibiting any amount of Red color are elusive. This piece displays full definition on all design elements, with blended orange-gold, lilac, and burgundy-brown hues over each side. Close examination reveals some faint, scattered carbon flecks on the obverse, though the eye appeal remains pleasing. Population: 49 in 65 (1 in 65+) Red and Brown, 19 finer (10/14). NGC ID# 22KY, PCGS# 3322

1916 Lincoln Cent, PR65 Red and Brown
Remarkable Presence of Red

3176 **1916 PR65 Red and Brown NGC. CAC.** Final issue in the matte proof series, only 600 coins were struck in three sets of 200 pieces each. This example retains a remarkable amount of original red, mostly darker cherry-red and we do not see any areas that are distinctly brown. This coin presents a remarkable opportunity for the astute collector. Census: 20 in 65 Red and Brown, 16 finer (10/14). NGC ID# 22KZ, PCGS# 3325

3177 **1936 Type One—Satin Finish PR64 Red and Brown PCGS. CAC.** The first proof coins of the modern era were produced with a satin finish, but the Mint switched to an all-brilliant finish later in the year. The original red surfaces of this sharply detailed Choice specimen have mellowed to light brown and violet in some areas. Population: 84 in 64 (1 in 64+) Red and Brown, 36 finer (10/14). NGC ID# 22L2, PCGS# 3331

3178 **1936 Type Two — Brilliant Finish PR65 Red PCGS.** This delightful Gem displays the all-brilliant finish used on proof coins later in the year, after the satin finish proved unpopular. The design elements are sharply defined and the original red surfaces show no mentionable distractions. NGC ID# 22L3, PCGS# 3335

3179 **1950 PR67 Red Ultra Cameo NGC.** While full Red examples of this proof issue are in abundance overall, only a limited number have been awarded an Ultra Cameo designation by NGC, and the present piece ranks as one of just 13 of those certified at the PR67 grade level, with none finer (10/14). Deep cherry-orange and coppery-red hues encompass the deep mirrors, leaving the sharp motifs well-contrasted. A must-have item for the Registry Set competitor. NGC ID# 22LA, PCGS# 93359

3180 **1951 Doubled Die Obverse, FS-101, PR68 ★ Red NGC.** Moderate die doubling on IN GOD WE TRUST identifies this *Cherrypickers'* variety. Designated on the NGC holder as VP-001. This eye-appealing example displays mint-fresh bloom, with deep mirrors and near-cameo contrast. A beautifully preserved, problem-free coin with vivid coppery-gold color. Census: 24 in 68* Red, 1 finer (10/14). PCGS# 38146

3181 **1952 PR67 Red Cameo NGC.** The sharply detailed design elements of this spectacular Superb Gem are unusually frosty, creating bold cameo contrast with the deeply mirrored fields. The well-preserved surfaces are blazing original red. Census: 25 in 67, 7 finer (10/14). NGC ID# 22LC, PCGS# 83365

3182 **1953 Doubled Die Obverse, FS-101, PR67 Red Ultra Cameo NGC.** Although not so-attributed on the holder, this Superb Gem Registry coin is a representative of the popular *Cherrypickers'* variety exhibiting mild die-doubling on the obverse lettering, most easily discernable on the 19 in the date. This coin is possibly the finest Ultra Cameo representative known of this variety, and even the date in general is rare with this bold contrast. A small tinge of deep cherry-red toning is seen near the TR in TRUST, but the coin is otherwise brilliant-orange. PCGS# 38153

3183 **1955 PR69 Red Cameo NGC.** It is truly a pleasure to observe the supremely smooth, flawlessly struck surfaces of this rare Superb Gem. A microscopic planchet flaw (as made) between the O and N of ONE, on the reverse side, is only perceptible with magnification, leaving the gorgeous, dark, deeply-mirrored fields, and the richly frosted, starkly contrasted devices to be the chief draw of the viewer's eye. A truly amazing proof specimen. *Ex: Central States Signature (Heritage, 5/2003), lot 5565.* NGC ID# 22LF, PCGS# 83374

3184 **1956 PR68 Red Ultra Cameo NGC.** NGC has encapsulated only 43 1956 proof cents in full Red Ultra Cameo grades, with only nine of those at the PR68 level and just 2 numerically finer (10/14). Visually, this high-end example is seemingly unrivaled, and the technical quality is equally supreme. Eye-catching field-motif contrast and profoundly deep mirrors complement the bold devices. An exceptional piece, fit for a high-ranking Registry Set. NGC ID# 22LG, PCGS# 93377

3185 **1957 PR68 Red Ultra Cameo NGC.** Only 11 full Red 1957 proof cents have been granted an Ultra Cameo designation from NGC, and this piece is tied numerically with just four others as the finest (10/14). Seemingly infinite depth of mirroring in the fields and bold, heavily frosted devices give the coin impressive eye appeal, while the surfaces exhibit impeccable preservation. NGC ID# 22LH, PCGS# 93380

3186 **1958 PR68 Red Ultra Cameo NGC.** A razor-sharp peach-gold specimen. The devices are luminous, and the fields are flawless and deeply mirrored, with tremendous eye appeal. *Ex: Central States Signature (Heritage, 4/2013), lot 1328.* NGC ID# 22LJ, PCGS# 93383

3187 **1960 Small Date PR68 Red Ultra Cameo NGC.** Fully mirrored amber-gold fields and frosty coppery-orange devices deliver outstanding contrast and eye appeal. The strike is bold, and there are no discernable contact marks or hairlines on this Registry-quality Superb Gem. Census: 12 in 68, 3 finer (10/14). NGC ID# 22LL, PCGS# 93392

TWO CENT PIECES

1864 Two Cent, MS65 Red and Brown
Scarcer Small Motto Variant

3188 1864 Small Motto MS65 Red and Brown PCGS. CAC. Orange-gold fills protected areas of this boldly struck Gem, while the high points and open fields are medium brown. The eye appeal is exceptional despite a trio of tiny reverse spots and a solitary tick near the right base of the large 2. The reverse displays a network of peripheral cracks. Population: 49 in 65 Red and Brown, 6 finer (10/14). NGC ID# 22N8, PCGS# 3580

3189 1864 Large Motto MS66 Red and Brown NGC. Although not as rare overall as its Small Motto counterpart, the 1864 Large Motto two cent piece is highly elusive in Premium Gem condition with any amount of remaining mint red. This piece displays well-balanced bronze-orange and burgundy hues, with sharply struck motifs. Only a few faint flecks are observed within the boundaries of the obverse shield stripes. Housed in a prior generation holder, with only three Red and Brown examples certified numerically finer at NGC (10/14). NGC ID# 22N9, PCGS# 3577

3190 1864 Large Motto MS65 Red PCGS. A Flynn-unlisted RPD variety with the crossbar of the 4 repunched south. Well struck and coruscating with scattered minute carbon and a few delicate obverse marks near 12 o'clock. NGC ID# 22N9, PCGS# 3578

3191 1864 Large Motto MS65+ Red PCGS. Two distinct varieties were featured during the initial year of the two-cent denomination, and this example is from the more available Large Motto type. This is an exceptional Gem example with fully struck design motifs and beautiful mint-red toning. NGC ID# 22N9, PCGS# 3578

3192 1865 Plain 5 MS66 Red and Brown PCGS. CAC. Plain 5. A peach-red Gem with slight mellowing of color on the obverse exergue. Mark-free and lustrous. The dies were somewhat out of parallel, causing an intricate strike on the left borders while the right margins show incompleteness. A plentiful date in most grades but not in the present quality. Population: 26 in 66 (1 in 66+) Red and Brown, 0 finer (6/14). PCGS# 38248

1871 Two Cent Piece, MS66 Red and Brown
Radiantly Luminescent

3193 1871 MS66 Red and Brown PCGS. Vibrant original luster illuminates well-balanced violet, burgundy, and coppery-red hues on each side of this eye-appealing Premium Gem. The strike is razor-sharp and the surfaces are devoid of discernable abrasions. This piece ranks as the sole finest at PCGS within with Red and Brown color category (10/14). NGC ID# 22NF, PCGS# 3610

PROOF TWO CENT PIECES

3194 1865 PR66 Red and Brown NGC. Plain 5. Rotation beneath a light displays iridescent orange-red and aquamarine shades. A fully struck and flashy Premium Gem. Carbon is confined to a fleck near the obverse rim at 12:30. Just 500 proofs were struck for this Civil War date. NGC ID# 274U, PCGS# 3628

3195 1867 PR65 Red and Brown Cameo NGC. CAC. The proof 1867 two cent piece was distributed to the tune of 625 examples via silver proof sets, plus an unknown number of pieces in minor proof sets, though the date is surprising elusive in higher grades of preservation and with true Cameo qualities. Each side of this attractive Gem displays distinct contrast, while mahogany hues prevail on the obverse, and the reverse is surprisingly close to full Red. Census: 5 in 65 Cameo, 4 finer (11/14). *Ex: Long Beach Signature (Heritage, 5/2008), lot 1108.* PCGS# 83634

3196 1868 PR65 Red and Brown PCGS. CAC. The 68 in the date is lightly recut within the upper loops. An exquisitely struck Gem with radiant gold and rose-violet colors. Well-preserved and decidedly scarce at this high grade level. Population: 43 in 65 Red and Brown, 15 finer (10/14).
Ex: ANA Signature (Heritage, 3/2003), lot 5279; Orlando Summer FUN (Heritage, 7/2010), lot 3192. NGC ID# 274X, PCGS# 3637

3197 1868 PR65 Red PCGS. From a mintage of approximately 600 proofs, this Gem shows iridescent orange color over smooth surfaces. The design elements are boldly impressed on each side and only a few wispy marks are noted. When tilted at the correct angle, the apparent proof contrast is impressive. Population: 21 in 65 Red, 9 finer (10/14). NGC ID# 274X, PCGS# 3638

3198 1872 PR65 Brown PCGS. CAC. The original red surfaces of this impressive Gem have mellowed to light brown and lilac in some areas, but about 50% of the original color remains. The design elements are sharply detailed and only a few microscopic carbon specks are evident. Population: 13 in 65 Brown, 3 finer (10/14). NGC ID# 2752, PCGS# 3648

1873 Two Cent, PR65 Red and Brown
Definitive Closed 3 Example

3199 1873 Closed 3 PR65 Red and Brown PCGS. The Open 3 and Closed 3 varieties of the proof 1873 two cent pieces can sometimes be difficult to differentiate, though this example is distinctly the latter. The fields are deeply reflective, displaying tan-gold and lilac-brown, while the devices show bold definition throughout. PCGS has awarded finer numeric grades to only 27 Red and Brown examples (10/14). NGC ID# 2753, PCGS# 3652

THREE CENT SILVER

3200 1852 MS66 PCGS. CAC. The central shield is not fully defined, but the strike is otherwise bold throughout. Thick mint frost illuminates pale olive-gold toning over each side, but reveals few detectable interuptions in the luster. Housed in an old green label holder. PCGS has certified only 18 numerically finer representatives (10/14). NGC ID# 22YZ, PCGS# 3666

3201 1854 MS64 PCGS. A dark toning spot on the upper ray of the obverse star provides an identifier for this gold-toned Choice Mint State three cent silver piece, representing the first year of the Type Two design. PCGS has certified 63 finer examples (10/14). NGC ID# 22Z3, PCGS# 3670

3202 1855 MS63 PCGS. This is a well-struck, satiny example of the short-lived Type Two design. Splashes of amber-gold, violet, and pale olive toning accent each side, masking any grade-limiting abrasions. Population: 19 in 63, 63 finer (10/14). NGC ID# 22Z4, PCGS# 3671

3203 1855 MS63 PCGS. This satiny, golden-gray example shows slight striking weakness on the right reverse stars, but is otherwise sharp throughout. Softly lustrous surfaces lack any singularly mentionable abrasions. Population: 19 in 63, 63 finer (10/14). NGC ID# 22Z4, PCGS# 3671

3204 1858 MS65 NGC. This lightly toned Gem exhibits an unusually bold shield and star for the type, with frosty original luster that highlights mottled shades of amber, blue, and sun-gold as it cartwheels beneath a light. Close examination fails to discern any mentionable abrasions. Census: 49 in 65, 33 finer (10/14). NGC ID# 22Z7, PCGS# 3674

1861 Three Cent Silver, MS67
Tack-Sharp, Tied for Finest at PCGS

3205 1861 MS67 PCGS. The strikingly bold design definition alone would make this Superb Gem highly desirable to three cent silver collectors, though its conditional rarity at the MS67 grade level further heightens its appeal. Shimmering, frosty luster on each side illuminates soft champagne centers, while the margins show deeper amber-orange and olive-gold hues. Population: 30 in 67, 0 finer (10/14). NGC ID# 22ZA, PCGS# 3679

1861 Three Cent Silver, MS67
Attractive, High-End Example

3206 1861 MS67 PCGS. CAC. The digits in the date show slight doubling on this piece, but this is the result of machine or strike doubling rather than a blundered die, and therefore is not one of Breen's doubled date varieties. This beautiful Superb Gem displays frosty silver luster beneath deep gold, russet, and steel toning, while the strike is pleasing and the surface preservation is immaculate. Population: 30 in 67, 0 finer (10/14).
Ex: Central States Signature (Heritage, 5/2007), lot 1367; Dallas Signature (Heritage, 11/2007), lot 194. NGC ID# 22ZA, PCGS# 3679

1863 Three Cent Silver, MS66
Prooflike Surfaces, Brilliant

3207 1863 MS66 NGC. The low mintage of 21,000 pieces may be only partially responsible for the rarity of this three cent silver issue, with the suspicion that many pieces of the mintage were melted. This survivor is brilliant, untoned, and prooflike. A glass reveals delicate hairlines, which are in part due to die polishing. The usual die clashing appears on both sides of the coin. A scarce and popular Civil War date, seldom available as a business strike in this Premium Gem condition. Census: 12 in 66, 6 finer (10/14). NGC ID# 22ZD, PCGS# 3682

3208 1864 MS62 NGC. Struck from strongly clashed dies. Most of this Civil War date was melted in 1873, but this is a pleasing Mint State survivor. Light gold and violet peripheral hues are faint almost to invisibility at the centers. Census: 10 in 62, 67 finer (10/14).
Ex: The Donald R. Frederick Collection of Early U.S. Coinage: Bayside Part II/Central States Signature (Heritage, 4/2010), lot 376. NGC ID# 22ZE, PCGS# 3684

3209 1865 MS62 NGC. Bold clash marks are immediately noticed, as is profound semiprooflike mirroring in the fields. The central regions exhibit slight striking deficiency, but the design elements are otherwise crisp. Very few marks are present for the grade. With a mintage of only 8,000 coins, this issue is decidedly scarce in all Mint State grades. NGC ID# 22ZF, PCGS# 3685

PROOF THREE CENT SILVER

3210 1862 PR64 Cameo PCGS. Vivid shades of lavender, slate-gray, and greenish-gold toning blanket the well-preserved surfaces of this sharply detailed Choice example. The frosty devices contrast boldly with the deeply reflective fields. Population: 7 in 64, 8 finer (10/14). PCGS# 83711

3211 1863 PR64 NGC. Just 460 proofs, along with 12,000 business strikes, were issued for this scarce Civil War date. This well struck specimen has flashy undisturbed fields and medium rose-gold and sea-green toning. Certified in an old pre-hologram holder. NGC ID# 22ZP, PCGS# 3712

3212 1868 PR65 PCGS. The design elements of this impressive Gem are well-detailed and the fields temperately reflective, under vivid shades of greenish-gold, cerulean-blue, and gray patina. From a small proof mintage of 600 pieces. Population: 47 in 65 (1 in 65+), 15 finer (10/14). NGC ID# 27CE, PCGS# 3718

3213 1873 PR63 PCGS. Bright, deeply mirrored fields frame satiny, boldly struck devices on this light golden-toned proof. A few minute marks in the fields limit the grade, but hardly affect the appeal to the unaided eye. NGC ID# 27CJ, PCGS# 3724

THREE CENT NICKELS

3214 1883 MS62 PCGS. This business strike issue had a meager mintage of 4,000 pieces, several thousand coins fewer than the proof mintage of the same date! Only a few dozen pieces have been rated in mint condition by PCGS and NGC combined. This example is well-struck, with light olive-gray coloration and blemish-free surfaces. Only somewhat subdued luster may have limited the grade of this otherwise impressive coin. Population: 12 in 62, 28 finer (10/14). NGC ID# 275E, PCGS# 3751

3215 1889 MS66 PCGS. CAC. From a small mintage of 18,100 pieces, this attractive Premium Gem displays well-detailed design elements and bright mint luster, with well-preserved surfaces under shades of nickel-gray and champagne-gold toning. Population: 33 in 66, 12 finer (10/14). NGC ID# 275J, PCGS# 3758

PROOF THREE CENT NICKELS

3216 1867 PR65 Cameo PCGS. CAC. An impressive Gem, with well-detailed design elements and deeply mirrored fields that contrast boldly with the frosty devices. Close inspection reveals a few planchet flaws and striations on both sides, as struck. Population: 28 in 65, 28 finer (10/14). PCGS# 83763

1867 Three Cent Nickel, PR66+ Cameo
Tied for Finest Cameo at PCGS

3217 1867 PR66+ Cameo PCGS. CAC. The proof 1867 three cent nickel's availability declines significantly when one crosses into the pursuit of Cameos. This Premium Gem showcases sharp, softly frosted devices set against moderately mirrored fields, with warm gold and powder-blue toning intermingling over each side. The surfaces are refreshingly free of the minor strike-throughs and excessive die polishing that typically affect proofs of this type. Population: 28 in 66 (2 in 66+), 0 finer (10/14). PCGS# 83763

1868 Nickel Three Cent, PR66 Deep Cameo
Eye-Catching Contrast

3218 1868 PR66 Deep Cameo PCGS. CAC. The thickly frosted devices and fully mirrored fields would provide stark white-on-black contrast, if not for a faint blush of light golden toning which adds a degree of warmth to each side. The strike is full and there are no discernable marks. Population: 8 in 66 (2 in 66+), 0 finer (10/14). PCGS# 93764

3219 1870 PR65 Cameo PCGS. CAC. Delicate gold and nickel-gray tints visit the shining surfaces of this delightful Gem. Pleasingly preserved with light, yet distinct contrast on each side. Population: 28 in 65 (1 in 65+), 12 finer (10/14).
Ex: FUN Signature (Heritage, 1/2008), lot 620. PCGS# 83766

3220 1877 — Environmental Damage — NGC Details. Proof. This issue saw a tiny total mintage of 900 coins, all of them proofs, making it a key date in the series. This piece is sharply struck with flashy mirrored fields and contact-free surfaces. A light layer of russet-colored specks on each side of the coin are characterized as environmental damage by NGC.

1877 Three Cent Nickel, PR64+ Cameo
Date Set Essential

3221 1877 PR64+ Cameo NGC. Pastel shades of jade-green, violet, and lavender-gold delicately grace each side of this near-Gem Cameo. The strike is razor-sharp throughout, and the surfaces are carefully preserved with only a few faint hairlines noted upon close study with a lens. This proof-only issue had a recorded mintage of just 900 coins, and is essential for a complete date set of nickel three cents. PCGS# 83773

3222 1878 PR66 Cameo PCGS. CAC. With a mintage of 2,350 pieces, the proof-only status of this issue brings it under increased market pressure from collectors. This is a brilliant, pristine example with razor-sharp definition and bold cameo contrast on both sides. PCGS# 83774

1879 Three Cent Nickel, PR68 ★
Brilliant With Frost on the Devices

3223 **1879 PR68 ★ NGC.** This gorgeous specimen displays razor-sharp striking definition throughout, and slight incompleteness on a few of the lower reverse design elements is merely the result of overzealous die polish. The untoned silver-gray surfaces are flashy and pristine, with glassy reflectivity in the fields and intense mint frost on the devices. A great proof example that is the only PR68 ★ coin at NGC, with none finer (10/14).
Ex: Central States Signature (Heritage, 4/2009), lot 1352; Long Beach Signature (Heritage, 6/2011), lot 3185. NGC ID# 275Z, PCGS# 3775

1879 Three Cent Nickel, PR67+
Deeply Mirrored Cameo

3224 **1879 PR67+ Cameo PCGS. CAC.** Faint traces of ice-blue and pale champagne toning grace otherwise brilliant mint bloom on each side of this Superb Gem Cameo. The strike is boldly executed, though excessive die polishing has partially effaced the reverse ribbon ends, as is typical of this type in general. No marks are present, affirming the lofty PR67+ grade from PCGS. Population: 40 in 67 (1 in 67+), 1 finer (10/14). PCGS# 83775

3225 **1882 PR67 NGC. CAC.** A beautifully toned Superb Gem. Orange, lemon-gold, and powder-blue shades endow fully impressed surfaces. Essentially immaculate, and certified in a former generation holder. NGC ID# 2764, PCGS# 3778

3226 **1884 PR67 Cameo PCGS. CAC.** A delightful Superb Gem, with sharply detailed frosty design elements that create bold cameo contrast with the deeply mirrored fields. Delicate shades of pale gold toning add to the terrific eye appeal. Population: 30 in 67 (1 in 67+), 2 finer (10/14). PCGS# 83780

3227 **1884 PR67+ Cameo PCGS. CAC.** Full cameo contrast delivers exceptional visual appeal on this carefully preserved proof type coin. The devices are boldly struck with a heavy coat of mint frost. A tiny strike-through in the field near the crook of Liberty's neck should not be mistaken for a contact mark, of which there are none. A faint blush of light golden toning adds a degree of warmth to each side. Population: 30 in 67 (1 in 67+), 2 finer (10/14). PCGS# 83780

SHIELD NICKELS

3228 **1866 Rays MS65 NGC.** An extremely popular type issue because of the short-lived Rays design. This attractive Gem offers well-detailed design elements and lustrous well-preserved surfaces with a few die cracks on both sides. NGC has graded 24 numerically finer examples (10/14). NGC ID# 22NX, PCGS# 3790

3229 **1866 Rays MS65 PCGS.** An almond-gold Gem with vibrant luster, unmarked surfaces, and attractive eye appeal. The strike is crisp except on a couple of the stars. Both sides exhibit several interesting cracks, and a triangular die break is prominent at 7 o'clock; a testament to the travails of the Mint coining the new copper-nickel alloy. NGC ID# 22NX, PCGS# 3790

3230 **1867 No Rays MS66 PCGS Secure.** The hard nickel alloy of the Shield nickel proved difficult to strike up fully, with the result that few surviving examples are sharp enough to qualify for a Premium Gem grade assessment. This piece is remarkably bold for the issue, with strong centrils on the stars and fully delineated shield stripes. Splashes of coppery-orange toning grace each side, while the underlying surfaces are nearly unabraded. Population: 16 in 66 (1 in 66+), 0 finer (10/14). NGC ID# 22NZ, PCGS# 3794

3231 **1868 MS66 PCGS. CAC.** Smooth surfaces reveal only a small mark below the 5, which prohibits an even higher grade. Pale gold toning and frosty luster cover both sides, resulting in a high degree of eye appeal. The strike is strong, with a die crack visible through the date. Population: 31 in 66 (4 in 66+), 1 finer (10/14). NGC ID# 22P2, PCGS# 3795

3232 **1869 MS66 PCGS.** With a mintage of more than 16 million pieces, the 1869 Shield nickel is not considered scarce in an absolute sense, but Premium Gem examples are. This piece is well-struck, with satiny, silver-gray luster and well-preserved surfaces. A late die state, as evidenced by a couple of forked die cracks on the upper obverse. Population: 14 in 66 (1 in 66+), 0 finer (10/14). NGC ID# 22P3, PCGS# 3796

3233 **1871 MS65 PCGS.** Pleasing shades of pale gold and lavender toning grace the well-preserved surfaces of this impressive Gem. Some recutting shows on the stars and the S in CENTS is incomplete, due to die polishing. The design elements are well-detailed and extensive die cracks show on the obverse. Population: 32 in 65, 12 finer (10/14). NGC ID# 22P5, PCGS# 3798

3234 **1871 MS65 PCGS. CAC.** The lower serif of the S in CENTS is broken. Softly struck as usual but with generous luster under a mix of peach and pale gray shadings. This minimally abraded Gem exhibits several obverse die cracks, the most noticeable running from the left (facing) arrow to the rim. Nickel production fell to just 561,000 pieces in 1871, as passage of a law permitting the Mint to reissue older minor coins that were redeemed by the banks drastically decreased the need for new production of those denominations. Population: 32 in 65, 12 finer (10/14). NGC ID# 22P5, PCGS# 3798

3235 **1873 Open 3 MS65 PCGS. CAC.** This is a splendid Gem example of the Open 3 Shield nickel. This issue had a sizeable mintage of 4.1 million pieces, nearly ten times more than its Closed 3 counterpart, but both varieties are scarce in high grades. This brilliant coin is highly lustrous and blemish-free, with bold strike definition and doubling noted on some of the obverse leaves. Population: 42 in 65 (2 in 65+), 9 finer (10/14). NGC ID# 276C, PCGS# 3800

1873 Open 3 Nickel, MS66
Fletcher-111, Doubled Die Obverse
Tied for Finest of the Date

3236 1873 Open 3, Doubled Die Obverse, Fletcher-111, MS66 NGC. A trace of almond-gold toning overlies lustrous slate surfaces. Sharply struck and nearly immaculate. Die doubled northwest, most apparent (as usual for the series) on the annulet. The lowest horizontal shield line is also strongly doubled. Also interesting for the heavy die crack along the left obverse border. Very similar to FS-101; nonetheless a different variety. NGC calls it VP-009 but we reference the Edward L. Fletcher, Jr. Shield nickel book. The sole business strike issue unavailable in proof format, although Closed 3 proofs were struck. Census of all 1873 Open 3 nickels: 4 in 66, 0 finer (10/14).
Ex: Boston Signature (Heritage, 8/2010), lot 4237. NGC ID# 276C, PCGS# 3800

3237 1876 MS65 PCGS. This impressive Gem displays a number of interesting die cracks on the obverse, with sharply detailed design elements and vibrant mint luster under delicate shades of pale gold toning. Population: 47 in 65 (1 in 65+), 14 finer (11/14). NGC ID# 22PB, PCGS# 3805

1880 Shield Nickel, Fine 15
Sharp for the Grade

3238 1880 Fine 15 PCGS. With a mintage of only 16,000 pieces, the 1880 Shield nickel is the major key issue in the series, carrying a strong premium over the common date in all grades. This evenly circulated, well-detailed example shows natural olive-gray patina on the obverse, with deeper reddish-gray color on the reverse. A pleasing mid-grade circulated example, ideal for the budget-minded collector. Population: 4 in 15, 61 finer (10/14). NGC ID# 276E, PCGS# 3810

1880 Shield Nickel, VF35
Appealing Mid-Grade Example

3239 1880 VF35 NGC. With a mintage of only 16,000 pieces (the lowest in the series), the 1880 Shield nickel is an undisputed key date in all grades. This is a highly pleasing mid-grade example, with even olive-gray patina and only light wear over each side. The design elements are boldly defined, though the extent of the wear and a lack of any detectable reflectivity in the crevices of the fields suggest a business strike origin. Census: 3 in 35, 28 finer (10/14). NGC ID# 276E, PCGS# 3810

3240 1881 MS65 PCGS. With a mintage of only 68,800 pieces, the 1881 is elusive in most grades, especially in the upper echelon of Mint State. Mottled slate-gray patina graces both sides of this lustrous and fully struck Gem. Population: 39 in 65 (1 in 65+), 20 finer (10/14).
Ex: Long Beach Signature (Heritage, 9/2008), lot 620. NGC ID# 276F, PCGS# 3811

3241 1883/2 FS-303 MS62 NGC. Once studied under a loupe, the base and central curve of the underdigit 2 is apparent between the 83 in the date. A middle die state with a rim-to-rim die crack that touches the base of the 18. A satiny, sharply struck, and unblemished wheat-gold and cream-gray example. PCGS# 38414

3242 1883 MS66 PCGS. CAC. A modest mintage of little more than 1.4 million coins was sufficient to allow moderate hoarding of this final-year issue, with the result that numerous Mint State pieces are available today, though this issue is widely sough-after as the first of three nickel types for the year. This is a boldly struck piece, though die wear has weakened the definition of several wreath leaves and the legend IN GOD WE TRUST. A number of the usual die cracks are also visible on each side near the borders. The coin is well-preserved and satiny, with a faint blush of golden toning on each side. PCGS has certified 13 numerically finer examples (10/14). NGC ID# 22PE, PCGS# 3813

PROOF SHIELD NICKELS

3243 1867 No Rays PR65 Cameo PCGS. CAC. The startling gold-on-black contrast on each side of this conditionally scarce Gem proof is outstanding, and the design motifs are fully struck. A beautiful, brilliant piece devoid of noteworthy surface flaws. This No Rays issue is not often seen in grades any finer than PR64. Population: 60 in 65 Cameo, 16 finer (10/14). PCGS# 83821

3244 1870 PR66 Cameo NGC. This untoned Premium Gem Cameo 1870 Shield nickel shows silver-gray fields with lighter silver-white high points amid surfaces that are virtually unmarked throughout, quite appealing and high-end for this elusive proof issue. These Shield nickel proofs seem considerably underrated at today's market levels. Census: 14 in 66, 2 finer (10/14). PCGS# 83824

3245 1876 PR66 Cameo PCGS. Noticeable cameo contrast is the hallmark of this Premium Gem proof, with a thin veil of light golden toning warming the deeply mirrored fields and sharp motifs. The entire obverse is lightly strike doubled, most noticeable on the date and motto. Population: 37 in 66 (5 in 66+), 6 finer (10/14). PCGS# 83830

3246 1878 PR65 PCGS. CAC. A proof-only Gem that boasts a bold strike and vibrant cartwheel sheen. Delicate ice-blue and almond-gold toning further increases the eye appeal. Certified in a first generation holder. NGC ID# 276V, PCGS# 3832

1878 Shield Nickel, PR67 Cameo
Problem-Free, Proof-Only Example

3247 **1878 PR67 Cameo NGC.** Often resembling a business strike more than a conventional proof, nevertheless the issue was marketed by the Mint as proofs, and thus they are known as such. This reflective example does justice to both its proof format and its Superb Gem condition, with mirrored areas between the shield lines and around the central devices. The reverse dies were more incompletely polished, with satiny, semiprooflike luster. This is a fully struck example from an early state of the dies, as indicated by a lump or similar artifact in the lower loop of the second 8. Census: 5 in 67, 0 finer (10/14). PCGS# 83832

3248 **1882 PR67 PCGS.** Lightly toned nickel-gray overall with elements of rose. This sharply struck Superb Gem offers noteworthy eye appeal, though contrast is minimal. Population: 37 in 67, 0 finer (10/14). *Ex: FUN Signature (Heritage, 1/2009), lot 675.* NGC ID# 276Y, PCGS# 3837

LIBERTY NICKELS

3249 **1883 With Cents MS66 PCGS. CAC.** This delightful Premium Gem was struck later in the year, after the design was altered to include the word CENTS. The design elements show a touch of the typical softness on the peripheral elements, but the central devices are sharply rendered. The well-preserved lustrous surfaces show delicate shades of pale gold toning. Population: 61 in 66 (5 in 66+), 2 finer (10/14). NGC ID# 22PH, PCGS# 3844

1885 Liberty Nickel, MS61
Pleasing Lower-End Mint State Example

3250 **1885 MS61 NGC.** The 1885 Liberty nickel's key date status drives widespread demand in all grades, but especially in Mint State. Just on the plus side of that grade threshold, this satiny, golden-gray example displays minimally abraded surfaces and pleasing appeal for the grade. Stars 1 through 3 are not fully brought up, though the strike is otherwise well-executed. NGC ID# 2773, PCGS# 3846

3251 **1886 MS62 NGC.** One of the key dates to the Liberty Head nickel series. The nickel-gray surfaces of this piece display occasional traces of deeper gray and tan. Generally well struck save for softness left of the bow knot. Moderate planchet laminations are visible on the left obverse rim. *Ex: ANA Signature (Heritage, 3/2010), lot 412.* NGC ID# 22PK, PCGS# 3847

3252 **1894 MS65 PCGS. CAC.** Warmly lustrous with peach and pink overtones. The strike is strong in the centers but erratic on the margins with a decently detailed left ear of corn in the reverse wreath but hit-and-miss obverse stars. Population: 55 in 65 (1 in 65+), 28 finer (10/14). NGC ID# 2779, PCGS# 3855

1912-S Liberty Nickel, MS65
Low-Mintage, Key Branch Mint Issue

3253 **1912-S MS65 PCGS.** While all previous Liberty nickels had mintages numbering in the millions of pieces, this series-ending issue (not including the 1913 anomaly) had a meager output of just 238,000 pieces. The current coin is a lovely Gem example this key San Francisco date. The surfaces are satiny and bright, with none of the dullness all too often seen on the issue. The strike is generally well-defined, the only exception being the left ear of corn on the reverse wreath. Minimal marks are present, as one would expect from the grade, and the coin offers a pleasing display of pale-lilac and rose toning. NGC ID# 277R, PCGS# 3875

PROOF LIBERTY NICKELS

3254 **1883 No Cents PR66+ Cameo PCGS. CAC.** A high-end Premium Gem specimen of the popular No CENTS design type, with sharply detailed frosty design elements that contrast boldly with the deeply mirrored fields. PCGS has graded 15 numerically finer examples (10/14). PCGS# 83878

3255 **1885 PR66 Cameo PCGS.** This is a beautiful piece with frosted champagne-gold devices and watery, deep green-gray fields. The impeccable strike definition on each side is revealed by razor-sharp design motifs. The desirability of this proof issue is tremendously enhanced by the low mintage of the 1885 business strikes. Population: 51 in 66 (3 in 66+), 11 finer (10/14). PCGS# 83883

1886 Liberty Nickel, PR67
Tied for Finest Known

3256 **1886 PR67 NGC.** Although far more available than high-grade business strikes for the date, Superb Gem proofs are rare and in high demand. This example is remarkably attractive. Reflective fields surround frosted devices with glimmering shades of lilac and peach-gold. The fully struck portrait is starkly contrasted to the unusually deep obverse mirrors. The reverse is a bit less reflective and contrasted, yet the surfaces reveal nearly no distractions. Neither PCGS nor NGC show a numerically finer proof representative. NGC Census: 20 in 67 (1 in 67+, 3 in 67 ★, 1 in 67+★), 0 finer (10/14). NGC ID# 277U, PCGS# 3884

3257 **1888 PR66+ PCGS. CAC.** Though the luster swirls as much as it reflects on this specimen, the sharp strike of a proof is unmistakable. Modest green-gold glimpses on the obverse lead to greater coverage on the reverse, particularly at the top. Population: 96 in 66 (3 in 66+), 5 finer (10/14). NGC ID# 277W, PCGS# 3886

1889 Liberty Nickel, PR68
Single Highest-Graded Specimen

3258 **1889 PR68 NGC.** This is the single highest-graded example from this proof issue of 3,336 pieces. This is a wonderfully preserved, seemingly pristine coin with flashy, reflective surfaces. The unusual but highly attractive coloration is light and slightly variegated between sky-blue, pale gold, and silvery-gray toning. Simply a great coin, virtually flawless. Census: 1 in 68, 0 finer (10/14). NGC ID# 277X, PCGS# 3887

3259 **1892 PR66+ Cameo PCGS.** A fully struck piece with bold field-to-device contrast noted on both sides. The surfaces are essentially flawless, with a tiny reddish-charcoal speck seen on Liberty's throat near the bust truncation. Population: 33 in 66 (6 in 66+), 5 finer (10/14). PCGS# 83890

3260 **1893 PR66 Cameo PCGS. CAC.** Shades of greenish-gold and cerulean-blue toning blanket the pristine surfaces of this spectacular Premium Gem, with sharply detailed design elements and deeply mirrored fields that contrast boldly with the frosty devices. Population: 45 in 66 (6 in 66+), 14 finer (11/14). PCGS# 83891

3261 **1897 PR67 PCGS. CAC.** Boldly defined design elements and moderately mirrored fields are among the pleasing attributes this Superb Gem has to offer. Faint sky-blue and pale golden toning accents the virtually flawless surfaces. Population: 23 in 67 (1 in 67+), 1 finer (10/14). NGC ID# 2787, PCGS# 3895

1897 Nickel, PR67 Cameo
Delicate Golden Patina

3262 **1897 PR67 Cameo PCGS.** Bold detail and stark field-device contrast deliver outstanding visual appeal on this Superb Gem Cameo. Warm golden toning accents each side, growing deeper toward the peripheries. The 1897 is a fairly plentiful proof issue overall, but high-grade Cameo examples are seldom available. Population: 18 in 67 (3 in 67+), 0 finer (10/14). PCGS# 83895

3263 **1905 PR67 PCGS.** Blended pastel hues seemingly melt into the highly reflective fields of this Superb Gem proof. The strike is needle-sharp and the fields are virtually free of the wispy hairlines that usually limit the grade. Population: 14 in 67, 1 finer (10/14). NGC ID# 278F, PCGS# 3903

3264 **1907 PR66 Cameo PCGS. CAC.** A mintage of 1,475 proof nickels was accomplished in 1907, but few survivors exhibit any degree of cameo contrast, and Gem or finer pieces featuring such are genuinely rare. This Premium Gem is one of just 18 PR66 Cameo representatives at PCGS, with only four certified numerically finer (10/14). The mark-free fields are deeply mirrored, and the devices display just enough frost to warrant the Cameo designation. A faint golden tint accents each side, while the only notable striking softness is seen on the lower left wreath leaves. PCGS# 83905

BUFFALO NICKELS

1913 Type One Nickel, MS67+
Superb Type Representative

3265 **1913 Type One MS67+ PCGS.** The Philadelphia issue is the most plentiful Type One Buffalo nickel in high grades, ideal for the type collector seeking a high-end piece for his set. This Plus-grade Superb Gem showcases shimmering golden luster and beautifully preserved surfaces. Some minor die erosion is noted in the recesses on each side, though the striking definition is not overly affected. Only 14 coins are numerically finer at PCGS (10/14). NGC ID# 22PW, PCGS# 3915

1913-D Type One Buffalo Nickel, MS67
A Superlative Representative

3266 **1913-D Type One MS67 PCGS. CAC.** The 1913-D Type One is generally a well-produced issue that shows strong mint luster. It offers extra appeal as part of a three-Mint set from a one-year type. This lovely Superb Gem displays reddish-gold tinted color and considerable satiny mint frost. The strike is uniformly strong throughout, and there are no significant marks on either side. Just two examples are certified in numerically finer condition by PCGS. Population: 57 in 67 (2 in 67+), 2 finer (10/14). *Ex: St. Louis CSNS Signature (Heritage, 5/2007), lot 1579; Orlando FUN Signature (Heritage, 1/2009), lot 775; Milwaukee CSNS Signature (Heritage, 4/2010), lot 1122.* NGC ID# 22PX, PCGS# 3916

3267 **1913-S Type One MS66 PCGS.** A satiny and beautiful Premium Gem with gold-green patina across parts of the otherwise nickel-white devices. Strong overall detail, though the bison's shoulder is a trifle soft. *Ex: Houston Signature (Heritage, 12/2009), lot 267.* NGC ID# 22PY, PCGS# 3917

3268 **1913-D Type Two MS65 PCGS.** The nickel-gray surfaces of this Gem display soft luster and just a few unobtrusive reverse marks. Well-struck except for minor weakness in the hair on the bison's head. *Ex: FUN Signature (Heritage, 7/2009), lot 241.* NGC ID# 22R2, PCGS# 3922

3269 **1913-D Type Two MS65 PCGS. CAC.** Light to medium rose-gold toning adorns this lustrous and unmarked early branch mint nickel. The centers show only minor incompleteness of strike. Housed in a green label holder. NGC ID# 22R2, PCGS# 3922

3270 **1913-S Type Two MS63 NGC. CAC.** Lovely blue, rose, and gold toning appears on both sides of this Select Mint State Buffalo nickel, with dusky gold at the upper obverse. NGC ID# 22R3, PCGS# 3923

3271 **1913-S Type Two MS64 PCGS. CAC.** The recessed mintmark and denomination on the reverse identifies the popular Type Two design. This well-detailed Choice example offers vibrant mint luster and highlights of pale gold toning. NGC ID# 22R3, PCGS# 3923

1914 Buffalo Nickel, MS67 ★
None Certified Finer at PCGS or NGC

3272 **1914 MS67 ★ NGC. CAC.** This lustrous Superb Gem is bathed in sun-gold and lime toning. The strike is unusually crisp, even on the hair above the braid. The LU in PLURIBUS is legibly clashed beneath the Indian's chin. Out of nine MS67 pieces known to NGC (with none finer), this is the only one to receive the Star designation. Nor are any certified numerically higher at PCGS (10/14).
Ex: Central States Signature (Heritage, 4/2008), lot 421; ANA Signature (Heritage, 7/2008), lot 1329; Long Beach Signature (Heritage, 6/2010), lot 383. NGC ID# 22R4, PCGS# 3924

3273 **1914/3 FS-101 MS63 ANACS.** The crossbar of a 3 is faintly apparent near the peak of the 4. Toned in pastel olive and rose shades. From late state dies with an orange-peel texture on the Indian's neck and the field near the profile. Due to the age of the small holder, designated with the obsolete FS-014.87 notation. PCGS# 147844

3274 **1914-S MS65 PCGS.** The 1914-S Buffalo nickel is an elusive issue in grades above the MS65 level. This impressive Gem exhibits sharply detailed design elements and vibrant mint luster throughout, under delicate shades of pale gold toning. NGC ID# 22R6, PCGS# 3926

1915-S Nickel, MS65
Scarce, Low-Mintage Issue

3275 **1915-S MS65 NGC.** Seldom available any finer, this Gem example shows a stronger strike than most representatives of this San Francisco date. Just over 1.5 million pieces were struck — fewer coins than even the more highly regarded 1921-S nickel. The fields display satin-smooth luster and pleasing iridescence with golden accents. The bold strike is especially strong on the bison and central hair detail, with only a touch of weakness at LIBERTY. NGC ID# 22R9, PCGS# 3929

3276 **1916-D MS65 PCGS.** Subtle gold and pink tints visit each side of this luminous Gem. A well-defined example with few superiors; PCGS has graded only 17 numerically finer examples (10/14).
Ex: Baltimore Signature (Heritage, 3/2009), lot 612. NGC ID# 22RB, PCGS# 3932

3277 **1916-D MS65 PCGS.** The 1916-D Buffalo nickel is scarce at the MS65 level, and finer coins are condition rarities. This attractive Gem exhibits sharply detailed design elements and vibrant mint luster throughout. PCGS has graded 17 numerically finer examples (10/14). NGC ID# 22RB, PCGS# 3932

3278 **1916-D MS65 PCGS. CAC.** Sharply detailed in most areas, with just the slightest touch of softness on the bison's shoulder, this delightful Gem offers satiny mint luster and hints of pale jade toning. PCGS has graded 17 numerically finer examples (10/14). NGC ID# 22RB, PCGS# 3932

1916-D Nickel, MS65+
Strong in All Areas, High-End Quality

3279 **1916-D MS65+ PCGS. CAC.** The 1916-D is all too often found weakly struck. This piece, however, is strongly detailed throughout with almost complete braid definition and full fur on the bison's head. The bright, satiny surfaces show just the slightest hint of pastel coloration and there are no mentionable marks. Truly a high-end coin. NGC ID# 22RB, PCGS# 3932

1916-S Buffalo Nickel, MS66
Superior Strike and Eye Appeal

3280 **1916-S MS66 NGC.** Warm golden-green toning embraces the clean, unmarked surfaces of this lustrous Premium Gem from San Francisco. Moderate die clash marks are noted on the obverse, most noticeably beneath the Indian's chin and lower hair feather. The nearly full strike definition is unusual for any business strike Buffalo nickel. Census: 14 in 66, 1 finer (10/14). NGC ID# 22RC, PCGS# 3933

3281 **1917-D MS65 PCGS.** Although the 1917-D is not quite as elusive in Gem condition as some of the later-series S-mint condition rarities, it is seldom seen finer than MS65; PCGS has certified only 19 examples numerically finer, and NGC eight (10/14). This example boasts quicksilver surfaces that are largely gold-tinged silver, save for an interesting swath of ice-blue down the buffalo's midsection. A well-struck and thoroughly delightful coin.
Ex: Long Beach Signature (Heritage, 9/2008), lot 740; Baltimore Signature (Heritage, 3/2009), lot 616. NGC ID# 22RE, PCGS# 3935

1917-S Nickel, Sharp MS65
Lightly Toned

3282 1917-S MS65 PCGS. The 1917-S is among the scarcer Buffalo nickel issues in the series in all Mint State grades, and Gems are especially difficult to locate. Striking deficiencies both at the margins and through the centers tend to preclude the typical Uncirculated survivor from surpassing the MS64 grade level. This solid Gem example is lightly toned and boasts uncommon sharpness in most areas, including the Indian's braid, the bison's horn and tail, and all peripheral lettering. Population: 90 in 65 (3 in 65+), 25 finer (10/14).
Ex: Heritage Signature (11/2003), lot 5814; Central States Signature (Heritage, 4/2006), lot 1052; FUN Signature (Heritage, 1/2007), lot 2265. NGC ID# 22RF, PCGS# 3936

3283 1918 MS65 NGC. Surprisingly, the 1918 Buffalo nickel is nearly as difficult to locate with a sharp strike as are many branch mint issues of the period. Pieces sharp and well-preserved enough to qualify for Gem status are only infrequently seen, and finer coins are scarce. This example is above-average in that regard, with only slight striking weakness on the centrals hair details. Blended olive-gold, turquoise, and pale lavender hues blanket each side, adding to the visual appeal. NGC ID# 22RG, PCGS# 3937

3284 1918 MS65 PCGS. This spectacular Gem exhibits well-detailed design elements with just a touch of the usual softness on the hair above the braid. The lustrous surfaces are blanketed in delicate shades of pale gold and ice-blue toning, with outstanding eye appeal. NGC ID# 22RG, PCGS# 3937

3285 1920-S MS63 PCGS. This attractive Select specimen exhibits well-detailed design elements, with just a touch of softness on the bison's shoulder, and satiny mint luster under shades of greenish-gold, ice-blue, and silver-gray toning. NGC ID# 22RS, PCGS# 3946

3286 1921 MS66 PCGS. A single trivial reverse mark prevents a higher grade to this impressive Premium Gem. Both sides are brilliant gray with delicate champagne toning. A powerful strike imparts bold design motifs. PCGS has only certified 23 finer examples (10/14). NGC ID# 22RT, PCGS# 3947

3287 1921 MS66 PCGS. Lovely quicksilver luster and solid definition are the prime attributes of this predominantly nickel-gray example. Excellent preservation makes this a coin that should appeal to the date collector.
Ex: FUN Signature (Heritage, 1/2008), lot 770. NGC ID# 22RT, PCGS# 3947

3288 1923 MS66 PCGS. The satiny, blemish-free surfaces display faint touches of die rust, under low magnification. Both sides are boldly struck save for typical weakness on the center of the obverse and the bison's hair. This Philadelphia issue is a common date, but Premium Gem and finer examples are scarce, and just 14 coins are rated higher by PCGS (10/14). NGC ID# 22RV, PCGS# 3949

3289 1923 MS66 PCGS. CAC. Sharply struck and well defined on the Indian's hair braid and knot. The lustrous surfaces exhibit pale champagne-gray, steel-blue, and antique-gold toning. A high-mintage common date in lower grades that becomes scarce at the Premium Gem level or finer. NGC ID# 22RV, PCGS# 3949

3290 1924 MS66 PCGS. The soft, swirling luster is lively beneath elegant champagne-gold shadings. A well-defined Premium Gem representative of this Roaring Twenties issue, carefully preserved and immensely appealing. Population: 98 in 66 (2 in 66+), 6 finer (10/14).
Ex: Central States Signature (Heritage, 4/2008), lot 459. NGC ID# 22RX, PCGS# 3951

3291 1924-D MS64 PCGS. Hints of ice-blue, lavender, and pale gold toning accent the well-preserved lustrous surfaces of this attractive Choice example. The design elements are well-detailed and eye appeal is quite strong. NGC ID# 22RY, PCGS# 3952

1924-D Buffalo Nickel, MS65
Seldom Available Any Finer

3292 1924-D MS65 PCGS. CAC. The name of the game is "strike" for this Denver issue, although most examples swing and miss. Perhaps fresh dies or a slightly thick planchet help this example deliver bold details on most of the motifs. Soft luster highlights iridescent hues over the predominant bronze-bold patina. The central strike is particularly bold for the issue. Just five coins are certified numerically finer by PCGS and NGC combined (10/14). NGC ID# 22RY, PCGS# 3952

1925-S Nickel, MS64
Thick Mint Luster

3293 1925-S MS64 PCGS. The 1925-S is one of the many mintmarked strike rarities from the 1920s with most examples seen weak on the bison's head as well as around the margins. The central devices show some of the expected softness on this piece, but the margins are particularly sharp as is the mintmark. The surfaces are remarkably smooth and lustrous beneath a light, even layer of gray-rose toning. NGC ID# 22S4, PCGS# 3956

1926 Nickel, MS67
Delicate, Silky Luster

3294 **1926 MS67 PCGS.** Shimmering, frosty luster illuminates delicate sky-blue and pale lavender toning on each side of this carefully preserved example. Slight striking weakness is present on the hair above the Indian's braid, though this is hardly noticed in comparison to the glowing patina. The 1926 nickel is readily available through the MS66 grade level, but it becomes genuinely rare in Superb Gem condition. Population: 36 in 67 (1 in 67+), 0 finer (10/14). NGC ID# 22S5, PCGS# 3957

1926-D Nickel
Richly Toned, Well-Struck Gem

3295 **1926-D MS65 NGC.** The 1926-D Buffalo nickel stands out in the series, usually for the wrong reasons as one of the most notable strike rarities. This piece boasts a wonderful strike for the issue, however, with a split tail, appropriately shaggy ruminant, and sharp details on the obverse. Both sides feature a thick layer of iridescent patina, largely golden-pink, but considerable luster shines forth nonetheless. Census: 31 in 65, 12 finer (10/14). NGC ID# 22S6, PCGS# 3958

1926-D Nickel, MS65
Lightly Toned, Above-Average Strike

3296 **1926-D MS65 PCGS.** Long recognized as a strike rarity in the series, this particular coin displays above-average definition, especially on the reverse. The obverse is just a bit soft on the Indian's braid. Mint luster is not a problem for this issue, and this piece is softly frosted with an overlay of light rose and lilac patina. NGC ID# 22S6, PCGS# 3958

3297 **1926-S AU50 PCGS.** With the lowest business strike mintage in the series, the 1926-S Buffalo nickel is an undisputed key date. This piece shows even, light khaki-gray toning with a couple of faint reddish-brown streaks noted on the reverse. A satiny, evenly worn representative that is virtually abrasion-free. NGC ID# 22S7, PCGS# 3959

1928-D Nickel, MS66
Tied for Finest at PCGS

3298 **1928-D MS66 PCGS. CAC.** Readily available in lower grades, the 1928-D nickel suddenly becomes rare in Premium Gem condition, and is virtually unknown finer. Glowing golden toning complements nearly undisturbed, satiny luster on this eye-appealing example. Above-average definition is seen overall, with only slight softness detectable on the bison's shoulder and the top of the Indian's braid. Population: 49 in 66, 0 finer (10/14). NGC ID# 22SC, PCGS# 3964

3299 **1930-S MS66 PCGS. CAC.** The 1930-S is a lower mintage and conditionally scarce branch mint issue. The present coruscating olive-gold representative is well struck except for the hair above the braid. Pristine aside from a trace of peripheral carbon on the reverse. Housed in a green label holder. NGC ID# 22SJ, PCGS# 3970

3300 **1931-S MS66 PCGS. CAC.** Boldly struck overall with softness noted only on the Indian's hair braid knot and the hair detail just above it. A vibrantly lustrous nickel with carefully preserved, blemish-free surfaces. NGC ID# 22SK, PCGS# 3971

3301 **1935 MS67 PCGS.** This piece is deeply satiny with pale lavender and sky-blue toning over each side. Some slight striking deficiency is noted on the hair immediately above the Indian's braid, though the strike is otherwise pleasing and the overall eye appeal is outstanding. PCGS has encapsulated only a single numerically finer representative (10/14).
Ex: FUN Signature (Heritage, 1/2007), lot 2355. NGC ID# 22SN, PCGS# 3974

3302 **1935 MS67 PCGS.** More than 58 million Buffalo nickels were struck at the Philadelphia Mint in 1935 and this sharply detailed Superb Gem is one of the finest survivors. The impeccably preserved surfaces radiate vibrant mint luster, under delicate hints of ice-blue and pale gold toning. PCGS has graded one numerically finer example (10/14). NGC ID# 22SN, PCGS# 3974

3303 **1937-D Three-Legged, FS-901, AU58 NGC.** The streaky dove-gray and almond-gold surfaces display lightly worn devices and a modicum of blemishes. A small area of minor granularity is noted in the Indian's hair. A famous and popular lapped die variety. PCGS# 38475

3304 **1937-D Three-Legged, FS-901, MS62 PCGS.** A lustrous tan-brown and dove-gray representative of the perennial collector favorite. Marks are virtually absent, but minor retained horizontal laminations (as made) are noted near the front hoof and above the bison's hump. PCGS# 38475

PROOF BUFFALO NICKELS

3305 **1936 Type Two — Brilliant Finish PR66 NGC.** The Mint resumed proof coinage in 1936 and the Brilliant Buffalo nickel proofs were struck later in the year, after the satin finish on earlier issues proved unpopular. This spectacular Premium Gem displays sharply detailed design elements and deeply reflective surfaces with no mentionable distractions. NGC ID# 278Y, PCGS# 3995

3306 **1937 PR66 PCGS.** A lovely piece struck with exacting precision on all of the design elements, as expected for a proof specimen. This Premium Gem is essentially brilliant, although touches of god color can be discerned near the borders as the coin rotates beneath a lamp. A well-preserved example with clean surfaces and considerable visual appeal. NGC ID# 278Z, PCGS# 3996

3307 **1937 PR67 NGC. CAC.** This would be an ideal type representative for the Buffalo nickel series. From a generous mintage of 5,769 proofs, the surfaces are fully defined and fully brilliant with mirrorlike reflectivity. NGC ID# 278Z, PCGS# 3996

JEFFERSON NICKELS

1942-D Nickel, MS62 Five Full Steps
D Over Horizontal D Variety

3308 **1942-D D Over Horizontal D, FS-501, MS62 Five Full Steps NGC.** Of all the major Jefferson nickel varieties, 1942-D/ Horizontal D is the rarest in Mint State grades. The mintmark was errantly entered into the die at a 90 degree rotation and then corrected, creating this unusual *Guide Book* curiosity. Satiny luster yields to pale lavender-gold toning on each side, while the strike is bold throughout. The surfaces are unusually well-preserved for the grade level, showing no obtrusive abrasions. PCGS# 38496

1943/2 Nickel, MS66 Full Steps
FS-101, *Guide Book* variety

3309 **1943/2-P Doubled Die Obverse, FS-101, MS66 Full Steps PCGS.** This popular *Guide Book* variety was created when an outdated 1942 die was rehubbed with the 1943 date. The second hubbing was not seated perfectly, resulting in the die doubling. The diagonal of the underlying 2 is evident within the lower loop of the 3 in the date. This example is sharply struck, with satiny luster and faint iridescent toning. PCGS# 38500

1943/2-P Nickel, MS66 Full Steps
FS-101, Overdate

3310 **1943/2-P Doubled Die Obverse, FS-101, MS66 Full Steps PCGS. CAC.** The remnants of an underlying 2 are evident within the lower loop of the 3 in the date. This popular *Guide Book* variety also features mild die doubling on all obverse lettering. The present example showcases vibrant, frost-white mint bloom and bold striking definition. The surfaces are free of any noticeable flaws, heightening this Premium Gem's immense visual appeal. PCGS# 38500

3311 **1945-P MS67 Full Steps NGC.** A fully struck Superb Gem example of this brief type, with a large P mintmark placed on the upper reverse field for Philadelphia Mint coins. This example shows crisply struck design motifs and intense mint luster. The bright silver surfaces display a few touches of russet color on the obverse, but both sides are otherwise essentially brilliant. Immaculately preserved and a great example with five full steps clearly evident on Monticello. Census: 4 in 67 (1 in 67 ★) Full Steps, 0 finer (10/14). NGC ID# 22TX, PCGS# 84025

PROOF JEFFERSON NICKELS

3312 **1942 Type One PR68 NGC.** Brilliant and untoned with superb definition and generally flawless surfaces. A transitional proof year that also saw the only production of proof silver nickels. This one is tied for the finest certified. Census: 9 in 68, 0 finer (10/14). NGC ID# 27A3, PCGS# 4179

3313 **1950 PR66 Deep Cameo PCGS.** Considered by many to be the key to the Cameo Jefferson nickel series, this 1950 has remarkably deep mirrors with noticeably contrasting mint frost over the devices. Both sides are draped in rich reddish-aqua patina. Remarkably few examples are known in high grades, nowhere near enough to satisfy collector demand. Population: 8 in 66 (1 in 66+), 8 finer (10/14). NGC ID# 27A5, PCGS# 94182

3314 **1950 PR66 Deep Cameo PCGS.** Razor-sharp definition is evident on all design elements and the deeply mirrored fields contrast profoundly with the frosty devices, creating a stunning cameo effect when this coin is tilted in the light. Population: 8 in 66 (1 in 66+), 8 finer (10/14). NGC ID# 27A5, PCGS# 94182

1954 Nickel, PR69 Ultra Cameo
Tied for the Finest Certified

3315 1954 PR69 Ultra Cameo NGC. Collectors of Ultra or Deep Cameo proof coinage may elect to complete a single series such as Jefferson nickels, a single year such as 1954, or a comprehensive collection. This nearly perfect example is a necessary component of all three collecting interests, and it is tied for the finest that NGC has certified. PCGS has never certified an example at this grade level. Both sides are brilliant and highly lustrous with extraordinary design definition and impressive contrast. Census: 3 in 69, 0 finer (10/14). NGC ID# 27A7, PCGS# 94186

3316 1955 PR69 Ultra Cameo NGC. This is an amazing Superb Gem, equal to the finest that has ever been certified. This piece has incredible field-to-device contrast with brilliant light gray surfaces. Census: 7 in 69, 0 finer (10/14).
Ex: Fort Worth Signature (Heritage, 3/2010), lot 549. NGC ID# 22YF, PCGS# 94187

3317 1956 PR67 Deep Cameo PCGS. A gorgeous proof Jefferson nickel with jet-black highly reflective fields and fully struck silvery-gray devices, producing stark Deep Cameo contrast on both sides. Impeccably preserved with a few tiny grayish specks on Jefferson's collar and jaw that are of little import. Population: 12 in 67, 6 finer (10/14). NGC ID# 22YG, PCGS# 94188

3318 1956 PR68 Ultra Cameo NGC. Stone-gray and pale ice-blue hues blanket the heavily frosted, needle-sharp devices of this deeply contrasted Superb Gem Cameo. The 1956 proof nickel is readily obtainable in most grades, but Ultra Cameo representatives are a distinct exception, being rare at all numeric levels. This piece represents an important opportunity for the Jefferson nickel Registry Set collector. Census: 4 in 68, 3 finer (10/14). NGC ID# 22YG, PCGS# 94188

3319 1959 PR68 Deep Cameo PCGS. The icy devices are exquisitely struck and provide outstanding contrast with the darkly mirrored fields. This piece is flawless aside from a couple of fully retained and nearly imperceptible laminations. There is no shortage of proof 1959 nickels without cameo contrast, but specimens such as this piece with a stunning white-on-black appearance are extremely rare. Population: 16 in 68, 1 finer (10/14). NGC ID# 27A9, PCGS# 94191

3320 1961 PR69 Deep Cameo PCGS. Quality reflectivity with just a hint of golden color. The frost over the devices does not have the granular quality sometimes associated with the best examples, but the Deep Cameo qualities of this piece are plain. A tiny imperfection to the left of Jefferson's nose contributes to the grade. Population: 13 in 69, 0 finer (10/14). NGC ID# 22YK, PCGS# 94193

3321 1971 No S PR68 Cameo PCGS. An important No S issue, mentioned in Scott Schechter and Jeff Garrett's *100 Greatest U.S. Modern Coins*, as entry number 30. This Superb example displays pinpoint-perfect striking definition and stark contrast between the richly frosted devices and the glassy, jet-black fields. The surfaces are pristine. Population: 66 in 68, 12 finer (10/14). NGC ID# 22YN, PCGS# 84204

BUST HALF DIMES

3322 1829 V-7, LM-1, R.2, MS64 NGC. Ocean-blue and autumn-gold grace this coruscating and unmarked Choice Capped Bust type coin. The strike is bold at the borders and incomplete at the centers. The D in UNITED is repunched. PCGS# 38612

3323 1830 V-3, LM-4.2, R.2, MS64 PCGS. Dappled mahogany-brown and aquamarine toning visits both sides, but is more prominent on the obverse. Lustrous, well struck, and unmarked. LM-4.2 is distinguished from LM-4.1 by a die chip in the left third of the upper loop of the second S in STATES. PCGS# 38642

1830 Half Dime, Satiny MS66
V-1, LM-14, Ex: Green-Newman

3324 1830 V-1, LM-14, R.3, MS66 NGC. Ex: "Col." E.H.R. Green, Eric P. Newman. Rich steel-gray fields and motifs are accompanied by walnut-brown and aquamarine margins. A lens fails to locate any perceptible abrasions. A precisely struck and satiny Premium Gem with a formidable pedigree. As of (6/14), NGC has certified seven 1830 half dimes as LM-14, with the present piece finest by two grades. PCGS# 38653

1835 V-4, LM-7 Half Dime, MS65
Elusive Die Pair; Large Date, Large 5C

3325 1835 Large Date, Large 5C, V-4, LM-7, R.3, MS65 PCGS. CAC. The LM-7 variety is quickly identified by the position of the scroll beneath the reverse legend, where it starts beneath the E of UNITED and ends beneath the left upright of M in AMERICA. Gem or finer examples are scarce both for the issue and the die pair. This lustrous example displays a thin circle of amber-gold at the rims surrounding brilliant, frost-white central motifs. The strike is extremely bold. A subtle area of die clash in front of Liberty's portrait appears as crescent of mint luster. A small area of deep toning sits near the rim at TE of UNITED. Population (all Large Date, Large 5C varieties): 35 in 65, 25 in 66, none finer (10/14). PCGS# 38711

SEATED HALF DIMES

1837 No Stars, Large Date Half Dime, MS66
An Excellent Type Coin

3326 **1837 No Stars, Large Date (Curl Top 1) MS66 PCGS.** An outstanding Premium Gem of the introductory Seated half dime issue, and an excellent choice for a high-grade type collection. Golden-brown and stone-gray blend across unabraded and lustrous surfaces. Well-struck except on the left-side dentils. Several interesting die cracks traverse the obverse. Population: 27 in 66, 2 finer (10/14). NGC ID# 232M, PCGS# 4311

1837 No Stars Half Dime, MS65+
Small Date Variant

3327 **1837 No Stars, Small Date (Flat Top 1) MS65+ NGC. CAC.** The scarcer of the two varieties, the Small Date 1837 Seated half dime is easily recognized by the flat upper flag of the 1 in the date. As a date, the 1837 is scarce in Gem condition and is seldom seen finer. The current piece is the sole Plus-graded Gem certified by NGC (10/14), displaying frosty cartwheel luster and boldly struck design elements. The obverse shows a hint of amber-gold color, though the reverse exhibits more vivid hues of the same, deepening toward the borders. A high-end, undeniably original No Stars type representative. NGC ID# 232M, PCGS# 4312

3328 **1838 Small Stars MS64 PCGS.** Both sides of this well-detailed Choice example exhibit dramatic clash marks but the lustrous, brilliant surfaces show only a thin horizontal obverse mark at 3 o'clock. The short-lived Stars, No Drapery subtype. Population: 7 in 64, 2 finer (10/14). NGC ID# 232R, PCGS# 4318

3329 **1857 MS66+ PCGS.** Shades of violet, silver-gray, golden-brown, and amber toning enhance the well-preserved surfaces of this high-end Premium Gem. The design elements are well-detailed and vibrant mint luster shines through the patina. Population: 31 in 66 (6 in 66+), 3 finer (10/14). NGC ID# 233S, PCGS# 4365

1860 Half Dime, MS67
Lustrous and Attractively Toned

3330 **1860 MS67 PCGS. CAC.** The year 1860 saw the production of 798,000 half dimes, and the issue often serves as a first-year type because of the addition of the obverse legend. This gorgeous Superb Gem features bright mint luster that shines through mostly violet-gray toning, with areas of peripheral ice-blue and sea-green color. Sharply struck and attractive. Population: 40 in 67, 4 finer (10/14). NGC ID# 2347, PCGS# 4377

3331 **1861/0 FS-301 MS65 PCGS.** Dove-gray motifs are framed by rich fire-red, apple-green, and tan-brown toning that deepens near the margins. Lustrous and nicely struck with minor obverse field grazes. Population: 2 in 65, 9 finer (10/14). PCGS# 145479

1861/0 Half Dime, MS66
High-End Overdate Example

3332 **1861/0 FS-301 MS66 PCGS. CAC.** This *Guide Book* variety exhibits the remnant of an underlying 0 to the lower-left of the second 1 in the date. Light golden patina visits both sides of this lustrous Premium Gem example. Only a few cereal grains on the upper-left wreath lack a full impression. Struck from clashed dies. Housed in a green label holder. Population: 4 in 66 (1 in 66+), 3 finer (10/14). PCGS# 145479

3333 **1871 MS66 PCGS.** A plentiful date in lower grades, the 1871 half dime becomes scarce in MS66 and is prohibitively rare any finer. This piece exhibits satiny luster amid peripheral pine-green and olive toning, with only a few minute ticks on the obverse device limiting the grade. The upper-left portion of the wreath is not fully defined, though the strike is otherwise pleasing. Population: 33 in 66 (5 in 66+), 1 finer (10/14). NGC ID# 234V, PCGS# 4398

PROOF SEATED HALF DIMES

3334 **1859 PR64 PCGS.** The ephemeral obverse subtype with hollow-centered stars and a different implementation of Liberty, credited to Anthony C. Paquet. The date is repunched. Fully struck and nicely mirrored with rich autumn-brown, ruby-red, and powder-blue patina. NGC ID# 235P, PCGS# 4438

3335 **1860 PR65 Cameo PCGS.** A delightful Gem Cameo proof, this example exhibits boldly defined and frosty devices with mirrored fields beneath delicate iridescent toning. This issue represents a new design type for the Seated half dime and dime, having the legend moved to the obverse. Population: 2 in 65, 7 finer (10/14). *Ex: T.W. Brown Collection (Heritage, 9/2010), lot 5044.* PCGS# 84443

1871 Half Dime, PR66 Cameo
Strong Contrast on Each Side

3336 **1871 PR66 Cameo PCGS. CAC.** Of the 960 proofs struck in 1871 of this unusual denomination, few are known in high grade and with such pronounced mint frost on the devices. The combination of each of these yields a starkly contrasted cameo proof. Most of each side is brilliant with just a hint of pale golden at the margins. Fully struck. Population: 6 in 66 (2 in 66+), 3 finer (10/14). PCGS# 84454

3337 **1872 PR65 PCGS.** An impressive Gem from a proof mintage of 950 pieces, this delightful specimen offers sharply detailed design elements and deeply mirrored fields under shades of champagne-gold and lavender-blue toning. Population: 20 in 65, 10 finer (10/14). NGC ID# 2369, PCGS# 4455

EARLY DIMES

3338 **1805 4 Berries, JR-2, R.2 — Reverse Scratched — NGC Details. XF.** Most 1805 dimes are from the JR-2 die variety, with four berries in the olive branch on the reverse. The only other variety has five berries. This dove-gray piece was obviously circulated before being saved by some early American numismatist, and it shows obvious wear along with slight rim damage in several locations. Most of the original design details remain evident. Several faint scratches are noted near the lower left and right peripheries.

3339 **1807 JR-1, R.2, Fine 12 PCGS.** The sole marriage for the final Draped Bust date. An earlier die state than usual, with clash marks limited to the field directly under Liberty's jaw. A circulated but problem-free representative with cream-gray fields and devices. Protected areas displays charcoal toning. PCGS# 38770

BUST DIMES

3340 **1824/2 JR-1, R.3, AU58 NGC.** This unmarked Borderline Uncirculated dime is mostly white despite peripheral dusky gray toning. Usual for the variety, the strike is somewhat soft at the centers, but border elements are crisp. PCGS# 38805

3341 **1836 JR-1, R.3, MS63 NGC.** A stone-gray representative with freckles of autumn-brown and sea-green near the rims. Crisply struck and unmarked with pleasing surfaces. The scarce JR-1 is attributed by the 0 in 10 C, which leans left. PCGS# 38888

SEATED DIMES

1838 Small Stars Dime, MS65
Attractively Toned and Lustrous

3342 **1838 Small Stars, Doubled Die Reverse, FS-801, MS65 NGC.** This is the late die state Small Stars variety, with prominent peripheral die cracks on each side. The reverse shows bold die doubling, most easily detected on the O and D in ONE DIME, as well as on the lower wreath leaves and bow. The relief elements are boldly impressed, and the surfaces show delicately preserved, frosty luster. Splashes of teal, gold, and pale lavender toning blanket each side, attesting to the originality of this immensely appealing No Drapery dime. Census: 9 in 65, 4 finer (10/14). NGC ID# 2TVT, PCGS# 145483

3343 **1838 No Drapery, Large Stars MS65 NGC.** A sharply detailed Gem representative of this popular type issue, with well-preserved lustrous surfaces under attractive shades of golden-brown and lavender toning. Census: 58 in 65 (2 in 65+), 42 finer (10/14). NGC ID# 237U, PCGS# 4568

1838 No Drapery Dime, MS65
Large Stars Variant

3344 **1838 No Drapery, Large Stars MS65 PCGS. CAC. Fortin-114, R.4.** Later uses of this obverse show die cracks through the lower-right base and down from the rim near star 7. This variety is uncracked on either side, though the reverse shows light die erosion above UNITED. Traces of light golden toning accent frosty, delicately preserved surfaces, while the strike is bold and the eye appeal is equally strong. As a date, the 1838 Large Stars dime is seldom available this well-preserved, and numerically finer examples are scarce, with only 18 such pieces certified by PCGS (11/14). NGC ID# 237U, PCGS# 4568

1839 No Drapery Dime, Satiny MS66+
Ex: Green, Newman

3345 **1839 No Drapery MS66+ NGC. CAC.** Ex: "Col." E.H.R. Green, Eric P. Newman Collection. Of the first four Philadelphia Seated dime dates, the 1839 is the only one not separated into multiple *Guide Book* varieties, leading many collectors to underrate the issue. This MS66+ example with its well-defined devices and satiny luster under pink, gold, and blue patina is a coin that rewards the numismatist who takes the time to inspect it closely. Census: 18 in 66 (1 in 66+), 21 finer (10/14). NGC ID# 237X, PCGS# 4571

1858-S Dime, AU55
Elusive in All Grades

3346 **1858-S AU55 PCGS. Fortin-103, R.4.** A mintage of only 60,000 coins and a proportionately low survival rate makes the 1858-S Seated dime an elusive semikey date in the series. The issue is scarce in all grades, and becomes rare at the AU level; Mint State pieces are exceedingly so. This Choice AU representative displays a bold strike with only slight friction over the high points of the design. Splashes of olive-gray toning accent luminous pewter-gray surfaces, leaving this piece with pleasing eye appeal. Population: 5 in 55, 9 finer (10/14). NGC ID# 2393, PCGS# 4618

1867 Dime, MS64 Prooflike
Scarce Semikey Issue

3347 **1867 MS64 Prooflike NGC. Fortin-102, R.5.** With a mintage of just 6,000 coins, the 1867 Seated dime is a scarce semikey issue, and is genuinely rare in Choice or finer condition. This near-Gem Prooflike example is boldly struck with strong field-motif contrast. Faint, parallel die striations in the fields do not inhibit the mirroring, while a thin veil of light golden toning adds a degree of warmth to the surfaces. NGC has certified only four Prooflike examples in all grades, with just one in MS64 and one numerically finer (10/14). NGC ID# 239U, PCGS# 4645

3348 **1871-CC — Scratch — PCGS Genuine. XF Details. Fortin-101.** Only one die pair is known for this key Carson City issue, with a mintage of only 20,100 coins. This lightly circulated example is well-detailed, with pale battleship-gray patina over each side. Some shallow, unobtrusive pinscratches in the fields preclude a numeric grade from PCGS. NGC ID# 23A5, PCGS# 4654

3349 **1872-CC — Repaired — PCGS Genuine. AU Details. Fortin-101.** The right obverse field has been repaired and smoothed, but is not outwardly obvious. The devices are well-detailed, while small specks of deep gunmetal-blue color are scattered over pale battleship-gray toning on each side. This Carson City issue is an important key date in the Seated dime series. NGC ID# 23A8, PCGS# 4657

1873-CC Arrows Dime, Original Good 6

3350 **1873-CC Arrows Good 6 NGC.** The 1873-CC is one of the better known series keys, not only among CC dimes but the series in general. Only 18,791 pieces were struck, and few survived in high grades. In fact, few survived unimpaired. This is an original piece with charcoal colored fields that establish a deep background for the pinkish tinged devices. A couple of shallow marks in the center of the reverse are the only defects worthy of mention. NGC ID# 23BH, PCGS# 4666

3351 **1875-CC Mintmark Below Bow MS64 PCGS. Fortin-106, R.3.** This variety is somewhat scarcer overall than its Mintmark Above Bow counterpart. PCGS has encapsulated only 18 examples in this grade, with just 11 numerically finer (10/14). This Choice example displays a blush of light champagne toning over each side, with minimal abrasions and frosty luster. Some minor striking weakness is seen on the upper-left portion of the wreath and the corresponding part of the obverse, as usual, though the motifs are otherwise sharp. Housed in an old green label holder. NGC ID# 23AD, PCGS# 4674

3352 **1877 MS66 NGC.** Type Two Reverse. This well-detailed Premium Gem exhibits just a touch of softness on Liberty's head and the ribbon bow. The pristine surfaces radiate vibrant mint luster under shades of champagne-gold and cerulean-blue patina. Census: 24 in 66 (1 in 66+, 1 in 66 ★), 8 finer (11/14). NGC ID# 23AL, PCGS# 4682

1877-CC Dime, Frosty MS66
Conditionally Scarce

3353 1877-CC MS66 PCGS. Fortin-105, R.3. The dies were nearing their retirement when this variety was struck; the obverse shows bold, circumnavigating die cracks and substantial die rust, while the reverse exhibits considerable erosion around the border denticles. A blush of light golden toning accents frosty, carefully preserved surfaces, giving this high-end Carson City dime excellent visual appeal. Some of the finer details, particularly on the obverse, are softened as a result of the late die state. Population: 50 in 66 (5 in 66+), 5 finer (10/14). NGC ID# 23AM, PCGS# 4683

1882 Seated Dime, MS67
None Finer at PCGS

3354 1882 MS67 PCGS. CAC. Attractive shades of bluish-gray and champagne-gold patina blanket the well-preserved surfaces of this impressive Superb Gem. The design elements are sharply detailed and vibrant mint luster shines through the toning. Eye appeal is terrific. Population: 20 in 67, 0 finer (10/14). NGC ID# 23AV, PCGS# 4690

1885 Seated Dime, MS67+
Conditionally Rare, Beautifully Toned

3355 1885 MS67+ NGC. CAC. Fortin-111, R.4. This beautifully toned 1885 dime ranks as the only Plus-graded MS67 example at NGC, with only one numerically finer (10/14). Both sides display concentric bands of ocean-blue, violet, mint-green, and sun-gold, with carefully preserved surfaces and unusually sharp design definition for the issue. Vibrant, frosty luster is observed when rotated beneath a light. NGC ID# 23AZ, PCGS# 4694

1886 Seated Dime, MS67
Tied for Finest Certified

3356 1886 MS67 PCGS Secure. CAC. This amazing Superb Gem has a delicate die crack at the top of the obverse. Both sides have frosty silver luster beneath medium golden-tan toning, and peripheral light blue and bright gold accents. Strongly and evenly struck throughout. Population: 8 in 67 (1 in 67+), 0 finer (10/14). NGC ID# 23B3, PCGS# 4696

3357 1887 MS67 NGC. Fortin-115, R.4. Boldly clashed dies, as is diagnostic of this variety. As a date, the 1887 dime is readily available in grades through MS66, but it becomes genuinely rare at the Superb Gem level. This piece is beautifully preserved with traces of light golden color over vibrant, frosty luster. A sharp strike completes the immense visual appeal. Census: 4 in 67, 2 finer (10/14). NGC ID# 23B5, PCGS# 4698

PROOF SEATED DIMES

1863 Dime, PR66 Cameo
Deeply Toned Throughout

3358 1863 PR66 Cameo PCGS. Fortin-101, R.4. This is the only die pair for 1863 Philadelphia dime coinage, as it was also employed for the short 18,000-coin business strike production of that year. This high-end proof example shows deep teal and violet toning in the mirrored fields, while the devices show lighter hues of the same with the occasional golden accent. The strike is bold, and only a few faint hairlines, well-hidden by the rich patina, limit the numeric grade. Population: 5 in 66 (1 in 66+), 1 finer (10/14). PCGS# 84756

1865 Dime, Toned PR66
Ideal for Date Representation

3359 **1865 PR66 PCGS. Fortin-101, R.5.** The Mint struck just 500 proof dimes in 1865, though even with such a low mintage the proof variant is slightly more available for date purposes than its business strike counterpart, which had a proportionately paltry mintage of only 10,000 coins. The present coin shows deeply reflective fields with beautiful hues of turquoise, blue, violet, and amber-gold. A bold strike completes the eye appeal. Population: 6 in 66, 2 finer (10/14). NGC ID# 23CN, PCGS# 4758

1865 Dime, PR65+ Cameo
Boldly Struck and Contrasted

3360 **1865 PR65+ Cameo NGC. Fortin-102, R.4.** This obverse die exhibits moderate rust in the recesses of the central device, though the frosty luster is not inhibited, and the field-motif contrast of this high-end Gem proof is unmistakable. The strike is needle-sharp, and both sides show a pale golden hue. The 1865 proof Seated dime is rare in all grades with a Cameo designation. Census: 5 in 65 (1 in 65+), 5 finer (11/14). PCGS# 84758

3361 **1867 PR65 Cameo NGC. Fortin-103, R.5.** The date numerals are repunched on this variety, the sole proof die marriage for the year. Although 625 examples were struck, Cameo survivors are scarce in any grade. This is a boldly contrasted, gold-tinted Gem example with sharply struck motifs. Some faint die polishing striations in the reverse fields should not be confused with hairlines. Census: 7 in 65, 8 finer (10/14). PCGS# 84760

3362 **1868 PR65 PCGS.** This proof Seated dime issue saw a small mintage of 600 pieces, and survivors are scarce at grade levels any finer than PR64. This sharply struck Gem exhibits dramatic, appealing turquoise-blue, rose, and champagne-gray toning. The surfaces are well-preserved and free of distractions. Population: 19 in 65 (1 in 65+), 5 finer (10/14). NGC ID# 23CS, PCGS# 4761

3363 **1870 PR66 NGC.** This Seated dime issue had a proof mintage of 1,000 pieces, but examples are rare at the current Premium Gem grade level. Deep hues of copper-rose, sea-green, and grayish-green patina adorn the clean, contact-free surfaces. Census: 14 in 66 (2 in 66 ★, 1 in 66+★), 2 finer (10/14). NGC ID# 23CU, PCGS# 4763

1871 Dime, PR67
Vividly Toned, Strong Mirrors

3364 **1871 PR67 NGC. Fortin-102.** The most common of three proof die pairs that were required to produce a small mintage of just 960 pieces, outnumbering the other two varieties combined. Vivid shades of orange, magenta, gold, and blue play across the mirrored surfaces in various combinations on both sides of the coin. A Superb Gem, with no obvious flaws and a bold strike. Census: 4 in 67 (1 in 67+), 1 finer (10/14). NGC ID# 23CV, PCGS# 4764

3365 **1877 PR66 NGC. CAC. Fortin-101.** Type Two Reverse. The E in DIME is die doubled. A peripheral band of ocean-blue toning frames the lightly toned centers. The portrait and much of the wreath exhibit cameo contrast. Housed in a prior generation holder. NGC ID# 23D2, PCGS# 4774

3366 **1880 PR65 PCGS.** Attractive shades of champagne-gold and cerulean-blue toning blanket the well-preserved surfaces of this sharply detailed Gem. The fields are brightly reflective under the patina. Population: 44 in 65, 45 finer (10/14). NGC ID# 23D5, PCGS# 4777

1885 Seated Dime, PR67 Cameo
Extraordinary Quality and Eye Appeal

3367 **1885 PR67 Cameo NGC. Fortin-101, R.3.** Extraordinary contrast meets the eye on this impressive Superb Gem Cameo proof, with gorgeous silver surfaces that show hints of peripheral champagne toning. Deeply mirrored fields provide a wonderful back drop for the intensely frosted devices. Census: 22 in 67 (1 in 67+, 1 in 67 ★), 7 finer (10/14). PCGS# 84782

1885 Seated Dime, PR67 Cameo
An All-Brilliant Type Coin

3368 **1885 PR67 Cameo PCGS.** This Superb Gem proof dime would make a wonderful type coin for some lucky collector. The surfaces are completely brilliant on each side. The devices display significant mint frost which contrast markedly against the deep mirroring seen in the fields. Population: 13 in 67 (1 in 67+), 2 finer (10/14). PCGS# 84782

1885 Dime, PR66 Ultra Cameo
Exceedingly Rare This Well-Contrasted

3369 **1885 PR66 Ultra Cameo NGC. Fortin-101, R.3.** Only one proof die pair is known for the 1885 issue, easily identified by light repunching on the upper flag of the 1 in the date and a couple heavy die lines in the upper wreath leaves. This Premium Gem is one of only five Ultra Cameos certified by NGC, with three in this grade and two numerically finer (10/14). The devices are sharply impressed, albeit showing light die rust, while the fields display full mirroring. A faint light golden tint precludes full brilliance. PCGS# 94782

1886 Seated Liberty Dime, PR67
Dramatically Toned Reflective Fields

3370 **1886 PR67 NGC. Fortin Unlisted.** The date position does not match one of the known proof die pairs, perhaps indicating a proof die later used for business strikes, or a new variety. Vivid orange and blue toning covers the obverse, while the reverse displays lavender, blue, and lemon-gold hues. Boldly struck, but not quite full at Liberty's head, and virtually mark-free. Scarce as a Superb Gem proof, with just one coin graded numerically higher at either service. NGC Census: 20 in 67, 1 finer (10/14). NGC ID# 23DB, PCGS# 4783

3371 **1890 PR65 PCGS. Fortin-101a, R.4.** The 1890 proof dime, with a limited mintage of just 590 pieces, is seldom available in high grades. This example is a refreshingly well-preserved, original specimen, with blended multicolor toning throughout the mirrored fields and bold, satiny devices. Population: 22 in 65, 22 finer (10/14). NGC ID# 23DF, PCGS# 4787

BARBER DIMES

3372 **1895-O — Cleaning — PCGS Genuine. AU Details.** A trace of friction from an old cleaning precludes a Mint State designation for this well-detailed key-date Barber dime. Pale pewter and blue-gray toning covers both sides, overlying subtle remnants of luster. NGC ID# 23DW, PCGS# 4807

1899-S Barber Dime, MS66
Conditionally Rare

3373 **1899-S MS66 PCGS.** Lightly toned in ice-blue and golden-brown hues with radiant luster shining through. The design motifs are strongly defined, especially on Liberty's hair and the lower wreath. Although the issue is plentiful in most grades, Premium Gems such as this are very rare. Population: 13 in 66 (1 in 66+), 3 finer (10/14). NGC ID# 23EB, PCGS# 4820

1902-S Dime, MS65
Ex: Duckor Collection

3374 **1902-S MS65 PCGS.** Ex: Duckor. The Barber dime collection of Dr. and Mrs. Steven L. Duckor is currently ranked #5 all-time on the PCGS Registry Set of the series and was auctioned by Heritage in January 2006. This fully struck Gem exhibits cream, tan, and sky-blue toning. The lustrous surfaces are devoid of contact. An outstanding example from a better date in the series. Population: 6 in 65, 10 finer (10/14).
Ex: Rosemont Central States (Heritage, 4/2008), lot 617. NGC ID# 23EL, PCGS# 4829

1905-O Dime, MS66
Wonderful Patina, Eye Appeal

3375 **1905-O MS66 PCGS. CAC.** Radiant luster shines through a veil of lavender and pale-blue patina with occasional golden-orange accents, accounting for the green label CAC approval sticker. This gorgeous Premium Gem is remarkably detailed, especially for a New Orleans coin, and features amazing surface preservation. Population: 19 in 66, 6 finer (10/14). NGC ID# 23EU, PCGS# 4836

3376 **1906-D MS66 NGC.** Attractive shades of greenish-gold and violet toning enhance the outstanding eye appeal of this sharply detailed Premium Gem. The well-preserved surfaces radiate vibrant mint luster throughout. Census: 6 in 66, 0 finer (10/14). NGC ID# 23EY, PCGS# 4839

1906-O Dime, MS67
Conditionally Rare

3377 1906-O MS67 PCGS. Dappled gold, green, and blue hues enrich the eye appeal of this late-date New Orleans Barber dime. Bold underlying luster forms a cartwheel pattern on the obverse and the peripheral reverse. The 1906-O dime is a condition rarity as a Superb Gem. Population: 7 in 67, 0 finer (10/14). NGC ID# 23EZ, PCGS# 4840

3378 1908-O MS65 PCGS. CAC. A softly lustrous late-date New Orleans dime, smothered in lavender-gray, orange-gold, and olive patina. The strike is above-average, and the surfaces are blemish-free. Population: 25 in 65, 15 finer (10/14).
Ex: FUN Signature (Heritage, 1/2007), lot 2656. NGC ID# 23F9, PCGS# 4848

3379 1910-S MS65 NGC. A better date in Mint State all grades, the 1910-S Barber dime becomes rare in Gem and finer condition. This example displays traces of golden peripheral toning around satiny, untoned centers. No significant abrasions are observed. Census: 7 in 65, 4 finer (10/14). NGC ID# 23FH, PCGS# 4856

1911 Barber Dime, MS67
Splendidly Toned and Preserved

3380 1911 MS67 PCGS. CAC. Registry Set enthusiasts are sure to take note of this beautifully toned Superb Gem. Sky-blue, apricot-orange, and lavender hues intermingle over the obverse and most of the reverse. The latter shows darker shades toward the upper-right margins. Booming luster percolates through the patina and heightens the already strong appeal. Crisply impressed and essentially void of noteworthy marks. Population: 16 in 67 (1 in 67+), 2 finer (10/14). NGC ID# 23FJ, PCGS# 4857

3381 1914-S MS66 PCGS. CAC. This is an impressive, conditionally rare Premium Gem with shimmering luster and only trace amounts of toning on the mostly stone-white surfaces. Few examples of this San Francisco issue have achieved this high grade, and only two Superb Gems are currently known at NGC and PCGS combined. Population: 16 in 66, 1 finer (10/14). NGC ID# 23FV, PCGS# 4867

PROOF BARBER DIMES

3382 1893 PR65 PCGS. This tack-sharp Gem showcases deep cobalt-blue and violet toning over deeply mirrored fields on each side. No contact marks are present, and any grade-limiting hairlines are well-hidden beneath the rich patina. Population: 29 in 65, 39 finer (10/14). NGC ID# 23G4, PCGS# 4877

3383 1894 PR65 Cameo PCGS. CAC. Champagne toning appears on both sides of this Gem. Small splashes of other colors are present as well, primarily on the reverse, among them teal and russet. The coin was sharply struck, creating impressive design details. Strong cameo contrast exists between the frosted motifs and deeply watery fields. Population: 21 in 65 (1 in 65+), 19 finer (10/14). PCGS# 84878

3384 1898 PR65 Cameo PCGS. Ex: Teich Family Collection. Light caramel-gold toning visits this nicely mirrored and well-preserved Gem. The devices are luminous and provide good contrast. Only 735 proofs were coined. Population: 16 in 65, 36 finer (10/14). *Ex: Jim Spaulding White Collection (Stack's, 2/1960), lot 795.* PCGS# 84882

3385 1900 PR65 NGC. Mostly brilliant with highly reflective fields and mildly frosted devices. There are a few light-colored spots on each side, and a lint mark is noted on the reverse, directly above the N in ONE, but there are no significant distractions to report. A conditionally scarce proof example from a low mintage of 912 pieces. NGC ID# 23GD, PCGS# 4884

1901 Dime, PR67
Deeply Mirrored Fields

3386 1901 PR67 NGC. From a proof mintage of 813 coins, this sharp Superb Gem displays deeply mirrored fields, with light frost seen over the obverse portrait. Intermingled blue, violet, and olive-gold hues accent the nearly perfect surfaces, adding to the visual appeal of this high-end representative. Census: 14 in 67 (1 in 67 ★), 2 finer (10/14). NGC ID# 23GE, PCGS# 4885

3387 1905 PR65 NGC. The 5 in the date is repunched. This Gem is one of 727 proof Barber dimes struck in 1905, and the issue is relatively available across most grade levels. Light contrast occurs over the obverse, while the reverse shows attractive ice-blue and light-orange toning. Census: 38 in 65, 55 finer (10/14). NGC ID# 23GJ, PCGS# 4889

3388 1914 PR65 PCGS. Delicate shades of pale gold and electric-blue toning visit the immaculate surfaces of this spectacular Gem, with sharply detailed design elements and deeply mirrored fields. Population: 30 in 65, 32 finer (11/14). NGC ID# 23GV, PCGS# 4898

1914 Barber Dime, PR67
Beautifully Toned

3389 1914 PR67 NGC. The Mint struck only 425 Barber dime proofs in 1914 — the lowest mintage in the entire series. A uniform layer of violet-gray patina covers the surfaces of this Superb Gem. The toning turns to attractive shades of lavender, orange, blue, and green when held beneath a lamp. Both sides are fully detailed and virtually pristine. Census: 10 in 67, 2 finer (10/14). NGC ID# 23GV, PCGS# 4898

1915 Barber Dime, PR67
Only 450 Pieces Struck

3390 1915 PR67 NGC. Mingled shades of greenish-gold, lavender, and cerulean-blue toning blanket the well-preserved surfaces of this spectacular Superb Gem, with more color on the obverse. The design elements are sharply detailed and the fields are deeply reflective under the patina. Census: 14 in 67 (1 in 67 ★), 0 finer (10/14). NGC ID# 23GW, PCGS# 4899

MERCURY DIMES

1916-D Dime, VF25
Deep Original Color

3391 1916-D VF25 PCGS. This key-date issue is most frequently seen in lower circulated grades, as much of the 264,000-coin mintage circulated extensively before falling into the hands of collectors. Pieces grading finer than this VF example are particularly challenging to locate. Tan-gray patina exhibits the occasional russet speck, while the design elements retain much detail. A couple old, faint pinstratches on the obverse do not concern the grade. NGC ID# 23GY, PCGS# 4906

1916-D Mercury Dime, VF25
Excellent Choice for a Mercury Dime Set

3392 1916-D VF25 NGC. The 1916-D Mercury dime is in demand in any level of preservation. The present mid-grade example offers prospective bidders an exceptional collecting opportunity. First, its surfaces display a pleasing soft grayish patina. Second, the design features exhibit relatively strong detail, including most of the lines in the fasces. Third, the rim is full. And fourth, both sides are free of the disturbing marks that often plague low and mid-grade representatives. This key-date coin is the perfect choice for a lower-grade Mercury dime collection. NGC ID# 23GY, PCGS# 4906

3393 1917 MS66 Full Bands PCGS. CAC. Frosty ice-blue luster illuminates tinges of champagne and golden-russet color around the margins. The strike is bold and there are no obtrusive surface flaws. PCGS has encapsulated only 23 numerically finer Full Bands examples (10/14). NGC ID# 23H2, PCGS# 4911

3394 1917-D MS66 PCGS. The design elements of this impressive Premium Gem are well-detailed, but the middle bands on the fasces are not completely split. The well-preserved surfaces show vibrant mint luster under attractive shades of champagne-gold and cerulean-blue toning. Population: 4 in 66, 1 finer (11/14). NGC ID# 23H3, PCGS# 4912

3395 1920-D MS64 Full Bands PCGS. CAC. Shades of golden-brown, lavender-gray, and amber toning visit the well-preserved surfaces of this impressive Choice example, with sharply detailed design elements, including Full Bands definition on the fasces. NGC ID# 23HC, PCGS# 4931

1921 Dime, MS64 Full Bands
Eye-Catching Original Luster

3396 1921 MS64 Full Bands NGC. A low mintage of little more than 1.2 million coins makes the 1921 Mercury dime a significant key date in the series. This is a high-end example for the Choice grade level, showing well-preserved, frosty luster beneath a veil of warm champagne toning. The strike is bold in the central regions, and weakens only slightly around the borders due to die wear. A shimmering coin with memorable eye appeal. NGC ID# 23HE, PCGS# 4935

1924 Dime, Vibrant MS67 Full Bands

3397 1924 MS67 Full Bands PCGS. CAC. Full Bands 1924 Mercury dimes can be located with patience through Premium Gem, but Superb Gem pieces are highly elusive and finer specimens are virtually unobtainable. PCGS and NGC have certified a mere 46 examples in MS67 Full Bands and only two numerically finer. Vibrant luster emanates from the untoned surfaces of the present offering that are impeccably preserved. *All* bands, including the diagonal ones, are fully struck. Fantastic overall eye appeal. Population: 32 in 67 (1 in 67+) Full Bands, 0 finer (10/14). NGC ID# 23HJ, PCGS# 4943

3398 1924-D MS66+ Full Bands NGC. A spectacular high-end Premium Gem, with razor-sharp definition on the design elements, including Full Bands definition on the fasces, and well-preserved brilliant surfaces that radiate vibrant mint luster. Census: 29 in 66 (1 in 66+) Full Bands, 6 finer (10/14). NGC ID# 23HK, PCGS# 4945

3399 **1924-S MS64 Full Bands NGC.** The central striking sharpness on this Choice example is unusually bold for a San Francisco issue from this period, with the reverse bands fully split and rounded. A faint blush of light golden color accents satiny luster on each side, while the surfaces are devoid of any obtrusive abrasions. Census: 40 in 64 Full Bands, 6 finer (10/14). NGC ID# 23HL, PCGS# 4947

3400 **1925 MS66 Full Bands PCGS. CAC.** Lange, in his *Complete Guide to Mercury Dimes*, says that nearly all coins of this date display an overall softness, both centrally and peripherally. This example is an exception. Aside from the designated fullness in the central reverse, the peripheral areas of both sides are sharply struck. Only the central obverse reveals minor weakness. Population: 52 in 66 (3 in 66+) Full Bands, 27 finer (10/14).
Ex: Long Beach Signature (Heritage, 6/2004), lot 8123. NGC ID# 23HM, PCGS# 4949

3401 **1926-D MS65 Full Bands PCGS.** This is a better-struck example than usually seen, for this poorly-produced Denver issue, with fully split central reverse bands and just a tiny bit of fadeaway noted on the tops of the reverse peripheral legends. A highly lustrous Gem with slight peripheral toning on each side and well-preserved surfaces. NGC ID# 23HS, PCGS# 4957

3402 **1926-S AU58 PCGS. CAC.** From a mintage of 1.5 million pieces, the 1926-S Mercury dime is an elusive issue in Mint State grades. This attractive near-Mint example shows just a trace of wear and the lightly abraded surfaces retain much of their original mint luster. NGC ID# 23HT, PCGS# 4958

3403 **1939-D MS68 Full Bands PCGS. CAC.** This is a marvelous Mercury dime, numbered among the highest-graded examples from this Denver mint issue. It is fully struck and shows deep coppery-orange, green, and red toning over most of the obverse, with lighter toning on the reverse. Impressively preserved and nearly pristine. NGC ID# 23JS, PCGS# 5019

3404 **1942/1 FS-101 AU58 PCGS. CAC.** Vivid shades of greenish-gold and lavender toning enhance the lightly abraded surfaces of this attractive near-Mint example. The well-detailed design elements show just a trace of wear and vibrant mint luster shines through the patina. Population: 92 in 58, 72 finer (10/14). PCGS# 145473

3405 **1945-S Micro S MS66 Full Bands PCGS. FS-512.** The Micro S mintmark differs in size and shape from the Knob Tail S seen on most examples of the 1945-S Mercury dime. This attractive Premium Gem is sharply detailed and brightly lustrous, with well-preserved surfaces under delicate shades of pale gold toning. NGC ID# 23KH, PCGS# 5063

PROOF MERCURY DIMES

3406 **1939 PR68 NGC.** This untoned high grade proof Mercury dime is thoroughly lustrous and essentially immaculate. The central bands are exquisitely defined, as are the letters near the rims. Neither major grading service has certified an example in a finer grade. Census: 77 in 68 (10 in 68 ★), 0 finer (10/14). NGC ID# 27DK, PCGS# 5074

3407 **1939 PR68 NGC. CAC.** The Mint produced 8,728 dimes in its third year striking Mercury proofs. This piece is exquisitely detailed and immaculately preserved. Two areas of golden-orange and purple-pink toning are confined to the obverse margins while a spot of violet coloration is seen to the left of the D in DIME. None numerically finer at NGC (10/14). NGC ID# 27DK, PCGS# 5074

1939 Mercury Dime, PR66
Rare Cameo Representative

3408 **1939 PR66 Cameo PCGS. CAC.** In the context of proof Mercury dimes, Cameo representatives are incredible rarities. PCGS has certified only 13 Cameo examples in the entire series, 11 of which reside within the 1939 proof issue (10/14). This Premium Gem example boasts brilliant, beautifully preserved surfaces, with noticeable field-motif contrast. The strike is bold, and the eye appeal is immense. Population: 4 in 66, 4 finer (10/14). PCGS# 85074

3409 **1940 PR68 NGC.** Splashes of sky-blue and creamy patination cascade over both sides of this Superb Gem. Crisply struck throughout and immaculately preserved. Census: 46 in 68 (5 in 68 ★), 2 finer (10/14). NGC ID# 27DL, PCGS# 5075

ROOSEVELT DIMES

1946 Roosevelt Dime, MS68 Full Torch
Major Condition Rarity, Registry Set Essential

3410 **1946 MS68 Full Torch NGC.** This radiantly frosty, high-end Superb Gem is offered from the current highest-rated NGC Registry Set of business strike Roosevelt dimes, and is a must-have coin for the advanced competitor. The reverse is essentially brilliant, though the obverse displays vivid sun-gold toning around the margins. Seemingly flawless surfaces showcase full design definition, giving this piece simply exceptional visual appeal. NGC has certified only two other Full Torch examples in this lofty grade (1 in 68 ★), and none finer (10/14).
From The Paul Kiraly #1 NGC Registry Roosevelt Dimes, Circulation Issue. NGC ID# 23KJ, PCGS# 85082

3411 **1946-S MS68 ★ Full Torch NGC.** Trumpet tail S. Exquisite fire-red, aquamarine, and olive-green toning adorn the borders of this lustrous and well struck first-year dime. Census: 7 in 68 (4 in 68 ★) Full Torch, none finer (10/14).
From The Paul Kiraly #1 NGC Registry Roosevelt Dimes, Circulation Issue. NGC ID# 23KL, PCGS# 85084

3412 **1947-S MS68 PCGS.** Sans Serif S. Russet-red, forest-green, and autumn-brown toning encompass the left borders of this high grade second-year Roosevelt dime. The surfaces display vibrant luster and only incidental contact. NGC ID# 23KP, PCGS# 5087

1949-D Dime, MS68 ★ Full Torch
Tied for the Finest Certified

3413 **1949-D MS68 ★ Full Torch NGC.** Vivid teal, crimson, and olive-gold toning graces the reverse periphery of this truly remarkable Superb Gem, while the obverse exhibits dappled olive and amber-gold hues around the margins. The design elements are fully defined, and the surface preservation is immaculate. This is an important opportunity for the Registry Set collector, as NGC has only certified six examples in MS68, with just five of those awarded Star designations, and none have graded numerically finer (10/14).
From The Paul Kiraly #1 NGC Registry Roosevelt Dimes, Circulation Issue. NGC ID# 23KV, PCGS# 85092

3414 **1950-D MS68 ★ Full Torch NGC.** Exquisite honey, apple-green, and rose-red hues embrace this nicely struck and highly lustrous Superb Gem. Census: 4 in 68 (2 in 68 ★) Full Torch, none finer (10/14).
Ex: Dr. S. Long Collection (Heritage, 1/2005), lot 1077.
From The Paul Kiraly #1 NGC Registry Roosevelt Dimes, Circulation Issue. NGC ID# 23KY, PCGS# 85095

3415 **1950-S MS68 ★ Full Torch NGC.** Exceptional ruby-red, jade-green, and lemon toning adorns Roosevelt's hair and the obverse periphery. The reverse displays similar but more subtle shades of color. Census: 8 in 68 (3 in 68 ★) Full Torch, 0 finer (10/14).
From The Paul Kiraly #1 NGC Registry Roosevelt Dimes, Circulation Issue. NGC ID# 23KZ, PCGS# 85096

1951-S Dime, MS68 ★ Full Torch
Seemingly Unmatched Quality and Appeal
Prime Registry Set Condition Rarity

3416 **1951-S MS68 ★ Full Torch NGC.** The importance of this premier Superb Gem to the Registry Set competitor cannot be overstated. NGC has encapsulated only three Full Torch examples in MS68, and this piece ranks as one of just two of those awarded a Star designation for superior eye appeal; none have been certified finer (10/14). The obverse showcases vivid bands of forest-green, crimson, and sun-gold around an iridescent ice-blue center, while the reverse shows amber-gold and lemon-yellow peripheral bands around an iridescent sky-blue and pale lavender center. The strike is razor-sharp and the surfaces are seemingly pristine.
From The Paul Kiraly #1 NGC Registry Roosevelt Dimes, Circulation Issue. NGC ID# 23L4, PCGS# 85099

3417 **1952-D MS68 Full Torch NGC.** This delightful Roosevelt dime exhibits mostly brilliant flawless surfaces with a few traces of greenish-gold toning. Full definition shows on the torch and vibrant mint luster radiates from both sides. Census: 2 in 68 (1 in 68 ★), 0 finer (10/14).
From The Paul Kiraly #1 NGC Registry Roosevelt Dimes, Circulation Issue. NGC ID# 23L6, PCGS# 85101

3418 **1954-D MS67+ Full Bands PCGS.** A high-end Superb Gem specimen, with razor-sharp definition on all design element, including the bands on the torch. The impeccably preserved lustrous surfaces show a few hints of apple-green and lavender toning. Population: 37 in 67 (4 in 67+) Full Bands, 0 finer (10/14). NGC ID# 23LC, PCGS# 85107

3419 **1956-D MS68 Full Torch NGC.** Just 229 examples of this Denver issue have received the Full Torch designation from NGC, and this coin is the single finest-graded of those, making it an obvious candidate for the finest Registry Set. It is fully struck with a light sprinkling of mottled patina on each side, turning to multicolored iridescent displays along the perimeters. Immaculately preserved and free of even the tiniest imperfection.
From The Paul Kiraly #1 NGC Registry Roosevelt Dimes, Circulation Issue. NGC ID# 23LJ, PCGS# 85113

1957-D Dime, MS68 ★ Full Torch
Registry Set Essential, Tied for Finest Certified

3420 **1957-D MS68 ★ Full Torch NGC.** Another selection from the current highest-rated Registry Set, this Star-designated Superb Gem showcases eye-catching obverse peripheral toning in concentric bands of forest-green, crimson, sun-gold, and deep olive around a luminescent champagne center. The reverse is largely untoned, save for a blush of light golden color. The coin is boldly struck and impeccably preserved, with an interesting tiny die break seen over Roosevelt's eye. NGC has seen only three Full Torch examples in MS68, all awarded the coveted Star designation for superior eye appeal (10/14).
From The Paul Kiraly #1 NGC Registry Roosevelt Dimes, Circulation Issue. NGC ID# 23LL, PCGS# 85115

3421 **1959 MS68 Full Torch NGC.** This brilliant, radiantly lustrous example is fully struck and impeccably preserved. The wispy lines on each side are raised die striations. As the single finest-graded example of this date, at NGC, this coin should pique the interest of the serious Registry Set specialist. Census: 1 in 68 Full Torch, 0 finer (10/14).
From The Paul Kiraly #1 NGC Registry Roosevelt Dimes, Circulation Issue. NGC ID# 23LP, PCGS# 85118

3422 **1970-D MS68 Full Torch NGC.** Impeccably preserved, the mostly brilliant surfaces of this magnificent Roosevelt dime show a few hints of greenish-gold toning at the peripheries. Full definition shows on the torch and both sides radiate vibrant mint luster. Census: 2 in 68 Full Torch, 0 finer (10/14).
From The Paul Kiraly #1 NGC Registry Roosevelt Dimes, Circulation Issue. NGC ID# 23MC, PCGS# 85138

3423 **1971-D MS68 Full Torch NGC.** This spectacular Roosevelt dime exhibits full definition on the torch and the impeccably preserved brilliant surfaces radiate vibrant mint luster throughout. Eye appeal is tremendous. Census: 2 in 68, 0 finer (10/14).
From The Paul Kiraly #1 NGC Registry Roosevelt Dimes, Circulation Issue. NGC ID# 23ME, PCGS# 85140

3424 **1980-D MS66 Full Torch NGC.** This is the sole 1980-D example with the Full Torch designation at NGC. PCGS has seen just two pieces with Full Bands, and only one coin similarly-graded at MS66, making this offering a prime candidate for a top Registry Set. Sharply struck and untoned, with gleaming luster and just a couple of trivial contact marks that keep it from grading even higher. Census: 1 in 66 Full Torch, 0 finer (10/14).
From The Paul Kiraly #1 NGC Registry Roosevelt Dimes, Circulation Issue. NGC ID# 23MZ, PCGS# 85158

3425 1982 No P MS67 Full Torch NGC. The mintmark was inadvertently omitted on this sought-after series rarity. This spectacular Superb Gem displays pinpoint definition on all design elements and the brightly lustrous surfaces are free of mentionable distractions. Census: 2 in 67, 0 finer (10/14).
From The Paul Kiraly #1 NGC Registry Roosevelt Dimes, Circulation Issue. NGC ID# 23N6, PCGS# 5162

3426 1994-P MS69 Full Torch NGC. A virtually perfect specimen, with impeccably preserved brilliant surfaces and vibrant mint luster on both sides. Razor-sharp definition is evident on the design elements, including full details on the torch. Census: 1 in 69, 0 finer (10/14).
From The Paul Kiraly #1 NGC Registry Roosevelt Dimes, Circulation Issue. NGC ID# 23NX, PCGS# 85186

3427 1996-W MS69 Full Torch NGC. Just a hint of golden-tan toning enhances the eye appeal of this incredible Roosevelt dime. The design elements are fully detailed throughout and vibrant mint luster emanates from impeccably preserved surfaces. Census: 14 in 69, 0 finer (10/14).
From The Paul Kiraly #1 NGC Registry Roosevelt Dimes, Circulation Issue. NGC ID# 23P2, PCGS# 85189

3428 1996-D MS69 Full Torch NGC. This incredible Roosevelt dime exhibits razor-sharp definition on all design elements, including full details on the torch. The pristine brilliant surfaces radiate vibrant mint luster on both sides, creating terrific eye appeal. Census: 2 in 69, 0 finer (10/14).
From The Paul Kiraly #1 NGC Registry Roosevelt Dimes, Circulation Issue. NGC ID# 23P3, PCGS# 85190

3429 1998-P MS69 Full Torch NGC. The fully detailed design elements of this magnificent MS69 specimen complement the impeccably preserved surfaces and vibrant mint luster. Eye appeal is incomparable. Census: 1 in 69, 0 finer (10/14).
From The Paul Kiraly #1 NGC Registry Roosevelt Dimes, Circulation Issue. NGC ID# 23P8, PCGS# 85195

PROOF ROOSEVELT DIMES

3430 1952 PR68 ★ Cameo NGC. Ocean-blue and golden-brown borders frame brilliant centers. A crisply struck and immaculate piece. The devices are frosty and contrast dramatically with the flashy fields. Census: 41 in 68 (4 in 68 ★), 2 finer (10/14). NGC ID# 27EL, PCGS# 85227

3431 1953 PR69 Cameo NGC. From an original proof mintage of 128,800 pieces. Relatively few have been certified with the Cameo designation, by both of the major services combined, and this example represents one of the six specimens at PR69 Cameo, all from NGC. Neither service has seen a PR70 Cameo coin, thus far. Fully detailed and near-pristine, the fields are profoundly reflective and the devices are attractively frosted. Census: 6 in 69, 0 finer (10/14). NGC ID# 27EM, PCGS# 85228

1954 Dime, PR68 Ultra Cameo
Tied for Finest Certified

3432 1954 PR68 Ultra Cameo NGC. Roosevelt dimes are not often seen with Deep or Ultra Cameo contrast, partly because the small coins have little room for fields, especially on the obverse where the central portrait dominates. To illustrate that point, it is instructive to note that just 17 proofs from 1954 have been designated as Deep or Ultra Cameo by PCGS and NGC combined, from an original mintage of 233,300 pieces. This example certainly seems well qualified, with amazingly deep reflectivity in the fields and sharply frosted ice-white devices. It is also immaculately preserved, and the design motifs are crisply impressed, as expected. Census: 3 in 68 Ultra Cameo, 0 finer (10/14). NGC ID# 27EN, PCGS# 95229

3433 1955 PR69 Ultra Cameo NGC. This delightful Roosevelt dime is one tick away from technical perfection, with fully detailed frosty design elements that contrast profoundly with the deeply mirrored fields. Census: 8 in 69, 0 finer (10/14). PCGS# 95230

3434 1955 PR69 Cameo NGC. This magnificent Roosevelt dime is one tick away from technical perfection. The design elements are sharply detailed and the brilliant fields are deeply reflective, with incredible eye appeal. Census: 46 in 69 (4 in 69 ★), 0 finer (10/14). PCGS# 85230

3435 1959 PR69 White Ultra Cameo NGC. The depth of contrast on both sides of this coin is exceptional for a 1950s proof. Brilliant and immaculate with a powerful strike and strong eye appeal. Census: 69 in 69 (2 in 69 ★), 0 finer (10/14).
Ex: V. A. Everest Collection (Heritage, 7/2003), lot 6875, which realized $1,495. NGC ID# 27EU, PCGS# 95234

3436 1961 PR70 Deep Cameo PCGS. A technically perfect Roosevelt dime, with fully struck design elements and deeply mirrored fields that contrast boldly with the frosty devices. The impeccably preserved surfaces are brilliant and untoned. Population: 4 in 70 (10/14). NGC ID# 27EV, PCGS# 95236

End of Session One

(1652) New England (NE) Shilling, AU55
Noe 1-A, Possibly the Finest Known

3437 **(1652) New England Shilling AU55 PCGS Secure. Noe 1-A, W-40, Salmon 1-B, R.7.** Ex: Newman Collection. 72.0 grains. On this remarkable shilling, alignment is just shy of 180 degrees. Similar to the sixpence, it shows russet patina on lovely light-gray surfaces. Minor radial cracking of the flan is evident on both sides, with trivial surface roughness. Very slight wear appears on the high-points of the NE and XII punches, with the second I weaker than the X, or the first I.

Design
Like the sixpence, the NE shillings had the origin and denomination stamps punched by hand on imperfectly round blanks. Three NE punches and four XII punches were combined to form six different varieties that are listed in Salmon's reference. He rates five of the varieties R.7, and one R.8. In the *Whitman Encyclopedia of Colonial and Early American Coins*, Bowers gives estimates ranging from URS-3 to URS-6, indicating between 44 and 76 known survivors.

Historical Observations
The silver used for the coin production was obtained locally, with a portion of the Mint Act of May 27, 1652 requesting that bullion be brought by "all persons whatsoever have liberty to bring into the mint house at Boston all bullion plate or Spanish coin." The pieces would be melted, assayed, refined, and then cast into strips by mint master John Hull in order to produce coins for the owner of the silver. The initial NE coinage was produced for only a short period, although a substantial number of coins were likely minted. The NE coins were replaced with the more elaborately designed pieces known as the Willow Tree series after the General Court issued orders to include a tree on one side of the new coins along with the word "Massachusetts," with the date and "New England" to appear on the reverse. The minimal style of the NE series, with simple designs, made them easily susceptible to clipping. Although the dates on the coins do not reflect it, except for the Oak Tree twopence, dated 1662, the Massachusetts Silver coinage was minted for approximately thirty years. Mint operations likely ceased a year or so prior to King Charles II annulling the Massachusetts Bay Colony's charter in 1694, establishing it as a royal colony.

Numismatic Commentary
An exceptional piece, the obverse of this Choice AU survivor exhibits the diagonal of N being thick, becoming thicker past the point where the right stand of the N intersects it. A die scratch extends from the middle bar of the E. The XII punch on the reverse is high, with the X being the highest and the second I being the lowest. The October 2005 Ford sale contained a single example of the Noe 1-A variety, with that piece described as "Choice Very Fine." Another outstanding collection of 180 Massachusetts silver coins, the Hain Family Collection, sold in January 2002, lacked the Noe 1-A combination. Numerous other well-known collections were absent a Noe 1-A specimen, including Roper and Norweb. This appearance provides an exceedingly rare opportunity to not only acquire a Noe 1-A example, but an extraordinary and noteworthy specimen as well.

Provenance
Ex: Eric P. Newman Numismatic Education Society. PCGS# 13

(1694) London Elephant Token, Diagonals, VF30
Rare Hodder 1-A Variety

3438 (1694) London Elephant Token, Diagonals VF30 PCGS. **Hodder 1-A, W-12000, High R.6.** The central reverse diagonal lines are faint on this example, but the right edges of them can be discerned with the aid of a strong magnifier. Much scarcer than the usual Hodder 2-B variety, which carries an R.2 designation. This reddish-tan example is well-struck and shows a few tiny planchet marks on the obverse, near the elephant's leg and head, and a smooth reverse. Listed on page 46 of the 2015 *Guide Book.* PCGS# 61

1778-1779 Rhode Island Ship Token
Betts-563, W-1740, MS62 Brown

3439 1778-1779 Rhode Island Ship Token, Wreath Below, Copper MS62 Brown PCGS. CAC. **Betts-563, W-1740, R.4.** The history of the Rhode Island ship medals is not known, including which country they were struck in and their intended message, with some believing they were one of many political and satirical medals struck by the Dutch. In any event, surviving examples are extremely popular and this is a particularly appealing specimen. Hues of brown and gold are present on this piece exhibiting a pleasing strike. The few marks present are minor in nature. Listed on page 50 of the 2015 *Guide Book.* Population: 4 in 62 Brown, 3 finer (10/14). PCGS# 576

Rhode Island Ship Token, MS60
Wreath Below, Pewter, Betts-563, W-1745

3440 1778-1779 Rhode Island Ship Token, Wreath Below, Pewter MS60 PCGS. **Betts-563, W-1745, High R.6.** Though scholars debate whether the Rhode Island Ship medals or tokens were pro-American or pro-British, there is little doubt that the audience for them was Dutch, both from the inscriptions and from historical evidence. John Kleeberg, in correspondence published with Q. David Bowers in the *Whitman Encyclopedia of Colonial and Early American Coins*, wrote: "We know that at least one piece did pass through Dutch hands, because the first publication took place in a Japanese book ... and at that period only the Dutch were permitted to trade with Japan (via Deshima)."

Further information on that book can be found in *The Shogun's Painted Culture*, a wide-ranging scholarly work by Timon Screech reflecting on the shogunate in Japan. He notes briefly, "Kutsuki Masatsuna, daimyo of Fukuchiyama, was ... one of the chief Westernists of his day. He was also an energetic numismatist and in 1787 published a large book called Western Coinage (Seiyō Senpu) which displayed, in a series of plates ordered by country, examples of tender from most European states and their colonies ..."

The nature of the *Seiyō Senpu* makes it impossible to tell what metal was used to make the Rhode Island Ship piece depicted, but it was almost assuredly copper or brass, as the pewter pieces, such as the example offered here, are far rarer today. Though it shows no trace of wear, certain areas of the pewter, including spots on the margins and the bow of the ship, show effects from the passage of time. Still, this is a generally bright representative with excellent eye appeal and great historical worth. Listed on page 50 of the 2015 *Guide Book.* Population: 1 in 60, 4 finer (10/14). *Ex: Los Angeles Signature (Heritage, 7/2009), lot 1010.* PCGS# 585

1787 Auctori Plebis Token, W-8770, AU58
The Finest-Graded Example at PCGS

3441 **1787 Auctori Plebis Token AU58 PCGS. CAC. Breen-1147, W-8770, R.3.** This is the usual late die state with a die crack in the upper reverse field. The Auctori Plebis tokens resemble Connecticut coppers, especially on the obverse. although they were struck in England. High-grade survivors are extremely rare, and this near-Mint specimen is the single-finest example that PCGS has certified (10/14). The olive and chocolate-brown surfaces show considerable luster with minimal marks. Listed on page 74 of the 2015 *Guide Book*. PCGS# 601

(1792-94) Kentucky Token, MS65 Red and Brown
Engrailed Edge, Breen-1162, W-8805

3442 **(1792-94) Kentucky Token, Engrailed Edge MS65 Red and Brown PCGS. W-8805, R.6.** 144.2 grains. Ex: Eric P. Newman. Struck in England circa 1792 to 1794 as part of the Conder token series, Kentucky tokens were widely collected by English numismatists, and are not known to have circulated in the United States. The reverse depicts a pyramid of 15 stars, representing the 15 United States; as Kentucky is seen at the peak, the piece is commonly called the Kentucky token. This Gem example represents the engrailed edge variety, which is among the rarer of the many varieties known. It is the finest of only three Red and Brown examples at PCGS by two full grade points (10/14), and displays substantial copper-red color beneath medium orange-brown patina on each side. Listed on page 75 of the 2015 *Guide Book*.
Ex: Selections from the Eric P. Newman Collection IV Signature Auction (Heritage, 5/2014), lot 30390, where it realized $5,287.50.
PCGS# 618

HALF CENT

1794 C-2a Half Cent, VF30
Small Edge Letters

3443 **1794 Normal Head, Small Edge Letters C-2a, R.3 VF30 PCGS.** Cohen-2a is the Small Edge Letters variety of the 1794 half cent with the Normal Head (Low Relief) obverse. The Small Edge Letters variant is somewhat more available than its Large Edge Letters counterpart (C-2b), although both varieties are scarce in VF30 or finer grades. The current example is an attractive, chocolate brown coin with moderate wear and a few minor slide marks on the upper neck and jawline, as well as a pair of faint intersecting lines above the date. The eye appeal is well above-average. Our EAC grade VG10. PCGS# 35024

3444 1831 Reverse of 1836 PR66 Red NGC. Breen-2, High R.5. The deeply mirrored fields and satiny, lustrous devices of this Premium Gem proof exhibit brilliant gold color with splashes and bands of cobalt-blue, violet, and mint green toning. There are no carbon spots or flecks on either side, and a few minuscule contact marks are all that separate this example from perfection.

The reverse was initially used for the 1836 Original and First Restrike half cents and later used for the 1831 First Restrikes, likely produced in the late 1850s or early 1860s. Richard Coleman records six die states and 31 known examples. This example is Coleman's Die State V with three known. Only one example of his terminal state, Die State VI, is known.

NGC has certified 11 examples in all grades (10/14), including two PR66 Brown, two PR66 Red and Brown, one PR66 Red (offered here), and one PR67 Red and Brown. PCGS has certified 21 examples, including three PR66 Brown, two PR66 Red and Brown, one PR66 Red, and one PR67 Brown.

In the last 20 years, we have only offered an 1831 First Restrike proof half cent on 12 different occasions, and at least five of those appearances are for a single coin. We believe that nearly three dozen examples are known today. Our EAC grade PR63.

Ex: David S. Wilson (S.H. Chapman, 3/1907), lot 1014; later, Larry Hanks; Garry Fitzgerald; Mid-American Rare Coin Auctions (5/1985), lot 9; Mid-American Rare Coin Auctions (9/1985), lot 9; Richard Gross; R.E. Naftzger, Jr.; Eric Streiner; Don Kagin and Andy Lustig; J. Treglia; Jim McGuigan; Bowers and Merena (8/1996), lot 7; Jim McGuigan (10/2000). PCGS# 1191

3445 1852 First Restrike, Small Berries PR66 Red and Brown NGC. B-2, R.5. Flashy orange-red surfaces display violet, magenta, green, and umber overtones. The N and T in CENT are noticeably doubled, as is the wreath ribbon below. While original proofs have Large Berries on the reverse, the restrikes are identifiable by Small Berries. The current coin is a nicely mirrored and technically well-produced proof, with no evidence of die pits or buckling, and therefore struck from the earliest state of the dies.

Current research suggests the 1852 First Restrike proofs were struck circa 1856, and indeed the reverse die is the same as that used for the 1856 proof half cents that went into sets for the year. This coin is apparently tied with one other PR66 Red and Brown NGC example for finest known (10/14). Our EAC grade PR63. NGC ID# 26ZT, PCGS# 1318

LARGE CENTS

1794 S-28, B-10 Cent, AU50
Sharp Motifs

3446 **1794 Head of 1794, S-28, B-10, R.2, AU50 PCGS.** Breen Die State III. A pleasing chocolate-brown example with the diagnostic single leaf opposite I of AMERICA, paired with the "finely treated locks" obverse showing five curls in a line (curls three through six, and curl eight). A few areas of darker porosity appear at the reverse legend, and prominent die clashing can be seen in and around the wreath. Several small rim irregularities are noted on both sides. Housed in a first generation PCGS holder. Our EAC grade VF30. PCGS# 35549

1798 Large Date Cent, AU53
Second Hair Style, S-165, B-31

3447 **1798 Second Hair Style, Large Date, S-165, B-31, R.4, AU53 NGC.** The Large Date variety only appears on S-165, 166, and 167 with the Second Hair Style, and S-165 is readily identified by the blundered second T in STATES that was first inverted, and then corrected. No clash marks or die cracks are evident on this Die State I example. Both sides of this attractive cent exhibit attractively blended golden-tan and olive-brown surfaces with excellent eye appeal. Our EAC grade VF30. PCGS# 36065

1814 Crosslet 4 Large Cent, S-294, AU58
Premium Quality for the Grade

3448 **1814 Crosslet 4, S-294, B-1, R.1, AU58 PCGS.** From a mintage of 357,830 pieces, perhaps restricted due to the hardships of the War of 1812, this early large cent issue was produced in just two die varieties: the Crosslet 4 and the Plain 4 (S-295). Struck slightly off-center toward 6 o'clock on the obverse, this deep lavender-brown example displays crisply struck central motifs. Modest high-point friction seems evident on the wreath leaves, but surface abrasions are nearly nonexistent. Our EAC grade AU50. Population: 25 in 58, 36 finer (10/14). PCGS# 36520

1814 Plain 4 Cent, S-295, AU58
Rich, Glossy Patina

3449 **1814 Plain 4, S-295, B-2, R.1, AU58 NGC.** Two varieties of the 1814 large cent are known, identified by having either a plain 4 or crosslet 4 in the date. The two are relatively similar in availability, though the Plain 4 variant is slightly scarcer overall. This Plain 4 example is an elusive near-Mint representative with no signs of the usual environmental impairments that affect this type. Deeply blended shades of burgundy, auburn, and chocolate-brown blanket glossy, problem-free surfaces on each side. The strike is above-average for the issue, while a small planchet flaw is noted on the rim near the ER in AMERICA. An immensely pleasing example for either date or type purposes. Our EAC grade XF40. PCGS# 36517

1839/6 Cent, Choice XF
N-1, Plain Cords

3450 **1839/6 Plain Cords, N-1, High R.3, XF45 PCGS. CAC.** Die State B, with a die crack from the obverse rim at 9 o'clock to Liberty's nose. In later die states this crack extends all the way across the obverse. This is the only use of this obverse, which is characterized by plain cords on Liberty's hair buns, rather than beaded cords. The remnants of an underlying 6 are also evident beneath the primary 9 in the date. This *Guide Book* variety is fairly scarce, and draws strong attention when preserved as well as the current piece. Both sides display moderately glossy chocolate-brown patina, with hints of auburn and burgundy in the recesses. Sharp detail remains on the central devices, though the stars lack their radial lines. A pleasing, problem-free example. Our EAC grade VF30. Population: 1 in 45, 4 finer (11/14). PCGS# 37261

1839 N-3 Cent, MS66 Brown
Head of 1838, Lustrous and Glossy

3451 **1839 Head of 1838, Beaded Cords, N-3, R.1, MS66 Brown PCGS. CAC.** Smooth and glossy, this Premium Gem cent displays umber-brown color interspersed with a generous amount of mint red around the stars, legends, and central motifs. Strong mint luster radiates in swirling waves across the surfaces. This Head of 1838, Beaded Cords cent shows diagnostic flowlining and intermittent weakness at the denticles. The line below CENT is thin and the berry beneath M is faint — all characteristic of the N-3 variety. Overall, the coin is sharply struck and beautifully preserved. Our EAC grade MS63. PCGS# 37228

PROOF FLYING EAGLE CENT

1858 Small Letters Cent, PR64
Very Scarce Proof Issue

3452 **1858 Small Letters PR64 PCGS. Snow-PR2.** Low Leaves reverse. Open E in ONE. The die markers for the present proof marriage are a nearly filled final A in AMERICA and a diagonal line in the dentils beneath the right ribbon end. The reverse die also struck Snow-4 1856 Flying Eagle cents. This sharply struck and satiny near-Gem is free from contact, although a loupe reveals a couple of tiny spots, below the A in STATES and above the E in ONE. Wheat-gold overall with a blush of peach-red on the left obverse. Population: 44 in 64 (2 in 64+), 9 finer (10/14). NGC ID# 227D, PCGS# 2043

INDIAN CENTS

1885 Indian Cent, MS66 Red
None Finer at PCGS or NGC

3453 **1885 MS66 Red PCGS.** Eagle Eye Photo Seal, card not included. Copious luster and rich copper-orange color are among the attributes this gorgeous Premium Gem, housed in a first generation holder, possesses. A few small splashes of orange appear on the reverse. The coin exhibits a sharp strike, adding to the appeal. The obverse displays only a few extremely minuscule marks, while the reverse is virtually pristine. Very few examples designated as Red are found at the upper grade levels, with PCGS having assigned the MS66 Red grade to 15 examples, with none finer and NGC having certified only two examples as MS66 Red, also with none (10/14). NGC ID# 228C, PCGS# 2153

1890 Cent, MS66 Red and Brown
Colorful Original Patina

3454 **1890 MS66 Red and Brown PCGS. CAC.** Glowing, frosty luster illuminates myriad toning hues including shades of sun-gold, amber, cherry-red, and olive-green. The headdress feathertips are not fully defined, though the strike is otherwise pleasing. The 1890 Indian cent is generally an available date, but this coin ranks as one of only two Red and Brown examples certified at the MS66 grade level at PCGS, with none finer (10/14). NGC ID# 228J, PCGS# 2176

3455 **1905 Cent — Struck on a $2 1/2 Gold Planchet — MS64 PCGS.** Weight: 64.5 grains, the standard weight of a quarter eagle. Exactly five Indian cents are known on gold planchets, according to information available to us. Among them are three dated 1900, this piece dated 1905, and an example dated 1906. The Judd pattern reference lists 1900 and 1907 gold cents in the section on mint errors. However, Andrew W. Pollock, III, listed the 1900 gold Indian cents as P-1990 in the regular pattern section of his reference. Pollock writes: "Listed in Judd as a mint error, but it is difficult to imagine that a Mint employee would be so careless as to feed gold planchets into a coinage press fitted with one-cent piece dies." Pollock suggests that these pieces may have been deliberately struck for one or more collectors.

The following Census of gold Indian cents and additional information about them is compiled from a variety of sources, including www.uspatterns. com, www.minterrornews.com, Donald Taxay's 1976 *Catalogue and Encyclopedia*, Andrew Pollock's 1994 *United States Patterns and Related Issues*, the Judd reference, and selected auction catalogs. Conversations with Fred Weinberg and Richard Snow provided additional background.

1900 MS65 PCGS. Col. E.H.R. Green; B.G. Johnson; John Beck (Abner Kreisberg Corporation, 1/1975), lot 609; Mike Byers; Auction '89 (Superior, 7/1989), lot 856; Bowers and Merena (8/1991), lot 4103; recently PCGS authenticated as a 1900 Indian cent struck on a gold $2.50 planchet, and graded MS65. The 1991 ANA catalog gives a weight of 65.8 grains, 1.3 grains too much for a quarter eagle planchet.

1900 AU55. Heritage (8/1993), lot 8000. The 1993 ANA catalog gives a weight of 4.35 grams (67.12 grains), 2.62 grains too much for a quarter eagle planchet.

1900. Michael Hodder reported in a May 14, 1996 letter to Q. David Bowers that he had personally seen three different pieces, all with weights in the range of 65.8 to 67.1 grains. See Bowers' *A Buyer's and Enthusiast's Guide to Flying Eagle and Indian Cents*, p. 427.

1905 MS64 PCGS. Apparently unknown to the numismatic community prior to it sale in the 2010 FUN Sale (Heritage, 1/2010), lot 2433. Weight: 64.5 grains, the standard weight for a quarter eagle planchet.

1906 AU58 NGC. Stack's (6/2004), lot 4097; Stack's (9/2009), lot 4299. Weight: 64.4 grains, within the 0.25 grain tolerance for a quarter eagle planchet.

1907. Listed in the Judd pattern book, and in Donald Taxay's *Catalogue and Encyclopedia [of] U.S. Coins*. The 1907 gold Indian cent is currently unlocated.

One example dated 1900 is also known in silver, from the identical dies as the 1900 gold Indian cents, suggesting they were all made at or near the same time. Rick Snow writes in *A Guide Book of Flying Eagle and Indian Head Cents* that "both the silver and gold examples are struck from the same dies, with light roughness on the reverse die, probably from die rust." That all three 1900 pieces have higher weights suggests that they were specially made, perhaps without the knowledge of Mint officials. Fred Weinberg explained to this cataloger that "the weights vary because in all probability, they were on planchets that might not have been filed down to the proper weight spread." Hand adjusting of individual gold planchets continued in the Mint until circa 1910. Those three pieces are almost certainly fancy pieces made for collectors, while the 1905 and 1906 examples, on correct weight planchets, are more likely pieces truly made in error, and substantially more important as such.

This example is slightly off-center toward 9 o'clock, the tops of UNITED STATES off the planchet. The strike is weak at the date, feather tips, RICA, the outer parts of the wreath, and the ribbon bow. The weakness seems counter to expectations of the soft gold, but the diameter is at least a full millimeter less than an Indian cent, meaning that the metal flowed out and was insufficient to accept the design from the deepest recesses of the dies. Both sides have bright yellow-gold surfaces with frosty mint luster. A few faint hairlines on the cheek prevent a Gem grade assignment. This stunning gold Indian cent is one of the truly amazing error coins we have ever handled. NGC ID# 2292, PCGS# 2220

1909-S Indian Cent, MS65 Red
Lustrous, Red-Orange Patina

1859 Indian Cent, PR66 Cameo
Stunning First-Year Indian

3456 1909-S MS65 Red PCGS Secure. Somehow, despite the fact that the 1909-S Indian cent shows only one-third the grading events of the higher-mintage 1909-S V.D.B. cent, it is valued at less than half as much. (So much for "relative rarity" as a predictor of value in numismatics.) Astute bidders will take note. This example is a richer red than most 1909-S Indian cents — which often tend to the straw-gold coloration — with a strong strike best-confirmed by the bold bust point and sharp shield details. Few marks exist anywhere on the coin. No spots are visible to the naked eye, and a glass reveals only a few microscopic evidences of carbon. Brilliant, orange-red luster floods the surfaces. Just 20 coins are certified numerically finer by PCGS (10/14). NGC ID# 2298, PCGS# 2240

3457 1859 PR66 Cameo PCGS. First year of issue for the Indian cent, the figure of Liberty is actually represented by a Caucasian female that is wearing a headdress of the Chippewa tribe. Only struck with this obverse and reverse combination in 1859, some 800 proofs were minted minus an unknown number that were melted at year's end. This is a bright, lightly toned example that appears to be fully original. Each side is lightly dusted with pleasant lilac-red patina, and for pedigree purposes, a lintmark is seen through the N of UNITED into the left obverse field. The fields are deeply reflective, and there is a significant amount of mint frost over the devices that gives the coin an appealing cameo contrast. Population: 6 in 66 Cameo, 0 finer (10/14).
Ex: Palm Beach signature (Heritage, 11/2004), lot 5287; Central States Signature (Heritage, 4/2009), lot 2099. PCGS# 82247

LINCOLN CENTS

1909-S VDB Lincoln Cent, MS66+ Red
Exceptional First-Year Series Key

3458 **1909-S VDB MS66+ Red PCGS. CAC.** The 1909-S VDB Lincoln cent is the most sought-after regular issue of the series, from a low first-year mintage of 484,000 pieces. The issue was saved to some extent because of its novelty value, but the supply of high-grade coins is still small compared to the enormous collector demand. The 1909-S VDB is scarce at the MS66 grade level, and very rare in finer grades.

This high-end Premium Gem displays well-detailed design elements and vibrant mint luster on both sides. The original red surfaces show only a few microscopic specks of carbon and the all-important designer's initials are bold. Eye appeal is terrific. PCGS has graded 11 numerically finer examples (10/14). NGC ID# 22B2, PCGS# 2428

1911-D Lincoln Cent, MS66 Red
Only One Numerically Finer Coin at PCGS

3459 **1911-D MS66 Red PCGS.** The 1911-D is the first Lincoln cent from the Denver Mint and examples in MS66 condition are quite rare. This delightful Premium Gem offers sharply detailed design elements and vibrant mint luster on both sides. The well-preserved original red surfaces are carbon-free. Population: 23 in 66 (1 in 66+) Red, 1 finer (10/14). NGC ID# 22B8, PCGS# 2446

1915-D Cent, MS66 Red
Among the Finest Certified

3460 **1915-D MS66 Red PCGS.** A delightful coin for the specialist who demands the finest available. Full Red appears on both sides with no noticeable fading, and only a few carbon flecks are noted near the O in ONE. The fields and surfaces are excellent, with a few tiny ticks found under scrutiny. Marks are absent save for a tick near Lincoln's forehead. Housed in an older green label PCGS holder. A prize for the Registry Set collector and a coin that is currently tied behind one numerically finer coin at PCGS. Population: 28 in 66 Red, 1 finer (10/14).
Ex: ANA Signature (Heritage, 7/2005), lot 10108, which realized $7,475. NGC ID# 22BL, PCGS# 2482

1916-D Cent, MS66 Red
Among the Finest Known

1922 No D Strong Reverse Cent, MS63 Brown
Rare in This Numeric Grade and Color

3461 **1916-D MS66 Red PCGS.** Shimmering orange-copper surfaces provide this exceptional Premium Gem cent with strong visual appeal. Neither PCGS nor NGC has awarded a grade of MS67 or finer to a single example, with PCGS certifying 15 in 66 Red and NGC grading 3 MS66 pieces (10/14). The few marks present on this coin are minuscule. The design elements exhibit strong definition, with only a touch of softness on the AM in AMERICA. The reverse reveals a couple of tiny splashes of blue-green color. Very few hints of carbon appear, all pinpoint in size. A desirable example in a rarely encountered grade, this piece will make a wonderful addition to an advanced collection. NGC ID# 22BP, PCGS# 2491

3462 **1922 No D, Strong Reverse, FS-401, MS63 Brown PCGS.** Die Pair 2. This is the only universally recognized No D variety, in which the D mintmark was deliberately and completely ground off in the process of removing some die damage that occurred in the coining press (per Bowers, 2008). Die Pairs 1 and 3, on the other hand, show a weakened D mintmark resulting from either heavy die polishing or from a grease-filled die.

This Select Brown example displays the diagnostics of Die Pair 2: the second 2 in the date is sharper than the first, all letters in TRUST are clearly delineated, and the reverse is very sharp, especially the lines and grains of the wheat stalks. Both sides display uniformly bluish-brown patination and reveal just a few minute grade-defining marks. PCGS has designated only 38 Brown examples as Mint State. Population: 10 in 63 Brown, 3 finer (10/14). PCGS# 37676

1924-S Lincoln Cent, MS65 Red
None Finer at PCGS

1972 Lincoln Cent, MS67 Red
FS-101, Doubled Die Obverse

3463 1924-S MS65 Red PCGS. Although the 1924-S Lincoln cent claims a large mintage of 11.6 million pieces, few high-quality examples were saved by contemporary collectors and the issue is one of the most challenging of the decade in high grade. It is likely that the 1924-S was not released into circulation until 1925, which might have caused collectors to miss it when they updated their collections in 1924.

The present coin is a delightful Gem, with impeccably preserved original red surfaces and blazing mint luster on both sides. Like most examples seen, the design elements are well-detailed, with just a touch of softness on the portrait. Population: 9 in 65 Red, 0 finer (10/14). NGC ID# 22CE, PCGS# 2557

3464 1972 Doubled Die Obverse, FS-101, MS67 Red NGC. CAC. Boldly doubled at the date, LIBERTY, and IN GOD WE TRUST, the secondary image broadly northeast of the primary motifs. The die pair is confirmed by a tiny die gouge above the D in UNITED. An abnormal number of doubled obverse die varieties exist for the Philadelphia date (a total of nine DDO variants), but this FS-101 variety is by far the most dramatic and desirable. Only the famous 1955 FS-101 doubled die is more obvious, although the 1969-S Doubled Die is a prominent one, too. This 1972 DDO cent is Registry Set-bound, with spot-free surfaces and deep, fire-orange color. The strike is bold. Listed on page 123 of the 2015 *Guide Book*. Census: 8 in 67 Red, 0 finer (10/14). PCGS# 38013

PROOF LINCOLN CENT

1990 No S Cent, PR69 Red Deep Cameo
Sought-After Modern Rarity

3465 **1990 No S, FS-101, PR69 Red Deep Cameo PCGS.** This intriguing and highly sought-after Mint error was created when cents were struck in San Francisco for the 1990 proof sets and Prestige proof sets, using a die that was missing the S mintmark. Such an error theoretically should not have been possible, as beginning in 1985, mintmarks were included on the master hubs, rather than being added after the fact. A feasible explanation, however, suggests that a regular Philadelphia die was polished and sand-blasted for proof coinage in San Francisco, thus explaining the missing mintmark.

This die is believed to have struck approximately 3,700 No S cents, with 145 confirmed to have been destroyed before leaving the mint. Schechter and Garrett, however, writing in *100 Greatest U.S. Modern Coins*, note:

> "To date (2011), only about 250 examples are known, less than 1/10 the number thought to be struck. The discovery rate is so low that some numismatists suggest that many fewer than 3,555 ever actually left the Mint."

This example is virtually flawless in both strike and preservation, and is tied with only a few dozen others as the finest certified. Ranked number 13 in Schechter and Garrett's book. PCGS# 408239

TWO CENT PIECES

1872 Two Cent, Red and Brown
Impressive Near-Gem
Final Business Strike Issue

3466 **1872 MS64 Red and Brown PCGS.** Only 65,000 business-strike two cent pieces were struck in 1872, the last regular-issue coinage of the series. This impressive Choice example offers sharply-detailed devices and lustrous surfaces that are patinated in shades of original red and light brown. An attractive, nicely balanced coin. Population: 31 in 64 (1 in 64+) Red and Brown, 16 finer (10/14). *Ex: New York Signature (Heritage, 12/2011), lot 3188.* NGC ID# 22NG, PCGS# 3613

1872 Two Cent, MS64 Red and Brown
Final Circulation Issue

3467 **1872 MS64 Red and Brown PCGS.** Deep reddish-orange and brick hues supply the Red, while dusky violet and blue overtones are the "Brown" on this Choice example from the last circulating two cent issue. This piece, from a business strike issue consisting of 65,000 coins, exhibits strong preservation and eye appeal. Population: 31 in 64 (1 in 64+) Red and Brown, 16 finer (10/14). *Ex: FUN Signature (Heritage, 1/2011), lot 4349.* NGC ID# 22NG, PCGS# 3613

PROOF TWO CENT PIECES

1865 Two Cent Piece, PR65 Red Cameo
Seldom Seen So Fine

3468 **1865 PR65 Red Cameo PCGS.** Plain 5. The mintage was 500 pieces, but few remain today in high grade and / or with full red color. This is a wonderful piece with yellowish centers that are surrounded by cherry-red at the margins. Significant contrast is apparent between the fields and devices on each side, and there are no detracting contact marks seen. Population: 7 in 65 (1 in 65+), 2 finer (10/14). PCGS# 83629

1873 Two Cent, PR65 Red and Brown
Later Open 3 Variant

3469 1873 Open 3 PR65 Red and Brown PCGS. CAC. It is believed that the Open 3 two cent proofs of 1873 are in actuality restrikes coined a few years later to supply collector demand for this final-year issue, as the date logotype is that which was used during that time period. The generally accepted mintage estimate is just 500 coins for this variety, and survivors become scarce in the finer grades. This Gem example displays fully struck motifs and moderately reflective fields. Largely orange-brown overall, though vivid cherry-red overtones appear when the fields catch a glint of light. Housed in an old green label holder. Population: 19 in 65 Red and Brown, 8 finer (10/14). NGC ID# 2754, PCGS# 3655

THREE CENT SILVER

1851 Three Cent Silver, MS67
None Numerically Finer

3470 1851 MS67 PCGS. CAC. The 1851 is a plentiful date overall, but becomes conditionally rare at the Superb Gem grade level. This example shows thick mint frost over each side, with impeccably preserved surfaces. Some striking softness on the high points of the shield is normal for the type, and the design elements are otherwise sharp. A highly appealing representative, with faint traces of olive-gold toning in the border recesses. Population: 14 in 67 (1 in 67+), 0 finer (10/14). NGC ID# 22YX, PCGS# 3664

PROOF THREE CENT NICKELS

1869 Three Cent Nickel, PR67 Ultra Cameo

3471 1869 PR67 Ultra Cameo NGC. Mint records report 600 1869 three cent nickel proofs having been distributed as part of silver proof sets, and it is likely that a small number of additional pieces were also sold in minor proof sets. Whatever the exact number, this issue's availability today is primarily limited to the Cameo and non-Cameo categories; Ultra Cameos are distinctly rare, and are exceedingly so when sought at the PR67 grade level. This stellar coin shows bold, heavily frosted devices and glassy mirroring in the fields. A blush of light golden toning warms each side, complementing the seemingly perfect surfaces. Census: 4 in 67 (1 in 67 ★), 0 finer (10/14). PCGS# 93765

1885 Three Cent Nickel, PR66 Deep Cameo
Tied for Finest at PCGS

3472 1885 PR66 Deep Cameo PCGS. A nominal mintage of 3,790 proof three cent nickels was accomplished in 1885 and Premium Gem examples, with Deep Cameo surfaces, are extremely rare. This delightful PR66 specimen displays sharply detailed frosty design elements that contrast boldly with the deeply reflective fields. Impeccably preserved surfaces add to the terrific eye appeal. Population: 3 in 66, 0 finer (10/14). PCGS# 93781

SHIELD NICKEL

1879 Shield Nickel, MS66
Among the Finest at PCGS

3473 1879 MS66 PCGS. A scarce semikey issue, with a mintage of only 25,900 coins. This Premium Gem example displays satiny silver-gray luster with hints of light golden color throughout. The strike is boldly impressed and the surfaces are devoid of the typical die cracks that usually affect examples of this type. Population: 26 in 66 (1 in 66+), 0 finer (10/14). NGC ID# 276D, PCGS# 3808

PROOF SHIELD NICKELS

1867 No Rays Shield Nickel
Bold PR66 Deep Cameo

3474 1867 No Rays PR66 Deep Cameo PCGS. Mint records report 600 proof No Rays Shield nickels having been sold as part of silver proof sets, and a small, unknown number of additional pieces were likely distributed in minor proof sets, as well. The survival rate is fair in the absolute sense, but the available population declines significantly when one crosses over into the pursuit of Cameo examples, and Deep Cameos are nothing short of rare. PCGS has encapsulated only five Deep Cameo representatives in all grades, with three in PR66 and none finer (10/14). This piece is simply magnificent in both technical and aesthetic appeal. Crisp white-on-black contrast exhibits warm champagne-gold toning over each side, with tack-sharp devices and seemingly flawless preservation. A beautiful coin in every respect. PCGS# 93821

1876 Nickel, PR66 Deep Cameo
One of the Finest Deep Cameos at PCGS

3475 1876 PR66 Deep Cameo PCGS. Few Deep or Ultra Cameo 1876 proof nickels are known from the surviving numbers of proofs. Indeed, of the 450 1876 proof nickels certified by PCGS a scant five (1%) are Deep Cameos. The deeply mirrored fields of the present Premium Gem strongly highlight the frosted motifs, all of which exhibit sharp design detail. Both sides have been very well cared for. Population: 3 in 66, 1 finer (10/14). PCGS# 93830

1877 Shield Nickel, PR67
Outstanding Key-Date Example

3476 1877 PR67 NGC. Ex: Simpson. Vibrant yellow toning intermingles with light blue accents on both sides of this carefully preserved Superb Gem. The strike is nearly full, as one would expect from a proof, and the surfaces appear pristine to the unaided eye. It would be virtually impossible to find a more attractive specimen. Census: 5 in 67, 0 finer (10/14).
Ex: ANA Signature (Heritage, 3/2003), lot 5357; ANA Signature (Heritage, 8/2010), lot 4259. NGC ID# 276U, PCGS# 3831

LIBERTY NICKEL

1912-S Nickel, MS65
Sole S-Mint Issue of the Series

3477 1912-S MS65 PCGS. CAC. A typically satiny example of this key San Francisco issue. A few tinges of pale gold and lavender toning accent each side, while the surfaces are attractively devoid of noticeable flaws. The 1912-S boasts the lowest mintage of the series (238,000 coins), and is genuinely rare in grades numerically finer than the present example, with just 18 so-graded coins certified at PCGS (10/14). NGC ID# 277R, PCGS# 3875

PROOF LIBERTY NICKELS

1884 Liberty Nickel, PR67 Cameo
Tied for Finest-Graded at PCGS

3478 **1884 PR67 Cameo PCGS. FS-301.** The base of 1 in the date is widely repunched. This fully struck, brilliant Superb Gem proof exhibits strong white-on-black contrast on both sides. It is tied for finest-graded in Cameo condition at PCGS with six other coins. Both sides of this example are exquisitely preserved and virtually pristine. Population: 7 in 67, 0 finer (10/14). PCGS# 83882

1887 Nickel, PR66+ Cameo
Delightful Eye Appeal

3479 **1887 PR66+ Cameo PCGS. CAC.** Cameo examples of this proof issue are decidedly rare, and are exceedingly so in Premium Gem and finer grades. This lightly contrasted example boasts bold design definition, with well-balanced cartwheel luster and prooflike mirroring in the fields. A blush of light golden toning adds a degree of warmth to the beautifully preserved surfaces. Population: 10 in 66 (3 in 66+), 1 finer (10/14). PCGS# 83885

1896 Liberty Nickel, PR67 Cameo
Pronounced White-on-Black Contrast
Only One Other Piece So Graded at PCGS

3480 **1896 PR67 Cameo PCGS.** Nickel coinage is often found with shallow mirrors in the fields, but that is certainly not the case with this proof. The fields display deepest mirroring, similar to the reflectivity one would find on a silver proof. The devices on this piece are also thickly frosted and present strong white-on-black contrast against the mirrored fields. Very rare. Population: 2 in 67, 0 finer (10/14). PCGS# 83894

1909 Liberty Nickel, PR67+ Cameo
Only One Finer Coin at PCGS

3481 **1909 PR67+ Cameo PCGS. CAC.** The sharply detailed frosty design elements contrast boldly with the deeply mirrored fields, creating a dramatic white-on-black cameo flash when this coin is tilted in the light. The mostly brilliant surfaces are impeccably preserved and delicate hints of pale gold toning enhance the terrific eye appeal. Population: 24 in 67 (3 in 67+), 1 finer (10/14). PCGS# 83907

BUFFALO NICKELS

1919-D Nickel, MS66
Struck From Fresh Dies
Unusually Sharp and Smooth

1920-S Nickel, MS65
Only One Numerically Finer at PCGS

3482 **1919-D MS66 PCGS. CAC.** The Denver Mint had significant difficulty producing sharp strikes during this period, a problem not helped by the hard alloy of the Buffalo nickel. The 1919-D nickel is not scarce in the absolute sense, but striking quality varies widely, and the collector may have to search a long time before having an opportunity to acquire a sharp example. The present coin is truly exceptional, as it is uncharacteristically well-defined on both sides with satiny golden-gray luster. The coin is struck from fresh dies, with no evidence of the usual die erosion in the recesses. As many nickel dies were used well-beyond their normal wear boundaries during this period, finding an example of any branch mint issue without flow lines and signs of die fatigue is a rare acquisition. Housed in an old green label holder, this piece is tied with just 17 others as the finest certified at PCGS (10/14). NGC ID# 22RM, PCGS# 3942

3483 **1920-S MS65 PCGS.** Nickel production at the San Francisco Mint topped 9.6 million coins in 1920, a rather substantial figure for a branch mint issue of the period. Most examples, however, are rather miserably struck, as working dies were frequently used well beyond their normal life expectancy and the hard nickel alloy of the planchets imparted significant abuse on the finer engraving details. This characteristic weakness accounts significantly for the rarity of Gem-quality survivors; the major certification services have seen hundreds of this issue in grades up to MS64, but at the Gem level, where strike quality begins to factor into the numeric grade, the population plunges dramatically, and finer coins are prohibitively rare.

This satiny MS65 example is slightly soft on the highest point of each side, though the definition is actually incredible for the issue. A few light grazes limit the grade, though they are well-hidden beneath iridescent golden-gray toning. Population: 19 in 65, 1 finer (10/14). NGC ID# 22RS, PCGS# 3946

1925 Buffalo Nickel
Well-Struck Superb Gem

1925-S Nickel, MS65
Prohibitively Rare Any Finer

3484 **1925 MS67 PCGS.** The 1925 is part of a string of high-mintage Philadelphia issues from the 1920s, heavily produced but also heavily spent. Though lesser Mint State coins are relatively available, Gems and better appear only in small quantities, and at the MS67 level, the emphasis is on "small," with just 11 other coins so-graded by PCGS and none numerically finer (10/14). This gleaming piece has frosty luster with occasional hints of peach patina over otherwise bright nickel-white surfaces. Sharply struck with a small planchet flake below the bison's body as the only flaw readily perceptible to the unaided eye.
Ex: Central States Signature (Heritage, 4/2009), lot 2146. NGC ID# 22S2, PCGS# 3954

3485 **1925-S MS65 PCGS.** In the 1920s, it was common practice at the branch mints to use the undated reverse dies well-past their normal life expectancy in an attempt to reduce production costs. The result was that many coins (especially prevalent among Buffalo nickels, due to the dense nickel alloy) were struck with strong obverses and weak reverses.

This 1925-S nickel is an excellent example of the phenomenon, with the obverse well-defined, but the reverse showing strong evidence of die erosion, particularly around the borders. The eye appeal remains pleasing, however, with soft champagne and sky-blue hues complementing satiny luster, and the surfaces are clean enough to easily qualify for the Gem grade level. Population: 27 in 65, 1 finer (10/14). NGC ID# 22S4, PCGS# 3956

1927-D Nickel, MS65
Refreshingly Well-Struck

3486   **1927-D MS65 NGC.** Striking problems plague the 1927-D nickel, with sharp, attractive pieces being scarce. Most of the rather dismal Mint State population is restricted to MS64 and lower grades, and any Gem or finer pieces can be considered conditionally rare. The present coin shows an area of minor softness on the bison's shoulder, but is otherwise unusually sharp for the issue. Iridescent golden-gray toning complements satiny luster, while closer examination reveals a scattering of tiny specks over each side. Census: 30 in 65 (1 in 65+), 6 finer (10/14). NGC ID# 22S9, PCGS# 3961

1935 Nickel, MS64
Doubled Die Reverse

3487   **1935 Doubled Die Reverse, FS-801, MS64 NGC.** Bold die doubling is evident on all reverse relief elements. This *Guide Book* variety is seldom seen in the upper circulated grades, and Mint State examples are genuinely rare at all levels. This representative shows pale golden and lavender-gray patina, with minimal abrasions and only a few faint flecks on either side. A touch of striking weakness is noted on the hair above the Indian's braid, though the devices are otherwise well-defined. No significant evidence of die erosion is present. Census: 3 in 64, 2 finer (11/14). PCGS# 38465

1937-D Buffalo Nickel, MS68
Exceptional Mintmark Type Coin

3488   **1937-D MS68 NGC.** The regular-issue 1937-D Buffalo nickel is an issue that will never be rare, but it does bask in the reflected glow from its illustrious variety sibling, the 1937-D Three-Legged Buffalo. It is also, for some reason, an issue that occasionally appears with stunning patina and remarkably well-preserved surfaces, as is the case with this MS68 NGC example. This amazing coin boasts concentric rings of lavender in the center, radiating outward to saffron, sunset-orange, magenta, and emerald at the rims, with a similar color palette on both sides. Well-struck surfaces are free of all but trivial marks. Census: 4 in 68 (2 in 68 ★), 0 finer (10/14). NGC ID# 22SW, PCGS# 3981

1937-D Three-Legged Nickel, MS63
Bold Strike, Smooth Satiny Appeal

3489   **1937-D Three-Legged, FS-901, MS63 PCGS.** The Indian's braid knot and upper hair detail is strong, although as always, a few areas on the reverse are slightly weak from the single die pair that was used to create the famous variety. A string of raised die lumps (rust pits) extend between the fore and hind legs, curving up from the mound top to the top of the left rear leg Lilac accents join golden highlights join satiny luster for nice eye appeal. One or two minor nicks and some planchet roughness on the Indian's neck determine the Select Uncirculated grade. PCGS# 38475

PROOF BUFFALO NICKEL

1937 Nickel, PR68
Light Champagne Toning

3490 1937 PR68 NGC. The quicksilver surfaces are flashy and gorgeous, completely pristine and lacking even the most picayune distractions, as would be expected for the Superb Gem grade. Only the 1936 and 1937 Buffalo nickels are available in proof format — save for some of the early issues — as the Philadelphia Mint made no Buffalos at all in 1938. Census: 46 in 68 (4 in 68 ★), 0 finer (10/14). *Ex: Long Beach Signature (Heritage, 5/2007), lot 607.* NGC ID# 278Z, PCGS# 3996

PROOF JEFFERSON NICKEL

1952 Nickel, PR68 Deep Cameo
Tied for Finest at PCGS

3491 1952 PR68 Deep Cameo PCGS. The Jefferson nickel Set Registry collector will immediately recognize the importance of this PCGS finest certified example. Both sides have extraordinary contrast between the highly lustrous devices and the fully mirrored fields on this untoned Superb Gem Deep Cameo proof. Population: 3 in 68, 0 finer (10/14). NGC ID# 27A6, PCGS# 94184

EARLY HALF DIMES

1800 Half Dime, V-1, LM-1, XF40
Pleasing Original Patina

3492 1800 V-1, LM-1, R.3, XF40 PCGS. An early die state example, before the rim cud develops below the 00 in the date. The design elements are well-struck, with strong central detail. The border denticles are complete on the obverse, but grow weak along the lower-right reverse rim. Blended gunmetal-blue and olive-gray hues encompass the recesses, yielding to lighter gray color over the relief elements. PCGS# 38601

1800 V-1, LM-1 Half Dime, MS63
Late Die State, Double Struck Both Sides

3493 1800 V-1, LM-1, R.3. MS63 PCGS. Strongly double struck on both the obverse and the reverse, most obviously on the scroll but also visible on virtually all the motifs. This is a Select Uncirculated example of the LM-1 die pair — the most available die marriage of 1800 — with a total mintage of 40,000 pieces for the date.

The strike displays weakness on the obverse, a result of the late die state, strong die clash, and likely die wear. Liberty's uppermost hair strands and several stars show doubling. A large die break and cud below the date and die clashing above the date are diagnostic of the late die state. The reverse is weak at the shield and the eagle's breast. Eye appeal is strong, however, with attractive orange, blue, and iridescent shades covering both sides of the coin. Population (all varieties): 17 in 63, 28 finer (10/14). PCGS# 38601

1805 Half Dime, V-1, LM-1, VF30
Lovely Toning on Both Sides

3494 1805 V-1, LM-1, R.4, VF30 PCGS. Only one die variety is known for this scarce issue, boasting a low mintage of only 15,600 pieces. The present example shows a typically uneven strike, with the lower and right-hand portions of the obverse border and the upper-right portion of the reverse ill-defined. The remaining details are sharp, most notably Liberty's hair curls, which are well-delineated. Vivid tinges of turquoise, gold, violet, and amber accent pale lavender-gray patina on each side. The remnants of some minor adjustment marks are observed in the fields, though these are partially masked by the rich patina. PCGS# 38611

BUST HALF DIMES

1831 Half Dime, V-5, LM-5, MS67
Superb Capped Bust Type Coin

3495 1831 V-5, LM-5, R.1, MS67 NGC. An available variety, well-suited for type representation. This beautifully preserved example displays razor-sharp devices and warm golden toning. A hint of semiprooflike mirroring accents the central fields, while the surfaces are otherwise softly frosted. Census: 18 in 67 (2 in 67+, 2 in 67 ★), 2 finer (11/14). PCGS# 38660

1832 Half Dime, V-6, LM-13, MS66
Pristine Type Coin

3496 1832 V-6, LM-13, R.3, MS66 PCGS. CAC. This is a luminous, carefully preserved example of this moderately available type coin. The hair curls and stars are fully defined, as are the shield lines and the eagle's talons. Blended olive-gray, lavender-gold, and deep russet toning attest to the originality of the satiny luster, while close study with a loupe fails to reveal any discernable abrasions. PCGS has seen only 41 submissions in this grade, with just 12 numerically finer (10/14). PCGS# 38684

SEATED HALF DIMES

1846 Half Dime, Patinated AU53
Seldom Available in Any Grade

3497 1846 AU53 PCGS. From a mintage of just 27,000 pieces, the 1846 Seated Liberty half dime is seldom encountered in any grade. PCGS has certified only 92 examples in all levels of preservation. Violet, electric-blue, and yellow-gold patination is slightly deeper on the obverse of this AU53 well-defined specimen. A faint, horizontal pinscratch from the shield to the left (facing) leg will help to pedigree the coin. Population: 4 in 53, 5 finer (10/14). NGC ID# 2338, PCGS# 4336

1848-O Half Dime, MS67
Snow-White, Frosted Surfaces

3498 1848-O MS67 PCGS. Large O mintmark. Three different mintmark sizes are known on the New Orleans issue: Large, Medium, and Small. Of these, the Large mintmark is seen more often than the Small, with the Medium O somewhere in between. We have offered just two or three Superb Gem examples in the past 20 years, underscoring the scarcity of the issue in MS67 condition or finer. Amazingly, this coin is as brilliant and frosty as the day it left the Mint — razor-sharp, with minimal weakness on a few dentils offset by bursting silver luster on both sides. Clearly among the finest known. Population: 5 in 67 (1 in 67+), 1 finer (10/14). NGC ID# 233C, PCGS# 4340

1868-S Half Dime, MS66
Tied for Finest Certified

3499 1868-S MS66 PCGS. CAC. The 1868-S half dime is a better date, especially at the upper grade levels. Areas of rich toning are present on this lustrous Premium Gem example, primarily at portions of the outer edges, including shades of dark russet, olive-gold, and flecks of amber-orange. Pronounced clash marks are noted upon further examination, though the strike is well-executed and the preservation is pleasing. Population: 4 in 66, 0 finer (10/14). NGC ID# 234P, PCGS# 4393

PROOF SEATED HALF DIMES

1852 Half Dime, PR65
Only a Handful of Proofs Known

1864 Half Dime, PR67 ★
One of the Finest-Graded Examples

3500 **1852 PR65 PCGS. CAC.** This carefully preserved, richly toned Gem proof comes from an estimated proof mintage of a mere 10 pieces. These proofs were struck several years prior to Mint Director Snowden's push to popularize proof coinage and make them more widely available to collectors. In 1852, proofs were still produced on an "as needed" basis, whenever requested by a collector.

Dense, obviously original sea-green and copper-red toning dominates on both sides, but iridescent accents of gold and purple-rose are also noteworthy. The design details are razor-sharp, and bright reflectivity becomes evident beneath the deep patina when the piece is rotated beneath a lamp. A few wispy die striations are noted on the obverse and reverse alike (creating the brightness in the fields), but the pleasing surfaces are free of bothersome contact marks. The proof 1852 is obviously a rare coin, and this is among the finest known as well as being the only Gem proof certified by PCGS. NGC has graded two coins at PR65, with one finer. PCGS has also encapsulated a single proof specimen at PR66 (10/14). *Ex: FUN Signature (Heritage, 1/2007), lot 854, where it brought $43,125.* NGC ID# 235K, PCGS# 4429

3501 **1864 PR67 ★ NGC.** This proof issue of 470 pieces had a low corresponding business strike mintage of 48,000 coins, increasing the market pressure on proofs. This Superb example, one of the finest-graded, displays vivid electric-blue peripheral toning that surrounds frosted silver-white and champagne-red central devices. A sharply detailed and seemingly pristine example of this better-date issue. Census: 1 in 67 ★, 1 finer (10/14). NGC ID# 235Z, PCGS# 4447

EARLY DIMES

1797 JR-1 Dime, MS62
16 Stars Obverse
Condition Census Quality

3502 1797 16 Stars, JR-1, R.4, MS62 PCGS. CAC. When we offered an MS62 NGC specimen as part of the Ed Price Collection in August 2008, we wrote that it was the second or third finest known behind an MS63 NGC coin that we handled a decade earlier. Since then, we have handled one piece graded MS64 NGC and a PCGS-certified MS65 in the 2013 FUN Auction. From examination of the auction records, it appears that only two or three finer pieces are known. This lovely specimen is easily in the Condition Census. Both sides are bright and lustrous with light silver surfaces and faint blue and gold toning. The strike is slightly weak in the centers, but nicely centered. The surfaces have few blemishes and excellent eye appeal. Population: 3 in 62, 4 finer (10/14). PCGS# 38748

1798/97 Dime, JR-1, MS60
Evenly Struck, Deeply Toned

3503 1798/97 16 Stars Reverse, JR-1, R.3, MS60 NGC. The underlying 7 is plainly visible beneath the primary 8 in the date. Minor weakness on the lower hair curls is from die lapping only, as the design elements are sharply struck on both sides, save for the central portion of the shield which is typically soft. Deep olive-gray and lavender-gold hues encompass each side, yielding to soft underlying luster. No singularly obvious abrasions are noted. This variety is highly intriguing for its overdate status, but it is also available enough to be considered for type. PCGS# 38750

1801 JR-2 Dime, AU58
Exceptional Strike and Surfaces

3504 1801 JR-2, R.5, AU58 PCGS. CAC. A common obverse die was paired with two reverses to strike the two varieties of this issue. JR-2, differentiated by the small size of the A in STATES, is slightly scarcer overall, and is also exceedingly rare in Mint State. The coin here offered is an impressive nearly Uncirculated representative, with hints of luster remaining in the recesses amid the warm amber-gold, and lavender-gray patina. Slight striking softness on the upper-right corner of the shield is normal for the variety, while the remaining design elements exhibit above-average definition. Complete dentils on each side attest to the well-centered, even strike. A must-have, problem-free coin. PCGS# 38757

1804 Dime, XF Details
JR-2, 14 Stars on Reverse

3505 **1804 14 Stars Reverse, JR-2, R.5 — Repaired, Whizzed — NCS. XF Details.** The 1804 is the key date of the Draped Bust series, which spans from 1796 to 1807. Just two 1804 varieties were struck, and each has a separate *Guide Book* listing due to different reverse star counts. JR-2, with 14 stars, is moderately rarer than its 13 Star JR-1 counterpart. This example is bright and granular from whizzing, and the obverse field has been carefully smoothed. *Ex: Dallas Signature (Heritage, 10/2008), lot 530.* PCGS# 38767.

1807 JR-1 Dime, MS63
Usual Late Die State

3506 **1807 JR-1, R.2, MS63 PCGS.** A typical 1807 dime, this example shows clash marks, die bulges, and other signs of die deterioration on both sides. A single obverse die was used to produce 165,000 dimes in 1807, and the reverse die was also used for quarter eagles. The strike is weak along the left side of the obverse and reverse as nearly always on these coins. Most of the central details are sharper, also typical of this issue. Trivial surface marks are present, with frosty silver luster and no obvious toning on either side. Population: 34 in 63 (1 in 63+), 28 finer (10/14). PCGS# 38770.

1807 JR-1 Dime, MS64
Highly Attractive, Upper-End for the Grade

3507 **1807 JR-1, R.2, MS64 PCGS.** Mint records report a mintage of 165,000 dimes in 1807, all delivered in the first two quarters of the year. However, only one die variety is known for the issue, and it is possible that about 40,000 to 50,000 of coins delivered in the first quarter were actually dated 1805. If accurate, though, this smaller mintage for the 1807 dime obviously did not affect its high-grade survival, as it is still the most plentiful variety of the Heraldic Eagle type.

The reverse die for the 1807 dime was previously employed for several quarter eagle coinages, specifically varieties of the 1805, 1806/4, 1806/5, and early 1807 issues. Its use for the dime of 1807 is its final use, as the quarter eagle and dime both underwent design changes in 1808 and 1809, respectively.

The present coin shows the usual clash marks on each side, though neither die is cracked, evidence of this piece having been struck early in the production run. The central devices are boldly struck, though the left obverse and reverse borders are poorly defined due to slightly uneven striking, as is normal for this issue. The centers exhibit pale golden-gray toning, while the margins show deeper aquamarine and olive-gold hues. The surfaces are unusually clean for the grade, giving this piece exceptional eye appeal. Population: 20 in 64 (1 in 64+), 12 finer (10/14). PCGS# 38770.

BUST DIMES

1823/2 Dime, JR-1, Toned MS64

3508 **1823/2 Small E's, JR-1, R.3, MS64 NGC.** Two obverse dies, both featuring the 1823/2 overdate, and two reverse dies were employed to strike three different die varieties of the 1823 dime. JR-1 is one of the two more plentiful of the three, with JR-2 being the only definably rare variety of the issue. This piece exhibits bold definition on both sides, with moderate reflectivity in the fields. Vividly intermingled teal, violet, and olive-gold encompass satiny luster on each side. A small, mint-made planchet flaw is noted on Liberty's chin, though the surfaces are otherwise devoid of significant marks. PCGS# 38802

1829 Capped Bust Dime, VG8
Elusive and Desirable
Curl Base 2, JR-10 Variety

3509 **1829 Curl Base 2, JR-10, FS-301, R.6, VG8 PCGS. CAC.** A substantial mintage of 770,000 Capped Bust dimes was accomplished in 1829, with 12 die varieties known for the date. This coin represents the JR-10 variety, with the Curl Base 2 in the date. The JR-10 is one of the most elusive varieties in the Capped Bust series and specialists prize examples in all grades and conditions. The variety was discovered in 1973 and most examples seen are in lower circulated grades. This was the only use of the obverse die, but the reverse was employed again in 1830, on the JR-2 variety.

The present coin is an evenly worn specimen, with legends, date, and LIBERTY all legible. The dove-gray surfaces show a moderate number of abrasions, mostly on the reverse, with a few hints of amber toning. This lot represents an important opportunity for the series enthusiast. Population: 6 in 8, 8 finer (10/14). PCGS# 38836

1835 JR-9 Dime, MS65
Bold Central Detail

3510 **1835 JR-9, R.2, MS65 PCGS.** The 3 in the date is boldly repunched, a diagnostic of the available variety. This highly lustrous dime shows scattered areas of charcoal-gray and russet toning that cover only a portion of the available surfaces, leaving most of the piece untoned and silvery-white. Carefully preserved, with bright, clean, mark-free surfaces. Struck from mildly worn dies, but with strikingly sharp definition in the centers. PCGS# 38887

1837 JR-4 Capped Bust Dime, MS66
From the Pittman Collection

3511 **1837 JR-4, R.1, MS66 NGC. Ex: Pittman.** A bisecting obverse die crack between 12 and 5 o'clock identifies the variety. Frosty luster shines through the beautiful rainbow toning with light silver devices. The obverse has light gold at the centers, changing to deeper gold, violet, russet, and cobalt-blue at the border. Reddish-gold at the central reverse changes to blue-green and gold at the border. The visual effect of the toning on this Premium Gem is stunning. Liberty's hair is a trifle soft, but the reverse is razor-sharp. An appealing example of this final-year Capped Bust dime. Struck from mildly rotated dies. Census: 5 in 66, 0 finer (10/14), for all 1837 Capped Bust varieties.
Ex: Barney Bluestone, 11/1943, sold for $2.50; John Jay Pittman Collection, Part One (David Akers, 10/1997), lot 577; Los Angeles Signature (Heritage, 8/2009), lot 450; Fort Worth Signature (Heritage, 3/2010), lot 595. PCGS# 38894

SEATED DIMES

1859 Seated Liberty Dime, MS67
Only One Numerically Finer Coin at PCGS

3512 **1859 MS67 PCGS. CAC. Fortin-107, R.3.** The 1859 Seated Liberty dime claims a reasonable mintage of 429,200 pieces, yet examples in MS67 are quite rare and finer coins are virtually unobtainable. This magnificent Superb Gem displays sharp detail, with satiny mint luster and surfaces that show just a hint of pink toning. Scattered tiny, "as-made" die lumps are present, primarily near the left obverse rim, and a tiny spot appears to the left of Liberty's head. Die chips appear near stars 2 to 8 and stars 12 and 13. Population: 15 in 67 (1 in 67+), 1 finer (10/14). NGC ID# 2394, PCGS# 4619

1873-CC Dime, AU Sharpness
Significant Carson City Rarity

3513 **1873-CC Arrows — Environmental Damage — PCGS Genuine. AU Details. Fortin-101.** Uniform granularity over both sides accounts for the Details grade from PCGS, though the devices remain sharply detailed and only slight wear is evident over the high points. The recesses exhibit pale olive-gray color, lightening to battleship-gray patina on the relief elements. The 1873-CC Seated dime is a major key date in the series, with a mintage of less than 19,000 pieces. The typical example is well-worn, and a well-detailed coin is challenging to locate in any condition. NGC ID# 23BH, PCGS# 4666

1874-CC Arrows Dime, AU Details
Classic Key Date

3514 **1874-CC Arrows — Environmental Damage — PCGS Genuine. AU Details.** The 1874-CC is a classic key-date issue of the Legend obverse type, here with Arrows at the date. The mintage was a mere 10,817 pieces and survivors are typically in low grade, with the average certified grade just VF25. Although both sides of this example are moderately corroded, that roughness is evenly distributed across the surfaces, resulting in a still pleasing example. The detail is exceptional. Collectors who seek a pleasing piece with bold design definition at an affordable price are strongly urged to consider this 1874-CC dime. NGC ID# 23BL, PCGS# 4669

1879 Dime, MS68
Blizzard-White Surfaces
None Finer at PCGS or NGC

3515 **1879 MS68 NGC. Fortin-102, R.3.** From a slim mintage of 14,000 pieces, the 1879 Seated Liberty dime is scarce in all grades. The present coin is a Superb Gem example of outstanding quality. The pristine fields are reflective — virtually prooflike — and all of the devices are deeply frosted, boldly struck, and supremely lustrous. Census: 3 in 68, 0 finer (10/14). NGC ID# 23AS, PCGS# 4687

Key 1885-S Dime, MS66
The Eliasberg Coin, Very Rare Even in Gem Grade
Finest Coin Ever Offered at Auction

3516 **1885-S MS66 PCGS. CAC. Fortin-101.** Ex: Eliasberg-Stellar. The U.S. coinage of 1885 is a study in blacks and whites. Some coins — the cent, Philadelphia dime, and Morgan dollars from four mints — were struck in amounts ranging well up into the millions, the high being the 1885 Morgan at nearly 18 million coins. Yet the double eagle was struck to the extent of only 751 pieces, making it among the lowest-mintage of all U.S. gold coins. The 1885-S Seated dime stands out not only due to its low mintage of 43,690 circulation strikes, but also because of its peculiar status as the only branch mint minor-coin issue for the entire year.

Described as a "Prooflike Gem" in the Eliasberg catalog, the present MS66 PCGS-certified 1885-S dime is either the sole finest graded, or tied for finest graded at a minimum, depending on whether the NGC example in the same grade is indeed a *different* coin. Our auction records for Heritage and other companies show no other offerings of an MS66 example of the 1885-S in MS66, and in fact there are precious few offerings even at the Gem level. There is certainly no record of a public offering of an MS66 NGC example, nor any hint of one.

This piece displays delicate gold patina on each side, accented with wisps of robin's-egg-blue and mint-green on the obverse. The surfaces are well-mirrored beneath the light layer of patina and boast an extremely sharp strike. There are no mentionable distractions on this remarkable coin. This is without question the *finest ever to be offered at a public auction.* *Ex: Louis E. Eliasberg, Sr. Collection (Bowers and Merena, 5/1996), lot 1228, where it was described as "MS-65, prooflike;" purchased from Joseph O'Connor (5/2004).* NGC ID# 23B2, PCGS# 4695

1886-S Dime, MS67
Outstanding High-End Example

3517 **1886-S MS67 PCGS. Fortin-101, R.4.** The 1886-S dime had a limited mintage of little more than 200,000 pieces, and is seldom seen in any Mint State grade. For the patient collector, however, a handful of impressive Superb Gems, such as the present offering, survive. This piece shows heavily frosted, radiant luster and carefully preserved surfaces. Delicate light golden toning complements boldly impressed design elements. Population: 4 in 67, 2 finer (10/14). NGC ID# 23B4, PCGS# 4697

PROOF SEATED DIMES

1846 Seated Dime, PR62
Exceedingly Rare as a Proof
Only 10 to 15 Known

3518 **1846 PR62 PCGS. Fortin-102, R.7.** No official records were kept of the number of proof dimes struck in 1846, though the mintage was undoubtedly minuscule. Only about 10 to 15 are believed to exist today in all grades. PCGS and NGC combined have encapsulated 15 examples, though it is possible a few of these reflect resubmissions of the same coin. This piece ranks as one of three for the grade at PCGS, with six finer (10/14). The devices are fully brought up, with deep mirroring in the fields. Largely untoned, with bright, steel-gray surfaces. NGC ID# 23C2, PCGS# 4733

1853 Arrows Dime, Toned PR66+
Finest Known Proof
From the Kaufman Collection

3519 1853 Arrows PR66+ PCGS. CAC. Undoubtedly the finest-known 1853 proof Arrows dime, this coin from the Kaufman Collection (and later from the exceptional Eugene H. Gardner Collection) has exceptional mirrors and amazing eye appeal, a treat for the connoisseur. While the number of proofs and the timing of the proof strikes has long been debated, it is generally agreed just five proofs of the Arrows dimes were made plus two proofs of the No Arrows variant. The current roster has not changed significantly in rank or known examples over the past fifteen or so years. It is believed that at least four of the following five appearances represent true proofs.

1. **PR66+ PCGS.** *From the Kaufman Collection.* This example is different from any of the following. **The present coin.**
2. **PR65.** *John Jay Pittman Collection (David Akers 10/1997), lot 615.*
3. **PR63 NGC.** *Hollinbeck Coin Co. (6/1953), lot 1997; Norweb Collection (Bowers 10/1987), lot 484; Lovejoy Collection (Stack's 10/1990), lot 270.*
4. **PR65 NGC.** *Superior (10/2000), lot 4345.* The cataloger implies that this is the Pittman coin when he states that it is the finer of two known proofs, identifying the Norweb coin as the other one. However, the plate clearly shows an entirely different coin from either of those pieces.
5. **Choice Proof.** *Kamal Ahwash (8/1981); unknown; Stack's (3/1996), lot 276.*

Earlier literature has suggested that the 1853 proofs are unintentional or "accidental" pieces struck from dies that were resurfaced and polished to remove clash marks. We feel strongly the pieces are indeed proofs, but there is no denying the muted clash marks that are present near Liberty's right leg and drapery, and inside the right branch of the wreath. Die resurfacing will remove these clash marks and other die defects, but an unavoidable consequence is the removal of shallow design elements. Careful observation of this proof shows complete design elements on each side, suggesting if die resurfacing was done, it was accomplished without compromising the strong detail of the motifs.

The exact timing and nature of the die pair used for the proofs is another matter. All genuine proofs show a diagnostic die lump above Liberty's right breast, and a smaller, less noticeable one near her right elbow. The proofs always display significant die clashing as discussed above. Another diagnostic, heretofore not mentioned in the literature, includes spikelike artifacts beneath Liberty's chin — apparently, an unfinished area of the die. All known proofs appear to show this feature as well.

Gerry Fortin makes a valid observation that the Fortin-120 obverse is of special interest. The date position is the same as the proofs, and the die lump above Liberty's breast and the one on the elbow are present, as is the unfinished die area beneath Liberty's chin. The date position is the same as the proofs — in fact, all diagnostics appear the same, except for the presence of die clashing. Might the proofs have been struck late in the year from the Fortin-120 die pair after it clashed, and that these dies were later prepared for proofs with a careful but non-effacing polishing? If so, Fortin-101 may be a late die state of the Fortin-120 dies.

We note that the obverses of at least two or three of the highest-graded proofs show what appears to be die rust above star 7 and on other areas at the peripheries, suggesting the dies sat idle for a period of time. It is a possibility worth future research.

Both sides of this boldly struck piece are sharp and complete. The mirrored fields are full and deep beneath bright champagne color with splashes of iridescent toning throughout. NGC ID# 23CE, PCGS# 4742

1856 Small Date Dime, Toned PR67
A Difficult Date in Proof

3520 1856 PR67 PCGS. CAC. Fortin-101. This date was struck in unknown but small numbers. Survivors are mainly in the lower numeric grades of PR60 to PR64, and number only in the 30 to 40-coin range per the PCGS website. The major services combined have certified 45 pieces in all grades, likely including a number of resubmissions. The present Superb Gem offering is the sole finest coin seen by PCGS, though NGC has graded a single PR68 Cameo (10/14).

The obverse die is boldly doubled north on the shield and within the lower gown folds, as is diagnostic of this proof die pair, while there is also a die defect on Liberty's left (facing) breast. On the reverse, a die line is seen from the rim to the R in AMERICA. Cobalt-blue and lavender obverse toning cedes to mostly cobalt-blue on the reverse. Sharply struck design elements further enhance the coin's beautiful eye appeal, as do the impeccably preserved surfaces. A difficult date to locate as a proof. NGC ID# 23CA, PCGS# 4745

1859 Dime, PR66 Cameo
Stark Field-Motif Contrast

3521 1859 PR66 Cameo PCGS. Fortin-101, R.4. The official recorded mintage of proof dimes in 1859 was 800 pieces, the largest production total up to that point. Surviving examples are occasionally available in the absolute sense, but few are known with Cameo contrast. This Premium Gem representative displays bold, frosty devices, with glassy mirroring in the fields. Splashes of sun-gold, pale violet, and aquamarine encompass the recesses, giving this carefully preserved proof exceptional eye appeal. Population: 7 in 66 (2 in 66+), 3 finer (10/14). PCGS# 84748

1881 Seated Dime, PR68 Cameo
Immaculate Mirrors
Tied for Finest-Certified in Cameo

3522 1881 PR68 Cameo PCGS. Fortin-101. An incredibly bold and attractive Superb Gem proof, with glittering silver surfaces surrounded by a blue and umber-gold borders. The fields are devoid of any lines or distractions even under magnification. The frost-white, fully struck devices contrast boldly with the watery-deep mirrors. Although 975 proofs were struck, just seven pieces qualify for this lofty Cameo grade by both services combined. PCGS Population: 2 in 68, 0 finer (10/14). PCGS# 84778

1884 Dime, PR67 Cameo
Lovely Multicolor Patina

3523 1884 PR67 Cameo PCGS. CAC. Fortin-101, R.3. The obverse of this carefully preserved proof displays concentric peripheral bands of royal-blue and violet around the warm sun-gold center. The reverse is more subtly toned, with a blend of lemon-gold and aquamarine. The devices are well-struck and frosty, with some light die rust observed upon close examination. The proof 1884 dime is an available issue overall, but Cameo examples are seldom seen, and are genuinely rare this well-preserved. Population: 20 in 67 (1 in 67+), 0 finer (10/14). PCGS# 84781

1885 Dime, PR67 Cameo
Delicate Peripheral Toning

3524 **1885 PR67 Cameo PCGS. CAC. Fortin-101, R.3.** Rich amber-gold peripheral toning surrounds brilliant, frosty devices on this deeply mirrored Cameo. The design elements are boldly impressed and the field-motif contrast is superb. This proof issue had a moderate mintage of 930 coins, but Cameo representatives are rarely seen at this lofty grade level. Population: 13 in 67 (1 in 67+), 2 finer (10/14). PCGS# 84782

1891 Dime, PR67
Delicate Multicolor Toning

3525 **1891 PR67 PCGS. CAC. Fortin-130, R.3.** Three different die pairs were employed for proof dime coinage in 1891, producing 600 coins in total. Of the three corresponding varieties, Fortin-130 is the most frequently encountered. This example displays well-struck devices and deep mirrors. Vivid sea-green, royal-blue, and violet hues encompass the reverse, and surround a light golden center on the obverse. As date, the 1891 is highly popular as the final-year proof issue, and is often encountered in type specialists' cabinets. Population: 9 in 67, 0 finer (10/14). NGC ID# 23DG, PCGS# 4788

BARBER DIMES

1895 Dime, Appealing MS66
Lowest-Mintage P-Mint Issue, Rare So Fine

3526 **1895 MS66 PCGS. CAC.** The 1895 Philadelphia Barber dime is the lowest-mintage P-mint issue in the series — only 690,000 pieces were struck — and the rarest P-mint in high grades and overall. This Premium Gem with CAC approval is an extremely appealing coin, showing a melange of mint-green, pinkish-gray, and copper-gold patina accompanying the full strike that this issue is known for. PCGS reports 11 in MS66 with four finer. CAC shows six in MS66 with four finer (10/14). NGC ID# 23DV, PCGS# 4806

1907-S Barber Dime, MS66
Second-Rarest S-Mint Barber Dime

3527 **1907-S MS66 PCGS. CAC.** An unheralded condition rarity within the Barber dime series, the 1907-S is quite rare in the higher Mint State grades despite its plentiful mintage exceeding 3.1 million coins. Among S-mint issues in the series in high grades, only the 1895-S is rarer (and excluding the 1894-S, of course). This Premium Gem 1907-S is one of eight such at PCGS, and there is one more at NGC. The CAC green approval sticker reduces the population to five in MS66-CAC (10/14). This splendid coin displays delicate pale mint, copper-gold, and dove-gray patina on each with sharply struck surfaces and excellent eye appeal. NGC ID# 23F6, PCGS# 4845

PROOF BARBER DIME

1895 Dime, PR67 Cameo
Lovely Peripheral Toning

3528 **1895 PR67 Cameo PCGS. CAC.** The collector will have little trouble acquiring a non-Cameo example of this proof issue, but Cameos such as this coin are decidedly challenging, especially in high grades. The obverse displays peripheral bands of royal-blue, violet, and amber around a pale champagne center, while the reverse is primarily light golden, with a multicolor crescent along the left-hand border. The strike is boldly executed, with deep mirroring in the fields. One of the ribbon ends on the obverse is segmented from the back of Liberty's head, a product of excessive die polishing. Population: 13 in 67 (1 in 67+), 0 finer (10/14). PCGS# 84879

MERCURY DIMES

1916-D Mercury Dime, MS66 Full Bands
Undisputed Key to This Popular Series

1921-D Mercury Dime, MS66 Full Bands

3530 1921-D MS66 Full Bands PCGS. CAC. Recession gripped the country in 1921 and 1922, resulting in reduced production at all three Mints. The Denver mint coined dimes only during the first half of the year, stopping at a mintage of just over 1 million pieces (the second-lowest mintage of the series behind the 1916-D issue). This example is softly lustrous and attractive. A thin band of orange toning attends the rims on both sides, with gleaming, silver-white centers. As expected with a Full Bands Premium Gem, the strike is bold overall. Just two coins are numerically finer — none at PCGS. Population: 21 in 66 (2 in 66+) Full Bands, 0 finer (10/14). NGC ID# 23HF, PCGS# 4937

1942/1 Mercury Dime, MS64
Popular Guide Book Variety

3531 1942/1 FS-101 MS64 PCGS. Among the keys to the series, this hubbing error is recognized by the overlapping last numerals in the date. Soft champagne-gold patina makes occasional visits to the lustrous surfaces of this near-Gem. The design elements are well-struck, including the middle bands that are a tad short of full. Housed in a green label holder. Population: 22 in 64, 11 finer (10/14). PCGS# 145473

3529 1916-D MS66 Full Bands PCGS. CAC. The 1916 introduction of the Winged Liberty or "Mercury" dime marked, according to numismatic art critic Cornelius Vermeule, "the first individual and imaginative design for this small denomination in American numismatic art." Between 1907 and 1921, during the Renaissance of American numismatic art, every U.S. coinage design from the Lincoln cent through double eagle was changed with a broad sweep of the brush — 10 new designs in all from the Lincoln cent through Saint-Gaudens double eagle. It is no accident that some of these series are among the most popularly collected today, with the Lincoln cent, Buffalo nickel, and Mercury dime likely near the top of the list.

While the Lincoln cent and Buffalo nickel series each has multiple key coins depending on condition (and color, in the case of cents), it is difficult to make a case for any issue other than the 1916-D dime being a key to the Mercury series. The low mintage made the issue an instant rarity, and attrition and extensive circulation took their toll on most of the emission. This example has been well cared for since the year of issue. The mint luster is bright and frosted, and each side displays a light accent of magenta patina with a thin sliver of blue at the margins. Population: 22 in 66 (2 in 66+) Full Bands, 7 finer (10/14). NGC ID# 23GY, PCGS# 4907

PROOF MERCURY DIME

1938 Mercury Dime, PR68
Fantastic Quality and Eye Appeal

3532 **1938 PR68 PCGS. CAC.** A fairly large number of the 8,728 proof dimes struck in 1938 have survived to the present day. PCGS has graded nearly 2,500 pieces, most in the near-Gem to Premium Gem levels of preservation. The population drops significantly at the MS67 level, and finer examples are extremely difficult to locate. Yellow-gold, violet, and green peripheral toning surrounds the luminous, pale-blue interiors of this razor-sharp specimen. Both sides have been wonderfully cared for, as might be expected from this lofty grade. The CAC sticker affirms the coin's magnificent eye appeal. Population: 9 in 68 (1 in 68+), 0 finer (10/14). NGC ID# 27DJ, PCGS# 5073

PROOF ROOSEVELT DIMES

1950 Dime, PR68 Ultra Cameo
Tomaska Plate Coin

3533 **1950 PR68 Ultra Cameo NGC.** As the first year of the newly restarted proofs, the 1950 is predictably a rare coin, especially with Ultra Cameo contrast. The PR68 designation makes it even more significant and makes this quite the purchase for a Registry Set collector. The field-device contrast could not be more profound. Each side is brilliant, the only exception being a faint streak of planchet granularity on the upper left of the reverse, a trait that identifies this as the plate coin on page 48 of Rick Tomaska's *Cameo and Brilliant Proof Coinage of the 1950 to 1970 Era* (1991). Census: 4 in 68, 0 finer (10/14). PCGS# 95225

1951 Roosevelt Dime
PR68 Ultra Cameo

3534 **1951 PR68 Ultra Cameo NGC.** This Superb Gem Ultra Cameo proof is an extraordinary untoned example that exhibits sharply detailed and satiny devices, seemingly floating over deeply mirrored fields. Such highly contrasted examples from the early 1950s are seldom encountered. Census: 4 in 68 (1 in 68 ★), 1 finer (10/14). NGC ID# 27EK, PCGS# 95226

TWENTY CENT PIECES

1876 Twenty Cent Piece
Beautifully Toned Gem Example

3535 **1876 MS65 NGC. BF-2, R.2.** The 1876 twenty cent comes from a low business strike mintage of 14,400 pieces. Concentric rings of violet, greenish-gold, electric-blue, and lavender patina adorn the lustrous surfaces of this Gem, and an exacting strike delivers strong definition to the design elements. Nicely preserved throughout. Census: 36 in 65, 20 finer (10/14).
Ex: Central States Signature (Heritage, 4/2009), lot 360; Long Beach Signature (Heritage, 2/2010), lot 1041. NGC ID# 23R8, PCGS# 5299

1876 BF-2 Twenty Cent, MS65
Rainbow-Toned, Bold Prooflike Example

3536 **1876 MS65 PCGS. BF-2, R.2.** The proper viewing angle is important to fully appreciate the reflective fields and vivid coloration of this dramatically toned twenty cent piece. Alternating bands of primary colors create a prismatic effect over both sides the coin. The surfaces are deeply prooflike — unusually so — and the bold details on the motifs suggest an early strike from polished ides. Just 14,640 circulation strikes were produced, the lowest mintage of the regular issue business strikes. Housed in a first generation holder. Population: 32 in 65, 16 finer (10/14). NGC ID# 23R8, PCGS# 5299

PROOF TWENTY CENT PIECES

1875 Twenty Cent, PR66
Beautiful Type or Date Candidate

3537 **1875 PR66 NGC. BF-2, R.4.** Proof twenty cent pieces are seemingly underappreciated as a collectible set, even though only four issues are needed and all are relatively available overall. The present coin is a visually exceptional representative of the 1875 issue, with fully struck, frosty devices and deeply reflective fields. Intermingled shades of olive-gray, lavender-gold, and aquamarine toning preclude a Cameo designation from NGC, but make up for it by contributing a lovely visual display. Census: 18 in 66, 1 finer (10/14). NGC ID# 27GZ, PCGS# 5303

1877 Twenty-Cent Piece, PR64 Cameo
Outstanding Conditionally Scarce Example

3538 **1877 PR64 Cameo PCGS. CAC.** This proof-only issue of 510 pieces saw an actual distribution only 350 coins, and examples that display noteworthy Cameo contrast are scarce. The current offering is an outstanding representative in every respect, from flawless strike definition to gorgeous deep peripheral toning in shades of golden-brown, dusky-green, and sky blue. The richly frosted devices are icy-white and starkly contrasted against watery fields. Population: 28 in 64 (1 in 64+), 13 finer (10/14). PCGS# 85305

1878 Twenty Cent Piece, PR64
Final Proof-Only Issue

3539 **1878 PR64 NGC.** The proof-only 1878 twenty cent piece was the last issue of the denomination, with a mintage of just 600 coins. Examples are popular with series specialists and type collectors. This Choice proof has attractive surfaces with fully mirrored fields beneath subdued gold and iridescent toning. A glass reveals only inconsequential contact marks and hairlines on this appealing example. NGC ID# 27H5, PCGS# 5306

1878 Twenty-Cent Piece, PR65
Low-Mintage Final Proof-Only Issue

3540 **1878 PR65 PCGS.** The twenty-cent piece was an unpopular type that was only produced for four years, from 1875 through 1878. The last two years of that span saw small proof-only issues from the Philadelphia Mint, including this final emission of just 600 coins. This is a pleasing Gem representative with razor-sharp strike definition. The undisturbed surfaces display light to medium-gray coloration enhanced on each side by strong accents of cobalt-blue, especially near the peripheries. Population: 27 in 65, 12 finer (10/14). NGC ID# 27H5, PCGS# 5306

EARLY QUARTER

1796 B-2 Quarter, VG Details
Single-Year Early Type Coin

3541 **1796 B-2, R.3 — Repaired — NGC Details. VG.** Nicely defined for the VG level, since all legends are bold and the right (facing) wing has ample plumage detail. A charcoal-gray example. Both sides are microgranular throughout. Portions of Liberty's hair are smoothed, behind her ear and on the neck curls. The right obverse field is likely also smoothed. Still an opportunity to acquire one of the rarest silver types. PCGS# 38920

BUST QUARTERS

1818/5 Quarter, Toned MS65
B-3, Overdated Obverse Die

1838 B-1 Quarter, MS64
End of the Capped Bust Type

3543 **1838 B-1, R.1, MS64 NGC.** The final Capped Bust date before replacement by the Seated type. Reportedly, a single die pair (B-1) was used to coin the entire 366,000-piece mintage — perhaps, some of those coins were actually dated 1837. The softly lustrous obverse has a tan-brown and silver-gray center framed by forest-green, blue, and reddish-lilac. The reverse is flashy and lightly toned with peripheral peach patina. A well preserved and satiny near-Gem, boldly struck and appealing. Census: 18 in 64, 6 finer (10/14).
Ex: New York Signature (Heritage, 7/2002), lot 7790; Fred Miller Collection (Heritage, 3/2004), lot 5631. PCGS# 39015

3542 **1818/5 B-3, R.3, MS65 NGC.** B-3 shares the same overdated obverse die as B-1, but the underlying 5 is no longer visible within the upper loop of the second 8 due to the die having been lapped prior to this second usage. On the present coin, however, a partial outline of the 5 is evident *on* the raised surfaces of the 8, as the 8 was not punched quite as deeply into the die face as the 5. B-3 is also the second use of this reverse, which was previously employed for B-2. Here it is seen clashed and lightly cracked (at the arrowheads) from its previous marriage.

This coin is remarkably well-preserved, as evidenced by the Gem grade, with shimmering original luster beneath rich, multicolor toning. The obverse shows hues of teal, olive-gold, and deep amber-violet, while the reverse shows the same in a much more even blend. Some of the finer design elements are weakly impressed, a typical characteristic of this variety, with both dies in their second use. Census of all 1818 quarters: 35 in 65, 17 finer (10/14). PCGS# 411648

SEATED QUARTERS

1846 Quarter Dollar, MS65
Underappreciated Early Seated Issue

3544 1846 MS65 PCGS. CAC. Briggs 2-D. The date is boldly repunched north, as is diagnostic of this variety. The 1846 quarter dollar comes from a mintage of 510,000 business strikes. The issue is a somewhat scarce date, evidenced in part by fewer than 160 examples certified in all grades by PCGS and NGC. Most examples are in the Extremely Fine to About Uncirculated levels of preservation. Uncirculated pieces in the MS60 to MS63 range can be located with patience and searching, while near-Gems will be more difficult to obtain. The two services combined have seen a mere three MS65 coins, including the present offering, and one Premium Gem graded by NGC (10/14).

A melange of deep reddish-gold, cobalt-blue, and purple toning fringes the borders of this lustrous example, complemented by boldly struck design features. An unobtrusive linear mark on Liberty's neck, one on the cheek, and two toning streaks to the lower left of the reverse shield identify the coin. NGC ID# 23SW, PCGS# 5409

1855 Arrows Quarter, MS65
Conditionally Rare Philadelphia Issue

3545 1855 Arrows MS65 PCGS. CAC. Briggs 2-B. The 1855 Arrows Seated Liberty quarter is a seemingly underappreciated Philadelphia issue. Its mintage of more than 2.8 million pieces would suggest it is plentiful, but the date is actually scarce in all grades. Mint State supplies are particularly limited, with the typical example grading no finer than MS63; Choice representatives are rare, and finer coins a even greater. This Gem example is one of just seven so-graded pieces at PCGS, with only three finer (10/14). The strike is crisp throughout, while the surfaces reveal minor, grade-consistent ticks. Shimmering, vibrant luster further increases the eye appeal, yielding to a veil of lavender-gold toning that deepens toward the borders. Struck from mildly rotated dies, this coin is a rare bidding opportunity for the advanced Seated quarter specialist. NGC ID# 23U8, PCGS# 5435

PROOF SEATED QUARTERS

1857 Seated Quarter, PR66
Ex: Kaufman, Tied for Finest Graded

3554 **1857 PR66 NGC. Briggs 7-G.** The exact number of proof quarters struck in 1857 is not known, as the Mint did not begin recording proof mintage data until the following year, but it was undoubtedly small. Survival estimates vary greatly, ranging from just 15 (Briggs, 1991) to as many as 100 (PCGS). The actual number is likely near the middle, as the two leading services show a combined population of 72 coins, including an unknown number of resubmissions.

This Premium Gem example, formerly in the Phil Kaufman Collection, is one of the three finest examples graded by NGC and PCGS combined (10/14). A medley of low-intensity cobalt-blue, golden-tan, orange, and yellow-green patination adorns the obverse, while deeper hues of the same palette adhere to the reverse. The sharp proof strike has created full detail throughout both sides. The preservation is flawless, engendering elegant eye appeal. A coin of high quality and rarity.
Ex: Phil Kaufman Collection / Baltimore ANA Signature (Heritage, 7/2008), lot 1828 NGC ID# 23WJ, PCGS# 5553

1867 Quarter, PR67 Cameo
Excellent Quality and Eye Appeal

3555 **1867 PR67 Cameo NGC. Ex: Eric P. Newman Collection.** The colors, surface quality, and overall preservation of this piece are consistent with other proof Seated quarters of this decade that are pedigreed to the Newman Collection. This coin is spectacular; it's a piece any collector would be eager to own. The strike is absolute insofar as we can tell, with somewhat deeper patina on the obverse. The cameo contrast is blatant, with the designation thoroughly well-deserved. Census: 3 in 67 (1 in 67 ★), 0 finer (10/14).
Ex: Eric P. Newman Numismatic Education Society. PCGS# 85566

1874 Arrows Quarter, Rare PR66 Cameo

3556 **1874 Arrows PR66 Cameo PCGS. Briggs 5-D.** With a mintage of 700 pieces, the 1874 proof quarter is no rarer overall than any other proof issue of the period, but Cameo representatives are another matter entirely. PCGS has awarded only 51 1874 proofs a Cameo designation, with this piece being tied with just nine others as the finest (10/14). An additional coin has been encapsulated as Deep Cameo by the same service, though this piece resides only at the PR63 grade level, making this eye-catching Premium Gem seem far superior from a technical standpoint. The deeply mirrored fields are home to shades of blue, violet, sea-green, and sun-gold, while the frosty central devices exhibit a pale champagne hue. The design elements are sharply impressed, and the corresponding eye appeal is outstanding. PCGS# 85575

1875 Quarter, PR66 ★ Cameo
Stark Field-Motif Contrast

3557 **1875 PR66 ★ Cameo NGC. Briggs 5-F.** The proof 1875 Seated quarter had a mintage of 700 coins, but Cameo representatives survive in remarkably limited numbers. This Premium Gem example displays sharp, frosty devices and deep mirroring in the fields. A suggestion of light golden color adds a degree of warmth to otherwise brilliant surfaces. Census: 2 in 66 (1 in 66 ★), 3 finer (11/14). PCGS# 85576

1882 Quarter, PR67+ ★
Outstanding Visual Appeal

3558 **1882 PR67+ ★ NGC. Briggs 2-B.** Beautifully preserved, this high-end Superb Gem proof exhibits vivid toning on the obverse in shades of golden-orange, teal, plum, pale yellow, and violet, with a commanding mirrored presence not often seen except on the finest proof coins. The reverse is more subtly toned but equally appealing in largely champagne-gold hues, with a pale splash of teal and electric-blue along portions of the left margin. As expected in this high grade, the coin displays an intricate strike and immaculate surfaces. Census: 16 in 67 (1 in 67 ★, 2 in 67+★), 4 finer (10/14). NGC ID# 23XE, PCGS# 5583

1891 Quarter, PR67 Deep Cameo
The Finest Deep Cameo Certified

3559 **1891 PR67 Deep Cameo PCGS. Briggs 1-A.** This amazing coin displays profoundly mirrored, jet-black fields that contrast nicely against the frosted, ice-white devices, producing the white-on-black appearance that collectors so desire in Deep Cameo/Ultra Cameo coinage. This fully struck coin is devoid of any other color, but the deep contrast should produce a frisson of excitement in the most jaded collector. The 1891 proof Seated quarter issue (600 specimens) was the last of the series, as the Barber design would be introduced in 1892. Population: 1 in 67, 0 finer (10/14).
Ex: FUN Signature (Heritage, 7/2010), lot 3596. PCGS# 95592

BARBER QUARTERS

1896-S Quarter, AU55
Popular Key Series Issue

3560 **1896-S AU55 NGC.** Just a touch of wear separates this attractive silver-gray piece from Mint State and a much higher price. A couple of small reeding marks on the cheek and at the bridge of the nose are the only mentionable contact, and the strike is quite well-executed throughout both sides (including the problematic upper-right shield corner). The 1896-S is a difficult issue to find in so nice a grade and with the lustrous aesthetics this piece possesses. Census: 4 in 55, 39 finer (10/14). NGC ID# 23Y9, PCGS# 5615

1901-S Barber Quarter, VG10
Rarest of the 'Big Three'

3561 **1901-S VG10 PCGS.** A classic key-date Barber quarter, the 1901-S is one of the "Big Three" in the series alongside the 1896-S and 1913-S quarters. Although a small number of Mint State examples survive, the typical 1901-S is well-worn, with little remaining detail. PCGS and NGC have combined to certify just over 1,000 submissions, with an average certified grade of just below 9. Only 129 of those submissions grade finer than the present piece, including just 91 finer examples at PCGS (10/14). This attractive pewter-gray example shows hints of magenta in the fields, and lighter silver-gray devices. An old scratch in the right obverse field is toned over, but the surfaces are generally exceptional for the grade, showing only trivial imperfections. NGC ID# 23YR, PCGS# 5630

1916-D Barber Quarter, MS67
Remarkable, Visually Pleasing Example

3562 **1916-D MS67 PCGS.** The scintillating mint luster exhibited by this Superb Gem is only one of its impressive attributes. It is also sharply struck and exquisitely preserved, showing immaculate, blemish-free surfaces. Each side displays a full coating of mottled patina: mostly champagne and gold on the obverse, and olive-green and russet-red on the reverse. A remarkable and visually pleasing piece, tied for finest-graded at PCGS. Population: 14 in 67, 0 finer (10/14). NGC ID# 2426, PCGS# 5674

PROOF BARBER QUARTERS

1894 Barber Quarter, PR68
Dazzling Visual Display

3563 **1894 PR68 NGC. CAC.** A nominal mintage of 972 proof Barber quarters was achieved in 1894 for inclusion in the proof sets of that year. Almost all 1894 silver proof sets were eventually broken up to provide date collectors with high-quality examples of the silver dollar, which had an unusually low business-strike mintage that year.

The 1894 proof quarter was a well-produced issue, but few survivors can match the technical quality and eye appeal of the present coin. The design elements exhibit razor-sharp definition throughout and the pristine fields are deeply mirrored. Spectacular shades of cerulean-blue and greenish-gold toning blanket the surfaces, creating a dazzling play of colors when this coin is rotated in the light. The eye appeal is incredible. Housed in a prior generation holder. Census: 5 in 68 (1 in 68+), 0 finer (10/14). NGC ID# 2429, PCGS# 5680

1897 Quarter, PR68 Cameo
Delicately Toned

3564 **1897 PR68 Cameo NGC.** A typical proof issue in the Barber quarter series, the 1897 is available in most grades, but becomes scarce with noticeable field device contrast. This is a visually superb Cameo, with swirling pastel hues in the fields and dusky silvery-gold toning over the relief elements. No contact marks or hairlines are discernable upon close examination. Census: 9 in 68 (5 in 68 ★), 0 finer (10/14). PCGS# 85683

1906 Barber Quarter, PR68
None Numerically Finer at Either Service

3565 **1906 PR68 NGC.** A small proof mintage of 675 Barber quarters was achieved in 1906. This magnificent PR68 specimen is one of the finest survivors. The fully struck design elements have a frosty texture that provides modest contrast with the pristine mirrored fields. The mostly brilliant surfaces are free of visible flaws and show a few hints of pale gold toning. Eye appeal is tremendous. Census: 12 in 68 (1 in 68+, 2 in 68 ★), 0 finer (10/14). NGC ID# 242M, PCGS# 5692

1911 Barber Quarter, PR68 Cameo
Impressive, Virtually Flawless Example

3566 **1911 PR68 Cameo NGC.** Exquisite and sure to delight high-quality proof type collectors, this coin is devoid of even the slightest toning. As such, one can fully appreciate the awe-inspiring cameo contrast between the frosty textured devices and deeply mirrored fields. Pinpoint striking definition is noted throughout, and there are no grade-limiting blemishes. Census: 12 in 68 (2 in 68 ★), 2 finer (10/14). *Ex: Long Beach Signature (Heritage, 2/2010), lot 1107.* PCGS# 85697

STANDING LIBERTY QUARTERS

1916 Standing Liberty Quarter, VG8
Pleasing Lower-Grade Example

3567 **1916 VG8 PCGS.** Pale olive and battleship-gray hues blanket each side of this moderately worn key-date quarter, with subtle iridescent accents seen when tilted beneath a light. The date is weak at the top, but clearly identifiable. Only 52,000 1916 Standing Liberty quarters were struck, and these were released into circulation alongside the first issuance of the 1917-dated pieces. As a result, most collectors mistakenly saved the 1917 coins as the first-year examples, and many 1916 quarters were left in circulation for long periods of time. This coin represents an excellent opportunity for the budget-minded collector. NGC ID# 242Y, PCGS# 5704

1916 Standing Liberty Quarter
AU Sharpness

3568 **1916 — Damage — PCGS Genuine. AU Details.** The 1916 Standing Liberty quarter is always in demand, widely viewed as the biggest key date in the series with a substantial premium over the common date even in low circulated grades. The present example shows strong detail for this poorly produced issue, with a clear date and only minor rub over the high points of the design. Soft golden toning blankets much of each side, while the reverse also exhibits deeper lavender-gray hues and a few scattered specks. A couple unobtrusive cuts, one on the B in LIBERTY and the other above the ME in AMERICA, as well as a few smaller nicks, account for the Details grade from PCGS, though these are not immediately obvious to the unaided eye. NGC ID# 242Y, PCGS# 5704

1923-S Quarter, MS65
Conditional and Absolute Rarity

3569 **1923-S MS65 PCGS. CAC.** The low-mintage 1923-S is an absolute and conditional rarity within the Standing Liberty quarter series, struck to the extent of only 1.36 million pieces, most of which circulated far and wide. This Gem PCGS example is frosty and largely untoned, showing a good strike overall and about 80% of the detail required for a Full Head designation. A few flecks of graying toning appear near the rims. PCGS has certified just 34 numerically finer non-Full Head examples (10/14). NGC ID# 243K, PCGS# 5744

1923-S Standing Liberty Quarter, MS67
Low-Mintage Key, None Finer at PCGS

3570 **1923-S MS67 NGC.** The 1923-S Standing Liberty quarter is a low-mintage key and few examples can match the quality and eye appeal of this remarkable Superb Gem. The well-detailed design elements show the slightest trace of softness on the head and a couple of shield rivets, but definition is sharp in most areas. The pristine brilliant surfaces display vibrant mint luster throughout, with outstanding eye appeal. Census: 4 in 67, 0 finer (10/14). NGC ID# 243K, PCGS# 5744

3571 1926-D MS67 Full Head PCGS. As Standing Liberty quarter specialist, J.H. Cline puts it: "The 1926-D is the classic in two categories: most available and most flat heads." The generally accepted reasoning for this issue's availability in lower Mint State grades is that many more bank-wrapped rolls of this date were saved than of any other. However, with Full Head examples, no amount of hoarding could preserve what hardly existed in the first place. Cline writes in the September 11th, 1998 edition of *The Coin Dealer Newsletter:*

> ". . . the 1926-D is a very common coin in MS62 through MS65, having an original mintage of 1,716,000. However, when struck with a Full Head and with that notation on the holder it becomes one of the rarest pieces in the series - more so than the 1916!"

Due to the rarity of high-grade survivors, Full Head 1926-D quarters make rather large jumps in value between Mint State grade levels, resulting in numerous resubmissions, which undoubtedly inflate the population data. In his book, *Standing Liberty Quarters,* fourth edition, Cline cites an occurrence when a friend of his resubmitted a single 1926-D at least seven times, hoping for an upgrade. He then estimates that as much as half of the population totals are the result of break-outs, which, if accurate, would mean that only about 62 Full Head 1926-D quarters are extant in all grades.

This exceptional Superb Gem is in a class by itself as the finest certified Full Head 1926-D quarter. Exceptionally sharp definition on Liberty's head, chain mail, shield rivets, and the leading edge of the eagle's right wing leaves no doubt as to the designation. Rich teal, violet, and golden accents grace portions of the peripheries, while frosty, brilliant luster blankets the remainder of the surfaces. A couple tiny, faint ticks are noted on Liberty's forward leg, but in no way disrupt the visual appeal of this piece. A truly remarkable example of this notoriously poor-quality issue. NGC ID# 243S, PCGS# 5757

1928 Quarter, MS67 Full Head
Significant Condition Rarity

1934-D Heavy Motto Quarter, MS67
Attractively Toned, Needle-Sharp

3572 1928 MS67 Full Head PCGS. Often considered a common date because of its 6.3 million-coin mintage, the 1928 Standing Liberty issue is scarce in Gem condition and very rare in Superb Gem when encountered with Full Head detail. PCGS has certified only seven submissions in MS67 Full Head and none finer (10/14).

This coruscant representative offers exceptional, razor-sharp devices. Liberty's head is strongly detailed, the shield lines are complete, and the chain mail is bold. Aside from occasional glimpses of golden-tan patina, the surfaces are brilliant. This impeccably preserved example is head and shoulders above any Registry Set coin at PCGS. NGC ID# 243X, PCGS# 5767

3573 1934-D Heavy Motto MS67 PCGS. CAC. The *Guide Book* lists Light Motto and Heavy Motto varieties for the Philadelphia-issued 1934 quarter but not for the Denver issue. The 1934-D Heavy Motto is also unlisted, thus far, in the *Cherrypickers' Guide*. As PCGS recognizes, however, Heavy Motto 1934-D quarters do exist and are important to completing a varieties-inclusive Registry Set. This Superb Gem is one of just four MS67 examples of the subtype certified by PCGS with none finer (10/14). Silver interiors, broader on the frosty reverse, give way to bold violet-orange and ocean-blue color around the margins, while the design definition is quite simply immaculate. PCGS# 85796

1937 Washington Quarter, MS65
Doubled Die Obverse

1962-D Quarter, MS67
Beautiful Obverse Toning

3574 **1937 Doubled Die Obverse, FS-101, MS65 PCGS.** This elusive *Guide Book* variety exhibits bold die doubling on all obverse elements, most obvious on the date, IN GOD WE TRUST, and the tip of Washington's nose. This variety is one of the most sought-after in the entire series, but is very seldom found, especially in Mint State. PCGS has attributed only 24 Uncirculated pieces, with just two in this grade and two numerically finer; NGC has only seen five Mint State examples, with none finer than MS64 (10/14). The present coin displays satiny golden luster, with a couple deep amber areas on Washington's neck and the along the lower obverse border. A small mark behind the eye is the only abrasions of note, and the strike is sharply executed. An attractive, high-end example of this important doubled die variety. PCGS# 145291

3575 **1962-D MS67 PCGS.** For the Registry Set collector, this Superb Gem is essentially the ultimate representative of the 1962-D quarter, as it is tied with just eight others as the finest certified at PCGS (10/14). It also ranks nearly half of a grade point finer than the example in the current highest-rated Registry Set. The obverse is awash in swirling rainbow hues, with warm champagne and deeper olive-gold shades residing amid the ribbons. The reverse is nearly brilliant, exhibiting only a trace of light golden toning. The technical appeal, however, rivals the immense visual attributes, boasting nearly flawless surfaces and bold design elements. The advanced Registry collector will want to bid accordingly. NGC ID# 246R, PCGS# 5873

EARLY HALF DOLLARS

1794 Flowing Hair Half Dollar, VF20
O-101a, Well-Detailed First-Year Issue

3576 **1794 O-101a, R.4, VF20 PCGS.** The early U.S. silver issues dated 1794 included 7,756 half dimes, 1,758 silver dollars, and 23,464 half dollars — by far, the half dollars were the most plentiful of the circulating coinage and it was the denomination most relied upon for commerce. As a result, most survivors are heavily worn, damaged, and many coins simply succumbed to attrition. Problem-free examples are scarce in all grades.

This lightly toned, silver-gray coin is an attractive and well-detailed. There are no Mint-related distractions. The smooth, hard planchet must have passed inspection for the correct weight, since there are no adjustment marks of any kind on the coin. The expected light marks from circulation are non-obtrusive an appropriate for the VF grade. Struck from the late state of the O-101 dies, with all of the diagnostic reverse die cracks distinctly visible. Attractive and always in demand. PCGS# 39201

1794 O-104 Flowing Hair Half, AU Details
Album-Toned, Nice Appeal Remains

3577 **1794 O-104, R.5 — Obverse Planchet Flaw, Improperly Cleaned — NCS. AU Details.** A scarce die marriage, particularly in lesser worn grades, that is attributed by its reverse, which has 9 berries on the left side of the wreath, and 10 berries on the right side. Heavy clash marks are evident at Liberty's nose. A prominent obverse planchet lamination extends from the forehead through the T in LIBERTY to the border on this lightly cleaned but still attractive 1794 half dollar. Both sides retain some luster with light gray centers and peripheral iridescence. The natural light blue and gold album toning provides heightened eye appeal. Minor reverse adjustment marks are evident.

1795/1795 3 Leaves Flowing Hair Half, VF20
O-111, Sole 3 Leaves Die Pair
Dramatic and Highly Desired Overton Variety

3578 **1795/1795 3 Leaves, O-111, High R.4, VF20 NGC.** The dramatic, 1795/1795 overdate appears on both the Overton O-111 and O-112 varieties, but only O-111 pairs it with the distinctive and highly desired Three Leaves reverse. Characterized by a bold, curving die break and sinking of the lower-left quadrant of the reverse, the three-leaves feature and adjacent motifs are always about 20 points bolder than the surrounding, more-exposed surfaces. Often seen only in impaired condition, this scarce variety exceeds its numeric rarity rating because of the intense demand from variety and type collectors. Original, attractive examples such as this coin are seldom available. The coin is thoroughly original with old silver-gray patina and lighter silver tones on the higher devices. Sharply detailed and appealing, the most noticeable marks include a toned-over scrape in the field near Liberty's forehead and some light, criss-crossing adjustment marks in the upper obverse fields and margins. PCGS# 39245

1807 Draped Bust Half, AU53
Sharp O-105 Variety

3579 1807 Draped Bust, O-105, R.1, AU53 PCGS. The Draped Bust design was retired partway through the year in 1807, but a substantial mintage of 301,076 pieces was accomplished before the design changed over to the Capped Bust motif. This attractive AU53 example retains almost all of its original design detail and traces of mint luster cling to the devices. The lightly abraded surfaces are toned in shades of lavender-gray and champagne-gold. Wavelike die clashing sits above the date, and two small digs on Liberty's chin are the most noticeable marks. Population, for the variety: 2 in 53, 4 finer (10/14). PCGS# 39343

BUST HALF DOLLARS

1814 Half Dollar, O-107, MS64
Eye-Catching Cartwheel Luster

3580 1814 O-107, R.2, MS64 PCGS. Heavy clash marks are observed on both sides, though the design elements are boldly impressed. Tinges of sun-gold, violet, and teal surround the peripheries, with light golden toning over the central regions. The luster is vibrant and undeniably original, with remarkably few abrasions. A highly appealing Choice example of this slightly better date. A small die lump in the N in UNITED aids in identifying the variety. PCGS# 39484

1815/2 Half Dollar, VF35
O-101, Album-Toned Example

3581 1815/2 O-101, R.2, VF35 PCGS. A generation of collectors saved Bust halves in coin boards and albums, many of them popularized by Wayte Raymond. The sulfur-infused cardboard tended to impart varying degrees of concentric, colorful toning over time. The 1815/2 issue is popular not only for its low mintage (just 47,150 pieces struck) but also from an historical perspective. The War of 1812 forced to the Mint to temporarily suspend operations. Later in 1815, order was restored and 1812 dies were overdated to produce a minimal production of half dollars. The day after the coins were delivered, the Mint burned and no more half dollars were struck until 1817. This Choice VF coin is attractive and nicely detailed for the grade, with a shallow-but-noticeable rim bump near star 5. PCGS# 39491

REEDED EDGE HALF DOLLARS

1836 Reeded Edge Half, GR-1, AU50
Impressive Color and Surfaces

3582 1836 Reeded Edge, GR-1, R.2, AU50 PCGS. Only one die variety is known for this elusive Reeded Edge half issue. This is a well-detailed AU representative, showing original golden-gray toning with deeper russet hues in the border recesses. No significant circulation scars are present, and tinges of luster remain in the protected areas. An ideal coin for the collector who appreciates natural coloration. PCGS# 531046

1837 GR-7 Bust Half, MS65
Top of the Condition Census for the Variety

3583   **1837 GR-7, R.2, MS65 NGC.** Struck from an early state of the dies with no cracks or weakening of the dentils, this smooth and lustrous example rates at the top of Dick Graham's Condition Census for the GR-7 variety. Not only a top example of the die pair, this lightly toned Gem is notable its "Inverted G" in AMERICA — a highly-sought anomaly by specialists of the series.

On the obverse, numerous die lines are visible in LIBERTY and in the hair below the headband, visible especially at L and E, a characteristic only seen on the obverse of this die pair. Champagne-gold toning is strongest at the margins and softly blends into silver centers on both sides of this brightly lustrous, boldly struck coin. The Condition Census in the 2012 *Registry of Die Varieties of Reeded Edge Half Dollars* for GR-7 is 65-65-64-62-62-61-58-58-55-53. PCGS# 531053

SEATED HALF DOLLARS

1855-O Arrows Seated Half, MS65
WB-101, Frosted Iridescence

3584   **1855-O Arrows MS65 PCGS. WB-101, Die Pair 6, R.3.** A boldly struck, iridescent Gem with frosted fields and devices. Multihued toning appears as the coin rotates in light, with rainbow shades near the obverse rims and deeper hues of blue, lilac, and silver-gray across the reverse. A huge mintage of more than 3.6 million pieces did not survive to any extent in high grades, with Gem Uncirculated and finer coins unquestionably rare. Population: 22 in 65, 6 finer (10/14). NGC ID# 24JP, PCGS# 6283

1870-CC Seated Half, VF30
WB-101, Natural Gray Patina

3585   **1870-CC VF30 NGC. WB-101, Die Pair 1, R.6.** An obtainable — but rare — key to the Seated Liberty series, this naturally patinated half is one of perhaps 200 known survivors of the Carson City date. Most were heavily circulated in the West, and many are impaired. This medium-gray example offers solid details and originality. Marks are primarily limited to some small nicks at the rims and a few planchet flaws, with a light streak of roughness across Liberty's knees and shield and some small planchet voids beneath the date. The sole NGC representative at this grade level. Census: 1 in 30, 29 finer (10/14). NGC ID# 24K2, PCGS# 6328

1883 Seated Half, MS66+
Largely Untoned, Well-Struck Throughout

3586   **1883 MS66+ PCGS. CAC.** One among a string of low-mintage issues, the 1883 half dollar saw only 8,000 business strikes coined. This MS66+ example displays silver-white, eye-appealing surfaces that are well-struck and largely untoned, save for a slight tinge of copper-gold around the rims. A single small luster graze in the left obverse field may be all that precludes an MS67 grade. Population: 19 in 66 (1 in 66+), 3 finer (10/14). NGC ID# 24KW, PCGS# 6365

PROOF SEATED HALF DOLLARS

1860 Seated Half, PR65
Brilliant and Untoned

3587 1860 PR65 NGC. Type Two Reverse. The reported proof mintage was 1,000 pieces, but many of the coins went unsold and were soon melted. Gem or finer examples are rare for the date, and Gem representatives are especially elusive for those who prefer an untoned, white proof. This coin displays deeply reflective mirrors and a nice amount of frosted cameo contrast with the motifs, although not so-designated on the older generation NGC holder (circa 1997 to 2001). Census: 14 in 65 (1 in 65+), 27 finer (10/14). NGC ID# 27TK, PCGS# 6414

1863 Seated Liberty Half
Low-Mintage, Rare Gem Proof

3588 1863 PR65 NGC. Recent research by John Dannreuther suggests that 1860 was the year when the Mint first charged a premium for proof coins, adding 13 cents per coin for silver proofs and 25 cents per coin for gold proofs. Mintages were large in 1860 and 1861 in anticipation of the demand, but customers balked at paying the premiums. Proof mintages in 1862 and 1863 were reduced by more than half as a result. The rarity of these dates is more a function of Mint economics than the Civil War or other factors. This Gem example is one of the few high-grade proofs from 1863. It displays attractive, multicolor iridescent toning and full details over mirrored surfaces. Census: 13 in 65, 8 finer (10/14). NGC ID# 27TP, PCGS# 6417

1868 Half Dollar, PR66
Appealing Multicolor Toning

3589 1868 PR66 PCGS. The availability of lower-grade proof 1868 half dollars leaves the rare high-grade pieces, such as this coin, seemingly underappreciated. Only one other non-Cameo PR66 example is certified at PCGS, and none are finer (10/14). A thin veil of dusky golden-gray patina graces more vivid hues of ocean-blue, violet, sun-gold, and mint-green. The strike is razor-sharp, and the fields are highly reflective, despite the rich patina. NGC ID# 27U3, PCGS# 6426

1876 Half Dollar, PR66 Cameo
Beautifully Toned, Deeply Mirrored

3590 1876 PR66 Cameo PCGS. CAC. The availability of this proof issue is primarily restricted to non-Cameo grades, as contrasted pieces are seldom seen. The current example is deeply toned, but the devices are frosty enough that the level of contrast is certainly noticeable. Both sides display blended hues of lavender, royal-blue, mint-green, and lemon-gold. The strike is sharp and any grade-limiting hairlines are fully masked by the rich patina. Population: 6 in 66 (1 in 66+) Cameo, 1 finer (10/14). PCGS# 86437

1880 Half Dollar, Powerfully Struck PR67

3591 1880 PR67 NGC. Wine, gold, and lavender patina on each side of this beautifully toned and powerfully struck Superb Gem proof contrasts with an open of silver-white in the central reverse area. Only 1,355 proofs were coined, along with 8,400 of the circulation strikes. No distractions are worthy of mention on this appealing Seated half proof. Census: 10 in 67, 0 finer (10/14). NGC ID# 27UF, PCGS# 6441

1882 Half Dollar, PR67
Conditionally Rare, Only One Numerically Finer

3592 **1882 PR67 NGC. WB-102.** An interesting variety example, this coin exhibits the tops of two errant 8s in the denticles below the date. Of the total mintage of 5,500 pieces for the year, 1,100 were proofs. This richly toned example includes shades of teal, copper, and peach-gold. Aside from minor weakness of the eagle's right claw, the strike is exemplary. Census: 4 in 67, 1 finer (10/14). NGC ID# 27UH, PCGS# 6443

1882 Half Dollar, PR66 Deep Cameo
Delicately Toned, Boldly Contrasted

3593 **1882 PR66 Deep Cameo PCGS.** Proof 1882 half dollars are in high demand due to the scarcity of high-grade business strikes. Deep Cameo examples, however, are rarely encountered. This piece showcases fully mirrored fields that display just a tinge of lavender-gold and pale blue toning. The devices are sharply impressed and heavily frosted, delivering exceptional contrast and eye appeal. Population: 5 in 66, 2 finer (10/14). PCGS# 96443

1885 Half Dollar, PR67
Vividly Toned in Myriad Rainbow Hues

3594 **1885 PR67 NGC.** Only 5,200 business-strike Liberty Seated half dollars were struck in 1885, making the slightly more available proofs of this date appealing to the date collector. Colorful cobalt-blue, lavender, and orange-gold patination resides on the lustrous surfaces of this Superb Gem. Well-struck devices and impeccable preservation complement these attributes. Census: 7 in 67 (1 in 67 ★), 3 finer (10/14). NGC ID# 27UL, PCGS# 6446

1886 Seated Liberty Half Dollar, PR65
Rare Deep Cameo Example

3595 **1886 PR65 Deep Cameo PCGS.** This delightful Gem exhibits razor-sharp definition on all design elements, and the devices display a rich coat of mint frost that creates profound cameo contrast with the deeply mirrored brilliant fields. From a proof mintage of 886 pieces. Population: 1 in 65, 2 finer (10/14). PCGS# 96447

1888 Seated Liberty Half, PR66 Cameo
No Numerically Finer Examples at PCGS

3596 **1888 PR66 Cameo PCGS.** An exquisitely struck Premium Gem, showing light golden patina on each side. The radiant and frosty devices deliver exceptional contrast with the unblemished, reflective fields. From a proof mintage of 832 pieces. Population: 4 in 66 (2 in 66+), 0 finer (10/14).
Ex: Long Beach Signature (Heritage, 2/2003), lot 7861; Baltimore Signature (Heritage, 7/2003), lot 7697. PCGS# 86449

BARBER HALF DOLLARS

1895-S Half Dollar, MS65
Challenging San Francisco Issue

3597 **1895-S MS65 NGC.** A frosty, solid Gem example of this highly challenging S-mint, one that possesses dazzling cartwheel luster in full brilliance on the obverse and reverse. Boldly struck and hard to find any finer, with only a handful of trifling flaws in the fields around the portrait. Census: 11 in 65, 6 finer (10/14). NGC ID# 24LU, PCGS# 6473

1906-O Barber Half Dollar, MS66
Delicate Golden Toning

3598 1906-O MS66 PCGS. Wisps of light golden color warm satiny, lustrous surfaces on this Premium Gem example. The design elements are sharply struck up, and Liberty's cheek is particularly clean. This New Orleans issue is somewhat challenging in Mint State when compared to some Philadelphia issues of the period, and is genuinely rare in Gem or finer condition. Population: 6 in 66, 3 finer (10/14). NGC ID# 24MW, PCGS# 6506

1910 Barber Half, MS66+
One of the Finest Known

3599 1910 MS66+ PCGS Secure. CAC. Ex: Duckor. The 1910 Barber half dollar, having a mintage of only 418,000 coins, is the fifth scarcest P-mint emission in the series behind the unheralded 1912 and the widely recognized 1913, 1914, and 1915 issues. This Premium Gem is sharply struck from perfect obverse and reverse dies showing no evidence of cracks or clash marks. Most design detail is full, although the claws are weak as usual. Both sides display fully brilliant and highly lustrous silver surfaces. A small splash of deep russet and steel toning appears on Liberty's neck. Population: 6 in 66 (1 in 66+), 0 finer (10/14).
Ex: Legend Numismatics (11/2003); Dr. and Mrs. Steven L. Duckor Barber Half Dollar Collection / Boston Signature (Heritage, 8/2010), lot 3230; purchased from Joseph O'Connor (10/2010). NGC ID# 24NB, PCGS# 6519

1911 Half Dollar, MS66
Underrated Date

3600 1911 MS66 PCGS. This stunning Barber half dollar exhibits fully brilliant and frosty silver luster with delicate champagne toning and splashes of steel-gray on the reverse. This is a scarce date, moreso than generally believed, and the present example is tied for the finest that PCGS has certified. Population: 11 in 66, 0 finer (10/14). NGC ID# 24ND, PCGS# 6521

PROOF BARBER HALF DOLLARS

1892 Half Dollar, Toned PR67
First-Year Type Example

3601 1892 PR67 NGC. The first year of Barber half dollar production experienced the highest proof mintage of the series (1,245 coins), making this issue ideal for type representation. The present coin boasts a full strike and deep, glassy fields. Splashes of ocean-blue, turquoise, amber, and pale gold toning encompass much of each side, precluding a Cameo designation from NGC, but providing equally strong eye appeal. Census: 15 in 67, 2 finer (10/14). NGC ID# 24NU, PCGS# 6539

1892 Barber Half, PR66 Ultra Cameo
Outstanding Deep-Mirrored Proof

3602 1892 PR66 Ultra Cameo NGC. A thin margin of clear-gold toning attests to the originality of this otherwise brilliant-white proof. The mirrored fields surround frosted motifs with dramatic depth and contrast. Were it not for a few scattered, delicate lines that are visible with a loupe, this Premium Gem proof may have achieved an even higher grade thanks to its considerable eye appeal and fully struck devices. PCGS and NGC combined have certified just seven numerically finer Deep or Ultra Cameo coins. NGC Census: 2 in 66, 5 finer (10/14). PCGS# 96539

1897 Half Dollar, PR68 Cameo
Deeply Toned, None Numerically Finer

3603 1897 PR68 Cameo PCGS. CAC. This extraordinary Superb Gem exhibits variegated toning with delicate gold and blue on the devices, and additional russet, blue-gray, and amber in the fields. The design motifs are exceptionally sharp. PCGS has certified only 12 proof 1897 Barber half dollars at the PR68 grade level, including five Deep Cameos, three Cameos, and four undesignated examples; no numerically finer representatives have been certified with any designation (10/14). The contrast on this piece is somewhat masked by the toning, which may have prevented a stronger Deep Cameo designation for this beautiful proof. A limited mintage of just 731 pieces was accomplished, making this issue conditionally rare in Superb Gem condition. PCGS# 86544

1900 Barber Half, PR67 Cameo
Sharply Detailed and Richly Frosted

3604 1900 PR67 Cameo NGC. The design elements of this delightful Superb Gem are sharply detailed and richly frosted, providing a stunning black-on-white cameo flash when the coin is tilted in the light. Free of any distractions or hairlines, the brightly reflective, deep fields show a few hints of pale gold toning and eye appeal is tremendous. Census: 11 in 67 Cameo, 3 finer (10/14). PCGS# 86547

WALKING LIBERTY HALF DOLLARS

1938-D Walking Liberty Half, MS67+
None Certified Finer by Either Service

3605 1938-D MS67+ PCGS. CAC. The low-mintage key to the mid-date series, and among the finest known of this always-popular Denver date. Just 491,600 pieces were struck, and while many coins were saved by savvy collectors, few examples are known in Superb Gem condition.

While most examples of the date are brilliant or lightly toned, the patina on this coin is superlative. Blazing orange hues rise with sun along the left obverse border, melding with blue, pink, lemon-yellow, and lilac tones bolstered by boisterous luster. Remarkably, the reverse toning is even more intense, with orange-gold and lemon shades surrounding lavender and magenta highlights. The strike is strong for the date, although a trifle incomplete at the centers as are all examples. Destined for the finest Walking Liberty collection or Registry Set. Population: 40 in 67 (3 in 67+), 0 finer (10/14). NGC ID# 24RV, PCGS# 6605

1939 Walking Liberty Half Dollar, MS68
Impeccably Preserved and Lightly Toned

3606 1939 MS68 PCGS. CAC. This magnificent Walking Liberty half dollar is impeccably preserved, with mostly brilliant surfaces that show a few highlights of greenish-gold toning and especially vibrant mint luster on both sides. The design elements are well-detailed with distinct separation between Liberty's thumb and finger. Population: 24 in 68 (3 in 68+), 0 finer (10/14). NGC ID# 24RW, PCGS# 6606

FRANKLIN HALF DOLLARS

1952 Franklin Half, MS67 Full Bell Lines
None Finer at PCGS

3607 1952 MS67 Full Bell Lines PCGS. CAC. A virtually immaculate Superb Gem that boasts potent luster and a good strike. The reverse displays rich peach-gold toning along with glimpses of mint-green and a peripheral scattering of russet patina. The obverse is comparatively lightly toned but exhibits iridescent lemon-gold, rose-red, and apple-green shades. Population: 14 in 67 Full Bell Lines, 0 finer (10/14). NGC ID# 24T3, PCGS# 86661

1962-D Half Dollar
Elusive Premium Gem, Full Bell Lines

3608 1962-D MS66 Full Bell Lines PCGS. This coin is numerically equal to another in the current highest-rated Registry Set, and indeed this 1962-D Franklin half ranks with just 14 others (1 in 66+) as the finest certified, Full Bell Lines example at PCGS (10/14). Frosty mint bloom illuminates a thin veil of light golden toning, while the motifs are boldly defined and the surfaces are free of major abrasions. *Ex: Dallas Signature (Heritage, 12/2007), lot 8985.* NGC ID# 24TS, PCGS# 86683

PROOF FRANKLIN HALF DOLLARS

1950 Franklin Half, PR66 Cameo
Impressive First-Year Proof Example

3609 1950 PR66 Cameo PCGS. CAC. This was the first year of proof coinage production at the Philadelphia Mint since 1942, and a low mintage of 51,386 proof Franklin half dollars was achieved. The unfamiliar proof process challenged Mint personnel, and few high-grade coins resulted. This example is fully struck and well-preserved, however, with minor cloudiness in the fields that fails to inhibit the bold cameo contrast that is evident on each side. An attractive and conditionally rare first-year Franklin proof. Population: 34 in 66, 9 finer (10/14). NGC ID# 27VA, PCGS# 86691

1952 Franklin Half, PR65 Deep Cameo
Entirely Untoned, Nice Contrast

3610 1952 PR65 Deep Cameo PCGS. Glittering, deep-silver mirrors surround frosted motifs for nice field-device contrast. The reverse strike is especially bold, while the obverse details show sharp definition and confirm the Gem grade. A whisper of lemon-gold on the rims does not intrude onto the untoned, silver surfaces. Population: 8 in 65, 9 finer (10/14). NGC ID# 27VC, PCGS# 96693

1795 Draped Bust Dollar, AU55
B-15, BB-52, Centered Bust

1795 Draped Bust Dollar, Choice AU
Centered Bust, B-15, BB-52

3611 **1795 Draped Bust, Centered, B-15, BB-52, R.2, AU55 NGC.**
Die State IV, with a finger-like die break in Liberty's hair curls
near the bow. Only two varieties are known for the 1795 Draped
Bust dollar, BB-51 and BB-52. Both are relatively available in the
VF grade range, but in AU grades, BB-52 emerges as significantly
scarcer, and is downright rare in Mint State. The present coin
is a lovely Choice AU example of this conditionally elusive
variety, with light silvery-gold toning and incredibly bold striking
definition throughout (another hallmark of this variety versus
BB-51). The denticles are complete and very broad, and the only
discernable adjustment marks are seen in the central reverse fields.
An intriguing coin, ideal for the date or variety enthusiast. PCGS#
39995

3612 **1795 Draped Bust, Centered, B-15, BB-52, R.2, AU55 NGC.**
Bowers Die State VI. B-15 is regarded as the second Draped Bust
die variety. Since no dies were shared with B-14, it is possible
that B-15 was struck first. However, numismatists assume that the
engraver learned from the blundered placement of the obverse bust
on B-14, because the bust is well centered on B-15. The present
Choice AU representative is noteworthy for its rich ruby-red,
jade-green, lemon-gold, and dove-gray toning. The borders are
especially colorful. The lightly circulated surfaces exhibit moderate
adjustment marks (as struck) between 9 and 12 o'clock on the
reverse periphery. Post-strike abrasions are inconsequential save for
a few small marks on the field near Liberty's chin. Census: 26 in 55,
48 finer (10/14). PCGS# 39995

1796 Silver Dollar, VF30
B-5, BB-65; Large Date

1797 Draped Bust Dollar, AU58
B-1, BB-73, Terminal Die State

3613 **1796 Large Date, Small Letters, B-5, BB-65, R.2, VF30 PCGS.** Bowers Die State II. The only Large Date logotype for 1796, utilizing the same size digits seen on 1797 dollars. The 6 in the date is noticeably doubled. This Large Date obverse is paired the Small Letters reverse showing a leaf under A of STATES, with a diagnostic die lump clearly visible at IC of AMERICA. Several leaves touch letters of the legend unlike any other reverse. Shades of silver-gray, orange, and blue with hints of golden luster cover both sides of this well-detailed early dollar. PCGS# 40002

3614 **1797 9x7 Stars, Large Letters, B-1, BB-73, R.3 AU58 PCGS. CAC.** Bowers Die State VI. The B-1, BB-73 dollar was struck from the latest state of the obverse die (with the B-2, BB-72 die pair its predecessor), and went through a progression of die states until its demise striking this coin and others like it. Late die state enthusiasts will find a seemingly unending melange of die cracks, clash marks, bulges, and other evidence of shattered dies in a terminal state. Despite the obvious weak points where the die is failing, other areas of this coin are remarkably well-struck and brightly lustrous. Some areas of heavy, charcoal-gray toning stand in stark contrast to the overall brilliant, silver-white surfaces that show very little wear. An interesting early dollar, a companion to the Baldenhofer-Ostheimer listed as sixth in David Bowers' list of notable specimens that was struck from the same Die State VI. CAC approval confirms the eye appeal and strong interest commanded by this near-Mint dollar. PCGS# 40003

1798 B-13, BB-108 Bust Dollar, XF45
Nice Remaining Luster

3615 **1798 Large Eagle, Pointed 9, 10 Arrows, B-13, BB-108, R.2, XF45 PCGS.** Bowers Die State II, the usual state with a diagnostic die crack toward the border from the right side of L in LIBERTY, and with the reverse cracked and lapped. Light silver-gray surfaces retain traces of luster on this Choice XF dollar. An area of roughness is noted at the center of the obverse, with faint adjustment marks at the center of the reverse. The reverse shows only 10 arrows, having been lapped to remove the "stick" — a headless arrow, seen on BB-107 in an earlier state of the die. PCGS# 40025

1798 Large Eagle Dollar, XF45
B-27, BB-113, Pointed 9

3616 **1798 Large Eagle, Pointed 9, Close Date, B-27, BB-113, R.2, XF45 PCGS.** Die State II. A fairly plentiful Heraldic Eagle variety, suitable for type representation. This piece is well-struck, with strong central detail remaining for the grade. Primarily lavender-gray toning yields to areas of deeper olive and sun-gold color in the border recesses. No adjustment marks are observed, though the denticles grow weak along the left reverse border, a product of a minutely off-center strike, rather than uneven die pressure. PCGS# 40030

1798 Large Eagle Dollar, AU55
B-27, BB-113, Pointed 9

3617 **1798 Large Eagle, Pointed 9, Close Date, B-27, BB-113, R.2, AU55 PCGS.** Bowers Die State II, as evidenced by a long die crack from the rim above the second S in STATES, through OF, to the rim above the first A in AMERICA. The border dentils are complete, though they are weak in spots, as is typical of this type, while the design elements are moderately well-struck, with only light wear seen over the high points. A touch of light golden toning graces otherwise bright, lustrous surfaces. Numerous varieties are known for the 1798 dollar, split between both the Small and Large Eagle reverse variants. BB-113 is among the more available varieties of the Heraldic Eagle reverse, but only moderately so. PCGS# 40030

1798 Large Eagle Bust Dollar, MS61
B-27, BB-113, Late Die State

3618 **1798 Large Eagle, Pointed 9, Close Date, B-27, BB-113, R.2, MS61 NGC.** This is a Close Date variety, the first of seven uses of the obverse die, with the 8 in the date much too high and leaning to the right. The reverse die was in its fourth and final use when this coin was struck. This MS61 example shows none of the die cracks expected for the die pair, which suggests the dies were lapped, since there are no known examples from a perfect state of the dies.

The reverse die, in particular, was near its demise. Close examination of the reverse shows multiple areas of weakness — particularly among the field stars and the last two clouds, as well as the F in OF. Die erosion is evident at the peripheries. Light golden overtones cover the softly lustrous, silver-gray surfaces of this nice dollar. Full details are seen on Liberty's hair strands and curls, although stars 1 through 7 are flat. The eagle's feather detail on the wings remain sharp despite the die lapping. An attractive, well-centered early dollar in Mint State. PCGS# 40030

1799 Dollar, AU58
B-15, BB-152, Irregular Date

3619 **1799 Irregular Date, 13 Stars Reverse, B-15, BB-152, R.3, AU58 PCGS.** Die State IV, as usual, with multiple obverse die cracks. BB-152 is significant as the only 1799 variety with the old "line pattern" star formation on the reverse. All other varieties of the 1799 Draped Bust dollar were struck with dies featuring a more graceful, arcing star formation, but this tail die shows the stars in a distinctly linear formation. This is the final use of this reverse, which was previously employed for the BB-123 and BB-124 1798 varieties. This obverse die, showing the so-called irregular date, is in its second use, previously employed for BB-151 and later for BB-153.

The present BB-152 example is rather well-struck for the variety, with much of the minor reverse weakness due to die lapping that was executed during its previous use for BB-124 of the 1798 coinage. Faint remnants of adjustment marks are noted along the lower-right obverse border, though the denticles remain complete on both sides. Pale lavender and golden-gray patina blankets each side, with hints of luster seen in the recesses when rotated beneath a light. Accompanied by a lot ID card from its sale in Bowers and Merena's 1995 sale of the Commodore Matthew C. Perry Collection.
Ex: The Commodore Matthew C. Perry Collection (Bowers and Merena, 1/1995), lot 2727. PCGS# 40045

1799 7x6 Stars Dollar, AU50
Scarce B-18, BB-154 Marriage

3620 **1799 7x6 Stars, B-18, BB-154, R.4, AU50 PCGS. CAC.** Bowers Die State IV. A heavy crack between the ED in UNITED promptly attributes this golden-brown and dove-gray early dollar. The centers show selected softness but the remainder of the strike is good. No marks are noteworthy. A better grade example of a scarce variety. *Ex: Baltimore ANA (Heritage, 7/2008), lot 760, which realized $8,050.* PCGS# 40046

1799 Draped Bust Dollar, XF40
B-16, BB-158; 7 x 6 Stars
Nice Luster Remains

3621 **1799 7x6 Stars, B-16, BB-158, R.2, XF40 PCGS.** Bowers Die State IV. Despite the late die state and a severely cracked obverse die, the central motifs exhibit bold detail including Liberty's hair strands and drapery folds. Some peripheral weakness at the star centers and eagle's wing tips can be attributed to die state as well as wear from moderate circulation. Both obverse and reverse show considerable die clashing. Delightful slate-gray, old-sliver patina covers both sides, which are surprisingly lustrous for the assigned grade and attractive. PCGS# 40050

1799 7x6 Stars Dollar, AU55
B-9, BB-166

3622 **1799 7x6 Stars, B-9, BB-166, R.1, AU55 NGC.** Die State V, terminal, with numerous die cracks in the right obverse field. A small die break near the second S in STATES quickly identifies this available variety. The present example is boldly struck, with notable definition on the obverse stars, Liberty's hair curls, and the central shield lines. The border denticles are complete, showing no evidence of adjustment marks. Deep lavender-gray patina blankets both sides, complementing glossy surfaces. PCGS# 40057

1800 B-19, BB-192 AMERICAI Dollar
Choice About Uncirculated Example
Rare Early Die State

3623 **1800 AMERICAI, B-19, BB-192, R.2, AU55 PCGS.** Bowers Die State I and rare as such. Well-centered and boldly struck on a good planchet, this attractive dollar shows minimal wear and considerable sharpness on all the motifs. Brassy-gold patina covers both sides, and nice remaining mint luster shines through. Virtually no marks of any note exist on the fields or devices — a notable departure from most examples that show die clashing above the date and die cracks at the reverse legend. *NOTE: a dark speck that appears in the field between stars 2 and 3 is on the inside of the holder, not on the coin.* The AMERICAI dollars are so-named for the distinctive "I" die scratch near the eagle's claw, and the variety is unfailingly popular with early dollar collectors. It is listed in the 2015 *Guide Book* on page 219. PCGS# 40082

1802/1 Silver Dollar, AU53
Wide Date, B-4, BB-232
Narrow (Close) Date Variety

3624 **1802/1 Narrow Date, B-4, BB-232, R.3, AU53 PCGS.** Bowers Die State II. Wonderful, high rims surround both sides with sharp dentils. Substantial mint luster remains among the devices and at the margins, resulting in iridescent tones across the old-silver patina. The BB-232 variety is confirmed by the 1 of the date firmly touching Liberty's curl, and the digits 02 are close together with both the 2 and the 8 leaning slightly right unlike any other 1802/1 overdate — the sole usage of this obverse die. A short die crack through the right side of the bust to star 13 confirms the Die State II. An attractive example of the overdate, with a few minor marks and a small planchet void on Liberty's neck, none of which diminish the coins original appeal. The variety is rare in AU or finer grades, with perhaps 10 to 15 known examples so fine. PCGS# 40092

SEATED DOLLARS

1859-S Seated Liberty Dollar, AU58
Low-Mintage, Heavily Exported Issue

3625 **1859-S AU58 PCGS.** The 1859-S Seated Liberty dollar claims a low mintage of just 20,000 pieces and most examples were exported in the China trade near the date of issue. The number of extant examples suggests that at least a small number of coins remained in domestic holdings, however. This attractive near-Mint specimen displays just a trace of wear on the well-detailed design elements and the lightly abraded silver-gray surfaces retain traces of original mint luster. Population: 18 in 58, 19 finer (10/14). NGC ID# 24YZ, PCGS# 6948

1870-CC Seated Dollar, AU50
Seldom Available Carson City Issue

3626 **1870-CC AU50 NGC.** The scarcity of Carson City Seated Liberty dollars is only fully understood when one realizes that the paltry 11,758-coin mintage of the 1870-CC is the highest in the series from this mint. Proportionately, the 1870-CC is also the most available, but is nonetheless scarce in all grades. This piece is boldly struck, with just slight wear over gold-tinted battleship-gray surfaces. Small remnants of semiprooflike mirroring remain in the protected regions, contributing to the overall appeal. NGC ID# 24ZE, PCGS# 6964

1870-CC Seated Dollar, AU55
Elusive Carson City Issue

3627 **1870-CC AU55 NGC.** At 11,758 pieces the 1870-CC Seated dollar had easily the highest mintage among the four Carson City issues of the type (1870, 1871, 1872, and 1873.) This is the most available date of the four, and should be favored by the high-end Carson City type specialist. This Choice AU coin exhibits mottled olive and lavender-gray toning. The design motifs are sharply struck, particularly over the centers, and only the obverse stars display partial incompleteness. Both sides are nearly mark-free, save for a handful of scattered nicks. A partial thumbprint on the upper right obverse is mostly concealed by the deep patina. Census: 25 in 55 (1 in 55+★), 38 finer (10/14). NGC ID# 24ZE, PCGS# 6964

1871-CC Seated Dollar, AU Details
Considerable Retained Luster

3628 **1871-CC — Improperly Cleaned — NGC Details. AU.** Although the NGC description of this piece is accurate, both sides exhibit considerable frosty silver mint luster with splashes of gold and blue-steel toning that intensifies near the obverse and reverse borders. Still an attractive example of this important Seated Liberty silver dollar. NGC ID# 24ZH, PCGS# 6967

1872-CC Silver Dollar
Choice VF, Original Coloration

3629 **1872-CC VF35 PCGS.** The San Francisco Mint produced only 3,150 silver dollars in 1872, making this issue one of the key dates in the Seated Liberty series. Most surviving examples show evidence of cleaning or are otherwise flawed, and fully original pieces are decidedly rare. This lightly circulated coin shows strong VF detail, with uniform lavender-gray patina and problem-free surfaces. An important opportunity for the Seated dollar collector. NGC ID# 24ZK, PCGS# 6969

1872-CC Seated Dollar, AU Details
Popular Nevada Mint Issue

3630 **1872-CC — Stained — NGC Details. AU.** Heather-gray surfaces exhibit hints of blue-steel patina on this pleasing, nicely detailed Seated Liberty dollar. A popular Carson City issue, this piece shows excellent surfaces for the grade. Amber staining at the central obverse accounts for the description.

1872-CC Seated Dollar, AU53
Important Carson City Issue

3631 **1872-CC AU53 NGC.** The four Carson City Seated dollar issues, all elusive and ranked from most to least important, are the 1873-CC, 1871-CC, 1872-CC, and 1870-CC. Mintages were 2,300; 1,376; 3,150; and 11,758; respectively, and all four issues are highly prized today. Although a number of Mint State examples are known of the 1872-CC, any AU piece is still highly collectible. This delicately toned silver-gray dollar has hints of champagne toning on each side, with considerable remaining luster. The strike is above average. An eye-appealing example for the advanced collector. Census: 8 in 53, 25 finer (10/14). NGC ID# 24ZK, PCGS# 6969

1872-CC Seated Dollar, AU58
Deep, Gunmetal-Gray Patina

3632 **1872-CC AU58 PCGS.** Perhaps more available than its tiny 3,150-piece mintage would suggest, most of the saved examples are in lower grades. The significance of mintmarks did not attract the collecting public until the 1890s, when the rarity was recognized and some coins were pulled from circulation. This deep, gunmetal-gray example spent very little time — if any at all — in commerce. Sharply struck and attractive, the coin shows only a few tiny abrasions and a bit of cloudiness over the underlying prooflike surfaces. Seldom offered in this near-Mint grade or finer. Population: 12 in 58, 12 finer (10/14). NGC ID# 24ZK, PCGS# 6969

1854 Seated Dollar, PR64
Extremely Rare as a Proof
Tied for Finest Non-Cameo at PCGS

3633 **1854 PR64 PCGS.** Apparently, the vast majority of business strike 1854 silver dollars were exported to the Orient to be used in trade, from where they never returned. As a result, the proofs are important to modern collectors as they can serve as a substitute for the rare business strikes. Of the 50 to 100 proofs estimated to have been struck, perhaps 25 to 40 are extant today; PCGS reports just 20 proofs in all grades (10/14), though this figure may include a number of resubmissions.

The surfaces of this piece have taken on a cloudy, grayish-blue patina, and the reflective fields contrast nicely with the moderately frosted devices. The design elements are sharply struck, with the only weakness occurring at the top of the eagle's right wing, which is typical for the issue. A few wispy handling marks are noted in the fields. This is a pleasing Seated dollar and a coin sure to generate much interest among bidders. Population: 4 in 64, 0 finer (10/14). *Ex: ANA Signature (Heritage, 7/2005), lot 10270.* NGC ID# 2528, PCGS# 6997

1859 Seated Dollar
Attractive PR63 Cameo

3634 **1859 PR63 Cameo PCGS. CAC.** Though light hairlines and a few areas of slight contact are noted in the fields, the overall eye appeal of this minimally toned, exquisitely detailed beauty holds strong. Powerful mirrors supply ample contrast with the moderately frosted devices. David Bowers suggests that the Mint was overly ambitious in the second year of officially offering proofs to the public, with a mintage of 800 pieces — of which at least 350 pieces were later melted as unsold. Population: 9 in 63 (1 in 63+), 12 finer (10/14). *Ex: Houston Signature (Heritage, 12/2008), lot 868.* PCGS# 87002

1867 Seated Dollar, PR64
Deep Mirrors, Exceptional Color

3635 **1867 PR64 PCGS.** Exceptional toning blankets both sides of this near-Gem proof without disturbing the deep, glassy mirrors or boldly struck motifs. Viewed at the proper angle, intricate color combinations gleam over the unmarked surfaces with intense purple, blue, orange, pink, and gold coloration that is both stunning and attractive. The surface quality and bold details are suggestive of a higher grade. Population: 60 in 64, 17 finer (10/14). NGC ID# 252N, PCGS# 7015

1871 Dollar, PR64+ Cameo
Delicate Golden Toning

3636 **1871 PR64+ Cameo PCGS.** The proof 1871 Seated dollar is one of several available proof issues from the late part of the series, but the certified population is largely limited to non-Cameo pieces. Contrasted coins are scarce in all grades, and Deep Cameos are nothing short of rare. The present near-Gem Cameo displays lovely champagne toning that deepens slightly toward the rims, while the fully mirrored fields reveal only a few faint hairlines and the boldly struck devices are free of marks. Cameo proof Seated dollars are some of the most beautiful 19th century issues in American numismatics, well-suited for type representation. Population: 12 in 64 (2 in 64+), 5 finer (10/14). PCGS# 87019

TRADE DOLLAR

1878-S Trade Dollar, MS66
Dazzling Luster, Conditionally Rare

3637 **1878-S MS66 PCGS.** Type Two Obverse and Reverse. Legislation for the abolishment of the troublesome Trade dollar and the reintroduction of the standard silver dollar (commonly known as the Bland-Allison Act) was passed in late February 1878, and the Philadelphia Mint promptly began production of the new Morgan dollars in early March. The branch mints in Carson City and San Francisco, however, did not receive working dies for the Morgan type until April, by which time the Carson City Mint had produced a small run of 97,000 Trade dollars, and the California branch had struck off more than 4.1 million examples.

As might be expected, the 1878-S is the most readily obtainable of the two 1878 business strike Trade dollar issues, and is a favorite among type and date collectors. Trade dollars were seldom well-preserved, however, and the issue's availability plummets significantly beyond the MS64 grade level.

The present coin is a rare Premium Gem example, showcasing radiant cartwheel luster and splendidly preserved surfaces. Peripheral tinges of aquamarine and amber-gold surround brilliant centers, while the design elements are attractively sharp. A visually supreme example from this historic year in numismatics. Population: 24 in 66 (10 in 66+), 3 finer (10/14). NGC ID# 253G, PCGS# 7048

PROOF TRADE DOLLARS

1873 Trade Dollar, PR63 Cameo
Remarkably Deep Mirrors

3638 1873 PR63 Cameo PCGS. The introductory year of the Trade dollar had a proof mintage of 865 pieces, and this issue remains moderately obtainable for the type collector who wishes to stray from the more plentiful proof-only issues of the later part of the series. This piece displays strong mirroring in the fields and satiny, well-struck devices. Contrast is subtle, but noticeable. A blush of violet and orange-gold toning graces the left-hand border on each side. Population: 17 in 63 (1 in 63+), 19 finer (10/14). PCGS# 87053

1877 Trade Dollar, PR65
Pleasingly Toned

3639 1877 PR65 NGC. Except for the unofficial strikings of 1884 and 1885 this date saw the lowest proof mintage of the Trade dollar series, at a mere 510 pieces. This fully struck Gem example displays sharply reflective fields and an attractive, variegated array of pastel coloration across both sides. A faint reeding mark to the left of star 13 is the only minor surface flaw detected with the aid of a standard loupe. Census: 15 in 65 (1 in 65+, 1 in 65 ★), 9 finer (10/14). NGC ID# 27YN, PCGS# 7057

1878 Trade Dollar, PR65
Impressive, Conditionally Scarce Example

3640 1878 PR65 NGC. This proof-only Trade dollar issue of 900 pieces is scarce in high grades any finer than PR64. The Gem offered here displays razor-sharp striking details and well-preserved surfaces that are deeply toned in variegated shades of gray-green, plum, and blue. An impressive specimen that will appeal to the specialist in this challenging series. NGC ID# 27YP, PCGS# 7058

1878 Trade Dollar, PR65 Cameo
Champagne-Gold and Attractive
Proof-Only Issue

3641 1878 PR65 Cameo NGC. The Philadelphia Mint ceased Trade dollar production for circulation and export in 1878, minting only 900 proofs for sale to collectors and dealers. The low, proof-only mintages would continue through 1883, not counting the surreptitious proofs that surfaced later dated 1884 and 1885. This excellent Gem example displays deeply mirrored champagne-gold surfaces, with the devices thickly frosted for bold Cameo contrast. The coin is fully struck, with only microscopic hairlines limiting the grade. Census: 25 in 65 (3 in 65 ★), 7 finer (10/14). PCGS# 87058

1882 Trade Dollar, PR65
Richly Toned, Proof-Only Issue

3642 1882 PR65 NGC. The 1882 Trade dollar was a proof-only issue from a generous mintage of 1,097 pieces. Medium-intensity orange and electric-blue toning adorns both sides of this Gem. Mirrored reflectivity clings most strongly to the edges of the design elements and the margins, with full revelation of color and the deep mirrors best seen when viewed at an angle. This is a crisply struck and nicely preserved example from the Mint's foray into more aggressive marketing of proof coins. Census: 66 in 65, 38 finer (10/14). NGC ID# 27YU, PCGS# 7062

1883 Trade Dollar, PR65
Elusive Proof-Only Issue

3643 1883 PR65 PCGS. The final Trade dollar except for the clandestine 1884 and 1885 issues, the 1883 was a proof-only issue with a mintage of just 979 coins. Only two other proof-only Trade dollars had lower mintages: 900 minted in 1878, and 960 minted in 1881. This lovely Gem has a sharp strike with fully mirrored fields beneath blue, violet, and iridescent toning on both sides. A reeding mark is noted to the left of Liberty's knees. Population: 50 in 65, 22 finer (10/14). NGC ID# 27YV, PCGS# 7063

MORGAN DOLLARS

1878 7/8TF Morgan, MS66
VAM-33A, Doubled Legs

3644 1878 7/8TF Weak VAM-33A, Doubled Legs, MS66 PCGS. The later die state with a clashed profile. The eagle's legs are die doubled, and the obverse is die doubled also, especially near 9 o'clock. A wisp of tan toning adorns this otherwise brilliant Premium Gem. Booming luster sweeps smooth surfaces. A well-struck and pleasing representative from the brief transitional period between the eight and seven tailfeather subtypes. Population: 4 in 66, 0 finer (10/14). PCGS# 134032

1878 Morgan Dollar, MS65+
7 Over 8 Tailfeathers, VAM-38

3645 1878 7/8TF Strong, VAM-38, MS65+ PCGS. CAC. Five tailfeather fragments emerge beneath the seven prominent feathers. A lustrous and brilliant Gem. The fields and cheek are smooth, and the strike is above average. Exceptional quality for this transitional first-year Morgan variety. As of (11/14), PCGS has certified just one coin finer as VAM-38. PCGS# 134035

1878 7/8TF VAM-41A Morgan Dollar
MS65 Deep Mirror Prooflike

3646 1878 7/8TF VAM-41A, 7/4 Weak MS65 Deep Mirror Prooflike NGC. The horizontal die line to the left of the bow (other die lines passing through the bow center) is a handy pickup point for this 7/4 Weak VAM variety. The bright, untoned surfaces exhibit deep contrast and superlative eye appeal, with minimal contact marks. The die lapping on the reverse in each wing, characteristic, is blatant and startling. An extremely appealing coin, worthy of premium bids from VAM specialists. PCGS# 40212

1878 7/8TF Morgan, MS62
VAM-44, Tripled Blossoms

3647 1878 7/8TF Tripled Blossoms, VAM-44, MS62 PCGS. CAC. A Top 100 Variety. This variety is widely regarded as the "King of VAMs." The obverse shows the clearest and widest tripled die in the Morgan dollar series, most famously evident on the cotton blossoms and leaves, hence the moniker "Tripled Blossoms." The reverse, however, is also die-doubled, with the spread most readily observed on the eagle's legs. This reverse, a "Weak" 7/8 tailfeathers die, was also employed for the VAM-33 variety, though VAM-44 is by far its rarer usage.

VAM-44 is very elusive in all grades, and is genuinely rare in Mint State. PCGS has attributed only eight Uncirculated examples, with just four in MS62 and only one finer; NGC has attributed only two Mint State examples, both MS62 coins (10/14). The current piece shows largely untoned surfaces, with just a few hints of golden color throughout. Semiprooflike mirroring in the fields frames softly frosted motifs, while grade-limiting abrasions are minor and evenly distributed. A touch of striking weakness is noted on the hair above Liberty's ear, though the design elements are otherwise well brought up. PCGS# 133829

1878 Morgan Dollar, MS66
Reverse of 1879
Tied for Finest Certified

1878-CC Morgan Dollar, MS66+
Incredible, Coruscating Mint Bloom
Conditionally Rare First-Year Survivor

3648 1878 7TF Reverse of 1879 MS66 PCGS. The Reverse of 1879 is a transitional variety of the 1878 Morgan dollars that followed the 8 Tailfeathers and 7 Tailfeathers coins. Michael "Miles" Standish writes in *Morgan Dollar, America's Love Affair With a Legendary Coin:* "It is assumed that the reverse of 1879 came into production later and is less common than the reverse of 1878." The new reference published earlier this year is a must-have book for the Morgan dollar aficionado.

This frosty and highly lustrous Premium Gem has brilliant silver surfaces with no evidence of toning. The strike is bold and the eye appeal is exceptional. This piece is tied for the finest certified at PCGS or NGC. Population: 17 in 66, 0 finer (10/14). NGC ID# 253L, PCGS# 7076

3649 1878-CC MS66+ PCGS. CAC. The Carson City received working dies for the new Morgan dollar in April 1878, and production began promptly with hundreds of thousands of ready planchets. By the end of the year, more than 2.2 million pieces had been produced, making the 1878-CC one of the highest-mintage issues in the series from this mint, trailing only the 1890-CC at 2.3 million coins. Nevertheless, the 1878-CC ranks as one of more challenging Carson City issues to locate above the Gem grade level today. The GSA sales of the early 1970s yielded only 60,993 examples of the issue; while this may seem like a large number, it is inherently small in comparison to the corresponding figures for the 1880 through 1885 Carson City issues, which range from hundreds of thousands to nearly 1 million coins each.

The present coin is a seldom seen Premium Gem example, with thickly frosted, brilliant luster and tack-sharp design definition. The luster cartwheels without interruption, though close scrutiny with a loupe detects a few nearly imperceptible grazes that PCGS felt precluded a full MS67 grade and a significantly higher market value. An exceptional coin, worthy of the finest Carson City Morgan dollar collection. PCGS has certified only six coins in finer numeric grades (10/14). NGC ID# 253M, PCGS# 7080

1879-CC Silver Dollar, MS64
Seldom Available Finer

3650 **1879-CC MS64 PCGS.** Although not heralded to the extent of the 1889-CC, the 1879-CC is a significant key issue among Carson City Morgan dollars. Many were likely melted under the terms of the Pittman Act of 1918, and only a little more than 4,000 pieces were offered in the GSA sales of the early 1970s, compared to tens of thousands of several other dates from this Mint. This piece displays subtle light golden toning over sharp, frosty devices. Substantial semiprooflike mirroring is seen in the fields, and only a few light marks on the cheek limit the grade. NGC ID# 253T, PCGS# 7086

1879-CC Dollar, MS65+
Limited High Grade Survival

3651 **1879-CC MS65+ PCGS. CAC.** The GSA holdings of the 1879-CC Morgan dollar were quite small in comparison to those of most other Carson City issues in the series; only 4,123 coins were distributed to collectors, or just 0.5 percent of the original 756,000-coin mintage. Since the GSA sales yielded many of the surviving Mint State Carson City dollars of all dates in the Morgan dollar series, the 1879-CC is, as a result, much scarcer in high grades than many lower mintage dates from this mint.

The present coin is devoid of any noticeable abrasions, with frosty luster and pale golden-gray toning. Slight striking deficiency is noted on the hair above Liberty's ear, though the viewer's eye is more readily drawn to Liberty's clean cheek. Only two examples are numerically finer at PCGS (10/14). NGC ID# 253T, PCGS# 7086

1879-CC Dollar, MS61
The 'Capped Die' Variety

3652 **1879-CC "Capped Die," VAM-3A, MS61 NGC.** A Top 100 Variety. The 1879-CC ranks as one of the more challenging Carson City issues in Mint State, behind only the key-date 1889-CC. While not so-attributed on the holder, this example represents the popular "Capped Die" variety, with doubling on the date numerals and moderate die chips around the mintmark. Frosty cartwheel luster resides beneath a blanket of light golden toning. Some minor striking weakness is seen at the centers, as usual, while light, scattered abrasions define the grade. PCGS# 133869

1879-CC Silver Dollar, MS62
VAM-3A, 'Capped Die'

3653 **1879-CC "Capped Die," VAM-3A, MS62 PCGS.** A Top 100 Variety. This piece is from the later die state of this popular *Guide Book* variety, with the G in GOD completely filled. This variety was created when a large mintmark was punched over a smaller one, with the former letters apparently partially effaced by minor chipping of the die around the mintmark. Doubling on the date numerals confirms the attribution. This example shows light golden toning and frosty luster. The eagle's breast and the hair above Liberty's ear are not fully defined, though the strike is otherwise pleasing. Scattered abrasions limit the grade. PCGS# 133869

1883-S Morgan Dollar
Brilliant Near-Gem

3654 **1883-S MS64 NGC. CAC.** Semiprooflikeness in the fields surrounds boldly struck devices to enhance the near-Gem status of this brilliant, untoned silver dollar. Potential bidders will want to weigh the considerable price jump into the next highest, full Gem grade, since this San Francisco issue is a legendary rarity when MS65 or finer. NGC has certified just 17 numerically finer coins (10/14). NGC ID# 254K, PCGS# 7148

1884 Morgan Dollar, MS67
Full Strike, Vibrant Luster

3655 **1884 MS67 PCGS.** The 1884 Morgan dollar is readily available in lower Mint State grades, but coins in Superb Gem condition are rare. Vibrant, frosty luster is the outstanding characteristic of this Superb Gem specimen, complemented by an exquisite strike and well preserved surfaces. Eye appeal is outstanding. Population: 44 in 67 (7 in 67+), 3 finer (10/14).
Ex: Palm Beach Signature (Heritage, 3/2005), lot 6098; Long Beach Signature (Heritage, 2/2008), lot 460; ANA Signature (Heritage, 8/2010), lot 5269, which realized $4,600. NGC ID# 254L, PCGS# 7150

1885 Morgan Dollar, MS67+
Impressive and Remarkably Attractive

3656 **1885 MS67+ PCGS. CAC.** This is an impressive, remarkably attractive example of this Philadelphia Mint issue. A relatively common date with a high mintage of 17.8 million pieces, this Morgan dollar issue is scarce at the Superb Gem level. Full striking definition is noted throughout, even on the traditionally difficult areas of the design. Soft, frosted mint luster radiates from each side, and variegated layers of gold, lavender, russet-brown and yellow-green reside mainly near the borders. Flawlessly preserved and pristine on both sides. Population: 8 in 67+, 2 finer (10/14). NGC ID# 254R, PCGS# 7158

1885-CC Silver Dollar, MS67
Bold Strike, Brilliant Appeal

3657 **1885-CC MS67 NGC.** One of the quintessentially popular Carson City dates, both for its availability in high grades and its high level of production quality. Only 228,000 pieces were minted, but few circulated and most remained in storage until the GSA sales of the early 1970s. Superb Gems are rare, however, and seldom available. This brilliant, frost-white coin is boldly struck with a mere handful of minor marks. Liberty's cheek and neck are clean and rounded. Full cartwheel luster blazes across the silver surfaces. Just six numerically finer coins are known by PCGS and NGC combined (10/14). NGC ID# 254S, PCGS# 7160

1885-CC Dollar, MS66+
Elusive Prooflike Example

3658 **1885-CC MS66+ Prooflike PCGS. CAC.** A beautifully preserved, deeply contrasted Prooflike example of this popular Carson City issue. The surfaces are devoid of significant abrasions, and a thin veil of light golden toning blankets each side, deepening toward the margins. Some minor softness is noted on the hair above Liberty's ear, though the flashy fields are the chief draw on the viewer's eye. Population: 43 in 66 (4 in 66+) Prooflike, 2 finer (10/14). NGC ID# 254S, PCGS# 7161

1886-S Silver Dollar, MS66
Conditionally Elusive

3659 **1886-S MS66 PCGS.** The 1886-S Morgan dollar had a mintage of just 750,000 pieces, and can only be termed available in MS64 and lower grades. This is a rarely seen Premium Gem example with brilliant, satiny luster and beautifully preserved surfaces. The strike is sharp and the eye appeal is excellent. Population: 47 in 66 (2 in 66+), 4 finer (10/14). NGC ID# 254X, PCGS# 7170

1888 Dollar, MS67
None Numerically Finer at PCGS

3660 **1888 MS67 PCGS.** Vibrant luster emanates from the essentially untoned surfaces of this Superb Gem Morgan dollar (though a small splash of orange-gold resides on the lower obverse near the rim). The hair above Liberty's ear and the eagle's breast feathers exhibit strong definition. Population: 29 in 67, 0 finer (10/14). NGC ID# 2555, PCGS# 7182

1889-CC Dollar, XF45
Pleasing, Lightly Circulated Example

3661 **1889-CC XF45 PCGS.** The 1889-CC Morgan ranks not only as the rarest Carson City issue in the series, but also as one of the major key dates overall. The issue is heavily pursued in all grades, and there is a strong demand for lightly circulated pieces with original patina. This Choice XF example is just such a coin. Remnants of mint luster reside in the protected regions, highlighting pale golden-gray toning and minimally scarred surfaces. Slight wear over the high points of the design limits the grade. NGC ID# 2559, PCGS# 7190

1889-CC Silver Dollar, AU58
Strong Coin for the Grade

3662 1889-CC AU58 PCGS. Four years after shutting down in early 1885 due to political opposition from newly elected, anti-silver President Grover Cleveland, the Carson City Mint was authorized to resume coinage operations in July 1889. Machinery repairs and the need for new officers, however, delayed actual production until October, which stunted the year's output of Morgan dollars to just 350,000 pieces. Large quantities of the issue were then paid into circulation before the turn of the century, leaving only limited numbers to be dispersed during the following decades. By the time of the early 1970s GSA sales, only a single example remained in federal holdings, which boldly reflects the 1889-CC's rarity in relation to other Carson City issues in the series, many of which survive by tens and even hundreds of thousands of coins. The issue's nickname "The King of the Carson City Morgans," therefore, is quite fitting.

This near-Mint example is boldly struck with just a touch of light wear over the high points of the design. Strong luster remains in the recesses, illuminating faint wisps of light golden toning over otherwise brilliant surfaces. Light, scattered abrasions accompany the grade, as usual. NGC ID# 2559, PCGS# 7190

1889-CC Dollar, Unc Details
Challenging Series Key

3663 1889-CC — Altered Surfaces — PCGS Genuine. Unc Details. A bright, unworn example of this key Carson City issue. The strike is sharp throughout and the surfaces are devoid of detracting marks. PCGS notes that the surfaces have been altered, with each side showing evidence of light polishing. A still-pleasing coin, and an important acquisition for the budget-minded Morgan dollar enthusiast. NGC ID# 2559, PCGS# 7190

The Carson City Mint

1889-CC Morgan Dollar, MS64
High-Caliber Carson City Rarity
Major Series Key

3664 **1889-CC MS64 NGC.** Four years following its closure after the election of anti-silver man Grover Cleveland to the presidency, the Carson City Mint was allowed to resume regular coinage in July 1889. Minor repairs of the building and machinery, however, delayed silver dollar production until October. This limited the year's Morgan dollar output to just 350,000 pieces, the third-lowest production total in the series from this mint (behind only the 1881-CC and 1885-CC). Its mintage figure, however, is hardly a reliable reflection of rarity, as the 1889-CC is many times more elusive than its lower mintage counterparts, especially in Mint State. Many thousands of 1889-CC Morgans were paid out into circulation before the turn of the century, while the 1881-CC and 1885-CC (as well as many other Carson City issues in the series) were largely stored long-term in government vaults.

Some small quantities of Mint State 1889-CC dollars turned up in the 1930s and shortly thereafter, but no large disbursements were made from Treasury holdings, and it is likely that a significant number were melted under the terms of the Pittman Act of 1918. When an inventory of government holdings was finally taken prior to the GSA sales of the early 1970s, only a single 1889-CC dollar remained in Treasury vaults. By contrast, the lower-mintage 1881-CC and 1885-CC issues were represented by nearly 150,000 examples each, having largely escaped the clutches of circulation and mass-melting.

With such a low survival rate, the 1889-CC is not only the rarest Carson City issue, but also one of the major key dates in the entire Morgan dollar series. Circulated examples are scarce, and Mint State coins are rare in comparison to the demand for them. The typical Uncirculated example, if indeed there is one, grades no higher than MS62. At the Choice level, the date is arguably more difficult to locate than it is to afford, and finer pieces are very nearly unobtainable.

The present coin is an eye-appealing reward for the patient pursuer of this legendary issue. Frosty luster and bold design elements reside beneath a thin veil of light golden toning, while the surfaces are devoid of any singularly noticeable abrasions. It may be several years before another 1889-CC dollar of this caliber is offered at auction. Census, including an unknown number of resubmissions: 44 in 64 (1 in 64 ★), 6 finer (10/14). NGC ID# 2559, PCGS# 7190

1890-O Morgan Dollar
Gem Deep Mirror Prooflike

3665 **1890-O MS65 Deep Mirror Prooflike PCGS.** The 1890-O Morgan dollars are far from common in Deep Mirror Prooflike format, and Gems such as this are downright rare. The strike is the least "prooflike" aspect of this piece, a touch soft on the hair over Liberty's ear, while a few long die polish marks are visible in the reverse fields. Even through partial milky and gold-gray patina, however, the coin's essential reflectivity remains intact. Light but distinct frost on the portrait completes the all-around eye appeal. PCGS has certified only 18 examples in MS65 Deep Mirror Prooflike and just one finer (10/14). NGC ID# 255E, PCGS# 97201

1892-O Dollar, MS65
Swirling Multicolor Patina

3666 **1892-O MS65 NGC.** The 1892-O Morgan dollar seldom makes the spotlight, partly due to its ample mintage of more than 2.7 million coins and moderate availability in grades through MS64. In reality, the date is conditionally scarce at the Gem grade level, and is genuinely rare any finer. This example shows vivid swaths of deep olive, forest-green, violet, and sun-gold over the obverse, with peripheral rings of the same surrounding dusky lavender-gray toning on the reverse. Some striking deficiency is noted in the extreme centers, as is typical of this New Orleans issue. NGC has certified only five numerically finer representatives (10/14). NGC ID# 255N, PCGS# 7216

1892-O Morgan Dollar, MS65
Scarce This Nice

3667 **1892-O MS65 PCGS Secure.** A marvelous Gem with a slight tinge of gold rim toning on the obverse. The reverse is fully brilliant over its frosty luster. The strike is typical for the New Orleans dollars from the 1890s, mostly sharp but with some weakness over the ear, and at the center of the reverse. The lustrous surfaces are free of all but the most inconsequential marks. PCGS and NGC combined have certified just 11 pieces numerically finer (10/14). *Ex: Long Beach Signature (Heritage, 6/2010), lot 1150.* NGC ID# 255N, PCGS# 7216

1892-O Silver Dollar, MS65
Rare Prooflike Representative

3668 **1892-O MS65 Prooflike ANACS.** The 1892-O Morgan is usually obtainable in the absolute sense, but cross over into the pursuit of Prooflike examples, and the issue becomes a major rarity. PCGS and NGC combined have certified only 27 Prooflike examples in all grades, with none finer than MS64 (10/14). This ANACS-certified coin ranks a full grade point finer than those, showing beautifully preserved surfaces and subtle field-motif contrast. A touch of striking weakness in the extreme centers is typical for the issue, and the overall eye appeal is exceptional. An important coin for the knowledgeable collector. NGC ID# 255N, PCGS# 7217

1892-S Morgan Dollar, AU55
Conditionally Elusive S-Mint Issue

3669 **1892-S AU55 PCGS.** Most of the 1.2 million silver dollars coined in San Francisco in 1892 were dispersed by the 1930s, making the issue significantly challenging and proportionately expensive in Mint State. This is a still-lustrous Choice AU example, with nearly complete detail. Subtle golden hues accent each side, but leave the surfaces with a largely brilliant appearance. An optimal grade for the date collector. NGC ID# 255P, PCGS# 7218

1893-CC Silver Dollar, MS62+
Nearly Prooflike

3670 **1893-CC MS62+ PCGS.** Substantial semiprooflike mirroring in the fields contrasts nicely with the frosted devices. Some lightness of strike is seen in the centers, as is typical of this issue, but the vibrant luster balances the appeal. Largely untoned, with grade-consistent abrasions. The 1893-CC is especially popular due to its status as the final Morgan dollar coined at the Carson City Mint, but it is also somewhat scarcer in Mint State than are some earlier issues from this mint, which were more substantially represented in the GSA sales of the early 1970s. NGC ID# 255S, PCGS# 7222

1893-CC Silver Dollar, MS63
Semiprooflike Fields

3671 **1893-CC MS63 PCGS.** Three Carson City Morgan dollar issues had the fate of being represented by only a single coin in the GSA sales of the early 1970s (1889-CC, 1892-CC, and 1893-CC), and all are either key or semikey issues in high grades as a result. Of these, the 1893-CC also carries with it the allure of being the final silver dollar issued at the Nevada branch mint. The present example shows virtually brilliant surfaces, with flashy, semiprooflike mirroring in the fields. The centers are weakly struck, as is typical of this issue, though the coin remains appealing for the grade. NGC ID# 255S, PCGS# 7222

1893-CC Silver Dollar, MS63
Last Year of the Carson City Dollars

3672 **1893-CC MS63 PCGS.** A fitting representative of the final CC-dollar issue, with partially prooflike fields, brilliant silver luster, a touch of toning on the rims, and a few of the trademark Carson City bagmarks. Scarce by demand, if not by mintage (677,000 pieces were struck), this example lacks boldness above Liberty's ear and on the eagle's center. Even so, eye appeal prevails. NGC ID# 255S, PCGS# 7222

1893-CC Dollar, MS63
Flashy, Nearly Prooflike Surfaces

3673 **1893-CC MS63 PCGS.** A remarkably attractive coin, especially for the grade, the fields of this piece are iridescent and semi-reflective, being just shy of Prooflike status (and a great deal more money). The obverse is toned in shades of lavender and gold, while the reverse is mostly brilliant with a light touch of the same alluring patina on that side. Weakly defined in the centers, as is often the case on '93-CC dollars. Marks are limited to a single scrape beneath Liberty's chin, minimized by the toning. NGC ID# 255S, PCGS# 7222

1893-O Morgan Dollar, MS62
Low-Mintage O-Mint Issue

3674 **1893-O MS62 PCGS.** The sharp and lustrous surfaces of this challenging O-Mint coin reveal scattered glimpses of faint orange and golden-brown shades at the margins. Light marks and abrasions are present, but do not pose a significant distraction. The reverse exhibits a few small pieces of debris. Only 300,000 pieces were struck, making it the lowest-mintage issue of the entire series produced at the New Orleans Mint. NGC ID# 255T, PCGS# 7224

1893-S Silver Dollar, VF20
Pleasing Mid-Grade Example

3675 **1893-S VF20 NGC.** The 1893-S Morgan dollar experienced extensive circulation following its issuance, with the result that a number of well-circulated examples are known today. This piece shows varying shades of gunmetal and olive-tan patina, with pleasing detail for the grade. An excellent, problem-free example for the budget-minded Morgan dollar enthusiast. NGC ID# 255U, PCGS# 7226

1893-S Dollar, VF25
Pleasing Mid-Grade Representative

3676 **1893-S VF25 NGC.** The entire 100,000-coin mintage of the 1893-S dollar was accomplished in the first month of the year, and the majority went straight into circulation. As a result, mid-grade circulated pieces comprise much of the surviving population of the date, and are ideal for the budget-minded collector. This example displays pale pewter-gray patina, with pleasing detail for the grade. NGC ID# 255U, PCGS# 7226

1893-S Dollar, Appealing VF25

3677 **1893-S VF25 PCGS.** A refreshingly original mid-grade example of this sought-after key date. Varying shades of olive and lavender-gray patina blanket each side, with grade-consistent wear and a lack of distractions. The 1893-S was a workhorse issue in Western commerce following its production, and circulated examples are usually obtainable for the date collector. Many have been cleaned, however, and finding a piece with original color can be a challenge. NGC ID# 255U, PCGS# 7226

1893-S Dollar, Well-Detailed VF25

3678 **1893-S VF25 PCGS.** Pale pewter-gray patina blankets both sides of this evenly worn mid-grade example. Most of the major details remain well-defined. This key-date Morgan issue is most plentiful in VF and lower grades, with these pieces being ideal for the budget-minded series collector. Above this level, the date becomes increasingly scarce and expensive. NGC ID# 255U, PCGS# 7226

1893-S Dollar, VF30
Deeply Patinated

3679 **1893-S VF30 PCGS.** Deep gunmetal and olive-gray toning encompasses each side of this lightly circulated representative. The devices are well-detailed and there are no singularly detracting marks. The 1893-S Morgan's key-date status draws substantial collector interest at all grade levels, with particular demand reserved for naturally toned examples. NGC ID# 255U, PCGS# 7226

1893-S Silver Dollar, AU Sharpness

3680 **1893-S — Cleaning — PCGS Genuine. AU Details.** This example is lightly cleaned, but retains subtle mint luster in the protected regions. A blush of golden toning accents each side, while the devices exhibit only slight high-point wear. Most 1893-S dollars are moderately well-worn from years in circulation, and AU or finer examples are seldom encountered. This piece will please many collectors. NGC ID# 255U, PCGS# 7226

1893-S Dollar, AU50
Seldom Seen in This Grade

3681 1893-S AU50 PCGS. Only 100,000 Morgan dollars were struck at the San Francisco Mint in 1893, this being the lowest production total in the entire series. The majority of these were soon distributed into circulation, with the result that the typical survivor grades only in the VF or lower range, with many damaged or otherwise not gradable examples also known. The date is infrequently available in XF, and AU coins are scarce; in Mint State, the 1893-S lives up to its name as a major key, as such examples are rare at all levels. This well-detailed About Uncirculated piece shows bright silvery-gray surfaces beneath a hint of light golden toning. A small, well-hidden mark on the eagle's lower breast is the only abrasion of note. This piece offers an important acquisition for the advanced Morgan dollar collector. NGC ID# 255U, PCGS# 7226

1894 Silver Dollar, MS64
High-End for the Issue

3682 1894 MS64 PCGS. The 1894 Morgan dollar had the second-lowest mintage of the series (110,000 coins), and ranks as the rarest Philadelphia issue in all grades. At the Choice level, this date becomes a significant semikey to the series. This is a well-struck example, with frosty, untoned luster and a lack of obtrusive abrasions. PCGS has encapsulated only 26 numerically finer examples, and NGC just four (10/14). NGC ID# 255V, PCGS# 7228

1894 Morgan, MS64
Vibrant, Frosty Luster

3683 1894 MS64 PCGS. The 1894 Morgan boasts the second-lowest business strike mintage in the series (just 110,000 coins), and is proportionately popular in Mint State. This frost-white example is highly attractive, with only minor, scattered surface grazes accounting for the grade. The eagle's breast and the hair above Liberty's ear show a touch of softness, though not enough to detract. NGC ID# 255V, PCGS# 7228

1894-O Dollar, MS64
Prohibitively Rare Any Finer

3684 1894-O MS64 PCGS. A challenging New Orleans issue, the 1894-O Morgan is seldom seen in Choice condition, and finer examples are exceedingly rare. This piece is free of major abrasions, with vibrant, frosty luster and a whisper of light golden toning over each side. Some striking deficiency is noted in the centers, likely contributing to the grade. PCGS has encapsulated only 11 numerically finer representatives (10/14). NGC ID# 255W, PCGS# 7230

1894-S Morgan Dollar, MS65
Conditionally Rare in Finer Grades

3685 **1894-S MS65 PCGS. CAC.** The 1894-S Morgan dollar is a semikey issue from a smallish mintage of 1.2 million pieces. Very scarce at the MS65 level, the 1894-S is a condition rarity in finer grades. This delightful Gem exhibits sharply detailed design elements and vibrant cartwheel mint luster throughout. The brilliant surfaces show no mentionable distractions and eye appeal is terrific. PCGS has graded only 14 numerically finer examples (10/14). NGC ID# 255X, PCGS# 7232

1896-O Morgan Dollar, MS63
Challenging Issue in High Grade

3686 **1896-O MS63 NGC.** An issue known for weak strikes, insipid luster, and excessive bagmarks, the 1896-O Morgan dollar is probably the most challenging date of the series in high grade. This well-struck Select example is a high-end representative for the date, with satiny mint luster and only a few minor contact marks on both sides. The surfaces display light golden-tan patina. NGC has graded only 14 coins in higher numeric grades (11/14). NGC ID# 2563, PCGS# 7242

1896-O Dollar, MS63
An Attractive Example of the Issue

3687 **1896-O MS63 NGC.** Ex: M L Moser Collection. Some interesting extra metal on the rim at 10 o'clock. A bit softly struck on the obverse but generally bold and crisply detailed on the reverse, this Select Mint State example displays smooth, satiny luster and mostly untoned surfaces that reveal subtle hints of sky-blue and almond-gold toning. Minor surface marks keep it from a higher grade. NGC has only graded 14 coins from this poorly-produced New Orleans issue any finer (10/14). NGC ID# 2563, PCGS# 7242

1897 Silver Dollar, MS67
None Numerically Finer

3688 **1897 MS67 PCGS. CAC.** A plentiful issue overall, benefiting from a mintage of more than 2.8 million coins, the 1897 Morgan becomes elusive in Premium Gem condition and is genuinely rare any finer. This Superb Gem representative showcases heavily frosted, untoned mint bloom and bold design definition. A few microscopic breaks in the luster are detected upon close examination, though the eye appeal is seemingly unrivaled for the issue. Population: 27 in 67 (1 in 67+), 0 finer (10/14). NGC ID# 2565, PCGS# 7246

1899 Silver Dollar, MS67
Carefully Preserved

3689 **1899 MS67 PCGS.** The 1899 has long been considered one of the key Philadelphia issues in the series, boasting a low mintage of only 330,000 pieces. This is a delightful Superb Gem example, with razor-sharp detail and carefully preserved surfaces. Traces of light golden toning warm otherwise brilliant, satiny luster on each side. Population: 19 in 67 (1 in 67+), 0 finer (10/14). NGC ID# 256B, PCGS# 7258

1900-O/CC Morgan, MS66
Popular *Guide Book* Variety

3690 **1900-O/CC VAM-12 MS66 PCGS. CAC.** A Top 100 Variety. Following the official close of the Carson City Mint in 1899 (coinage operations had been ceased since 1893), the remaining equipment and unused dies were shipped back to the Philadelphia Mint. Several of the reverse dies, however, already marked with the Carson City mintmark, were repunched with an O mintmark and then sent to the mint in New Orleans the following year. Dollars struck from these tail dies, commonly known as the O/CC varieties, are immensely popular among Carson City specialists and VAM collectors alike.

Ten different VAMs are known exhibiting the overmintmark, of which VAM-12 shows the clearest remnants of the underlying CC. It is also one of the more available varieties overall, much to the delight of collectors. This Premium Gem example displays satiny luster with hints of light golden color throughout. Some usual minor striking deficiency is noted on the hair immediately above Liberty's ear, though the devices are otherwise sharp and the preservation is excellent. PCGS has certified only two numerically finer 1900-O/CC dollars (10/14). PCGS# 133964

1901 Silver Dollar, MS62
Elusive in Mint State

3691 **1901 MS62 PCGS.** The 1901 Morgan is well-known as one of the most conditionally challenging issues in the series, being readily available in circulated grades, but distinctly scarce in Mint State. This example reveals few abrasions for the MS62 grade level, and shows an above-average strike for the issue. Traces of light golden color accent otherwise brilliant, satiny luster on each side. NGC ID# 256J, PCGS# 7272

1903-S Dollar, MS63
Aesthetically Superior for the Grade

3692 **1903-S MS63 PCGS.** The 1903-S Morgan had a mintage of only a little more than 1.2 million coins, most of which were distributed before the Treasury releases of the early 1960s. As a result, the issue is challenging in most grades, and is especially prized in pleasing Mint State condition. This is an unusually appealing coin for the MS63 level, exhibiting only a few light, scattered luster grazes on each side. Some minor striking softness on the eagle's breast and the hair above Liberty's ear is not detracting, and the satiny surfaces are essentially brilliant, save for traces of light golden color that are seen when turned beneath a light. NGC ID# 256T, PCGS# 7288

1903-S Dollar, AU50
Scarce Small S, VAM-2

3693 **1903-S Small S, VAM-2, AU50 NGC. CAC.** A Top 100 Variety. The undersized mintmark punch was likely intended for Barber quarters, but also impressed a single reverse die of the better date 1903-S. Also known as the Micro S variety. An unblemished and pleasing silver-gray AU example that exhibits plentiful tan-tinged luster across the borders and motifs. PCGS# 133967

1904-S Silver Dollar, MS64
Seldom Encountered This Nice

3694 **1904-S MS64 NGC.** The 1904-S Morgan dollar was not well-represented in either the Treasury releases of the early 1960s, or the Redfield hoard of the 1970s, and is seldom encountered in pleasing Mint State condition. This Choice example displays a touch of semiprooflike mirroring in the fields, with a faint blush of light golden color overall. Some minor striking deficiency is noted on the eagle's breast and the hair above Liberty's ear, as usual, but the surfaces are devoid of any obtrusive abrasions. NGC has encapsulated only 36 numerically finer representatives (10/14). NGC ID# 256W, PCGS# 7294

1904-S Dollar, MS64
Semiprooflike Fields

3695 **1904-S MS64 PCGS. CAC.** Moderate mirroring in the fields highlights essentially brilliant centers on this Choice example, while a thin ring of light golden color surrounds the extreme outer peripheries. Slight striking weakness is noted in the centers, though the unusually clean surfaces balance the eye appeal. The 1904-S Morgan is a slightly better date in Mint State grades, and is scarce above the MS64 grade level. NGC ID# 256W, PCGS# 7294

1921-S Morgan Dollar, MS66
None Numerically Finer at PCGS

3696 **1921-S MS66 PCGS.** Of the three 1921 Morgan dollar issues, the 1921-S is far and away the most difficult to locate in Gem and finer condition. This is a thickly frosted, brilliant Premium Gem, with above-average definition on the central design elements. A few faint luster grazes on the obverse limit the technical grade, but hardly inhibit the eye appeal. Population: 65 in 66 (2 in 66+), 0 finer (10/14). NGC ID# 256Z, PCGS# 7300

PROOF MORGAN DOLLARS

1881 Morgan Dollar, PR66 Cameo
'One of the Very Finest in Existence'

3697 **1881 PR66 Cameo PCGS. CAC.** Ex: Eliasberg. Of the 984 proofs struck this year a surprising number are still known, some even in higher grades. However, few are extant in both high grade and with cameo contrast. This is an exceptional coin. In the Eliasberg catalog it was described as, "... one of the very finest in existence." The centers are almost completely brilliant while the margins are tinted in light golden. The cameo contrast is strong on each side. Population: 8 in 66 (2 in 66+), 7 finer (10/14).
Ex: Chapman Brothers (1/1900); J.M. Clapp; John H. Clapp; Clapp Estate, 1942, to Louis E. Eliasberg, Sr.; Eliasberg Collection (4/1997), lot 2260. PCGS# 87316

1887 Dollar, PR65
First Generation Holder

3698 **1887 PR65 PCGS.** The 1887 is one of the more challenging proof Morgan dollar issues to locate in high grades, partly due to a diminished mintage of only 710 pieces (down from a peak of 1,100 coins in 1882). The typical example is well-struck, and this coin is a prime example in that regard. A lack of marks or obtrusive hairlines in the mirrored fields also contributes to the overall appeal, while golden-gray toning deepens toward the margins on each side, yielding to tinges of blue around the peripheries. Housed in a first generation holder. Population: 29 in 65, 17 finer (10/14). NGC ID# 27ZG, PCGS# 7322

1889 Morgan, Bold PR66+ Cameo
Exceptional Visual Appeal

3699 **1889 PR66+ Cameo PCGS. CAC.** The needle-sharp design definition and profound white-on-black contrast of this Plus-graded Premium Gem seem to belie Bowers' assessment of this proof issue: "Average strike, usually flat at the centers. Medium to low cameo contrast." The frosted devices beautifully accent incredibly deep mirroring in the fields, while a faint golden tint adds just a tinge of warmth to each side. Contact marks are nonexistent, and the few wispy hairlines in the fields that preclude an even finer grade assessment are detectable only upon close examination with a lens. Population: 5 in 66 (1 in 66+), 3 finer (10/14). PCGS# 87324

1893 Dollar, PR65 Deep Cameo
Uncharacteristically Bold Contrast

3700 **1893 PR65 Deep Cameo PCGS. CAC.** Ex: Teich Family Collection. The Mint produced 792 proof Morgan dollars in 1893, these being coined in several "batches" throughout the course of the year. Little attention, however, was paid to striking quality, as most examples are lacking somewhat in central sharpness, and it is a rarity to locate a piece with Deep Cameo contrast. The present coin showcases fully mirrored fields with a tinge of amber toning, while the devices are heavily frosted with above-average definition. The PCGS population report shows this to be one of only nine Deep Cameo representatives certified at that service, with the other eight coins being numerically finer (10/14). PCGS# 97328

1897 Silver Dollar, PR65 Cameo
Elusive in Finer Grades

3701 1897 PR65 Cameo NGC. Most 1897 proof dollars are boldly struck with deep cameo contrast, although the present coin is properly graded as a regular Cameo. The deep-mirrored fields are in full bloom, however, with lavender hues that contrast with the lightly frosted motifs. Delicate lines (particularly in the left obverse field) are a factor but do not diminish the overall appeal of this elusive Gem proof. Census: 9 in 65, 27 finer (10/14). PCGS# 87332

PEACE DOLLARS

1924 Peace Dollar, MS67
Sharp Luster, Smooth Surfaces

3702 1924 MS67 PCGS. Intense, snow-white mint luster rolls across the frosted surfaces in blazing cartwheels. This is an extremely rare coin in this Superb Gem grade, with fully untoned, silver fields and devices that show no hint of the golden patina that often attaches itself to this Philadelphia issue. Detail on the devices is sharp but not bold, with evidence of worn dies visible mostly at the edges. Only a few tiny, non-distracting marks are seen with a glass. Housed in a green label holder. PCGS and NGC combined have certified just two coins in a numerically higher grade. PCGS Population: 28 in 67, 1 finer (10/14). NGC ID# 257J, PCGS# 7363

1927 Peace Dollar, MS65
Lightly Toned, Lower-Mintage Issue

3703 1927 MS65 PCGS. CAC. This sharply struck representative lacks only a touch of definition in Liberty's tresses, with essentially flawless satin surfaces and glowing luster. The surfaces appear brilliant at first glance, but closer inspection reveals attractive shades of pale gold and powder blue. Certified in a green-label holder.
Ex: Portland Signature (Heritage, 3/2004), lot 6825; ANA Signature (Heritage, 8/2010), lot 5439. NGC ID# 257S, PCGS# 7370

1934-S Peace Dollar, MS64
Glowing Original Mint Frost

3704 1934-S MS64 PCGS. CAC. This semikey Peace dollar is devoid of obtrusive abrasions, being limited in grade only by some faint luster grazes that are seen when tilted beneath a light. The strike is sharp, with thickly frosted cartwheel luster residing beneath a thin veil of light golden toning. A popular late-series issue, the 1934-S is seldom available finer than this eye-appealing near-Gem. NGC ID# 257Z, PCGS# 7377

1935 Peace Dollar, MS66+
Remarkable High-End Premium Gem

3705 1935 MS66+ PCGS. This final-year example has a rich satiny sheen and well-struck design motifs, with a vivid copper-orange band along the left side peripheries of obverse and reverse alike. The carefully preserved surfaces are nearly mark-free. Population: 9 in 66+, 0 finer (10/14). NGC ID# 2582, PCGS# 7378

GOLD DOLLARS

1853 Gold Dollar, Frosty MS66
Premium Type One Representative

3706 1853 MS66 PCGS. The 1853 gold dollar is one of the most plentiful issues of the period, ideal for representing the Type One design. The present coin is sharply struck with frosty green-gold luster. The surfaces are devoid of significant abrasions, with only a few faint grazes precluding an even finer grade from PCGS. As it stands, this piece is conditionally scarce, as PCGS has so-graded only 33 coins (1 in 66+), and 11 finer (10/14). NGC ID# 25BU, PCGS# 7521

1853-C Gold Dollar, MS62
Final Type One Charlotte Issue

3707 **1853-C MS62 NGC. Variety 1.** The 1853-C gold dollar is only marginally available in the context of Charlotte issues, with 200 to 300 examples believed extant. The typical piece is lightly or moderately worn, grading in the lower AU and XF range. Doug Winter estimates no more than 25 truly Mint State pieces exist, a number far smaller than the combined certified population totals (71 coins); the latter figure certainly includes resubmissions.

This example shows satiny green-gold luster and minimally abraded surfaces. The central relief elements are weakly impressed, as is characteristic of this poorly produced issue. A small, mint-made planchet void in the central reverse should not be mistaken for damage. Census: 16 in 62 (2 in 62+), 16 finer (10/14). NGC ID# 25BV, PCGS# 7522

1855-C Gold Dollar, AU53
The Only Type Two Charlotte Issue

3708 **1855-C AU53 NGC. Variety 2.** The "ugly duckling" award goes to this Charlotte date, which is almost never well-struck or attractive, and one that is subject to bad planchets and die clashing. While the current coin is not a raving beauty, the planchet is better than most and die clashing is visible only lightly on the obverse. The reverse is unclashed. A soft strike at the centers is typical for the issue. The surfaces display natural medium-gold appeal, with glimpses of orange at the margins. A rare coin, always in demand by date and type collectors despite the nearly unavoidable strike and planchet issues. NGC ID# 25C5, PCGS# 7533

1855-D Gold Dollar, AU Details
Key, Low-Mintage Dahlonega Issue

3709 **1855-D — Scratched, Cleaned — NGC Details. AU. Variety 7-I.** The 1855-D gold dollar was rare when Franklin Pierce was president — only 1,811 pieces were struck. Of that number it is estimated that today a mere 75-100 coins are known in all grades. The 8 in the date is weak, as usual, but otherwise the devices are well detailed for a Dahlonega product. The surfaces are hairlined, and there are several small, scattered scratches scattered about, most are seen on the reverse. NGC ID# 25C6, PCGS# 7534

1858-S Gold Dollar, MS61
Only Two Finer Coins at PCGS

3710 **1858-S MS61 NGC.** Only 10,000 gold dollars were struck at the San Francisco Mint in 1858, and few examples were saved by contemporary collectors, making the issue scarce-to-rare in all grades today. This attractive MS61 example offers sharply detailed design elements and vibrant mint luster with excellent eye appeal. Census: 7 in 61, 2 finer (10/14). NGC ID# 25CK, PCGS# 7550

1863 Gold Dollar, AU55
Scarce Philadelphia Issue

3711 **1863 AU55 PCGS.** A paltry 6,200 business strike gold dollars were produced in Philadelphia in 1863, and survivors are seldom seen in any grade. This Choice AU piece retains substantial mint luster in the semiprooflike fields, while the rich orange-gold patina beautifully accents the boldly struck design elements. Population: 6 in 55, 28 finer (10/14).
From The J.S. Morgan Collection of Gold Dollars. NGC ID# 25CX, PCGS# 7562

1884 Gold Dollar, MS64
Deep Prooflike

3712 1884 MS64 Deep Prooflike NGC. Although NGC has certified 227 Mint State 1884 gold dollars, only 38 of those have mirrored surfaces, and just five are deeply mirrored. This boldly defined light yellow-gold example has excellent eye appeal, with lustrous devices that contrast nicely against the mirrored fields. Census: 3 in 64 Deep Prooflike, 0 finer (10/14). PCGS# 97585

1886 Gold Dollar, MS67 Prooflike
Rich Gold Color and Flashy Luster

3713 1886 MS67 Prooflike NGC. CAC. The flashy luster on this Superb Gem provides many visual pleasures, as does the rich gold coloration. The strike is exceptional. No contact marks are seen, and a few wispy hairlines are minor. The reverse is rotated a few degrees counterclockwise. From a mintage of 5,000 coins. Census: 5 in 67 Prooflike, 0 finer (10/14), but this is the sole example in this grade with the CAC green approval sticker.
Ex: FUN Signature (Heritage, 1/2008), lot 3708. PCGS# 77587

PROOF EARLY QUARTER EAGLE

1831 Quarter Eagle, BD-1, Proof
Attractive, Razor-Sharp Example

3714 1831 — Tooled — PCGS Proof Genuine. Unc Details. BD-1, R.7 as a proof. This date had an unknown proof mintage that was undoubtedly small, with 10 pieces as the most optimistic estimate that we have heard. Akers stated that there are five or six proofs known, according to PCGS Coinfacts. Five unimpaired specimens have been graded by NGC (3) and PCGS (2), in grades ranging from PR63 to PR66.

While there has been much controversy over prooflike coins being rated as proofs of this date, the present piece shows undeniable evidence of being one of the few known proofs. The strike definition is razor-sharp on virtually every design detail, save for a small area of softness on the eagle's upper left (facing) wing, just to the left of the shield (this feature was also recognized on an NGC PR63 coin that we sold in our 2009 Central States auction in Cincinnati). The fields are glassy and highly reflective on the obverse, while the reverse fields seemingly show the "Tooling" indicated by PCGS, and have a satiny, faintly granular appearance.

CLASSIC QUARTER EAGLES

1834 Quarter Eagle, MS61
Small Head, Variety 1

3715 **1834 MS61 PCGS. Breen-6138, Variety 1, R.1.** Small Head. The 1834 is a fairly plentiful issue in the Classic Head quarter eagle series, and is often represented in type collections. This lower-grade Mint State example shows a touch of semiprooflike mirroring in the fields, with pale green-gold patina overall. The hair curls around Liberty's face exhibit considerable weakness, though the stars and the central reverse are sharply impressed. NGC ID# 25FS, PCGS# 7692

1834 Classic Quarter Eagle, MS62
Breen-6140, Variety 3

3716 **1834 MS62 PCGS. Breen-6140, Variety 3, R.4.** Large Head. A scarce variety of this popular first-year Classic Head issue. This example displays bright green-gold patina with semiprooflike fields. Some minor striking weakness is noted in the centers, though all major details are plain. The 1834 Classic Head quarter eagle had a mintage in excess of 112,000 pieces, and is often chosen for type purposes. NGC ID# 25FS, PCGS# 7692

1836 Classic Head Quarter Eagle, MS63
Variety 11, Script 8 Variant

3717 **1836 Script 8 MS63 PCGS. Variety 11, R.2.** An impressive Select example from a late state of the dies. A bisecting die crack is evident from the rim through star 6, across the bust, and through the field to the rim between stars 12 and 13. Both sides show some incomplete detail, due to lapping. The lustrous orange-gold surfaces show only minor signs of contact. Population: 32 in 63 (1 in 63+), 14 finer (10/14). NGC ID# 25FU, PCGS# 7694

1839-C Quarter Eagle, AU55
Winter-2, Variety 22

3718 **1839-C AU55 NGC. Breen-6150, Winter-2, Variety 22, R.4.** Recut 39. A middle die state with lengthy cracks above the left (facing) wing and through the beak, but without the eventual bold crack across the portrait from star 2 to 9. Nicely struck and untoned with moderate contact near the chin and UNITED. The 1839-C is eagerly pursued for its low mintage and Charlotte Mint origin. *Ex: FUN Signature (Heritage, 1/2008), lot 3814.* NGC ID# 25G4, PCGS# 7699

LIBERTY QUARTER EAGLES

1841-C Liberty Quarter Eagle, AU58
Very Rare Issue in Higher Grades

3719 **1841-C AU58 NGC. Variety 1.** The 1841-C Liberty quarter eagle is a challenging issue from a poorly produced mintage of 10,281 pieces. This attractive near-Mint specimen displays a better-than-average strike, with just a trace of actual wear on the design elements. The pleasing yellow-gold surfaces are lightly abraded and retain much of their original mint luster. Census: 24 in 58 (1 in 58 ★), 6 finer (10/14). NGC ID# 25GE, PCGS# 7721

1842-D Quarter Eagle, XF45
Scarce Low-Mintage Issue

3720 **1842-D XF45 PCGS. Variety 3-F.** A scant mintage of only 4,643 quarter eagles at the Dahlonega Mint in 1842 resulted in the survival of only 85 to 105 examples in all grades today, per the research of Doug Winter. The typical coin resides in the XF or lower range, with anything finer being particularly elusive; only four pieces have been certified as Mint State, all NGC coins. The present piece is from a late die state, with the repunching on the bottom of the 1 and 8 in the date slightly faded. Subtle orange-gold overtones accent bright, green-gold surfaces, while the devices are well-struck with only light wear. A pleasing Choice XF example of this seldom seen Dahlonega issue. Population: 15 in 45, 24 finer (10/14). NGC ID# 25GJ, PCGS# 7725

1844-C Quarter Eagle, MS61
Lustrous, Above-Average Example

1846 Quarter Eagle, MS63
Top-Drawer Condition Census Example

3721 **1844-C MS61 PCGS. Variety 1.** This challenging issue is one of the most difficult quarter eagles from the Charlotte Mint to acquire in Mint State. Most examples are long gone, victims of a small mintage of 11,622 pieces or lost to years of circulation in the South prior to the Civil War. Indifferent production at the Charlotte Mint often causes even technically Uncirculated examples difficulty passing muster at the grading services.

The strike on the stars and eagle is typically weak on the present coin, but luckily the luster is extensive, bright, and somewhat prooflike. Honey-gold color laced with traces of lavender and light green delivers a consistent patina throughout both sides. A couple of pinpoint ticks show on the cheek, but these are appropriate for the grade, especially since the remainder of the surfaces are splendidly clean. This is really a nice, above-average coin for the issue and the grade designation. Population: 3 in 61, 3 finer (10/14).
Ex: ANA Signature (Heritage, 7/2005), lot 10316; Dallas Signature (Heritage, 11/2005), lot 2369; FUN Signature (Heritage, 1/2006), 3417. NGC ID# 25GU, PCGS# 7735

3722 **1846 MS63 PCGS.** The 1846 quarter eagle, sporting a mintage of 21,598 pieces, can be located in circulated grades with a degree of effort. Uncirculated examples, however, are a true condition rarity. The two major grading services have seen a little over 30 specimens in mint condition, none finer than MS63.

The Select piece offered in this lot is one of the three finest seen at either service. When viewed from directly overhead the partially prooflike surfaces yield a mild gold-on-black appearance. Sharply struck throughout, accentuating somewhat the field-motif contrast. The few marks are relatively light and within the parameters of the designated grade. Really a nice coin for an MS63. Population: 2 in 63, 0 finer (10/14). NGC ID# 25GZ, PCGS# 7740

1846-C Two and a Half, XF40
Appealing Original Patina

3723   **1846-C XF40 PCGS. Variety 1.** This low-mintage Charlotte issue (only 4,808 pieces struck), is seldom seen in any grade. Doug Winter suggests just 100 to 125 examples are extant, with only a small number of those retaining natural coloration. The present coin is an important piece in that regard, with original olive-gold patina overall and deeper coppery-orange hues in the recesses. Slight striking softness on the central reverse is of little concern at this grade level. Population: 11 in 40, 46 finer (10/14). NGC ID# 25H2, PCGS# 7741

1847-C Two and a Half, MS62
Sharply Struck C-Mint Type Coin

3724   **1847-C MS62 PCGS. Variety 1.** The only die pair. The obverse shows the characteristic die line that connects stars 12 and 13, and the diagonal die line crosses through MER on the reverse. The 1847-C is the most frequently seen Charlotte quarter eagle, even though only 23,226 pieces were minted. Three or four dozen Uncirculated coins are believed known, making this the logical choice for a high-grade type set. The surfaces are bright yellow and green-gold with bright, semireflective fields. Sharply struck throughout and problem-free. Population: 8 in 62, 12 finer (10/14). NGC ID# 25H6, PCGS# 7745

1852 Quarter Eagle, MS66
Major Condition Rarity

3725   **1852 MS66 PCGS.** Overall, the 1852 is one of the more plentiful quarter eagle issues from the 1850s, benefiting from a mintage in excess of 1.1 million coins. However, most Uncirculated representatives are heavily abraded, as is typical of gold issues from this period, grading no finer than MS62; in comparison to collector demand, MS63 and MS64 coins are scarce, and anything finer is a major rarity. PCGS has certified only two examples in MS66, and just one numerically finer (10/14). Fully struck motifs and frosty green-gold luster are the hallmarks of this Premium Gem, delivering truly impressive eye appeal. A few minute ticks on the obverse are all that preclude an even finer grade. NGC ID# 25HR, PCGS# 7763

1854-C Quarter Eagle, AU58
Appealing Originality
Rare at This Grade Level

3726 **1854-C AU58 PCGS. Variety 1.** The Charlotte Mint struck only 7,295 quarter eagles in 1854, and as few as 105 to 145 are believed extant. Doug Winter suggests of this issue: "It is scarce in the lower AU grades and rare in properly graded AU55 to AU58." This near-Mint representative displays deep olive-gold color overall, with small orange overtones seen in the protected regions. Some typical lightness of strike is seen on the central devices, though a degree of reflectivity in the fields balances the visual appeal. Population: 7 in 58 (1 in 58+), 6 finer (10/14). NGC ID# 25HY, PCGS# 7770

1860-C Quarter Eagle, AU58
Final Charlotte Mint Two and a Half

3727 **1860-C AU58 NGC. Variety 1.** From a mintage of just 7,469 pieces, the 1860-C is the last quarter eagle from the Charlotte Mint. Like most examples seen, the obverse design elements of this attractive near-Mint specimen are sharper than the reverse devices. The lustrous greenish-gold surfaces are lightly abraded and only a trace of actual wear shows on the high points. Census: 23 in 58, 11 finer (10/14). NGC ID# 25JT, PCGS# 7792

The Charlotte Mint

1868-S Quarter Eagle, Radiantly Lustrous MS64
One of the Three Finest Certified

3728 **1868-S MS64 PCGS. CAC.** Most of the 34,000 quarter eagles produced at the San Francisco Mint in 1868 entered circulation. Enough circulated pieces remain to satisfy collector demand, but Mint State examples are another matter. PCGS and NGC have graded a total of 28 Uncirculated examples (10/14), the finest being three near-Gems at PCGS, one of which we offer here.

Intense luster radiates from the honey-gold surfaces that exhibit sharply struck design elements, save for the typically soft arrow feathers and adjacent claw. Both sides are free of bothersome marks. Two small milling marks on Liberty's upper jaw determine the grade and serve to help identify the coin. Pleasing overall eye appeal. NGC ID# 25KC, PCGS# 7808

1900 Quarter Eagle, MS67
Tied for Finest at PCGS

1905 Quarter Eagle, MS67
Exceptional Fully Struck Example

3729 **1900 MS67 PCGS. CAC.** Defects are virtually nonexistent on this Superb Gem business strike. Satin-smooth surfaces are evenly frosted and free of abrasions. Strong mint luster seems to radiate from behind Liberty's fully struck portrait and the equally bold eagle. The 67,000-piece mintage makes this date a popular type choice as well as for Registry Set collectors, and this example ranks high among the finest candidates. Population: 11 in 67, 0 finer (10/14). NGC ID# 25LR, PCGS# 7852

3730 **1905 MS67 PCGS.** This is a remarkable Superb Gem example with intensely lustrous honey-gold surfaces and exceptional, full strike definition that includes precise delineation of the eagle's talons, arrows, arrow fletchings, and leg feathers. Both sides of the coin are impressively preserved and virtually immaculate. Population: 69 in 67, 2 finer (10/14). NGC ID# 25LW, PCGS# 7857

1859 Quarter Eagle, PR64 Cameo
Possibly Unique Specimen with Type II Reverse
Ex: Byron Reed Collection

3731 1859 PR64 Cameo NGC. Ex: Byron Reed Collection. Some confusion seems to exist with respect to this extremely rare issue. All of the published authorities agree that the proofs from this date are rare, with approximately eight to ten examples extant. The confusion arises with regard to the reverse style for these pieces, which were struck in a transitional year for the new or Type II reverse. Walter Breen originally contended that all 1859 proofs were from the New Reverse hub, in his 1977 proof *Encyclopedia*, but when his *Complete Encyclopedia* appeared in 1988 he had reversed his opinion. Paul Taglione, in 1986, stated that all of the 1859 proof quarter eagles were made using this newer reverse design, but more recent commentators disagree.

According to the Second Edition of Garrett and Guth's *Encyclopedia of U.S. Gold Coins* (2008): "Nearly all of the Proof 1859 quarter eagles were struck with the Old Reverse style. **The Byron Reed example was struck with the New Reverse and is possibly unique**. The coin sold for $25,300 in 1996, an incredible bargain in retrospect."

This is the Byron Reed specimen referred to by Garrett and Guth, and it is a remarkable piece in several respects. In addition to being unique, or possibly so, it is a coin of remarkable beauty and overall quality. The striking impression is sharp and nearly full, save for a slight degree of softness on the first two or three obverse stars. The Y in LIBERTY is recut. The orange-gold devices are richly frosted and the sea-green fields are watery and pleasingly reflective.

When the coin was sold as part of the Byron Reed Collection, by Spink America and Christie's, it was described in the auction catalog as follows:

"Quarter-Eagle, 1859, type II reverse, arrowheads small and far from CA of AMERICA, *some tiny handling marks and hairlines, Proof with a pleasing cameo effect, just eighty Proofs of the date are thought to have been struck, many of which were later melted as unsold*, Breen (Encyclopedia, 6245), *makes no mention of the Type II reverse Proofs, Akers (Volume II, page 120) noted, 'a small number of Proofs, probably less than ten are known'*"

The following roster of known examples is adapted from that in Breen's *Encyclopedia* (1988):

1. Ex: United States Mint; Smithsonian Institute.
2. Ex: J. P. Morgan; American Numismatic Society.
3. Ex: F. C. C. Boyd; World's Greatest Collection Sale (Numismatic Gallery, 1/46), lot 127; Memorable Sale (Numismatic Gallery, 3/48), lot 118; Wolfson Sale (Stack's, 10/62), lot 179; Spring Sale (Stack's, 4/78), lot 805; Ed Trompeter; Ed Trompeter Collection Sale (Superior, 2/92), lot 39; Orlando Sale (Superior, 8/92), lot 562; Baltimore Sale (Superior, 8/92), lot 851.
4. Ex: David S. Wilson Sale (S. H. Chapman, 3/07); John H. Clapp; Louis E. Eliasberg, Sr.; Louis E. Eliasberg, Jr.; United States Gold Coin Collection Sale (Bowers & Ruddy, 10/82), lot 186; Dr. Jerry Buss Collection Sale (Superior, 1/85), lot 1714; H. W. Blevins Estate and George Bodway Collections Sale (Superior, 6/88), lot 6624, where it realized $19,800.
5. William Cutler Atwater Sale (B. Max Mehl, 6/46), lot 1963; Amon Carter Collection Sale (Stack's, 1/84), lot 553.
6. John Jay Pittman; John Jay Pittman Collection Sale (Akers, 10/97), lot 834, as part of an 1859 proof set.
7. Private Collection.
8. Byron Reed; Omaha City Library; Byron Reed Collection Sale (Spink America, 10/96), lot 55. **The present example.**

The current offering represents an amazing opportunity to acquire a coin which may represent the sole proof example known to display the so-called "New Reverse", also called Reverse Type II.
Ex: The Byron Reed Collection of Important American Coins and Manuscripts (Spink America, 10/1996), lot 55. NGC ID# 25M2, PCGS# 87885

1898 Quarter Eagle, PR63 Deep Cameo
Commanding Visual Presence

1900 Two and a Half, PR67 Deep Cameo
Two Points Finer Than the Smithsonian Proof

3732 **1898 PR63 Deep Cameo PCGS.** A combination of exceptionally deep mirrors and exquisite border toning makes this scarce proof memorable. Sky-blue patches at the margins counterbalance sunset-gold color at the centers, with residual glints of teal and magenta adding extra pizzazz. Brilliant luster focuses the eye on frosted, fully struck motifs. A few delicate hairlines are visible with a glass, but they do not hinder the main attraction, which is the outstanding, reflective coloration. Just 165 proofs were struck. Population: 8 in 63, 20 finer (10/14). NGC ID# 288M, PCGS# 97924

3733 **1900 PR67 Deep Cameo PCGS.** Only 205 proof quarter eagles were struck in this turn-of-the-century year. It is reliably estimated that today only 100 or so pieces exist today in all grades. This one of the finest, certainly at PCGS. That service has only certified three other pieces in PR67 and with Deep Cameo contrast, with a mere two pieces finer (11/14). This is an extraordinary coin that displays even reddish-gold color and strong field-device contrast on each side. As one might expect from a PR67, there are no obvious contact marks on either side. As a sidenote, the coin in the Smithsonian is "only" a PR65 Deep Cameo. NGC ID# 288P, PCGS# 97926

INDIAN QUARTER EAGLES

1908 Quarter Eagle, MS66
Luminous, Richly Colored Surfaces

3734 **1908 MS66 PCGS.** Incomplete engraving of the reverse die resulted in all examples of the 1908 quarter eagle being struck with rather weak definition on the eagle's wing feathers, even though the obverse may be razor-sharp. This Premium Gem represents an important opportunity for both the date and type collector, as only two coins have graded numerically finer at PCGS (10/14). Rich orange-gold color highlights radiant mint luster, while the design elements, save for the eagle's wing, are needle-sharp. NGC ID# 288Y, PCGS# 7939

1911-D Quarter Eagle, AU55
Natural Coloration

3735 **1911-D AU55 PCGS.** Strong D. Many AU examples of this key Denver issue have been cleaned or otherwise brightened, and it can be difficult to secure a piece with natural patina. The present example is an important coin in that regard, showing deep orange-gold color over the high points on each side, with lighter bronze-gold in the recesses. The strike is sharp and only a brush of actual wear is evident. NGC ID# 2894, PCGS# 7943

1911-D Two and a Half, AU58
Nice, Problem-Free Surfaces

3736 **1911-D AU58 NGC.** The 1911-D is the undisputed key to the Indian quarter eagle series, and just a glance at the low mintage figure explains why. This is an attractive, problem-free AU with just a hint of high-point friction. The mintmark is a bit soft but clearly discernible. Sharply struck throughout. NGC ID# 2894, PCGS# 7943

1911-D Indian Quarter Eagle, MS62
Sought-After Series Key

3737 **1911-D MS62 NGC.** An impressive MS62 example of this low-mintage key, with sharply detailed design elements throughout and vibrant mint luster on both sides. The light orange-gold surfaces show a few scattered contact marks, but none are unduly distracting and eye appeal is quite strong for the grade. NGC ID# 2894, PCGS# 7943

1913 Quarter Eagle, MS65
Conditionally Scarce

3738 **1913 MS65 PCGS.** The 1913 Indian quarter eagle had a substantial mintage of 722,000 pieces, but its availability declines sharply at the Gem grade level, and finer examples are rare. This representative exhibits sharp design elements and satiny, lemon-gold luster. A few light, scattered surface grazes limit the grade, but hardly inhibit the eye appeal. Only seven coins are numerically finer at PCGS (10/14). NGC ID# 2897, PCGS# 7945

1914 Two and a Half
Collectible Choice Example

3739 **1914 MS64 NGC.** Behind the key-date 1911-D, the 1914 Indian quarter eagle is the next issue in the series to pose a challenge for the date collector. In Gem condition, it is very nearly as scarce as the 1911-D, but enough Choice examples are certified that the date can still be acquired in pleasing condition without emptying the pocket book. This piece shows luminous bronze-gold luster and well-struck design elements. A few light, scattered marks limit the grade, but do not inhibit the overall appeal. Only 47 coins are numerically finer at NGC (10/14). NGC ID# 2898, PCGS# 7946

1914 Quarter Eagle, MS64
Smooth, Satiny Surfaces

3740 1914 MS64 NGC. The 1914 Indian quarter eagle boasts the second-lowest mintage of the series (240,000 pieces), and is not surprisingly the second-rarest overall, trailing only the key-date 1911-D. This example displays soft, wheat-gold luster, and is devoid of any individually noticeable abrasions. The devices are sharply impressed, giving this coin ample visual appeal for the grade. NGC has certified only 47 numerically finer examples (10/14). NGC ID# 2898, PCGS# 7946

1914 Quarter Eagle, MS64
Challenging Series Date

3741 1914 MS64 NGC. While the mintage is about four times that of the key 1911-D date, the 1914 Philadelphia issue is scarce in its own right. Because the Indian Head quarter eagle series has no uncollectible rarities, this date is the second-most challenging (financially) of the series to acquire. It is eminently affordable in near-Gem condition, however, and this well-produced example would be a wise selection. Lustrous amber-gold surfaces are fully struck with only minor marks of any kind. NGC ID# 2898, PCGS# 7946

1914 Quarter Eagle, MS64
Underrated Philadelphia Issue

3742 1914 MS64 PCGS. Both the 1914 and 1914-D quarter eagles prove to be elusive for series collectors in near-Gem or finer grades. They are also somewhat neglected by the collecting public, with substantial mintages but relatively few high-grade survivors. While nearly equal in population at the Gem level, the 1914 Philadelphia issue is nearly twice as scarce in near-Gem than its Denver counterpart. This example is a lustrous, green-gold coin with just a few light marks and a sharp strike. NGC ID# 2898, PCGS# 7946

1914 Quarter Eagle, MS64+
Shimmering Original Luster

3743 1914 MS64+ PCGS. CAC. Pleasing luster emanates from both sides of this high-end near-Gem, each of which displays soft reddish-gold patina that assumes slightly deeper hues on the reverse. The design features are well-struck, including the eagle's shoulder feathers. A few minuscule marks, largely visible through UNUM on the reverse, are of little consequence. The 1914 is challenging to locate numerically finer, as PCGS has graded only 59 such pieces and NGC 47 (10/14). NGC ID# 2898, PCGS# 7946

1914-D Quarter Eagle, An Exceptional MS65
The Premier Rarity in Gem and Finer Grades

1914-D Indian Quarter Eagle, MS65
Notably Rare in High Grades

3744 1914-D MS65 NGC. The 1914-D quarter eagle can be located without too much difficulty through near-Gem, but it is the premier rarity in the series in Gem and finer condition. NGC and PCGS combined have graded just 89 examples in MS65 and a solitary specimen finer (an NGC MS67). The issue is one of the most poorly struck, if not *the* worst struck, in the series. Many come with numerous marks, and many show mint-made spots.

This Gem displays coppery-gold color laced with traces of rose on its lustrous surfaces. It is much better-struck than typically seen, especially on the Indian's hair and headdress and the eagle's plumage, including that on the shoulder. The mintmark is also strong. Both sides are quite clean, lacking the marks and spots typically seen. Census: 42 in 65, 1 finer (10/14). NGC ID# 2899, PCGS# 7947

3745 1914-D MS65 NGC. The 1911-D and the 1914-D have long been regarded as the keys to the Indian quarter eagle series, because of their low mintage and their scarcity even in lower grades. At the MS65 level, however, the 1914-D emerges as a notable conditional rarity. Just 42 pieces have achieved the Gem grade at NGC as of (10/14), significantly fewer than the 1911-D. Much of the reason for this is that the 1914-D "may well be the worst struck Indian Head Quarter Eagle," according to Michael Fuljenz in his 2010 reference, *Indian Gold Coins of the 20th Century*. The present piece is crisply struck, however, and only thorough examination reveals a few tiny areas of softness within the headdress. The lustrous lemon-gold surfaces are unabraded except for a couple of tiny ticks near the U in UNITED.
Ex: Long Beach Signature (Heritage, 2/2005), lot 7706. NGC ID# 2899, PCGS# 7947

1926 Quarter Eagle, MS66
Exceptionally Clean Surfaces

3746 1926 MS66 PCGS. Two and a half and five dollar Indian gold pieces are exceptionally difficult to locate in high grade, primarily because these coins were struck with sunken relief. This means the fields are the high points of these coins, leaving them wide open to abrasions. This is a remarkably clean example with thick, frosted mint luster and even reddish-gold color. Population: 42 in 66, 0 finer (10/14). NGC ID# 289C, PCGS# 7950

1927 Quarter Eagle, MS66
Splendid High-Grade Gold Type

3747 1927 MS66 PCGS. A popular date for type purposes, the 1927 Indian quarter eagle is usually available in high-grade condition. Moreover, it is one of the better-produced and more attractive dates from this series as most are sharply struck and quite lustrous.

The peach-gold surfaces of this highly lustrous Premium Gem display hints of light green. Sharp definition is seen on the design features, including the Indian's hair and headdress feathers and the eagle's shoulder and leg plumage. A few minute, insignificant ticks are within the parameters of the grade designation. Population: 21 in 66, 0 finer (10/14). PCGS# 7951

THREE DOLLAR GOLD PIECES

1854 Three Dollar Gold, MS64
Shimmering Original Luster

3748 1854 MS64 PCGS. A delightful near-Gem example, this coin represents the first year of the three dollar gold denomination. Peach-gold coloration displays hints of light green, all overlying lustrous surfaces. The design features are well brought up, and just a few light ticks are consistent with the grade. PCGS has seen only 33 pieces numerically finer (10/14). NGC ID# 25M3, PCGS# 7969

1854 Three Dollar Gold Piece, MS64
Even Yellow-Gold Color

3749 1854 MS64 PCGS. The mintage of 138,618 pieces makes the 1854 one of the most readily obtainable three dollar issues in the entire 35-year series. This is a lovely example with bright, even yellow-gold color. The strike is strong, except on the bottom of the middle two digits in the date, and there are no significant marks on either side. NGC ID# 25M3, PCGS# 7969

1854 Three Dollar Gold, MS64
Popular, First Year of Issue

3750 1854 MS64 PCGS. The 1854 is often dismissed as "common" within the context of the three dollar series; but when it can be acquired for a common date price it makes quite a type coin when compared to an 1878 or 1874. This is a bright yellow-gold example with a remarkably strong strike on each side. No obvious or detracting abrasions are seen. NGC ID# 25M3, PCGS# 7969

1855 Three Dollar Gold, MS63
Highly Appealing, Conditionally Scarce

3751 1855 MS63 PCGS. Due to a fairly substantial mintage in the context of the series (50,555 coins), the 1855 three dollar piece is not considered to be one of the absolutely elusive issues overall, but it is still not counted among the "common" dates because of its inherent scarcity in Mint State grades. The present example is a lovely, lustrous example, with sharp design elements and blended yellow and honey-gold color. A few small abrasions define the grade. Population: 60 in 63 (2 in 63+), 27 finer (10/14). NGC ID# 25M6, PCGS# 7972

1855-S Three Dollar, AU55
Seldom Located Finer

3752 1855-S AU55 NGC. *Ex Manhattan Collection.* This issue is virtually unobtainable in mint condition — only five Uncirculated examples have been seen by PCGS and NGC combined — and better AU examples such as this are always in demand by collectors. Hints of prooflike reflectivity frame the devices, where glimpses of mint luster remain. Light abrasions are seen on both sides of the coin, yet none are severe or individually important. The yellow-gold surfaces display a sharp strike, now a bit softened by wear. Census: 18 in 55, 14 finer (10/14). NGC ID# 25M7, PCGS# 7973

1857 Three Dollar Gold, MS63
Scarce Issue in Mint State

3753 1857 MS63 PCGS. The 1857 three dollar gold piece claims a mintage of 20,891 pieces, but the vast majority entered circulation, with few set aside in Mint condition. Only 45 to 60 Uncirculated pieces are believed known. A lovely Select example, this coin exhibits a strong level of detail overall, with just a touch of softness on the ribbon bow. Bright satiny mint luster adds to the eye appeal. A few minor contact marks appear on both sides. Population: 28 in 63, 5 finer (10/14). NGC ID# 25MA, PCGS# 7976

1858 Three Dollar, AU58
Low-Mintage Early P-Mint Issue

3754 1858 AU58 PCGS. The mintage of the 1858 three dollar was a meager 2,133 circulation strikes, a series low for P-mint issues that would persist until the 1865, at 1,140 coins. This near-Mint State 1858 shows much prooflike reflectivity throughout each side, especially in the protected areas around the devices. Otherwise, the apricot-gold surfaces show what we would characterize as light field chatter rather than singular contact marks. Population: 13 in 58, 10 finer (10/14). NGC ID# 25MC, PCGS# 7978

1860-S Three Dollar Gold, AU53
Scarce San Francisco Issue

3755 1860-S AU53 NGC. In the context of the three dollar gold series, a small mintage of just 7,000 coins is not all that exciting, as many low-mintage issues from this series were heavily saved and are disproportionately available today. The 1860-S, however, is the exception to the rule. The date is scarce in all grades and extremely rare in Mint State. This About Uncirculated piece is immensely attractive for the grade, showing remnants of original luster beneath rich orange-gold patina. The surfaces are devoid of obtrusive abrasions. Census: 12 in 53, 40 finer (10/14). NGC ID# 25MF, PCGS# 7981

1863 Three Dollar Gold, MS62
Better Philadelphia Issue

3756 1863 MS62 PCGS. The 1863 three dollar piece had a typically low mintage for the series (only 5,000 coins), but Mint State examples are also somewhat scarcer than are those of later, more heavily saved dates. The present coin displays medium green-gold patina, with semiprooflike fields and minimal abrasions. The bow knot is ill-defined, as usual, though the strike is otherwise sharp throughout. Population: 10 in 62, 24 finer (10/14). NGC ID# 25MJ, PCGS# 7984

1867 Three Dollar, MS62
Mint State Rarity

3757   1867 MS62 PCGS. Just 2,600 pieces were struck — most of them prooflike from the lightly-used dies. This reflective example is rare and attractive despite light wisps in the fields and a few tiny marks. An overall bold strike and medium-gold patina add to the appeal. Always a "target date" for series collectors, the issue is seldom seen at auction in Mint State. Population: 10 in 62, 9 finer (10/14). NGC ID# 25MN, PCGS# 7988

1868 Three Dollar, Well-Struck MS62
A Low-Mintage, High Survival Rate Date

3758   1868 MS62 PCGS. Despite the low mintage of 4,850 pieces, the 1868 three dollar has a relatively high survival rate, evidenced by the 673 examples seen in all grades by the two major services, nearly 200 of which are in Mint condition. The lustrous yellow-gold surfaces display hints of rose and exhibit well-struck devices. A few minute marks account for the grade. Population: 45 in 62 (1 in 62+), 43 finer (10/14). NGC ID# 25MP, PCGS# 7989

1878 Three Dollar Gold, MS62 Prooflike
Rare With Mirrored Surfaces

3759   1878 MS62 Prooflike NGC. Only the 1854 three dollar issue had a higher mintage than the 1878, and the NGC *Census Report* clearly indicates that this is a plentiful issue, with more than 5,000 examples certified. The same report also illustrates the considerable rarity of prooflike specimens, as only 13 coins have received the NGC Prooflike designation. Nearly all surviving examples of this issue have frosty luster. This brilliant yellow-gold specimen has fully mirrored fields around its satiny devices with scattered grade-consistent marks. The strike lacks the level of detail that would normally be found on proofs, and that slight weakness confirms the circulation strike format. Census: 5 in 62 Prooflike, 5 finer (10/14). PCGS# 78000

1879 Three Dollar Gold, MS62
Exceptionally Attractive, High-End Example

3760   1879 MS62 PCGS. The strike impression is razor-sharp, with stronger-than-usual definition on the central design motifs. This light green-gold example is prooflike (although not designated as such on the holder) and highly attractive, with few wispy marks noted on each side. This issue had a scant mintage of 3,000 pieces, but not many were circulated, and quite a few coins were saved by collectors and coin dealers. NGC ID# 25N2, PCGS# 8001

1880 Three Dollar Gold, MS65+
Beautifully Preserved Condition Rarity

3761 **1880 MS65+ NGC.** The 1880 three dollar gold piece had a meager mintage of only 1,000 coins. While in most cases such a low production figure would translate into extreme rarity in all grades, in the case of the 1880 (and many other low-mintage issues in the three dollar series), it prompted the saving of numerous examples by dealers and speculators. As a result, the 1880 is somewhat more collectible than it theoretically should be, but still cannot be considered plentiful. Most of the surviving Mint State examples are somewhat limited in technical quality, being lightly abraded or showing traces of rub from poor handling. Gem examples are decidedly rare, and finer coins are exceedingly so.

This Plus-graded representative is boldly struck, with warm honey-gold surfaces and semiprooflike mirroring in the fields. A few minute ticks preclude a full Premium Gem grade, though the unaided eye finds nothing of distraction. A beautiful coin that delivers a unique combination of flash and shimmer when tilted beneath a light. Census: 16 in 65 (1 in 65+, 1 in 65 ★), 5 finer (10/14). NGC ID# 25N3, PCGS# 8002

1884 Three Dollar Gold, MS61 Prooflike
Scarce, Low-Mintage Issue

3762 **1884 MS61 Prooflike NGC.** At first glance, this beauty looks just like a proof, but only on closer examination do the tell-tale signs of a circulation strike become obvious. The strike is excellent, but falls short of full. The fields are mirrored, but fail to show the depth of true proofs. The die was undoubtedly polished, but the planchet was probably unpolished. The tiny field spaces inside the ribbon bows show satin luster, but are not mirrored.

With a mintage of only 1,000 circulation strikes, examples are rare and desirable in either format. This lovely piece has bright yellow surfaces and few minor marks that prevent a higher grade. Census: 1 in 61 Prooflike, 3 finer (10/14).
Ex: Long Beach Signature (Heritage, 9/2008), lot 3553. PCGS# 78006

James B. Longacre, designer of the three dollar gold piece.

1886 Three Dollar Gold, MS63
Elusive Low-Mintage Issue

3763 1886 MS63 PCGS. A remarkably low mintage of just 1,000 three dollar gold pieces was accomplished in 1886, but enough examples were saved by dealers and speculators that the issue is moderately obtainable overall today. Still, the typical piece grades only in the XF and AU range; Mint State coins are occasionally seen, but are primarily restricted to MS62 and lower levels. Any example certified at MS63 is a significant rarity, and finer coins are prohibitively elusive. This piece is one of only 10 pieces for the grade at PCGS, with just six numerically finer (10/14). Warm honey-gold patina yields to semiprooflike mirroring in the fields and sharp design definition on the devices. No significant abrasions are present, though a few small marks in the fields contribute to the grade. NGC ID# 25N9, PCGS# 8008

1887 Three Dollar Gold, MS62
Unusually Appealing for the Grade

3764 1887 MS62 PCGS. A typical late-series issue, the 1887 three dollar piece had a paltry mintage (only 6,000 coins), but enough examples were saved early on that the date is moderately collectible today. This example has soft yellow-gold luster and boldly struck motifs. No significant abrasions are present, though a loupe reveals some faint grazes and luster disturbances in the fields on each side. NGC ID# 25NA, PCGS# 8009

1887 Three Dollar Gold, MS63
Salient Original Mint Bloom

3765 1887 MS63 PCGS. This late-series issue had a predictably low mintage of only 6,000 coins, but experienced a fairly high survival rate and is moderately collectible today. Still, it is not nearly as plentiful as are the 1888 and 1889. This example displays radiant yellow-gold mint bloom with deeper orange-gold overtones seen in the recesses. The wreath bow knot is lacking slightly in definition, though the design elements are otherwise well brought up. No mentionable abrasions are present. NGC ID# 25NA, PCGS# 8009

1887 Three Dollar, Conditionally Scarce MS65
Highly Lustrous and Sharply Struck

3766 **1887 MS65 PCGS.** While Mint records indicate that 6,000 business strikes were produced of the 1887 three dollar gold piece, the net distribution may have been less because of meltings in the Mint. Mint State examples can be located through near-Gem with some degree of searching. Gems are very scarce and higher-grade examples are rare.

Bright luster exudes from the yellow-gold surfaces of this MS65 example and a solid strike imparts crisp definition to the design elements. Both sides have been very well cared for. These attributes add up to giving this piece pleasing eye appeal. Population: 26 in 65, 9 finer (10/14). NGC ID# 25NA, PCGS# 8009

1888 Three Dollar Piece, MS63
Appealing Original Type Coin

3767 **1888 MS63 PCGS.** This late-series issue had a scant mintage of only 5,000 coins, but survives in large enough quantities to be considered for type representation. This well-struck Select example shows rich apricot-gold luster with flashy semiprooflike mirroring in the fields. No obtrusive abrasions are noted, as the grade seems to be limited only by some faint field chatter seen when tilted beneath a light. NGC ID# 25NB, PCGS# 8010

1889 Three Dollar Gold, MS62
Attractive Final-Year Example

3768 **1889 MS62 PCGS.** In this final year of the three dollar gold denomination just 2,300 pieces were struck, but Mint State survivors are surprisingly numerous, making this issue a good choice for the type specialist seeking an attractive and affordable example. This piece is well-struck with vibrant satiny mint luster and light green-gold toning that yields to pink-rose peripheral accents on each side. NGC ID# 25NC, PCGS# 8011

1889 Three Dollar Gold, MS62
Sharply Struck Type Coin

3769 **1889 MS62 PCGS.** This final-year issue is highly popular among type specialists. Only 2,300 examples were struck, but an unusually high survival rate makes this issue obtainable for the patient collector. The present example shows hues of honey and green-gold over each side, with semiprooflike mirroring in the fields. Bold definition is enjoyed on the relief elements, even the bow knot, which is almost always weak. NGC ID# 25NC, PCGS# 8011

PROOF THREE DOLLAR GOLD PIECE

1884 Three Dollar, PR62 Cameo
Low Total Mintage Date

3770 **1884 PR62 Cameo PCGS.** Rare in both proof and business strike formats; only 106 proofs were struck and a tiny emission of 1,000 business strikes was minted. A number of small and individually insignificant contact marks account for the PR62 grade. What is remarkable here is the strong eye appeal created by the stark field-device contrast seen on each side. Slight orange-peel effect is seen in the fields, a common occurrence on 19th century proof gold. Population: 2 in 62, 14 finer (10/14). NGC ID# 28AT, PCGS# 88048

1805 Half Eagle, BD-1, MS61
Undeniably Original Luster

1807 Bust Right Half Eagle, BD-6, MS61
Semiprooflike Fields

3771 1805 MS61 PCGS. Close Date, BD-1, High R.3. Bass-Dannreuther Die State c/b. A very early stage of this die state, with the crack above UNITED just beginning. This is the only use of this reverse die, as the aforementioned crack later develops into a large cud and the die is retired. This obverse developed a bisecting die crack through the 0 in the date early, but did not completely fail and was thus also employed for the next variety, BD-2. BD-1 is the most plentiful of the five 1805 half eagle varieties, ideal for date representation. The present example displays shimmering, original luster beneath warm honey-gold patina. The strike is well-executed, with the inner portion of the eagle's left (facing) wing and a few obverse stars showing the only discernable weakness. No significant abrasions are present, with only light chatter in the fields limiting the grade. NGC ID# 25P4, PCGS# 8088

3772 1807 Bust Right MS61 PCGS. Large Date, BD-6, High R.4. Bass-Dannreuther Die State b/c, with die lapping on each side. This is the only use of this obverse die and the third and final use of this reverse. Neither die is known to have failed completely, and it is possible that they were only retired to make way for the new Capped Bust Left type of the same year. Overall, BD-6 is a plentiful variety (if only in the context of the Bust Right 1807 half eagle), tied with BD-1 as the most frequently seen; Dannreuther estimates about 80 to 100 examples survive in all grades, though Mint State representatives are only a distinct minority.

This example is boldly struck, with bright yellow-gold surfaces and a degree of semiprooflike mirroring in the fields. No significant abrasions are present, though some light chatter in the fields precludes a finer grade assessment from PCGS. A highly appealing example for the grade. NGC ID# 25P8, PCGS# 8092

1807 Draped Bust Half Eagle, MS62
BD-4, Small Date
Outstanding Original Color

1807 Bust Left Half Eagle, MS62
Rare BD-7 Variety

3773 1807 Bust Right MS62 NGC. Small Date, BD-4, High R.4. Small Obverse Stars, Large Reverse Stars. Bass-Dannreuther Die State c/a. BD-4 is one of the more plentiful 1807 Draped Bust half eagle varieties, though it is still itself scarce, with only 75 to 90 pieces believed to still exist in collections. This is the second and final use of this obverse, and the first of three uses of this reverse die, which was later paired with two different obverses and employed for the final two varieties of the Draped Bust type (BD-5 and 6).

The present coin is a rare Mint State example, with original honey-gold luster amid shades of yellow and orange-gold patina. The strike is well-executed and centered, with only a few faint adjustment marks still visible across the central obverse. Abrasions are minimal, leaving this piece with outstanding eye appeal. Census: 23 in 62, 24 finer (10/14). NGC ID# 25P8, PCGS# 8092

3774 1807 Bust Left MS62 NGC. BD-7, High R.5. Bass-Dannreuther Die State b/c, likely terminal for the reverse, with two radial die cracks from the rim near 12 o'clock. As a date, the Bust Left 1807 half eagle is one of the most plentiful early gold issues overall, and is frequently seen at auction and on the bourse. However, nearly all known examples are representative of the plentiful BD-8 die variety; the BD-7 variety, here offered, is a significant rarity, with only 30 to 40 pieces believed known. Both varieties share a common obverse, though the reverse die employed for BD-7 cracked early on and was quickly retired, possibly after as few as 3,000 examples were struck. This is an important Mint State survivor, with luminous green-gold surfaces and boldly struck design elements. Some faint adjustment marks are observed along the lower reverse rim, not uncommon for gold issues of this period, while the die state-consistent clash marks are present in the fields on each side. NGC ID# 25P9, PCGS# 8101

LIBERTY HALF EAGLES

1839-D Half Eagle, AU58
Sharply Struck and Impressive

1847-O Five Dollar, XF40
The Scarcest O-Mint Half Eagle

3775 1839-D AU58 NGC. Variety 2-A. The 1839-D issue is a distinct and important one-year type as the sole Liberty Head half eagle from the Dahlonega mint facility to bear an obverse mintmark. This is the more common of two known die varieties, with a tilted mintmark that is over 39 in the date. According to Doug Winter, writing in the third edition of his *Gold Coins of the Dahlonega Mint:* "This date is very rare in About Uncirculated-58 and it is extremely rare in Uncirculated, with just four to six known."

The current offering is a near-Mint coin with impressively sharp strike definition and light green-gold coloration over each side. The piece displays considerable mint luster, and there are only occasional wispy marks noted on the smooth surfaces. High-point friction is minimal. Census: 16 in 58, 4 finer (10/14). NGC ID# 25S9, PCGS# 8193

3776 1847-O XF40 PCGS. Variety 1. The 1847-O half eagle is the scarcest O-mint five, both in terms of absolute as well as condition rarity. Only 12,000 pieces were struck with a mere 40-50 coins believed extant in all grades. Just over a dozen examples are estimated in XF condition, and no more than 10 examples are finer. This is a well-struck, problem-free piece that displays bright, subtly variegated pale rose and yellow patina. NGC ID# 25TR, PCGS# 8235

1853 Half Eagle, Rare MS64+
Shimmering Mint Luster

3777　**1853 MS64+ PCGS.** The 1853 half eagle's mintage of more than 305,000 pieces ranks among the highest of period, but surviving examples of this Philadelphia issue are only plentiful in circulated grades, as few Mint State coins were set aside for contemporary collectors. The typical Uncirculated example is heavily abraded, grading no finer than MS62, and finer examples are decidedly rare and seemingly underappreciated in comparison to some branch mint issues of the period. The present offering is the only Choice example certified by PCGS, with just two numerically finer (10/14). Rose and honey-gold hues blanket softly frosted luster on each side, leaving the surfaces remarkably void of noticeable abrasions. Some slight striking weakness is noted on the eagle's right (facing) talons, though the motifs are otherwise sharply impressed. NGC ID# 25UD, PCGS# 8253

1854-D Half Eagle, MS60
Natural, Orange-Gold Coloration

3778　**1854-D Large D MS60 PCGS. Variety 36-AA.** The Large D mintmark is lightly repunched south on this variety. The mintage of 56,413 pieces was substantial for Dahlonega in the mid-1850s — not the highest production, but far from the decade's lowest in 1859. As a result, the issue is one of the more-available candidates for branch-mint gold specialists and type collectors alike. Smooth, semiprooflike surfaces gleam with vibrant, orange-gold patina. Softness on the high-points of the eagle prevents a higher Mint State award. Population: 3 in 60, 22 finer (10/14). NGC ID# 25UK, PCGS# 8258

The Dahlonega Mint

1857-O Half Eagle, MS63
Sole Finest Known, Ex: Ashland City

1861-C Five Dollar, AU55
Final Charlotte Issue

3779 1857-O MS63 PCGS. Variety 1. Ex: Ashland City. This is the finest certified 1857-O half eagle, the finest currently known, and likely to remain so for the foreseeable future. It is the only one certified MS63 at PCGS with none finer, and there are none its equal at NGC (10/14). It was unlisted in Douglas Winter's 1992 reference on the series, but in his 2006 revision it is listed as the finest known by two grade points. *Winter specifically cites this coin as the "undisputed finest known example."*

The New Orleans Mint half eagles of the 1850s are historic and numismatically significant pieces in their own right. The 1857-O was the last O-mint half eagle minted before the Civil War, the last produced for some 35 years until the 1892-O.

This is truly an exceptional coin. The surfaces are softly frosted, with a glimmer of reflectivity in the fields. A bold strike shows full star centers and a complete beaded hair cord. A touch of softness appears on the upper hair bun and below the coronet, and on the reverse there is a bit of blending on the eagle's right (facing) claw and on the arrow fletchings. The central shield and wing feather details are extremely well delineated. The second vertical stripe in the first pair is broken, a die diagnostic of the issue. Each side exhibits a rich accent of golden-orange patina. The surfaces are remarkably clean for a coin of this grade. A thin, straight scrape runs from behind Liberty's eye downward to her chin, useful for pedigree purposes. A memorable coin, and a must-have for Registry Set collectors or those desiring an historic, high-grade example of New Orleans gold.
Ex: Ashland City Collection (Heritage, 1/2003), lot 4800, which brought $40,250; Delaware Valley Rare Coins; Long Beach Signature (Heritage, 2/2008), lot 2536, FUN Platinum Night (Heritage, 1/2011), lot 5115. NGC ID# 25V5, PCGS# 8274

3780 1861-C AU55 NGC. Variety 1. Die State III, showing a faint die crack that connects the tops of AMERI. Only 150-175 examples are believed known of the 1861-C, an issue that only had 6,879 pieces struck at the time of minting. Three to four dozen AU coins are believed extant. This is a pleasing example for this final (and scarce) Charlotte half eagle issue. Rich yellow-gold luster radiates from each side, and though a number of fine abrasions are apparent, neither the fields nor the devices show the "choppy" appearance noted by Winter. Modest wear crosses the high points.
Ex: Baltimore Signature (Heritage, 3/2009), lot 2952. NGC ID# 25VL, PCGS# 8289

1864-S Half Eagle, XF45
Premier San Francisco Rarity
Only 20 to 30 Examples Known

1868-S Five Dollar, MS61
Remarkable S-Mint Rarity

3781 **1864-S XF45 PCGS.** In discussions of major rarities within the Liberty half eagle series, the 1864-S is often overlooked, when in fact it is one of the absolute rarest issues overall. It significantly outpaces every Charlotte and Dahlonega date in the series, and is *about on par with the equally rare but much more valuable 1854-O and 1856-O double eagles.* Mint records report a mintage of 3,888 coins, a small mintage to be sure, but the survival rate is even more surprisingly low. The accepted belief is that only 20 to 30 coins are extant in all grades, an estimate that directly mirrors the certified population figures which count just 25 coins at PCGS and NGC combined (10/14). The Smithsonian contains an additional piece, but the coin grades only Fine 15 (per Garrett and Guth) and is one of the lowest-grade gold pieces in that entire collection. With such a low surviving population, there is little wonder as to why.

This Choice XF coin is one of the finer-known representatives of the date. Small remnants of original luster illuminate warm honey-gold patina on each side, while the design elements retain much of their finer details. An old, faint, V-shaped pinscratch on Liberty's neck and a couple small ticks in the field below the eagle's beak serve as pedigree identifiers. The branch mint gold specialist should not pass this one up. Population: 1 in 45, 5 finer (10/14). NGC ID# 25VV, PCGS# 8297

3782 **1868-S MS61 NGC.** Many of the S-mint half eagles from the 1850s and 1860s are unknown — or virtually unknown, depending on the issue — in Uncirculated condition. The 1868-S half eagle saw an increase over the meager mintages of the previous San Francisco issues, to some 52,000 pieces, but its rarity in Mint State is in no way lessened. NGC and PCGS combined show just five grading events in Mint State with four NGC MS61 coins being the finest.

The present 1868-S is among the finest certified of the issue. As expected for the MS61 grade level, this piece shows a few bagmarks and ticks. However, the reddish-orange surfaces accented with lilac tinges show a surprisingly robust strike for an S-mint half eagle of this vintage, and strong eye appeal is furthered by a pleasing amount of mint luster on both sides. An important offering of this S-mint conditional rarity. Census: 4 in 61, 0 finer (10/14). NGC ID# 25W6, PCGS# 8316

1871-CC Half Eagle, Choice AU
Significant Carson City Condition Rarity

3783 1871-CC AU55 NGC. CAC. Variety 1-B. Produced in only the second year of the fabled Carson City Mint's short lifespan, the 1871-CC half eagles were made to the extent of only 20,770 pieces. That was a fairly generous number for the series and the era; compare it with the 7,675 coins that facility managed to make in its first year. The Carson City Mint was a demand-driven establishment. The need for a local mint — rather than distant San Francisco — drove its creation, and its products were readily snapped up to feed the needs of regional commerce. CC-mint pundit Rusty Goe estimates a survival rate below 1% for the issue, or 140-175 coins in all grades. In AU55 this piece is one of only eight so-graded at NGC, with nine coins finer (10/14). The apricot-gold surfaces are relatively free of singular abrasions, with excellent eye appeal. A hint of strike softness appears on the high points of each side, but otherwise there are few distractions.
Ex: Dallas Signature (Heritage, 10/2009), lot 1450. NGC ID# 25WD, PCGS# 8323

1880 Half Eagle, MS65+
Impressive High-Grade Example

3784 1880 MS65+ NGC. As noted by Garrett and Guth, the 1880 half eagle saw an increased mintage from the prior year, and this date is common in grades up to MS63, becoming scarce any finer. Peach overtones enhance the honey-gold toning of this lustrous, well-struck Gem. There are only a handful of distributed, tiny surface marks, and none of them are readily apparent to the unaided eye. Census: 8 in 65+, 2 in 65 ★, 2 finer (10/14). NGC ID# 25XA, PCGS# 8351

1883-CC Half Eagle, AU58
Still-Lustrous, Original Surfaces

3785 1883-CC AU58 PCGS. CAC. Variety 1-A. A small mintage of only 12,598 half eagles was accomplished in 1883, almost all of which experienced extensive circulation. This near-Mint example is a rarity, and represents an important opportunity for the Carson City gold enthusiast. Remnants of original luster illuminate honey and rose-gold hues on each side, while the strike is sharp and has been subjected to only slight friction. No major abrasions are observed. Population: 19 in 58, 4 finer (10/14). NGC ID# 25XL, PCGS# 8362

1886 Half Eagle, MS65
One of the Finest-Known

3786 1886 MS65 PCGS. One of the five highest-graded examples of this scarce issue, with impressively sharp strike definition throughout, and appealing, blended rose and terra cotta toning. The surfaces are nearly mark-free. This issue is rare any finer than the MS63 level of preservation, despite a moderate mintage of 388,300 pieces. Population: 2 in 65, 1 finer (10/14). NGC ID# 25XU, PCGS# 8369

1893-CC Half Eagle, Sharp MS62

3787 **1893-CC MS62 NGC. CAC. Variety 1-A.** A pleasing Mint State example of this final-year Carson City issue. Frosty green-gold luster complements sharp devices, while the surfaces show only light chatter to limit the grade. The 1893-CC half eagle had a limited mintage of 60,000 pieces, and is rarely seen above the MS62 grade level. NGC has encapsulated only 31 such pieces (10/14). NGC ID# 25YB, PCGS# 8384

1893-CC Five, Variety 1-A, MS63
Flashy, Conditionally Scarce Example

3788 **1893-CC MS63 PCGS. Variety 1-A.** This is a popular low-mintage final-year Carson City issue with 60,000 pieces originally produced. Mint State coins are scarce and examples grading finer than MS62 are rare. This Select Uncirculated representative is flashy and highly lustrous, with lovely apricot-gold toning and nicely preserved surfaces. Population: 12 in 63, 4 finer (10/14). NGC ID# 25YB, PCGS# 8384

1893-O Five Dollar, Seldom-Seen MS64
Lustrous Surfaces, Razor-Sharp Strike

3789 **1893-O MS64 NGC. Variety 2,** showing the date about centered between the denticles and bust truncation, scarcer than Variety 1 with the date lower. The 1893-O half eagle mintage was a fairly skimpy 110,000 coins, and most of the survivors are well-circulated. Most of the surviving mintage is in the XF to AU range. This near-Gem is one of only two such submissions at NGC, and a single piece is finer (10/14). The mellow golden-orange surfaces are highly lustrous and problem-free, with a razor-sharp strike a pleasant surprise. NGC ID# 25YC, PCGS# 8385

1896-S Half Eagle, MS63
Lightly Patinated and Attractive

3790 **1896-S MS63 PCGS.** A healthy mintage of 155,400 makes this an available San Francisco issue, but it becomes rare in Select Mint State or finer. Some chatter and minor abrasions in the left obverse field and on the portrait limit the grade of this boldly struck half eagle, which has splendid eye appeal and bountiful mint luster. Rich, honey-gold surfaces have a Mint-fresh quality. Rare this nice. Population: 5 in 63, 4 finer (10/14). NGC ID# 25YL, PCGS# 8393

<table>
<tr>
<td>

PROOF LIBERTY HALF EAGLE

1878 Half Eagle, PR63+ Deep Cameo
Sole Finest Deep Cameo at PCGS

</td>
<td>

INDIAN HALF EAGLES

1911 Half Eagle, MS65
Uncharacteristically Sharp and Attractive

</td>
</tr>
</table>

3792 1911 MS65 PCGS. The 1911 Indian half eagle had a generous mintage of 915,000 coins, but like most issues in the series, it becomes conditionally scarce at the Gem grade level. Mike Fuljenz notes that this issue is also one of the most difficult to find well-struck with pleasing luster, another factor that contributes to the low Gem availability. The piece here offered is truly exceptional in every respect, showcasing bold definition throughout the headdress and the eagle's feathers, with satiny luster that travels around each side in soft cartwheels when turned in-hand. A few light surface grazes preclude an even finer grade, but none of the usual deep abrasions are present on this example. Population: 60 in 65 (3 in 65+), 1 finer (10/14). NGC ID# 28DP, PCGS# 8520

1912 Indian Half Eagle, MS65
None Graded Finer at PCGS

3791 1878 PR63+ Deep Cameo PCGS. CAC. Only 20 proofs of this half eagle issue were reportedly struck, and it is a certainty that fewer survive today, likely only about half. PCGS and NGC combined have encapsulated just 13 examples in all grades and levels of contrast, though this figure undoubtedly includes resubmissions.

This Select proof is the sole finest Deep Cameo certified at PCGS. The surfaces are lovely orange-gold color with good overall reflectivity and marked field-device contrast. The strike is well-executed, although a trifle soft on the high points of Liberty's hair. A few thin scrapes appear in the obverse right field around stars 11 to 13, with another in the left obverse field, and a couple of small ticks appear on the profile, together accounting for the grade.

Our auction archives show just four previous appearances by a proof 1878 half eagle, and all are earlier offerings of this same exact coin. The specialist will want to bid accordingly, as another representative may not become available for a very long time. *Ex: Fort Lauderdale Bullet Auction (Heritage, 3/2000), lot 546; Central States Signature (Heritage, 5/2000), lot 7717; FUN Signature (Heritage, 1/2003), lot 4841; Internet Auction (Heritage, 11/2003), lot 11650.* NGC ID# 28CF, PCGS# 98473

3793 1912 MS65 PCGS. The 1912 Indian half eagle boasts a reported mintage of 790,000 pieces, and the issue was produced to a high standard of quality. As a result, the 1912 is not too difficult to locate in high grade and often trades as a type coin. The 1912 is very scarce at the MS65 level, however, and finer specimens are virtually unobtainable.

The present coin is a delightful Gem, with pinpoint definition on all design elements. The well-preserved yellow-gold surfaces show attractive highlights of green, with vibrant mint luster on both sides. Eye appeal is outstanding. This coin is a prime Registry Set candidate. Population: 52 in 65, 0 finer (10/14). NGC ID# 28DS, PCGS# 8523

1913 Indian Eagle, MS65
Terrific Eye Appeal
Registry Set Candidate

3794 1913 MS65 PCGS. With a reported mintage of 915,901 pieces, the 1913 Indian half eagle is not too difficult to locate in high grade, making it a popular choice for both type and date collectors. The present coin exhibits razor-sharp definition on all design elements, with fine detail on the lower headdress feathers and other usual trouble spots. The well-preserved yellow and rose-gold surfaces radiate vibrant mint luster from both sides and no mentionable distractions are evident. Eye appeal is terrific and this coin is definitely a Registry Set candidate. Population: 52 in 65, 1 finer (10/14). NGC ID# 28DT, PCGS# 8525

1915-S Half Eagle, MS64
Major Series Condition Rarity
Only One Coin Numerically Finer

3795 1915-S MS64 NGC. The 1915-S half eagle had a fairly small mintage of 164,000 pieces, and a comparably low survival rate. Mint State examples are genuinely scarce, and are typically only seen in the MS62 and lower grade range. MS63 coins are exceedingly scarce, and Choice examples are undeniably rare. The 1915-S is also the only issue in the entire series with only a single representative certified in Gem or finer condition, an NGC MS65 coin. In that light, the present Choice example, one of only 13 (1 in 64+) certified by NGC (10/14), becomes a significant condition rarity and an important acquisition for the advanced Indian gold collector. Satiny bronze-gold luster gives a glowing appearance to each side, while no significant abrasions are present. Slight striking weakness is seen on the lower headdress feathers, though the motifs are otherwise well-detailed. NGC ID# 25ZR, PCGS# 8531

1916-S Five, MS63
Final S-Mint Indian Half Eagle

3796 1916-S MS63 PCGS. A minor hoard yielded a few hundred Mint State coins many years ago, and they add to the availability of this San Francisco issue. Mint luster is a bit reserved over the frosted, slightly granular surfaces, but a bold strike at the centers saves the day. The mintmark is characteristically mushy and filled for this final S-Mint issue of the series. NGC ID# 28DY, PCGS# 8532

EARLY EAGLES

1795 BD-1 Eagle
Type One Small Eagle, 13 Leaves

3797 1795 13 Leaves — Damaged — PCGS Genuine. BD-1, High R.3. Bass-Dannreuther Die State b/a. Damage is the reason, or perhaps one of the reasons, that PCGS deemed this coin not gradable. In our opinion, this coin has the details of an AU specimen that has been cleaned and retoned. The surfaces show several unnatural orange spots and perhaps a small area of smoothing, although much pleasing detail remains. Several pinprick-size marks, lumps, and tiny abrasions are distributed across the otherwise sharp fields and devices. This is the 13 Leaves variety, 10 x 5 Stars, the most available die pair for the date yet still scarce, with only 200 to 225 pieces known. The coin displays a bright, yellow-gold color and a diagnostic die crack to the left of Y in LIBERTY. NGC ID# 25ZT, PCGS# 8551

1799 Capped Bust Right Eagle, AU Details
Popular Small Stars, BD-7 Variety
Interesting Intermediate Die State

3798 1799 Small Stars Obverse — Repaired, Whizzed — NGC Details. AU. Irregular Date, BD-7, R.3. Bass-Dannreuther Die State d/d. Repaired on the reverse field near the arrowheads, above the left (facing) shield tip, and near the stem of the olive branch. Whizzed and cleaned with small marks along Liberty's profile. The devices display a wealth of detail, and the yellow-gold surfaces retain indications of luster. With 250 to 350 examples believed extant, BD-7 is one of the more plentiful varieties of this type, ideal for type representation.
Ex: FUN Signature (Heritage, 1/2011), lot 7001.

First Philadelphia Mint

1801 BD-2 Ten Dollar
Near-Mint State Example

3799 **1801 AU58 NGC. BD-2, R.2.** Bass-Dannreuther Die State a/a. Up to 90% or so of the 44,344 eagles dated 1801 are this BD-2 variety, easily identifiable by the large, less-chunky stars with longer, spindly tips (called the Type III stars by Bass), of which star 8 is positioned much closer to Liberty's cap than the scarcer BD-1 variety. Most of the BD-2 variety display nine vertical spines in the cap, an anomaly acquired on the obverse die early in its life judging by the number of examples that display the peculiarity.

This example is lightly abraded with a touch of wear. Nominal strike weakness exists at stars 1 and 2 on the obverse, as well as on two of the field stars on the reverse. No evidence of die clash is seen on either side of the coin. Pleasing, green-gold color shows amber accents near the rims. Remaining mint luster surrounds the obverse stars and is plentiful on the reverse, making this a nice, near-Mint selection for early gold eagle collectors and for gold type enthusiasts alike. NGC ID# 2627, PCGS# 8564

1801 BD-2 Ten Dollar
Uncirculated Details

3800 **1801 — Damage — PCGS Genuine. Unc Details. BD-2, R.2.** A well struck and prooflike yellow-gold representative. The left obverse field is granular, and a few minor pinscratches are noted on Liberty's neck and the field near the bust tip. Most examples of BD-2 display nine vertical spines in the cap, from unknown damage to the die similar to that seen on the "Spiked Chin" 1804 half cent. But the present coin is an unlisted early die state without the spines, before the obverse die was accidentally damaged. Nonetheless clashed above the right shield corner and about the star near the beak. NGC ID# 2627, PCGS# 8564

LIBERTY EAGLES

1839 Type of 1838, Large Letters Ten, XF45
Attractive, Sharply Struck Example

3801 **1839 Type of 1838, Large Letters XF45 NGC.** Easily distinguished by the sharp bust truncation pointing above star 13, the Type of 1838 is one of two varieties produced in this transitional year, along with the so-called Type of 1840. Approximately two-thirds of the years' mintage of 25,801 coins were of the Type of 1838.

This example displays excellent striking sharpness, only showing weakness on the obverse peripheral stars. It is typically worn for the grade, with a number of small-to-moderate abrasions evident on each side. An attractive Choice XF coin for this popular *Guide Book* variety. NGC ID# 262E, PCGS# 8576

1842-O Eagle, AU55
Scarce New Orleans Issue

3802 **1842-O AU55 NGC. Variety 2.** From the mintage of 27,400 pieces there are relatively few survivors, and just over 400 grading events are recorded by NGC and PCGS, including likely resubmissions. The majority of those coins are rated between VF and AU, and Mint State pieces are rare. The current Choice AU example is a well-struck piece with smooth, unabraded surfaces and light khaki-green toning. A few wispy hairlines are noted on both sides. Census: 36 in 55, 27 finer (10/14). NGC ID# 262N, PCGS# 8587

The New Orleans Mint

1846 Liberty Ten, AU58
Underrated and Underappreciated

3803 **1846 AU58 PCGS.** While the mintage of 20,095 coins suggests that the 1846 is only a moderately scarce Liberty eagle issue, the population data suggests that it is quite rare, with an average certified grade of just over XF45. PCGS has only certified 78 examples in all grades, and only one of those is finer than the present piece, with only one other AU58 example, and only four that grade AU55 (10/14). David Akers wrote: "In my opinion, few other U.S. coins are as underrated and underappreciated for their true rarity as this one." A few trivial marks appear on each side of this attractive yellow-gold eagle. The strike is adequate and the fields retain nearly full prooflike reflectivity. NGC ID# 262W, PCGS# 8594

1854-S Eagle, AU58
First-Year San Francisco Issue
Rare Any Finer

3804 **1854-S AU58 NGC.** The newly-opened San Francisco Mint focused on three denominations in its first year of operations: gold dollars, eagles, and double eagles. Only token mintages of the quarter eagle and half eagle were struck, and today those issues are fabulous rarities.

Although more than 123,000 1854-S eagles were struck, evidently most of the survivors were plucked from circulation; as a result, certified examples average between Choice XF and AU, and Mint State pieces are quite rare. This near-Mint State NGC piece represents a true collector opportunity, showing lustrous orange-gold surfaces with much reflectivity and eye appeal. Census: 56 in 58, 5 finer (10/14). NGC ID# 263K, PCGS# 8615

1854-S Eagle, AU58
Conditionally Scarce First-Year Example
From the San Francisco Mint

3805 **1854-S AU58 NGC.** In its first year of operations, the San Francisco mint facility struck 123,826 ten dollar gold coins, but most of those pieces were seemingly lost to heavy circulation and survivors are scarce, especially in Mint State where fewer than 10 examples have been seen by NGC and PCGS combined.

This is a lovely piece that boasts exceptional eye appeal for the grade. The smooth, orange-gold surfaces are enhanced by noticeable accents of lilac color near the centers and the peripheral devices. Surface marks are slight and non-distracting. Census: 67 in 58, 5 finer (10/14). NGC ID# 263K, PCGS# 8615

1855-O Eagle, AU55
Boldly Struck Orange-Gold Example

3806 **1855-O AU55 NGC. Variety 1.** Slanted 5s. The 1855-O eagle mintage has exactly the same mintage as the 1852-O production, each at 18,000 coin. Coincidence? At any rate, one big difference between the two issues is that minor silver was again circulating by the time the 1855-O was struck, due to the lower-content Arrows coinage. This Choice AU 1885-O ten offers a bold strike over orange-gold surfaces that show no major marks and lots of eye appeal. Probably underrated at this level. Census: 15 in 55, 9 finer (10/14). NGC ID# 263M, PCGS# 8617

1857-O Ten, AU53
Scarce, Low-Mintage Issue

3807 **1857-O AU53 PCGS. Variety 1.** The bright surfaces display light khaki-gold coloration and well-struck, evenly worn motifs. Superficial marks and hairlines are seen on both sides of this lightly-circulated example. A scarce, low-mintage issue that is difficult to locate any finer than the currently-offered AU coin. Population: 10 in 53, 8 finer (10/14). NGC ID# 263U, PCGS# 8623

1860-O Ten Dollar, AU55
Elusive Southern Gold Issue

3808 **1860-O AU55 NGC. Variety 2.** Two different obverse dies were paired with a single reverse to strike just 11,100 gold eagles at the New Orleans Mint in 1860. This was the final issuance of that denomination in New Orleans until 1879, when the branch mint finally resumed post-war operations. This is an appealing Choice AU example with remnants of semiprooflike mirroring in the fields. Slight high-point wear leaves pleasing detail and warm honey-gold color overall. Scarce at the AU grade levels, the 1860-O is prohibitively rare in Mint State. Census: 34 in 55, 29 finer (10/14). NGC ID# 2645, PCGS# 98631

1860-O Ten Dollar, AU55
Fully Original Patina

3809 **1860-O AU55 NGC. Variety 1.** The New Orleans Mint produced only 11,100 gold eagles in 1860, almost all of which experienced extensive circulation in Southern commerce. Extant examples are scarce in all grades, and prohibitively rare in Mint State. For the budget-minded collector, a patient search will turn up a pleasing AU example, but finding a piece with original patina can be exceedingly difficult. This Choice example, however, is just such a coin. Undeniably original olive-gold patina blankets each side, retaining subtle hints of luster in the recesses and displaying smooth, problem-free surfaces. All major details remain bold. Census: 34 in 55, 29 finer (10/14). NGC ID# 2645, PCGS# 98631

1861-S Ten Dollar, Problem-Free XF40

3810 **1861-S XF40 NGC. CAC.** Even though 15,500 pieces of the ten dollar gold piece were struck in San Francisco mint this year, almost all of them entered circulation and stayed there. This piece shows even, light wear over the high points and each side displays smooth, reddish-gold patina. NGC ID# 2648, PCGS# 8634

1876-CC Eagle, AU50
Scarce and Important Carson City Issue

1877 Ten Dollar, AU53
Major Philadelphia Rarity
Fewer Than 65 Examples Believed Known

3811 1876-CC AU50 PCGS. CAC. Variety 1-A. The 1876-CC eagle had a paltry mintage of just 4,696 pieces, all of which was dumped into circulation where it remained, for the most part, until the coins were well-worn or completely lost. The typical survivor of this issue, therefore, grades in the VF to XF range; AU coins are decidedly rare, and none are known to survive in any condition that can be labeled as Mint State by the grading services. The present AU coin, with remnants of semiprooflike mirroring in the fields and original orange-gold color, is undeniably of great importance to the quality-conscious branch mint gold collector. Slight friction leaves much detail to be appreciated, which complements traces of luster in the border recesses. Another chance to bid on such an appealing example of this date may be long in coming. Population: 11 in 50, 9 finer (10/14). NGC ID# 265D, PCGS# 8675

3812 1877 AU53 PCGS. The 1877 eagle is the last of three consecutive Philadelphia issues with paltry mintages of fewer than 1,000 coins, in this case, just 797 pieces. Furthermore, the 1877's survival rate did not benefit from hoarders and speculators, as virtually all examples were distributed into circulation. PCGS estimates only 50 to 65 examples are extant in all grades, making the 1877 slightly rarer than its much more valuable Carson City counterpart, which also had a significantly higher mintage (3,332 pieces). In that light, the 1877 is seemingly underappreciated, especially in the higher grades.

PCGS and NGC combined report having graded just 68 pieces at all numeric levels, likely counting an unknown number of resubmissions. The typical example grades in the XF and AU categories, with just three Mint State pieces (all PCGS coins) certified. This example retains remnants of original luster and prooflike mirroring in the recesses, with natural orange-gold patina overall. Some light surface chatter accompanies the grade, though no obtrusive abrasions are present. Slight high-point friction does not impede the sharp strike. Population: 2 in 53, 15 finer (10/14). NGC ID# 265F, PCGS# 8677

1879 Liberty Eagle, MS64
Only Three Numerically Finer at PCGS

3813   **1879 MS64 PCGS.** Lustrous peach-gold surfaces with hints of green-gold provide this near-Gem with a lovely appearance. In addition, the coin exhibits a sharp strike. A couple of tiny alloy spots are present on the reverse. Although scattered signs of contact appear, including a few tiny hair thin marks, they are minor. Population: 9 in 64 (1 in 64+), 3 finer (10/14). NGC ID# 265M, PCGS# 8683

1894-O Ten, MS63
Famously Rare in Select or Finer Grades

3814   **1894-O MS63 NGC. Variety 4.** A six-figure mintage makes this New Orleans date easily available in lower grades, yet MS63 examples or finer coins are true condition rarities. This Select Uncirculated example is lustrous and boldly struck for an O-Mint eagle. Attractive and frosty medium-gold patina displays a pale ring of olive-gold at the margins. Just 25 coins are graded in MS63 condition by both services combined, and a mere four coins are certified numerically finer. NGC Census: 12 in 63, 3 finer (10/14). NGC ID# 2676, PCGS# 8730

1894-O Ten Dollar, MS63
Significant Condition Rarity

3815   **1894-O MS63 PCGS. Variety 3.** The 1894-O eagle is one of most easily obtainable New Orleans tens in circulated condition, but Mint State examples are disproportionately scarce, and are genuinely rare at the MS63 level. This is an immensely attractive piece with shimmering honey-gold luster that shows tinges of green-gold in the border recesses. The strike is bold, and only some minor chatter in the obverse fields preclude an even finer grade assessment from PCGS. Population: 13 in 63, 1 finer (10/14). NGC ID# 2676, PCGS# 8730

1897 Eagle, MS66
Incredible Quality, True Condition Rarity

3816   **1897 MS66 PCGS.** An amazing, deeply frosted and wonderfully patinated Premium Gem eagle. Lilac, olive, and rose-red accents swirl across the undisturbed surfaces. Vibrant mint luster flashes over the orange-gold base toning, and a bold strike delivers essentially full details to the motifs.

This Philadelphia issue is one of the "sleeper" late-date tens in high Mint State. The coin is virtually without distractions, with just three or four tiny marks widely scattered and of negligible significance. The eye appeal is off the charts. PCGS has certified just three pieces as MS66 with none finer. NGC reports six MS66 examples and one coin in MS67 (10/14). NGC ID# 267D, PCGS# 8737

1903-O Liberty Ten, MS64
Only One Piece Finer at PCGS

3817 **1903-O MS64 PCGS. Variety 2.** The 1 in the date centered between denticles attributes this variety. The 1903-O ten dollar, from a production of 112,771 pieces, is the most common New Orleans eagle, yet Garrett and Guth say, "MS63 examples are not too difficult to locate, but anything finer is a great rarity." Intense luster radiates from both sides of this MS64 example, which displays soft yellow-gold and rose patination. All design elements are well brought up, further enhancing the coin's pleasing eye appeal. A few minuscule marks preclude Gem classification. PCGS and NGC have each certified just one coin in a higher numeric grade. Population: 20 in 64, 1 finer (10/14). NGC ID# 267W, PCGS# 8753

1903-O Eagle, MS64
Rare This Fine

3818 **1903-O MS64 PCGS. Variety 3.** The 1 in the date is centered directly over the dentil and the mintmark is low relative to the tip of the tailfeathers. In 1903, the New Orleans Mint struck 112,771 eagles, making it among the most available O-Mint ten dollar issues. The availability is relative, though, given the issue's rarity in Choice grades and higher. The motifs are sharply defined and frosty luster cascades over each side. The intense, yellow-gold surfaces show a few scattered abrasions on the obverse, as is typical, while the reverse is nearly devoid of distracting marks. Population: 20 in 64, 1 finer (10/14). NGC ID# 267W, PCGS# 8753

1906 Liberty Head Ten, MS65
Beautiful, Conditionally Rare Example

3819 **1906 MS65 PCGS.** This early 20th century issue had a relatively modest mintage of 165,497 pieces, but it is easily available in Mint State grades of 60 to 62, where more than 1,750 coins have been rated by the two major services. Far fewer are known at the MS63 to MS64 levels, and examples are rare any finer.

This remarkable Gem exhibits bright, intensely lustrous surfaces adorned by lovely hues of peach-gold and sun-gold. The design motifs are sharply struck and nearly full, and just a few trivial blemishes are noted on both sides of the coin. Population: 8 in 65, 4 finer (10/14). NGC ID# 2684, PCGS# 8759

INDIAN EAGLES

1907 Indian Ten, MS64
Beautiful First-Year Type

3820 **1907 No Periods MS64 NGC.** Charles E. Barber pulled out all the stops (literally) in his No Periods revision of the Saint-Gaudens ten dollar gold, and despite the compromises in design, a workable, production-ready eagle coin was the result. The modifications were meant to be an improvement to its Rolled Rim predecessor, which Barber had ordered to be melted en masse. Among other changes, the rims were adjusted to be sharper. However, they remain distinctly "rolled" on this example. The mint luster is outstanding over the smoothly frosted surfaces. As usual, some softness at the centers is the result of the new design, an area that was improved upon later in the series. This is a beautiful, near-Gem example of the No Periods first-year type. NGC ID# 28GF, PCGS# 8852

1907 Indian Eagle, MS66+
Popular First-Year No Periods Variant

1908-D Indian Eagle, MS64
First Year With Motto

3821   **1907 No Periods MS66+ PCGS. CAC.** Although it was preceded by two limited-mintage patterns (the Rolled Edge and Wire Rim issues), the 1907 No Periods was the first variety of Saint-Gaudens' acclaimed Indian design actually seen by most numismatists and the general public. The No Periods issue claims a mintage of 239,400 pieces, and some high-quality examples were saved for their novelty value, but the coins are rare in grades above MS66.

This high-end Premium Gem displays well-detailed design elements and impeccably preserved orange-gold surfaces with vibrant mint luster throughout. Eye appeal is tremendous. PCGS has graded nine numerically finer examples (10/14). NGC ID# 28GF, PCGS# 8852

3822   **1908-D Motto MS64 PCGS.** Although the 1908-D Indian eagle claims a large mintage of 836,500 pieces, it is surprisingly difficult to locate in high grade. Apparently, the novelty had worn off after the first year of the Indian design, and few high-quality examples of this second-year issue were saved. Of course, this issue does represent the first year of the Motto subtype, an important consideration for type collectors.

This impressive Choice specimen exhibits sharply detailed design elements and the well-preserved orange-gold surfaces radiate vibrant mint luster on both sides. Eye appeal is outstanding. Population: 24 in 64, 22 finer (10/14). NGC ID# 28GK, PCGS# 8860

1908-S Indian Eagle, MS63
Low-Mintage, Early Series Issue

3823 **1908-S MS63 PCGS.** The 1908-S Indian eagle claims a mintage of 59,850 pieces, a low production total for any 20th century coin. The coins were struck later in the year, and all examples show the motto IN GOD WE TRUST, unlike the coins issued earlier in the year by the other mints. The 1908-S is scarce-to-rare in all Mint State grades today, but a few high-quality specimens, such as the present coin, were set aside by contemporary collectors. This coin exhibits well-detailed design elements and lightly marked orange-gold surfaces that show highlights of rose and lilac. Frosty mint luster radiates from both sides, adding to the outstanding eye appeal. This piece should find a home in a fine collection or type set. Population: 46 in 63 (1 in 63+), 70 finer (10/14). NGC ID# 28GL, PCGS# 8861

1909 Indian Ten, MS64
Challenging Philadelphia Issue

3824 **1909 MS64 PCGS.** The 1909 Indian eagle claims a smallish mintage of 184,789 pieces and the date is one of the more challenging Philadelphia issues of the series. This impressive Choice example displays sharp definition on all design elements and the well-preserved yellow-gold surfaces are brightly lustrous throughout. Population: 87 in 64 (1 in 64+), 29 finer (10/14). NGC ID# 28GM, PCGS# 8862

1909-D Ten Dollar, MS63
Daunting Denver Date

3825 **1909-D MS63 PCGS.** Unlike its half eagle counterpart, the 1909-D ten dollar piece is only available in MS62 and lower grades; Select examples are scarce, and finer pieces are seldom seen. This piece shows bold striking definition throughout the eagle's feathers and the Indian's headdress, with soft rose and green-gold patina over each side. A scattering of abrasions contributes to the grade. PCGS has encapsulated 41 numerically finer representatives (10/14). NGC ID# 28GN, PCGS# 8863

1909-D Ten Dollar, MS63
Better Denver Issue

3826 **1909-D MS63 NGC.** The Denver Mint produced a limited number of gold eagles in 1909 (little more than 121,000 pieces), and extant representatives are somewhat elusive overall. The typical Uncirculated piece is heavily abraded, grading no finer than MS62; MS63 coins are scarce, and finer pieces are borderline rare. This Select example shows sharp design definition and rich orange-gold luster. A few small ticks on the cheek preclude a finer grade, but hardly detract from the overall appeal. Census: 60 in 63 (1 in 63+), 31 finer (10/14). NGC ID# 28GN, PCGS# 8863

1909-D Indian Eagle, MS63+
Underrated Issue in High Grade

3827 **1909-D MS63+ NGC.** From a mintage of 121,540 pieces, the 1909-D Indian eagle is a challenging issue in high grade. This high-end Select example offers sharply detailed design elements and vibrant mint luster throughout. The pleasing yellow-gold surfaces show only scattered minor contact marks and eye appeal is outstanding. NGC ID# 28GN, PCGS# 8863

1910 Indian Eagle, MS65
Remarkable Eye Appeal

3828 **1910 MS65 NGC.** This beautifully struck Gem example displays softly frosted mint luster and lovely yellow-gold toning accompanied by pleasing rose accents, noticed mainly within the feathers of the headdress. A visually impressive Indian eagle with mattelike surface textures and remarkable eye appeal. NGC ID# 28GR, PCGS# 8865

1910-S Ten Dollar, MS64
Deep Multihued Patina
Important Condition Rarity

3829 **1910-S MS64 NGC.** The 1910-S Indian eagle's mintage of 811,000 coins, the highest production total from the San Francisco Mint in the series, is somewhat deceiving as to this issue's actual rarity. The date's availability was drastically decreased in the mid-1930s, when most of the original mintage was destroyed during the massive gold melts brought about Roosevelt's Executive Order 6102, which prohibited the private ownership of monetary gold. Mint State survivors are seldom available and typically grade only in the MS62 and lower range. The date is genuinely scarce in MS63, and rare at the Choice level. Finer pieces are prohibitively elusive. The present example is a visual delight for the collector who enjoys original patina. Both sides show frosty luster beneath deep orange, lilac, and lavender-gold hues. The design elements are sharply impressed, and only a few minute ticks preclude full Gem status. Census: 21 in 64, 5 finer (10/14). NGC ID# 268D, PCGS# 8867

1911 Ten Dollar, MS65
Bright Yellow-Gold Mint Luster

3830 **1911 MS65 NGC.** The 1911 is a well-produced issue among early P-mint ten dollar Indians. This is an attractive Gem with bright yellow-gold surfaces and no noticeable or mentionable abrasions. The strike details are remarkably strong also, the only hint of softness seen at the top of the eagle's wing. NGC ID# 28GT, PCGS# 8868

1911 Eagle, MS65+
Colorfully Toned, Strong Strike

3831 **1911 MS65+ PCGS.** The issue is normally attractive and sharply produced, but this beautifully patinated Gem with the Plus rating from PCGS scores extra points for eye appeal. Rich red accents enliven the medium-gold base toning at the centers, and lilac overtones flash over the boldly struck devices. Frosty, lustrous surfaces show the fine granularity that typifies most 1911 gold issues, and makes them a favorite for both type and series collectors. NGC ID# 28GT, PCGS# 8868

1911-D Ten Dollar, AU58
Popular Denver Key

3832 **1911-D AU58 NGC.** With a mintage of only 30,100 pieces, the 1911-D gold eagle is a significant key date in the Indian ten series. This nearly Uncirculated example shows substantial honey-gold luster in the recesses beneath mottled olive-gold patina and scattered field chatter. A bold strike enhances the overall appeal, and the only noteworthy mark is seen across the back of Liberty's jaw. Finer pieces are elusive. NGC ID# 28GU, PCGS# 8869

1911-D Eagle, MS61
Key Denver Issue

3833 **1911-D MS61 PCGS.** Much of the fanfare about 1911-D gold issues goes to the quarter eagle, which ranks as the only major key date in its respective series, but the 1911-D eagle is actually a significantly rarer issue in all grades, especially Mint State. Only 30,100 pieces were struck, most of which wound up in circulation. This piece grades near the lower end of the Mint State spectrum, as do nearly all examples of this date that can be termed Uncirculated, but the grade-limiting abrasions are evenly dispersed so as to cause minimum distraction. The devices are sharply brought up with the dies, and the satiny surfaces display original honey-gold luster. This is an important bidding opportunity for the Indian gold collector. NGC ID# 28GU, PCGS# 8869

1911-D Indian Eagle, MS63
Challenging Low-Mintage Issue

1912-S Indian Eagle, MS62
Brightly Lustrous Surfaces

3834 1911-D MS63 PCGS. Mintage is far from the sole determinant of rarity in late-date American gold, but with just 30,100 pieces struck, the 1911-D ten dollar gold is one of the most challenging Saint-Gaudens issues. Even Select examples are condition rarities. Garrett and Guth (2006) attached considerable importance to this issue, proclaiming that "[a]ll Indian Head eagle collections are judged to some degree on the quality of the 1911-D issue."

A stately glow emanates from the surfaces of this luminous piece — predominantly yellow-gold, with a touch of wheat. Liberty's cheek is clean and at first glance, the piece appears much finer than its Select designation. Only on closer inspection does one identify the wispy, grade-defining abrasion present in the left obverse field. The reverse is rotated approximately 20 degrees counterclockwise. Population: 34 in 63, 17 finer (10/14).
Ex: Dallas Signature (Heritage, 11/2007), lot 452. NGC ID# 28GU, PCGS# 8869

3835 1912-S MS62 PCGS. An attractive MS62 example of the popular Indian design from a mintage of 300,000 pieces. This pleasing example offers well-detailed design elements and vibrant mint luster, with a scattering of minor contact marks on the bright yellow and rose-gold surfaces. Eye appeal is quite strong for the grade. NGC ID# 28GX, PCGS# 8872

1912-S Ten Dollar, MS65
Major Condition Rarity

3836 **1912-S MS65 NGC.** The old saying, "Don't judge a book by its cover," might be applied to the 1912-S Indian eagle; the date had a moderately substantial mintage of 300,000 pieces, but surprisingly ranks as one of the premier condition rarities in the Indian eagle series. Mint State examples are elusive in all grades, with the typical piece exhibiting heavy abrasions. Active searching can yield an MS63 or Choice example with patience, but Gems are nothing short of rare.

The present piece is radiantly frosty with smooth golden luster, while the surfaces are devoid of obtrusive abrasions. Minor striking softness seen on the upper portion of the eagle's wing is characteristic of this poorly produced issue, though the detail is better than is usually seen. NGC shows a population of only nine coins in this grade, with two finer (10/14). NGC ID# 28GX, PCGS# 8872

1913-S Eagle, MS61
Radiant Original Luster

3837 **1913-S MS61 NGC.** A close rival to the 1911-D, the 1913-S Indian eagle is also an important key date in the series, boasting a low mintage of only 66,000 coins. This Mint State example shows scattered light chatter, rather than obtrusive abrasions, with deep honey-gold luster and well-defined design elements. NGC has encapsulated only 48 numerically finer representatives (10/14). NGC ID# 28GZ, PCGS# 8874

1914 Indian Eagle, MS64
Excellent Candidate for Type

3838 **1914 MS64 PCGS.** The substantial mintage of 151,050 pieces survived in sufficient numbers and quality to make this issue available in virtually all collector grades. The surface quality, strike, and eye appeal of this coin would fit nicely in any high-grade date or type set. The finely textured, orange-gold surfaces display bold detail on the portrait, and the eagle appears three-dimensionally feathered. This lustrous, near-Gem example is not only beautifully preserved, but it is at the precise grade that offers optimum collectibility. Any finer, and the price triples. NGC ID# 28H2, PCGS# 8875

1914-S Ten Dollar, Eye-Appealing MS64
Seldom Available This Nice

3839 1914-S MS64 NGC. The popularity of the Indian eagle series as a pursuable collection imparts significant demand on high-grade examples of all dates, but especially the early branch mint issues, many of which are conditionally rare. The 1914-S is a prime example in that regard; Mint State representatives are frequently available in grades through MS62, but Choice examples are distinctly scarce, and anything finer is a significant rarity. This piece boasts sharp detail and above-average, honey-gold luster. A few unobtrusive surface ticks, largely hidden in the eagle's feathers and Liberty's hair curls, are all that preclude a Gem grade assessment from NGC. Census: 29 in 64, 14 finer (10/14). NGC ID# 28H4, PCGS# 8877

1915 Indian Ten, PR66
Exquisite Sandblast Proof Finish
Tied for Finest at PCGS

3840   1915 PR66 PCGS. The controversy over matte and sandblast finishes for proof gold and other coinage has hardly lessened in the intervening years from when the Mint embarked on its "great experiment" with proof coins that were issued early in the 20th century. The subject is taken up by numismatists young and old even today, with proponents in each corner.

However, the debate was never stronger than in 1914 and 1915, when the Mint employed a coarser, more dramatic "sandblast" matte finish that was nearly unanimously derided by the public. Today, many collectors (but not all) are drawn to the expert production, strike, and distinctive finish of the proofs.

The 1915 proof Indian ten vies with the 1912 issue for rarity within the eight-coin eagle proof series. The number of known 1915 survivors is less than 25 coins. At Gem or finer levels, the 1915 issue appears to be the rarest of the eight collectible dates, although the balance can be tipped by one or two coins either way. Reported mintages of proof Indian eagles are somewhat meaningless because so many coins were melted as unsold for several of the dates.

Within the series, 1909 and 1910 eagle proofs are normally found with Roman finishes — a result of public outcry against the dark matte finish of the 1908 proofs — while the Mint experimented with other matte finish techniques on the 1911 through 1915 proof issues. The aim of the Mint was to create a subtle-yet-dynamic finish, the result of light reflection from microscopic, multifaceted surfaces created by sandblast process at the particulate level of the coin's surface.

The resultant "look" of the 1915 issue is one of mattelike texture with slight granularity and a velvety, refined visual aspect. Some describe the color of the 1915 proofs as ranging from orange-gold to green-gold, and different examples do indeed vary in coloration. The present coin is remarkable in its appearance. The patina is a stunning combination of an opaque, deep-goldenrod color over olive-gold (often described as khaki-gold), but the color is more intense than that. Napa Jack's incredible gourmet Amber Beer Mustard comes to mind when viewing the coloration of the coin.

This example offers an exquisite full strike and immaculate surfaces. It is difficult to locate a single pedigree marker to differentiate the coin from the other finest examples of the date. A tiny "beauty mark" — no more than a raised dot visible under magnification — exists near Liberty's mouth, but it is difficult to see either in hand or photographically. There are no other singular marks to mention and no shiny grazes are seen.

The coin is currently tied for finest-known with one other PR66 coin at PCGS, while NGC reports seven such Premium Gems and two finer at PR67 (10/14). There are undoubtedly duplications and resubmissions at the upper end of the population reports. NGC ID# 28HJ, PCGS# 8897

LIBERTY DOUBLE EAGLES

1850 Double Eagle, AU50
Green Label Holder

3841 1850 AU50 PCGS. The overall availability of the 1850 double eagle, coupled with its first-year issue status, makes the date a favorite for type representation. This AU example displays original yellow-gold patina with tinges of deeper orange-gold near the borders. Scattered abrasions accompany the grade, as can be expected at this level, but none are individually bothersome. Housed in an old green label holder. NGC ID# 268F, PCGS# 8902

1850 Liberty Twenty, AU55
Some Remaining Mint Luster

3842 1850 AU55 PCGS. This is a well-detailed, Choice AU representative of this popular first-year issue. Original green-gold patina overall yields to tinges of remaining mint luster in the recesses. The 1850 double eagle was produced in substantial numbers (more than 1.1 million pieces), but these circulated extensively, making the issue challenging in the upper AU and Mint State grades. NGC ID# 268F, PCGS# 8902

1851 Twenty Dollar, AU58
Attractive Type One Representative

3843 1851 AU58 NGC. The Philadelphia Mint struck more than 2 million double eagles in 1851, being the workhorse facility for the denomination until the new San Francisco Mint took over in 1854. This near-Mint example shows pale yellow-gold color, with remnants of original luster in the recesses. The strike is sharp, and no significant circulation scars are noticed on either side. NGC ID# 268H, PCGS# 8904

1851-O Liberty Twenty Dollar, XF45
Moderate Circulation, Smooth Appeal

3844 1851-O XF45 NGC. Variety 2. Double eagle production at the New Orleans Mint started strong in 1850 but slumped in 1853 and skidded to a halt in 1861, not to resume until a meager mintage in 1879. The 1851-O twenties represent the top O-Mint production for any one year. Available in circulated grades, this Choice XF example offers pleasing green-gold color and relatively few noticeable abrasions. A shallow dig near star 6 deserves mention. Otherwise, moderate wear softens high point detail as well as any bagmarks for a smooth, appealing example of the grade. NGC ID# 268J, PCGS# 8905

1852 Double Eagle, AU58
Attractive and Lustrous

3845 1852 AU58 PCGS. More than two million double eagles were coined at the Philadelphia Mint in 1852, and this is a common Type One issue. The vast majority of graded examples are circulated, however, and Mint State pieces are extremely scarce. This near-Mint survivor is still lustrous, with a satiny sheen that enlivens the pale wheat-gold and pastel rose surfaces. Faint high-point friction and a number of trivial abrasions are evident on each side. NGC ID# 268K, PCGS# 8906

1853-O Double Eagle, AU Details
Elusive O-Mint Twenty

3846 1853-O — Improperly Cleaned — NGC Details. AU. Variety 1. Significantly less available than the 1851 or 1852 New Orleans twenties, circulated examples of the 1853-O exist to a certain extent from the original mintage of just 71,000 pieces. Uncirculated coins are rare. The current coin shows About Uncirculated sharpness, but a few too many hairlines account for the grade. A shallow scrape near star 2 and a mark near the R of America are the most noticeable abrasions. The coin retains pleasing green-gold coloration with a touch of luster despite the cleaning. NGC ID# 268N, PCGS# 8910

1857 Liberty Head Twenty, MS62
Seldom Available in Finer Grades

3847 1857 MS62 NGC. Reddish-gold accents visit the recesses of this sharply lustrous and original double eagle. Just 28 survivors of this scarce Philadelphia date were pulled from the *S.S. Central America* and *S.S. Republic*, slightly altering the available population yet the issue remains rare in Mint State.

The present coin is shows no evidence of seawater surface, with lustrous, frosted apricot-gold patina and a scattering of small marks that determine the grade. The strike is slightly weak at the centers, with rounding of Liberty's high-point curls. PCGS and NGC combined have certified just seven numerically finer coins. NGC Census: 14 in 62, 3 finer (10/14). NGC ID# 2693, PCGS# 8920

1857-S Twenty Dollar, MS61
Attractive Type One Example

3848 1857-S MS61 NGC. Obviously not from the *Central America*, the mintmark is too low and positioned too far right to match any of the known varieties from that salvage effort. The surfaces are bright and lustrous with pleasing golden-rose-lilac patina. The strike is strong throughout and there are no mentionable abrasions in spite of the grade. NGC ID# 2696, PCGS# 8922

1857-S Double Eagle, MS61
Sharply Detailed and Lustrous

3849 1857-S MS61 PCGS. Like all Type One double eagles, the 1857-S was extremely rare in Mint State before recent shipwreck finds augmented the small supply of high-grade examples. This attractive Mint State specimen offers vivid orange-gold surfaces with a few dark alloy spots on the reverse, and bright mint luster throughout. The 1857-S is listed among the *100 Greatest U.S. Coins*. NGC ID# 2696, PCGS# 8922

3850 1859-O AU50 PCGS. Variety 1. Heritage cataloger Brian Koller has identified three different die varieties for the 1859-O double eagles. This one has the 1 of the date centered over two denticles, and the mintmark close to the tailfeathers, and centered over the N in TWENTY. The crossbar of the A in STATES is handcut.

All New Orleans double eagles minted after 1853 are rare, due to decreased gold deposits after the San Francisco Mint opened in 1854. The 1859-O, coming from a mintage of only 9,100 pieces, has the third lowest total PCGS population behind the ultra-rare 1854-O and 1856-O double eagles. In AU and finer grades, the total PCGS population of the 1859-O is tied with the 1860-O and 1879-O for fourth place behind the 1854-O, 1855-O, and 1856-O issues.

This AU50 example displays apricot-gold coloration with high-point glints of hazel-gray. The date shows orange accents in the background. Considerable prooflike reflectivity remains in the protected areas around the date, peripheral stars, and recesses of the portrait. This attribute is similar around the reverse elements. A loupe reveals a few singular contacts, including a small patch of reeding marks inside the small circle of reverse stars, and a second patch of such marks between the Y in TWENTY and D. Occasional light field chatter is also visible. All in all, this is a nice, attractive coin for having been in circulation for a short period of time. Indeed, we suggest that it possesses above-average eye appeal for an issue that is typically below-average in that regard. Population: 8 in 50, 19 finer (10/14). NGC ID# 269B, PCGS# 8927

1859-S Twenty, AU55
Lustrous, Type One Issue

3851 1859-S AU55 NGC. CAC. Gold from British Columbia supplemented California bullion supplies for the San Francisco issue, resulting in a mintage of 636,445 pieces. Nice luster remains on this Choice About Uncirculated example, with natural, medium-gold surfaces and olive-gold highlights. Numerous minor nicks and abrasions are distributed across the fields and devices, but none are overly significant for the assigned grade. Sharp detail remains. NGC ID# 269C, PCGS# 8928

1860-S Double Eagle, AU58
Premier Quality for the Grade

3852 1860-S AU58 NGC. This San Francisco issue is readily available in circulated grades, but Uncirculated examples are rare. This near-Mint representative comes close to a Mint State designation, with plentiful luster and a slight degree of friction noted on the high points. The obverse is moderately abraded, while the reverse displays fewer marks. NGC ID# 269F, PCGS# 8931

1861 Double Eagle, MS61
Relatively Unabraded Surfaces

3853 1861 MS61 NGC. This lustrous orange-gold Type One double eagle offers fewer abrasions than might be expected given the grade; the only singular mark is along Liberty's jawline. The well-struck surfaces beam with bountiful luster, creating top-notch eye appeal and a generous quotient of collectibility. NGC ID# 269G, PCGS# 8932

1866-S No Motto Twenty, AU Sharpness
One of the Rarest Issues in the Series

3854 1866-S No Motto — Improperly Cleaned — NGC Details. AU. The noted cleaning has dimmed the luster noticeably and given the piece a rather flat appearance, even though there is some color shift around the device outlines. Scattered abrasions include a rather deep, straight one running diagonally right and up from the last 6 in the date, and another noticeable mark and graze near the chin. Nonetheless this is a singularly rare issue in the entire Liberty Head series, second among S-mint issues behind the 1861-S Paquet Reverse, and this piece should afford some collectors the opportunity to obtain an example at an advantageous price.

1866 Double Eagle, AU55
First P-Mint With Motto Issue

3855 1866 AU55 NGC. Medium yellow-gold color, a bold strike, and only a light sprinkling of abrasions on each side make this an attractive example of the first P-mint With Motto issue. The addition of the motto ushered in the Type Two era, which would endure for only a decade until the modification of the denomination to TWENTY DOLLARS in 1877 would make the commencement of the Type Three coins. NGC ID# 269X, PCGS# 8949

1866 Twenty Dollar, Appealing MS61
Frosty Original Luster, Condition Rarity

1869-S Double Eagle, AU58
Elusive Type Two S-Mint Date

3856 **1866 MS61 PCGS.** The first Type Two issue from this mint, the 1866 double eagle had a fairly substantial mintage of nearly 700,000 pieces, but it is somewhat scarcer overall than one might be led to believe. Domestic circulation at the time of production was not the primary cause of attrition, as many pieces were exported for trade; those that survived melting and have returned to the numismatic marketplace typically show light wear and are heavily abraded. Mint State pieces are rare, with virtually all restricted to the MS60 and MS61 levels; finer pieces are prohibitively rare.

This representative is among the few genuinely appealing examples known, showing frosty rose and honey-gold luster, and sharp design elements. Light chatter in the fields accounts for the grade, as no singularly obtrusive abrasions are present. An excellent acquisition for the collector of conditionally rare gold. Population: 29 in 61, 6 finer (10/14). NGC ID# 269X, PCGS# 8949

3857 **1869-S AU58 PCGS.** The California branch mint produced more than 686,000 double eagles in 1869, but nearly all experienced moderate circulation. Mint State survivors are seldom encountered, and typically command strong prices at auction. This near-Mint coin offers the collector with a still-attractive, much more affordable alternative. Substantial original mint luster remains in the recesses, with warm wheat-gold color. Scattered abrasions are present, as is expected at this grade level. PCGS has encapsulated only 48 numerically finer pieces (10/14). NGC ID# 26A6, PCGS# 8956

1870-CC Double Eagle, AU50
First-Year-of-Issue, Extreme Carson City Rarity
Only Auction Appearance of This Coin in Nearly 30 Years

3858 **1870-CC AU50 PCGS. Variety 1-A.** The Comstock Lode provided the necessary impetus to open a new Mint in Carson City, Nevada — capital of the Territory — just fifteen miles distant from the silver and gold deposits needed to make the venture viable. Unhardened dies were shipped from Philadelphia to Carson City in October, 1869 to prepare for the initial production of coins. However, little bullion was on hand to commence operations. In early January, the first mintage of silver dollars was achieved, followed by limited quantities of gold eagles and half eagles. On March 10, 1870 the first delivery of 1870-CC double eagles was accomplished to the tune of 1,332 coins.

The newly-minted coins immediately entered circulation, followed by another 2,457 double eagles later in the year for a total mintage of just 3,789 coins. All entered channels of commerce — there was no collector demand for CC-Mint coins (or for any mintmarked coins, for that matter) and the issue was not recognized as a rarity until many years later. As a result, no Uncirculated 1870-CC double eagles are known to this day.

Just 35 to 45 examples are thought to exist, although estimates vary. Rusty Goe thinks as many as 55 to 65 coins may survive, most of which were poorly produced by the inexperienced Mint. Many show evidence of cleanings, heavy abrasions, or severe scrapes and scratches. Most coins suffer a combination of all the maladies to one extent or another.

This AU50 example resides in an earlier generation blue label holder and compares favorably with the finest-known coins in the current roster of the issue. There are, of course, small abrasions as typical for the first-year twenties from rough handling and transport. There are no heavy marks of any kind, though, and it is difficult to isolate a single "pedigree marker" deep or noticeable enough to be individually significant.

Wonderful, orange-gold patina attests to the obvious originality of the coin. The strike is soft on all examples of the Carson City date, especially on the star centers, but the current coin is at least the equal of any other known representative of the issue. Considerable luster remains over the surfaces, with prooflike flash in virtually all of the protected areas. It would not be hard to imagine this example inching up the grading scale based on its overall quality and eye appeal compared to the other high-grade coins. The only known previous auction appearance for this coin is a January, 1985 Stack's sale of Selections from the Estate of Joseph Bellini and other consignments. No information in the catalog links the coin specifically to the Bellini estate or any other collection.

Roster of High-Grade 1870-CC Double Eagles

1. **AU58 NGC.** The finest-known specimen, recently discovered and shortly thereafter stolen during a Brinks transport on October 19, 2011. Unrecovered.

2. **AU55 NGC.** Baltimore Auction (Bowers and Merena, 3/2009), lot 3909, realized $414,000.

3. **AU53 PCGS.** Doug Winter; Nevada collection; Universal Coin and Bullion; Isaac Edmunds Collection (Bowers and Merena, 6/2002), lot 2371; FUN Signature (Heritage, 1/2004), lot 3129, realized $368,000; Bently Collection (Heritage, 3/2014), lot 30435, realized $411,250.

4. **AU53 NGC.** Denver Signature (Heritage, 8/2006), lot 5645, realized $359,375; Philadelphia ANA Sale (Stack's Bowers, 8/2012), lot 11039, realized $345,000.

5. **AU53 NGC.** Long Beach Signature (Heritage, 9/2003), lot 8296; Pre-Long Beach Sale (Ira and Larry Goldberg, 5/2010), lot 1712; Chicago ANA Sale (Stack's Bowers, 8/2011), lot 7762.

6. **AU50 PCGS.** This piece matches none of the other coins on the roster. Public Auction Sale (Stack's, 1/1985), lot 1118; private collection. **The present coin.**

7. **AU50 PCGS.** Lee Minshull and Casey Noxon; James E. Haldan Collection (Sotheby's, 6/1996), lot 146; Universal Coin & Bullion; private collection; CSNS Signature (Heritage, 4/2014), lot 5821, realized $305,500.

8. **AU50 PCGS.** FUN Signature (Heritage, 1/2014), lot 5541, realized $329,000.

9. **AU50 PCGS.** Classics Sale (American Numismatic Rarities, 1/2004), lot 546.

10. **AU50 NGC.** Richmond Collection (David Lawrence, 7/2004), lot 2288.

11. **AU50 Cleaned, Uncertified.** Baltimore Auction (Bowers and Merena, 2/2008), lot 2749.

12. **AU50 Details ANACS.** New York Signature (Heritage, 2/2014), lot 5418, realized $164,500. NGC ID# 26A8, PCGS# 8958

1872-S Double Eagle, MS61
Seldom Seen in Mint State

3859 **1872-S MS61 PCGS.** This Type Two S-mint is a rarity in Mint State, where gold gurus Jeff Garrett and Ron Guth opine that fewer than 200 pieces survive. This yellow-gold example shows full luster but shows a peppering of abrasions that constitute the grade, most notably a series of reeding marks in the left obverse field and on Liberty's lower lip. There is no trace of high-point rub. Population: 36 in 61, 14 finer (10/14). NGC ID# 26AF, PCGS# 8965

1874-S Type Two Twenty, MS62
Small Squat S Mintmark

3860 **1874-S MS62 PCGS.** Small Squat S. At least three different mintmark styles were used on 1874-S twenties. The Block S and Broad S are approximately equal in scarcity, but the present mintmark size is rare for the issue, and likely from a single holdover reverse die. This apricot-gold double eagle has good luster and the expected number of obverse abrasions. None are noticeable aside from a narrow scratch between the first two stars. Population: 59 in 62, 4 finer (10/14). NGC ID# 26AR, PCGS# 8972

1875-S Double Eagle, MS62
Impressive, Conditionally Scarce Example

3861 **1875-S MS62 PCGS.** Pleasing hues of mint-green, peach, and sky-blue are blended together on the surfaces of this Mint State example. Impressive cartwheel luster radiates from both sides. The obverse is typically marked for the grade, while the reverse is much smoother. Most of the Uncirculated examples of this issue are found in MS60 and MS61 holders. MS62 examples are scarce and finer pieces are rare. NGC ID# 26AU, PCGS# 8975

1876 Twenty, MS63
Lustrous, Conditionally Scarce Example

3862 **1876 MS63 PCGS.** This Philadelphia Mint issue had a substantial mintage of 583,905 coins, and examples are plentiful in AU and Mint State grades up to MS62. Select Uncirculated examples like this one are extremely scarce, and coins rated any finer than MS63 are rare.

Outstanding, intense mint frost is the hallmark of this piece. The surfaces exhibit scattered small marks and lovely peach-gold and rose toning. Population: 39 in 63 (2 in 63+), 12 finer (10/14). NGC ID# 26AV, PCGS# 8976

1876-CC Twenty, MS60
Popular Carson City Issue

3863 **1876-CC MS60 NGC.** Variety 3-A. Warm honey-gold luster flows over each side of this basal Mint State 1876-CC twenty, kept from a higher grade by a combination of abrasions, including a few on the large side, along with luster grazes and smaller marks. This is a popular issue combining the Centennial year with the Carson City mintmark, one of 138,441 coins struck. NGC ID# 26AW, PCGS# 8977

1878-CC Twenty Dollar, XF40
Low Mintage of 13,180 Coins

3864 **1878-CC XF40 NGC.** Variety 1-A. The Carson City Mint managed to eke out only 13,180 examples of the Liberty Head double eagle during 1878, the year that it first pumped out more than 2.2 million Morgan silver dollars. Interestingly, that mintage of double eagles required two different obverses and two different reverses, this being the variety with wide CC mintmark on the reverse and a diagonal long, straight die line on Liberty's neck. The moderate wear seen on this attractive amber-gold coin is consistent with the grade. NGC ID# 26B4, PCGS# 8986

1883-CC Twenty Dollar, AU55
Seldom-Seen Variety 1-B

3865 **1883-CC AU55 NGC. Variety 1-B,** a scarcer variety showing the second C in the mintmark left of the D in DOLLARS, diagonal die lines within the lower shield, and a diagonal die line near star 13 on the obverse. Orange-gold surfaces show plenty of luster and good eye appeal on this lightly circulated Choice AU 1883-CC twenty, one of nearly 60,000 struck. NGC ID# 26BH, PCGS# 8999

1884-CC Liberty Twenty, MS61
Popular Type Three Carson City Issue

1884-S Liberty Double Eagle, MS63
Seldom Encountered in Finer Grades

3867 **1884-S MS63 PCGS.** The 1884-S Liberty double eagle enjoyed a substantial mintage of 916,000 pieces, but the issue was released into circulation and few examples were saved by contemporary collectors. This attractive Select example displays well-detailed design elements and lightly marked orange-gold surfaces with frosty mint luster on both sides. PCGS has graded 23 numerically finer examples (10/14). NGC ID# 26BL, PCGS# 9002

3866 **1884-CC MS61 PCGS. Variety 1-A.** Among Carson City double eagles of the 1880s, the 1884-CC is the most available issue, making it a favorite of mintmark type collectors seeking a Type Three example from the famous Western mint. The reported mintage was a relatively generous 81,139 pieces and the surviving population probably numbers 1,250-1,500 pieces in all grades. Examples in lower Mint State grades can be located with patience, but high-grade pieces are rare.

The present coin is an attractive MS61 example, with sharply detailed design elements and vibrant mint luster. The pleasing yellow and rose-gold surfaces show a few highlights of green and a scattering of minor contact marks does little to detract from the considerable eye appeal. NGC ID# 26BK, PCGS# 9001

3868 **1885-CC AU53 NGC. Variety 1-A.** Carson City double eagles from the 1880s and 1890s are typically available in XF and AU grades, due to substantial numbers being discovered in overseas hoards. The 1885-CC, however, is curiously lacking in most listings. With a scant mintage of only 9,450 pieces and a proportionately low survival rate, one begins to realize why. The typical piece grades no finer than XF, and About Uncirculated examples are the finest usually available; a small number of Mint State pieces have been certified, though these are decidedly rare. The present example displays original bronze-gold patina, with tinges of original orange-gold luster in the recesses. Slight wear over the high points of the design precludes a Mint State assessment, though the surfaces are largely free of the scattered heavy abrasions that typically affect examples in this grade. An important opportunity for the Carson City double eagle collector. NGC ID# 26BN, PCGS# 9004.

1885-S Double Eagle, MS65
Radiant Saddle Ridge Example
Tied With One Other for the Finest Known

3869 **1885-S MS65 PCGS.** The 1885-S double eagle benefits overall from a substantial mintage of 683,500 coins, the largest production of the year for this denomination by a staggering margin. However, the issue's availability follows the general pattern of most Type Three San Francisco issues from this mint, being plentiful in grades through MS62, but decidedly scarce finer. Furthermore, Jeff Garrett and Ron Guth question the accuracy of the certified population reports, especially for the MS63 grade level, due to numerous resubmissions brought about by the rather dramatic increases in value that the 1885-S makes at each succeeding Mint State grade. At the Choice Mint State level, PCGS reports just 34 grading events (1 in 64+), while NGC shows only 11 (10/14). Take into account a small number of likely resubmissions, and the rarity of this issue in high grades becomes blatantly apparent.

Only two Gems have been certified (both PCGS coins), these being the undisputed finest known of the date. One is likely the Dallas Bank Collection coin, which last sold at auction back in 2001, uncertified, for the then impressive sum of $21,850. The other, offered here, although not pedigreed on its holder, traces its origin to the fabulous Saddle Ridge Hoard, discovered in California in early 2013. The Hoard yielded 20 examples of the 1885-S, of which this piece is the sole finest.

Heavily frosted, uninhibited mint bloom radiates from both sides in lovely rose-gold hues. The design elements are boldly brought up, with little evidence of the excessive die lapping that often affects branch mint double eagles of this period. A faint, thread-like, coppery-red alloy mark near Liberty's chin serves as a pedigree identifier, while the surfaces are largely devoid of all but the lightest of luster grazes on the cheek and below the eagle's tailfeathers. An immensely attractive coin, and the single finest example of this Type Three San Francisco issue that we have ever offered at auction. NGC ID# 26BP, PCGS# 9005.

1888-S Double Eagle, MS63
Original Color, Nice Surfaces

3870 **1888-S MS63 PCGS. CAC.** The ready availability of the San Francisco date and the notable surface quality make this Select Uncirculated twenty especially desirable. Reddish-gold highlights enhance the original, orange-gold color. The strike is about normal for the San Francisco Mint in this era, with a bit of blending on Liberty's hair and some softness at the eagle's head. Only scattered, minor abrasions appear on the brightly lustrous surfaces. Eye appeal trumps all, and this double eagle has it. NGC ID# 26BU, PCGS# 9009

1889 Double Eagle, MS62
Scarce Low-Mintage Issue

3871 **1889 MS62 PCGS. CAC.** The 1889 double eagle mintage was a low one, at 44,070 coins, and survivors are scarce at all grade levels. This example is highly lustrous, with bright peach-gold toning and much better eye appeal than its MS62 designation might imply. It is sharply struck with grade-consistent abrasions that are mostly confined to the field areas. NGC ID# 2695, PCGS# 9010

1889-S Twenty Dollar, MS63
Rare Any Finer

3872 **1889-S MS63 NGC.** Well-defined on Liberty's hair and the eagle's plumage, far from a guarantee for this San Francisco issue. Rolling cartwheel luster with a faintly frosty sheen has a yellow-gold base with lighter and deeper variations. Assorted light abrasions and a few rim bumps combine to account for the grade. Rare any finer. NGC ID# 26BW, PCGS# 9012

1889-S Double Eagle, MS64
Conditionally Scarce

3873 **1889-S MS64 PCGS.** The 1889-S double eagle had a substantial mintage of more than 774,000 coins, and is moderately available overall. However, most Mint State survivors are significantly abraded, residing only in MS62 and lower grades. Choice examples are positively scarce, and only a handful of finer coins are known. This piece shows frosty rose and honey-gold luster over largely undisturbed surfaces. Liberty's hair curls and the stars are well brought up, also contributing to the overall excellent eye appeal. A high-end example for the grade. Population: 37 in 64 (5 in 64+), 0 finer (10/14). NGC ID# 26BW, PCGS# 9012

1889-S Twenty, MS64
Smooth and Attractive

3874 1889-S MS64 PCGS. The collecting landscape has changed considerably for this San Francisco date since the discovery of more than 300 1889-S double eagles in the Saddle Ridge Hoard. With the influx of several high-grade coins, the upper-end of the population report shows a number of new entries.

In our opinion, the current coin is not one of the Hoard coins. The deep, rich-gold color shows orange accents and deep-seated mint luster that rolls over the super-smooth, mint-fresh surfaces. A few tiny, wispy abrasions account for the near-Gem grade. The strike is full throughout. Population (includes Saddle Ridge coins): 73 in 64 (15 in 64+), 5 finer (10/14). NGC ID# 26BW, PCGS# 9012

1889-S Liberty Twenty, MS64
None Numerically Finer at PCGS

3875 1889-S MS64 PCGS. The 1889-S Liberty double eagle claims a mintage of 774,700 pieces but the issue circulated heavily in the regional economy and the channels of foreign trade at the time of issue. Most examples seen show heavy wear from circulation or excessive surface marks from storage and transport., Until approximately 300 pieces surfaced in the famous Saddle Ridge Hoard, the 1889-S was a rare issue in any Mint State grade. It is still quite elusive at the MS64 grade level and finer examples are virtually unobtainable.

This delightful Choice example offers sharply detailed design elements and the well-preserved yellow-gold surfaces radiate vibrant mint luster on both sides. Overall eye appeal is outstanding. Population: 37 in 64 (5 in 64+), 0 finer (10/14). NGC ID# 26BW, PCGS# 9012

1889-S Twenty Dollar, MS64+
Eye-Catching Mint Bloom

3876 1889-S MS64+ PCGS. The availability of the 1889-S double eagle was significantly increased by the discovery of the Saddle Ridge Hoard in February 2013, but its conditional scarcity at the Choice grade level should not be written off. The Hoard about doubled the supply of MS64-graded coins at PCGS, though that service still only shows 68 examples in this grade (15 in 64+), and only five finer (10/14). The present coin, with noticeable semiprooflike mirroring and dazzling apricot-gold luster, rivals the Saddle Ridge Hoard coins in eye appeal, which is significant considering how the latter are among the most eye-appealing examples of this issue known to collectors. The strike is sharp and only a few tiny marks on the cheek preclude a full Gem grade. NGC ID# 26BW, PCGS# 9012

1889-S Double Eagle, MS64+
Exceptional, Conditionally Rare Example

3877 1889-S MS64+ NGC. CAC. The recently-discovered Saddle Ridge Hoard, an amazing group of coins that received widespread coverage in the national media, produced around 300 examples of this San Francisco date. Approximately 225 of those coins graded either MS62 or MS63, while just 31 were rated at MS64. Five pieces graded out at MS65.

Outstanding luster quality and razor-sharp strike definition are the most noteworthy attributes of this visually exceptional near-Gem (which is not pedigreed to the Saddle Ridge Hoard). Light honey-gold toning and exceptionally clean surfaces also contribute to the overall desirability of this conditionally rare double eagle. Census: 7 in 64+ (1 in 64+★), 3 finer (10/14). NGC ID# 26BW, PCGS# 9012

1889-S Double Eagle, MS63+
Ex: Saddle Ridge Hoard

1889-S Liberty Twenty, MS64
Ex: Saddle Ridge Hoard

3878 **1889-S Saddle Ridge Hoard MS63+ NGC.** NGC awarded this coin a rather limited grade of MS63+, though close examination with a loupe is needed to find any surface flaws that preclude a Choice assessment, these seen only in the form of a few light luster grazes on Liberty's cheek, as usual; the reverse is seemingly pristine. Frosty green and rose-gold luster enhances the appeal of the razor-sharp design elements. Pedigreed to the famous Saddle Ridge Hoard, this piece carries with it a great deal of numismatic and historical appeal. PCGS# 109012

3879 **1889-S Saddle Ridge Hoard MS64 NGC.** The Saddle Ridge Hoard yielded some of the most well-preserved and eye-appealing 1889-S double eagles known to collectors. Buried for more than a century in California's gold region, one can only awe at the superb preservation and outstanding luster of these coins, some of which are now the finest known of the date. The present example is exceptional in all regards, and might have received a full Gem grade assessment, save for a small, faint luster graze near star 3. A bold strike only increases the already immense visual appeal. Census of all 1889-S double eagles: 34 in 64 (7 in 64+, 1 in 64+«), 2 finer (10/14). PCGS# 109012

1889-S Double Eagle, MS64
Ex: Saddle Ridge Hoard

1889-S Double Eagle, MS64+
Ex: Saddle Ridge Hoard

3880 **1889-S Saddle Ridge Hoard MS64 NGC.** In February 2013, on a private homestead located in what was once the gold hills of the California Gold Rush, more than 1,400 gold coins were literally unearthed in old, rusted cans, where they had been buried for more than a century. The cache, now dubbed the Saddle Ridge Hoard, is arguably the greatest buried treasure discovery in the recorded history of the North American continent, yielding some of the finest known examples of numerous 19th century San Francisco double eagles.

The 1889-S was represented by more than 300 coins, with many grading in Choice or better condition. This representative displays bold detail and radiant honey-gold luster. No significant abrasions are observed, and the eye appeal is exceptional. Census of all 1889-S double eagles: 34 in 64 (7 in 64+, 1 in 64+★), 2 finer (10/14). PCGS# 109012

3881 **1889-S Saddle Ridge Hoard MS64+ NGC.** Many examples of the 1889-S double eagle were among the coins discovered in the Saddle Ridge Hoard, but the date's scarcity in Choice condition was only marginally affected. Even after the disbursal of the Hoard coins, NGC has encapsulated only 34 examples in MS64 (7 in 64+, 1 in 64+★), and just two finer (10/14). The present coin must have just missed a Gem grade assessment, as the surfaces are largely devoid of imperfections and the fields display subtle semiprooflike mirroring beneath warm wheat-gold luster. The devices are boldly impressed, and the visual appeal is seemingly unmatched for the grade. PCGS# 109012

1889-S Twenty Dollar, MS64+
Radiant Saddle Ridge Hoard Coin

1890-CC Double Eagle
Lustrous Near-Mint Example

3882 **1889-S Saddle Ridge Hoard MS64+ NGC.** The Mint State availability of the 1889-S double eagle was noticeably affected by the discovery of more than 300 examples in the Saddle Ridge Hoard of February 2013, but the date remains scarce at the Choice level, and is distinctly rare in finer grades. The present example showcases vibrant honey-gold mint bloom and razor-sharp design elements. A couple tiny marks on Liberty's cheek preclude a full Gem grade assessment from NGC, though the impressive eye appeal beautifully displays the superior quality and preservation that contribute to the Saddle Ridge Hoard coins' immense popularity. Census of all 1889-S double eagles: 34 in 64 (7 in 64+, 1 in 64+«), 2 finer (10/14). PCGS# 109012

3883 **1890-CC AU58 NGC. CAC. Variety 1-A.** The usual late die state example, with the eagle's right-side tailfeathers partially effaced by die lapping. This piece shows original orange-gold patina, with remnants of luster in the recesses. The design elements are sharply impressed, with only slight friction over the high points. The 1890-CC is a fairly plentiful date in the context of Carson City twenties, ideal for the collector seeking a single representative from this mint. NGC ID# 26BY, PCGS# 9014

1891-CC Double Eagle, AU53
Semikey Carson City Twenty

3884 1891-CC AU53 NGC. Variety 1-A. The Carson City double eagles from the 1890s are generally available in AU and lower Mint State grades, with the sole exception of the 1891-CC. Its mintage of just 5,000 coins, produced with a single die pair, is the second-lowest in the series from this mint, trailing only the legendary 1870-CC. A patient search will turn up a few examples in the XF and lower circulated grades, but this issue becomes genuinely scarce in AU, and Mint State coins are distinctly rare. The present example exhibits original orange-gold patina over both sides, with tinges of vibrant luster remaining in the protected regions. Light high-point wear leaves sharp detail in most areas, and the surfaces show only minor marks. NGC ID# 26C3, PCGS# 9017

1892 Double Eagle, AU50
Scarce in All Grades

3885 1892 AU50 PCGS. A paltry mintage of only 4,430 double eagles at the Philadelphia Mint in 1892 accounts for the scarcity of this issue in all grades. PCGS and NGC combined show a population of just 231 coins across the entire spectrum, and it is likely even this small figure includes a number of resubmissions. The present coin is a sharply detailed AU example, with original honey-gold patina and tinges of luster in the recesses. Scattered abrasions are present, as usual, though the eye appeal is above-average for the issue. NGC ID# 26C5, PCGS# 9019

1892-CC Double Eagle, AU55
Attractive Semiprooflike Fields

3886 1892-CC AU55 PCGS. Variety 1-A. Remnants of semiprooflike mirroring in the fields and impressively sharp detail for the grade give this Choice AU representative eye-catching appeal. A few light abrasions are present, but these are of little significance. The 1892-CC is one of more plentiful double eagle's from the Carson City Mint in circulated grades, but becomes scarce and proportionately more expensive across the Mint State threshold. NGC ID# 26C6, PCGS# 9020

1893-CC Twenty Dollar, AU55
Last-Year Double Eagle From Carson City

3887 1893-CC AU55 NGC. Variety 1-A. The meager mintage of this last-year Carson City double eagle was only 18,402 pieces, making it popular among Western gold specialists. This Choice AU example shows orange-gold surfaces retaining considerable luster amid scattered light marks that help account for the grade. NGC ID# 26C9, PCGS# 9023

1894 Double Eagle, MS64
Pleasing and High-End for the Grade

3888 1894 MS64 PCGS. CAC. This high-mintage issue is easily available in lower grades, up to MS63, but near-Gems are very scarce, and Gems are downright rare with fewer than 10 known. This example is remarkably attractive and highly lustrous, with lovely light coloration and relatively slight abrasions for the grade. The CAC sticker confirms this coin's high-end status. NGC ID# 26CB, PCGS# 9025

1896 Double Eagle
Brilliant, Deeply Frosted Near-Gem

3889 1896 MS64 PCGS. One of the "fooler" late-series twenties, which are common in lower grades but much more elusive at higher Uncirculated levels. This Philadelphia date is a condition rarity in MS65 and decidedly scarce in near-Gem condition such as the current coin. Only a few minor grazes are seen anywhere on the boldly struck, thickly frosted surfaces. Lilac and olive overtones flash with the deep-seated luster. The eye appeal and technical merit suggest an even higher grade. PCGS has certified just six numerically finer coins (10/14). NGC ID# 26CF, PCGS# 9029

1902 Twenty Dollar, MS62
High-End for the Grade

3890 1902 MS62 PCGS. A limited mintage of only 31,140 pieces accounts for the scarcity of this issue overall. The date is most often seen in MS62 and lower grades, as finer examples are rare. This piece displays sharp detail with frosty green-gold luster overall. Grade-limiting abrasions are light and evenly dispersed, posing little distraction. An immensely appeal representative for the grade. NGC ID# 26CU, PCGS# 9041

1905 Twenty Dollar, MS64+
Oft-Overlooked Condition Rarity

3891 1905 MS64+ NGC. In discussions of conditionally rare Liberty double eagles, 20th century issues are often overlooked, since so many are generally just considered plentiful type coins. Amid the common dates, however, resides the 1905: a Philadelphia issue with a small mintage of only 58,919 coins, and a certified Mint State population that is insufficient to supply the needs to collectors. NGC has certified only four examples at the Choice grade level, and this piece is one of only two of those awarded a Plus designation; just one numerically finer coin is known, an NGC-graded Gem (10/14).

This piece is pleasantly sharp throughout, with frosty wheat-gold luster that delivers a soft shimmering effect when turned beneath a light. A few insignificant marks on the cheek limit NGC's numeric opinion, though the eye appeal is hardly inhibited. NGC ID# 26D2, PCGS# 9047

1903 Double Eagle, PR61
Pleasing Lower-Grade Proof

Select 1907 High Relief Twenty
Wire Rim Variant

3892 1903 PR61 PCGS. The 1903 is one of the more plentiful proof issues in the Liberty double eagle series, though this is only in the comparison to other proof issues in the series, many of which are prohibitively rare. The Mint struck only 158 examples, and it is believed only about 50 to 60 pieces are extant in all grades. PCGS and NGC combined show a population of 87 examples, though this figure undoubtedly includes a number of resubmissions. The present example shows a fair number of faint hairlines in the fields, limiting the grade, but is nonetheless a pleasing, moderately affordable example of the immensely popular proof Liberty double eagle. Deep mirrors frame boldly struck devices, while the obverse exhibits subtle field-motif contrast — a rarity on this issue. Population: 2 in 61, 25 finer (10/14). NGC ID# 26ER, PCGS# 9119

3893 1907 High Relief, Wire Rim MS63 PCGS. When viewing a High Relief, it is obvious that the design was produced by a sculptor. It is radically different in concept from all that preceded it, which were coins that were designed by mint personnel. The only previous design that approaches Saint-Gaudens' concept was the radically different depiction of a modified Britannia on the Gobrecht dollar, which was based on sketches by noted artists Titian Peale and Thomas Sully.

The three-dimensional quality of the High Relief is a compelling feature on this coin. On this particular piece, the fullness of strike gives the figure of Liberty and the eagle a directness not seen on any other American coin. The satiny surfaces have a rich yellow-gold color with a slight tinge of reddish patina. Minimally abraded for an MS63. NGC ID# 26F2, PCGS# 9135

1907 High Relief, Wire Rim Twenty, MS64
Bright Mint Luster and Crisp Detail

1907 Flat Rim High Relief Twenty
Superior Select Uncirculated Example

3894 **1907 High Relief, Wire Rim MS64 NGC.** Six years ago the Mint struck the 2009 Ultra High Relief double eagle, a project from a century ago that fulfilled the vision of Augustus Saint-Gaudens, but in a form accessible to more than just a handful of fortunate numismatists. The program also brought the original High Relief twenties increased popularity. The present Choice piece shows a strong obverse wire rim and uncommonly strong luster across the lemon-gold fields. Boldly impressed as always with a profound, sculptural quality to the well-preserved central devices.
Ex: FUN Signature (Heritage, 1/2009), lot 4167. NGC ID# 26F2, PCGS# 9135

3895 **1907 High Relief, Flat Rim MS63 PCGS.** To say Chief Engraver Charles E. Barber objected to the Augustus Saint-Gaudens High Relief design may be an understatement. Partly from professional jealousy, and certainly from a technical standpoint, Barber's reaction to the project could be at times mean-spirited and truculent, yet he deserves a share of the credit for the mintage of what is generally regarded as the pinnacle of American coinage. A case in point is the difficulty from excessive metal flow between the dies and collar that resulted in a vulnerable Wire Rim on the earliest High Relief strikings. Barber's tenacity eventually solved the problem, resulting in the beveled-edge, Flat Rim solution that was minted in relatively small numbers at the end of 1907.

This example of the Flat Rim High Relief offers exceptional quality for the Select Uncirculated grade. The surfaces are smooth and attractive, with sumptuous yellow-gold color and a strong strike. Only a few tiny marks are widely scattered, and even then they need sharp eyes with an assist from a glass to be visible. The Flat Rim variant is considerably scarcer than the Wire Rim, adding to the appeal. It would be hard to improve upon this superior High Relief double eagle for the assigned grade. PCGS# 9136

1907 Double Eagle, MS65
Flat Rim High Relief
Warm, Satiny Mint Luster

3896 1907 High Relief, Flat Rim MS65 NGC. Augustus Saint-Gaudens is universally considered the greatest American sculptor of the 19th and early 20th centuries. But work did not come easy in his early years. His son Homer recounts that after his father returned to New York after his first residency in Rome, it was with "great persistence" that he obtained commissions in those early years. As examples of Saint-Gaudens' need for work in the early 1870s he mentions two commissions:

> "One of these commissions for a large semi-circular panel for the Adams Express Company Building in Chicago, represented a bull-dog, with revolvers and bowie knives to assist him, guarding a couple of safes. Another, for a silver candelabra, which Tiffany was to place in the Gordon Bennett yacht *Mohawk*, was a figure of an Indian dancing with knife and scalp."

Even though commissions were difficult to come by in these early years and caused him "intense nervous stress" Saint-Gaudens made time to teach his brother Louis and three others how to cut cameos, a craft he had learned beginning at age 13. His skill as a cameo cutter acquainted him with some of the demands of sculpting, especially when working in a small area, a skill that would serve him well when he was later called upon to redesign the nation's coinage.

By the time he was called upon by President Roosevelt to redesign the ten and twenty dollar gold pieces, he was certainly more secure in commissions than in his early years. However, Saint-Gaudens had difficulty turning down commissions throughout his life, even when completion was years away. His previous experience as a cameo cutter and sculptor are abundantly evident in the design of the High Relief twenty dollar. This particular coin shows an almost completely flat rim around each side, just a trace of extruded metal can be seen on the reverse. The surfaces exude a warm, satiny mint luster that is lightly accented by light reddish patina, and there are no obvious contact marks on either side. PCGS# 9136

1907 Saint-Gaudens Double Eagle, MS65+
Scarcer Flat Rim Variant

3897 1907 High Relief, Flat Rim MS65+ NGC. CAC. The 1907 High Relief Saint-Gaudens double eagle has been acknowledged as America's most beautiful regular-issue coin. A limited mintage of 12,367 examples was accomplished, and early strikes feature a fin, or Wire Rim, around the edges of the coins, caused by metal being extruded through the tiny gap between the collar and the dies. Considered a liability, mint personnel adjusted the planchet dimensions and milling to eliminate this feature. As a result, coins struck later in the year display a Flat Rim, like the present coin. The Flat Rim variant is much scarcer than its Wire Rim counterpart.

This high-end Gem displays the usual sharply detailed central design elements, with well-preserved yellow and rose-gold surfaces and vibrant mint luster on both sides. Eye appeal is outstanding. Census: 93 in 65 (4 in 65+), 90 finer (10/14). PCGS# 9136

3898 **1907 High Relief PR64 NGC.** Extraordinary, bright satiny mint luster is seen over the surfaces of this specially produced High Relief twenty. Extra sharpness of strike, including a sharp inner border on each side help distinguish proofs from business strikes. Additionally, the berries on the olive branch and rounded, all the details are brought up on the Capitol building, and the eagle's tail feathers are all distinct. The swirling die polish marks that are always seen on High Reliefs can easily be found in the clean fields of this piece. An unknown number of these special coins were struck in late 1907. The only area that shows any trace of contact is in the reverse field below UN in UNITED, and magnification will be required to pick this up. PCGS# 9132

3899 **1908 No Motto, Wells Fargo Nevada MS67 PCGS.** Nearly all the high-grade survivors of the 1908 Philadelphia No Motto twenty are traced to the amazing Wells Fargo Nevada Gold hoard, which was discovered in the 1990s. Nearly 20,000 gold double eagles rested undisturbed in a Wells Fargo bank vault since 1917, and nearly all the representatives graded in Gem or finer condition. The hoard yielded the highest-graded, non-high relief double eagles known to this day: 10 incredible, MS69 coins that are still the finest Saint-Gaudens double eagles of any regular-relief date. While slightly below that seldom-attained caliber, this Superb Gem example is typically attractive and marvelously produced. Strong mint luster radiates beneath frosted, rich-gold surfaces with a bold strike throughout. PCGS# 99142

1908 No Motto Twenty, MS68
Wells Fargo Hoard Example

3900 **1908 No Motto, Wells Fargo Nevada MS68 NGC.** The 1908 No Motto Saint-Gaudens double eagle represents the final year of the popular two-year design type, an important distinction for type purposes. Adding to the issue's popularity is the fact that it is readily available in high grades. More than 19,000 high-quality examples (including the present coin) were discovered in the vaults of a Wells Fargo Bank in Nevada and marketed by Ron Gillio in the 1990s. The coins had been stored in sealed bags, safe from the ravages of circulation, since 1917.

This magnificent MS68 example is well-detailed, with vibrant mint luster and pleasing orange and greenish-gold surfaces. Close examination with a loupe reveals no visible surface flaws and eye appeal is tremendous. Only 10 coins, all from the Wells Fargo Hoard, have been certified in higher grade by either of the leading grading services (10/14). PCGS# 99142

1909 Saint-Gaudens Twenty, MS64
Rare in Finer Grades

3901 **1909 MS64 PCGS.** The 1909 double eagle had a minimal mintage of little more than 160,000 coins, and is decidedly rare above the Choice grade level. This example exhibits bold striking definition, with satiny apricot-gold luster. Light, scattered ticks preclude full Gem status, though none are singularly discernable. Only 25 coins are numerically finer at PCGS (10/14). NGC ID# 26FB, PCGS# 9150

1909/8 Saint-Gaudens Twenty, Lustrous MS64

3902 **1909/8 MS64 PCGS. FS-301.** "This overdate was created when the engraver struck a 1908-dated die with a 1909 hub, creating at least one overdate die," according to Garrett and Guth (2008). The total business strike mintage for this date was 161,282 coins, approximately half of which were overdates.

This near-Gem is exceptionally lustrous, with a bright satiny sheen that radiates from rim-to-rim on each side of the coin. The lovely honey-gold toning is imbued with slight undertones of pale green. Relatively few examples of this popular variety are known at the MS64 grade level, and coins rated even finer are rare. PCGS has seen just 25 high-graded pieces as of (10/14). NGC ID# 26FC, PCGS# 9151

1911 Double Eagle, MS65
Rarely Encountered Finer

3903 **1911 MS65 PCGS.** The 1911 is one of the scarcer Philadelphia issues in the Saint-Gaudens double eagle series. A mintage of 197,250 pieces was accomplished, but Mint State survivors are usually only available in MS62 and lower grades, with Select and Choice coins being challenging. At the Gem level, this issue is genuinely scarce, and finer pieces are rare. This example displays razor-sharp design definition, with satiny green-gold luster and a lack of significant abrasions. Overall, a highly appealing example of an issue that often lacks attractive features. Population: 43 in 65 (1 in 65+), 11 finer (10/14). NGC ID# 26FJ, PCGS# 9157

1911 Twenty Dollar, MS65
Striking Mint Bloom

3904   1911 MS65 PCGS. Like several other Philadelphia issues from this period, the 1911 Saint-Gaudens double eagle is moderately available in grades through MS64, but the Gem condition barrier is broken by very few examples. The present coin is not only certified MS65, but is also firmly near the upper end of that numeric grade, with beautifully preserved surfaces that are seemingly devoid of noticeable flaws. The strike is crisp throughout, with special attention given to Liberty's left (facing) fingers, which are sharply delineated. The 1911 double eagle is seen with varying degrees of luster with the majority being somewhat below average in eye appeal, but this remarkable coin is refreshingly vibrant and frosty. Genuinely rare this high-end. Population: 43 in 65 (1 in 65+), 11 finer (10/14). NGC ID# 26FJ, PCGS# 9157

1912 Twenty Dollar, MS64+
Thickly Frosted Luster, Smooth Surfaces

3905   1912 MS64+ PCGS. CAC. At first glance, this coin appears to be a full Gem, with eye-catching frosty, wheat-gold luster and remarkably clean fields. Close examination is needed to detect the light, grade-limiting surface grazes present on the figure of Liberty and amid the eagle's feathers. A boldly struck piece, certain to impress even the most quality-conscious bidder. The 1912 double eagle is only marginally scarce in Choice Mint State condition, but finer pieces are rarely seen. PCGS has seen only 43 numerically finer submissions (10/14). NGC ID# 26FM, PCGS# 9160

1912 Saint-Gaudens Twenty, MS65
Rarely Seen Finer

3906   1912 MS65 PCGS. There was little need for double eagles in the national economy in 1912 and none were struck at the branch mints. A smallish mintage of 149,750 business-strike examples was accomplished at the Philadelphia Mint, and many of these coins were used in foreign trade. While a limited number of these coins were repatriated in later years, the 1912 remains an elusive issue in high grade, and the date is a prime condition rarity above the MS65 level.

   This attractive Gem displays sharply detailed design elements and well-preserved yellow and rose-gold surfaces, with vibrant mint luster on both sides. Eye appeal is terrific. Population: 38 in 65, 5 finer (10/14). NGC ID# 26FM, PCGS# 9160

1915 Double Eagle, Lustrous MS64
Seldom Seen in Gem Condition

3907 1915 MS64 PCGS. This near-Gem 1915 double eagle may prove appealing to many collectors of this series, as Gems are seldom seen and difficult to obtain. Warm luster over honey-gold surfaces complements a decent strike, but a few scattered marks, most notably just left of the bottom of Liberty's torch, account for the grade. PCGS shows only 47 submissions numerically finer (10/14). NGC ID# 26FV, PCGS# 9167

1915 Saint-Gaudens Twenty, MS64+
Vibrantly Lustrous

3908 1915 MS64+ PCGS. This Philadelphia issue is usually available in Choice and lesser grades, but finer examples are distinctly scarce. This Plus-graded near-Gem exhibits radiant orange-gold luster and sharply impressed design elements. A few minute ticks on each side limit the grade, but are not obtrusive to the unaided eye. Only 47 coins are numerically finer at PCGS (10/14). NGC ID# 26FV, PCGS# 9167

1916-S Twenty Dollar, MS66
None Numerically Finer at PCGS

3909 1916-S MS66 PCGS. This San Francisco issue had a moderate mintage of 796,000 coins, but surviving Mint State examples are not nearly as plentiful as they theoretically should be. This is a seldom encountered Premium Gem representative, ranking among the finest certified of the date at PCGS. The strike is bold, and radiant orange-gold mint luster highlights excellent surface preservation. NGC ID# 26FX, PCGS# 9169

1920-S Saint-Gaudens Double Eagle, AU Details
Rare Heavily Melted Issue

3910 1920-S — Mount Removed — PCGS Genuine. AU Details. The 1920-S Saint-Gaudens double eagle is the earliest series rarity that owes its elusive nature to the massive melts of the 1930s. This vivid lemon-yellow example shows a touch of wear on the high points of the well-detailed design elements. Some minor marks on the rim and a vertical scratch in the left obverse field indicate this coin may have been removed from a jewelry mount. NGC ID# 26FZ, PCGS# 9171

3911 **1921 MS62 NGC.** The Saint-Gaudens series has its share of rare issues — some are absolute rarities as a result of low mintages, but many are rarities by political happenstance.

Gold coinage for the year was limited to only the 1921 double eagles, with 528,500 pieces struck. A small portion of the mintage circulated in the postwar economy, which was sluggish and in decline. Jobs were scarce in the cities and farmers were in trouble due to falling prices. It would be years before the Roaring 20s hit full swing. While pennies, nickels, and dimes were struck in reasonable quantities, few quarters or half dollars were struck. Only Morgan dollars were struck in large quantity.

Franklin D. Roosevelt's controversial 1933 gold recall played havoc with the survivorship of many late-date Saints, but also with middle dates that were not heavily exported, but put aside in storage at the Treasury such as the 1920-S and 1921 twenties. Those coins were melted, along with many coins recalled from dealers and the public.

As a result, perhaps only 150 or so 1921 double eagles survive today — most of them in circulated condition. Few coins of the date returned from foreign hoards, and the population of certified coins in MS62 or finer has actually declined by two coins in the past five years. In fact, it can be argued the 1921 issue is the rarest Saint-Gaudens twenty in MS62 or finer condition (excluding the ultra-rare 1927-D and 1933 dates), making it the premier condition rarity of the series.

This example displays frosty orange-gold surfaces and a bold strike. Light abrasions account for the assigned grade, with the most noticeable mark being a shallow scrape beneath the branch stem. Cartwheel mint luster shines beneath the frosted patina. Census: 13 in 62, 8 finer (10/14). NGC ID# 26G2, PCGS# 9172.

1922-S Twenty, MS64
Radiantly Lustrous

3912 **1922-S MS64 PCGS.** A scarcer San Francisco issue, the 1922-S double eagle is only marginally available in MS64, and finer pieces are genuinely rare. This example displays frosty rose and green-gold hues over each side, with sharp design elements. Light, scattered surface grazes limit the grade, but none are individually noteworthy. PCGS has encapsulated only 16 numerically finer representatives (10/14). NGC ID# 26G4, PCGS# 9174

1924-D Twenty, MS63
Lustrous and Appealing

3913 **1924-D MS63 PCGS.** Coins grading MS64 of this scarce issue are about as nice as practicable, but MS63 coins are seen fairly often in the marketplace, even though all survivors of the issue are considered scarce. This piece shows some alternating areas of brilliant and frosty luster, with good cartwheel luster and areas of greenish-gold near the peripheries. An attractive, Select Uncirculated coin. *Ex: FUN Signature (Heritage, 1/2008), lot 5108.* NGC ID# 26G8, PCGS# 9178

1924-S Double Eagle, MS62
Challenging S-Mint Issue

3914 **1924-S MS62 PCGS.** In stark contrast to its Philadelphia counterpart, which is available in staggering numbers, the 1924-S double eagle is conditionally scarce in all Mint State grades. This example shows blended rose and green-gold hues over frosty luster. The gown lines on Liberty's torso are not fully defined, though the strike is otherwise sharp. Each side displays light, scattered surface chatter, rather than obtrusive abrasions. NGC ID# 26G9, PCGS# 9179

1924-S Saint-Gaudens Twenty, MS63
Soft, Original Mint Luster

3915 **1924-S MS63 NGC.** A luminous, orange-gold example of this better San Francisco issue. The strike is well-executed, and only some minor chatter on Liberty's torso limits the grade. Frosty luster delivers a pleasing cartwheel affect when turned in-hand. Finer pieces are scarce, and are virtually unobtainable in Gem condition. NGC ID# 26G9, PCGS# 9179

1925-D Saint-Gaudens Double Eagle, MS63
Heavily Melted Issue

3916 **1925-D MS63 PCGS.** The vivid orange and rose-gold surfaces of this attractive Select example show highlights of green and vibrant mint luster throughout. The design elements are well-detailed and only minor signs of contact are evident. Overall eye appeal is quite strong. The 1925-D claims a substantial mintage of 2.9 million pieces, but the issue was heavily melted in the 1930s. NGC ID# 26GB, PCGS# 9181

1925-S Double Eagle, MS61
High Mintage, Heavily Melted
Scarce in Mint State

3917 **1925-S MS61 NGC.** The huge mintage of 3,776,500 pieces counts for little these days, because the surviving number of Mint State coins from the 1933 gold recall is only a tiny fraction of the original production. The few European hoard coins that returned to the states are assimilated into the market, and the San Francisco date remains scarce-to-rare when Uncirculated. This example is lustrous and attractive, with only tiny marks and abrasions distributed over the brilliant, medium-gold surfaces and sharp motifs. NGC ID# 26GC, PCGS# 9182

1926 Saint-Gaudens Twenty, MS66
FS-101, Tripled Die Obverse

1929 Saint-Gaudens Double Eagle, MS64+
Elusive Late-Series Issue

3918 **1926 Tripled Die Obverse MS66 PCGS. FS-101.** Boldly struck and lustrous, the smooth surfaces and outstanding visual appeal of this Premium Gem twenty earn greater accolades than the tripled die, which is visible on Saint-Gaudens' initials and to a lesser extent on the date. Reddish-gold highlights swirl across the brilliant, medium-gold surfaces. A terrific example for type, with the FS-101 variety a nice bonus. PCGS# 145744

3919 **1929 MS64+ NGC. CAC.** The 1929 Saint-Gaudens double eagle claims a mintage of nearly 1.8 million pieces, but only a tiny fraction of that impressive total survives today. Most of the coins were held in banks or Treasury vaults to act as currency reserves, and only about 25,000 examples were actually released into circulation before the Gold Recall of 1933. Once that Presidential Order took effect, the coins in storage were easily gathered up and turned in. Later, the coins were melted and stored as gold bars at the Gold Bullion Repository at Fort Knox. This fate was a common one for the later issues in the Saint-Gaudens series, and all the issues struck after 1929 are rare today.

While the 1929 is not as rare in an absolute sense as the later issues in the series, it is more difficult to locate than such acclaimed dates as the 1931 and 1932 in higher Mint State grades. This indicates that some of the 25,000 coins released into circulation in 1929 survived, while almost no examples of the later dates ever escaped from government control. A few high-quality coins were saved by contemporary collectors, providing the small supply of high grade specimens we know about today. David Akers estimates 175-230 examples survive in all Mint State grades. NGC has certified a total of 130 pieces in all grades, while PCGS has graded 183 all-told (10/14). The population data include an unknown number of resubmissions and crossovers. Whatever the true population of the 1929 double eagle is, it is definitely not adequate to supply all the collectors who want one.

The present coin is a high-end Choice example, with well-preserved yellow and rose-gold surfaces. Vibrant mint luster radiates from both sides and the design elements are sharply detailed. Eye appeal is outstanding. Census: 64 in 64 (1 in 64+), 6 finer (10/14). NGC ID# 26GL, PCGS# 9190

1908 Saint-Gaudens Double Eagle, PR65 Satin
Extremely Rare Satin Finish Proof
Ex: Bigelow, Morse

3920 **1908 Motto PR65 Satin NGC.** Ex: Ferrari Collection. Both 1907 and 1908 issues of double eagles saw variants in both design and finishes. The 1908 coins are most notable for the No Motto and With Motto designs. All proofs from that year are With Motto coins. These pieces characteristically are found with deep khaki-green coloration and pronounced matte surfaces. However, of the 101 proofs struck, at least one "Satin" or "Roman Gold" proof is known. The coin offered here shows razor-sharp definition on Liberty's fingers, sandal, and toes, as well as the stars and torch, with broad squared off rims. It was clearly struck on a medal press as a proof. However, the surfaces are bright, orange-gold with a semireflective sheen in the fields, much different from the dark, granular surfaces of the matte proofs. In short, this coin is a "Roman Gold" proof.

One would think that this piece was struck late in the year as a prototype for the "Roman Gold" finish used in 1909 and 1910. However, research done by the staff at Sotheby's in 1997 indicates that this piece was actually presented to the Boston Museum of Fine Arts by William Sturgis Bigelow on June 11, 1908. The museum's catalog card for the coin states: "One of the first coins struck after this legend was restored." This information was supplied to the museum by Frank Leach, Mint Director at the time of the coin's striking.

This piece first appeared at public auction after it was deaccessioned by the Boston Museum of Fine Arts in the 1976 ANA catalog (Stack's). Both a double eagle and an eagle with a Roman Finish were consigned to that sale, and both brought surprisingly high prices for the time: $7,500 for the ten dollar and $10,000 for the double eagle. Close examination of the plate in the 1976 ANA catalog and the 1997 Sotheby's catalog show that this is the same coin. There are a couple of "shiny spots" that show on the photos that are also present on this coin.

The real question is whether there is only one coin. Until recently that was the consensus of opinion among experts like David Akers and Walter Breen, but Jeff Garrett and Ron Guth suggest as many as four examples may be extant. When one looks at the population data from PCGS and NGC, the answer would appear to be a resounding 'no.' NGC shows that six coins have been certified (three in PR65), while PCGS shows none, although this coin was certified as PR64 PCGS at the time of the Phillip Morse Collection sale in November of 2005. Do others actually exist? Is this a case of multiple resubmissions of the same coin? We are not in a position to answer these questions, but they are provocative. Nevertheless, this is the Boston Museum of Fine Arts coin and the one piece that has been consistently recognized in the literature as a Roman Finish proof. An exceptional opportunity for the specialist to acquire what is possibly a unique example of the Roman Finish from 1908. Census: 3 in 65, 0 finer (10/14).

Ex: Dr. William Sturgis Bigelow (from Theodore Roosevelt?) after May 18, 1908; Bigelow to The Boston Museum of Fine Arts, June 11, 1908; 1976 ANA Sale (Stack's, 8/1976), lot 3302, where it brought $10,000, and was purchased by Jim Halperin/NERCA; 1987 GNA Sale (Mid-American, 5/1987), lot 1115, where it realized $69,300; Sotheby's (12/1997), lot 268, where it realized $253,000; Phillip H. Morse Collection (Heritage, 11/2005), lot 6557, realized $276,000. NGC ID# 26GV, PCGS# 9205

1893 Isabella Quarter, MS66+
Lovely Toning, Dazzling Luster

3921 **1893 Isabella Quarter MS66+ NGC.** A sharply struck, impressively preserved example of this first commemorative quarter issue. Radiant, frosty luster highlights shades of violet and royal-blue on each side, giving this piece tremendous eye appeal. The Isabella quarters were issued in conjunction with the World's Columbian Exposition, held in Chicago in 1893, and had a limited distribution of just 24,214 pieces. NGC has seen 60 coins numerically finer than this Plus-graded example (10/14). NGC ID# 28HR, PCGS# 9220

Mrs. Potter Palmer
"Grande Dame" of the World's Columbian Exposition

1893 Isabella Quarter, MS67
Outstanding, Multihued Example

3922 **1893 Isabella Quarter MS67 PCGS. CAC.** The Isabella quarter, issued in conjunction with the World's Columbian Exposition, held in Chicago in 1893, was issued in much smaller numbers than its half dollar counterpart, and was more actively saved by collectors due to a steady market for the coins that ensued following the Exposition. While the half dollars lost much of their numismatic value and eventually ended up in circulation in large numbers, the Isabella quarter sustained a market value equal to or slightly higher than its issue price of one dollar. In the latter half of the 20th century, however, the demand for this first commemorative increased dramatically, especially for high-grade examples such as this representative.

The design elements are sharply impressed, and the beautifully preserved surfaces are awash in vibrant, frosty luster. Attractive multicolor toning in shades of teal, pale violet, and olive-gold blankets each side, giving this high-end example exceptional visual appeal. An eye-appealing and conditionally scarce example of this long-popular early commemorative. Population: 40 in 67 (5 in 67+), 6 finer (10/14). NGC ID# 28HR, PCGS# 9220

1936 Cincinnati Half, MS67
Tied for the Finest Certified

3923 1936 Cincinnati MS67 PCGS. This stunning Superb Gem has distinctive peripheral gold and iridescent toning on the obverse, with mottled gold toning over much of the reverse. Both sides exhibit satiny silver luster. Tied for the finest certified with eight at PCGS and four at NGC (10/14). An important opportunity for the commemorative connoisseur. NGC ID# 28JZ, PCGS# 9283

1936 Cincinnati, MS67
Tied for Finest at PCGS and NGC

3924 1936 Cincinnati MS67 PCGS. Satin luster covers pearl-gray silver surfaces, enhanced by lilac highlights and russet-gold accents at the margins. Far-better produced and preserved than most examples of this commemorative issue, created on behalf of the Cincinnati Music Center and paying tribute to adopted native son Stephen Foster, "America's Troubadour." Softly lustrous and boldly struck. Population: 9 in 67 (1 in 67+), 0 finer (10/14). NGC ID# 28JZ, PCGS# 9283

1892 Columbian Half Dollar, MS67
Frosty, Highly Lustrous

3925 1892 Columbian MS67 PCGS. Well-saved following its issue in conjunction with the World's Columbian Exposition, held in Chicago in 1893, the 1892 Columbian half dollar is readily available in most grades, but becomes conditionally rare at the MS67 grade level. This frosty, nearly untoned example displays well-detailed motifs and beautifully undisturbed luster in the fields. Population: 28 in 67 (5 in 67+), 0 finer (10/14). NGC ID# 26H5, PCGS# 9296

1893 Columbian Half Dollar, MS67
Beautiful Rainbow Toning

3926 1893 Columbian MS67 PCGS. The 1893 Columbian half dollar is slightly more available than its 1892 counterpart in lower grades, but becomes somewhat scarcer at the finer Mint State levels. This Superb Gem example boasts sharp design definition and moderate semiprooflike mirroring in the fields. The obverse showcases vivid rainbow peripheral toning around a nearly brilliant center, while the reverse shows more dispersed hues of the same beneath a veil of dusky golden-gray patina. Population: 17 in 67 (2 in 67+), 0 finer (10/14). NGC ID# 26H6, PCGS# 9297

1922 Grant Half Dollar, MS65
With Star Variant

3927 1922 Grant With Star MS65 NGC. The Grant With Star half dollar is an important commemorative variant that boosted sales at the time these coins were issued. It is believed that the variety was unrequested, but created at the Mint for unknown reasons. This Gem has satiny luster as always, with delicate peripheral iridescence. NGC ID# 28KC, PCGS# 9307

1936-S Oregon Trail Half Dollar, MS68
Among the Finest Certified

3928 1936-S Oregon MS68 NGC. The Oregon Trail half dollar is one of the most popular issues in the silver commemorative series and the 1936-S claims a low distribution of 5,006 pieces. This magnificent MS68 specimen exhibits sharply detailed design elements and satiny mint luster under attractive shades of lavender and golden-brown toning. Census: 14 in 68 (2 in 68 ★), 0 finer (10/14). NGC ID# 28L4, PCGS# 9346

1939-D Oregon Trail Half, MS68
None Numerically Finer at PCGS or NGC

3929 1939-D Oregon MS68 PCGS. An immensely appealing representative of this popular commemorative, this 1939-D Oregon Trail half dollar displays rich, satiny luster and beautiful iridescent toning in shades of ice-blue, olive-gold, and pale amber. The strike is crisp, save for the very rear upright of the wagon, which is minimally soft, and the surfaces are seemingly flawless. Population: 23 in 68 (3 in 68+), 0 finer (10/14). NGC ID# 28LA, PCGS# 9353

1915-S Panama-Pacific Half Dollar, MS67
Ex: Eliasberg

3930 1915-S Panama-Pacific MS67 NGC. Ex: Eliasberg. The 1915-S Panama-Pacific half dollars were produced in large numbers, but few survivors can match the technical quality and eye appeal of the present coin. This delightful Superb Gem offers well-detailed design elements and vibrant mint luster under shades of pink and golden-brown toning. Census: 3 in 67 (1 in 67 ★), 0 finer (10/14). NGC ID# 26H7, PCGS# 9357

1927 Vermont Sesquicentennial Half
Attractive Superb Gem Example

3931 1927 Vermont MS67 PCGS. CAC. An extremely well-executed example of the highest-relief design of the entire commemorative series, unmarked and attractively toned in iridescent "candy" colors: lime-green, lemon-yellow, pink, lavender, and orange. The mint luster is outstanding. The Vermont commemorative celebrates the turning-point Battle of Bennington, with the idealized portrait of Ira Allen (brother to Ethan Allen, the gunsmith leader of the Green Mountain Boys) and with a catamount pictured on the reverse, although the depiction resembles a mountain lion more than the true Vermont catamount, which is the short-tailed Canada lynx. Population: 32 in 67 (2 in 67+), 1 finer (10/14). NGC ID# 28M6, PCGS# 9401

1946-D Booker T. Washington Half
Vividly Toned Premium Gem

3932 1946-D Booker T. Washington MS66 PCGS. CAC. A mintage of 50,000 pieces makes the 1946-D one of the more obtainable issues in the Booker T. Washington commemorative half series, excellent for type representation. This Premium Gem example displays rich, blended hues of amber, crimson, and olive-gold over much of the reverse and around the obverse margins, with mottled lavender-gray toning on the remainder of each side. The strike is sharp, and the preservation is excellent. PCGS has encapsulated 47 numerically finer representatives (10/14). NGC ID# 28M8, PCGS# 9405

COMMEMORATIVE GOLD

1915-S Panama-Pacific Quarter Eagle
Radiant Superb Gem Example

3933 1915-S Panama-Pacific Quarter Eagle MS67 NGC. Examples of this popular Panama-Pacific commemorative were generally well cared for following their issuance, with many Gem and Premium Gem representatives known today. At the MS67 grade level, however, scarcity prevails, and this issue is downright difficult to acquire. The present example shows beautiful, frosty golden luster and sharp design elements. A must-have coin for the advanced collector of classic commemorative gold issues, with none certified numerically finer (10/14). NGC ID# 26HK, PCGS# 7450

1995-W Silver Eagle, PR70 Ultra Cameo
The Key to the Series

1850 Moffat & Co Five Dollar, MS64
K-7a Large Eagle Reverse
Likely the Third-Finest Known

3934 **1995-W Silver Eagle PR70 Ultra Cameo NGC.** Every series has its key date, even the Silver Eagle bullion coins. The 1995-W proof Silver Eagle was only distributed as part of the special American Eagle bullion program 10th anniversary proof sets, for which a collector had to shell out some $999. The rather high initial cost of these sets likely had a dampening affect on the number sold, which ended up totaling only 30,125 sets. This low figure was by extension the entire production total for the proof 1995-W Silver Eagle, making this issue the king of Silver Eagles.

This Ultra Cameo example is tied for the finest known, showing bold white-on-black contrast and perfect preservation. A must-have item for the advanced collector of American Silver Eagles. NGC ID# 28WZ, PCGS# 9887

3935 **1850 Large Eagle Moffat & Co. Five Dollar MS64 NGC. K-7a, R.4.** Brilliant and lustrous, this early Gold Rush issue is a notable rarity for both its near-Gem grade and its historic private maker, Moffat & Company. John L. Moffat was a pioneering San Francisco smelter and assayer, the senior member of a company that included Joseph R. Curtis, Philo H. Perry, and Samuel H. Ward. Originally striking gold ingots, Moffat & Co. branched out into minting circular coins in 1849 and soon became perhaps the most important private issuer of California gold coinage. Eventually, Moffat & Co. entered into a quasi-partnership with the U.S. Assay Office and was awarded a coining contract.

The 1850 Moffat fives were strictly a private issue, struck with both small eagle and large eagle motifs. They circulated "at par," while other private issues often were taken only at a discount. Somewhat crudely engraved, the Large Eagle reverse on this coin shows a prominent die break at the denomination. The coin is amazingly lustrous, smooth, and semireflective, with attractive yellow-gold coloration and a mere handful of insignificant marks scattered across the surfaces. Listed on page 384 of the 2015 *Guide Book*. *Current* PCGS and NGC population reports show just three finer examples, although one of those is a crossover duplication from NGC to PCGS. NGC Census: 1 in 64, 2 finer (10/14). PCGS# 10243

1852 Assay Office Fifty Dollar, MS64
900 Thous., K-14, Ex: Zabriskie
Tied for Finest Certified

3936 **1852 Assay Office Fifty Dollar, 900 Thous. MS64 PCGS Secure. CAC. K-14, High R.5.** The firm of Moffat & Co. was dissolved on February 14, 1852, when John Little Moffat sold his interest to his three partners, Joseph R. Curtis, Philo H. Perry, and Samuel H. Ward. The remaining partners immediately established their new firm as the United States Assay Office of Gold and continued the federal contract to issue gold coinage in California. Augustus Humbert remained in his position as United States Assayer, and Customs Collector T. Butler King was authorized by Secretary of the Treasury Thomas Corwin to accept the firm's coins for customs payments. The summer passed uneventfully, but an economic bombshell was dropped when a federal law prohibiting the acceptance of gold coins under .900 fineness for customs dues was passed on August 31, 1852. Since the U.S. Assay Office coins were only .880, .884, and .887 fine, this virtually deprived the region of all legal tender currency.

Although the Assay Office coins were of lesser fineness than their federal counterparts, they compensated by being heavier. The intrinsic value of the coins met, or even exceeded, their face value, but Congress feared that the lesser fineness might damage the credibility of the United States if they were used in international trade. The reaction of the people of California to this destructive policy was outlined in an article in the *National Intelligencer* on September 14, 1852:

> "Perhaps a more unnecessarily severe and wanton injury has never been committed upon an entire community by the National Legislature, than this enactment, comprised in two lines, has inflicted upon the people of California."

In this emergency situation, local merchants and businessmen petitioned Curtis, Perry, and Ward to issue coins of the new fineness, which Customs Collector King took it upon himself to accept for customs payments. The Assay Office complied, issuing coins of the new fineness in several denominations, with most of the gold coming from the lesser fineness coins which were turned in for recoinage. A total of 13,800 fifty dollar slugs of the K-14 variety were issued in January 1853, followed by 10,000 more in February 1853, all bearing the old 1852 date and the new fineness 900 THOUS. on the ribbon. The coins were accepted by King and circulated widely in the channels of commerce, both in California and abroad, until the opening of the San Francisco Mint in 1854 gave the people of California a dependable federally sanctioned medium of exchange.

The present coin is the only MS64 at PCGS. It is likely that the coin was preserved by U.S. Assayer Augustus Humbert himself at the time of issue, although this cannot be proven with absolute certainty. The coin has certainly never been in circulation, and Humbert is the most likely candidate for its preservation. Humbert kept an extensive collection of private gold coinage until his death, when his coins passed to his brother, Pierre. Pierre, in turn, retained his brother's collection until his death in 1901, at which time Captain Andrew C. Zabriskie was able to purchase as much of the collection as he desired from the executors. Zabriskie was probably the biggest collector of Territorial gold in the early 20th century, and this coin made its first auction appearance in lot 360 of Henry Chapman's catalog of his collection, which was sold on June 3 and 4, 1909:

> "1852 $50. Defiant eagle to left, head turned to right, a U.S. shield which rests on rocks, and three arrows in right talon, while from the base of right wing starts a ribband inscribed LIBERTY and passing on through the eagle's beak, terminates in right field, around UNITED STATES OF AMERICA FIFTY DOLLS. above on scroll 900 THOUS this central device enclosed in a beaded circle, outside of which and following the octagon shape of the coin is UNITED STATES ASSAY OFFICE OF GOLD SAN FRANCISCO CALIFORNIA 1852. R. Engine turned. Edge, milled. Octagonal. Extremely fine. Sharp impression. Very rare. See plate."

The lot realized $220 to an unknown buyer. We have not been able to trace its history over the next several decades, so it is likely it found a home in one of the great early 20th century collections, like those of Colonel James W. Ellsworth or Virgil Brand, that were later mainly dispersed through undocumented private transactions. The coin finally surfaced again in lot 820 of the Baltimore Auction (Superior, 7/1993), where it realized $50,000.

This remarkable Choice example exhibits much sharper detail than is usually seen on this issue, with all letters in the legend plainly legible and fine definition on the eagle's feathers. These large gold coins are typically found with excessive bagmarks, but this piece shows only minor signs of contact in the fields, and displays none of the large edge bumps that often plague this issue. The most remarkable visual characteristic of this coin is its vibrant mint luster, which radiates intensely from both sides, with a few hints of prooflike reflectivity in selected areas. The vivid orange-gold surfaces add to the extraordinary eye appeal. This coin combines the highest available technical quality and eye appeal with unmatched historic interest and an illustrious pedigree. There is simply no comparable example for the finest collection of Territorial gold. Listed on page 387 of the 2015 *Guide Book*. Population: 1 in 64, 0 finer (10/14).

Ex: Possibly Augustus Humbert; Humbert Estate; Captain Andrew C. Zabriskie; Zabriskie Collection (Henry Chapman, 6/1909), lot 360; unknown intermediaries; Baltimore Auction (Superior, 7/1993), lot 820. PCGS# 10019

1852 Assay Office Ten Dollar, K-12a
AU Sharpness

3937 **1852 Assay Office Ten Dollar — Improperly Cleaned — NGC Details. AU. K-12a, R.4.** A minimally abraded green-gold and apricot representative of this scarce variety, among the first struck by the U.S. Assay Office after Moffat's exit. The fletchings display wear but the wings remain sharply defined. Mildly subdued by a wipe, with hairlines noted on the obverse rim. Listed on page 387 of the 2015 *Guide Book*. PCGS# 10001

1852 K-12a Assay Office Ten Dollar, AU50
884 Thous, Attractive Example

3938 **1852 Assay Office Ten Dollar AU50 PCGS. CAC. K-12a, R.5.** Faint beads on the reverse rim. This issue was struck during the early days of the United States Assay Office of Gold, when the office transitioned from a contractual agreement with Moffat & Company to a similar relationship with the firm (and former Moffat assistants) Curtis, Perry & Ward. An acute shortage of lower denomination circulating gold coins was temporarily relieved by these .884 fine pieces, which were struck in ten dollar and twenty dollar denominations. Naturally alloyed with silver, the issue did not conform to the required .900 fineness specified by law, because the Assay Office lacked the required copper and parting acids to prepare the correct composition. Rather, the weight was adjusted to compensate for the sub-fineness.

Most Assay Office pieces exhibit problems of one kind or another, but this example is both untroubled and attractive, as confirmed by the CAC approval. The green-gold patina displays orange accents over lightly abraded surfaces. Strong feather details remain on the eagle's breast, with minor weakness of the shield and arrows. Listed on page 387 of the 2015 *Guide Book*. PCGS# 10001

1850 Baldwin Five Dollar, K-2, AU53
Important Gold Rush Coiner

3939 **1850 Baldwin Five Dollar AU53 PCGS. K-2, R.5.** A lightly circulated green-gold example from the famous early Gold Rush coiner. The strike is even and the surfaces display no more than the expected number of small to moderate marks. An intermediate die state with a break at star 12 but without a break above star 9. The blundered reverse with the second A in CALIFORNIA entered over an inverted V. George Baldwin and Thomas Holman were the principals of Baldwin & Co., a firm dissolved promptly after it was discovered that their output was underweight. Baldwin coins were plentiful in San Francisco in their day, but most were melted following the firm's repudiation. K-2 is rare, yet the most available Baldwin variety and is often selected to represent the maker within pioneer gold type sets. Listed on page 391 of the 2015 *Guide Book*. Population: 3 in 53, 8 finer (10/14). PCGS# 10025

1855 Wass, Molitor Fifty, K-9, XF Details
Popular Round Private Gold Issue

1849 Mormon Five Dollar, K-2, XF45
Rare, Heavily Melted First-Year issue

3940 1855 Wass Molitor Fifty Dollar — Damaged — NGC Details. XF. K-9, R.5. Wass, Molitor & Co. was mainly an assaying firm with a reputation for strict honesty and scrupulous quality control. The firm was petitioned to issue private gold coinage on several occasions because the region had no dependable medium of exchange to service the booming economy. The California State Legislature forbade the issuance of paper money in the area, so the large fifty dollar coins issued by Wass, Molitor & Co. in 1855 were especially popular for use in settling large transactions.

This orange-gold specimen displays XF sharpness on the design elements, but the surfaces show extensive porosity and the usual number of abrasions for a large gold coin. Traces of original mint luster remain intact.

3941 1849 Mormon Five Dollar XF45 PCGS Secure. K-2, R.5. The Mormon gold five dollar coins were the longest-lived of the four denominations they struck, as examples were struck in 1849, 1850, and again in 1860 with a revised design. The other three denominations — quarter eagle, eagle, and double eagle — are known only with the 1849 date. The early Mormon gold was discredited as being underweight in assays as early as mid-January 1850, along with the private gold coins issued by the Pacific Co. Determined to be underweight by as much as 20 percent, the Mormon gold coinage circulated in Utah, but in California it was either refuse outright or else accepted only at very high discounts from par value. For a coin graded Choice XF, this piece radiates considerable luster underneath yellow-gold surfaces that show mostly extensive field chatter but no singular marks, save for one tiny planchet indent to the right of the bishop's miter. Listed on page Population: 24 in 45, 30 finer (10/14). PCGS# 10262

1860 Clark, Gruber & Co Five Dollar
Choice AU, Kagin-2

3942 **1860 Clark, Gruber & Co. Five Dollar AU55 NGC. K-2, R.4.** A lightly abraded sun-gold example. The wings and borders are well struck although the high relief portrait shows softness on the curls near the ear. Unlike its ten and twenty dollar cousins, the five dollar Clark, Gruber merely imitates Federal types. The private coiner's operations were purchased by the U.S. Treasury, which operated the facility as an assay office before its eventual replacement by the Denver Mint. Listed on page 398 of the 2015 *Guide Book*. PCGS# 10136

1861 Clark, Gruber & Company Ten Dollar, AU50
K-7, Attractive and Scarce Example

3943 **1861 Clark, Gruber & Co. Ten Dollar AU50 PCGS. K-7, R.4.** Struck by the most prominent of the Colorado Gold Rush banking and assaying companies, this piece displays very decent striking quality for a privately-issued coin, with some softness apparent on the design's high points. The green-gold surfaces display wispy hairlines in the fields and remnants of reddish mint luster that cling to some of the peripheral devices. Listed on page 399 of the 2015 *Guide Book*. Population: 18 in 50, 56 finer (10/14). PCGS# 10141

1861 Clark, Gruber & Co. Twenty, MS61 Brown
Copper Die Trial, K-12c

3944 **1861 Clark, Gruber $20 Copper Die Trial MS61 Brown NGC. K-12c, R.6.** This copper pattern represents the adopted design for the 1861 Clark, Gruber & Co. twenty dollar gold piece with a reeded edge and shows the usual recutting of the date and the N in TWENTY. The V in DENVER was recut over an errant N. This attractive Mint State specimen offers well-detailed design elements and lightly marked chocolate-brown surfaces. Census: 3 in 61, 4 finer (10/14). PCGS# 10153

CALIFORNIA FRACTIONAL GOLD

1863 Liberty Octagonal 25 Cents, BG-733, MS61
One of Only Five Examples Known

3945 **1863 Liberty Octagonal 25 Cents, BG-733, High R.7, MS61 NGC.** An extremely rare variety. Breen-Gillio suggests that there are only five known examples, and one of those is in the Smithsonian. This piece is typically struck for the type and variety, with somewhat flat strike definition. The light green-gold surfaces are a trifle subdued, but are unmarked on both sides. Slight purple-rose color appears on the lower reverse, the result of an imperfect alloy mixture. Census: 1 in 61, 0 finer (10/14). PCGS# 10560

1874 Octagonal Half Dollar, MS63
Excessively Rare BG-944A Variety

3946 **1874 Indian Octagonal 50 Cents, BG-944A, Low R.8, MS63 PCGS.** An extremely rare gold half dollar variety, made by Christopher Ferdinand Mohrig of San Francisco. A die line connecting the 7 and 4 in the date, as well as numerous cracks and lines on the face identify this die pair. Likely no more than three or four examples are known. This variety was discovered by Richard Montgomery with PCGS in 1994. The present example is well-preserved, with deeply prooflike fields and well brought up motifs. Bright yellow-gold color engulfs each side. Population: 2 in 63, 0 finer (10/14). PCGS# 10825

1881 Octagonal Half Dollar, BG-956
MS67 Deep Prooflike
The Single Finest Certified

3947 **1881 Octagonal 50 Cents, BG-956, High R.4, MS67 Deep Prooflike NGC.** State II. A scarce octagonal half dollar variety, made by Christopher Ferdinand Mohrig in San Francisco. The strike is well-executed, save for the hair curls immediately behind the ear, which are always weak on this variety. Bright yellow-gold surfaces deliver full cameo contrast and showcase exceptional preservation. Struck with a 90 degree die rotation. This piece ranks as the sole finest certified of the variety (10/14). PCGS# 910814

1871 Liberty Octagonal Dollar
BG-1109 MS66 Deep Prooflike
Remarkably Eye-Appealing Example

3948 **1871 Liberty Octagonal Dollar, BG-1109, Low R.4, MS66 Deep Prooflike NGC.** An astonishing example of this scarce octagonal dollar variety that is well-struck, with rich yellow-gold toning and glassy, deeply-mirrored fields. Both sides are remarkably preserved and distraction-free, save for hints of scattered die rust. In terms of sheer eye appeal, this is likely the finest-known example of this issue. PCGS# 710920

COINS OF HAWAII

1883 Hawaii Half Dollar, PR63
Extremely Rare and Reflective

3949 **1883 Hawaii Half Dollar PR63 PCGS Secure.** Ex: Forsythe Collection. This Select proof PCGS-certified 1883 Hawaii half dollar is an extremely rare and important item for the collector of Hawaiian coinage. Reliable references give the proof mintage of the silver dime, quarter, half dollar, and dollar at just 26 pieces each in proof sets, along with 20 examples of the one-eighth dollar pattern, a coin that was replaced with the dime and never saw regular production. The present Select proof half dollar retains considerable reflectivity throughout each side, underneath light layers of pinkish-gold and pastel-blue patina. A few contact marks and light field hairlines determine the grade, but this is a coin of noteworthy rarity and good eye appeal. Population: 3 in 63, 1 finer (10/14). PCGS# 10993

1883 Hawaii Dollar
Attractively Toned, Near-Gem Kalakaua Issue

3950 **1883 Hawaii Dollar MS64 NGC. CAC.** An attractive near-Gem example of the King Kalakaua I dollar, designed by Charles Barber and struck at the San Francisco Mint. The progressive King Kalakaua sought to create a stable form of currency for the island chain after taking power. When Hawaii became a U.S. territory in 1900, the coins' legal tender status was revoked. Most were withdrawn and melted (especially the dollar, with its high silver content).

This example displays lovely forest-green toning with orange-gold and royal-blue accents. Mint luster gleams beneath the toning. Fully struck and well-preserved, the coin shows only a few tiny abrasions on the smooth, lustrous fields and motifs. The eye appeal of the CAC-approved dollar is excellent. Certified in a prior generation holder. Census: 14 in 64, 19 finer (10/14). PCGS# 10995

PATTERNS
1870 Standard Silver Half in Copper
PR64 Red and Brown, Judd-990

3951 **1870 Standard Silver Half Dollar, Judd-990, Pollock-1119, High R.7, PR64 Red and Brown PCGS. CAC.** Standard Silver design. Liberty faces right wearing a headband with a single star, a scroll below, and UNITED STATES OF AMERICA above. The reverse is similar to that used in 1869 with 50 CENTS in the center, surrounded by a wreath of oak and laurel, with 1870 below and STANDARD SILVER above. Struck in copper with a plain edge. This fully struck and unabraded specimen retains ample orange-gold, especially on the obverse, while the borders exhibit shades of aquamarine and rose-red at the borders. A few specks of carbon appear on each side. PCGS# 71236

Golden-Tinged, Reflective Gem Proof
1871 Indian Princess Quarter, Judd-1099
Four or Five Known

3952 **1871 Quarter Dollar, Judd-1099, Pollock-1235, High R.7, PR65 NGC. CAC.** The obverse bears the seated Indian Princess design of James B. Longacre, with 13 stars around the rim. The reverse is the normal With Motto quarter dollar dies. Struck in silver with a reeded edge. This is a lovely, problem-free, well-contrasted Gem example with a suggestion of gold toning over silver-white surfaces. When we cataloged the Lemus-Queller Collection we provided a roster of four pieces known to us. This may or may not be a fifth specimen, but in any case this is an extremely rare pattern. The Lemus-Queller piece was a PR64 NGC example that brought $5,750 (FUN Signature, Heritage, 1/2009, lot 1799). PCGS# 61358

1879 Washlady Quarter, PR66 Red and Brown
Struck in Copper, Judd-1591

3953 **1879 Washlady Quarter Dollar, Judd-1591, Pollock-1784, Low R.7, PR66 Red and Brown PCGS.** The Society Lady, better-known as the Washlady, here in the quarter denomination. Charles Barber's obverse depicts a Liberty head with her hair bound up behind. IN GOD WE TRUST appears in small letters at the upper border with the date below and stars seven left, six right. An eagle on the reverse has wings displayed, holding an olive branch and three arrows in the dexter and sinister claws, respectively, with the wings passing in front of both. UNITED STATES OF AMERICA and E PLURIBUS UNUM are at the upper border with QUAR. DOLLAR below. Struck in copper with a reeded edge. The Washlady patterns are admired far more today than they were in the late 19th century; the pejorative moniker dates to the sale of the New York Coin & Stamp sale of Doughty Collection in April 1891, the term likely given by David Proskey. Perhaps 12 to 15 of the copper pieces survive today. This glowing Premium Gem Red and Brown proof offers sunset-orange and violet-red fields on each side that contrast nicely with the deeper red-brown devices. A few scattered lilac flecks appear throughout, but there are no mentionable distractions, and the eye appeal is excellent. This piece is the sole finest of just five examples certified by PCGS (10/14). *Ex: Purchased from Stanley Kesselman, August 30, 1971; Harry W. Bass, Jr. Research Foundation.* PCGS# 71968

1883 Liberty Head Five Cents in Pure Nickel
Judd-1704, Pollock-1908, PR67 Ultra Cameo

3954 **1883 Liberty Head Five Cents, Judd-1704, Pollock-1908, Low R.6, PR67 Ultra Cameo NGC.** The obverse is similar in design to the Liberty nickel adopted this year, except the stars are replaced with the legend UNITED STATES OF AMERICA. The reverse has a central inscription that reads PURE NICKEL, surrounded by a wreath of cotton and corn. FIVE CENTS is separated above and below with seven stars left and six right. Struck in pure nickel with a plain edge, which makes examples magnetic and difficult to strike properly. Only a few more than a dozen examples are known, making any representative a rare and important acquisition. This deeply contrasted silvery-gray piece is tied with just one other as the finest certified at NGC (10/14). The design elements are fully brought up, devoid of contact marks or other flaws. A highly appealing example of this rare pattern. PCGS# 962120

GSA DOLLARS

1879-CC Silver Dollar, MS63
Minimally Toned Example

3955 **1879-CC GSA MS63 NGC.** A splash of orange-gold toning on the reverse adds personality to this otherwise brilliant-white, Normal CC (Clear CC) Select Uncirculated dollar. The fields appear nearly unmarked and semiprooflike, while the motifs show numerous marks across both Liberty's portrait and the eagle's high points — the result of coin-to-coin contact during bag transport and storage. Housed in its original GSA holder with the blue NGC hologram band. There is no box or certificate included. PCGS# 518848

1879-CC GSA Dollar, MS64
Challenging Carson City Issue

3956 **1879-CC GSA MS64 NGC.** Large Normal Mintmark. Conceivably, the Normal Mintmark (also called the Perfect CC or Clear CC) variant is scarcer than the Capped Die overmintmark variety, which shows a large CC repunched over a crudely effaced small CC. The population reports are of no help clarifying how many of each mintmark variety exist, because reporting them separately is a fairly recent occurrence.

This untoned, heavily frosted near-Gem example is less abraded in the fields than it is on the central motifs. Both Liberty's portrait and the eagle show numerous small marks. The strike is bold for he issue, however, and bright luster visits the semiprooflike surfaces. NGC has seen just eight GSA Hoard coins in numerically finer condition from nearly 600 pieces certified (10/14). Band-certified in the black GSA holder of issue and offered alone (no box or paperwork). PCGS# 518848

1881-CC Morgan Dollar
Lightly Toned Superb Gem
GSA-Holdered With Frosty Silver Luster

1884-CC Morgan Dollar, MS67
Attractively Toned GSA Hoard Coin

3957 1881-CC GSA MS67 NGC. A low mintage of 296,000 pieces — even less than the mintage for the rare 1889-CC issue — were struck at Carson City in 1881. Yet the issue is one of the most easily obtained dollars in high Mint State grades in the CC series. In truth, issue is rare only in worn grades, which is one of the numismatic quirks that amaze and amuse collectors of Carson City dollars.

Few pieces of the original mintage went into circulation at all, and most were stored. As late as 1964 nearly 50% of the mintage remained in government hands, finally to be issued as part of the GSA releases. Remarkably, this coin survived all the years of shifting and storage in nearly pristine, Superb Gem condition. Only a few minuscule luster grazes on the eagle mark the surfaces, and they are minor in nature and non-distracting. A slight glint of orange toning between 6 and 9 o'clock on the obverse accents the creamy-white surfaces of this exceptional, boldly struck dollar.

The coin is band-certified in the black GSA holder of issue and offered without its packaging (no box or paperwork). NGC has certified only 26 1881-CC dollars as MS67 in GSA holders — with none finer — from more than 8,000 such pieces certified (10/14). PCGS# 518863

3958 1884-CC GSA MS67 NGC. The GSA Hoard releases introduced nearly a million more 1884-CC coins into the numismatic marketplace, or nearly 85% of the original mintage. Such a glut would seemingly cause the value to plummet, but instead it introduced a whole new generation of Morgan dollar enthusiasts to the hobby.

As with the 1881-CC and 1885-CC issues, Mint State coins are by far more available than worn, circulated ones. Even so, the 1884-CC issue is conditionally rare in Superb Gem condition because most of the GSA Hoard coins were heavily marked by transport and years of storage and counting. This attractively toned example displays gunmetal-blue bands alternating with reddish-orange shades on the obverse, with a complementary crescent of color on the reverse. A sharp, nearly-full strike supports the lofty grade. NGC has seen just one numerically finer coin, GSA Hoard or otherwise (10/14). Housed in its original GSA holder, but no box or certificate accompanies the coin. PCGS# 518872

1945 New York Assay Office Gold Ingot
26.94 Ounces, 999.8 Fine Gold

3959 **1945 New York Assay Office Gold Ingot. 26.94 Ounces.** The assay office at New York City was opened in 1854, and continued operations until 1982. Mr. Sigmund Solomon (1887-1948) was the assayer in charge when this ingot was manufactured in 1945. Solomon entered the post in 1936, and remained there until his death. All official United States Assay Offices operated under the U.S. Mint.

Representative of the countless gold ingots produced there over the years is this 26.94 ounce ingot of 999.8 fine gold. The face of the ingot contains the round date-stamped hallmark of the U.S. Assay Office in New York, along with the fineness. The right side has the weight, and control numbers 288 and 196 are punched in the top and bottom sides, respectively. Approximate measurements are 36 mm. x 55 mm. x 21 mm. Prior to this offering, we have auctioned 18 New York Assay Office gold ingots dated between 1930 and 1969, and weighing between 5.34 ounces and 28.70 ounces.

End of Session Two

SESSION THREE

TWENTY CENT PIECES

3960 **1875-CC AU55 ANACS. BF-2, R.1.** Lavender, forest-green, and tobacco-brown toning graces the borders of this lightly abraded and partly lustrous Carson City type coin. The eagle's breast and Liberty's knee indicate a cursory stint in Old West commerce. NGC ID# 23R6, PCGS# 5297

3961 **1875-CC AU55 ANACS. BF-2, R.1.** This lustrous Carson City type coin approaches Mint State, although the eagle's breast and the crest of the left (facing) wing are incompletely brought up. Minimally abraded for the designated grade. Richly toned sea-green with blushes of plum-red on the obverse. NGC ID# 23R6, PCGS# 5297

3962 **1875-CC — Artificial Toning — NGC Details. Unc. BF-2, R.1.** Only two twenty-cent issues emerged from the mint facility in Carson City, and this one is by far the more available of the two. This piece is sharply struck throughout, save for a touch of softness on the eagle's head and left (facing) wing. The dramatic turquoise-blue toning over the obverse has been deemed artificial by NGC.

3963 **1875-CC MS62 PCGS. BF-2, R.1.** Medium wheat-gold toning visits the obverse of this lustrous Carson City type coin. The reverse is nearly brilliant. A good strike except on the crest of the left (facing) wing. Lustrous and surprisingly void of marks. NGC ID# 23R6, PCGS# 5297

1875-S Twenty Cent Piece, MS65
Lustrous and Attractively Toned

3964 **1875-S MS65 PCGS. CAC.** Mint luster is thick and a dominant feature on this odd-denomination type coin, even though each side is covered in layers of multicolored toning. The strike is strong overall, the only area of weakness localized to the upper left (facing) wing of the eagle. NGC ID# 23R7, PCGS# 5298

3965 **1876 MS63 NGC. CAC. BF-2, R.2.** Golden-brown borders encompass pearl-gray centers. A highly lustrous and sharply struck representative. Only 14,400 pieces were issued, although Philadelphia dealers likely secured a few hundred Uncirculated coins. NGC ID# 23R8, PCGS# 5299

EARLY QUARTERS

3966 **1804 B-1, R.3 — Graffiti — ANACS. AG3 Details.** Tompkins Die State 2/2, both sides clashed. Each side displays a pair of intersecting pinscratches, perhaps test marks entered by a mid-19th century owner unfamiliar with the Heraldic Eagle design. The obverse margin has occasional minor abrasions. The date is bold, the silver-white types are well outlined, and the fields are charcoal-gray. AMERICA and UNITED are well-worn. PCGS# 38921

1806 B-3 Quarter, XF45
Ex: Jules Reiver

3967 **1806 B-3, R.1, XF45 NGC.** Ex: Jules Reiver Collection. Tompkins Reverse Die State 4. The I and T in LIBERTY are broken, and the 5 in the denomination is clear of all devices. The date is clashed within ATES, and a die crack forms from the rim to the first S in STATES. The surfaces are bright and lustrous, displaying silver-gray and traces of peripheral gold. The irregular strike is typical of the issue, showing weakness on Liberty's curls and the eagle and stars. A small rim nick appears over the E of UNITED. Great eye appeal and quality for the grade.
Ex: Julian Leidman (3/1987); Jules Reiver Collection (Heritage, 1/2006), lot 22317. PCGS# 38929

BUST QUARTERS

3968 **1819 Large 9, B-2, R.3, XF40 PCGS.** Delicate olive-green and cream-gray toning adorns this unblemished XF Bust quarter. Traces of luster emerge from the plumage, legends, and other design elements. PCGS# 38957

3969 **1834 O Over F in OF, B-1, FS-901, R.1, MS61 NGC.** OF is obviously repunched, as is the first A in AMERICA and the eagle's left (facing) claw. This nicely struck and moderately abraded example has golden-brown and navy-blue peripheral patina. PCGS# 38992

3970 **1834 B-3, R.3, MS62 NGC.** A dove-gray representative that boasts a sharp strike and only unimportant marks. Moderately subdued but the eye appeal is good. Die cracks above the eagle and through the top of the cap identify the Browning marriage. PCGS# 38994

3971 **1835 B-2, R.2, AU55 PCGS. CAC.** A charming golden-brown and dove-gray example. Only briefly circulated and free from consequential contact. Luster fills the legends, plumage, and curls. Clashed shield lines beneath Liberty's ear indicate a later die state. PCGS# 38998

3972 **1838 B-1, R.1, AU55 PCGS.** The final Capped Bust quarter die variety is ideal for type purposes, as it is collectible and often encountered with a sharp strike on the motifs. The present pearl-gray example displays substantial luster and is smooth except for an obverse rim mark near star 6. PCGS# 39015

SEATED QUARTERS

3973 1838 No Drapery AU58 PCGS. Briggs 1-A. Larry Briggs suggests the head, stars, and obverse dentils are poorly struck for the first-year No Drapery Philadelphia issue, but all of those areas are sharp on this frosty and lustrous near-Mint coin. LIBERTY is bold on the scroll. With only glimpses of silver-gray patina, the virtually brilliant surfaces are exceptionally well produced, attractive, and free of abrasions. Population: 14 in 58, 70 finer (11/14). NGC ID# 23SE, PCGS# 5391

3974 1841-O MS63 NGC. Briggs 2-C. A heavily die-doubled obverse quickly identifies this variety, with the spread most easily seen on the shield, LIBERTY, and the stars. On the reverse, all vertical shield lines extend boldly into the the horizontal lines and below into the eagle's feathers. As a date the 1841-O quarter is seldom seen with original coloration, and is especially challenging in Mint State. This example displays well-detailed design elements, with satiny luster illuminating natural olive-gray toning. Census: 11 in 63, 6 finer (10/14). NGC ID# 23SL, PCGS# 5400

3975 1843-O Large O, FS-501, VF20 PCGS. This variety could very well be called Huge O, as the mintmark is quite prominent, likely intended for an 1843-O half dollar instead. The cream-gray and charcoal surfaces are void of evident marks. Population: 2 in 20, 9 finer (10/14). PCGS# 395927

1844-O Seated Quarter, MS63
Recut Date, Extra Digits in Dentils

3976 1844-O MS63 PCGS. Briggs 1-A. This New Orleans quarter is both conditionally rare and numismatically intriguing. The date is noticeably recut north, with evidence of the underdigits most visible at the lower sides of the crosslets. Extra digits — apparently, a 1 and an 8 — are visible in the dentils. The fields show areas of prooflikeness, with deep teal and red-gold toning, interspersed with shades of dark-charcoal gray. The coin is boldly struck except for the star centers on either side of Liberty's head. Rare in this Select Uncirculated condition. Population: 6 in 63, 5 finer (10/14). NGC ID# 23SU, PCGS# 5407

1847-O Quarter, Conditionally Rare AU53

3977 1847-O AU53 PCGS. Briggs 1-A. When Larry Briggs published his encyclopedic reference in 1991, he was aware of only one Uncirculated example of this challenging New Orleans issue, and wrote "quite rare in grades XF/AU." Current population reports show only 10 Mint State coins at PCGS and NGC combined, with less than 30 About Uncirculated examples. The present coin is lightly toned with amber-gold accents. Weakness at Liberty's head and the adjacent stars is typical of the issue. An appealing example, seldom available. Population: 4 in 53, 10 finer (10/14). NGC ID# 23SY, PCGS# 5411

1849-O Seated Quarter, VF30
Unknown Mintage, Rare

3978 1849-O VF30 NGC. Briggs 1-A. The mintage is unknown for this New Orleans date and it is assumed to be included in the production of the 1850-O quarters. Based on population data, not many 1849-O pieces were struck. Larry Briggs estimates the mintage as 16,000 coins, with few survivors. Areas of reddish-gold luster remain among the stars and legends of this solid VF example, which features an original, deep silver-gray color and sharp details for the grade. Nice, wide rims surround problem-free surfaces. Census: 3 in 30, 22 finer (10/14). NGC ID# 23T3, PCGS# 5414

3979 1849-O — Reverse Repaired — NGC Details. XF. Briggs 1-A. An elusive key-date issue, the 1849-O is widely sought in all grades and conditions. This lightly circulated piece shows pleasing detail and deep gunmetal-gray toning. The upper-left reverse field is noticeably repaired, precluding a numeric grade from NGC. This is an excellent opportunity for the budget-minded collector to acquire a well-detailed example of this rare date.

1852-O Quarter, AU Details
Rare in XF or Finer Grades

3980 1852-O — Improperly Cleaned — NGC Details. AU. Briggs 1-A. Larry Briggs mentions in his reference, "Three or four coins that would normally classify as AU or choice UNC. have a microscopic grainy surface, giving them 'saltwater surface' appearance." This coin matches that description, although the graininess may be exacerbated by cleaning. Even so, the coin is now nicely toned in reddish-gray hues and it retains a large measure of appeal. A rarity despite the net NGC grade.

1853 Arrows and Rays Quarter, MS64
Great Type Representative

3981　**1853 Arrows and Rays MS64 PCGS.** The Briggs reference describes the 119 obverse dies and 120 reverse dies needed to accomplish a substantial mintage of more than 15 million pieces — the second-highest mintage of the long series, exceeded only by the 17.8 million pieces produced in 1876. This lustrous example is boldly struck and lightly toned, with silvery surfaces and golden-gray overtones. A great selection for type. PCGS has seen only 25 submissions in higher numeric grades (10/14). NGC ID# 23U4, PCGS# 5426

3982　**1854-O Huge O, Briggs 1-A, FS-501, VG10 PCGS.** A circulated but problem-free example of the well-known Huge O variety. The mintmark is unusual for its irregular broad outline and high relief. IBERT is bold and the L and Y are partial. PCGS# 395933

3983　**1854-O Huge O, Briggs 1-A, FS-501, Fine 15 NGC.** The elusive variety with the "Yap stone" mintmark, which specialists believe was handcut into the dies. This Choice 15 collector coin retains the rims and all major design elements intact in outline. Most letters in LIBERTY are bold. PCGS# 395933

1854-O Quarter, VF20
FS-501, 'Huge O' Variety

3984　**1854-O Huge O, Briggs 1-A, FS-501, VF20 PCGS.** This intriguing *Guide Book* variety is inherently difficult to find with pleasing eye appeal, as most examples are well-worn and suffer from varying degrees of die fatigue. The present coin is lightly circulated, but retains detail worthy of the VF grade level. Original pewter-gray patina overall yields to deeper toning in the recesses, giving this piece a distinct old-time appearance. An old, faint pinscratch in the right obverse field does not affect the grade assessment from PCGS. PCGS# 395933

1854-O FS-501, Quarter, VF25
'Huge O' Mintmark

3985　**1854-O Huge O, Briggs 1-A, FS-501, VF25 PCGS.** This highly popular *Guide Book* variety is decidedly scarce in all grades, and is rarely seen above the VF level. This example shows soft pewter-gray patina with hints of gold and lavender throughout. Strong detail is present for the grade, making this piece one of the more appealing examples of this variety available in the VF grade range. An important acquisition for the Seated quarter enthusiast. PCGS# 395933

3986　**1867 XF45 PCGS. Briggs 1-A.** Overly aggressive grinding of the obverse die eliminated much of LIBERTY from the scroll on the obverse shield, an instant clue to the business strike status of this coin and others like it. Other motifs are well brought up, however, confirming the Choice XF grade. Luster remains at the margins of this lightly toned, silver-gray coin. Just 20,000 business strikes were issued. Population: 8 in 45, 32 finer (11/14). NGC ID# 23UD, PCGS# 5470

1877-CC Quarter, MS66
Richly Toned

3987　**1877-CC MS66 NGC. Briggs 3-C.** Vibrant frosty mint luster shines through attractive shades of cobalt-blue and golden-lavender toning on the well-preserved surfaces of this spectacular Premium Gem. The design elements are sharp, save for stars 7 and 8, and the eye appeal is outstanding. The 1877-CC is among the most plentiful Carson City issues in the series overall, but pieces achieving the Premium Gem grade level are seldom seen. Census: 12 in 66 (1 in 66+), 6 finer (10/14). NGC ID# 23V6, PCGS# 5505

3988　**1877-S Over Horizontal S, FS-501, MS63 NGC. CAC.** The S mintmark was initially punched into the die horizontally, then corrected. This lustrous representative is brilliant save for a slender arc of golden toning on the lower reverse margin. The reverse is exceptionally unabraded for the Select level, and the obverse is nearly as smooth. NGC ID# 23V7, PCGS# 5507

PROOF SEATED QUARTERS

3989 1866 Motto PR64 PCGS. Sharply struck and richly lustrous, with deep rainbow iridescence on the reverse, and a typical number of small abrasions, for a near-Gem. Population: 27 in 64 (1 in 64+), 12 finer (10/14).
Ex: Dallas Bullet Sale (Heritage, 12/2004), lot 1819. NGC ID# 23WX, PCGS# 5565

3990 1866 Motto PR64 NGC. Briggs 2-B. The proof mintage of 725 pieces was not saved despite the addition of the Motto to the reverse. A single set of dies accomplished entire proof output, characterized by a diagnostic spur on a dentil below the final 6 and a long, well-hidden die line on the obverse shield through the scroll at R. This richly patinated near-Gem proof is fully struck with deep blue and bronze-gold toning. There are no significant marks. Census: 44 in 64 (1 in 64+), 35 finer (11/14). NGC ID# 23WX, PCGS# 5565

1868 Quarter, Toned PR65

3991 1868 PR65 PCGS. Briggs 2-B. The obverse of this Gem proof exhibits full cameo contrast, though the reverse is a bit too deeply toned to qualify for the designation from PCGS. The obverse shows a swath of royal-blue and mint-green toning along the left-hand border, with light champagne and violet over the right-hand portions. The reverse is more deeply toned in blended shades of green-gold, blue, and purple. A sharply struck, eye-appealing representative. Population: 11 in 65 (1 in 65+), 5 finer (10/14). NGC ID# 23WZ, PCGS# 5567

3992 1870 PR64 Cameo PCGS. CAC. Briggs 2-B. The scattering of delicate lines on the obverse are visible under magnification and account for the near-Gem grade, although visually in-hand this frost-white example is attractive without qualification. Boldly contrasted with the mirrored fields, a mere suggestion of pale gold toning touches a few frosted high points and enhances the appeal. A few microscopic marks on the portrait do not distract. Population: 25 in 64 (1 in 64+), 7 finer (11/14). PCGS# 85569

3993 1874 Arrows PR63 PCGS. Briggs 5-D. The obverse, while attractive, is a bit more restrained in color than the vividly toned reverse. A mintage of 700 proofs was well-produced, although Briggs notes weakness at Liberty's head that does not appear on this fully struck coin. The head, star centers, gown lines, and eagle are extremely sharp and the fields deeply reflective. Turquoise and rose hues cover the obverse, while the reverse shows spectacular tones of violet, orange, magenta, and gold. Excellent quality for the Select grade, with only a few wispy lines beneath the obverse toning. NGC ID# 23XS, PCGS# 5575

3994 1877 PR64 PCGS. Briggs 1-B. A deeply mirrored proof with attractive, teal-blue toning at the margins surrounding silver-gold centers. The fully struck devices show a slight degree of mint frost for pleasing contrast with the reflective fields. One or two tiny marks are visible with a glass beneath the lovely patina. Population: 37 in 64, 25 finer (11/14). NGC ID# 23X9, PCGS# 5578

3995 1882 PR64 Cameo PCGS. CAC. This Choice Cameo proof has impressive field-to-device contrast beneath gorgeous rose, violet, sea-green, and blue toning. Population: 19 in 64 (1 in 64+), 34 finer (10/14). PCGS# 85583

1890 Quarter, PR66 Cameo
Delicate Light Golden Toning

3996 1890 PR66 Cameo PCGS. Briggs 3-C. This late-series proof issue is moderately available in the absolute sense, though Cameo examples are seldom seen in any grade. This Premium Gem representative showcases heavily frosted devices set against deeply mirrored fields. A blush of pale champagne toning over each side complements the beautifully preserved surfaces. From a limited mintage of just 590 proofs. Population: 5 in 66, 4 finer (10/14). PCGS# 85591

1891 Seated Quarter, PR67
Two-Sided Patina

3997 1891 PR67 NGC. Beautiful ocean-blue, amber-gold, and autumn-orange prevail on the obverse of this Superb Gem proof, while the reverse offers alternating mint-green and pale blue tinges. Both sides show a bold strike, and no mentionable marks appear on either side. A great-looking example of this last-year Seated quarter issue. NGC ID# 23XP, PCGS# 5592

BARBER QUARTERS

3998 1896-S Fine 12 NGC. This is an appealing mid-grade example of this major key-date issue, with original battleship-gray patina overall and deeper olive-gray color in the border recesses. LIBERTY grows weak on BER, though the inscription is complete, as is required by the Fine grade level. NGC ID# 23Y9, PCGS# 5615

1896-S Quarter Dollar, VF35
Low-Mintage, Key-Date Issue

3999 1896-S VF35 PCGS. The 1896-S Barber quarter, with a low mintage of 188,039 coins, is one of three key dates in the series along with the 1901-S and the 1913-S. This example reveals a coating of gray patina over the obverse with olive accents at the margins, while the reverse shows silver-gray color on the design's high points and mostly forest-green toning in the fields and at the borders. Several shallow marks are noted on the obverse, and a couple more are present on the reverse. NGC ID# 23Y9, PCGS# 5615

4000 1897 MS65 NGC. An exacting strike completes the design elements on this wonderful Gem. White surfaces exhibit full luster, and are devoid of significant marks. Census: 23 in 65, 11 finer (10/14). *Ex: Long Beach Signature (Heritage, 2/2008), lot 395; FUN Signature (Heritage, 1/2009), lot 2468.* NGC ID# 23YA, PCGS# 5616

4001 1897-S AU58 PCGS. The sharply detailed design elements of this impressive near-Mint example show just the slightest touch of high-point friction and the surfaces display prooflike reflectivity throughout, with only minor signs of contact. Population: 6 in 58, 59 finer (11/14). NGC ID# 23YC, PCGS# 5618

4002 1901-S AG3 NGC. A major key date in the series, always in demand. This example is well-circulated, displaying full rims on the obverse, but showing more extensive wear on the reverse. The coin is original, with olive-gray color blending to deeper gunmetal-gray hues in the recesses. No obtrusive abrasions are noted, making this piece highly appealing for the grade. NGC ID# 23YR, PCGS# 5630

4003 1909 MS66 PCGS. The impeccably preserved surfaces of this sharply detailed Premium Gem exhibit dappled shades of lavender-gray, greenish-gold, and amber toning, with vibrant mint luster underneath. Population: 20 in 66 (2 in 66+), 3 finer (11/14). NGC ID# 23ZG, PCGS# 5653

4004 1911 MS66 PCGS. Thick mint frost covers this carefully preserved example. This Premium Gem offers delicately golden surfaces and sharply detailed devices. A few trivial ticks do nothing to affect the eye appeal. Population: 15 in 66, 1 finer (11/14). NGC ID# 23ZN, PCGS# 5659

1913 Quarter Dollar, Well-Struck MS65
A Low-Mintage Issue

4005 1913 MS65 PCGS. CAC. The 1913, with a mintage of just 484,000 pieces, is the lowest-mintage Philadelphia issue in the series and is very scarce in Gem condition. This piece displays glowing golden-gray luster and well-struck design elements, save for the usual softness in the upper-right shield corner and the claws. The surfaces are void of any notable abrasions. Population: 38 in 65 (2 in 65+), 9 finer (10/14). NGC ID# 23ZU, PCGS# 5664

1913 Quarter, MS65
Thick Mint Frost

4006 1913 MS65 PCGS. CAC. The 1913 Barber quarter is arguably the most elusive Philadelphia issue in the series; it is scarce in Gem condition, and genuinely rare any finer. Frosty luster reveals only a few minute disruptions on this example, while the devices are well-defined. Light amber-gold toning graces each side, attesting to the originality of the surfaces. Population: 38 in 65 (2 in 65+), 9 finer (10/14). NGC ID# 23ZU, PCGS# 5664

4007 1915-D MS65 PCGS. Wisps of honey-gold color overlay the light dove-gray patina. A lustrous Gem that has a good strike and a nearly immaculate reverse. The portrait displays faint luster grazes. Certified in a green label holder. *Ex: Baltimore Signature (Heritage, 7/2003), lot 7016, which realized $948.75.* NGC ID# 2423, PCGS# 5671

4008 1916-D MS66 ★ NGC. CAC. A brilliant and flashy high grade quarter whose semiprooflike surfaces are likely the reason this coin secured a Star designation from NGC. The strike is good save for blending near the fletchings. Census: 64 in 66 (2 in 66+, 6 in 66 ★), 14 finer (10/14). NGC ID# 2426, PCGS# 5674

PROOF BARBER QUARTERS

1892 Quarter, Patinated PR66

4009 1892 PR66 PCGS. CAC. Type Two Reverse. Rich cherry-red, jade-green, and peach-gold toning endows this fully struck Premium Gem. Evaluation beneath a loupe fails to locate any detractions. Interest in the new Barber designs led to the highest proof mintage of the type, but the median certified piece grades only PR64. Population: 28 in 66 (1 in 66+), 16 finer (10/14). NGC ID# 2427, PCGS# 5678

4010 1893 PR66 PCGS. Attractive shades of cobalt-blue and lavender-gray toning blanket the pristine surfaces of this delightful Premium Gem. The design elements are sharply detailed and the fields are deeply mirrored. Population: 33 in 66 (1 in 66+), 20 finer (10/14). NGC ID# 2428, PCGS# 5679

4011 1895 PR65 NGC. A needle sharp Gem proof, this deeply mirrored example showcases vivid blue and violet peripheral toning around sun-gold centers. No contact marks are present, and any grade-limiting hairlines are well-hidden by the rich patina. From a mintage of 880 pieces. NGC ID# 242A, PCGS# 5681

4012 1901 PR66 Cameo PCGS. Splendid golden-brown, rose, and sea-green colors endow this typically struck and gorgeously preserved specimen. The head of Liberty is frosty and provides pleasing contrast with the flashy fields. One of a mere 813 proofs struck. Population: 16 in 66 (1 in 66+), 11 finer (10/14).
Ex: Palm Beach Signature (Heritage, 11/2004), lot 3593. PCGS# 85687

4013 1902 PR66 NGC. Iridescent splashes of pink, jade-green, sky-blue, and apricot color the lightly toned surfaces of this Premium Gem proof Barber quarter. A bold strike augments the desirability of this piece. Census: 40 in 66 (1 in 66+, 1 in 66+★), 21 finer (10/14). NGC ID# 242H, PCGS# 5688

4014 1907 PR66 PCGS. Only 575 proof Barber quarters were struck in 1907. This delightful Premium Gem offers well-detailed design elements and well-preserved deeply reflective fields with outstanding eye appeal. Population: 12 in 66, 14 finer (10/14). NGC ID# 242N, PCGS# 5693

4015 1908 PR65 NGC. A tinge of deep violet and russet toning along the right obverse border expands to cover the entire reverse in luminous color, leaving the remaining portion of the obverse brilliant. Satiny devices accent the mirrored fields, and the eagle's right (facing) talons show the only indication of striking deficiency. Census: 32 in 65, 59 finer (10/14). NGC ID# 242P, PCGS# 5694

4016 1912 PR64 PCGS. From a small proof mintage of 700 pieces, this impressive Choice example displays sharply detailed frosty design elements and deeply mirrored fields under shades of champagne-gold and lavender toning. Population: 57 in 64 (1 in 64+), 64 finer (10/14). NGC ID# 242U, PCGS# 5698

1913 Quarter Dollar, PR67+
Eric P. Newman Collection Provenance

4017 1913 PR67+ NGC. Ex: Eric P. Newman Collection. Modest field-motif contrast shows on this high-end Superb Gem. Whispers of gold-brown concentrate at the borders, while Liberty's cap assumes multicolored toning. The design elements are solidly struck and close examination reveals no mentionable marks. From a relatively small mintage of 613 pieces the 1913 proof quarter is notably rare in the higher numerical grades, and this is the sole coin with the NGC Plus designation at the grade level. Census: 16 in 67 (1 in 67+), 5 finer (10/14). NGC ID# 242V, PCGS# 5699

STANDING LIBERTY QUARTERS

4018 1917 Type One MS66 Full Head NGC. The Type One 1917 quarter is known for being well-struck overall, though the present example is particularly sharp. In addition to a bold Full Head and crisp shield lines, the outer edge of the shield is complete over Liberty's bust, the stars are boldly defined, and the leading edge of the eagle's left (facing) wing is minutely detailed. A touch of light golden luster accents the lustrous matte-like surfaces of this Premium Gem type representative. NGC ID# 242Z, PCGS# 5707

4019 1917-D Type One MS65 Full Head PCGS. Two design types were produced of this type in 1917, with approximately four times as many Type Twos struck at the Denver mint compared to the Type Ones. This is a splendid Gem with gleaming satiny luster and mostly-untoned silver-gray surfaces that reveal a slight degree of mottled olive and tan patina near the reverse peripheries. NGC ID# 2432, PCGS# 5709

4020 1917-D Type One MS66 Full Head PCGS. The well-preserved surfaces of this impressive Premium Gem display vibrant mint luster throughout, with highlights of champagne-gold and amber toning. The design elements are sharply detailed and PCGS has graded 22 numerically finer examples (11/14). NGC ID# 2432, PCGS# 5709

1917-S Type One Quarter
Gem Full Head Example

4021 1917-S Type One MS65 Full Head PCGS. CAC. The 1917-S is the most difficult Type One quarter to acquire with Full Head detail (save for the key-date 1916), and is genuinely scarce with such above the Gem grade level. This piece exhibits pale olive-gold toning over each side with the matte-like luster that is characteristic of the Type One issues. The strike is well-executed throughout, save for the leading edge of the eagle's left (facing) wing which is almost always soft on San Francisco issues in this series. Only a few minute ticks in unobtrusive places limit the grade. NGC ID# 2433, PCGS# 5711

1918-S Quarter, MS64 Full Head
Satiny Mint Luster

4022 1918-S MS64 Full Head NGC. Quality control at the San Francisco Mint slipped further in 1918, and the 1918-S quarter is, up to this point, the most challenging S-mint issue with Full Head detail. The present example displays sharp head detail and a bold date, though the shield rivets and the eagle's breast feathers show some of the usual striking deficiency. A suggestion of light golden color precludes full mint brilliance on this piece, while the surface are free of obvious detractions. Census: 56 in 64 (1 in 64+) Full Head, 22 finer (10/14). NGC ID# 2439, PCGS# 5725

1918/7-S Quarter
Sole Overdate of the Series

4023 1918/7-S FS-101 PCGS Genuine. The PCGS number ending in .92 suggests Cleaning as the reason, or perhaps one of the reasons, that PCGS deemed this coin not gradable. In our opinion, this coin has the details of an XF specimen that has been cleaned. Pale golden-gray patina blankets both sides. Some striking deficiency is noted on Liberty's head, the shield, and eagle's breast, as usual, though the overdate feature remains bold. PCGS# 395949

4024 1919-S AU53 PCGS. This pleasing AU53 example exhibits just a trace of wear on the high points of the design elements, and the lightly abraded surfaces retain much of their original mint luster. The 1919-S Standing Liberty quarter is one of the most challenging issues of the series. NGC ID# 243D, PCGS# 5732

1920-D Quarter, MS63 Full Head
Unusually Sharp Throughout

4025 1920-D MS63 Full Head PCGS. The branch mint issues of 1920 are some of the most poorly produced in the entire Standing Liberty quarter series, and are undeniably difficult to locate with Full Head detail, regardless of numeric grade. This example of the Denver issue is an unusually well-struck representative, showing a sharp Full Head and above-average definition on the shield rivets, gown lines, and eagle's feathers. Pale sun-gold toning warms satiny luster on each side, while the underlying surfaces show only minute grazes and ticks. NGC ID# 243F, PCGS# 5737

4026 1921 AU58 PCGS. Well-defined shield lines and rivets attest to the exactness of the strike on this near-Mint key-date quarter. The date numerals are slightly flat, but are clearly defined, and the eagle's feathers are sharply detailed. A trace of friction prevents a Mint State grade assessment from PCGS, though the surfaces retain substantial satiny luster beneath a tint of iridescent golden toning. NGC ID# 243H, PCGS# 5740

4027 1921 MS64 PCGS. This key-date quarter displays frosty, carefully preserved luster beneath just a hint of ice-blue toning. The strike is boldly executed, with notable sharpness seen on the shield lines and rivets, the leading edge of the eagle's left (facing) wing, and Liberty's head, which is nearly full. No singularly noticeable abrasions are observed. NGC ID# 243H, PCGS# 5740

4028 1923-S XF45 NGC. This is a fine Choice XF example of the low-mintage key 1923-S Standing Liberty quarter that seems high-end for the grade. Boldly struck and untoned, with relatively light, even high-point wear and just a couple of superficial pin marks on the reverse. NGC ID# 243K, PCGS# 5744

1923-S Quarter, MS62 Full Head
Excellent Collecting Grade

4029 1923-S MS62 Full Head PCGS. This key-date quarter is certified in an ideal grade for the budget-minded collector of Full Head Standing Liberty quarters. The shield and leading edge of the eagle's left (facing) wing are lacking slightly in striking quality, but the head and date numerals are bold. A few wisps of light gold and pale blue toning accent bright, satiny surfaces, while few noticeable abrasions are present. NGC ID# 243K, PCGS# 5745

4030 **1924-S MS63 Full Head PCGS.** A typical San Francisco issue for this poorly produced series, the 1924-S Standing Liberty quarter is elusive with Full Head detail. This example is well-struck on the head and date numerals, though the shield rivets and the eagle's breast feathers show the usual softness. Unusually luminous, frost-white luster engulfs each side, giving this piece exceptional visual appeal for the grade. Singularly significant abrasions are seemingly nonexistent, though close-examination reveals grade-limiting contact on the figure of Liberty and the high points of the eagle. Struck from worn dies, with several cracks and parallel die striations observed on the obverse. NGC ID# 243N, PCGS# 5751

1926-S Quarter, MS66
Conditionally Rare

4031 **1926-S MS66 PCGS. CAC.** Disproportionate to its mintage (2.7 million coins), the 1926-S quarter is seldom available in Mint State, and is genuinely rare at the Premium Gem grade level. This example displays frosty luster beneath soft golden-gray and ice-blue patina, with deeper olive accents seen around the peripheries. Liberty's head shows nearly complete definition, and the surfaces are free of any significant abrasions. Population: 18 in 66, 0 finer (10/14). NGC ID# 243T, PCGS# 5758

4032 **1928 MS66 Full Head NGC.** This delightful Premium Gem exhibits a better-than-average strike, with a little softness on the shield rivets and on Liberty's head, but full definition on Liberty's head. The pristine surfaces radiate vibrant mint luster and show a few hints of lavender and amber toning. Census: 15 in 66 Full Head, 13 finer (11/14). NGC ID# 243X, PCGS# 5767

4033 **1929 MS66 Full Head PCGS.** Light golden toning encompasses much of this Premium Gem Full Head example, while a crescent of beautiful rainbow colors is also seen along the lower obverse, spilling over onto the corresponding reverse border. The shield lines and rivets show a touch of the usual softness, though Liberty's head is sharp and the surfaces are devoid of noticeable abrasions. PCGS has encapsulated only seven numerically finer Full Head pieces (11/14). NGC ID# 2442, PCGS# 5773

1930 Quarter, MS67 Full Head
Vividly Toned Throughout

4034 **1930 MS67 Full Head NGC.** A beautifully preserved, boldly struck Superb Gem, this final-year type coin displays sharp definition throughout Liberty's head and gown lines, as well as the eagle's feathers and the stars. The shield rivets and lines are not fully defined, though the sharpness is greater than is usually seen. Radiant, frosty luster illuminates a blanket of aquamarine, lemon-gold, amber, and olive toning on the obverse, while the reverse shows splashes of the same plus pale lavender-blue and deeper forest-green color. An immensely appealing representative. Census: 32 in 67 (1 in 67 ★) Full Head, 0 finer (10/14). NGC ID# 2445, PCGS# 5779

4035 **1930-S MS66 Full Head PCGS.** This well-detailed Premium Gem shows Full Head definition, with just a touch of softness on the central obverse. The well-preserved surfaces are brightly lustrous, with a few hints of golden-brown toning. Population: 88 in 66 (2 in 66+) Full Head, 20 finer (10/14). NGC ID# 2446, PCGS# 5781

WASHINGTON QUARTERS

4036 **1932 Doubled Die Obverse, FS-101, MS66 PCGS.** Washington's earlobe is nicely die doubled. Key to a date collection of the series, the 1932 is seldom encountered as a Premium Gem. Lustrous and lightly toned with pleasing surfaces and a crisp strike. *Ex: Long Beach Signature (Heritage, 2/2007), lot 3783.* PCGS# 145629

4037 **1932-D MS62 PCGS.** An attractive MS62 example of the most elusive issue in the Washington quarter series, this piece exhibits sharply detailed design elements and lustrous surfaces with highlights of pale gold toning. A nearly vertical scratch in the right obverse field is the only mark of note. NGC ID# 2448, PCGS# 5791

4038 **1932-D MS63 PCGS.** Pleasing shades of lavender-gray, golden-brown, and amber toning visit the lightly marked surfaces of this sharply detailed Select specimen. The 1932-D Washington quarter is an elusive series key. NGC ID# 2448, PCGS# 5791

4039 **1932-D MS64 PCGS.** One of just two major keys in the Washington quarter series, the 1932-D is seldom encountered above the MS64 grade level. This Choice example displays sharp central definition and is devoid of noticeable abrasions. Light golden and pale lavender toning blankets both sides, complementing the satiny luster. NGC ID# 2448, PCGS# 5791

4040 **1932-D MS64 PCGS. CAC.** Of the two big key dates in the Washington quarter series (the 1932-S and 1932-D), the 1932-S has the lower mintage (408,000 versus a little more than 436,000 pieces), but the 1932-D is the rarer coin in high grades. This example of the latter displays satiny luster beneath tinges of amber-gold toning. The strike is bold and there are no singularly detracting marks. NGC ID# 2448, PCGS# 5791

4041 **1932-S MS64+ NGC. CAC.** A few tiny ticks on the obverse portrait preclude a full Gem grade assessment from NGC, though the overall preservation is well-deserving of the assigned Plus designation. The luster is vibrant and beautifully illuminates light golden toning on each side. Washington's hair and the eagle's breast feathers exhibit uncharacteristically sharp definition, a feature that makes this coin superior to most numerically equal examples. NGC ID# 2449, PCGS# 5792

1932-S Quarter, MS65
Deep Multicolor Toning

4042 **1932-S MS65 PCGS.** The 1932-S is widely sought-after for its key date status, but is seldom found in Gem condition. This frosty example shows dusky golden-gray toning over the obverse, with vivid rainbow hues around the reverse margins. A few tiny ticks on the cheek and the eagle's breast limit the grade, but hardly inhibit the eye appeal. PCGS has seen only four numerically finer submissions (10/14). NGC ID# 2449, PCGS# 5792

4043 **1934-D Medium Motto MS66 PCGS.** Dappled forest-green and ruby-red toning dominates the borders. The centers are mostly silver-gray. Lustrous and crisply struck with marks confined to a pair of faint field lines near the top of Washington's nose. NGC ID# 244C, PCGS# 5796

1936-D Quarter, MS67
Conditionally Rare Registry Coin

4044 **1936-D MS67 NGC.** Available in lower grades, the 1936-D quarter is a significant series rarity in Superb Gem condition. This Registry Set example is tied with just six others as the finest certified at NGC (10/14). Light golden color accents frosty luster on each side, while a couple splashes of amber and teal toning are also seen on the obverse. A sharp, carefully preserved representative (10/14). NGC ID# 244H, PCGS# 5801

4045 **1938 MS67 PCGS. CAC.** The well-preserved surfaces of this spectacular Superb Gem are enhanced by shades of apple-green, silver-gray, and amber toning. The design elements are well-detailed and frosty mint luster shines through the patina. Population: 53 in 67 (4 in 67+), 0 finer (10/14). NGC ID# 244N, PCGS# 5806

4046 **1942-D Doubled Die Obverse, FS-101, MS62 NGC.** The date digits are extraordinarily thick, GOD and TRUST are die doubled south, and LIBERTY is widely doubled in a clockwise direction. Among the most dramatic of the many doubled die varieties in the Washington series. A satiny example with russet and lavender toning in protected regions. PCGS# 145011

1954-D Quarter, MS67
Among the Finest Certified

4047 **1954-D MS67 PCGS.** PCGS has certified only 13 examples of the 1954-D quarter in MS67 (1 in 67+), with none finer (10/14), and as the Plus-graded piece is housed in the current highest-rated Registry Set, this coin is literally one of the finest obtainable examples of the date. Frosty luster in shades of pale gold and ice-blue enliven much of each side, with deep sun-gold and amber-brown crescents seen along the lower obverse and upper reverse peripheries. The strike is well-executed, and the surfaces are seemingly flawless. NGC ID# 2468, PCGS# 5856

EARLY HALF DOLLARS

1795 Flowing Hair Half, VF20
O-119, Two Leaves

4048 **1795 2 Leaves, O-119, R.4, VF20 PCGS.** A die lump near star 13 and a heavy, short die line at the end of the eagle's right (facing) wing tip are diagnostic of this variety. The present example also displays a small planchet lamination (as made) near the U in UNITED. Wear is evenly distributed, and the surfaces display dusky golden-gray and olive toning. A small patch of dark verdigris is noted on the obverse near star 3, though this is otherwise a pleasing type representative. PCGS# 39236

4049 **1803 Large 3, Large Reverse Stars, O-103, R.3, VF35 PCGS.** The large 3 in the date paired with the Large Stars reverse identifies the O-103 variety. This Choice VF example retains more interior detail in the drapery than usually seen on coins in this grade. Shades of mottled lavender-gray and golden-tan toning blanket the lightly abraded surfaces. Population for the variety: 2 in 35, 5 finer (10/14). PCGS# 39273

4050 **1805 O-111, R.2, XF40 PCGS.** Extensive reverse die cracks, most obvious in the right margin, are characteristic of this fairly plentiful variety. The present coin is well-detailed for the grade, though some minor die fatigue is evident amid the right reverse stars. The border denticles are complete, with no evidence of adjustment marks. Dusky lavender-gray and bright olive-green toning blankets each side. PCGS# 39285

1805 O-111 Draped Bust Half, XF45
Original Patina, Sharp Motifs

4051 **1805 O-111, R.2, XF45 NGC.** Lovely, old silver-gray toning yields to smooth, light-gray patina on the high points of this sharply struck, attractive early half. Liberty's hair strands are virtually complete and the eagle's feather detail is bold. The only marks are a collection of rim disturbances on the obverse, with the most noticeable bump located between stars 12 and 13. A long, curving die crack from STATES through AMERICA with intersecting radial cracks confirm the variety. PCGS# 39285

1806 O-109 Draped Bust Half, AU50
Pointed 6, No Stem
Much Luster Remains

4052 1806 Pointed 6, No Stem, O-109, R.1, AU50 NGC. Attractive silver luster is abundant across the surfaces on both sides of this sharp early half. Liberty's hair strands are bold and lustrous. The reverse displays lively shades of lilac and silver-gray patina. Light wear appears on Liberty's high points — the uppermost hair detail and ribbons — as well as on the bust drapery lines. A small area of dark toning or residue sits on the rim to the right of the date. A Draped Bust half with great eye appeal and originality. PCGS# 39310

BUST HALF DOLLARS

1808 Half Dollar, AU55
O-103, Lightly Toned Example

4053 1808 O-103, R.1, AU55 PCGS. A missing serif on the 1 in the date confirms the obverse die, with AM of AMERICA solidly joined at the base to help identify the reverse. The fact that nearly all 1808 half dollars are weakly struck makes the technical grade a challenge for both collectors and the grading services. This properly graded Choice AU coin is characteristically weak at the rims and blended on the central details, but nearly full satin luster remains. Attractive umber-gray toning visits the rims. PCGS# 39364

1810 O-105 Capped Bust Half, AU58
Partial Milling, Sharp Luster

4054 1810 O-105, R.2, AU58 PCGS. The variety is confirmed by a diagonal line extending upward through the crossbars from the first line of the sixth shield stripe. Other lines extend into the crossbars as well, and star 13 nearly touches Liberty's curl. Sharply struck, although almost all Overton-105 examples lack at least some of the dentilation on both sides. This near-Mint example is brightly lustrous and virtually untoned, with a mere hint of pale gray patina on the attractive, silver surfaces. PCGS# 39411

4055 1811 Small 8, O-111, R.1, AU55 PCGS. Close to O-111a, but the crack through OF AMERICA does not extend left through the ES in STATES. A chestnut-gold and silver-gray representative with ample luster and light high point wear. Refreshingly free from abrasions. PCGS# 39436

4056 1812 Large 8, O-104, R.1, AU55 PCGS. A horizontal die line through the left (facing) wing is diagnostic for the collectible Overton-104. A brilliant and lightly marked Choice AU half dollar with bright luster throughout the borders and eagle. Certified in a green label holder. PCGS# 39447

4057 1818 O-114, R.3, AU58 PCGS. CAC. The lowest point of star 1 is repunched, the pick-up point for Overton-114. Narrow bands of golden-brown and navy-blue patina frame stone-gray and chestnut fields and motifs. A few marks are noted on the central obverse. PCGS# 39532

4058 1823 O-108a, R.3, AU58 PCGS. This late die state of the obverse has all the die cracks of O-108a. The first A is perfect, and a reverse center dot is clearly visible, confirming the O-108 attribution. Specialists always get a little excited when they see the die crack across the bust, which also appears on the O-109 rarity. This near-Mint example has satin luster with light silver surfaces and delicate champagne toning on the obverse. Splashes of deep gold appear on the reverse. PCGS# 39613

4059 1827 Square Base 2, O-106, R.2, AU58 PCGS. Many Bust half collectors believe that the AU58 grade provides the best balance between value and quality. The present near-Mint coin confirms that judgment, since the lightly toned surfaces are partly lustrous and nearly free from visible marks. PCGS# 39698

1827 O-126 Half Dollar, MS63
Square Base 2
Endearing Originality

4060 1827 Square Base 2, O-126, R.2, MS63 PCGS. CAC. Square Base 2. Lustrous ice-blue margins surround frosted central devices of this sharply original, Select Uncirculated half. Rose-gold accents glow beneath the thick, warm-gray crust with a natural appeal that endears similarly toned Bust halves to series enthusiasts. Only rated R.2 on the rarity scale, yet numerous MS63 examples are seen in the Condition Census for the O-126 variety, and this coin certainly ranks with them. A prominent die break interrupts the lower curl and multiple shield stripes extend into the crossbars to confirm the die pair. PCGS# 39725

1829/7 Half Dollar, O-101, MS63
Bold Overdate, Attractively Toned

4061 **1829/7 O-101, R.1, MS63 NGC.** All four digits show evidence of recutting, but especially on the 9, where the upright of an underdigit 7 is clearly visible beneath the primary numeral. Strangely, the O-101 variety shows the 18 recut south while the 29 is repunched north. A large, bold 5 in the denomination confirms the die pair, as does E PLURIBUS UNUM lettering being notably recut right in its entirety. Rose-gray patina covers both sides, with a sharp strike except at the top of Liberty's cap. PCGS# 39807

4062 **1834 Large Date, Large Letters, O-101, R.1, AU58+ PCGS.** A late die state example, with the recutting on the 5 in 50C no longer visible. As appropriate for the AU58+ grade assigned by PCGS, this coin displays vibrant, frosty mint luster, with essentially brilliant, minimally marked surfaces. The obverse stars and a portion of the eagle's left (facing) wing are not fully defined, though the strike is otherwise pleasing. Just a suggestion of friction on the highest points of the hair curls precludes a Mint State grade from PCGS (10/14). PCGS# 39905

4063 **1834 Small Date, Small Letters, O-113, R.1, MS61 NGC.** Light to medium tan-gold and silver-gray toning visits this satiny half dollar. A couple of thin marks near the upper left stars, but otherwise free from contact. A trace of struck-in grease is noted beneath the shoulder curl. PCGS# 39917

REEDED EDGE HALF DOLLARS

4064 **1837 GR-14, R.1, MS61 NGC.** A descending die crack through the date is characteristic of GR-14. The reverse border and left-side stars are also cracked. Chestnut-gold and stone-gray toning encompass this lustrous and lightly marked representative. A two-year type. PCGS# 531060

4065 **1839-O GR-1, R.1, XF45 PCGS.** The familiar '39-O die pairing with heavy reverse die cracks and a lightly repunched mintmark. Noticeable luster fills the legends and eagle. The borders display classic sea-green and golden-brown peripheral "album" toning. PCGS# 531106

SEATED HALF DOLLARS

4066 **1839 Drapery MS62 PCGS. WB-102.** Gunmetal-blue accents add appeal to the primary slate-gray patina, with slight iridescence visible where the underlying mint luster shines through. A bold strike on the motifs is slightly weaker at the borders, seen on several star centers and at the reverse legend, especially on STATES. An attractive, highly original-looking example. Population: 11 in 62, 30 finer (10/14). NGC ID# 24GL, PCGS# 6232

4067 **1841 MS62 PCGS. WB-101.** An attractive example of this challenging early date. The coin is boldly struck on Liberty's head and the surrounding star centers, with just a hint of blending on the eagle's leg — although the strike is far above-average for this early issue. Pleasing original toning covers both sides in shades of orange-tan and gunmetal-blue. Silver luster peaks through the toning. Population: 4 in 62 (1 in 62+), 11 finer (11/14). NGC ID# 24GR, PCGS# 6236

4068 **1848-O AU58 PCGS. WB-101, Die Pair 16, R.5.** An antebellum New Orleans issue with a fairly high mintage, but most survivors are in Fine to XF grades. Borderline Uncirculated examples, such as the present piece, are very scarce. Well struck and flashy with light autumn-gold and ocean-blue toning. NGC ID# 24HD, PCGS# 6261

4069 **1852 XF45 PCGS. WB-101.** A prized Philadelphia date for Seated half collectors, with a low mintage of just 77,130 pieces. The issue is notably scarce in any grade. This example is lightly iridescent and glossy over silver-bronze surfaces. Strong detail and glimpses of mint luster remain for the Choice XF grade. Population: 9 in 45, 69 finer (11/14). NGC ID# 24HL, PCGS# 6268

4070 **1855-O Arrows MS63 PCGS. WB-101, Die Pair 4, R.3.** A delicate die crack through star 4 seals the attribution. A satiny pearl-gray and almond-gold New Orleans No Motto half dollar. Free from relevant marks but slightly subdued. Certified in an old green label holder. NGC ID# 24JP, PCGS# 6283

4071 **1866 Motto MS63 PCGS. WB-104.** Liberty's outer hair strands are doubled, as is the pole above the hand. This lustrous coin shows the Motto reverse hub type one, with a lower split berry. An untoned, brilliant-white coin, with fully struck devices. Wispy lines in the fields determine the Select Uncirculated grade. Population: 10 in 63, 24 finer (11/14). NGC ID# 24JS, PCGS# 6319

4072 **1873 Arrows MS63 PCGS. WB-106.** Large Arrows. Open 3. Boldly struck and frosted, this sharp Select Uncirculated example displays cartwheel luster beneath mostly untoned silver surfaces. Few marks of any note are seen on either side. More than 1.8 million pieces were struck of the Open 3 Arrows varieties. Population: 33 in 63, 48 finer (10/14). NGC ID# 24L7, PCGS# 6343

1873 Arrows Half Dollar, MS64
Lightly Toned, Lustrous Example

4073 **1873 Arrows MS64 PCGS. WB-106.** A relatively plentiful date in the absolute sense, the 1873 With Arrows half dollar finally becomes scarce at the Choice grade level, and finer pieces are rarely seen. This example displays sharply struck design elements and satiny original luster. Lightly mottled olive-gold, lavender, and aquamarine toning colors each side, with the deeper hues more prevalent on the obverse. Population: 34 in 64 (1 in 64+), 15 finer (10/14). NGC ID# 24L7, PCGS# 6343

1873-CC Arrows Half Dollar, AU50
Evenly Toned, Silver-Gray Example

4074 **1873-CC Arrows AU50 PCGS. WB-103, Die Pair 6, Low R.4.** Large CC Mintmark. Perennially a collector favorite as a scarce, two-year type, this Open 3 Large Arrows example features evenly toned, silver-gray patina with occasional glimpses of remaining mint luster. Even though the Closed 3, No Arrows type is somewhat scarcer than the Open 3 With Arrows coins, both issues are eagerly sought by type, date, and Carson City collectors and are notably elusive. Population: 16 in 50, 43 finer (10/14). NGC ID# 24L8, PCGS# 6344

4075 **1874-CC Arrows VG10 PCGS. CAC. WB-101, R.4.**
Aquamarine and golden-tan toning encompass this lightly abraded rare date half dollar. All letters in IN GOD WE TRUST are at least partly present. A meager 59,000 pieces were struck, fewer than any other Carson City issue of the series aside from the first-year 1870-CC. NGC ID# 24LB, PCGS# 6347

1875-S Seated Half, MS65
Pleasing Luster

4076 **1875-S MS65 PCGS. WB-101, Die Pair 6, R.3.** Mint State 1875-S half dollars are scarce through MS65 and are a significant condition rarity any finer. Rich luster remains beneath a patina of gray-green, golden-brown, rose-pink, and orange-gold on this pleasing Gem example. The design elements display strong detail. Population: 60 in 65 (2 in 65+), 22 finer (10/14). NGC ID# 24KF, PCGS# 6351

4077 **1877-S MS64 NGC. WB-104, Die Pair 35, R.3.** Type Two Reverse. Very Small S. Golden-brown and forest-green toning visits the borders. The flashy fields and frosty motifs are brilliant. Sharply struck and well preserved with substantial eye appeal. NGC ID# 24KM, PCGS# 6357

1879 Seated Half, MS66
Outstanding Visual Appeal

4078 **1879 MS66 NGC. WB-102, R.2.** Congress passed the Bland-Allison Act on February 28, 1878, mandating that the Treasury Department purchase 2 to 4 million dollars worth of silver bullion each month and coin it into standard silver dollars. This dramatic shift in priorities at the Mint resulted in remarkably low half dollar production beginning in 1879, when only 4,800 halves were coined. Thus, the 1879 is highly elusive in all grades, though a small number of high-grade specimens survive for those who are patient searchers. This razor-sharp piece displays excellent preservation with vibrant, semiprooflike luster shining through rich teal, violet, and amber-gray patina. Census: 34 in 66 (1 in 66+, 3 in 66 ★, 1 in 66+★), 10 finer (10/14). NGC ID# 24KS, PCGS# 6361

4079 **1880 MS64 PCGS. CAC. WB-102.** An attractive, densely iridescent piece showing gray-tan toning and olive-green peripheral coloration. Several prooflike areas break through, especially on the reverse, where approximately half of the surface areas are ice-blue and glassy, in a mottled arrangement. Boldly struck and abrasion-free on both sides. Population: 26 in 64, 41 finer (11/14). NGC ID# 24KT, PCGS# 6362

PROOF SEATED HALF DOLLARS

4080 **1859 PR62 Cameo PCGS.** Razor-sharp definition is evident on all the design elements and the deeply mirrored fields contrast boldly with the frosty devices. A few hints of champagne-gold toning enhance the outstanding eye appeal. Population: 7 in 62, 22 finer (10/14). PCGS# 86413

4081 **1860 PR63 NGC.** Attractive shades of cerulean-blue and pale gold toning blanket the lightly marked surfaces of this impressive Select example. The design elements are sharply detailed and the fields are deeply mirrored throughout. Census: 36 in 63, 57 finer (11/14). NGC ID# 27TK, PCGS# 6414

1866 Seated Half, PR65
First Year With Motto

4082 **1866 Motto PR65 PCGS. WB-101.** Few Gem or finer proofs exist for collectors wanting to add the first-year With Motto type to their set. This exceptional example is sharply produced and wonderfully toned. The deep-mirrored obverse fields display a blending of ocean-blue and mango-orange toning; equally attractive, the reverse is reflective with medium shades of pale orange-gold. There are no distracting marks or flaws worth mention. Population: 12 in 65, 4 finer (10/14). NGC ID# 27TZ, PCGS# 6424

1867 Half Dollar, PR64 Cameo
Needle-Sharp Motifs

4083 **1867 PR64 Cameo PCGS.** A limited mintage of 625 proof half dollars was accomplished in 1867, and Cameo survivors are rarely seen in any grade. This example shows pleasing field-device contrast, with warm golden toning over both sides. The design elements are fully brought up, giving this piece exceptional eye appeal, despite a few faint, grade-consistent hairlines in the fields. Population: 11 in 64 (1 in 64+), 15 finer (10/14). PCGS# 86425

1873 Arrows Half Dollar, PR63 Cameo
Two-Year Proof Subtype

4084 **1873 Arrows PR63 Cameo PCGS. CAC. WB-106.** Brilliant reflective fields, particularly on the reverse, are among the considerable attributes of this Select proof example. The devices display bold definition and an attractive layer of mint frost, providing noticeable contrast. A few minor, milk-white toning spots and wispy hairlines are present. Population: 12 in 63, 15 finer (10/14). PCGS# 86434

4085 **1880 PR64 PCGS.** Gorgeous turquoise-blue and salmon toning adorns the obverse. The reverse displays lighter hues of reddish-tan and gray-green. A sharply struck near-Gem proof that seems conservatively graded. NGC ID# 27UF, PCGS# 6441

4086 **1881 PR63 NGC.** Type Two Reverse. This low total-mintage date saw a mere 10,000 business strikes and just 975 proofs emerge from the Philadelphia Mint. This example boasts exceptional eye appeal, showing purple-violet toning across each side, along with vibrant electric-blue peripheral iridescence. Fully struck with few surface flaws, and seemingly high-end for the grade. NGC ID# 27UG, PCGS# 6442

4087 **1884 PR64 NGC.** A popular proof issue, due to the scarcity of high-grade business strikes. This example exhibits deeply mirrored fields around sharp, satiny devices. A thin veil of light golden toning warms each side, masking any grade-limiting hairlines. NGC ID# 27UK, PCGS# 6445

1890 Seated Half, PR65
Intense Mirrors and Indigo Hues

4088 **1890 PR65 NGC.** One of the low-mintage, late-series dates in the long run of Seated halves. Just 12,000 business strikes and a skimpy 590 proofs were struck for the year. This intensely mirrored proof displays marvelous blue shades and indigo hues within gold peripheral margins. A glittering Gem proof, fully struck and perfect for an advanced set of the late-date subseries 1879 through 1891. Census: 32 in 65 (1 in 65+), 28 finer (10/14). NGC ID# 27US, PCGS# 6451

BARBER HALF DOLLARS

4089 **1892 MS64+ NGC. CAC.** This high-end Choice example exhibits razor-sharp definition on all design elements and the well-preserved brilliant surfaces radiate vibrant mint luster on both sides. Eye appeal is terrific. NGC ID# 24LF, PCGS# 6461

1892 Barber Half, Bold, Patinated MS66

4090 **1892 MS66 NGC.** This lovely Premium Gem 1892 half dollar, the first of the new Barber design, is an attractive example for date or type purposes, as it is fully struck throughout both sides. Neither the often-weak juncture of the hair with the forehead of Liberty, nor yet the eagle's right (facing) claw and right shield corner and wing, betray the slightest sign of weakness. A further complement to the broad appeal is deep original patina, orange-gold and gunmetal-gray with glints of jade on each side. Census: 34 in 66 (1 in 66+, 2 in 66 ★), 9 finer (10/14).
Ex: Long Beach Signature (Heritage, 6/2006), lot 1709; Long Beach Signature (Heritage, 9/2011), lot 4047; December Auction (Heritage, 12/2011), lot 3653. NGC ID# 24LF, PCGS# 6461

4091 **1892 Tripled Die Reverse, FS-801, MS63 NGC.** The reverse legend is die tripled throughout. One of several doubled die varieties found on first-year Barber issues, reminiscent of similar problems the Mint had with the 1878 Morgan dollars. The present lustrous piece displays splashes of peach-gold toning. The central reverse is brilliant. A few delicate slide marks on the cheek determine the grade. PCGS# 145290

1894 Half Dollar, MS65
Upper-End for the Grade

4092 **1894 MS65 NGC.** The 1894 Barber half dollar does not receive as much acclaim as do its San Francisco and New Orleans counterparts, but it is relatively on par with them overall when it comes to Mint State rarity. This Gem displays frosty luster beneath attractive olive and golden-gray toning. The strike is sharply executed, and the blatant lack of perceptible surface flaws makes one have to search to find any grade-limiting imperfections. Census: 16 in 65, 9 finer (10/14). NGC ID# 24LN, PCGS# 6468

4093 **1894-S MS63 PCGS.** Despite a high mintage in excess in four million coins, this San Francisco issue is absolutely scarce at all grade levels, and conditionally scarce in mint condition. This Select Mint State representative is well-struck with smooth satin luster and clean surfaces that are nearly blemish-free. Light mottled and streaky toning occurs on each side. Population: 26 in 63, 57 finer (10/14). NGC ID# 24LR, PCGS# 6470

4094 **1895 MS64 NGC.** Variegated layers of ash-gray, cobalt-blue, gold-orange, and purple-rose toning adorn both sides of this conditionally scarce near-Gem Barber half. Well-struck with pleasing satin luster and a few wispy, barely noticeable marks on Liberty's cheek that keep it from grading even higher. Census: 25 in 64, 14 finer (10/14). NGC ID# 24LS, PCGS# 6471

4095 **1896 MS63 PCGS.** The mint luster is deep and coruscating over the frosted surfaces of this Select Uncirculated Barber half. A full strike on the eagle confirms the bold details seen elsewhere on the coin. The mild, silver-gray patina is more a function of heavy mint frost than overt toning of any kind. Population: 31 in 63 (1 in 63+), 49 finer (10/14). NGC ID# 24LV, PCGS# 6474

1900 Barber Half, MS65
High Technical and Visual Quality

4096 **1900 MS65 PCGS. CAC.** This lustrous Gem receives high marks for both technical and visual quality. The strike is bold throughout, providing a suitable palette for the pastel and rainbow hues that roll across the gleaming, frosted surfaces. Housed in an old green label holder, CAC affirms the merits of the coin — an excellent choice for the discriminating type collector or for a high-end Barber half specialist. Population: 35 in 65 (2 in 65+), 10 finer (10/14). NGC ID# 24M9, PCGS# 6486

4097 **1904 MS64 PCGS.** Brilliant and untoned, this near-Gem half is brightly lustrous and Choice. A bold strike starts with the eagle's right (facing) side, where shield junction and eagle's leg show nice detail. A scrape on the leg is the only noticeable mark and accounts for the assigned grade. Few coins are certified numerically finer. Population: 40 in 64, 19 finer (10/14). NGC ID# 24MM, PCGS# 6498

4098 **1905-O MS64 PCGS.** The 1905-O is a low-mintage (just over half a million pieces) New Orleans issue that is among the more difficult O-mints in the entire Barber half dollar series at the Uncirculated level. This piece is especially well-struck on the obverse and shows only minor bluntness at the center of the reverse. Light gray patina overlays each side. Population: 37 in 64 (1 in 64+), 23 finer (11/14).
Ex: FUN Signature (Heritage 1/2001), lot 7832; Long Beach Signature (Heritage, 2/2005), lot 7148. NGC ID# 24MS, PCGS# 6502

4099 **1908-D MS65 PCGS.** An attractive Gem example with satiny surfaces that are well-preserved and distraction-free. Mottled olive patina decorates the peripheries and clings to some of the central devices. Population: 28 in 65 (1 in 65+), 12 finer (10/14). NGC ID# 24N5, PCGS# 6513

4100 **1909-O MS63 PCGS.** The mostly brilliant centers of this attractive Select specimen yield to shades of greenish-gold, lavender-gray and amber toning at the peripheries, with vibrant mint luster and well-detailed design elements. Population: 14 in 63, 51 finer (10/14). NGC ID# 24N9, PCGS# 6517

4101 **1911 MS64 PCGS. CAC.** Lustrous with blended layers of multicolored patina across each side, this is a pleasing near-Gem example with clean, distraction-free surfaces. Boldly struck and a solid, high-end coin for the grade. NGC ID# 24ND, PCGS# 6521

4102 **1912-D MS64 NGC.** This is an attractive near-Gem example of the 1912-D Barber half dollar, from a mintage of 2.3 million pieces. The creamy-silver surfaces are lustrous and well-preserved, with minimal marks and sharply struck design motifs. NGC ID# 24NH, PCGS# 6525

4103 **1915-S MS64 PCGS.** Portions of the peripheries exhibit dark amber toning on this otherwise lightly toned near-Gem. The strike is sharp overall, though a few areas of weakness are present, including a few of the stars and the eagle's left talon. A pleasing degree of luster appears. Population: 95 in 64 (1 in 64+), 52 finer (10/14). NGC ID# 24NT, PCGS# 6534

PROOF BARBER HALF DOLLARS
1894 Half Dollar, PR65 Cameo
Vivid Reverse Toning

4104 **1894 PR65 Cameo PCGS.** The Mint struck an adequate number of proof half dollars in 1894 (972 coins), but Cameo survivors are disproportionately difficult to locate in high grades. This piece shows tack-sharp detail and deeply mirrored fields, though its primary visual allure stems from the vivid blue, violet, and orange-gold peripheral bands that surround the reverse, complementing warm sun-gold toning over the remainder of each side. Population: 16 in 65, 26 finer (10/14). PCGS# 86541

1895 Half Dollar, PR66 Cameo
Richly Contrasted Surfaces

4105 **1895 PR66 Cameo NGC.** The surfaces of this Premium Gem proof 1895 Barber half show only a faint hint of golden patina at the extreme rims, but generous contrast is set up on each side between the richly frosted devices and deeply reflective fields. A faint dark spot appears on one of the upper olive leaves in Liberty's wreath. The strike is sharp throughout if not quite full. Census: 18 in 66 (1 in 66+) Cameo, 24 finer (10/14). PCGS# 86542

1900 Half Dollar, PR65 ★ Cameo
Bold Field-Device Contrast

4106 **1900 PR65 ★ Cameo NGC.** Dramatic contrast between the icy devices and the glass-like fields provides eye appeal worthy of the NGC Star designation. A whisper of gold patina on the portrait denies absolute brilliance. A lovely Gem of this scarce turn-of-the-century issue. Census: 9 in 65 (1 in 65 ★, 1 in 65+★), 38 finer (10/14). *Ex: FUN Signature (Heritage, 1/2007), lot 4622.* PCGS# 86547

4107 **1901 PR63 Cameo PCGS.** The sharply detailed frosty design elements contrast boldly with the deeply mirrored fields to create a dramatic cameo effect when this coin is tilted in the light. A few hints of pale gold toning enhance the terrific eye appeal. Population: 7 in 63, 50 finer (10/14). PCGS# 86548

1906 Barber Half, All-Brilliant PR66

4108 **1906 PR66 NGC.** Bright, watery mirrors are completely untoned and even boast a hint of contrast on an issue that normally displays the all-brilliant finish utilized over much of this decade. Examination with a loupe reveals a couple of minor slidemarks on Liberty's cheek. Census: 34 in 66 (1 in 66+, 1 in 66 ★), 25 finer (10/14). *Ex: Long Beach Signature (Heritage, 6/2005), lot 6412.* NGC ID# 24PA, PCGS# 6553

1908 Barber Half, PR65
Sharply Struck With Iridescent Patina

4109 **1908 PR65 NGC.** From a tiny mintage of 545 pieces, the 1908 proof Barber half dollar is very scarce in Gem condition. The present coin is patinated in iridescent shades of pale green and light pink, with deeply reflective fields underneath the toning. The strike is sharp in most areas, despite some characteristic lack of detail at the juncture of the shield and eagle's wing on the reverse. Census: 25 in 65, 48 finer (10/14). *Ex: Long Beach Signature (Heritage, 9/2010), lot 4194.* NGC ID# 24PC, PCGS# 6555

1910 Barber Half, Toned PR66

4110 **1910 PR66 NGC.** Blended forest-green, lavender-red, sun-gold, and aquamarine toning engulfs both sides of this Premium Gem proof type coin. The design elements are boldly impressed, and any grade-limiting surface flaws are well-masked by the rich patina. From a limited mintage of just 551 proofs, and proportionately elusive in high grades. Census: 27 in 66 (1 in 66+), 25 finer (10/14). NGC ID# 24PE, PCGS# 6557

4111 **1911 PR63 Cameo PCGS.** Sharply detailed frosty design elements contrast boldly with the deeply reflective fields, under delicate shades of champagne-gold and lavender toning. From a proof mintage of 543 pieces. Population: 5 in 63, 58 finer (10/14). PCGS# 86558

1913 Half Dollar, PR65 Cameo
Pronounced Contrast

4112 **1913 PR65 Cameo NGC.** The low business-strike mintage of the 1913 Barber half dollar (188,000 pieces) places added pressure on the proofs, of which NGC has certified fewer than 200 examples, few of which grade Gem Cameo or finer. Pronounced field-motif contrast shows over both sides, each of which exhibits sharply struck design elements. There are no marks worthy of individual mention. Census: 2 in 65, 8 finer (10/14). PCGS# 86560

WALKING LIBERTY HALF DOLLARS

4113 **1916-D MS64+ PCGS.** This first-year Walking Liberty half dollar displays softly frosted mint luster and smooth, unmarked, stone-white surfaces. The devices are somewhat weakly struck, as typically seen on examples from this Denver mint issue. NGC ID# 24PM, PCGS# 6567

4114 **1916-D MS65 PCGS. CAC.** Lively mint luster engulfs each side of this Gem first-year Walker, with just a touch of delicate golden toning overall. The strike is bold, with notable definition on Liberty's head, branch hand, and the eagle's rear leg feathers. The rich, matte-like luster fails to reveal any significant abrasions when studied with a loupe. Finer examples are scarcely encountered. NGC ID# 24PM, PCGS# 6567

4115 **1917-D Obverse MS64 PCGS.** From a mintage of only 765,400 pieces, this Choice Mint State example displays strong, satiny luster, with tinges of golden-orange and lavender toning throughout. Some typical softness is noted on Liberty's thigh and the eagle's central feathers, though it is minor. NGC ID# 24PR, PCGS# 6570

4116 **1917-D Obverse MS64 PCGS. CAC.** Soft, satiny luster exhibits a few hints of pale golden color, with largely unabraded surfaces. The design definition is sharp throughout, including bold detail on Liberty's head and branch hand. Overall, the Obverse Mintmark variant is slightly more available than its Reverse Mintmark counterpart, though both issues are elusive above the Choice grade level. NGC ID# 24PR, PCGS# 6570

4117 **1917-S Obverse AU50 NGC.** The low-mintage 1917-S Walking Liberty half dollar, with the prominent obverse mintmark, is prized by type collectors and series enthusiasts alike. This lightly abraded AU specimen shows just a touch of wear on the well-detailed design elements and traces of original mint luster cling to the pleasing surfaces. NGC ID# 24PT, PCGS# 6572

1919-D Half Dollar, AU55
Semikey Denver Issue

4118 **1919-D AU55 NGC.** Only a trace of actual wear is observed, as much of the softness in the centers is primarily due to deficient striking, an often-seen characteristic on this poorly produced Denver issue. Remnants of luster remain in the recesses beneath dusky golden-gray toning. This issue is most often encountered in lower circulated grades, as AU and Mint State coins are elusive. NGC ID# 24PZ, PCGS# 6578

4119 **1920 MS64+ PCGS. CAC.** This high-end Choice specimen exhibits a better-than-average strike with clear separation showing between Liberty's thumb and finger on the wreath hand. The well-preserved lustrous surfaces show highlights of pale gold toning and eye appeal is outstanding. NGC ID# 24R3, PCGS# 6580

4120 **1921-D — Improperly Cleaned — NGC Details. XF.** Luster rolls across the plumage and legends of this dusky stone-gray key date half dollar. Thorough evaluation finally locates delicate obverse hairlines. The lowest mintage business issue of the series, undoubtedly due to the exceptional mintage of silver dollars that year. NGC ID# 24R7, PCGS# 6584

4121 **1921-S VF30 PCGS. CAC.** The 1921-S Walking Liberty half dollar claims a low mintage of 548,000 pieces. This VF30 example retains most interior detail on the skirt lines, but the breast and right arm show some wear. The lightly abraded surfaces are visited by shades of lavender-gray and golden-brown toning. NGC ID# 24R8, PCGS# 6585

4122 **1921-S — Cleaning — PCGS Genuine. XF Details.** This is a still-pleasing, lightly circulated example of this elusive key date. Shades of sky-blue and pale lavender visit light golden-gray patina on each side, while deeper, scattered russet areas are seen in the reverse recesses. Lightly cleaned, but retaining pleasing detail. NGC ID# 24R8, PCGS# 6585

4123 **1927-S AU58 NGC.** This charming near-Mint specimen exhibits well-detailed design elements with just a trace of friction on the high points. The brilliant surfaces radiate vibrant mint luster with no mentionable abrasions. NGC ID# 24RA, PCGS# 6587

4124 **1927-S MS63 PCGS.** The 1927-S is a somewhat overlooked San Francisco issue, seldom offered in pleasing Mint State condition. This example is weakly struck in the centers, as is usual, but exhibits few noticeable abrasions. A faint, light golden hue blankets each side, attesting to the originality of the satiny luster. NGC ID# 24RA, PCGS# 6587

1927-S Walking Liberty Half, MS64
Strong Eye Appeal

4125 **1927-S MS64 PCGS. CAC.** The typical softness at Liberty's head, branch hand, and gown lines is matched by weakness at the eagle's trailing leg as always seen for this date, but that is the only limiting factor to keep this attractive, near-Gem coin from an even higher grade. The eye appeal is terrific, with smooth fields and vivid colors lightly dispersed around the margins and behind the central devices. Satiny luster rolls across the mark-free surfaces. NGC ID# 24RA, PCGS# 6587

4126 **1929-D MS65 NGC.** This attractive Gem displays well-detailed design elements, with just the slightest trace of softness on the eagle's leg, and vibrant mint luster on both sides. The well-preserved surfaces show a few highlights of golden-tan toning. Census: 86 in 65 (3 in 65+), 15 finer (11/14). NGC ID# 24RC, PCGS# 6589

4127 **1933-S MS63 PCGS.** This brilliant, silver-white half dollar exhibits remarkably crisp strike definition, especially over the perennially-soft branch hand of Liberty. A couple of faint marks in the right obverse field are all that prevent a finer grade assessment. NGC ID# 24RE, PCGS# 6591

1935-D Walker, MS66
None Numerically Finer

4128 **1935-D MS66 PCGS.** Frosty luster resides beneath shades of powder-blue, champagne, and orange-gold toning. Liberty's head is softly struck, as is characteristic of this issue in general, though the central regions show better-than average detail for a branch mint issue. The 1935-D is scarcely seen in MS66, and none have been certified numerically finer (10/14). NGC ID# 24RK, PCGS# 6596

1935-S Walking Liberty Half, MS66
Full Frosted Luster

4129 1935-S MS66 PCGS. A condition rarity of the middle-date series, with relatively few Premium Gem coins certified despite a 3.8 million-piece mintage. This example if boldly struck for the issue, with minor central blending but less than normally seen. A primarily brilliant, snow-white example, with tiny crescents of amber and violet toning near the date and above the eagle's wings. PCGS and NGC have seen a total of just six numerically finer coins (10/14). NGC ID# 24RL, PCGS# 6597

4130 1937 MS67 PCGS. CAC. A spectacular Superb Gem with well-detailed design elements and vibrant mint luster. The impeccably preserved surfaces show delicate shades of champagne-gold toning. PCGS has graded five numerically finer examples (11/14). NGC ID# 24RR, PCGS# 6601

4131 1938-D MS65 PCGS. A wisp of olive-gold toning graces this lustrous and splendidly preserved Gem. Liberty's head is well struck, although the branch hand shows blending. A popular low mintage issue. Certified in an old green label holder. NGC ID# 24RV, PCGS# 6605

4132 1940-S MS66 PCGS. Although central weakness is noted on both sides, the strike is actually finer than usual for this poorly-produced issue. Both sides have frosty silver luster with wispy traces of champagne toning. Only eleven examples of this San Francisco issue are rated higher than MS66 by PCGS (10/14).
Ex: Beverly Hills Signature (Heritage, 11/2011), lot 3715. NGC ID# 24S2, PCGS# 6610

4133 1941-D MS67+ NGC. CAC. The impeccably preserved surfaces of this high-end Superb Gem display vibrant mint luster and attractive shades of orange-gold toning on both sides. The design elements are well-detailed and overall eye appeal is extraordinary. NGC has graded three numerically finer examples (11/14). NGC ID# 24S4, PCGS# 6612

4134 1941-S MS66 PCGS. This San Francisco issue of 8.1 million coins was well-produced, and many high-grade examples remain available to collectors. This is a lovely Premium Gem with boldly struck devices and shimmering mint luster over untoned surfaces. Both sides of the coin are mark-free. NGC ID# 24S5, PCGS# 6613

4135 1941-S MS66 PCGS. This well-detailed Premium Gem shows just a touch of the usual softness on the eagle's leg and Liberty's wreath hand, but the well-preserved surfaces show attractive highlights of champagne-gold toning and vibrant mint luster throughout. PCGS has graded nine numerically finer examples (10/14). NGC ID# 24S5, PCGS# 6613

4136 1943-S MS66+ PCGS. Typical of the late-date San Francisco Walking Liberty halves, this issue almost always displays an indifferent strike at the center. The present coin is no exception, with soft detail through the middle of Liberty's head, hand, and leg. The eagle's trailing leg lacks detail as well. Otherwise, the coin is virtually without fault with lemon-gold toning interspersed with silver-blue accents. It earns the PCGS Plus for eye appeal. NGC ID# 24SB, PCGS# 6620

1943-S Half Dollar, MS67
Pure Silver Luster

4137 1943-S MS67 NGC. A blinding-white coin with a rare bold strike for the issue. This Superb Gem is entirely untoned with brilliant, satin-smooth luster. Struck from obviously polished dies, the motto is lightly die-doubled. The devices are for all purposes unimprovable for the San Francisco date, which is normally soft at the centers. Neither PCGS nor NGC have certified a numerically finer example. Census: 25 in 67 (1 in 67 ★), 0 finer (10/14). NGC ID# 24SB, PCGS# 6620

1943-S Walking Liberty Half Dollar, MS67 ★
Notable Condition Rarity

4138 1943-S MS67 ★ NGC. Few examples of the San Francisco issue display outstanding eye appeal — and virtually no coins are boldly struck — accounting for the dearth of Superb Gem representatives despite a mintage of more than 13 million coins. This example earns the sole NGC Star for visual impact. Russet and gold toning embrace the rims, surrounding pearlescent-silver centers. Iridescent colors are more subtly present amid glowing, satin luster. The central details are less impressive, but overall the motifs are above-average for this strike-challenged issue. Census: 25 in 67 (1 in 67 ★), 0 finer (10/14).
From The Paul Kiraly #1 NGC Registry Roosevelt Dimes, Circulation Issue. NGC ID# 24SB, PCGS# 6620

4139 1946-D MS67 PCGS. This spectacular Superb Gem exhibits sharply detailed design elements with clear separation between Liberty's thumb and finger on the wreath hand. The impeccably preserved surfaces radiate vibrant mint luster. Population: 65 in 67 (1 in 67+), 0 finer (10/14). NGC ID# 24SK, PCGS# 6628

PROOF WALKING LIBERTY HALF DOLLARS

1936 Half Dollar, PR66
Scarcest Walking Liberty Proof
Bold Visual Appeal

4140 1936 PR66 NGC. Vivid orange and lemon-yellow toning visits the deeply mirrored surfaces of this brilliant proof, the first and arguably the most-desired date of the series in proof format. The reverse is particularly impressive, with a full strike on the eagle and blazing orange highlights sparkling among lemon and chartreuse shadings. A slight haze on the obverse restrains the underlying iridescence, but the mirrors are strong and the strike fully worthy of Premium Gem status. NGC ID# 27V4, PCGS# 6636

4141 1940 PR68 NGC. Only 11,279 proof Walking Liberty half dollars were struck in 1940 and few survivors can match the quality of this incredible PR68 example. The design elements offer razor-sharp definition throughout, with deeply reflective fields and pristine surfaces that show highlights of greenish-gold toning. Census: 59 in 68 (4 in 68 ★), 0 finer (11/14). NGC ID# 27V8, PCGS# 6640

4142 1940 PR68 NGC. This magnificent PR68 example has fully brilliant silver surfaces of impeccable quality, with slight traces of cameo contrast on each side, yet not enough to receive such a designation. In fact, full Cameo proof Walking Liberty half dollars are extremely rare. Census: 59 in 68 (4 in 68 ★), 0 finer (11/14). NGC ID# 27V8, PCGS# 6640

FRANKLIN HALF DOLLARS

4143 1949-D MS66 Full Bell Lines PCGS. A boldly detailed Registry Set candidate, this Full Bell Lines Franklin half dollar displays frosty golden-gray luster beneath lightly mottled shades of forest-green, amber-red, and olive-gold toning. No significant abrasions are observed. Population: 48 in 66 (3 in 66+) Full Bell Lines, 0 finer (10/14). NGC ID# 24SU, PCGS# 86654

1949-D Half Dollar, MS66 Full Bell Lines
Rare This Nice, Lightly Toned

4144 1949-D MS66 Full Bell Lines PCGS. A dusting of almond-gray toning — more prominent on the reverse than the obverse — adorns the essentially silver-white surfaces of this lustrous, boldly struck Premium Gem half. The Denver issue is rare in MS66 condition with or without Full Bell Lines (most high-grade examples show FBL), and neither PCGS nor NGC have certified any coins numerically finer than the current example. Population: 48 in 66 (3 in 66+) Full Bell Lines, 0 finer (10/14). NGC ID# 24SU, PCGS# 86654

4145 1949-S MS66+ Full Bell Lines PCGS. CAC. Vibrant satiny mint luster illuminates a full coating of speckled copper-orange and olive patina across both obverse and reverse. Fully struck with carefully preserved surfaces that are nearly pristine. Population: 12 in 66+ Full Bell Lines, 6 finer (11/14). NGC ID# 24SV, PCGS# 86655

4146 1953-D MS66+ Full Bell Lines NGC. Shades of sea-green, silver-gray, and amber patina visit the immaculate surfaces of this high-end Premium Gem. The sharply detailed design elements include Full Bell Lines definition. Census: 23 in 66 (1 in 66+ Full Bell Lines, 2 in 66 ★ NGC ID# 24T7, PCGS# 86665

1954-D Franklin Half, MS66+ Full Bell Lines
Conditionally Challenging Issue

4147 1954-D MS66+ Full Bell Lines PCGS. CAC. While easy enough to locate in lower grades, even MS65 FBL, examples of the 1954-D are difficult to find in MS66 condition. This Plus-designated coin is brilliant throughout (with none of the often-seen spots) and the mint luster is thick and frosted. No obvious abrasions are seen on either side. NGC ID# 24TA, PCGS# 86668

1961-D Franklin Half, MS66 Full Bell Lines
None Numerically Finer

4148 1961-D MS66 Full Bell Lines PCGS. This beautifully preserved, frosty Premium Gem is one of just 19 examples certified at the MS66 grade level at PCGS (1 in 66+), with none finer (10/14), and is also numerically equal to the coin represented in the current highest-rated Registry Set. A pale golden hue graces vibrant luster on each side, while the strike is sharp, as evidenced by the Full Bell Lines designation from PCGS. A small reed mark, well-hidden within Franklin's hair strands, appears to be the grade-limiting factor for this piece, but is hardly detectable to the unaided eye. NGC ID# 24TP, PCGS# 86681

4149 1962 MS65 Full Bell Lines PCGS. CAC. A spectacular Gem with well-preserved brilliant surfaces and vibrant mint luster throughout. The design elements are sharply detailed, with Full Bell Lines definition. PCGS has graded only six numerically finer examples (10/14). NGC ID# 24TR, PCGS# 86682

4150 1963 MS65 Full Bell Lines NGC. Remarkable cherry-red, apple-green, and autumn-gold toning dominates the reverse but leaves a window of brilliance on the bell. The obverse is stone-white. Lustrous and well preserved. NGC ID# 24TT, PCGS# 86684

PROOF FRANKLIN HALF DOLLARS

4151 **1955 PR67 Deep Cameo PCGS. CAC.** Frost-white devices set against fully mirrored fields deliver incredible white-on-black contrast on this beautifully preserved Deep Cameo. The strike is full and the surfaces are devoid of color. A prime Registry Set contender. Population: 57 in 67 (1 in 67+), 20 finer (10/14). NGC ID# 27VF, PCGS# 96696

4152 **1960 PR68 Deep Cameo PCGS. CAC.** A magnificent Franklin half dollar, with razor-sharp definition on the design elements and deeply mirrored fields that contrast profoundly with the frosty devices. The brilliant surfaces are virtually perfect and eye appeal is terrific. Population: 75 in 68, 5 finer (10/14). NGC ID# 24TY, PCGS# 96701

1961 Doubled Die Reverse, FS-801, PR65
Dramatic, Rare Doubled-Die Variety

4153 **1961 Doubled Die Reverse, FS-801, PR65 PCGS.** Dramatic die doubling is readily apparent on UNITED, E PLURIBUS UNUM, and HA in HALF on this important proof Doubled Die Reverse variety. This is a brilliant, fully struck Gem with highly reflective fields and well-preserved surfaces. A single, small milky spot appears on the crack in the Liberty Bell. Population: 5 in 65, 9 finer (10/14). PCGS# 145292

1961 FS-801 Half Dollar, PR66
Boldest Doubled Die of the Series

4154 **1961 Doubled Die Reverse, FS-801, PR66 PCGS. CAC.** The die doubling is remarkable on this proof, with dramatic doubled lettering on all letters of the left side reverse visible with the naked eye. The variety is pictured on the Fivaz-Stanton *Cherrypickers' Guide*, an indication of the importance this modern-day proof rarity commands. Seen here on a brilliant, untoned Premium Gem coin, the technical quality matches the visual impact. Listed in the 2015 *Guide Book* on page 211. Population: 25 in 66 (2 in 66+), 11 finer (10/14). PCGS# 145292

PROOF KENNEDY HALF DOLLAR

4155 **2014-W Gold, 50th Anniversary, PR70 Ultra Cameo NGC.** Ex: Chicago ANA August 2014. A technically perfect example of this incredibly popular issue, with fully detailed, richly frosted design elements struck in high relief. The impeccably preserved, deeply mirrored fields provide profound cameo contrast with the frosty devices. Eye appeal is terrific. PCGS# 530186

EARLY DOLLARS

4156 **1795 Flowing Hair, Three Leaves, B-7, BB-18, R.3 — Plugged, Retoned — NCS. Fine Details.** No plug is readily evident, but the silver-gray and charcoal surfaces are moderately granular, and the scattered small pits are accompanied by scratches. The centers are faintly hairlined. A scarcer die variety. PCGS# 39973

1795 Draped Bust Dollar, VF Details
Off Center Bust, B-14, BB-51
Planchet Flaw, Counterstamped

4157 **1795 Draped Bust, Off-Center, B-14, BB-51, R.2 — Damage — PCGS Genuine. VF Details.** Described as a Mint Error on the PCGS holder, but the only Mint-related factor is a planchet flaw at star 6. The counterstamp "5" was applied sometime after the coin was minted by an unknown person, with unknown significance. Perhaps an inspector number, gunsmith or toolmaker mark.

Otherwise, this is a wonderful Small Eagle early dollar with smooth, unabraded surfaces, nice rims, full dentils, and a strong strike. Attractive olive-gray toning covers the sharply detailed surfaces.

1795 Draped Bust Dollar, VF Details
B-15, BB-52, Centered

4158 **1795 Draped Bust, Centered, B-15, BB-52, R.2 — Improperly Cleaned — NGC Details. VF.** Die State IV, with a knife-like die break in Liberty's hair to the right of the ribbon. Only two 1795 Draped Bust dollar varieties are known, and both are moderately obtainable in the absolute sense for type purposes. This BB-52 example shows strong borders and moderate central detail for the grade. The surfaces are unnaturally bright, due to past cleaning, though the recesses have reacquired pale battleship-gray patina. PCGS# 39995

1796 B-4, BB-61 Dollar, VF Details
Large Letters, Small Date

4159 **1796 Small Date, Large Letters, B-4, BB-61, R.3 — Improperly Cleaned — NGC Details. VF.** Bowers Die State I. Both sides are predominantly gray, but the obverse has rose-red tints while the reverse exhibits powder-blue undertones. This Small Eagle collector coin displays ample design detail and lacks any mentionable abrasions. Though designated as cleaned by NGC, the surfaces are only mildly glossy. PCGS# 40000

4160 **1797 9x7 Stars, Large Letters, B-1, BB-73, R.3 — Filed Rims — PCGS Genuine. Fine Details.** A slender mark on the rim above the LI in LIBERTY is accompanied by file marks, which also affect the edge in the vicinity. The traces of lacquer residue are most apparent near the R in AMERICA. Overall, though, this steel-gray and slate example will satisfy many collectors. PCGS# 40003

4161 **1798 Large Eagle, Knob 9, 5 Vertical Lines, 10 Arrows, B-6, BB-96, R.3 — Cleaning — PCGS Genuine. XF Details.** Bowers Die State V. Die cracks on the lower left obverse allow prompt attribution. A subdued steel-gray representative with a hint of granularity and only a couple of faded marks on the field above the hair ribbon. PCGS# 40011

4162 **1798 Large Eagle, Pointed 9, Wide Date, B-22, BB-104, R.4 — Graffiti — PCGS Genuine. VF Details.** Bowers Die State V. Deep olive-brown and dove-gray toning embraces this better variety early silver dollar. Several pinscratches intersect on the portrait, and three additional vertical pinscratches ascend near the eagle's beak. Less conspicuous marks are noted west of the 7 in the date. PCGS# 40021

4163 **1798 Large Eagle, Pointed 9, 10 Arrows, B-13, BB-108, R.2, Fine 15 PCGS.** Bowers Die State II. A die break near the L in LIBERTY attributes this deeply toned Heraldic Eagle dollar. The gunmetal-gray fields contrast with lighter lavender high points. Lightly abraded except for a noncontiguous mark beneath the T in LIBERTY. PCGS# 40025

4164 **1798 Large Eagle, Pointed 9, Wide Date, B-15, BB-112, R.3 — Improperly Cleaned — NGC Details. XF.** Bowers Die State III. The curls and wings exhibit noticeable luster, and the high points display tan toning. The fields are mildly bright, but the only reportable mark is a brief horizontal line above the arrows. A small flan flaw rests above the eagle's head.

1798 Draped Bust Dollar, VF35
B-8, BB-125
Sharp and Original

4165 **1798 Large Eagle, Pointed 9, Four Berries, B-8, BB-125, R.2, VF35 PCGS.** Bowers Die State II. Actually an earlier die state than normally encountered, with no die weakness at the stars or on letters N and E of UNITED. Devoid of die cracks save for the omnipresent light crack from the lower right serif of E in LIBERTY to the hair. Diagnostic Four Berries reverse and vertical die flaw in the left obverse field confirm the variety. This originally toned dollar is remarkably sharp for a die pair plagued by weakness and multiple reverse die breaks. An attractive olive-bronze patina covers both sides of this Choice VF example. Minor scrapes by the date and between STATES OF are the only mentionable marks. PCGS# 40042

1798 Large Eagle Dollar, VF35
B-8, BB-125, Four Berries

4166 **1798 Large Eagle, Pointed 9, Four Berries, B-8, BB-125, R.2, VF35 NGC.** Die State II. This is the only use of both dies, with four large berries on the reverse branch. The present coin shows strong detail for the grade and original gunmetal-gray patina overall. An appealing Draped Bust type representative of a moderately available variety. Seldom seen with original surfaces. PCGS# 40042

1799/8 13 Stars Reverse Early Dollar, XF40
B-2, BB-143

4167 **1799/8 13 Stars Reverse, B-2, BB-143, R.4, XF40 NGC.** Bowers-Borckardt Die State II. This bright, untoned example of the 1799/8 early dollar shows a few faint hairlines and minor pinscratches on each side, but large or deep abrasions are absent. The reverse displays 13 stars above the eagle, and a thick die crack down through the curved part of D, distinguishing it from the two other 1799/8 varieties. A few scattered die lumps are also noted on the obverse. PCGS# 40066

4168 **1799 Irregular Date, 13 Stars Reverse, B-15, BB-152, R.3, VF30 NGC.** Bowers Die State IV. The first 9 was entered as if the date would be curved, but the second 9 was entered in line with the first two digits. Deep golden-brown and steel-gray encompasses this midgrade early dollar. Smooth aside from several tiny marks on the shield. PCGS# 40045

4169 **1799 7x6 Stars, B-7, BB-156, R.4 — Cleaning — PCGS Genuine. XF Details.** A narrow vertical granular streak beneath Liberty's chin is accompanied by a patch of hairlines. Otherwise, a nicely defined early dollar with slate-gray centers and sea-green margins. A scarce Bolender variety interesting for several prominent die cracks on the reverse. PCGS# 40048

4170 **1799 7x6 Stars, B-5, BB-157, R.2 — Cleaning — PCGS Genuine. VF Details.** Bowers Die State III. Iridescent plum-red, yellow-gold, electric-blue, and olive-gold patina encompasses this lightly abraded Draped Bust dollar. Slight rim dings near OF and obverse star 12 are of only minor concern. PCGS# 40049

1799 Dollar, Choice VF
7x6 Stars, B-11, BB-161

4171 **1799 7x6 Stars, B-11, BB-161, R.3, VF35 PCGS.** Die State IV, unlisted, with a die chip below the eagle's beak and a heavy die crack from the reverse rim near the D in UNITED. For the grade, this Choice VF coin retains substantial detail. The strike is bold and evenly executed, with complete border denticles on each side and sharp central devices. Splashes of tan-gray color interrupt deep gunmetal-gray and steel-blue patina. PCGS# 40052

4172 **1799 7x6 Stars, B-8, BB-165, R.3, VF25 PCGS.** The left side of the drapery is worn, but this attractive Draped Bust dollar retains much of its interior design detail and the pleasing silver-gray surfaces show only minor abrasions. Population for the variety: 1 in 25, 9 finer (10/14). PCGS# 40056

4173 **1800 B-16, BB-187, R.2, VF25 NGC.** Bowers Die State III. Steel-blue and walnut-brown toning alternates this charming early silver dollar. All letters in E PLURIBUS UNUM are perceptible, and most are clear. Marks are minimal for the grade aside from a thin line beneath the Y in LIBERTY. PCGS# 40073

4174 **1800 B-16, BB-187, R.2, VF25 PCGS.** Bowers Die State IV. A stone-gray Heraldic Eagle type coin. Abrasions are minor for the grade, despite a minor reverse rim ding near 2:30 and a faded thin field mark beneath the chin. A flan flaw above the R in LIBERTY is of mint origin. PCGS# 40073

1800 Silver Dollar, B-16, BB-187, XF40

4175 **1800 B-16, BB-187, R.2, XF40 PCGS.** Bowers Die State III. A primarily silver-gray example of this relatively common die pair, often available in circulated grades but hardly ever seen in Uncirculated state. This is a somewhat bright coin with moderate wear. Glimpses of silver luster remain among the stars and legend, with few abrasions of any size, but a bit of roughness is visible on the portrait and right obverse field. PCGS# 40073

1800 Dollar, AU Details
B-16, BB-187

4176 **1800 B-16, BB-187, R.2 — Cleaning — PCGS Genuine. AU Details.** Die State III, with a long curving die crack from the second 0 in the date through Liberty's bust to star 10. The strike is bold and even, with complete border denticles and sharply impressed, very lightly worn central devices. A small patch of crisscrossing adjustment marks is noted in the lower-right obverse field. PCGS notes evidence of light cleaning, though each side has since retoned shades of olive and pewter-gray. PCGS# 40073

4177 **1800 10 Arrows, B-15, BB-195, R.4, VG8 PCGS.** Die State I. This is a well-worn example, but it retains strong border and central detail for the grade. The dentils are complete, and there are no obtrusive adjustment marks. Olive-gray and deep golden patina blankets each side, revealing small tinges of blue and lavender when turned in-hand. PCGS# 40080

1801 Draped Bust Dollar, VF35
Scarce B-4, BB-214 Variety

4178 **1801 B-4, BB-214, R.4, VF35 PCGS. CAC.** Bowers-Borckardt Die State III. This is the scarcest of four known die varieties for the 1801 silver dollars. This Choice VF example displays pleasingly smooth surfaces with a deep layer of green-gray toning across each side. A few grade-consistent marks are noted near the center of the obverse. PCGS# 40086

4179 **1802 Narrow Date, B-6, BB-241, R.1, VG10 ANACS.** This Heraldic Eagle type coin is mostly slate-white but shows charcoal toning in design crevices. No marks are consequential except for minor rim bumps near the 02 in the date and the IT in UNITED. PCGS# 40088

1802 Dollar, B-6, BB-241, VF25
Attractive Original Patina

4180 **1802 Narrow Date, B-6, BB-241, R.1, VF25 PCGS. CAC.** Die State III, as usual. Undeniably original patina yields primarily gunmetal-gray hues, though lighter shades of pewter and lavender-gray are seen over portions of the relief elements. The strike is bold, showing complete border denticles and sharp central devices, while only minor wear is evident over the high points. Housed in an old green label holder. PCGS# 40088

GOBRECHT DOLLAR

1836 Gobrecht Dollar, Fine Details
Judd-60, Die Alignment I

4181 **1836 Name on Base, Judd-60 Original, Pollock-65 — Repaired — NGC Details. Fine.** Silver. Plain Edge. No Stars Obverse, Stars Reverse. Die Alignment I (coin turn, center of Liberty's head opposite DO in DOLLAR). There is no evidence of the diagonal clash mark above the eagle's wing, but it is inconclusive whether it was there at one point or not because of the problems on the coin. The fields show extensive smoothing, a hole appears to have been plugged at 3 o'clock, reengraving is seen on several of the letters on the reverse, and several random scratches are noted on the reverse also. Murky gray-rose toning covers each side. PCGS# 11225

SEATED DOLLARS

1841 Seated Dollar, MS62
Delicately Toned

4182 **1841 MS62 PCGS.** In the context of No Motto Seated dollars, the 1841 is one of the more plentiful early dates overall, but it is still scarce in Mint State. The present coin displays subtle ice-blue and pale champagne hues over each side, with a few deeper tinges of gold and olive-gray near the borders. Some minor striking deficiency is noted on the eagle's left (facing) leg and upper wing feathers, as is typical of this issue, though the design elements are otherwise well brought up. A softly lustrous, minimally abraded type coin. Population: 21 in 62, 22 finer (10/14). NGC ID# 24YB, PCGS# 6927

4183 **1842 AU55 PCGS. CAC.** Blended shades of golden-brown, cerulean-blue, and dove-gray toning blanket the lightly abraded surfaces of this Choice AU specimen. The well-detailed design elements show just a trace of wear on the high points. NGC ID# 24YC, PCGS# 6928

1844 Silver Dollar, AU58
Popular Low-Mintage Issue

4184 **1844 AU58 PCGS.** This issue is slightly more challenging in high grades than the dates immediately preceding it, but is still available enough to be collectible. The limited 20,000-coin mintage was apparently accomplished with just one die pair, which shows bold die doubling on the obverse shield lines. On the reverse, numerous crisscrossing die file striations are seen in the fields adjacent to the eagle's body, as well as within the recesses of the shield stripes. This example is sharply struck, with only slight friction over the high points of the design. Dusky golden-gray toning blankets each side, revealing subtle hints of luster in the protected regions. Population: 21 in 58, 32 finer (10/14). NGC ID# 24YE, PCGS# 6930

4185 **1846 AU55 PCGS.** The 1846 is one of the more plentiful Seated dollar issues from the 1840s, though it is not seen as often as the more popular type dates from 1841 to 1843. This is a boldly detailed Choice AU representative, with subtle semiprooflike mirroring beneath a thin veil of light golden color. Slight high-point friction precludes a Mint State grade. NGC ID# 24YG, PCGS# 6932

4186 **1846 AU58 PCGS.** The lightly abraded surfaces of this attractive near-Mint example retain much of their original mint luster, under shades of lavender, gray, and pale gold toning. The well-detailed design elements show just a trace of wear. Population: 50 in 58, 71 finer (11/14). NGC ID# 24YG, PCGS# 6932

1855 Silver Dollar, XF45
Low Mintage, Few Survivors

4187 **1855 XF45 PCGS.** Seated dollars from the 1850s functioned as unofficial "trade dollars," while few coins actually circulated domestically. Exported and subsequently melted in the China trade, relatively few examples of the 1855 issue remain in any condition. This choice XF coin shows rainbow shades at the borders and reflective, silver-gray centers. Sharp detail remains with a hint of luster around the devices. The rims are strong and unmarked. Only tiny abrasions visit the partially prooflike fields; none are significant for the grade. Population: 8 in 45, 79 finer (10/14). NGC ID# 24YU, PCGS# 6943

4188 **1859-O — Reverse Scratched — NGC Details. Unc.** 1859-O dollars are slightly scarcer than their 1860-O successors, and both issues are known for lustrous but bagmarked white surfaces. The present piece is typical for an Uncirculated 1859-O except for a slender diagonal mark on the field above the eagle's head. NGC ID# 24YY, PCGS# 6947

4189 **1862 — Cleaning — PCGS Genuine. AU Details.** Mildly glossy from a wipe, but the motifs show only minor wear. Generally toned pearl-gray, although recesses display jade-green and butter-gold. A thin field mark is noted near the D in UNITED. Only 11,540 pieces were struck. NGC ID# 24Z5, PCGS# 6952

4190 **1866 Motto XF45 NGC.** A Choice XF representative of this popular type issue, from a mintage of 48,900 pieces. This coin retains complete detail on the shield stripes and the eagle's eye is bold. The lightly abraded surfaces show a few traces of original mint luster. NGC ID# 24Z9, PCGS# 6959

4191 **1866 Motto MS61 NGC.** The 1866 Seated Liberty dollar with the motto IN GOD WE TRUST is always popular with first-year type collectors. This impressive MS61 example offers well-detailed design elements and lustrous surfaces that show a scattering of minor contact marks, under attractive shades of greenish-gold toning. Census: 4 in 61, 29 finer (10/14). NGC ID# 24Z9, PCGS# 6959

1868 Seated Dollar, MS61
Attractive Original Toning
FS-301, Misplaced Date

4192 **1868 Misplaced Date, FS-301, MS61 PCGS.** A seldom seen With Motto issue, genuinely rare in Mint State with original color. This example is boldly struck with well-balanced gunmetal-blue and lavender-gray toning. Slight reflectivity remains in the fields, as is characteristic of the Seated type in general. No significant abrasions are present, despite the lower Mint State grade. This coin represents an interesting *Cherrypickers'* variety, with the upper loop of a misplaced 8 (or 6) seen in the dentils below the 6 in the date. Population: 3 in 61, 23 finer (10/14). NGC ID# 24ZB, PCGS# 6961

4193 **1869 AU53 PCGS.** The sharply impressed design elements of this attractive AU53 specimen show just a trace of wear on the high points and the lightly abraded surfaces exhibit semiprooflike reflectivity in sheltered areas. Population: 14 in 53, 89 finer (10/14). NGC ID# 24ZC, PCGS# 6962

4194 **1870-CC — Cleaning — PCGS Genuine. XF Details.** A still-attractive representative of this sought-after, low-mintage issue, with light wear on the design elements and lightly abraded surfaces that show somewhat flat luster, the result of a light cleaning. NGC ID# 24ZE, PCGS# 6964

4195 **1870-CC — Environmental Damage — NGC Details. AU.** Breen-5485, Variety 3-C. Breen's "CC closely spaced" variety, which he considered rare. The first issue struck at the legendary Carson City Mint, the 1870-CC has a low mintage of 12,462 pieces. The present example has only light wear but the deeply toned borders are moderately granular, and the stone-gray centers display several small spots. NGC ID# 24ZE, PCGS# 6964

4196 **1872 AU55 NGC. CAC.** Deep layers of bluish-brown patina blanket both sides of this Choice AU example. It is well-struck and lightly worn, with minimal marks for a circulated coin. This date had the highest business strike mintage of its type, at 1.1 million pieces, and it is extremely popular as a type issue. NGC ID# 24ZJ, PCGS# 6968

4197 **1872 MS62 NGC.** From a mintage of 1.1 million pieces, the 1872 Seated Liberty dollar is an available date and a popular type issue. This pleasing MS62 example offers well-detailed design elements and lightly marked surfaces under attractive shades of greenish-gold toning. Census: 31 in 62 (1 in 62+), 41 finer (10/14). NGC ID# 24ZJ, PCGS# 6968

4198 **1872-CC — Improperly Cleaned — NGC Details. VG.** A well-worn example of this key Carson City issue that retains all major design elements in outline, with some interior detail, date, and lettering still intact. The dove-gray surfaces show no large or distracting marks, with some signs of light cleaning. NGC ID# 24ZK, PCGS# 6969

1872-CC Dollar, VF20
Scarce in All Grades

4199 1872-CC VF20 PCGS. Scarce at all grade levels, the low-mintage 1872-CC Seated dollar has seen a total of 213 grading events at PCGS, including an unknown number of resubmission (10/14). This VF example resides in an older PCGS holder with a light-green label. The evenly worn cream-gray surfaces are free of significant distractions. The letters LI-RTY in LIBERTY are visible. An attractive example of this important key issue for the grade. NGC ID# 24ZK, PCGS# 6969

1872-CC Seated Dollar, XF Sharpness
A Collectible Example, Low-Mintage Issue

4200 1872-CC — Cleaned — NGC Details. XF. Strong rims and sharp XF details are redeeming factors for this lightly worn Seated dollar, which retains considerable appeal despite the noted cleaning. The hairlines are well-concealed and a thin skin of golden toning softens the resultant brightness. A small group of abrasions beneath star 8 comprise the most noticeable marks on the otherwise smooth surfaces. Always in demand as a challenging, low-mintage Carson City issue.

1873-CC Seated Dollar, Fine Details
Rarest Carson City Issue

4201 1873-CC — Repaired — NGC Details. Fine. Smokey-silver toning covers the moderately worn surfaces of this rare Carson City dollar, disguising the exact area(s) of smoothing and repair. Several small rim bumps are seen on each side. Even so, this example is not without its appeal to those who wish to fill the challenging "hole" in their collection and for Carson City specialists who realize how few examples of this date exist in any condition. NGC ID# 24ZN, PCGS# 6972

PROOF SEATED DOLLARS

1860 Seated Dollar, PR62
Noticeable Field-Device Contrast

4202 1860 PR62 PCGS. CAC. Housed in an old green label holder, this piece is not designated as a Cameo, though the field-motif contrast is unmistakable. Sharp definition on the stars and eagle's feathers complements deeply mirrored fields, while a thin veil of light champagne toning adds a degree of warmth to each side. Highly appealing for the grade, as affirmed by the CAC green label. NGC ID# 252E, PCGS# 7003

1865 Seated Dollar, Toned PR61

4203 1865 PR61 ANACS. Deep gunmetal-blue and lavender-gray toning precludes a cameo designation for this piece, though the incredible sharpness of the devices and lack of heavy abrasions confirms its proof status. The proof 1865 Seated dollar had a limited mintage of just 500 pieces, but in high grades, these are more easily obtainable than their rare business strike counterparts, and are ideal for date representation. NGC ID# 252K, PCGS# 7008

1865 Dollar, PR62 Cameo
Pleasing Lower-Grade Proof

4204 1865 PR62 Cameo PCGS. The 1865 is a moderately available proof issue overall, but Cameo representatives are scarce, regardless of numeric grade. This piece is certified near the lower end of the proof grade spectrum, but nonetheless exhibits outstanding eye appeal and contrast. The strike is bold, and only a few wisps of light golden color are present to preclude full brilliance. Faint, scattered hairlines, seen only with a glass, contribute to the grade. Population: 13 in 62, 38 finer (10/14). PCGS# 87008

4205 **1868 — Questionable Color — PCGS Proof Genuine. Unc Details.** A crisply struck and unworn specimen. The glossy surfaces display consistent caramel-gold toning. A lens reveals only infrequent small contact marks. One of only 600 proofs issued. NGC ID# 252P, PCGS# 7016

4206 **1868 PR61 PCGS.** Fully struck as expected for the well-produced proof format, with light contrast between the central devices and the brilliantly untoned, strongly reflective fields. Delicate hairlines are readily apparent when viewed at an angle, yet the coin offers dramatic, deep-mirrored silver appeal. NGC ID# 252P, PCGS# 7016

1868 Seated Dollar, PR62 Cameo
Brilliant, High-Contrast Example

4207 **1868 PR62 Cameo PCGS.** A brilliant-white, deep-mirrored proof — entirely untoned, save for a small spot near Liberty's knee. The motifs are fully struck and frosted. Many proofs of this era show delicate lines in the fields, as does this coin, most of which require a glass to view. An attractive, high-contrast proof for the assigned grade. Population: 7 in 62, 34 finer (10/14). PCGS# 87016

1869 Seated Dollar, PR63 Cameo
Full Reverse Scroll

4208 **1869 PR63 Cameo PCGS.** Surprisingly, three obverse dies and two reverse dies were used to strike the 1869 proofs despite a mintage of just 600 pieces. The most commonly used reverse was lapped, resulting in weakness of the scroll above the eagle. This example, however, is fully struck, suggesting a less-available die pair with the date lower and further left than the other varieties. Hazy powder-gold toning covers both sides of this Choice proof, although deep reflective mirrors are visible at the proper viewing angle. Mint frost covers the boldly struck devices. Population: 13 in 63 (1 in 63+), 21 finer (10/14). PCGS# 87017

4209 **1870 — Improperly Cleaned — NGC Details. Proof.** The frosty design elements of this Seated Liberty dollar are sharply detailed and show no actual wear, but the reflective fields show the flat aspect that usually indicates a light cleaning. Shades of apple-green, gray, and blue toning visit the surfaces. NGC ID# 252S, PCGS# 7018

TRADE DOLLARS

1874 Trade Dollar, MS64
Flashy Original Luster

4210 **1874 MS64 PCGS.** Type One Obverse and Reverse, period after FINE. The 1874 Trade dollar is only marginally available in Mint State grades, and is genuinely rare above the Choice level. This coin is free of any significant abrasions, displaying a blend of warm gold and amber toning over each side. The strike is sharp, and the surfaces exhibit a balanced combination of frosty luster and semiprooflike mirroring. Population: 35 in 64, 8 finer (10/14). NGC ID# 252Z, PCGS# 7034

4211 **1874-S MS61 PCGS.** Medium S. No period after FINE. Light chestnut toning adorns this well struck and thoroughly lustrous silver type coin. The obverse field displays minor marks, but the eye appeal is unquestionably superior for the MS61 level. NGC ID# 2533, PCGS# 7036

4212 **1875-CC Type Two Reverse MS61 PCGS.** Type One Obverse, Type Two Reverse. The rare Type Two Reverse, with no berry under the claw. This well-detailed MS61 example displays satiny mint luster and delicate shades of champagne-gold toning. Population for the variety: 1 in 61, 1 finer (10/14). PCGS# 40109

4213 **1875-S Type One Reverse MS63 NGC.** Large S. This coin's eye appeal seems to belie its numeric grade. Boldly struck with radiant luster, the coin exhibits rich sea-green, violet, and blue peripheral toning around fiery sun-gold in the margins and lighter champagne in the centers. Grade-limiting abrasions are minor and evenly dispersed. A truly lovely coin in all respects. PCGS# 510101

4214 **1875-S Type One Reverse MS63 PCGS.** Lustrous and well-produced, with pleasing hues of champagne and silver displayed across each side. This Select Mint State specimen is somewhat conditionally scarce, and finer-graded examples are scarce-to-rare. PCGS# 510101

4215 **1875-S Type One Reverse MS63 NGC.** Large S. Light wheat-gold and powder-blue toning graces this lustrous silver type coin. The strike is bold aside from blending on the eagle's right (facing) claw. Only minor field marks determine the grade. PCGS# 510101

1875-S Trade Dollar, MS64
Richly Toned, S-Mint Type Coin

4216 **1875-S Type One Reverse MS64 PCGS.** Large S. A production of nearly 4.5 million coins and a high survival rate make the 1875-S one of the more available Trade dollar issues in the series and an appropriate choice for inclusion in a type set. This is a richly toned example with pinpoint definition on the stars in particular. Liberty's head and the eagle's right claw are a touch incomplete. PCGS has graded only 35 numerically finer submissions (10/14). PCGS# 510101

4217 **1875-S Type Two Reverse MS61 PCGS.** A thin ring of rainbow toning graces the extreme outer peripheries on this minimally abraded example, with pale champagne color seen over the remainder of each side. The top of Liberty's head and portions of the eagle's plumage are not fully defined, though the strike is otherwise pleasing. PCGS# 510102

4218 **1876 Type One Obverse, Type One Reverse, MS62 PCGS.** A brilliant, untoned Centennial-year example of this collector favorite featuring a bold strike and minimally marked fields. The eagle's plumage is extra-bold. Housed in a first generation holder, the lack of abrasions, strong strike, and sharp luster are all suggestive of an even higher grade. PCGS# 40110

4219 **1876-S Type One Obverse, Type One Reverse, MS63 NGC.** Large S. Dusky gunmetal-gray and walnut-brown toning blend throughout this satiny and inoffensively abraded Select Trade dollar. A well struck Centennial-year example. PCGS# 40114

4220 **1876-S Type One Obverse, Type One Reverse, MS63 NGC.** Large S. An impressive silver type coin that boasts dynamic cartwheel sheen and original apricot-gold and steel-blue toning. The strike is good and marks are minimal aside from a vertical hairline west of the arrowheads. Housed in a former generation holder. PCGS# 40114

1878-S Trade Dollar, MS64
Minor Tripled Die Obverse

4221 **1878-S — Tripled Die Obverse — MS64 PCGS.** Noted by PCGS to have die doubling on the obverse, though the signs are subtle. Some minor doubling is also noted on the reverse lettering, though this is not one of the varieties listed in the *Cherrypickers'* reference. This piece displays brilliant, radiant centers with thin rings of golden-orange and aquamarine toning around the periphery. The strike is well-executed, and the surfaces are only minimally abraded for the grade. NGC ID# 253G, PCGS# 7048

PROOF TRADE DOLLARS

4222 **1874 — Scratch — PCGS Proof Genuine. Unc Details.** Two pinscratches extend from star 3 to the rim near 7 o'clock. The fields are only faintly hairlined. Sharply struck and nicely mirrored with substantial cameo contrast. Just 700 proofs were issued. NGC ID# 27YK, PCGS# 7054

1875 Trade Dollar, PR64 Cameo
Frosty Devices, Flashy Mirrors

4223 **1875 PR64 Cameo PCGS.** Type One Obverse, Type Two Reverse. Ice-white motifs rise in full detail above glassy fields. Brilliant and beautiful with only inconsequential hairlines. Minor die doubling is present on E PLURIBUS UNUM. From the proof mintage of 700 pieces, relatively few remain with comparable eye appeal. Population: 22 in 64 (2 in 64+), 7 finer (10/14). PCGS# 87055

1876 Trade Dollar, PR63
Two-Toned Color Palette

4224 **1876 PR63 PCGS.** Type One Obverse, Type Two Reverse. An interesting medley of colors interplays on each side of this Select proof 1876 Trade dollar, comprising chiefly pale yellow-gold in the fields and deep mauve around the device outlines on each side. Scattered hairlines and thin contact marks in the fields account for the grade. A scarce issue in proof format. Population: 54 in 63 (1 in 63+), 71 finer (10/14). NGC ID# 27YM, PCGS# 7056

4225 **1883 PR53 NGC.** Type Two Obverse and Reverse. For the budget-minded collector, this lightly circulated final-year proof retains substantial eye appeal with subtle hints of mirroring still residing in the fields. Both sides are deeply toned in original gunmetal-gray, aquamarine, and golden hues. An unusually attractive proof for the grade. NGC ID# 27YV, PCGS# 7063

1883 Trade Dollar, PR63
Deep Original Toning

4226 **1883 PR63 PCGS.** Type Two Obverse and Reverse. Business strike Trade dollar production ceased in 1878, following congressional legislation that demonetized the denomination, but proof examples continued to be made for collectors through 1883. The present example of this final-year issue displays deep gunmetal-gray, olive, and amber-gold toning over mirrored fields and crisply struck design elements. Housed in an old green label holder, with any grade-limiting hairlines well-hidden by the rich patina. NGC ID# 27YV, PCGS# 7063

MORGAN DOLLARS

4227 **1878 8TF Polished Ear, VAM-14.2, MS65 PCGS.** The peach-gold obverse center is framed by slender peripheral arcs of cherry-red and sky-blue. The reverse is brilliant save for a band of faint gold toning near 1 o'clock. Well struck and exceptionally smooth. The obverse is prooflike and the reverse exhibits cartwheel luster. PCGS# 133797

4228 **1878 8TF Broken R&B, VAM-21, MS65 PCGS.** The bases of the R and B in PLURIBUS are broken. This Gem eight tailfeather dollar has light golden toning and a prooflike reverse. The obverse displays cartwheel luster. Well struck and impressively preserved. PCGS# 133822

4229 **1878 8TF Broken R&B, VAM-21, MS65 PCGS.** The entire reverse is lightly die doubled on this variety, with the evidence most easily seen on the wreath leaves, the upper arrowhead, and much of the lettering. The obverse exhibits broken feet on the R and B in PLURIBUS. Both sides exhibit heavy die polishing, another feature of this variety. This example displays boldly struck design elements and exhibits only a few minor ticks on the cheek. Radiant cartwheel luster illuminates blended multicolor toning on each side, revealing hues of lemon-gold, aquamarine, amber-red, violet, and forest-green. A must-have coin for either the toning or VAM enthusiast. PCGS# 133822

4230 **1878 7/8TF 7/3 Weak, VAM-32, MS64 Prooflike PCGS.** A Top 100 Variety. A rare die variety distinguished a die line within the right side of the eagle's lapped tail. Brilliant save for a glimpse of russet and navy-blue toning at 12 o'clock on the reverse. VAM-32 Population: 4 in 64 Prooflike, 4 finer as 64 Deep Mirror Prooflike (11/14). PCGS# 40205

1878 7/8 Tailfeathers Dollar, MS65+
Strong 7/5 TF, Boldly Doubled Obverse

4231 **1878 7/8TF Strong, VAM-38, R.4 MS65+ NGC.** LIBERTY is strongly doubled left, the broadest shift of this kind known. Other doubling is seen on the left and right stars, as is the date — most obviously, at the 1 and the 7, which are doubled right. Five tail feather ends show beneath the primary feathers. Brilliant and frost-white, this nearly mark-free, untoned coin earns the NGC Plus designation. PCGS and NGC combined show just 15 coins certified in a higher numeric grade for all 7/8 TF Strong dollars, and this coin is certainly among the finest known of the interesting VAM-38 variety (10/14). PCGS# 134035

4232 **1878 7/8TF 7/5 Strong, VAM-39A, MS65 PCGS.** A Hit List 40 variety, due to its prominently doubled tailfeathers. A lustrous Gem with an intricate strike and only a trace of golden patina. Well preserved and undoubtedly elusive in the present quality. PCGS# 134036

1878 7TF Morgan Dollar, MS66
Reverse of 1878, Among the Finest at PCGS

4233 **1878 7TF Reverse of 1878 MS66 PCGS.** The 1878 seven tailfeathers, Reverse of 1878 is a rather accessible issue through Gem condition. At the Premium Gem level, however, it becomes markedly rare. This fully brilliant MS66 representative exhibits slight doubling on several obverse stars and notable die clash marks in the left reverse fields. A touch of strike softness occurs over the central motifs, but the design definition is otherwise strong. Lustrous and devoid of mentionable marks. Population: 38 in 66 (4 in 66+), 0 finer (10/14). NGC ID# 253K, PCGS# 7074

4234 **1878 7TF Reverse of 1879 MS65 PCGS.** The slanted top arrow feather identifies the Reverse of 1879. This attractive Gem is sharply detailed throughout, with well-preserved surfaces and vibrant mint luster. PCGS has graded 17 numerically finer examples (10/14). NGC ID# 253L, PCGS# 7076

4235 **1878 7TF Reverse of 1879 MS64 Prooflike PCGS.** Both obverse and reverse of this brilliant, untoned dollar show only minor marks and abrasions on the prooflike fields. Liberty's cheek, neck, and facial features are unmarked and frosted. Minor blending in the hair above Liberty's ear is the only departure from a bold strike. A Choice near-Gem coin, scarce in prooflike format. Population: 36 in 64 Prooflike, 6 finer (10/14). NGC ID# 253L, PCGS# 7077

4236 **1879 MS66 PCGS.** This is a conditionally scarce Premium Gem, with brilliant surfaces and intense cartwheel luster. Liberty's cheek is entirely smooth, and the few trivial nicks are located away from focal areas. This issue is rare any finer. NGC ID# 253S, PCGS# 7084

1879 Silver Dollar, MS66
Radiant Frost-White Luster

4237 **1879 MS66 PCGS. CAC.** Frosty, untoned luster is devoid of significant interruptions as it cartwheels around each side of this beautifully preserved Premium Gem. Slight softness is noted on the hair immediately above Liberty's ear, though the strike is otherwise sharp. The 1879 Morgan is a fairly plentiful date in lower grades, but it becomes scarce at the Premium Gem level. PCGS has certified only four numerically finer representatives (10/14). NGC ID# 253S, PCGS# 7084

1879-CC Dollar, AU55
Normal Mintmark

4238 **1879-CC AU55 PCGS.** Nice luster remains over the silver-gray surfaces of this lightly circulated dollar, second only to the 1889-CC as the scarcest Carson City issue. Just 756,000 pieces were struck. This is the Normal Mintmark (Clear CC) variety, less available yet strangely less popular than the more often-seen Capped Die overmintmark variant. Well-struck but lightly bagmarked with scuffy abrasions across both sides. NGC ID# 253T, PCGS# 7086

1879-CC Dollar, AU55
Pleasing for the Grade

4239 **1879-CC AU55 NGC.** Normal Mintmark. Moderate luster remains in the recesses of this well-detailed Choice AU representative. The coin appears brilliant at first glance, though closer examination reveals subtle hints of gold color. No significant marks are present. The 1879-CC trails only the key-date 1889-CC in overall rarity among Carson City Morgan dollars. NGC ID# 253T, PCGS# 7086

1879-O Morgan Dollar, MS65
Well-Produced New Orleans Issue

4240 **1879-O MS65 PCGS.** Rare any finer, this New Orleans issue was conscientiously produced and carefully preserved. Brilliant, silver-white surfaces are frosted and attractive. Bagmarks are always a danger for the issue, but this coin escaped with only a few. Small ticks surround Liberty's eye and minor grazes are seen at the chin and neck truncation. A boldly struck O-Mint coin, with nice hair detail above the ear and a full-feathered eagle. PCGS shows just 16 numerically finer examples (10/14). NGC ID# 253V, PCGS# 7090

1879-O Silver Dollar, MS65
Conditionally Elusive O-Mint Issue

4241 **1879-O MS65 PCGS.** A challenging issue in Gem condition, the 1879-O Morgan becomes genuinely rare any finer. This frosty, essentially untoned representative boasts sharp striking definition and superior eye appeal for the issue. Only a few minute ticks on Liberty's cheek preclude any even finer grade. PCGS has certified only 16 numerically finer examples (10/14). NGC ID# 253V, PCGS# 7090

4242 **1880/79-CC Reverse of 1878, VAM-4, MS65 PCGS.** A Top 100 Variety. Desirable both for the Reverse of 1878 and for the strong 89/79 overdate. The reverse displays a Small CC mintmark and parallel arrow feathers. Brilliant and frosted, this attractive Gem example shows slight blending over the ear but the eagle's talons are bold. PCGS# 133876

4243 **1880/79-CC Reverse of 1878, VAM-4, MS65 PCGS.** A Top 100 Variety. The most prominent overdate of the series is paired with an obsolete Second Reverse. Only a hint of golden toning visits this lustrous and well struck Gem. Careful examination reveals occasional small marks. PCGS# 133876

4244 **1880-CC 8 Over High 7, VAM-5, MS65 PCGS.** A Top 100 Variety. The undertype 7 is visible high in the loop of the second 8 in the date. This attractive Gem is sharply detailed and brightly lustrous with well-preserved surfaces that show a few hints of pale gold toning. PCGS# 133877

1880-CC Morgan, MS66
Brilliant-White; VAM-5, 8 Over High 7

4245　**1880-CC 8 Over High 7, VAM-5, MS66 PCGS.** A Top 100 Variety. Fully struck and strongly lustrous, the frosted motifs show only slight grazes while the smooth, brilliant fields display only a two or three minimal abrasions. Otherwise pristine, this Premium Gem is a high-grade example of the VAM-5 variety with an underdigit 7 punched high beneath the primary second 8, with the crossbar visible inside the upper loop and the stem within the lower loop. The first 8 is doubled, and the second 8 microscopically tripled left. A bold die gouge runs between the top arrow feather and the branch on the reverse. PCGS# 133877

4246　**1880-CC 8 Over High 7, VAM-5, MS65 Prooflike PCGS.** A Top 100 Variety. Liberty's cheek is clean and the coin presents a bold strike on motifs surrounded by prooflike fields. Vestiges of three serifs from the underdigit 7 are prominent above and to the side of the second 8, and the balance of a 7 shows in the loops below. This 8/7 High Overdate variety is scarce and desirable, particularly with the prooflike designation. Population: 27 in 65 Prooflike, 1 finer (10/14). PCGS# 41133

4247　**1880-CC 8 Over Low 7, VAM-6, MS65 PCGS.** A Top 100 Variety. The undertype 7 is visible low in the upper loop of the second 8 and the base shows below the bottom of the primary digit. This impressive Gem offers well-detailed design elements and virtually pristine lustrous surfaces. PCGS# 133878

4248　**1880-CC MS65 PCGS.** This is a lovely stone-white Gem with bold strike definition and just a trace of weakness above the ear. There are a few wispy marks on the obverse but none at all on the reverse. An appealing example from this readily available Carson City issue. NGC ID# 2542, PCGS# 7100

4249　**1880-CC MS66 PCGS. VAM-3, R.3.** The VAM-3 variety shows a "dash" beneath the second 8 (the remnant tail of a 7) and has slight doubling of the first 8 inside the lower loop. This Premium Gem example is brilliant, frosted, and lustrous with a bold strike for the issue. A slight graze on Liberty's chin and in the field nearby are the most noticeable marks. PCGS has certified just 30 numerically finer coins (10/14). NGC ID# 2542, PCGS# 7100

4250　**1880-CC MS65 Prooflike PCGS.** This is an impressive Prooflike example with snow-white surfaces and boldly struck devices. Trivial field marks keep it from grading even higher, while mint-made die striations only increase the coin's flashy reflectivity. NGC ID# 2542, PCGS# 7101

4251　**1880-O MS64 PCGS.** Small O Mintmark. Brilliant and boldly struck. Remarkably few abrasions are seen, with only tiny high-point marks on Liberty's jawline and beneath the eye. This is a silver-white near-Gem, at its optimal collecting grade because just 35 pieces have been certified numerically finer by PCGS (10/14). NGC ID# 2543, PCGS# 7114

1880-O Silver Dollar, MS64+
Rarely Encountered Finer

4252　**1880-O MS64+ PCGS. CAC.** A plentiful issue in lower grades, the 1880-O Morgan suddenly becomes rare at the Gem grade level. This Plus-graded near-Gem displays untoned, frosty cartwheel luster and above-average striking sharpness for the issue. A few faint surface grazes on the cheek preclude full Gem status, but leave this piece with substantial appeal for the grade. Only 35 coins are numerically finer at PCGS (10/14). NGC ID# 2543, PCGS# 7114

4253　**1880-O 8 Over 7 Ear, VAM-6A, MS64 PCGS.** A Top 100 Variety. The "Ear" above the left side of the second 8 in the date is actually the left-side fragment of the crossbar of a 7. Traces of the 7 also appear on the upper left loop of the 8. In addition, a few letters are faintly clashed. Lustrous and virtually brilliant with potent luster and pleasing preservation. PCGS# 133883

4254　**1880-O 8 Over 7 Ear, VAM-6A, MS64 PCGS. CAC.** A Top 100 Variety. The "check mark" and "ear" from the underdigit 7 is apparent on the second 8 in the date. Lustrous and lightly toned with a good strike and exceptional preservation for the MS64 level. Designated as VAM-6C by PCGS, but only a single clash from the wing is present in front of Liberty's neck. PCGS# 133883

4255　**1880-S MS67 PCGS.** Large S. Comprehensive fire-red and apple-green occupies the obverse. The reverse is brilliant aside from peripheral arcs of golden-brown, powder-blue, and ruby-red. A lustrous high grade type representative. NGC ID# 2544, PCGS# 7118

4256　**1880/79-S Medium S, VAM-8, MS67 NGC.** A Top 100 Variety. Medium S. Sharply struck and shining with traces of the overdate visible under magnification. Whispers of peach-gold patina appear at the margins, while the centers are predominantly silver-gray. *Ex: Long Beach Signature (Heritage, 5-6/2007), lot 1439; Long Beach Signature (Heritage, 2/2008), lot 1160.* PCGS# 133886

4257　**1881 MS66 PCGS.** The 1881 Morgan dollar is very scarce in MS66 condition, and finer examples are very rare. This sharply detailed Premium Gem displays spectacular shades of golden-brown, silver-gray, and electric-blue toning over well-preserved lustrous surfaces. PCGS has graded four numerically finer examples (10/14). NGC ID# 2546, PCGS# 7124

4258　**1881-CC MS66+ PCGS. CAC.** Bold relief elements compliment thickly frosted, radiant luster which is devoid of significant abrasions. The coin has the overall appearance of full mint brilliance at first glance, though closer examination reveals faint traces of light golden color on both sides. Seldom available in higher numeric grades. NGC ID# 2547, PCGS# 7126

1881-CC Dollar, MS66 Prooflike
Exceptional Quality and Appeal

4259 **1881-CC MS66 Prooflike PCGS.** The eye appeal is extremely high for this untoned and brilliant, prooflike dollar. The motifs show thick mint frost with only minor areas of contact. Liberty's cheek is rounded and unabraded. Fully struck on the devices, this example exudes quality over the reflective fields as well, and there are no numerically finer coins at PCGS. Population: 36 in 66 (2 in 66+) Prooflike, 0 finer (10/14). NGC ID# 2547, PCGS# 7127

4260 **1881-O MS65 PCGS.** The 1881-O Morgan dollar is not too difficult to locate at the Gem level, but finer coins are decidedly elusive. This sharply detailed MS65 example displays pristine surfaces with vibrant mint luster and highlights of champagne-gold toning. NGC ID# 2548, PCGS# 7128

4261 **1881-O MS65 PCGS.** The 1881-O Morgan dollar is conditionally rare in grades above the MS65 level. This sharply detailed Gem exhibits well-preserved brilliant surfaces with vibrant mint luster throughout. PCGS has graded 26 numerically finer examples (10/14). NGC ID# 2548, PCGS# 7128

4262 **1881-O MS65 PCGS.** The well-preserved surfaces of this spectacular Gem radiate vibrant mint luster on both sides and the design elements are well-detailed, with just a touch of the usual softness on the hair above the ear. NGC ID# 2548, PCGS# 7128

4263 **1881-O MS65 PCGS.** This delightful Gem exhibits sharply detailed design elements and vibrant mint luster throughout and the well-preserved surfaces show a few hints of greenish-gold toning at the peripheries. PCGS has graded 26 numerically finer examples (10/14). NGC ID# 2548, PCGS# 7128

4264 **1881-S MS67+ PCGS. CAC.** A high-end Superb Gem example of one of the most popular type issues of the series, this magnificent coin exhibits sharply detailed design elements and immaculate surfaces with vibrant cartwheel mint luster. NGC ID# 2549, PCGS# 7130

1882 Silver Dollar, MS66+
Thick Mint Frost

4265 **1882 MS66+ PCGS.** Cartwheel luster beams brightly from both sides of this Premium Gem dollar. Thickly frosted surfaces show only the most minor marks, with none to distract from the high-end appeal of this untoned and brilliant-white example. Although MS66 representatives of this date are often available, few receive the Plus designation from PCGS indicating superior quality and appeal. Just eight examples are certified numerically higher by PCGS (10/14). NGC ID# 254A, PCGS# 7132

1882 Silver Dollar, MS66+
Coruscating Mint Bloom

4266 **1882 MS66+ PCGS. CAC.** Unlike the San Francisco and Carson City issues of this year, the 1882 Philadelphia Morgan dollar is seldom available at the Premium Gem grade level, and is rarely seen finer. This Plus-graded example exhibits thick, brilliant mint frost and sharp design elements, while a lack of noticeable surface flaws completes the immense eye appeal. Only eight coins are numerically finer at PCGS (10/14). NGC ID# 254A, PCGS# 7132

4267 **1882-CC MS66+ PCGS. CAC.** The 1882-CC is a plentiful issue in grades up to the MS66 level, but finer examples are very scarce. This spectacular Premium Gem exhibits sharply defined devices and vibrant mint luster, with pristine brilliant surfaces. NGC ID# 254B, PCGS# 7134

4268 **1882-CC MS66+ PCGS. CAC.** Lavish mint frost and sharp strike definition endow this brilliant Premium Gem with considerable visual appeal. A superficial luster graze in the left obverse field and a couple of faint, milky toning streaks on the upper reverse fail to detract from this coin's exceptional appearance. NGC ID# 254B, PCGS# 7134

4269 **1882-CC MS66 Prooflike PCGS.** The 1882-CC Morgan dollar is an available issue in high grade, but sharply detailed Premium Gem examples with reflective prooflike surfaces, like the present coin, are quite elusive. Population: 91 in 66 (5 in 66+) Prooflike, 1 finer (10/14). NGC ID# 254B, PCGS# 7135

4270 **1883-CC MS66+ PCGS. CAC.** Thick mint frost and beautifully preserved, brilliant surfaces are the hallmarks of this high-end Premium Gem, though a well-executed strike also contributes to the immense visual appeal. Few examples have been certified numerically finer. NGC ID# 254H, PCGS# 7144

4271 **1883-CC MS66+ PCGS. CAC.** Vibrant frost-white mint bloom captivates the viewer's eye as this high-end Carson City dollar is rotated beneath a light. The strike is razor-sharp and the surfaces are devoid of both color and significant abrasions, with only a few faint luster grazes on the obverse preventing a full MS67 grade from PCGS. NGC ID# 254H, PCGS# 7144

4272 **1883-CC MS65 Deep Mirror Prooflike PCGS.** The 1883-CC is a plentiful date in the context of Carson City Morgan dollars, but Deep Mirror Prooflike examples are seldom seen in high grades. This Gem representative boasts substantial cameo contrast between the deep mirrors and thickly frosted devices. The strike is sharp and there are no individually obvious abrasions. Housed in an old green label holder, with hints of light golden color over both sides. NGC ID# 254H, PCGS# 97145

1883-O Silver Dollar, MS64
VAM-22A, Partial E Reverse

1883-S Dollar, MS64
Rarely Encountered Finer

4273 **1883-O Partial E Reverse, VAM-22A, MS64 PCGS.** A Hot 50 Variety. Clashed dies feature a partial E on the reverse below the eagle's tailfeathers, transferred from LIBERTY on the obverse. This variety is very difficult to find in high grades, as most examples are moderately abraded and suffer from varying degrees of striking deficiency. The present coin displays frosty luster beneath delicate sun-gold and lavender-blue toning. The peripheral legends and stars are weakly impressed, as is characteristic of this die pair, though the central devices are sharp. The surfaces are exceptionally well-preserved, putting this coin firmly among the finer-known examples of the variety. Population: 3 in 64, 1 finer (10/14). PCGS# 148715

4274 **1883-S MS61 PCGS.** This Mint State 1883-S Morgan dollar exhibits sharply detailed design elements and vibrant frosty mint luster on both sides. A scattering of minor contact marks explains the grade and a few hints of champagne-gold toning visit the surfaces. NGC ID# 254K, PCGS# 7148

4275 **1883-S MS62 PCGS.** A brilliant and flashy better date dollar. The strike is good and marks are mostly relegated to the lower cheek and the fields near the shoulder curl and arrows. Encapsulated in an old green label holder. NGC ID# 254K, PCGS# 7148

4276 **1883-S MS62 PCGS. CAC.** Brilliant silver luster combines with semiprooflike flash for strong visual impact. A bold strike throughout offsets busyness in the fields, which accounts for the assigned grade. CAC approved for its impressive eye appeal. NGC ID# 254K, PCGS# 7148

4277 **1883-S MS63 PCGS.** The surfaces of this attractive Select Morgan dollar are lightly marked and show a mix of satiny luster and semiprooflike reflectivity. The design elements are well-detailed and just a trace of golden-tan toning visits the peripheries. NGC ID# 254K, PCGS# 7148

4278 **1883-S MS63 PCGS.** More than 6.2 million pieces were struck, yet few Mint State survivors withstood the ravages of time or rough handling during transport, and few Treasury releases augmented the supply. This Select Uncirculated example displays deep, interspersed orange and gunmetal-blue toning in the recesses and at the margins. Dusky silver luster glows from the centers. A sharp example with a tangible old-West appeal. NGC ID# 254K, PCGS# 7148

4279 **1883-S MS64 PCGS.** The 1883-S Morgan is a slightly better date in Mint State grades, and is only marginally available through the MS64 level. Finer pieces decidedly rare, and proportionately expensive for the budget-minded collector. This Choice example displays a sharp strike and radiant, frosty luster. A few wisps of light golden color accent each side, while the surfaces are devoid of any significant abrasions. PCGS has certified only 18 numerically finer representatives (10/14). NGC ID# 254K, PCGS# 7148

4280 **1884-CC MS65 Deep Mirror Prooflike PCGS. CAC.** Dazzling field reflectivity ensures the eye appeal of this brilliant Carson City Gem. The strike is precise and the cheek is unperturbed by contact. Encapsulated in an old green label holder. NGC ID# 254M, PCGS# 97153

4281 **1884-O MS67 PCGS.** The 1884-O Morgan dollar is scarce in MS67 condition, and finer examples are virtually unobtainable. This delightful Superb Gem displays sharply detailed design elements and impeccably preserved surfaces with vibrant mint luster. PCGS has graded only one numerically finer example (10/14). NGC ID# 254N, PCGS# 7154

4282 **1884-S AU58 PCGS.** A lovely near-Mint piece featuring light golden-gray and lavender toning with orange accents. Trace amounts of friction is seen over otherwise sharply struck devices. A nice example of an elusive issue in Uncirculated condition. NGC ID# 254P, PCGS# 7156

4283 **1884-S AU58 PCGS.** The fields of this nearly Uncirculated 1884-S dollar exhibit well-balanced luster and semiprooflike mirroring, with only a hint of light golden color seen when tilted beneath a light. Only a trace of high-point friction is present, giving this piece the overall visual appeal of lower-grade Mint State coin. NGC ID# 254P, PCGS# 7156

4284 **1884-S AU58 NGC.** The 1884-S Morgan is widely sought in the upper AU grades by budget-conscious series collectors, as Mint State examples are seldom available and significantly more expensive. This piece retains substantial original luster beneath a thin veil of light golden toning. Wear is limited to a couple small flat spots on the hair above Liberty's ear and the eagle's breast, while the only noticeable abrasion is a small reed mark in the right reverse field. NGC ID# 254P, PCGS# 7156

4285 **1884-S AU58 PCGS. CAC.** A lustrous near-Mint representative of the 1884-S Morgan dollar, with sharply detailed design elements that show just the slightest trace of friction on the high points and lightly marked pleasing surfaces. NGC ID# 254P, PCGS# 7156

4286 **1885-CC MS66 PCGS.** A sharply detailed Premium Gem representative of this popular Carson City issue, with vibrant mint luster and well-preserved brilliant surfaces throughout. Eye appeal is exceptional. NGC ID# 254S, PCGS# 7160

4287 **1885-CC MS66+ PCGS.** A high-end Premium Gem example from the charismatic Carson City Mint, this coin exhibits razor-sharp definition on all design elements and the impeccably preserved brilliant surfaces radiate vibrant mint luster. NGC ID# 254S, PCGS# 7160

4288 **1885-CC MS64 Ultra Deep Mirror Prooflike ANACS.** This piece is a full cameo with exceptional visual appeal. Tinges of sun-gold, violet, and blue surround portions of the peripheries, with light champagne color over the remainder of each side. Some minor striking weakness is noted on the lower wreath leaves and the eagle's talons, though the eye appeal is hardly affected. An immensely appealing example of this popular Carson City issue. NGC ID# 254S, PCGS# 97161

4289 **1885-O MS67 PCGS.** The 1885-O is readily available in grades through MS66, but its availability declines somewhat at the Superb Gem level. This piece displays radiant, frosty luster with a warm champagne hue. The strike is sharp and the surfaces are devoid of noteworthy flaws. PCGS has certified only a single numerically finer representative (11/14). NGC ID# 254T, PCGS# 7162

4290 **1886 MS67 PCGS. CAC.** The satiny, light golden luster of this Superb Gem illuminates beautifully preserved surfaces and boldly struck design elements. The eye appeal is truly outstanding. PCGS has certified only six numerically finer examples of this available Philadelphia issue (11/14). NGC ID# 254V, PCGS# 7166

4291 **1886-O MS62 PCGS.** Despite a large mintage of 10.7 million pieces, the 1886-O Morgan dollar is a challenging issue in higher Uncirculated grades. This well-detailed MS62 example shows a number of minor contact marks on each side, but the lustrous surfaces display attractive shades of gold and pink toning. NGC ID# 254W, PCGS# 7168

4292 **1886-S MS65 PCGS.** This San Francisco issue becomes challenging in Gem condition and scarce any finer, as confirmed by the population reports and prices realized from recent auction appearances. Brilliant silver luster enlivens clear fields and a full, clean cheek on Liberty. Bold details define Liberty's hair strands and the eagle's plumage. The coin is white except for hints of lilac on the central high points. NGC ID# 254X, PCGS# 7170

4293 **1886-S MS65 PCGS.** This delightful Gem exhibits sharply defined design elements and well-preserved brilliant surfaces with vibrant mint luster on both sides. The 1886-S Morgan dollar is a scarce issue in higher grades. NGC ID# 254X, PCGS# 7170

1887 Silver Dollar, AU58
VAM-1B, Partial E Reverse

4294 **1887 Partial E Reverse, VAM-1B, AU58 PCGS.** A Hot 50 Variety. Clashed E varieties are uniquely popular among VAM specialists, and are typically elusive in high grades. This VAM-1B example shows a partial E below the eagle's tailfeathers, as transferred from the E in LIBERTY on the obverse die. A thin die crack through the date numerals confirms the attribution. The strike is well-executed, with only slight wear over the central high points on each side. Tinges of deep amber and orange-gold are seen periodically around the peripheries, while the central regions display lighter champagne color. Substantial mint luster remains, giving this piece the overall eye appeal of a lower-grade Uncirculated piece. Population: 2 in 58, 2 finer (10/14). PCGS# 134003

4295 **1888-O MS66 PCGS.** The availability of this moderately plentiful issue is restricted to Gem and lower grades, as MS66 examples are seldom available. This example displays sharp motifs and radiant luster. Varying shades of lemon-gold toning encompass the obverse and spill over on the reverse peripheries, and the underlying surfaces are free of any major abrasions. None have been certified numerically finer at PCGS (11/14). NGC ID# 2556, PCGS# 7184

4296 **1888-O Hot Lips, Doubled Die Obverse, VAM-4, AU55 PCGS.** A Top 100 Variety. Blatant die doubling on Liberty's profile explains the nickname for this dramatic *Guide Book* VAM. Partly lustrous and minimally toned with moderate facial contact. Unattainable in better Uncirculated grades. Choice AU examples are well above average for the variety. PCGS# 133919

4297 **1889 MS66 PCGS. CAC.** Vivid shades of cerulean-blue, lavender-gray, and greenish-gold toning enhance the outstanding eye appeal of this delightful Premium Gem. The design elements are sharply detailed and the well-preserved surfaces radiate vibrant mint luster. PCGS has graded only four numerically finer examples (11/14). NGC ID# 2558, PCGS# 7188

4298 **1889-CC VF25 PCGS.** A collectible example of this key Carson City dollar, with much design detail remaining intact on the hair and ear, but the eagle's breast feathers worn smooth. Shades of pink, blue, and apple-green toning blanket the lightly abraded surfaces. NGC ID# 2559, PCGS# 7190

4299 **1889-CC VF30 PCGS.** A pleasing VF30 example of this key Carson City issue. This coin retains three quarters of the detail on the hair between Liberty's ear and forehead and the ear remains bold. The lightly abraded surfaces show hints of champagne-gold and silver-gray toning. NGC ID# 2559, PCGS# 7190

4300 **1889-CC VF35 ANACS.** According to the *Official Register of the United States* for 1889, listing all individuals in the government service on July 1, Charles Colburn was the coiner at Carson City, George Keith was the assistant coiner, and George McLaughlin was the pressman. They were assisted by two "helpers," Richard Brown and Samuel Fairbanks. That team created the 1889-CC dollar rarities, along with double eagles, the only other coins minted in Carson City during the year. After it was struck, this piece entered circulation where it received considerable wear, and acquired pewter-gray patina and gold toning. NGC ID# 2559, PCGS# 7190

1889-CC Morgan, XF40
Refreshingly Original Patina

4301 **1889-CC XF40 NGC.** The 1889-CC ranks as the king of the Carson City Morgan dollars due to its overall scarcity in relation to other dates from not only this mint, but the entire series. The famous GSA sales of the early 1970s, which yielded many thousands of examples of other dates, offered only a single example of the 1889-CC, as most representatives of this issue were paid into circulation or melted decades before. The present coin is lightly circulated, but exhibits choice original color in varying shades of battleship and pewter-gray. The detail is sharp and the eye appeal is excellent for the grade. NGC ID# 2559, PCGS# 7190

4302 **1889-CC — Repaired — NGC Details. XF.** The 1889-CC Morgan dollar is the most elusive issue of the Carson City series and collectors prize examples in all grades and conditions. This lightly worn and lightly abraded example shows evidence of some minor repair in the upper reverse field. NGC ID# 2559, PCGS# 7190

4303 **1889-CC XF40 ANACS.** Olive accents are seen periodically across the natural gunmetal-gray surfaces of this lightly circulated 1889-CC Morgan. A very pleasing and well-detail example for the grade. This issue was only produced to the extant of 350,000 pieces, its production limited by the fact that the Carson City Mint did begin striking the denomination that year until October, following the completion of repairs to the building and machinery. NGC ID# 2559, PCGS# 7190

4304 **1889-CC — Cleaning — PCGS Genuine. XF Details.** A lightly worn and lightly abraded example of the rarest Morgan dollar from the Carson City Mint, this coin retains a trace of mint luster, but the unnatural sheen indicates a light cleaning in the past. NGC ID# 2559, PCGS# 7190

4305 **1889-CC — Improperly Cleaned — NGC Details. XF.** Luster fills the plumage and legends of this key date Carson City Morgan. The hairlined obverse field and portrait are silver-gray, while the remainder of the coin has retoned sea-green and rose-gold. NGC ID# 2559, PCGS# 7190

4306 **1889-CC — Repaired — NGC Details. AU.** The design elements show just a touch of actual wear and the surfaces retain a trace of mint luster under hints of pink toning. The 1889-CC is the most elusive CC-mint Morgan. Some pin-scratches in the obverse field are not overly obtrusive. NGC ID# 2559, PCGS# 7190

4307 **1889-CC — Cleaning — PCGS Genuine. AU Details.** The 1889-CC Morgan dollar is the key to the Carson City series. This still-attractive specimen shows evidence of a light cleaning in the past, but the design elements show just a touch of wear and the surfaces are lightly abraded. NGC ID# 2559, PCGS# 7190

1889-O Morgan Dollar, MS65
Bold Strike, Lightly Toned

4308 **1889-O MS65 PCGS.** The prodigious mintage of nearly 12 million pieces resulted in a large number of poorly struck coins, caused by a combination of factors including die wear, die spacing, and careless attention to quality. This Gem example, however, shows a bold strike for the New Orleans issue with only minor blending above the ear. The light toning is more prevalent on the obverse, with blue and russet shades strongest at the margins and thinly dispersed elsewhere. Nice luster illuminates minimally marked surfaces. PCGS has certified just 10 numerically finer examples (10/14). NGC ID# 255A, PCGS# 7192

1889-O Silver Dollar, MS65
Colorfully Toned, Condition Rarity

4309 **1889-O MS65 PCGS.** The New Orleans Mint made the most of their dies for this high-mintage issue, wearing them out with more than 11.8 million silver dollars produced. As a result, PCGS has seen fewer than 200 Gem examples, and a mere 10 coins are certified finer (10/14). Quality of strike is a factor, with nearly all coins struck softly over the ear and on the eagle's breast. This iridescently toned Gem is relatively well-struck and visually appealing. The surfaces are devoid of distracting bagmarks or abrasions. NGC ID# 255A, PCGS# 7192

4310 **1890 MS65 PCGS.** This delightful Gem is sharply detailed in most areas, with just a touch of softness on the hair above Liberty's ear. The surfaces are brightly lustrous, with highlights of pale gold toning. PCGS has graded four numerically finer examples (10/14). NGC ID# 255C, PCGS# 7196

4311 **1890 MS65 PCGS.** This issue is only marginally available in Gem condition, and finer pieces are exceedingly rare, with just four such coins certified at PCGS (11/14). This example displays softly frosted, untoned luster and well-preserved surfaces. Some minor lightness of strike is noted on the eagle's breast, though the motifs are otherwise well brought up. NGC ID# 255C, PCGS# 7196

4312 **1890 MS65 PCGS. CAC.** This is a gloriously radiant-white Gem from the Philadelphia Mint, housed in an old green label PCGS holder. Trace amounts of gold-orange peripheral patina emerge on the obverse. A small number of wispy nicks, also on the obverse, seemingly prevent an even finer grade designation. Just four examples are rated higher at PCGS. NGC ID# 255C, PCGS# 7196

4313 **1890-CC MS64 PCGS.** Delicate hints of pink and pale gold toning enliven the lightly marked surfaces of this attractive Carson City dollar. The design elements are sharply rendered and satiny mint luster emanates from both sides. NGC ID# 255D, PCGS# 7198

4314 **1890-CC MS64 PCGS. CAC. VAM-3.** The 90 in the date is lightly repunched southwest. This lustrous scarcer date Carson City dollar has superior preservation for the designated grade, along with only a wisp of tan toning. One small spot noted on the eagle's left (facing) leg. NGC ID# 255D, PCGS# 7198

4315 **1890-CC MS63 Deep Mirror Prooflike PCGS.** Ice-white devices rise in virtually full detail above untoned mirrored fields. Minor roller marks (as made) are noted, but the preservation is exceptional for the MS63 level. Certified in an old green label holder. NGC ID# 255D, PCGS# 97199

1890-O Dollar, MS65 Prooflike
Delicately Toned Cameo

4316 **1890-O MS65 Prooflike PCGS.** Fully prooflike fields deliver pleasing cameo contrast on this Gem 1890-O Morgan dollar. Slight striking softness on the hair above Liberty's ear does not inhibit the eye appeal, and the surfaces are free of any significant abrasions. Essentially brilliant at first glance, but with pale champagne color seen upon closer examination. Population: 41 in 65 (1 in 65+) Prooflike, 3 finer (10/14). NGC ID# 255E, PCGS# 7201

1890-S Morgan, MS66
Radiant Mint Luster

4317 **1890-S MS66 PCGS.** A light sheen of reddish-gold patina covers the obverse fields, while Liberty's portrait is virtually untoned and silver-white. The reverse shows a narrow vignette of complementary gold around the margin and through the legends. A boldly struck and attractive Premium Gem, with just eight coins certified numerically finer by PCGS and NGC combined (10/14). NGC ID# 255F, PCGS# 7202

4318 **1890-S MS65 Prooflike PCGS. CAC.** Fully struck and brilliant, this remarkable Gem offers sharp contrast between the deeply-mirrored fields and the lightly frosted devices. An exceptionally attractive, conditionally rare example of this San Francisco mint issue. Population: 19 in 65 Prooflike, 3 finer (10/14). NGC ID# 255F, PCGS# 7203

4319 **1891-CC MS64 PCGS. CAC.** Frosty, untoned luster and well-preserved surfaces are the hallmarks of this Choice Carson City dollar. Slight striking softness is noted on the hair above Liberty's ear, though the eye appeal is hardly inhibited. Housed in a first generation holder with a green CAC label for excellent quality. NGC ID# 255H, PCGS# 7206

4320 **1892 MS64 Prooflike NGC.** The 1892 Morgan dollar is an elusive date in high grade, especially with prooflike surfaces. This well-detailed Choice example offers brilliant reflective fields with only minor signs of contact. Census: 28 in 64 (1 in 64+) Prooflike, 9 finer (10/14). NGC ID# 255L, PCGS# 7213

4321 **1892-CC MS63 PCGS.** Attractive shades of burnt-orange, lavender-gray, and violet toning blanket the lightly marked surfaces of this pleasing Select example, with sharply detailed design elements and vibrant mint luster under the patina. NGC ID# 255M, PCGS# 7214

1892-CC Silver Dollar, MS64
Brilliant, Frost-White Appeal
VAM-4B Repunched Mintmark

4322 **1892-CC MS64 PCGS. VAM-4B, R.5.** Extensive die cracks on the reverse and the multiply clashed N of IN are equally pronounced as the repunched CC/CC Down mintmark. A smooth, lustrous, and frost-white near-Gem example, with brilliant cartwheel luster and a bare minimum of minor marks determining the grade. An attractive example of this interesting VAM variety. NGC ID# 255M, PCGS# 7214

1892-CC Dollar, MS64+
High-End Example

4323 **1892-CC MS64+ PCGS.** Always in demand, this Carson City issue often displays high-quality, attractive surfaces and a bold strike. This borderline Gem coin is a sharp example, with nice frosted detail on the motifs and clear, unabraded fields. A couple of small marks above the eagle's head do not detract significantly from the appeal. Brilliant, save for a glint of champagne-gold at the rims. NGC ID# 255M, PCGS# 7214

4324 **1892-CC MS62 Prooflike PCGS.** This fully Prooflike example exhibits moderate cameo contrast between the fields and the frosty, sharply struck devices. A scattering of minor abrasions on Liberty's cheek limits the grade, but the eye appeal is nonetheless pleasing for the MS62 level. NGC ID# 255M, PCGS# 7215

4325 **1892-S AU50 PCGS.** About Uncirculated examples of this semikey San Francisco issue are not truly scarce themselves, but collector demand for them is remarkably strong due to the prohibitive rarity of pleasing Mint State examples. This coin shows original golden-gray patina with hints of luster in the recesses. A pleasing, well-detailed example for the series collector. NGC ID# 255P, PCGS# 7218

1892-S Dollar, AU55
Attractive for the Grade

4326 **1892-S AU55 NGC.** Although 1.2 million examples were struck, the 1892-S Morgan is nonetheless one of the most difficult issues in the series to locate in Mint State. For the casual date collector, a number of pleasing AU examples are known, such as this still-lustrous Choice example. Warm golden and pale aquamarine peripheral toning surrounds light champagne centers, while only a touch of wear is evident on the eagle's breast and the hair above Liberty's ear. NGC ID# 255P, PCGS# 7218

1893 Silver Dollar, MS64
Vivid, Two-Sided Toning

4327 **1893 MS64 PCGS. CAC.** Strong mint luster resides beneath the dynamically toned surfaces of this low-mintage Morgan dollar. Just 389,792 pieces were struck in the wake of new legislation repealing parts of the Sherman Silver Purchase Act. This example displays indigo-blue and reddish-gold shades on the obverse, with vivid electric-blue and orange-gold hues on the reverse. A few obverse scrapes are disguised in the toning and minor central weakness account for the near-Gem grade. NGC ID# 255R, PCGS# 7220

4328 **1893-CC — Improperly Cleaned — NGC Details. AU.** This still-attractive, but lightly cleaned, Morgan dollar represents the last year of coinage operations at the Carson City Mint. The design elements show light wear on the high points and the surfaces display only minor abrasions. NGC ID# 255S, PCGS# 7222

1893-CC Dollar, Unc Sharpness
Limited High Grade Survival

4329 **1893-CC — Improperly Cleaned — NGC Details. Unc.** The scarcity of the 1893-CC Morgan in relation to other issues from this mint can be attributed to the fact that nearly all examples of this date were distributed long before the GSA sales of the early 1970s, where just a single coin was represented. The present piece is lightly cleaned, but retains moderate luster and has retoned a light golden hue. The strike is above-average for the date, and surface abrasions are minimal. NGC ID# 255S, PCGS# 7222

4330 **1893-O AU58 PCGS.** The 1893-O is the lowest mintage Morgan dollar from the New Orleans Mint. This well-detailed near-Mint example displays lightly abraded lustrous surfaces, with hints of greenish-gold toning. NGC ID# 255T, PCGS# 7224

4331 **1893-S Good 6 NGC.** The 1893-S is the most sought-after regular issue of the Morgan dollar series. This well-worn example retains the legends, date, mintmark and major design elements intact in outline, with some interior detail still evident. NGC ID# 255U, PCGS# 7226

4332 **1893-S — Improperly Cleaned — NGC Details. VG.** A cream-gray key date dollar with glimpses of charcoal toning in protected regions. No marks are singularly noticeable. Minor hairlines cross the portrait but they are not out of place for the VG level. NGC ID# 255U, PCGS# 7226

4333 **1893-S — Bent — NGC Details. VG.** Collectors prize the 1893-S Morgan dollar in all grades and conditions. This typically worn example retains some interior design detail in the hair and wing feathers and shows some rim dings and evidence of slight bend on the upper obverse rim.

1893-S Silver Dollar, VF Sharpness

4334 **1893-S — Improperly Cleaned — NGC Details. VF.** The frequent appearances of 1893-S dollars at auction tend to diminish the perceived rarity of the issue, but the low mintage always confirms the underlying rarity of this San Francisco date. Demand continues unabated for all examples, even when impaired such as this cleaned coin. Unnaturally glossy and flat at the centers (above the ear and on the eagle's breast), the marks are light for the grade level and some hopeful glimpses of golden-gray toning improve this coin's prospects.

4335 **1894 VF25 PCGS.** A nice collectible example of this low-mintage Philadelphia key, this coin retains much interior detail on Liberty's hair and ear, but the feathers on the eagle's breast are worn. The surfaces are lightly abraded and problem-free. NGC ID# 255V, PCGS# 7228

4336 **1894 VF35 PCGS.** Bits of orange and blue luster remain at the margins of this low-mintage Morgan. Deep old-silver toning covers both sides. Choice for the VF condition, with nice originality. A tiny cut near Liberty's ear and a few small, scattered rim marks are inconsequential for the grade. NGC ID# 255V, PCGS# 7228

4337 **1894 VF35 NGC.** This Choice VF specimen retains about three-fourths of the design detail in Liberty's hair and the lightly toned surfaces show only minor abrasions. Traces of original mint luster remain on both sides. NGC ID# 255V, PCGS# 7228

4338 **1894 — Improperly Cleaned — NGC Details. AU.** A still-attractive specimen of this low-mintage issue, with well-detailed design elements that show just the slightest trace of wear and lightly marked surfaces that exhibit slightly subdued mint luster, due to a light cleaning. NGC ID# 255V, PCGS# 7228

4339 **1894 AU53 NGC.** An attractive AU53 example of this low-mintage Morgan dollar, with just a touch of wear on the well-detailed design elements and lustrous, lightly abraded surfaces that show a few hints of pale gold and lavender toning. NGC ID# 255V, PCGS# 7228

4340 **1894 AU55 NGC.** The 1894 Morgan dollar is a sought-after issue because of its mintage of 110,000 pieces. This Choice AU example shows just a trace of high-point wear and lustrous, lightly abraded surfaces with highlights of apple-green and pink toning. NGC ID# 255V, PCGS# 7228

4341 **1894 AU58 NGC.** A few hints of pink toning enliven the lightly abraded surfaces of this low-mintage Morgan dollar. The well-detailed design elements show just a trace of wear and vibrant mint luster radiates from both sides. NGC ID# 255V, PCGS# 7228

1894 Silver Dollar, MS62
Elusive in all Grades

4342 **1894 MS62 NGC.** A sparse Philadelphia mintage of just 110,972 pieces accounts for across-the-board scarcity of this issue. Even so, enough examples survive to tantalize collectors in nearly every auction. The quality of the current coin is at least one point finer than the stated grade if not for a noticeable graze on Liberty's forehead, cheek, and jawline. Few other marks are seen anywhere on the surfaces of this sharply struck, attractive coin. A brief crescent of orange toning enhances the lustrous, frosted fields and motifs. NGC ID# 255V, PCGS# 7228

4343 **1894-S MS63 PCGS.** The surfaces of this attractive Select example show a scattering of minor contact marks and vibrant mint luster on both sides. The design elements are sharply detailed throughout and a few hints of golden-tan toning enhance the visual appeal. NGC ID# 255X, PCGS# 7232

4344 **1895-S AU58 PCGS.** A charming near-Mint Morgan dollar with just the slightest trace of friction on the design elements and lightly abraded surfaces that retain most of their original mint luster. A few hints of pale gold toning add to the considerable eye appeal. NGC ID# 255Z, PCGS# 7238

4345 **1895-S/S VAM-3 AU50 PCGS.** A Hot 50 Variety. The VAM is undesignated on the insert. This low-mintage San Francisco issue saw just 400,000 pieces produced, a very small number for the Morgan dollar series. This is an appealing, untoned example showing wispy hairlines but no disturbing abrasions on the bright surfaces. PCGS# 134020

1896-O Silver Dollar, MS62
Strong Cartwheel Luster

4346 **1896-O MS62 PCGS.** The 1896-O is a slightly better New Orleans issue in Mint State grades. This example is frosty with a tinge of pale gold color over each side. Slight softness is seen on the hair immediately above Liberty's ear, though the strike is otherwise well-executed. Light, scattered surface chatter accounts for the grade, as no singularly obvious abrasions are present. NGC ID# 2563, PCGS# 7242

1896-O Dollar, MS62+
Scarce This Nice

4347 **1896-O MS62+ NGC.** The 1896-O has a poor reputation when it comes to eye appeal and strength of strike. Few attractive coins exist in any grade, as confirmed by the reluctance of the grading services to certify hardly any examples higher than MS63. This coin received a MS62 with the Plus designation from NGC, yet there are nearly no marks of any significance on the coin and the mint luster is above average for the issue. Typical strike weakness above the ear is balanced by sharp details elsewhere on the coin. The wise bidder will ignore the "Plain Jane" reputation of the issue and bid instead according to this coin's considerable, silver-white appeal. NGC ID# 2563, PCGS# 7242

1896-S Morgan Dollar, MS63
Lustrous-White Example

4348 **1896-S MS63 PCGS.** This coin displays the brilliance and luster of a higher grade, while numerous bagmarks and abrasions account for the Select Uncirculated designation. Entirely untoned, brilliant, and frosted, the coin was susceptible to marks and grazes from transport and Mint handling. Slight softness over the ear and at the eagle's legs is typical of this scarce, heavily melted San Francisco issue. NGC ID# 2564, PCGS# 7244

4349 **1897-O MS61 NGC.** With minimal releases from the Treasury and few hoard coins to supplement the supply of Mint State coins, this New Orleans issue is somewhat scarce and seemingly undervalued. The current coin is sharp for the assigned grade, with nice cartwheel luster and a stronger strike than expected. The few obverse field marks are light and unobtrusive. NGC ID# 2566, PCGS# 7248

4350 **1897-O MS61 PCGS.** Despite a high mintage in excess of four million coins, this New Orleans issue is scarce in Mint State, and rare any finer than MS63. This untoned, creamy-white example displays fine satiny luster and scattered small marks that define the grade. NGC ID# 2566, PCGS# 7248

4351 **1897-O MS62 PCGS.** This attractive MS62 Morgan dollar displays vibrant mint luster and well-detailed design elements throughout, and the pleasing surfaces show only minor signs of contact, with subtle hints of golden-tan toning. NGC ID# 2566, PCGS# 7248

4352 **1897-O MS62 PCGS.** The lustrous surfaces of this attractive MS62 example show a scattering of minor contact marks and hairlines, under shades of lavender and greenish-gold toning. The design elements are sharply detailed in most areas, with a touch of softness on the hair above the ear. NGC ID# 2566, PCGS# 7248

1898 Dollar, MS67
Frosty Type Representative

4353   1898 MS67 PCGS. Tinges of amber-gold toning grace the peripheries of this frosty Superb Gem, while the strike is well-executed and the surfaces are devoid of mentionable abrasions. The 1898 Morgan is readily obtainable in grades through MS66, but finer coins are scarce. None have been certified numerically finer than this piece (10/14). NGC ID# 2568, PCGS# 7252

4354   1898 MS66 Prooflike NGC. CAC. This Philadelphia Mint issue is common in Mint State grades, but Prooflikes are considerably scarcer. This boldly struck Premium Gem example is essentially untoned with snow-white frosted devices and highly reflective charcoal-gray fields. A couple of wispy luster breaks are noted on Liberty's neck area. Census: 10 in 66 (1 in 66 ★) Prooflike, 2 finer (10/14). NGC ID# 2568, PCGS# 7253

4355   1898-S MS65 PCGS. This delightful Gem offers well-detailed design elements and vibrant mint luster throughout, with well-preserved surfaces under shades of greenish-gold , lavender, and blue toning. NGC ID# 256A, PCGS# 7256

4356   1899-S MS65 PCGS. Traces of greenish-gold and violet toning visit the mostly brilliant surfaces of this spectacular Gem, with vibrant mint luster and sharply detailed design elements throughout. Eye appeal is terrific. NGC ID# 256D, PCGS# 7262

4357   1900 MS66+ PCGS. CAC. An intensely frosty, essentially brilliant example, this high-end Premium Gem also boasts sharp design definition and a distinct lack of discernable surface abrasions. The 1900 Morgan dollar is usually obtainable in MS66, but finer representatives are genuinely scarce. PCGS has encapsulated only 37 numerically finer examples (11/14). NGC ID# 256E, PCGS# 7264

1900-O Silver Dollar, MS67
None Certified Numerically Finer

4358   1900-O MS67 PCGS. This New Orleans issue was produced in quantity (more than 12.5 million pieces), but its availability plummets at the MS67 grade level. This lustrous example is well-struck with excellent preservation. Mottled amber-gold, olive, and dusky lavender toning blankets much of each side. Population: 58 in 67 (3 in 67+), 0 finer (10/14). NGC ID# 256F, PCGS# 7266

4359   1900-O/CC MS65 PCGS. VAM-11. A Top 100 Variety. The primary mintmark is centered and punched over the undertype CC. This sharply detailed Gem offers well-preserved brilliant surfaces with vibrant mint luster throughout. NGC ID# 256G, PCGS# 7268

4360   1900-O/CC VAM-11 MS65 NGC. A Top 100 Variety. A sharply detailed Gem example of this popular overmintmark variety, with well-preserved surfaces that display a few highlights of pale gold toning and vibrant mint luster on both sides. PCGS# 133963

4361   1900-S MS65 PCGS. This delightful Gem exhibits sharply detailed design elements throughout, but the reverse was struck from a new hub that shows shallower detail on the breast feathers. The brilliant surfaces are lustrous and well-preserved. NGC ID# 256H, PCGS# 7270

4362   1900-S MS65 NGC. No mentionable distractions are evident on this delightful Gem, suggestive of an even higher grade. The design elements are sharply defined everywhere except the hair above the ear, where some parallel die striations are not completely struck out. Vibrant mint luster adds to the outstanding eye appeal. NGC ID# 256H, PCGS# 7270

4363   1900-S MS65 PCGS. VAM-8. The 90 in the date is repunched, with curves of extra metal above and left of the digits. The fields have numerous lengthy raised die lines, as struck. Lustrous and mildly prooflike with a good strike. The cheek has faint roller marks, as struck, but the surfaces are extremely well preserved. A scarce issue as a Gem. NGC ID# 256H, PCGS# 7270

4364   1900-S MS65 PCGS. A sharply detailed Gem representative of this popular turn-of-the-century issue, with well-preserved surfaces that show dappled shades of lavender-gray and greenish-gold toning. Prooflike reflectivity shines through the patina in many areas. NGC ID# 256H, PCGS# 7270

4365   1900-S MS65 PCGS. CAC. VAM-9. The mintmark is minutely repunched, but of greater interest are the several lengthy die cracks, including a vertical crack across Liberty's nose. Brilliant, lustrous, and well struck. Housed in an old green label holder.
Ex: Long Beach Signature (Heritage, 5/2003), lot 7711; St. Louis Signature (Heritage, 5/2005), lot 9945. NGC ID# 256H, PCGS# 7270

1900-S Morgan, MS65 Prooflike
Flashy and Nearly Brilliant

4366   1900-S MS65 Prooflike PCGS. CAC. A wisp of canary-gold toning enriches the borders of this otherwise brilliant better date Gem. The strike is sharp aside from the extreme centers and cartwheel luster adds to the eye appeal. A few scattered marks appear on each side. Encapsulated in an old green label holder. Population: 20 in 65 Prooflike, 6 finer (10/14). NGC ID# 256H, PCGS# 7271

4367   1901 AU58 PCGS. An attractive near-Mint example of this turn-of-the-century Morgan dollar, with lightly abraded, lustrous surfaces and well-detailed design elements that show just a trace of wear. NGC ID# 256J, PCGS# 7272

4368   1901 Doubled Die Reverse, VAM-3, AU53 PCGS. The VAM-3 "Shifted Eagle" is an extremely popular *Guide Book* variety that shows doubling on the eagle's tail feathers, arrows, olive branch, and other design elements on the reverse. This well-detailed AU53 example is lustrous and lightly abraded, with just a touch of wear. PCGS# 133965

4369 1901-S MS64 NGC. Bolstered by the rarity of the 1901-S quarter and, to a lesser extent, the 1901-S half dollar, the dollar enjoys a degree of respect, too, especially in higher Uncirculated grades. This near-Gem example is frosty and attractive. A tinge of russet-red toning at the margins merges with lustrous silver centers. The strike is a bit soft above the ear as usually seen. A shallow pinscratch follows Liberty's jawline. NGC ID# 256L, PCGS# 7276

4370 1901-S MS64 PCGS. This impressive Choice Morgan dollar offers sharply detailed design elements and lightly marked surfaces with frosty cartwheel mint luster. A few hints of pale gold toning enhance the considerable eye appeal. NGC ID# 256L, PCGS# 7276

4371 1901-S MS64 PCGS. The 1901-S Morgan dollar is a better date, especially in high grade. This attractive MS64 example offers well-detailed design elements and lustrous lightly abraded surfaces on both sides. NGC ID# 256L, PCGS# 7276

4372 1902-O MS66+ PCGS. The eye appeal of this high-end Premium Gem can only be fully appreciated when one realizes that the 1902-O Morgan is one of the most poorly struck and typically lackluster issues in the latter half of the series. This piece showcases uncharacteristically frosty luster and far-above-average design definition. Traces of light golden toning are seen over each side, though close examination is required to observe any grade-limiting surface imperfections. Only 15 coins are numerically finer at PCGS (11/14), from an original mintage in excess of 8.6 million pieces. NGC ID# 256N, PCGS# 7280

4373 1902-O MS64 Deep Mirror Prooflike PCGS. This impressive Choice example displays deeply mirrored fields that contrast boldly with the well-detailed frosty design elements. The mostly brilliant surfaces show a few hints of pale gold toning, with only minor signs of contact. Population: 25 in 64 Deep Mirror Prooflike, 4 finer (10/14). NGC ID# 256N, PCGS# 97281

4374 1903 MS66+ NGC. CAC. The well-preserved brilliant surfaces of this high-end Premium Gem radiate vibrant cartwheel mint luster and the sharply detailed design elements add to the terrific eye appeal of this popular late-series issue. NGC ID# 256R, PCGS# 7284

4375 1903 MS66+ PCGS. CAC. The 1903 Morgan dollar is typically more satiny in appearance, than deeply frosty, and the current example is a beautiful representation of this. A faint suggestion of pale champagne toning accents clean surfaces, while the central motifs show above-average striking detail. Numerically finer pieces are seldom available. NGC ID# 256R, PCGS# 7284

1903 Dollar, MS67
None Numerically Finer at PCGS

4376 1903 MS67 PCGS. CAC. Soft hues of blue, violet, and sun-gold encompass the obverse, while the reverse shows just a light golden hue. Some usual softness is noted on the eagle's breast and the hair above Liberty's ear, though the surfaces are attractively free of noticeable abrasions. The 1903 Morgan is available in lower grades, but becomes conditionally scarce at the MS67 level. None have been certified numerically finer at PCGS (10/14). NGC ID# 256R, PCGS# 7284

4377 1903-O MS66+ PCGS. CAC. The 1903-O Morgan dollar is not a scarce date, but it is challenging at the current MS66+ grade level or finer. The strike definition is full, while the radiantly lustrous surfaces are snow-white and minimally marked. Population: 24 in 66+, 71 finer (10/14). NGC ID# 256S, PCGS# 7286

4378 1903-S AU55 PCGS. This is a pleasing Choice AU example of this semikey San Francisco issue. Light golden toning on each side complements remnants of original luster in the recesses, while only slight high-point wear is evident over the central motifs. NGC ID# 256T, PCGS# 7288

4379 1903-S Micro S, VAM-2, XF40 PCGS. A Top 100 Variety. Also called the Small S variety. Any 1903-S dollar is elusive, but the Micro S is rare, since only one die bears the wrong mintmark punch, intended for a smaller-diameter coin. A slate-gray example with moderate wear and a small obverse rim ding at 5 o'clock. PCGS# 133967

4380 1921 MS64 Deep Mirror Prooflike NGC. A splendid representative of the single-year subtype. The strike is intricate and the fields are flashy. Lightly dappled rose-gold and blue-green toning congregates near the rims. A reed mark is noted on the eagle's belly. Certified in a prior generation holder. NGC ID# 256X, PCGS# 97297

4381 1921-S MS65 PCGS. An impressive Gem representative of the final year of the Morgan dollar design, this coin offers sharply detailed design elements and well-preserved satiny surfaces under delicate shades of lavender toning. NGC ID# 256Z, PCGS# 7300

PROOF MORGAN DOLLARS

1879 Morgan Dollar, PR64
Only 1,100 Proofs Struck

4382 1879 PR64 PCGS. From a reported mintage of 1,100 proofs, the 1879 issue is one of the more challenging proof dates in the Morgan dollar series. CoinFacts estimates that only 180 representatives survive in all grades. This near-Gem example features a layer of dusky violet-gray patina with iridescent accents that become more prominent when held at the correct angle beneath a proper light source. Shades include blue, green, and orange. PCGS has certified only 35 finer pieces in higher numeric grades (10/14). NGC ID# 27Z2, PCGS# 7314

4383 1882 PR62 PCGS. Substantial mirroring in the fields complements bold design definition on this lower-grade proof Morgan. Close examination reveals scattered hairlines in the fields, but the field-motif contrast is still distinct. Pale sun-gold toning blankets each side, with a few deeper tinges in the upper obverse regions and around the reverse borders. NGC ID# 27Z6, PCGS# 7317

1885 Morgan Dollar, PR63
Moderate Cameo Contrast

4384 **1885 PR63 PCGS.** Subtle cameo contrast resides beneath a thin veil of pale golden toning on each side, the color deepening toward the borders. The devices are sharply impressed, and the fields exhibit only a few faint, grade-determining hairlines. Proofs of this date were generally well-produced, making them an excellent choice for type or date representation. NGC ID# 27ZE, PCGS# 7320

PEACE DOLLARS

4385 **1921 MS65 PCGS.** Most first-year Peace dollars have a mushy central impression, but the present Gem has a surprisingly bold strike. The pastel wheat-gold and ice-blue toning further increases the eye appeal. Encapsulated in an old green label holder. NGC ID# 2U4E, PCGS# 7356

4386 **1922-D MS66 NGC.** The 1922-D Peace dollar is not too difficult to locate in MS66 condition, but finer examples are rare. This sharply detailed Premium Gem displays well-preserved brilliant surfaces with vibrant mint luster. NGC has graded 16 numerically finer examples (10/14). NGC ID# 257D, PCGS# 7358

4387 **1922-D MS66 NGC.** Intense mint luster illuminates delicately preserved surfaces on this Premium Gem example. The strike is sharp and the eye appeal is further heightened by a veil of warm golden toning that deepens toward the borders. NGC has encapsulated only 16 numerically finer representatives (11/14). NGC ID# 257D, PCGS# 7358

1923 Peace Dollar, MS67
Dazzling Mint Brilliance

4388 **1923 MS67 NGC. CAC.** For the collector who must simply have only the best, this Superb Gem is tied for the finest certified at NGC and PCGS, displaying radiant, frost-white luster and impeccably preserved surfaces. The strike is bold, and the eye appeal is simply exceptional. The 1923 Peace dollar is by far the most plentiful date in the series in high grades, ideal for type representation. Census: 97 in 67, 0 finer (10/14). NGC ID# 257F, PCGS# 7360

4389 **1925-S MS64 PCGS. CAC.** The 1925-S Peace dollar is not difficult to locate in grades up to the MS64 level, but finer examples are seldom encountered. This well-detailed Choice specimen displays vibrant mint luster and lightly marked surfaces with a few hints of golden-tan toning. NGC ID# 257M, PCGS# 7366

4390 **1926-D MS66 PCGS.** Sharply struck at the centers with minor incompleteness of impression near the rims. Hints of wheat-gold patina visit this lustrous and high grade Denver Mint dollar. Encapsulated in an old green label holder.
Ex: Long Beach Signature (Heritage, 10/2000), lot 8521. NGC ID# 257P, PCGS# 7368

4391 **1927 MS65 PCGS.** Radiant mint bloom propels around both sides of this Gem example in vibrant, brilliant cartwheels. The strike is razor-sharp and the surfaces are devoid of any noticeable imperfections. The 1927 is a better date in Mint State grades, and is decidedly rare finer than the Gem level, with only nine coins so-graded by PCGS (10/14). NGC ID# 257S, PCGS# 7370

4392 **1927-S MS64 NGC. CAC. VAM-1H.** Golden-brown toning graces the margins of this lustrous, smooth, and nicely struck near-Gem. The dies clashed and were lapped. Both fields display polish lines, and rays near the O in DOLLAR were touched up on the working die by a mint worker. Certified in a former generation holder. NGC ID# 257U, PCGS# 7372

4393 **1927-S MS64+ PCGS. CAC.** A high-end Choice example of this low-mintage issue, with sharply detailed design elements and vibrant mint luster on both sides. The well-preserved brilliant surfaces enhance the outstanding eye appeal. NGC ID# 257U, PCGS# 7372

1928 Dollar, Conditionally Scarce MS65

4394 **1928 MS65 PCGS.** This key-date Peace dollar claims a series-low mintage of 360,649 pieces. Mint State examples are readily available through near-Gem, but Gems are scare and finer pieces are very rare. Light gold color visits the lustrous surfaces of this Gem and the design elements are well-struck. Small marks are visible on Liberty's neck and cheek. PCGS has seen only 14 examples numerically finer (10/14). NGC ID# 257V, PCGS# 7373

1934 Peace Dollar, MS66
Delicately Toned

4395 **1934 MS66 PCGS.** The 1934 Peace dollar is one of just four issues in the series with a mintage of less than 1 million coins (954,057 pieces), and is seldom available in high grade. This Premium Gem example displays beautifully preserved surfaces, with sharp design elements and softly frosted luster. Pastel rainbow hues blend over much of each side, giving the overall appearance of a pale golden-blue patina at first glance, but revealed in their entirety when tilted beneath a light. Housed in an old green label holder, with just three pieces numerically finer at PCGS (10/14). NGC ID# 257X, PCGS# 7375

4396 **1934-D MS65 PCGS.** Micro D. Dazzling luster, a good strike, and smooth surfaces confirm the quality of this better date silver dollar. Light tan toning adorns the fields. A costly acquisition above the MS65 level. NGC ID# 257Y, PCGS# 7376

4397 **1934-D MS65 PCGS.** Micro D. Dappled almond-gold toning graces the reverse of this nicely struck Gem. The obverse is close to brilliant. Lustrous and minimally abraded. A costly acquisition any finer. NGC ID# 257Y, PCGS# 7376

4398 **1934-S Doubled Tiara, VAM-3, AU58 NGC.** A Top 50 Variety. The rays on Liberty's tiara are lightly die doubled. This example exhibits slight friction over the high points of the design, but the surfaces retain substantial, untoned mint luster. The strike is sharp and the detail is essentially complete. Census: 2 in 58, 2 finer (10/14). PCGS# 133782

1935 Peace Dollar, MS66
Frosty, Luminous Surfaces

4399 **1935 MS66 PCGS. CAC.** Lime-green and butter-gold blend across this lustrous and beautifully preserved low-mintage final-year Premium Gem. The strike is good, although the centers lack a complete impression, as usual. Encased in a green label holder. PCGS is yet to certify any numerically finer representatives (10/14). *Ex: Central States Signature (Heritage, 4/2011), lot 5977.* NGC ID# 2582, PCGS# 7378

4400 **1935-S MS65 NGC.** Four rays below ONE. Delicate tan toning endows this thoroughly lustrous and well struck final-year Gem. The fields are beautifully preserved and the cheek exhibits minor abrasions. NGC ID# 2583, PCGS# 7379

4401 **1935-S MS65 PCGS. CAC.** Four rays beneath ONE. Light straw-gold toning embraces this lustrous and boldly struck Gem. Incidental distributed grazes correspond to the grade. Difficult to procure any finer. NGC ID# 2583, PCGS# 7379

4402 **1935-S Doubled Reverse, VAM-4, MS65+ PCGS. CAC.** A Top 50 Variety. Four rays below ONE. Delicate wheat-gold and powder-blue toning visits this lustrous and carefully preserved Gem. The cheek is smooth and the strike is good. The eagle's branch is lightly die doubled south. The variety is undesignated on the PCGS holder. PCGS# 133783

EISENHOWER DOLLAR

Top-Graded 1972-S Silver Ike, MS69
Formidable Registry Set Candidate

4403 **1972-S Silver MS69 PCGS.** This 40% silver Eisenhower Dollar is unavailable in a higher numeric grade at either service, and it may be unimprovable in business strike format. A mere two dozen coins have achieved this lofty grade, which requires pristine surfaces and an undeniable full strike. There are no interruptions to the amazing mint bloom or incredibly smooth silver surfaces. Population: 18 in 69, 0 finer (11/14). NGC ID# 2589, PCGS# 7411

MODERN ISSUES

4404 **1987-W Constitution Gold Five Dollar PR70 Ultra Cameo NGC. Five-Coin Lot.** All five Constitution gold five dollar pieces are encapsulated in mid-generation NGC holders, with a common grade of PR70 Ultra Cameo. The coins are essentially identical in appearance, exhibiting heavily frosted devices and fully mirrored fields. The strikes are bold and the eye appeal is unrivaled. These were struck in commemoration of the 200th anniversary of the adopting of the United States Constitution.(Total: 5 coins)

4405 **2011-W Lucy Hayes Half-Ounce Gold Ten Dollar MS70 NGC.** This technically perfect specimen commemorates Lucy Hayes, who married Rutherford B. Hayes in 1852 and served as First Lady from 1877 to 1881. From a limited mintage of only 2,263 Uncirculated examples. PCGS# 506968

4406 **2012-W Frances Cleveland Half-Ounce Gold Ten Dollar, First Term PR70 Deep Cameo PCGS.** The First Spouse bullion series is known for its low-mintage issues, and the proof First Term Frances Cleveland issue is no exception, with just 3,158 pieces struck. The present example displays fully mirrored, black fields set against frosty, glowing devices. The strike is bold and the coin is technically flawless. PCGS# 512932

MODERN BULLION COINS

4407 **1989-P Half-Ounce Gold Eagle PR70 Ultra Cameo NGC.** This proof issue features the Roman numeral date, as was seen on the original High Relief double eagles using Saint-Gaudens' majestic design. This piece is boldly struck with stark contrast and exceptional eye appeal. NGC ID# 28YB, PCGS# 9833

4408 **1991 Quarter-Ounce Gold Eagle MS70 NGC.** The strike is tack-sharp, with frosty golden luster overall. A perfect coin in regards to both technical and aesthetic appeal. From a mintage of only 36,100 pieces. NGC ID# 26M7, PCGS# 9850

4409 **1991-W One-Ounce Gold Eagle PR70 Ultra Cameo NGC.** From a lower-mintage of 50,411 coins, this is a beautiful, flawlessly preserved example with razor-sharp striking definition and amazingly deep cameo contrast on both sides. NGC ID# 28Z2, PCGS# 9855

4410 **1992-W One-Ounce Gold Eagle PR70 Ultra Cameo NGC.** Intensely frosted golden devices seem suspended above glassy, jet-black fields. A fully struck and immaculately preserved example of this one-ounce fifty-dollar gold proof. NGC ID# 28Z3, PCGS# 9865

1993 Half-Ounce Gold Eagle, MS70
Technically Flawless, Eye-Appealing

4411 **1993 Half-Ounce Gold Eagle MS70 PCGS.** The Mint struck 73,324 half-ounce Gold Eagles in 1993, and MS69 is far and away the most-awarded grade at PCGS. The same service, however, shows a mere 12 grading events in MS70. This is a technically flawless and eye-appealing representative with attractive lemon-gold color and needle-sharp design detail. NGC ID# 26NE, PCGS# 9872

4412 **1993-W One-Ounce Gold Eagle PR70 Ultra Cameo NGC.** This fifty-dollar proof gold issue had a low mintage of 34,369 pieces. This pristine representative exhibits flawlessly-struck design motifs and spectacular deeply-mirrored fields. NGC ID# 28Z5, PCGS# 9875

4413 **1994-P Silver Eagle PR70 Deep Cameo PCGS.** The fully struck design elements of this magnificent specimen display a rich coat of mint frost that contrasts dramatically with the deeply mirrored fields to create a stunning cameo effect. A technically perfect example of this low-mintage issue. NGC ID# 26JM, PCGS# 9877

4414 **1999-W Quarter-Ounce Gold Eagle — Struck From Unfinished Proof Dies — MS69 PCGS.** Although prepared for proof production with the West Point mintmark, the dies that struck this popular *Guide Book* variety were left unfinished and employed for regular business strike production. The result was a coin with deeply satiny luster and tack-sharp detail. This example is nearly perfect in preservation with rich golden color. Only one coin has been certified numerically finer at PCGS (10/14). NGC ID# 26MG, PCGS# 99942

4415 **2001-W One-Ounce Gold Eagle PR70 Ultra Cameo NGC.** Rich golden luster complements the stark white-on-black contrast of this beautifully produced and preserved Ultra Cameo. This West Point proof issue had a small mintage of only 24,555 pieces. NGC ID# 28ZD, PCGS# 99958

4416 **(5) 2005 Quarter-Ounce Platinum Eagles MS70 NGC.** All five quarter-ounce platinum bullion coins are housed in mid-generation NGC holders, with a common numeric grade of MS70, attesting to both perfect preservation and flawless manufacture. Frosty, silvery-white luster blankets each piece, which contains a quarter-ounce of .9995 pure platinum.(Total: 5 coins)

4417 **(5) 2006 Half-Ounce Platinum Eagles, Early Releases MS70 NGC.** All five 2006 half-ounce platinum bullion coins are encapsulated in NGC Early Releases holders, with a common numeric grade of MS70. The coins are flawless in both strike and preservation, with brilliant, frosty luster and appropriately strong eye appeal. Each coin contains a half-ounce of .9995 pure platinum. (Total: 5 coins)

4418 **2008-W Quarter-Ounce Gold Buffalo, .9999 Fine MS70 PCGS.** The American Buffalo bullion series is highly popular due to the accurate reproduction of James Earle Fraser's iconic Buffalo nickel design. The current quarter-ounce ten dollar coin is boldly struck and flawlessly preserved. PCGS# 399928

4419 **2008-W Quarter-Ounce Gold Buffalo PR70 Deep Cameo PCGS.** From a low mintage of 13,125 pieces, this technically perfect example offers fully struck design elements and deeply reflective fields that contrast profoundly with the richly frosted devices. PCGS# 399934

4420 **2008-W Half-Ounce Gold Buffalo MS70 PCGS.** Struck in .9999 fine gold and boldly detailed throughout, this half-ounce American Buffalo bullion coin is a visual treat for the collector of modern bullion issues. Close study with a lens fails to find any surface flaws on either side. PCGS# 399930

4421 **(5)2008 Quarter-Ounce Platinum Eagles MS70 NGC.** All five quarter-ounce platinum bullion coins are certified in mid-generation NGC holders, with a common numeric grade of MS70. Confirming the grade, the coins are fully struck with flawless preservation. Free of toning, each piece showcases frosty, silvery-white luster. Each example contains a quarter-ounce of .9995 pure platinum.(Total: 5 coins)

2008-W One-Ounce Gold Buffalo
PR70 Deep Cameo

4422 **2008-W One-Ounce Gold Buffalo PR70 Deep Cameo PCGS.** Quite literally among the finest in existence, this perfectly preserved Deep Cameo American Buffalo boasts fully struck motifs and eye-catching contrast. Struck at the West Point Mint, from a mintage of just 13,125 pieces. The one-ounce American Buffalo proofs are immensely popular among bullion coin enthusiasts, due to the accurate reproduction of James Earle Fraser's famous Buffalo nickel designs. PCGS# 393329

4423 **2009 One-Ounce Gold Ultra High Relief Twenty Dollar Uncertified.** The acclaimed Saint-Gaudens Ultra High Relief design appears in small format on this coin, much as it was featured on the original reduced diameter, double thickness patterns (Judd-1917) that now reside at the Smithsonian. This delightful example is housed in the original government-issue box with certificate of authenticity. It is accompanied by the separately mailed booklet, still in original shrinkwrap. NGC ID# 26S4, PCGS# 407404

COINS OF HAWAII

1847 Hawaii Cent, MS64 Red and Brown
Medcalf 2CC-2, Crosslet 4

4424 **1847 Hawaii Cent MS64 Red and Brown PCGS. Medcalf 2CC-2. Crosslet 4.** The most plentiful variety, easily attributed by the placement of a berry below the first A in HAWAII. This is a boldly struck, well-preserved representative, with substantial coppery-red luster in the recesses. A few minute specks are observed upon close examination, though the surfaces are otherwise devoid of distractions. Population: 22 in 64 (1 in 64+) Red and Brown, 1 finer (10/14). PCGS# 10966

4425 **1883 Hawaii Quarter MS63 PCGS.** A boldly struck, essentially untoned example of this popular Hawaiian issue, design by Charles Barber and struck at the San Francisco Mint in 1883. Radiant luster illuminates each side, giving this piece ample visual appeal. No significant abrasions are observed. PCGS# 10987

4426 **1883 Hawaii Quarter MS64 PCGS.** A mintage of 500,000 quarters (including 26 proofs) was accomplished for the 1883 Hawaiian quarter dollar at the San Francisco Mint. However, when Hawaii became a U.S. territory in 1900, the legal tender status of these pieces was revoked, and many were later withdrawn and melted. This Choice survivor displays vibrant mint bloom beneath faint traces of amber-gold toning. The strike is needle-sharp, and there are no singularly obvious abrasions. PCGS# 10987

GSA DOLLARS

1878-CC Morgan Dollar, MS64 Prooflike
From the Historic GSA Hoard

1880-CC GSA Dollar, MS66
Strong for the Grade

4427 **1878-CC GSA MS64 Prooflike PCGS.** This impressive Choice example represents the first year of the Morgan design, with sharply detailed design elements and well-preserved brilliant surfaces and brightly reflective prooflike fields. The coin and its original black holder are encapsulated and certified by NGC. Population: 3 in 64 (1 in 64+) Prooflike, 0 finer (11/14). PCGS# 518846

4428 **1880/79-CC GSA, Reverse of 1878, MS65 PCGS. VAM-4.** A Top 100 Variety. The undertype 79 is visible below the final primary digits in the date and the parallel top arrow feather identifies the Reverse of 1878. This sharply detailed Gem is lustrous and well-preserved, The coin in its original black case is encapsulated and certified by NGC. Population: 1 in 65, 1 finer (11/14). PCGS# 518922

4429 **1880-CC GSA, 8 Over High 7, VAM-5, MS65+ NGC.** A Top 100 Variety (not mentioned on the NGC band certification). The second 8 is repunched over a 7, with the remnants of an original 7 high with "ears" above the 8, the crossbar in the upper loop, and the stem of the 7 visible in the lower loop. The first 8 is lightly doubled, visible at the top of the lower loop. A high-end Gem example, sharply struck, with brilliant-silver luster and few marks. No box or certificate accompanies, but housed in its original GSA holder. PCGS# 518857

4430 **1880-CC GSA MS65 PCGS.** Thickly frosted, delicately preserved mint luster dominates both sides of this Gem Carson City Morgan. The extreme outer rims exhibit a touch of light golden color, but the surfaces are otherwise brilliant. Bold design definition completes the eye appeal. Encapsulated in its original GSA hard plastic holder. The number of GSA dollars remaining in their original holders is rather minimal at this grade level, with PCGS having so-certified only 10 examples, with just four numerically finer (11/14). PCGS# 518851

4431 **1880-CC GSA MS65+ NGC.** Thick mint frost blankets brilliant, carefully preserved surfaces on this high-end Gem GSA dollar. More than 130,000 examples of this issue were distributed through the GSA sales, but few remain in their original black GSA holders. This survivor has been awarded a Plus designation by NGC, attesting to its superb strike and eye appeal. PCGS# 518851

4432 **1880-CC GSA MS66 NGC.** As a date, the 1880-CC Morgan dollar is not prohibitively rare in MS66, but only a small number of coins in this grade are still housed in their original GSA holders. The present example also boasts thickly frosted cartwheel luster beneath just a few faint wisps of light golden color. There are no distracting abrasions and only trivial striking weakness is seen on the hair above Liberty's ear. NGC has certified 25 1880-CC dollars in a finer numeric grade, but only one of those also remains in its original GSA holder (10/14). PCGS# 518851

4433 **1881-CC GSA MS66 NGC.** Silver cartwheel luster rolls across nearly unblemished surfaces of this dazzling white Premium Gem. A few minor luster grazes are visible on the the high points of Liberty's hair, yet the semiprooflike fields are virtually clear of distractions. NGC reports more than 8,000 grading events for 1881-CC GSA dollars, with just 26 coins granted a numerically finer grade (10/14). Band-certified in its original GSA holder, but no box or certificate accompanies the coin. PCGS# 518863

4434 **1881-CC GSA MS66 NGC.** An extremely appealing Premium Gem — untoned and snow-white, with lively silver luster. The frosted fields and devices display a full strike and nearly unimprovable quality, while a collection of spidery die cracks circle the reverse legends. Few GSA releases are certified finer for the issue. The eye appeal is terrific. Band-certified in the black GSA holder of issue and offered without box or paperwork. PCGS# 518863

4435 **1882-CC GSA MS66 PCGS.** The 1882-CC is an available Carson City issue, but examples such as this piece that are certified by the leading services in their original GSA packaging are seldom seen at the MS66 grade level, and are rare any finer. This piece is heavily frosted with a light golden hue over each side. Only a few faint luster grazes limit the grade, and the design elements are boldly impressed. Population: 12 in 66 (5 in 66+), 1 finer (11/14). PCGS# 518866

4436 **1885-CC GSA MS65 NGC.** The original GSA holder with box and paperwork is a powerful plus for this Gem dollar with the band-certified NGC certification. Untoned, brilliant, and attractive on both sides, the frosty silver luster complements a bold strike. Marks are limited to a few light grazes as often seen on these otherwise mint-fresh GSA dollars. PCGS# 518875

1885-CC GSA Dollar, MS66
Eye-Catching Cartwheel Luster

4437 **1885-CC GSA MS66 NGC.** The 1885-CC had one of the lower mintages in the Carson City Morgan dollar series (just 228,000 coins), but an incredible 64.9 percent of these survived in Treasury vaults and were distributed to collectors through the GSA sales of the early 1970s. Challenging for collectors, however, is finding a high-grade example that is still housed in its original GSA holder. The present coin is just such a piece, with frosty, untoned mint bloom and bold design definition. A lack of noticeable abrasions warrants the lofty MS66 grade. Only 16 numerically finer GSA Hoard dollars have been certified by NGC (10/14). PCGS# 518875

1885-CC GSA Hoard Dollar
Snow-White Premium Gem

4438 **1885-CC GSA MS66 NGC.** Stored in 1,000-coin boxes at the U.S. Bullion Depository at West Point, chances for coin-to-coin contact were many and Premium Gem survivors were few. This sharp, brilliant-white MS66 coin offers snowy mint frost on the devices and gleaming, slightly reflective untoned fields. Tiny chatter marks take the form of minor luster grazes on the obverse, while the reverse shows a pair of reeding marks, one under each wing. The 1885-CC is the lowest-mintage Carson City dollar at just 228,000 pieces struck. 65% of the mintage ended up in the GSA Hoard distributions. Band-certified in the black GSA holder of issue and offered alone (no box or papers). PCGS# 518875

1885-CC GSA Dollar, MS66
Seldom Seen So Nice in Original GSA Holder

4439 **1885-CC GSA MS66 NGC.** Due to the distribution of more than 148,000 coins through the GSA sales of the early 1970s, the 1885-CC Morgan dollar is readily collectible today. Most high-grade examples, however, have been cracked out of their original GSA holders for certification, making the limited number of Premium Gems that survive in their original packaging highly sought-after by Carson City specialists. This representative showcases the potent, frosty luster that this issue is known for, with few of the small handling abrasions that typically affect coins from the GSA sales. NGC has certified only 16 numerically finer coins in their original GSA holders (10/14). PCGS# 518875

1890-CC Morgan Dollar, MS62
Scarce Carson City Issue

4440 **1890-CC GSA MS62 NGC.** Although this Carson City date had the largest mintage of any CC-minted silver dollar at more than 2.3 million pieces, it also shows the smallest GSA Hoard distribution in the range of about 3,600 pieces. This MS62 representative is a bit soft at the centers and moderately abraded. Bright cartwheel luster shines on both sides. Housed in its original GSA holder with the blue NGC hologram band, but no box or paperwork included. PCGS# 518878

4441 **1891-CC GSA MS61 PCGS.** More than 5,600 Uncirculated examples of this issue remained in inventory following the Treasury releases of the early 1960s, and were later distributed through the famous GSA sales of the early 1970s. Frosty cartwheel luster graces each side of this well-struck example, while scattered abrasions define the grade. The second-lowest distribution in the GSA sales (the 1890-CC dollar had the lowest). Encapsulated by PCGS in its original plastic GSA holder but no box is included. PCGS# 518881

4442 **1891-CC Spitting Eagle, VAM-3, MS63 NGC GSA Hoard.** A Top 100 Variety. The ubiquitous but popular "Spitting Eagle" variety, with the oblong die gouge in its usual place beneath the eagle's beak. Perhaps more interesting is the other significant diagnostic for the variety, with slight doubling of the CC mintmark at the tops of the Cs. This Select Uncirculated example is boldly struck, brilliant, and frosty. Light abrasions account for the assigned grade. Housed in its original GSA holder with the blue NGC hologram band, but no box or certificate is included. PCGS# 518881

ALASKA TOKENS

4443 **1911 Parka Head, 1/2 Alaska Gold, MS63 NGC. Gould-Bressett 176.** Part of the M.E. Hart "Coins of the Golden West" series, sold by Farran Zerbe in San Francisco circa 1915 to 1916, during the Panama-Pacific Exposition or shortly later. An unabraded honey-gold example with an interesting Y-shaped die crack on the lower obverse. Listed on page 402 of the 2015 *Guide Book*. PCGS# 661160

4444 **1911 Parka Head, 1/4 Alaska Gold, MS65 NGC. Gould-Bressett 177.** Part of the M.E. Hart "Coins of the Golden West" series sold in San Francisco around the time of the Panama-Pacific Exposition. This caramel-gold Gem appears pristine except for a tiny spot between stars 4 and 5. Listed on page 402 of the 2015 *Guide Book*.

GOLD CHARM

4445 **1914 Montana Gold (One) MS64 NGC.** A member of the popular M.E. Hart "Coins of the Golden West" series, distributed at the Panama-Pacific Exposition held in San Francisco in 1915. A satiny and unblemished green-gold representative. The strike is bold except on the tops of MONTANA.

ERRORS

1888 Three Cent Nickel, PR65 Cameo
Split Planchet After Strike

4446 **1888 Three Cent Nickel — Split Planchet — PR65 Cameo NGC.** This Gem Cameo proof three cent nickel neatly split into two pieces after the strike, due to alloy impurities in the strip used to stamp planchets. Both pieces have survived together, and are housed in separate but identically graded NGC holders. The smaller piece (0.4 gm) is a thin layer from the upper half of the obverse. The larger piece (1.5 gm) has a normal reverse while the obverse retains the lower half of the design. The reverse of the first fragment, and the upper obverse of the second piece, display the striated dark gray surface expected of the coin interior. (Total: 2 coins)

Undated Kennedy Half
Struck on a Cent Flan
MS60 Red and Brown

4447 **Undated Kennedy Half — On a Cent Planchet — MS60 Red and Brown ANACS.** Though the date is off the flan, this is a 1964 Philadelphia half dollar, since it has a Type One Reverse and no mintmark is near the branch stem. Aligned with the collar at 10:30, most of the portrait and eagle are present though the peripheral legends are largely absent. Those letters that are here, such as the B in LIBERTY, are distorted from collar-unrestrained metal flow. Toned olive-brown with plentiful brick-red within design recesses.

4448 **1911 Indian Eagle — Struck-Through Reverse — MS64 PCGS.** A noticeable string-like strike-through is observed on the lower-right reverse, overlapping the tip of the eagle's tailfeathers. The design definition is overall razor-sharp, with frosty honey-gold luster and no obtrusive abrasions. An immensely appealing 1911 gold eagle, with an added allure from the reverse strike-through.

4449 **1922 Grant No Star Gold Dollar — Obverse Struck Through Grease — MS63 PCGS.** A significant portion of Grant's hair lacks definition due to the excess grease that remained on the dies. The rest of the design, however, is sharply detailed. Shimmering satiny luster enhances the yellow-gold surfaces.
Ex: Los Angeles Signature (Heritage, 8/2009), lot 2233.

CERTIFIED MODERN PROOF SET

4450 **1939 Five-Piece Proof Set, PR65 to PR67.** The set includes: **cent PR65 Red,** deeply mirrored fields accent sharp devices amid blended coppery-orange and cherry-red hues, with a few minute specks; **nickel PR67,** traces of pale champagne accent largely ice-blue surfaces, with deeply mirrored fields and a full strike; **dime PR66,** fully struck, with beautifully preserved surfaces and iridescent, light golden toning; **quarter PR66,** light golden in color, with sharp motifs and deeply mirrored fields; **half dollar PR65,** similar in appearance to the dime and quarter, showing light golden color and fully struck devices. All five coins are encapsulated in old green label holders with consecutive serial numbers. A well-matched, fully original set.(Total: 5 coins)

End of Session Three

SESSION FOUR

PATTERNS

1867 Nickel, PR65
Judd-566, Longacre-Designed Liberty

4451 **1867 Five Cents, Judd-566, Pollock-627 PR65 PCGS.** The obverse resembles the issued three cent nickel. Liberty is wearing a coronet inscribed LIBERTY. Around, the legend UNITED STATES OF AMERICA and below, the date. On the reverse, the denomination 5 CENTS is enclosed within a laurel wreath, with the motto IN GOD WE TRUST above. Struck in nickel with a plain edge. A well struck and nicely mirrored caramel-gold and cream-gray Gem. The undisturbed and unblemished surfaces possess pleasing eye appeal. PCGS# 60776

1867 Five Cent Pattern in Nickel, PR62
Judd-570, Pollock-638

4452 **1867 Five Cents, Judd-570, Pollock-638, R.5, PR62 PCGS.** A bust of Liberty wearing a coronet and facing left dominates the obverse design. UNITED STATES OF AMERICA is around the periphery with the date below. The top of the 7 is distant from the curl. The reverse shows 5 CENTS centered within a laurel wreath with the motto IN GOD WE TRUST at the top. CENTS is in a curved line. Struck in nickel with a plain edge. This is a pleasing lower-grade example with pale golden-gray and ice-blue toning. The fields show moderate mirroring, while the frosty devices are sharply defined. No major contact marks are observed. PCGS# 60780

1867 Five Cent Pattern in Nickel
Judd-570, PR63

4453 **1867 Five Cents, Judd-570, Pollock-638, PR63 PCGS.** A bust of Liberty wearing a coronet and facing left dominates the obverse design. UNITED STATES OF AMERICA is around the periphery with the date below. The top of the 7 is distant from the curl. The reverse shows 5 CENTS centered within a laurel wreath with the motto IN GOD WE TRUST at the top. CENTS is in a curved line. Struck in nickel with a plain edge. This is an attractive and relatively inexpensive pattern with more than 30 examples known. The nickel-gray surfaces are covered with pale golden patina over each side. PCGS# 60780

1870 Standard Silver Quarter in Aluminum
Judd-923, Pollock-1028, PR65 Cameo

4454 **1870 Standard Silver Quarter Dollar, Judd-923, Pollock-1028, High R.7, PR65 Cameo PCGS. CAC.** The obverse shows Liberty facing right, the hair tied in a loose bun behind the head, with additional flowing curls across the shoulder. The headband is inscribed LIBERTY with a star above the forehead. The reverse is the usual Standard Silver design with the denomination inside a wreath, the date below. Struck in aluminum with a plain edge. Less than a half dozen of this variety are known, making this Gem Cameo an important and rare acquisition for the advanced specialist. Pale ice-blue toning accents frosty devices and deeply mirrored fields. Some lightness of strike is noted on the reverse bow, though the motifs are otherwise sharp. PCGS# 800082

1884 Perforated Cent Pattern, PR66 Cameo
Judd-1721, Pollock-1929

4455 **1884 One Cent, Judd-1721, Pollock-1929, R.5, PR66 Cameo PCGS. CAC.** Eastman Johnson's "holey" design for the cent with the center perforated with an irregular circumference. These experimental pieces were intended to make small denomination coinage easier to distinguish by the blind, and thereby to "remedy the inconvenience of similarity in our small coin." The obverse bears the legend UNITED STATES OF AMERICA about the upper rim and the date at the bottom. The reverse shows the denomination ONE CENT at the top with an inverted shield and two laurel sprigs below. Struck in nickel with a plain edge. This brightly mirrored specimen is spot-free and can be identified by a lint mark beneath RI in AMERICA.
Ex: Long Beach Signature (Heritage, 6/2005), lot 7453; ANA Signature (Heritage, 8/2007), lot 2766. PCGS# 391598

GOLD DOLLARS

1851-C Gold Dollar, Sharply Struck MS61

4456 **1851-C MS61 NGC. Variety 1.** The 1 in the date centered below the O, heavy doubled stars, and a die crack atop F AM confirm the variety. The 1851-C gold dollar, with a mintage of 41,267 pieces, is the most plentiful issue of any denomination from Charlotte. Yellow- and greenish-gold surfaces exhibit sharply struck design elements, and scattered light marks do not detract. Nice for the designated grade. NGC ID# 25BL, PCGS# 7514

1851-C Gold Dollar, MS62
Strikingly Sharp Throughout

4457 **1851-C MS62 NGC. Variety 3.** Ideal for the collector seeking a single representative from this mint, the 1851-C gold dollar is one of the more plentiful Charlotte issues in the series and is also one of the better-struck, as a rule. Still, a number of examples are known with minor weakness on Liberty's head and some of the stars, putting the fully struck examples in higher demand. Winter estimates 125 to 175 pieces survive in the various Mint State grades, which gives a decent representation of this date's availability in comparison to the other, conditionally rare issues from this mint.

The present coin shows incredible detail, with no evidence of striking weakness on either side. Frosty orange-gold luster reveals few disruptions, and the overall eye appeal is more in line with a Philadelphia issue, than what is typically seen from this Southern branch mint. Housed in a prior generation holder. Census: 34 in 62, 27 finer (10/14). NGC ID# 25BL, PCGS# 7514

4458 **1853 MS64+ PCGS.** A tack-sharp Type One representative, this high-end Choice example boasts frosted honey and green-gold hues over each side, with only a few minor surface grazes here and there. A small, mint-made planchet void near star 2 should not be confused with damage. NGC ID# 25BU, PCGS# 7521

4459 **1853-O MS63 NGC. Variety 1.** The 1853-O gold dollar had a rather substantial mintage of 290,000 coins, but its corresponding availability declines above the MS62 grade level. This piece shows well-struck devices and frosty green-gold luster. No singularly obvious abrasions are noted. NGC has encapsulated 52 numerically finer representatives (10/14). NGC ID# 25BX, PCGS# 7524

4460 **1853-O MS63 PCGS. Variety 2.** The centered date variety, rarer than the high date Variety 1. A fully struck, lustrous, and pleasing sun-gold representative. The fields display only inconsequential grazes. A popular New Orleans type issue. NGC ID# 25BX, PCGS# 7524

4461 **1855 MS61 NGC.** The Type Two gold dollar design was only produced from 1854 to 1856, making it an important target for type collectors. The 1854 and 1855 Philadelphia mintages were easily the highest, making these two dates the most popular. This is a nicely-struck example with pale peach-gold toning and minimally marked surfaces for the grade. NGC ID# 25C4, PCGS# 7532

4462 **1855 MS62 NGC.** Although the 8 in the date is not fully struck, due to being opposite the high relief portrait, the strike is otherwise exemplary. This light matte-golden representative offers extensive luster and nearly unmarked surfaces. Struck from boldly clashed dies, which is typical for this short-lived and desirable type.
Ex: Long Beach Signature (Heritage, 9/2005), lot 4248. NGC ID# 25C4, PCGS# 7532

4463 **1855 MS62 NGC.** An attractive MS62 example of this popular type issue, with well-detailed design elements and some dramatic clash marks on both sides. The lustrous orange-gold surfaces show a few minor signs of contact. NGC ID# 25C4, PCGS# 7532

1855-O Gold Dollar, AU55
Sole Type Two New Orleans Issue

4464 **1855-O AU55 NGC. Variety 2.** The 1855-O is not only popular for its scarcity in high grades, but also for its status as the only Type Two gold dollar produced at New Orleans. This Choice AU example displays pale green-gold luster and smooth, problem-free surfaces. The 8 in the date is not fully struck, though the remainder of each side shows strong detail. NGC ID# 25C7, PCGS# 7535

4465 **1856-S/S FS-501 XF45 NGC.** The mintmark is widely repunched, with the secondary impression seen to the upper-left of the primary. As a date, this issue is seldom available due to a small 24,600-coin mintage, and is highly popular as the only Type Two issue struck after 1855. This piece shows grade-consistent wear, but is otherwise problem-free with rich olive-gold color. PCGS# 145703

4466 **1858-S AU58 NGC.** A well-detailed near-Mint example, with lightly abraded orange and rose-gold surfaces that retain traces of original mint luster. From a mintage of 10,000 pieces. Census: 32 in 58, 10 finer (11/14). NGC ID# 25CK, PCGS# 7550

1861 Gold Dollar
Frosted, Mark-Free Gem

4467 **1861 MS65 NGC.** There are virtually no post-mint marks on this gleaming orange-gold Gem dollar, with mint-related characteristics the only mentionable distractions. Die clashing is clearly evident on both sides, and two areas of planchet porosity are noted above Liberty's headdress. In hand, the coin displays tremendous eye appeal from the bold strike, frosted luster, and delightful gold patina. Census: 34 in 65 (1 in 65 ★), 10 finer (10/14). NGC ID# 25CU, PCGS# 7558

4468 **1862 MS65 PCGS.** The bright yellow-gold surfaces are frosty and radiant, with faint touches of pastel rose color adding to the coin's eye appeal. A well-struck, carefully preserved Gem. NGC ID# 25CW, PCGS# 7560

4469 **1864 MS61 PCGS.** The 1864 gold dollar had a limited mintage of only 5,900 pieces, and Mint State survivors are genuinely scarce in all grades. The present coin displays deep orange-gold luster and minimally abraded surfaces. The central obverse is not fully brought up, with the result that some minor adjustment marks remain on the highest point of the portrait. Population: 7 in 61, 37 finer (11/14). NGC ID# 25CY, PCGS# 7563

1866 Gold Dollar, MS64+★
Flashy Semiprooflike Fields

4470 **1866 MS64+ ★ NGC.** The sought-after combination of the Plus and Star designations from NGC puts this high-end Choice 1866 gold dollar remarkably close to full Gem technical quality, though the eye appeal is seemingly unlimited. The devices display sharp definition and frosty golden luster, set against radiant, semiprooflike fields. A few minute ticks are observed upon close scrutiny with a lens, though these are of little significance. From a mintage of only 7,100 pieces. Census: 14 in 64 (1 in 64+★), 11 finer (10/14). NGC ID# 25D2, PCGS# 7565

1867 Gold Dollar, MS64 ★
Semiprooflike Fields

4471 **1867 MS64 ★ NGC.** Only 5,200 gold dollars were struck in Philadelphia in 1867, few of which survive in any grade. The present offering is a beautifully preserved Choice example, with semiprooflike fields and sharp, frosty devices. No noticeable abrasions are present, giving this piece substantial eye appeal, as evidenced by the NCG Star designation. The dies are heavily clashed, with LIBERTY fully transferred to the reverse field below the date. Census: 10 in 64 (1 in 64+, 1 in 64 ★), 7 finer (10/14). NGC ID# 25D3, PCGS# 7566

4472 **1868 MS62 Prooflike NGC.** Despite being somewhat more available than the surrounding dates, this issue remains scarce in all grades and particularly so with prooflike surfaces. A copper alloy mark between A and T of STATES is the most noticeable mark on the coin, with a few light abrasions widely scattered over the reflective surfaces. Attractive medium-gold fields and devices are boldly struck with no evidence of die clashing. PCGS# 77567

1873 Open 3 Gold Dollar, MS66
Uninhibited Mint-Fresh Luster

4473 1873 Open 3 MS66 NGC. Thickly frosted, shimmering luster engulfs each side of this beautifully preserved Open 3 example. The devices are boldly struck, set against an eye-catching yellow-gold back drop. A thin, faint mark near Liberty's neck is the only discernable surface flaw. This issue is readily available in grades through MS64, but the certified population plummets in Gem and finer grades. Census: 11 in 66, 1 finer (10/14). NGC ID# 25DB, PCGS# 7573

4474 1878 MS62 Prooflike NGC. Strikingly reflective fields and mildly frosted devices enable a nice cameo-like effect on each side. Wispy hairlines in the fields and a pair of faint slide marks on the portrait limit the grade. Just 3,000 business strikes were produced. Census: 3 in 62 Prooflike, 5 finer (10/14). PCGS# 77579

1880 Gold Dollar, MS65 Prooflike
Low-Mintage Late-Series Issue

4475 1880 MS65 Prooflike NGC. The Mint struck only 1,600 gold dollars in 1880, but enough examples were saved by dealers and speculators that the issue is moderately obtainable in high grades today. Despite the high survival rate, however, NGC has awarded few examples a Prooflike designation. This Gem example shows pleasing field-device contrast and radiant rose-gold luster. Some minor striking softness is noted on the bow knot, though the motifs are otherwise well-defined. Census: 6 in 65 Prooflike, 32 finer (10/14). PCGS# 77581

1880 Gold Dollar, MS66 ★ Prooflike
Mirrored Fields, High-Contrast Devices

4476 1880 MS66 ★ Prooflike NGC. CAC. Despite a tiny mintage of 1,600 business strikes and 36 proofs, hundreds of this issue were hoarded — many in prooflike condition. Soon, high-end business strikes were masquerading as the much-rarer proofs. Today, the grading services have done much to sort things out. The present coin has a strong prooflike presence, but small areas of porosity along the rims and at the legends are a tip-off to its business strike status. Still, it is a spectacular Premium Gem with the NGC Star and CAC endorsement for quality. Struck without any die clashing, this glittering, yellow-gold coin offers exceptional, prooflike eye appeal. PCGS# 77581

4477 1886 MS65 NGC. A mintage of just 5,000 pieces ensures the scarcity of the 1886, and only a small portion of survivors are Gems. A lustrous and well struck orange-gold example with clashed fields and exemplary preservation. Encapsulated in a former generation holder. NGC ID# 25DR, PCGS# 7587

1888 Gold Dollar, Lustrous MS67

4478 1888 MS67 PCGS. The rich orange-gold patination is accented by traces of light green on this boldly struck Superb Gem gold dollar. Close examination reveals no marks worthy of special note on the highly lustrous surfaces. Very scarce in this grade and extremely rare any finer. Population: 44 in 67 (1 in 67+), 5 finer (10/14). NGC ID# 25DT, PCGS# 7589

4479 1889 MS66 PCGS. An immensely attractive final-year type coin, this Premium Gem gold dollar showcases intermingled mint-gold, rose, and fiery-orange luster, with sharp motifs and frosty surfaces. Close examination fails to reveal any mentionable surface flaws. NGC ID# 25DU, PCGS# 7590

1889 Gold Dollar, MS67
Superb Final-Year Type Coin

4480 1889 MS67 NGC. An ideal issue for type purposes, the 1889 gold dollar had a fairly limited mintage of only 28,950 coins, but a disproportionately high survival rate. This piece displays beautiful, frosty yellow-gold luster and bold design definition. NGC has encapsulated only 16 numerically finer representatives (10/14). NGC ID# 25DU, PCGS# 7590

1889 Gold Dollar, MS67
Only Four Coins Numerically Finer at PCGS

4481 1889 MS67 PCGS. The 1889 was widely saved as a final-year issue, and is proportionately available for type purposes. The present Superb Gem is awash in frosty orange-gold luster, with boldly struck design elements. A tiny planchet void (as made) is noted near the first S in STATES, but the surfaces are devoid of discernable abrasions. PCGS has certified only four numerically finer representatives (10/14). NGC ID# 25DU, PCGS# 7590

CLASSIC QUARTER EAGLES

4482 1834 AU58 PCGS. Breen-6138, Variety 1, R.1. The finer details remain bold, despite slight high-point friction. Substantial semiprooflike mirroring in the fields complements deep apricot-gold patina, giving this first-year Classic Head type coin ample visual appeal for the grade. NGC ID# 25FS, PCGS# 7692

4483 1834 AU58 NGC. Breen-6140, Variety 4, R.3. A lovely lemon-gold Borderline Uncirculated Large Head example. Devoid of remotely relevant marks, and the strike is excellent for the Classic type. Luster illuminates the motifs and margins. NGC ID# 25FS, PCGS# 7692

4484 1836 Script 8 AU58 PCGS. CAC. Breen-6143, Variety 11, R.2. Head of 1835. Remaining mint luster illuminates the recesses, while each side displays original lemon-gold patina. Some minor striking softness is noted in the centers, not unusual for a late die state example. This piece displays a prominent die crack down from the obverse rim at 11 o'clock. NGC ID# 25FU, PCGS# 7694

4485 1837 AU53 NGC. Breen-6145, Variety 16, R.2. Apricot toning graces this lightly circulated and typically struck scarcer date quarter eagle. The few minor marks on the upper reverse field are expected of the grade.
Ex: Orlando FUN Signature (Heritage, 1/2008), lot 3787. NGC ID# 25FX, PCGS# 7695

4486 1839-C — Improperly Cleaned — NGC Details. AU. Breen-6150, Variety 22, R.4. The 3 in the date is widely repunched south. The slightly granular straw-gold surfaces are only minimally marked. Nicely struck except on the stars and the left shield border. A misaligned collar die causes a steep railroad rim on the obverse near 2 o'clock. NGC ID# 25G4, PCGS# 7699

LIBERTY QUARTER EAGLES

4487 1841-C — Reverse Planchet Flaw — NGC Details. AU. Variety 1. This early Charlotte Mint rarity has pleasing sharpness and unmarked straw-gold surfaces. Luster brightens design recesses. A partially retained lamination affects the upper reverse. NGC ID# 25GE, PCGS# 7721

4488 1843-C Large Date, Plain 4 XF45 PCGS. Variety 1. Both the date and mintmark are lightly repunched. An olive-gold Choice XF Charlotte quarter eagle with unblemished surfaces. The strike at the centers is incomplete, but the stars are sharply defined. NGC ID# 25GN, PCGS# 7728

4489 1846-D — Scratch — PCGS Genuine. AU Details. Variety 7-L (formerly 7-K). The same die pair as the 1846-D/D, but a later state with the initial errant mintmark no longer present. A well struck and only lightly circulated honey-gold Dahlonega example. Clusters of pinscratches are on the field near the right (facing) wing, and a lesser pinscratch is concealed beneath the bust. NGC ID# 25H3, PCGS# 7742

4490 1846-O AU58 NGC. Variety 1. A clean canary-gold near-Mint New Orleans example. The strike is bold except on the eagle's leg and the ER in LIBERTY. The leftmost mintmark placement for the issue. 62,000 pieces were struck, from a single obverse die paired with three different reverses. NGC ID# 25H4, PCGS# 7743

4491 1856-C — Improperly Cleaned — NGC Details. AU. Variety 1. A prooflike apricot-gold Charlotte example with a few rose alloy spots above the hairbun and a cluster of minor marks near the profile. As is usual for the issue, mint-made strike-throughs are prominent on the field near the chin, and on the reverse field near the arrows and the eagle's head. NGC ID# 25J8, PCGS# 7778

4492 1857-D — Improperly Cleaned — NGC Details. AU. Variety 21-N. Just one die variety is known from the scant mintage of 2,364 pieces. The strike is good given the Dahlonega origin, but the neck feathers display merging. The wheat-gold surfaces are a bit bright but are free from relevant abrasions. NGC ID# 25JD, PCGS# 7783

1860 Type One Gold Dollar, MS61
Semiprooflike Fields

4493 1860 Old Reverse, Type One, MS61 NGC. Differentiated by a more oval-shaped O in OF, the Old Reverse (or Type One) 1860 quarter eagle is much scarcer than its New Reverse counterpart, and is genuinely rare in Mint State. This representative displays rich bronze-gold luster with subtle rose overtones in the recesses. The fields showcase near-prooflike reflectivity and the devices are essentially bold, save for the eagle's right (facing) talons. An immensely appealing example for the grade. Census: 7 in 61, 3 finer (10/14). PCGS# 97791

4494 1861 Old Reverse, Type One, MS61 NGC. The Old Reverse variety of the 1861 quarter eagle is many times rarer than its New Reverse counterpart from the same date, and only a limited number of pieces are known of the former type. This scarce Mint State example displays bright, semi-prooflike surfaces and pale yellow-gold toning. Wispy hairlines and a few minuscule contact marks limit the grade. Census: 23 in 61, 19 finer (10/14). NGC ID# 25JW, PCGS# 97794

1869 Quarter Eagle, Well-Struck MS61
Rare in Mint Condition

4495 1869 MS61 NGC. The 1869 quarter eagle had a low mintage of 4,320 pieces. Mint State examples are rare with none certified better than near-Gem. The NGC census of 17 MS61 examples is likely inflated by resubmissions. The yellow-gold surfaces are imbued with traces of apricot and red and exhibit well-struck design elements. Several scattered marks determine the grade. Census: 17 in 61, 5 finer (10/14). NGC ID# 25KD, PCGS# 7809

4496 1871-S MS62 NGC. A mintage of 22,000 Liberty quarter eagles was accomplished at the San Francisco Mint in 1871, small in absolute terms, but not unusual in the context of the series. This impressive MS62 survivor exhibits well-detailed design elements, with a touch of softness on the reverse. The lustrous orange and rose-gold surfaces show only minor contact marks. Census: 2 in 62, 11 finer (10/14). NGC ID# 25KJ, PCGS# 7814

1875-S Quarter Eagle, MS61
Underrated in Mint State

4497 1875-S MS61 NGC. CAC. Luminous orange-gold luster illuminates minimally abraded surfaces for the grade. The eagle's left (facing) leg is not fully struck, though the design elements are otherwise sharply impressed. The 1875-S quarter eagle had a paltry mintage of only 11,600 pieces, and is rarely seen in Mint State. Census: 20 in 61, 9 finer (10/14). NGC ID# 25KT, PCGS# 7823

4498 1878 MS64 PCGS. CAC. The mintage of quarter eagles increased significantly at the Philadelphia Mint in 1878, indicating an increased demand for small gold coinage. This sharply detailed Choice example offers well-preserved peach-gold surfaces with vibrant mint luster on both sides. NGC ID# 25KY, PCGS# 7828

4499 1880 MS62 NGC. From a tiny mintage of 2,960 pieces, the 1880 Liberty quarter eagle is scarce-to-rare in all grades. This attractive MS62 example is well-detailed, with prooflike greenish-gold surfaces that show a scattering of minor contact marks. Census: 14 in 62, 13 finer (10/14). NGC ID# 25L4, PCGS# 7832

4500 1887 MS63 PCGS. From a mintage of just 6,160 pieces, this well-detailed Select specimen displays lightly marked orange-gold surfaces with vibrant mint luster and highlights of lilac. Population: 26 in 63, 20 finer (10/14). NGC ID# 25LB, PCGS# 7839

1888 Quarter Eagle, MS65
Attractive, Frosty Mint Luster

4501 1888 MS65 NGC. Shimmering rose-gold mint frost delivers outstanding visual appeal on this Gem 1888 quarter eagle. Light clash marks are noted on the reverse, as is some minor striking weakness on the eagle's left (facing) leg. A few tiny marks in the left obverse field preclude a finer grade. This Philadelphia issue had a limited mintage of 16,001 pieces, and is rarely seen at the Gem grade level. Census: 27 in 65 (2 in 65+), 6 finer (10/14). NGC ID# 25LC, PCGS# 7840

4502 1895 MS64 PCGS. Tinges of honey accent frosty green-gold luster on each side of this boldly struck Choice example. Grade-limiting abrasions are minor and evenly distributed in non-focal areas. Population: 31 in 64, 24 finer (10/14). NGC ID# 25LK, PCGS# 7847

1903 Quarter Eagle, MS67
Gorgeous Eye Appeal

4503 1903 MS67 NGC. Warm, yellow-gold color blankets the near-pristine surfaces, accented by touches of light-green. This high-end Superb Gem exhibits a remarkably full strike and vivid, frosty luster, which further enhance its visual appeal. Despite a high-mintage and availability in most Mint State grades, examples as fine as this prove challenging. NGC has graded 5 numerically finer pieces (10/14) NGC ID# 25LU, PCGS# 7855

4504 1905 MS65 NGC. A spectacular Gem representative of this popular type issue, with razor-sharp definition on the design elements and vibrant mint luster throughout. The well-preserved peach-gold surfaces add to the outstanding eye appeal. NGC ID# 25LW, PCGS# 7857

4505 1905 MS65 NGC. CAC. The 1905 Liberty quarter eagle is a plentiful issue in high grade, making it a favorite choice of type collectors. This delightful Peach-gold Gem exhibits sharply detailed design elements and well-preserved lustrous surfaces. NGC ID# 25LW, PCGS# 7857

4506 1906 MS66 PCGS. Sharply struck with remarkably clean fields and bright yellow-gold luster. A couple of shallow nicks near the center of the obverse are only discernible with the aid of a loupe. NGC ID# 25LX, PCGS# 7858

1906 Quarter Eagle, MS67
Frosted Full Strike

4507 **1906 MS67 PCGS.** A Superb Gem in every way, this highly lustrous quarter eagle possesses a full strike with devices that boldly rise above glowing, satiny fields. The rich, yellow-gold surfaces radiate lilac and orange hues when rotated under light, unhindered by abrasions or copper stains sometimes seen on this issue. A wonderful type coin, seldom available any finer. Population: 53 in 67, 2 finer (10/14). NGC ID# 25LX, PCGS# 7858

4508 **1907 MS66 PCGS.** A shimmering orange-gold type coin, with frosty luster and carefully preserved surfaces. Save for slight weakness on the eagle's left (facing) leg, the devices are boldly brought up. Housed in an old green label holder. NGC ID# 25LY, PCGS# 7859

INDIAN QUARTER EAGLES

1908 Quarter Eagle, MS65
First-Year Type Coin

4509 **1908 MS65 PCGS.** The 1908 is one of the most plentiful Indian Head quarter eagles in Gem grades, largely due to it being well-saved as a first-year issue. The type collector has many examples from which to choose, so cherrypicking for quality is advised. In that regard, the present Gem example is impressively high-end, even for the MS65 grade; the satiny, lemon-gold surfaces are delicately preserved, with only a few insignificant ticks on the reverse limiting the grade. The eagle's wing feathers are ill-defined, as always on this issue, though the strike is otherwise sharp. NGC ID# 288Y, PCGS# 7939

4510 **1910 MS63 PCGS.** Frosty luster and bold design elements reside beneath deep orange and honey-gold hues on each side of this pleasing Select example. The surfaces are devoid of any obtrusive abrasions, giving this piece substantial eye appeal for the grade. NGC ID# 2892, PCGS# 7941

4511 **1910 MS64 NGC.** This near-Gem quarter eagle features reddish-gold coloration and satiny luster. Pleasing detail is noted on the eagle's breast and leg feathers as well as the Indian's headdress. Minimally abraded with only a thin graze from the T in UNITED to the L in PLURIBUS. NGC ID# 2892, PCGS# 7941

1910 Quarter Eagle, MS65
Rarely Encountered Finer

4512 **1910 MS65 NGC.** The 1910 quarter eagle has a mintage of 492,682 coins, and survivors are plentiful in lower Mint State grades. However, Gem examples are scarce, and their high-grade rarity falls in the top half of the series, ranking seventh out of 15 issues for NGC certification in MS65 and finer grades. This frosty honey-gold example has brilliant luster with trivial marks that prevent an even higher grade. There are no copper spots evident on either side. NGC has seen 14 numerically finer submissions (10/14). NGC ID# 2892, PCGS# 7941

1910 Two and a Half, MS65
Luminous Original Luster

4513 **1910 MS65 PCGS.** Gem examples of any Indian Head quarter eagle are scarce, with perhaps the sole exception of the 1908 which was well-saved as a first-year issue. This 1910 example shows soft, frosty luster over honey-gold, carefully preserved surfaces. If studied closely, some minor striking weakness is observed in the lower headdress feathers, though the remainder of each side if sharply impressed. Only 11 coins are numerically finer at PCGS (10/14). NGC ID# 2892, PCGS# 7941

1910 Two and a Half, MS65
Rarely Seen Finer

4514 **1910 MS65 NGC.** Jeff Garrett and Ron Guth report an average certified grade of 60.5 and an average auction grade of 63.8. The average certified grade is tied for sixth out of 15 issues, and the average auction grade is tied for fifth. This attractive yellow-gold example features frosty mint luster with the usual minuscule marks expected for the grade. NGC has only certified 14 numerically finer examples (10/14). NGC ID# 2892, PCGS# 7941

1910 Indian Quarter Eagle
Richly Patinated MS65

4515 **1910 MS65 PCGS.** The 1910 quarter eagle is an excellent type candidate for the collector who seeks an early representative of the design rather than one of the plentiful issues from the late 1920s. Deep orange-gold color, with hints of red and green, provides this Gem with strong eye appeal. A pleasing strike adds to the attractiveness of this piece. NGC ID# 2892, PCGS# 7941

1910 Quarter Eagle, MS65
Delicately Preserved, Frosty Luster

4516 **1910 MS65 NGC.** Softly frosted, shimmering luster gives this Gem 1910 quarter eagle impressive visual appeal. The strike is boldly executed, complementing the original honey-gold patina. Close examination with a loupe fails to reveal any discernable abrasions, with only a few small luster grazes present to limit the grade. NGC has encapsulated only 14 numerically finer representatives (10/14). NGC ID# 2892, PCGS# 7941

4517 **1911 MS64 PCGS.** Not a great rarity like its 1911-D counterpart, but a scarce issue any finer than the current MS64 grade level. Rich sun-gold toning yields to lime-green and lilac accents near the centers. A small purple alloy spot covers the first U in UNUM. A lustrous and well-struck example, free of distracting surface marks. NGC ID# 2893, PCGS# 7942

4518 **1911 MS64 NGC.** The pleasing orange-gold surfaces of this attractive Choice specimen offer vibrant mint luster on both sides and show only minor signs of contact. The design elements are sharply defined and overall eye appeal is terrific. NGC ID# 2893, PCGS# 7942

4519 **1911 MS64 NGC.** The well-preserved orange-gold surfaces of this attractive Choice example are brightly lustrous and the sharply detailed design elements add to the outstanding eye appeal. NGC ID# 2893, PCGS# 7942

1911 Two and a Half, MS65
Bold Strike for the Issue

4520 **1911 MS65 PCGS.** The surface granularity often associated with this issue does not appear on this smooth and inviting Gem. Nor are the typical areas of strike weakness visible, with the eagle's wing tips bold and all but one or two of the headdress feathers fully detailed. Strong luster emanates from the green-gold surfaces for excellent appeal. PCGS and NGC combined have certified just eight numerically finer examples (10/14). NGC ID# 2893, PCGS# 7942

1911 Quarter Eagle, MS65
Few Certified Finer

4521 **1911 MS65 NGC.** The 1911 Indian quarter eagle is the sixth-rarest issue of the series in high grade. This delightful Gem is sharply detailed throughout, and the pleasing greenish-gold surfaces are lustrous and free of mentionable distractions. Eye appeal is quite strong on this piece, and NGC has graded only seven coins in higher numeric grades (10/14). NGC ID# 2893, PCGS# 7942

1911 Quarter Eagle, MS65
Shimmering Mint Frost

4522 **1911 MS65 NGC.** Although not to the extent of its Denver counterpart, the 1911 quarter eagle is a scarce issue in Gem condition, with most Mint State examples showing moderate abrasions and scrapes throughout the exposed fields. This frosty straw-gold representative is a refreshing exception in that regard, and also boasts superb definition on the eagle's wing the headdress feathers. An immensely eye-appealing representative in every respect. NGC has seen only seven numerically finer examples (10/14). NGC ID# 2893, PCGS# 7942

4523 **1911-D — Improperly Cleaned — NGC Details. AU.** A caramel-gold key date quarter eagle with minimal wear and mildly bright surfaces. The mintmark is clear and there are no consequential marks. Nicer than suggested by the NGC designation. NGC ID# 2894, PCGS# 7943

1911-D Quarter Eagle, Well-Detailed AU55

4524 **1911-D AU55 NGC.** This piece represents the Weak D variety, though the mintmark is easily detectable with a low-power loupe. Each side exhibits even bronze-gold color, with just a touch of wear over the high points of the design. The fields are free of any major abrasions, making this piece a pleasing example of this low-mintage Denver issue. NGC ID# 2894, PCGS# 7943

1911-D Quarter Eagle, AU55
Appealing Strong D Example

4525 **1911-D AU55 PCGS.** Strong D. Many 1911-D quarter eagles in the AU grade range are cleaned or otherwise unnaturally bright, and of little interest to collectors who appreciate old-time patina. This Choice example is a refreshing exception, with luminous green-gold color and smooth, problem-free surfaces. The design elements remain sharply detailed, despite slight high-point friction. NGC ID# 2894, PCGS# 7943

4526 **1912 MS63 NGC.** This sharply detailed Select specimen presents attractive orange-gold surfaces that show highlights of rose and yellow, with vibrant mint luster and only minor signs of contact. Eye appeal is quite strong. NGC ID# 2896, PCGS# 7944

1912 Two and a Half, MS64+
Lustrous and Sharply Stuck

4527 **1912 MS64+ PCGS.** The 1912 is a conditionally elusive date in the series that tends to get lost among the more prominent 1911-D, 1914, and 1914-D. In fact, even the well-resourced collector will require patience to locate an example finer than this attractive near-Gem. Coruscating luster and butter-gold coloration typify the clean, sharply struck surfaces. PCGS has awarded the Plus designation to just 26 coins in MS64, and the service reports 72 examples finer (10/14). NGC ID# 2896, PCGS# 7944

4528 **1913 MS64 NGC.** An impressive Choice example of this popular issue, with vivid orange-gold surfaces that show only minor signs of contact and ample mint luster. The design elements are sharply detailed and eye appeal is terrific. NGC ID# 2897, PCGS# 7945

4529 **1913 MS64 NGC. CAC.** The sizeable mintage of 722,000 pieces yielded few attractive, minimally abraded coins in high Mint State grades, increasing the desirability of this sharp and lustrous example. CAC endorsement accompanies the near-Gem grade, and appealing orange-gold color trumps the normal light, yellow-gold patina seen most often for the date. NGC ID# 2897, PCGS# 7945

1913 Quarter Eagle, MS65
Conditionally Scarce, Rare Any Finer

4530 **1913 MS65 NGC.** Gem Indian quarter eagles are always in demand, as the nature of the sunken relief design significantly inhibited the survival rate of high-grade representatives. As the coins had no protective rims, their exposed fields were easily scarred by such minuscule tasks as stacking in a bank vault. This 1913 example shows shimmering honey-gold luster and unusually clean fields. The strike is boldly impressed, leaving nothing unsightly for the eye. NGC has seen just six numerically finer pieces (10/14). NGC ID# 2897, PCGS# 7945

1913 Quarter Eagle, MS65
Rarely Encountered Finer

4531 **1913 MS65 PCGS.** This Philadelphia issue is readily available in grades through MS64, but Gems are scarce and finer pieces are decidedly rare. This representative displays satiny green-gold luster and sharp design definition on the headdress feathers and the eagle's wing. A few minute ticks preclude an even finer grade, but do not inhibit the eye appeal. PCGS has seen only seven numerically finer representatives (10/14). NGC ID# 2897, PCGS# 7945

1913 Two and a Half, MS65
Seldom Seen in Higher Grades

4532 1913 MS65 NGC. This is an appealing Gem example with bold striking characteristics, straw-gold coloration, and swirling luster. Each side features remarkably clean surfaces considering the absence of raised rims, which made coins vulnerable to impairment from stacking. From a substantial mintage of 722,000 pieces, the issue is scarce in this lofty grade, and NGC has certified only six submissions numerically finer (10/14). NGC ID# 2897, PCGS# 7945

1913 Quarter Eagle, MS65
Delightful, Conditionally Scarce Example

4533 1913 MS65 NGC. From the mintage of 722,000 pieces, survivors are plentiful in circulated and lower Mint State grades, ranging all the way through MS64. Gems are very scarce, however, and coins rated finer than MS65 are so rare as to be virtually unobtainable for the average collector. This is a delightful Gem representative with light honey-gold toning and remarkably clean surfaces. NGC ID# 2897, PCGS# 7945

4534 1914 MS62 PCGS. This attractive MS62 specimen displays sharply defined design elements and lightly marked orange-gold surfaces with highlights of lemon-yellow. Both sides display radiant mint luster, adding to the considerable eye appeal. NGC ID# 2898, PCGS# 7946

1914 Quarter Eagle, MS63
Second-Lowest Mintage in the Series

4535 1914 MS63 PCGS. The 1914 is the second-rarest quarter eagle in an absolute sense, and also stands among the rarest in high grades. This pleasing Select example exhibits the excellent device definition that is characteristic of the issue, with lustrous yellow-gold surfaces and a lack of major abrasions. NGC ID# 2898, PCGS# 7946

1914 Two and a Half, Wheat-Gold MS63

4536 1914 MS63 PCGS. Warm wheat-gold color greets the viewer on surfaces brimming with luster. This Select Mint State 1914 is among the scarcer issues in the series — the second-rarest overall behind the 1911-D — its scarcity beginning with the moderate 240,000-coin mintage. The MS64 grade level is the finest frequently seen. A few ticks on the Indian's cheek and the obverse field nearby account for the grade. NGC ID# 2898, PCGS# 7946

1914 Quarter Eagle, MS63
Rich Original Patina

4537 1914 MS63 PCGS. Deep amber and olive overtones accent the satiny lemon-gold luster of this minimally abraded Select Mint State example. Some slight incompleteness is noted on the lower headdress feathers, though the strike is otherwise sharp. The 1914 quarter eagle had the second-lowest mintage of the series (240,000 coins), and is one of the scarcer dates overall in Mint State grades. NGC ID# 2898, PCGS# 7946

1914-D Quarter Eagle, MS64
Seldom Seen in Finer Grades

4538 1914-D MS64 NGC. An attractive example of this conditional rarity within the Indian Head quarter eagle series, obtainable at the near-Gem level of the present coin but far more elusive in Gem and finer grades, where NGC and PCGS report 43 and 47 submissions finer, respectively (10/14). Appealing patina in shades of orange-gold and minimal marks on each side contribute to the grade. NGC ID# 2899, PCGS# 7947

1914-D Quarter Eagle, MS64+
Exceptionally Vibrant, High Appeal

4539 **1914-D MS64+ NGC.** Known as the second-rarest issue in the Indian quarter eagle series at grades of MS65 or better, this Denver date stands out as a major "condition rarity" overall. The coin displays an exceptionally high degree of flash and deep, vibrant orange-gold toning seldom seen on coins of even a higher numeric grade. A couple of wispy lines on the upper reverse do not detract from the immense appeal of this rare quarter eagle. 44 in 64+, 4 in 64 ★, 43 finer (8/14). NGC ID# 2899, PCGS# 7947

1915 Quarter Eagle, MS65
Luminous, Eye-Catching Patina

4540 **1915 MS65 NGC.** The 1915 quarter eagle is not an especially rare issue in the context of the series, but it does become elusive at the Gem grade the level. The true allure of this piece, however, lies not only in its technical condition, but also in its aesthetic appeal. Original lilac, olive-gold, and luminous apricot luster engulfs each side in frosty radiance. The strike is bold and the surfaces are devoid of significant distractions. Only eight coins are numerically finer at NGC (10/14). NGC ID# 289A, PCGS# 7948

1915 Two and a Half, MS65
Only Four Coins Numerically Finer at PCGS

4541 **1915 MS65 PCGS.** Deep honey and olive-gold hues encompass the satiny luster of this elusive Gem example. The strike is bold and the surfaces are distinctly free of any obtrusive abrasions, with a few minute luster grazes on the reverse being the only grade-limiting factor. PCGS has encapsulated just four numerically finer representatives (10/14). NGC ID# 289A, PCGS# 7948

1915 Quarter Eagle, MS65
Excellent Type Candidate

4542 **1915 MS65 PCGS.** The 1915 quarter eagle is the most available issue in the Indian Head series save for the debut 1908- and 1909-dated coins, making it a popular target for the type-collecting community. This Gem exhibits great surface appeal through its combination of orange-gold color, soft yet thorough luster, and minimal abrasions. PCGS has seen only eight submissions technically finer, four each in MS65+ and MS66 (10/14). NGC ID# 289A, PCGS# 7948

4543 **1926 MS65 PCGS.** An attractive Gem type coin, this late-series Indian quarter eagle shows blended shades of olive, apricot, and sun-gold color, with frosty luster and sharp motifs. A few grade-consistent surface grazes are observed upon close examination. NGC ID# 289C, PCGS# 7950

1927 Quarter Eagle, MS65+
Fresh Mint Bloom

4544 **1927 MS65+ NGC. CAC.** Indian quarter eagles are rarely seen this eye-appealing, regardless of date or grade. Both sides display radiant, frosty mint bloom and bold design definition, giving this piece the overall appearance of a freshly struck Gem. A few faint luster grazes, observed only upon close examination, are all that limit the technical grade of this immensely attractive type coin. NGC has seen only 10 numerically finer examples (10/14). NGC ID# 289D, PCGS# 7951

4545 **1929 MS65 NGC.** A lovely Gem example, highly lustrous with pleasing wheat-gold toning and virtually unmarked surfaces. This final-year issue in the Indian quarter eagle series is relatively abundant at the MS65 grade level, making it an ideal choice for a Gem type set. Only four pieces have been rated even finer by NGC (10/14). NGC ID# 289F, PCGS# 7953

1929 Quarter Eagle, Sharply Struck MS65
The Highest Grade Likely to be Located

4546 **1929 MS65 NGC.** The 1929 quarter eagle is a plentiful issue through near-Gem, with several thousand pieces certified by NGC and PCGS. The population drops precipitously at the Gem level to about 375 examples, the highest grade that will likely be encountered as the two services have seen fewer than 10 coins finer (10/14). Pleasing luster emanates from the orange-gold surfaces that exhibit sharply struck design elements, including the eagle's shoulder feathers. A few small marks are visible over each side, including one on the Indian's cheek. NGC ID# 289F, PCGS# 7953

1929 Quarter Eagle, MS65
Fresh, Frosty Mint Bloom

4547 **1929 MS65 PCGS.** The 1929 is the most elusive of the late-series issues in Gem and finer condition, but it is still plentiful enough to be considered for type representation. This piece displays frosty wheat-gold luster, with only a few scattered ticks limiting the grade. Some striking deficiency is noted on the lower headdress feathers, though the devices are otherwise sharp. Only four coins are numerically finer at PCGS (10/14). NGC ID# 289F, PCGS# 7953

1929 Two and a Half, MS65
Attractive Final-Year Type Coin

4548 **1929 MS65 PCGS.** Unlike its half eagle counterpart, which was heavily melted in the mid-1930s, the 1929 quarter eagle is an available date overall, ideal for type representation. This piece is well-struck, with rich apricot-gold luster. A few small ticks are observed upon close examination, though none are out of line for the grade. Only four coins are numerically finer at PCGS (10/14). NGC ID# 289F, PCGS# 7953

1929 Quarter Eagle, MS65
Strong Eye Appeal

4549 **1929 MS65 PCGS. CAC.** Both the quarter eagle and half eagle Indian Head series came to an end in 1929. The 1929 half eagle claims a higher mintage than its quarter eagle counterpart, yet the half eagle is rare, while the quarter eagle is more accessible. At the MS65 level, however, the 1929 two and a half is undeniably scarce. This shimmering Gem offers a bold strike, clean surfaces, and pleasing eye appeal. PCGS has certified just four pieces finer (10/14). *Ex: Long Beach Signature (Heritage, 6/2010), lot 1578.* NGC ID# 289F, PCGS# 7953

THREE DOLLAR GOLD PIECES

4550 **1857-S VF30 PCGS.** Almost the entire mintage of 14,000 pieces was apparently placed into circulation, making higher-grade examples of this San Francisco issue extremely scarce. This VF example displays intermingled hues of rose and khaki-green. The surfaces are moderately worn with a few noticeable abrasions. NGC ID# 25MB, PCGS# 7977

4551 **1858 — Reverse Damage — NGC Details. AU.** A few tiny digs are noted on the reverse near 3, 6, 7, and 11 o'clock. A pair of short vertical marks extend from the upper right cotton leaf. Both sides have traces of struck-in grease, but this butter-gold low mintage example shows only light circulation wear. NGC ID# 25MC, PCGS# 7978

4552 **1859 AU58 PCGS.** The well-detailed design elements of this attractive near-Mint specimen show just a trace of wear on the high points and the lightly abraded yellow-gold surfaces retain much of their original mint luster. NGC ID# 25MD, PCGS# 7979

4553 **1860 AU55 PCGS.** Original bronze-gold patina yields tinges of deeper orange-gold in the recesses on each side, complementing subtle remnants of luster in the crevices. The strike is bold and only slight wear is evident over the high points of the design. From a low mintage of only 7,036 pieces. NGC ID# 25ME, PCGS# 7980

1860 Three Dollar Gold, MS61
Elusive Early P-Mint Issue

4554 **1860 MS61 NGC.** While many late-series issues were well-saved in high grades, the low mintage of the 1860 three dollar piece (7,036 coins) translates into genuine scarcity in Mint State. This example shows luminous green-gold surfaces, with just light chatter in the fields rather than noticeable abrasions. The bow knot is lacking slightly in striking weakness, though the design elements are otherwise well brought up. Census: 29 in 61, 35 finer (10/14). NGC ID# 25ME, PCGS# 7980

1867 Three Dollar, Choice AU
Better Philadelphia Issue

4555 **1867 AU55 PCGS.** While many later low-mintage dates in the three dollar gold series were heavily saved, the 1867 (only 2,600 pieces produced) experienced moderate circulation and is rarely seen in high grades. This Choice AU example shows original olive-gold patina with hints of luster remaining in the recesses. Slight friction precludes a Mint State grade, but does not dull the level of detail. Population: 25 in 55, 32 finer (10/14). NGC ID# 25MN, PCGS# 7988

4556 **1874 AU58 NGC.** A lustrous example with lime-gold toning and peach border accents. The fields are peppered with small abrasions and the high points display mild high-point friction. NGC ID# 25MX, PCGS# 7998

1874 Three Dollar Gold, MS62
Rare Prooflike Example

4557 **1874 MS62 Prooflike NGC.** The 1874, one of the three issues in the series most often chosen for type purposes (the others being the 1854 and 1878), becomes a distinctly rare date if one focuses his search on pieces certified as Prooflike. NGC has only so-graded 28 examples in all grades, with just three in MS62 and only two numerically finer (10/14). This example showcases bright yellow-gold color and deeply mirrored fields with subtle cameo contrast. The bow knot is deficiently struck, but the design elements are otherwise sharp. A small planchet void (as made) is noted near the obverse rim at 10 o'clock. PCGS# 77998

1883 Three Dollar Gold, Luminous AU58
Only 900 Pieces Struck

4558 **1883 AU58 NGC. CAC.** Much original luster illuminates shades of orange, honey, and green-gold on each side of this smooth, attractive near-Mint example. Slight friction does not inhibit the sharpness of the design elements. The 1883 three dollar gold piece had a rather paltry mintage of only 900 coins, though enough were saved by dealers and speculators that the date is moderately collectible today. NGC ID# 25N6, PCGS# 8005

1886 Three Dollar Gold, AU55
Flashy Prooflike Example

4559 **1886 AU55 Prooflike NGC.** This sharply struck and briefly circulated three dollar piece retains much of its initial mint flash. Tiny abrasions are distributed, and we note a solitary pinscratch in the left obverse field. A mere 1,000 pieces were struck, and no more than one-third of that production has survived. Census: 1 in 55 Prooflike, 29 finer (10/14). PCGS# 78008

1888 Three Dollar, MS62
Excellent Late-Series Type Coin

4560 **1888 MS62 PCGS.** The 1888 three dollar piece had a limited mintage of only 5,000 coins, but enough Mint State examples survive to make the date suitable for type representation. This example shows well-struck devices, with soft honey-gold luster. No significant abrasions are present, making this piece highly appealing for the grade. NGC ID# 25NB, PCGS# 8010

EARLY HALF EAGLE

1806 Half Eagle, BD-6, AU Details
Luminous Original Surfaces

4561 **1806 Round Top 6, 7x6 Stars — Graffiti — PCGS Genuine. AU Details. BD-6, R.2.** Bass-Dannreuther Die State d/e, with a rust lump on the R in LIBERTY. BD-6 is a plentiful variety, if any early gold variety can be so-considered, ideal for type representation. This is the only use of this "Knobbed 6" obverse, though this reverse was previously employed for BD-5. The present coin is slightly soft on the upper-left corner of the shield, but is otherwise boldly struck. Original orange-gold luster encompasses much of each side, and there is only very slight evidence of rub on the highest points of the design. Several old, thin pinscratches on each side account for the Details grade from PCGS, but these are not immediately obvious to the unaided eye. NGC ID# 25P5, PCGS# 8089

CLASSIC HALF EAGLES

4562 1834 Plain 4 AU55 NGC. Breen-6501, McCloskey 3-B, R.1. A straw-gold Choice AU representative with ample bright luster across the margins and motifs. The forehead curls display minor wear, but field marks are unimportant for the grade. NGC ID# 25RR, PCGS# 8171

4563 1836 AU53 PCGS. Breen-6510, McCloskey 3-C, R.2. Breen's "Third Head" variety with an open mouth and a short forehead curl. The R in LIBERTY is repunched north. A boldly struck and unblemished butter-gold Classic type coin. NGC ID# 25RY, PCGS# 8174

4564 1838 AU53 PCGS. Breen-6514, McCloskey 1-A, R.2. The Large Arrows, Small 5 variety. A well struck peach-gold and olive-green representative. The wingtips display light wear but luster fills the legends and outlines individual stars. Marks are relatively minor and clustered beneath the left (facing) wing. NGC ID# 25S4, PCGS# 8176

4565 1838 AU55 NGC. Breen-6515, McCloskey 2-B, R.1. Small Arrows, Large 5. Ample luster fills the borders and devices of this straw-gold Classic type coin. Unimportant abrasions are distributed, including a tick below star 8. NGC ID# 25S4, PCGS# 8176

1838 Small Arrows, Large 5 Half Eagle
McCloskey 2-B, Sharply Struck MS63

4566 1838 MS63 PCGS. Breen-6515, McCloskey 2-B, R.1. The D in the denomination centered below the branch stem characterizes the Small Arrows, Large 5 reverse, one of two known varieties for this last year of the 1838 Classic Head fives. The lustrous yellow-gold surfaces of this Select specimen exhibit sharply struck design elements, while scattered light marks determine the grade. A small, light copper-alloy spot is visible on the lower neck below the curl. Population: 15 in 63, 24 finer (10/14). NGC ID# 25S4, PCGS# 8176

LIBERTY HALF EAGLES

4567 1841-C XF45 PCGS. Variety 1. Better struck than the usual Charlotte half eagle, this well defined example has luminous butter-gold surfaces. Minimally abraded aside from a cluster of small marks on the upper reverse field. From a scant mintage of 21,467 pieces. NGC ID# 25SP, PCGS# 8203

4568 1842-D Small Date XF45 NGC. Variety 7-E. This pumpkin-gold Dahlonega five is mildly granular and exhibits the expected number of individually minor abrasions. The wings are well detailed but Liberty's hair is lightly brought up. NGC ID# 25SX, PCGS# 8210

4569 1846-D VF35 NGC. Variety 15-H (formerly 14-I). The high date, leftmost mintmark die pairing. Typically struck on the major devices, but glimpses of luster remain, and the eagle's wings and shield are sharp for the assigned grade. Marks are minor except on Liberty's neck.
Ex: Long Beach Signature (Heritage, 6/2006), lot 3300, which realized $1,955. NGC ID# 25TH, PCGS# 8228

1847 Half Eagle, MS62
Appealing for the Grade

4570 1847 MS62 NGC. The 1847 half eagle had a substantial mintage of nearly 1 million coins, but remarkably few survive in Mint State condition. This example is sharply struck, with bright yellow-gold patina and semiprooflike mirroring in the fields. An interesting, bisecting die crack is seen on the obverse from 11:30 to 6:30. No distinct abrasions are present, though some light field chatter limits the grade. Census: 43 in 62 (1 in 62+), 37 finer (10/14). NGC ID# 25TL, PCGS# 8231

1847 Half Eagle, MS62+
Luminous Original Surfaces

4571 1847 MS62+ NGC. In the context of the series, the 1847 is the most plentiful half eagle from the 1840s in Mint State grades, but from an absolute standpoint, the date is still scarce at this level. This Plus-graded example shows original orange-gold luster, with well-struck devices and ample visual appeal. No singularly obvious abrasions are present, though some light chatter in the fields accounts for the limited numeric grade. Census: 43 in 62 (1 in 62+), 37 finer (10/14). NGC ID# 25TL, PCGS# 8231

4572 1852-D — Cleaned, Lacquered — ANACS. XF Details, Net VF30. Variety 33-V. A few light hairlines are noted behind Liberty's neck, but the piece is only mildly cleaned. Translucent ice-blue lacquer residue outlines design elements. The strike is soft on Liberty's curls and the eagle's fletchings, as usual for the mint. *Ex: Steve Glenn Collection (Heritage, 4/2006), lot 2710.* NGC ID# 25UC, PCGS# 8252

1856-C Half Eagle, AU55
Scarce Charlotte Mint Issue

4573 1856-C AU55 NGC. Variety 1. Only 150 to 200 coins from this Charlotte issue are estimated to survive, from the mintage of 28,457 pieces. This is an impressive Choice AU example showing light green-gold surfaces that are free of any significant distractions. An evenly worn half eagle with surprisingly few trivial surface marks for a lightly-circulated example from the 1850s. Census: 22 in 55, 38 finer (10/14). NGC ID# 25UW, PCGS# 8267

1859-D Half Eagle, AU58
Medium D Variant

4574 **1859-D Medium D AU58 NGC. Variety 44-HH.** The Medium D is the more often seen of the two 1859-D half eagle varieties, but this is of little consequence, since the issue is relatively scarce overall, with only 175 to 225 pieces believed known. The typical coin grades in the XF to lower AU range, and and Mint State coins are rare. This near-Mint example displays luminous apricot-gold patina, with only slight high-point friction and minimal surface abrasions. Some slight striking softness is noted on the hair curls around Liberty's face and the central eagle's feathers, though the sharpness is nonetheless above-average for this poorly produced issue. Census: 38 in 58 (1 in 58+), 12 finer (10/14). NGC ID# 25VD, PCGS# 8282

1866-S Motto Five, AU Sharpness
Challenging Issue in any Condition

4575 **1866-S Motto — Improperly Cleaned — NGC Details. AU.** Scarce in all grades, the 1866 Motto five is unknown in Mint State and rare in About Uncirculated condition. This example was lightly cleaned but not to a glossy sheen, and the surfaces retain a pleasing, medium-gold color. Softness from wear and strike is noted on the high points of Liberty's hair and the eagle's head. Abrasions are small and scattered, with a few minor rim marks noted but no major distractions. A scarce coin with this much detail and an opportunity despite the cleaning. NGC ID# 25W2, PCGS# 8312

1873-S Half Eagle, AU55
Low-Mintage S-Mint Issue

4576 **1873-S AU55 NGC.** In addition to an already low mintage of 31,000 coins, the 1873-S half eagle had a moderately high attrition rate. The date is scarce in all grades, and only a single Mint State piece has been certified (an MS61 NGC coin). This is a well-detailed AU representative, with natural green-gold patina overall and hints of original luster in the recesses. Census: 18 in 55, 3 finer (10/14). NGC ID# 25WM, PCGS# 8332

1875-CC Half Eagle, AU Sharpness
Challenging in All Grades

4577 **1875-CC — Polished — PCGS Genuine. AU Details. Variety 1-B.** The 1875-CC half eagle had a low mintage of only 11,828 pieces, and is proportionally scarce in all grades; AU examples are considered high-end for the issue, and only two Mint State pieces are shown on the certified population reports. This example shows nearly complete detail, with a small area of striking weakness seen on the right reverse shield stripes. Lightly polished in the past, the surfaces show unnaturally bright, yellow-gold color, though a lack of major abrasions makes this piece moderately appealing. NGC ID# 25WU, PCGS# 8337

1875-S Half Eagle, AU50
Elusive San Francisco Issue

4578 **1875-S AU50 NGC.** The 1875-S half eagle had a low mintage of only 9,000 coins, and circulated heavily to the point that surviving examples in any grade are scarce, and Mint State pieces are prohibitively rare. This softly lustrous AU representative is sharply struck, save for the lower portion of the reverse ribbon, which is characteristically weak. An old, well-hidden scratch in the obverse field adjacent to Liberty's nose is the only surface flaw of note. Census: 9 in 50, 20 finer (10/14). NGC ID# 25WV, PCGS# 8338

4579 **1877 — Cleaning — PCGS Genuine. AU Details.** The rare date 1877 has a business mintage of only 1,132 pieces. The PCGS Population is 34 examples in all grades, although that roster excludes the present coin, as it is moderately bright from a wipe. Generally orange-gold, although the portrait displays lavender shades. NGC ID# 25WZ, PCGS# 8342

4580 **1880-S MS64 NGC.** The light orange and rose-gold surfaces of this attractive near-Gem display satiny mint luster mixed with semiprooflike reflectivity in sheltered areas. A scattering of minor contact marks prevents an even higher designation. NGC has graded 17 numerically finer examples (10/14). NGC ID# 25XC, PCGS# 8353

1881-S Half Eagle, MS65
Condition Rarity

4581　**1881-S MS65 NGC.** Gem examples of this San Francisco issue are remarkably rare in comparison to the date's substantial mintage of nearly 1 million coins, and finer examples are very nearly unknown. Frosty orange-gold luster on this piece reveals few abrasions when rotated beneath a light. The hair curls around Liberty's face are not fully delineated, though the stars and the eagle's feathers are sharply defined. Census: 22 in 65, 1 finer (10/14). NGC ID# 25XF, PCGS# 8357

4582　**1882 MS64 PCGS.** Lovely rose-gold luster shimmers over both sides of this sharply struck Choice example. Abrasions a minor, with none individually noteworthy. The 1882 is an available date in grades through MS64, but finer pieces are rare, with just 15 such coins certified by PCGS (10/14). NGC ID# 25XG, PCGS# 8358

4583　**1882-S MS64 NGC.** The 1882-S Liberty half eagle is an underrated issue in high grade. This attractive Choice example is sharply detailed and brightly lustrous, and the yellow and rose-gold surfaces show a few minor contact marks in the fields. NGC ID# 25XJ, PCGS# 8360

1884-S Half Eagle, MS64
Conditionally Rare

4584　**1884-S MS64 PCGS.** A seldom available San Francisco issue, the 1884-S becomes genuinely rare at the Choice grade level, and finer pieces are prohibitively so. This example displays well-struck devices and frosty apricot-gold luster. Minute, scattered surface ticks limit the grade, but hardly deprive the viewer from the overall appeal. Population: 13 in 64 (1 in 64+), 1 finer (10/14). NGC ID# 25XR, PCGS# 8366

4585　**1885 MS64+ NGC.** Although more than 600,000 pieces were struck, this Philadelphia issue is scarce in Gem condition and nearly unobtainable any finer. The current borderline Gem is close to full Gem condition, with bountiful mint luster over richly frosted, medium-gold surfaces. A few minor marks do not detract and the strike is full. NGC ID# 25XS, PCGS# 8367

4586　**1886 MS64 NGC. CAC.** This frosty Choice example displays blended hues of rose and green-gold luster, while the design elements are boldly brought up. A few minute ticks limit the grade, but are not detracting to the unaided eye. This issue is conditionally scarce at the Choice level, and finer pieces are rare. Census: 17 in 64 (1 in 64 ★), 3 finer (11/14). NGC ID# 25XU, PCGS# 8369

1886-S Half Eagle, Sharply Struck MS65+
Virtually Unobtainable Any Finer

4587　**1886-S MS65+ NGC.** The enormous mintage exceeding 3.2 million coins is responsible for the survival of high-grade Gem examples such as this compelling coin. Higher-grade specimens are virtually unobtainable. Orange-gold centers cede to mint-green near the rims on each side, and a finer grade is precluded only by a couple of scattered reeding marks. The strike is sharp throughout. Census: 52 in 65 (2 in 65+, 1 in 65 ★), 1 finer (10/14). NGC ID# 25XV, PCGS# 8370

4588　**1892 MS64 NGC.** The 1892 Liberty half eagle is a scarce issue in MS64 condition. This attractive Choice example displays lightly marked orange-gold surfaces with well-detailed design elements and vibrant mint luster. Census: 79 in 64 (2 in 64+), 60 finer (10/14). NGC ID# 25Y6, PCGS# 8379

1892 Half Eagle, MS65
Softly Frosted Mint Luster

4589　**1892 MS65 PCGS.** Plentiful in lower grades, the 1892 half eagle becomes scarce at the Gem level, and is rarely seen finer. This example displays frosty rose-gold luster and boldly struck design elements. A few faint surface grazes interrupt the cartwheel effect, but hardly inhibit the eye appeal. Population: 29 in 65 (1 in 65+), 23 finer (10/14). NGC ID# 25Y6, PCGS# 8379

4590　**1893 MS65 NGC.** The attractive orange-gold surfaces of this delightful Gem display a few hints of red and lilac, with vibrant mint luster and few signs of contact. The design elements are well-detailed and eye appeal is outstanding. Census: 64 in 65 (5 in 65+), 10 finer (10/14). NGC ID# 25YA, PCGS# 8383

1893 Half Eagle, MS65+
Conditionally Scarce

4591 1893 MS65+ NGC. Produced to the extent of more than 1.5 million coins, the 1893 half eagle is plentiful in grades through MS64, but Gems are scarce and anything finer is decidedly rare. This Plus-designated representative is sharply struck, with frosty rose-gold luster and impressively preserved surfaces. Census: 64 in 65 (5 in 65+), 10 finer (11/14). NGC ID# 25YA, PCGS# 8383

4592 1894 MS64 PCGS. The lustrous orange-gold surfaces of this attractive Choice example show a few minor contact marks, mostly on the reverse. The design elements are well-detailed and eye appeal is outstanding. Population: 41 in 64, 5 finer (11/14). NGC ID# 25YE, PCGS# 8387

4593 1895-S MS61 NGC. Splashes of red-orange and peach colors are scattered on this honey-gold example of a better date in the series that was released into circulation rather than housed in overseas banks. As expected at this grade level, numerous marks are present. A granular area appears near the arrows, but the devices are sharply detailed and the surfaces retain much original mint luster. Census: 16 in 61, 7 finer (10/14). NGC ID# 25YJ, PCGS# 8391

4594 1895-S MS62 PCGS. The population reports provide a telling story about this San Francisco issue. An adequate mintage of 112,000 pieces was struck, but most entered circulation immediately after production and virtually no Mint State coins were saved. PCGS and NGC combined have certified just 10 examples in MS62 and nine piece numerically finer (10/14). This example is obviously original and undeniably attractive. The bold surfaces display a deeply frosted, orange-gold patina, with only minor marks determining the assigned grade. NGC ID# 25YJ, PCGS# 8391

4595 1896-S MS61 NGC. The 1896-S Liberty half eagle is seldom encountered in Mint State grades. This attractive MS61 example exhibits well-detailed design elements and bright mint luster, with the expected number of minor contact marks for the grade. Census: 40 in 61, 39 finer (11/14). NGC ID# 25YL, PCGS# 8393

4596 1897 MS65 NGC. An attractive Gem specimen from a mintage of 867,883 pieces, this coin exhibits sharply detailed design elements and vibrant mint luster on both sides. The pleasing peach-gold surfaces show only minor contact marks and luster grazes. Census: 73 in 65 (1 in 65 ★), 8 finer (10/14). NGC ID# 25YM, PCGS# 8394

4597 1899-S MS64 PCGS. Only minor ticks and tiny marks appear anywhere on this coin, seemingly too few to prevent a higher grade given the powerful eye appeal of this lustrous near-Gem half eagle. Sky-blue highlights encircle the margins of this gleaming, honey-gold coin. A full strike completes the appeal. NGC ID# 25YT, PCGS# 8399

4598 1899-S MS62 Prooflike NGC. A high mintage, high melt issue, with few attractive Mint State examples to satisfy collectors. Philadelphia Mint coins of the date outnumber San Francisco examples at the grading services by a ratio of about 20 to 1 despite relatively similar mintages. A scattering of light lines in the prooflike fields are less frequent than expected for the grade. NGC has certified just nine prooflike examples in all grades. Census: 5 in 62 Prooflike, 2 finer (10/14). PCGS# 78399

4599 1901/0-S FS-301 MS64 NGC. An undertype 0 is visible below the final 1 in the date, identifying the popular FS-301 variety. This impressive Choice specimen displays well-preserved peach-gold surfaces with vibrant mint luster and sharply detailed design elements. Census: 65 in 64 (1 in 64+), 28 finer (10/14). PCGS# 145720

1901/0-S Half Eagle, MS65
FS-301, *Guide Book* Overdate

4600 1901/0-S FS-301 MS65 PCGS. A genuine 20th century overdate, this popular *Guide Book* variety exhibits the upper loop of an underlying 0 in the date beneath the upper portion of the second 1. This variety is seldom available at the Gem grade level, and is rare any finer. The present coin shows frosty lemon-gold luster and sharply struck design elements. A few faint disturbances in the cartwheel effect preclude an even finer grade. Population: 19 in 65, 2 finer (10/14). PCGS# 145720

1903 Half Eagle, MS65
An Undervalued Date

4601 1903 MS65 PCGS. Although the marketplace values the 1903 Liberty half eagle as a type coin, the low mintage and similarly low population suggest it should be valued higher. This sharply defined and satiny Gem has brilliant yellow luster with excellent eye appeal. The obverse shows a thin planchet lamination from the eye to the nose and the left field. Free of copper stains that frequently plague this issue. Population: 23 in 65, 12 finer (10/14). NGC ID# 25Z2, PCGS# 8407

4602 1903-S MS64+ PCGS. CAC. This high-end Choice example offers lightly marked orange-gold surfaces with a minor rim bruise at 1 o'clock on the obverse.. The design elements are sharply detailed and vibrant mint luster adds to the considerable eye appeal. NGC ID# 25Z3, PCGS# 8408

4603 1903-S MS65 PCGS. The design elements of this spectacular Gem are sharply detailed and some faint die cracks connect the upper stars. The well-preserved peach-gold surfaces radiate vibrant mint luster. PCGS has graded 19 numerically finer examples (10/14). NGC ID# 25Z3, PCGS# 8408

1903-S Half Eagle, Frosty MS66

4604 **1903-S MS66 PCGS.** An available date in the absolute sense, the 1903-S half eagle becomes something of a rarity at the Premium Gem grade level. This example boasts delicately preserved, frosty luster in shades of rose, honey, and green-gold. The strike is sharp and the eye appeal is correspondingly high. Population: 19 in 66 (2 in 66+), 0 finer (10/14). NGC ID# 25Z3, PCGS# 8408

4605 **1906-D MS65 PCGS.** The 1906-D Liberty half eagle is very scarce in MS65 condition. This impressive Gem exhibits well-detailed design elements and vibrant mint luster, with well-preserved orange-gold surfaces. Population: 54 in 65 (2 in 65+), 7 finer (10/14). NGC ID# 25ZA, PCGS# 8414

INDIAN HALF EAGLES

4606 **1908 MS63 NGC.** Always popular as the first year of the Indian design, the 1908 is in demand from type collectors as well as series specialists. This brightly lustrous Select example is well-detailed and lightly marked. NGC ID# 28DE, PCGS# 8510

4607 **1908 MS63+ NGC.** Plus-graded by NGC, this first-year Indian Head half eagle is a sharp Select Uncirculated coin. A bit of softness on the eagle's shoulder and a few microscopic field marks define the grade. Nice luster glows beneath the medium-gold surfaces. The Indian headdress and central obverse details are bold. NGC ID# 28DE, PCGS# 8510

4608 **1908 MS64 NGC.** The 1908 Indian half eagle is an available date in high grade and a popular choice of type collectors. This attractive MS64 example displays well-preserved yellow-gold surfaces with highlights of green and vibrant mint luster on both sides. NGC ID# 28DE, PCGS# 8510

4609 **1908 MS64 NGC.** Sharply struck with exceptional eye appeal, this near-Gem, first-year Indian half eagle offers an excellent opportunity for the type specialist. Beautifully preserved, the surfaces reveal only a few scarcely visible grazes that preclude full Gem status, but are virtually undetectable to the unaided eye. Radiant, satiny mint luster blankets both sides with rich green-gold patina. NGC ID# 28DE, PCGS# 8510

4610 **1908-D MS63 NGC.** The 1908-D Indian half eagle is an underrated issue in higher Mint State grades. This attractive Select specimen exhibits well-detailed design elements and brightly lustrous orange-gold surfaces that show only minor signs of contact. NGC ID# 28DF, PCGS# 8511

4611 **1908-D MS64 NGC.** The Denver mint struck 148,000 half eagles in 1908, and while survivors in lower Mint State grades are encountered with some frequency, Gem-quality examples can only be described as rare. This Choice Uncirculated piece displays well-struck design elements, with satiny orange-gold luster over each side. Light, scattered abrasions define the grade. Only four examples have graded numerically finer at PCGS (10/14). NGC ID# 28DF, PCGS# 8511

4612 **1908-D MS64 PCGS.** A bold strike and soft, satiny luster are the chief draws of the viewer's eye on this Choice 1908-D half eagle. Rose, honey, and apricot-gold hues blend over each side, giving this piece excellent visual appeal. A few light grazes in the left obverse field are seemingly all that keep this coin from a full Gem grade. PCGS has encapsulated just 11 numerically finer representatives (10/14). NGC ID# 28DF, PCGS# 8511

4613 **1909 MS64 NGC.** Glowing, satiny mint luster radiates from the surfaces of this near-Gem in shades of peach, rose, and straw-gold. The surfaces are free of even minor distractions in almost all areas, and a single, faint scratch behind the eagle's head seems to be all that precludes full Gem status. As a date, the 1909 half eagle is among the more available early issues of the series, though Gem-quality pieces are conditionally scarce. NGC ID# 28DH, PCGS# 8513

4614 **1909 MS64 PCGS.** This satiny example looks high-end for the grade, despite the lack of a "+" grade. The headdress feathers and the eagle's breast, wing, and leg feathers are boldly rendered. The light khaki-gold surfaces display few marks for a near-Gem designation. NGC ID# 28DH, PCGS# 8513

1909 Half Eagle, Bold MS64
Reddish-Gold Surfaces

4615 **1909 MS64 PCGS. CAC.** The 1909 half eagle is among the more accessible issues in its series and remains available for a price at the MS64 level, though finer coins are conditionally scarce. Rich reddish-gold color shows hints of light green, and a solid strike is most prominent on the lower headdress and upper wing feathers. Great overall eye appeal. NGC ID# 28DH, PCGS# 8513

4616 **1909-D MS64 PCGS. CAC.** This intensely lustrous example displays sharp strike definition, with a bold, clear mintmark. The satiny honey-gold surfaces reveal few marks. NGC ID# 28DJ, PCGS# 8514

4617 **1910 MS64 NGC.** The pleasing reddish-gold surfaces of this attractive Choice specimen show a few microscopic alloy spots on the obverse and satiny mint luster on both sides. The design elements are well-detailed and eye appeal is quite strong. NGC ID# 28DK, PCGS# 8517

1910 Half Eagle, MS64
Green Label Holder

4618 **1910 MS64 PCGS.** The 1910 half eagle's status as a plentiful issue holds true through the MS63 grade level, but the issue's availability declines in MS64, and finer pieces are seldom seen. This example, housed in a green label holder, is beautifully preserved, with a tiny mark behind the eagle's head being the only flaw of note. The strike is sharp, while rich honey and green-gold hues blanket each side. PCGS has encapsulated only 24 numerically finer representatives (10/14). NGC ID# 28DK, PCGS# 8517

1910-D Half Eagle, Satiny MS63

4619 **1910-D MS63 NGC.** Denver half eagle production declined in 1910 to just 193,600 coins (down from more than 3.4 million pieces the previous year). Appropriately, the 1910-D half eagle is also somewhat more elusive than the 1909-D, being infrequently seen in MS63 and rare finer. This piece displays sharp design elements and satiny orange-gold luster. A few light abrasions contribute to the grade. NGC has certified only 33 numerically finer representatives (10/14). NGC ID# 28DL, PCGS# 8518

4620 **1910-S MS61 PCGS.** The 1910-S half eagle had a fairly substantial mintage of more than 770,000 pieces, but the vast majority experienced light to moderate circulation; Mint State examples are elusive, particularly above the MS61 grade level. This sharply struck piece displays deep olive overtones over satiny yellow-gold luster. Scattered abrasions limit the grade. NGC ID# 28DM, PCGS# 8519

4621 **1910-S MS61 NGC.** Elusive in mint condition, the 1910-S half eagle is actually rare any finer than MS62, despite a moderately high mintage of 770,200 coins. Rich honey-gold toning, with occasional coppery accents, increases the eye appeal of this lustrous example. The mintmark is softly defined, but easy to identify under low magnification. NGC ID# 28DM, PCGS# 8519

1910-S Half Eagle, MS62
Undeniably Original Coloration

4622 **1910-S MS62 NGC.** The 1910-S Indian half eagle had a fairly substantial mintage of more then 770,000 pieces, but Mint State survivors are disproportionately scarce, and are rarely seen above the MS62 grade level. This sharply struck coin is lightly abraded, but is nonetheless appealing for its undeniably original patina that includes shades of olive, honey, and russet. Only 35 pieces are numerically finer at NGC (10/14). NGC ID# 28DM, PCGS# 8519

4623 **1911 MS64 PCGS.** This high-mintage issue of 915,000 pieces is available through the current Choice Mint State grade level, but examples are scarce any finer. This piece displays exceptionally clean surfaces and vibrant mint luster. A few minuscule marks are noted on the upper right reverse. NGC ID# 28DP, PCGS# 8520

1911-D Half Eagle, AU58
Scarce Denver Issue

4624 **1911-D AU58 NGC.** Uncharacteristically, the mintmark is weak on this near-Mint Indian half eagle, an unusual state of affairs for the Denver issue that is usually sharply struck in all areas. A few light field abrasions and a touch of blending on the eagle's shoulder confirm the assigned grade, which still offers substantial eye appeal and nice remaining luster. A scarce, key date in series, with just 72,500 pieces minted. NGC ID# 28DR, PCGS# 8521

4625 **1911-S MS62 NGC.** Despite a high mintage of 1.4 million coins, the 1911-S half eagle is conditionally scarce in grades any higher than MS62. This is a pleasing, boldly struck representative with shimmering mint luster and attractive light coloration. NGC ID# 25ZM, PCGS# 8522

4626 **1912 MS63 NGC.** An attractive Select specimen of this popular date, with well-detailed design elements and lustrous reddish-gold surfaces that show a few minor contact marks on close inspection. NGC ID# 28DS, PCGS# 8523

1912 Five Dollar, MS64
Challenging in Higher Grades

4627 **1912 MS64 PCGS.** The 1912 is a popular issue among type collectors because of its sharp strike and lively luster. Light butter-gold color and typically vibrant luster embrace each crisply impressed side. A small linear depression adjacent to star 2 is likely all that prohibits a Gem designation. NGC ID# 28DS, PCGS# 8523

4628 **1912 MS64 PCGS.** With a rather substantial mintage of 790,000 pieces and a reputation for being well-made, the 1912 half eagle is a popular choice for type representation, though it becomes scarce at the Gem grade level and finer pieces are virtually unobtainable. This near-Gem exhibits bold design definition and satiny peach-gold luster overall. The surfaces are generally well-preserved, with only a few small marks in the reverse fields precluding a finer grade. NGC ID# 28DS, PCGS# 8523

4629 **1912 MS64 PCGS.** While the mintage of 790,000 coins, might suggest otherwise, the 1912 is a definite condition rarity that is elusive in finer grades. PCGS has only certified 52 pieces better than this Choice Mint State specimen (10/14). Both sides have deep orange luster with lilac accents, strong design details, and frosty surfaces. NGC ID# 28DS, PCGS# 8523

4630 **1912 MS64 PCGS.** The 1912 half eagle's availability declines in MS64, and finer pieces are rare in comparison to the demand for them. This Choice example shows satiny yellow-gold luster and minimal abrasions for the grade. Some minor incompleteness is noted on the eagle's upper wing feathers, though the strike is otherwise well-executed. PCGS has seen 52 numerically finer representatives (10/14). NGC ID# 28DS, PCGS# 8523

4631 1913 MS63+ PCGS. This attractive, olive-gold representative is well-struck with soft, satiny luster. A few small ticks and grazes are observed upon close examination, but the surfaces are devoid of any singularly obtrusive abrasions. As a date, the 1913 half eagle is fairly plentiful in lower Mint State grades, but its availability declines somewhat above the MS63 level. NGC ID# 28DT, PCGS# 8525

1913 Indian Half Eagle, MS64
Lustrous and Appealing

4632 1913 MS64 PCGS. The bright satiny mint luster exhibited by this attractive near-Gem example is exceptional, and considerably enhances the coin's overall appeal. The motifs are sharply struck, and the well-preserved surfaces exhibit pleasing orange-gold coloration. This issue becomes extremely scarce at the Gem grade level or finer. NGC ID# 28DT, PCGS# 8525

1913 Half Eagle, MS64
Upper-End for the Grade

4633 1913 MS64 NGC. CAC. Like many Philadelphia issues in the Indian half eagle series, the 1913 is a plentiful date in grades through MS64, but its availability plummets drastically at the Gem level. This near-Gem offers the date collector with an affordable, yet appealing representative. Satiny green-gold luster and bold design elements draw the viewer's focus, though grade-limiting abrasions are difficult to locate even upon close study with a loupe. NGC shows a population of 42 numerically finer representatives (10/14). NGC ID# 28DT, PCGS# 8525

1913-S Five Dollar, MS61
Conditionally Elusive Date

4634 1913-S MS61 PCGS. CAC. A typical San Francisco issue from the early part of the Indian half eagle series, the 1913-S is seldom seen in Mint State, and becomes increasingly scarce in grades finer than MS61. The present piece shows original olive-gold color and a clear mintmark. Some minor striking softness is noted on the lower headdress feathers, though the design elements are otherwise sharp. Light, scattered abrasions account for the grade. NGC ID# 25ZP, PCGS# 8526

4635 1915 MS63 NGC. The 1915 Indian half eagle was a well-produced issue and this impressive Select specimen offers sharply detailed design elements and lustrous rose-gold surfaces that show a few darker alloy spots. NGC ID# 28DX, PCGS# 8530

1915 Half Eagle, MS64
Nicely Toned Example

4636 1915 MS64 PCGS. This frosty near-Gem is a lovely example of the Indian half eagle design with sharp details and brilliant, yellow luster. Both sides of this beautiful piece have wispy blue-green overtones. The 1915 is a common date, but rarely seen in higher grades. PCGS has certified only 48 numerically finer examples (10/14). NGC ID# 28DX, PCGS# 8530

1915 Five Dollar, MS64
Top Selection for Type

4637 1915 MS64 PCGS. The Philadelphia Mint took extra care producing half eagles for the year, with bold strikes and attractive coloration the norm for the issue. This apricot-gold example shows nice luster and few marks, with orange accents within the recesses of the sharply struck motifs. The central details are particularly bold. Scarce any finer. NGC ID# 28DX, PCGS# 8530

1915 Half Eagle, Eye-Appealing MS64

4638 1915 MS64 NGC. CAC. The 1915 half eagle can be located in near-Gem with patient searching. Higher-grade coins are elusive with fewer than 90 such pieces seen by NGC and PCGS (10/14). Orange-gold surfaces exude strong luster and exhibit well-struck design features. Scattered light marks preclude Gem classification. Nice eye appeal, affirmed by the CAC endorsement. NGC ID# 28DX, PCGS# 8530

1915 Half Eagle, MS64
Well-Preserved for the Grade

4639 **1915 MS64 PCGS. CAC.** The 1915 half eagle's availability drops off sharply above the MS64 grade level, making high-end Choice examples, such as this coin, highly popular among series collectors. Bold detail and satiny straw-gold luster deliver pleasing eye appeal, while the surfaces are refreshingly devoid of any significant abrasions. PCGS has encapsulated just 48 numerically finer representatives (10/14). NGC ID# 28DX, PCGS# 8530

1916-S Half Eagle, MS62
Essential Date Representative

4640 **1916-S MS62 PCGS.** The 1916-S half eagle's popularity stems in part from its status as the final branch mint issue struck of the denomination, but the date is also essential for a complete date set, as no other mints produced half eagles in 1916. This example shows well-struck devices and bright yellow-gold luster. Light, scattered abrasions contribute to the grade. NGC ID# 28DY, PCGS# 8532

LIBERTY EAGLES

4641 **1842-O XF40 PCGS. Variety 2.** Two mintmark size and placement varieties are known and are approximately equal in rarity. The second New Orleans ten dollar issue has a mintage of only 27,400 pieces. A nicely defined and luminous honey-gold representative that displays the expected number of minor field abrasions. NGC ID# 262N, PCGS# 8587

4642 **1842-O — Reverse Scratched — NGC Details. AU. Variety 1.** A scarcer date from the New Orleans mint facility, especially in higher grades, from a low mintage of 27,400 coins. This piece exhibits substantial AU Details, and even green-gold toning over both sides. A pair of scratches are noted on the upper reverse, one of them directly above the eagle's head. NGC ID# 262N, PCGS# 8587

4643 **1842-O AU50 NGC. Variety 2.** The broad mintmark variant of this lower mintage New Orleans issue. A well defined butter-gold representative. Moderate marks are distributed, but only a vertical field line near the profile merits mention. NGC ID# 262N, PCGS# 8587

4644 **1845-O Repunched Date XF45 NGC. Variety 1.** The 84 in the date is repunched south, and the top of the second vertical shield stripe has a small circular area absent. This mint-made feature is undoubtedly related to the "Shield Ring" varieties found on selected 1848 to 1853 issues. Ruby-tinted luster clings to device outlines, but the moderately marked surfaces are primarily yellow-gold. *Ex: Long Beach Signature (Heritage, 6/2007), lot 2443.* PCGS# 88593

4645 **1846-O XF45 PCGS. Variety 3.** The usual die variety for the issue, sometimes called an 1846/'5'-O due to a defective date punch. Nicely detailed with even khaki-gold coloration and wispy hairlines. A few minuscule marks are noted, but none of these are readily apparent to the unaided eye. A scarce New Orleans issue, rare any finer than this pleasing Choice XF representative. Population: 13 in 45, 14 finer (10/14). NGC ID# 262X, PCGS# 8595

4646 **1847 AU55 PCGS Secure.** The 1847 Liberty eagle is a popular No Motto type coin that is relatively available in the context of the series. This Choice AU example displays well-detailed design elements with just a touch of wear and lustrous orange-gold surfaces with an average number of minor abrasions for the grade. Population: 36 in 55, 44 finer (10/14). NGC ID# 262Z, PCGS# 8597

4647 **1847-O AU55 NGC. Variety 2.** The base of the 1 in the date is repunched, and both sides have several spindly die cracks. This yellow-gold New Orleans type coin is mildly luminous and free from any mentionable abrasions. Luster is prevalent on the legends, curls, and eagle. NGC ID# 2632, PCGS# 8598

4648 **1853-O XF45 NGC. Breen-6908, Variety 3.** Breen-6908, small hollow ring atop second vertical stripe within shield. This issue is usually seen without a shield ring, unlike the 1851-O which always has a ring present. A butter-gold example with surprisingly unmarked fields and motifs. Just 51,000 pieces were struck. NGC ID# 263F, PCGS# 8612

4649 **1860 XF45 PCGS.** Six-fold or "bulging" bun subtype. The more available of the two varieties from the meager mintage of 15,055 pieces. A well-defined wheat-gold example with distributed small to moderate marks. NGC ID# 2644, PCGS# 8631

4650 **1866-S Motto — Improperly Cleaned — NGC Details. AU.** A mintage of 11,500 pieces ensures the rarity of the first Motto San Francisco ten. The NGC Census lists 36 examples in all grades, although that number excludes the present green-gold coin, which has a subdued area on the field beneath Liberty's chin. NGC ID# 264K, PCGS# 8650

4651 **1867 VF35 PCGS.** Only 3,140 Liberty eagles were struck at the Philadelphia Mint in 1867, making the date quite elusive in all grades. This Choice VF specimen retains much of its original design detail and traces of original mint luster. The orange-gold surfaces are lightly abraded and problem-free. Population: 6 in 35, 29 finer (10/14). NGC ID# 264L, PCGS# 8651

1868-S Ten Dollar, AU53
Nice Appeal for the Grade

4652 **1868-S AU53 NGC.** With a Mint State population of zero, this attractive AU example gains considerably in stature. Abundant luster remains, and the expected gathering of small abrasions seems less severe than implied by the grade. Some central weakness on Liberty's highest curls and the eagle's head is the result of combined light wear and soft strike. An attractive example of this rare, low-mintage issue. Census: 11 in 53, 24 finer (10/14). NGC ID# 264P, PCGS# 8654

4653 1870-S VF20 NGC. This low-mintage issue had a meager production of just 8,000 coins, and examples are scarce at all grade levels. The light green-gold surfaces of this VF example display orange-rose luster remnants near some of the devices, especially on the obverse. A noticeable puncture mark resides near the center of the horizontal shield stripes on the reverse. Census: 2 in 20, 53 finer (11/14). NGC ID# 264V, PCGS# 8659

1874-CC Ten Dollar, VF20
Deep Original Coloration

4654 1874-CC VF20 PCGS. Variety 1-A. The 1874-CC eagle's mintage of just 16,767 pieces was actually one of the more substantial production figures of the period for the Carson City Mint, though this does not translate into availability for the 1874-CC ten. The issue is seldom seen in any grade, but is most plentiful in the VF to XF range. AU examples are scarce, and Mint State coins are almost nonexistent. The present coin is a must-have example for the collector who appreciates old-time patina; both sides exhibit a deep orange and coppery-gold "crust," with a few tinges of violet throughout. Wear is evenly distributed, and the surfaces are attractively problem-free. A rare, fully original example. NGC ID# 2658, PCGS# 8670

1876 Ten Dollar Gold, AU Details
One of 732 Pieces Struck

4655 1876 — Obverse Damage, Improperly Cleaned — NCS. AU Details. Following a tiny mintage of just 100 business strikes and 20 proofs in 1875, the Philadelphia Mint produced another meager mintage in 1876. Just 687 business strikes and 45 proofs were made. The present coin survived but not without problems. The surfaces are heavily hairlined and overly bright, and a small dig in the right obverse field near star 2 is of unknown cause. Few examples of the date are available to collectors, however, and a coin in this condition will still command considerable interest. NGC ID# 265C, PCGS# 8674

1879-O Ten Dollar, AU Details
Key New Orleans Issue

4656 1879-O — Harshly Cleaned — NGC Details. AU. Variety 1. The Civil War closed the doors of the New Orleans Mint in 1861, but the facility re-opened in 1879 to assist in the unprecedented production of Morgan dollars needed to fulfill the Bland-Allison Act. That year, New Orleans also struck 1,500 eagles, the first gold coins from the facility since its was controlled by the Confederacy. Perhaps 100 pieces survive, generally in XF and AU grades. The present piece has minimal actual wear, but both sides are thickly hairlined and unnaturally lusterless.
Ex: Central States Signature (Heritage, 4/2010), lot 3741.

4657 1880-S MS63 NGC. Breen-7000. Tall S. Two different mintmark sizes and placements were used on the '80-S eagle. The Tall S is more available than its Tiny S counterpart. A sea-green and orange-gold example with good luster, a crisp strike, and the expected number of small marks. Census: 47 in 63, 4 finer (10/14). NGC ID# 265V, PCGS# 8690

4658 1881 MS64 NGC. Despite the ample mintage of 3.8 million pieces, the 1881 Liberty eagle is an elusive issue in MS64 condition. This attractive Choice example is sharply detailed, with well-preserved orange-gold surfaces. Census: 34 in 64 (2 in 64+), 2 finer (11/14). NGC ID# 265W, PCGS# 8691

1881-S Ten Dollar, MS63
Only Two Coins Finer at NGC

4659 1881-S MS63 NGC. Demand for high-grade examples from this San Francisco issue is perennially strong and continually exceeds supply. While a mintage of 970,000 coins makes the date relatively available in lower grades, NGC has seen just 28 coins in MS63 (one in MS63 ★) and only two pieces finer (10/14). This Select peach-gold coin displays abundant mint frost over typically struck and lightly marked surfaces. NGC ID# 265Z, PCGS# 8694

4660 1882 MS63 NGC. CAC. A popular type issue from a mintage of 2.3 million pieces, this attractive Select example offers well-detailed design elements that show some incompleteness on the central reverse, due to die polishing. The lustrous orange-gold surfaces are lightly marked. NGC ID# 2662, PCGS# 8695

4661 **1882 MS64 PCGS.** One of the notable strike rarities of the entire Liberty Head eagle series. The large mintage of 2.3 million pieces yielded many examples through MS63 grades, yet incredibly few near-Gems for the mintage and virtually no finer coins. This sharply lustrous, frosty example offers a bold strike and original yellow-gold coloration with olive and orange highlights. A few tiny field marks define the grade. Population: 41 in 64 (1 in 64+), 1 finer (10/14). NGC ID# 2662, PCGS# 8695

4662 **1883 MS63 NGC.** This Philadelphia Mint issue is scarce any finer than the MS62 grade level, and rare any finer than MS63. PCGS and NGC have only seen six MS64 coins, and none better. This is a lovely, frosty Select Mint State representative with light coloration and an intense, radiant sheen across both sides. Census: 94 in 63, 4 finer (11/14). NGC ID# 2666, PCGS# 8699

1886 Ten Dollar, Elusive MS63

4663 **1886 MS63 PCGS.** This Select 1886 eagle shows a razor-sharp strike, even though it is perhaps just a shade away from full. Impressive luster exudes from the surfaces on both sides, complementing the attractive peach-gold coloration. Distributed marks determine the grade. The 1886 can be located in the lower levels of Mint State, but MS63s and finer specimens are elusive. Population: 34 in 63, 8 finer (10/14). NGC ID# 266F, PCGS# 8708

1886-S Ten Dollar, MS64
Frosty Original Luster

4664 **1886-S MS64 PCGS.** Before the discovery of the Saddle Ridge Hoard, this Choice 1886-S eagle was tied for the finest certified of the date at PCGS. A handful of numerically finer coins are now known, though this piece remains conditionally rare. Frosty green-gold luster exhibits tinges of coppery-orange and rose in the central reverse, while the design elements are boldly impressed and the surfaces are free of any obtrusive detractions. Population: 24 in 64 (1 in 64+), 4 finer (10/14). NGC ID# 266G, PCGS# 8709

4665 **1887-S MS63 NGC.** This issue is much scarcer in Uncirculated condition than its mintage of 817,000 pieces might imply. This example displays satiny luster and exceptionally crisp strike definition. Scattered tiny marks limit the grade of the piece but allow it to retain a significant degree of visual appeal. Census: 70 in 63, 12 finer (10/14). NGC ID# 266J, PCGS# 8711

4666 **1888-S MS63 NGC.** The 1888-S Liberty eagle is scarce in MS63 condition and finer examples are very rare. This sharply detailed Select example displays vibrant mint luster and only minor signs of contact. Census: 81 in 63 (1 in 63+), 4 finer (10/14). NGC ID# 266M, PCGS# 8714

1889 Ten Dollar Gold, MS61
Just 4,440 Pieces Struck

4667 **1889 MS61 PCGS.** Tucked between high-mintage issues of eagles from the San Francisco Mint, this anomalously low-mintage Philadelphia date seems underrated and overlooked. Population data supports the absolute rarity and it is unlikely the issue will continue to be ignored. This example has some busyness in the fields and bagmarks, but it is fully struck and brightly lustrous. Mint-fresh sun-gold color offers excellent eye appeal. Population: 27 in 61, 6 finer (10/14). NGC ID# 266N, PCGS# 8715

4668 **1891-CC/CC FS-501 AU50 NGC. Variety 3-C.** The mintmark is nicely repunched. FS-501 constitutes about one-third of the issue, but the variety went unreported prior to a Steve Ivy's 1982 Phoenix auction. The present example has ample peripheral luster and lightly marked sun-gold surfaces. PCGS# 145728

4669 **1892 MS64 PCGS.** This Philadelphia Mint issue, with a moderately high mintage of 797,400 pieces, was not saved from circulation in great numbers and high-grade examples are scarce. This is an attractive, well-struck piece with vibrant luster and lovely light-orange and rose coloration. Population: 15 in 64 (1 in 64+), 11 finer (10/14). NGC ID# 266V, PCGS# 8721

4670 **1892-CC AU55 NGC. FS-101, Variety 1-A.** IN GOD WE TRUST is die tripled, as seen on all examples of the low mintage issue. This well struck Carson City ten offers rich pumpkin-gold toning and is lightly abraded for the grade and type. NGC ID# 266W, PCGS# 8722

4671 **1894 MS63 Prooflike NGC.** This issue is a very common date, with thousands of Mint State examples known. Prooflike pieces are extremely scarce, however, and this coin is among the finest available in Prooflike condition. The dark fields are glassy and deeply-mirrored, while the motifs are well-struck and sharply frosted. Census: 14 in 63 (2 in 63+ Prooflike, 1 in 63 ★), 1 finer (10/14). PCGS# 78729

4672 **1895 MS63 NGC.** An attractive Select specimen of this popular date, with well-detailed design elements, vibrant mint luster, and peach-gold surfaces that show a scattering of minor contact marks on both sides. NGC ID# 2678, PCGS# 8732

4673 **1895 MS61 Prooflike NGC.** The 1895 Liberty eagle is seldom encountered with the Prooflike designation. This attractive MS61 example exhibits razor-sharp definition on all design elements and the deeply mirrored fields show a scattering of minor contact marks on both sides. Census: 10 in 61 Prooflike, 8 finer (10/14). PCGS# 78732

4674 **1896-S MS61 PCGS.** From a mintage of 123,750 pieces, the 1896-S Liberty eagle is a scarce issue in Mint State. This attractive MS61 specimen is well-detailed and lustrous, with a scattering of minor contact marks on both sides. Population: 21 in 61, 33 finer (10/14). NGC ID# 267C, PCGS# 8736

1896-S Eagle, MS62
Rare This Well-Preserved

4675 **1896-S MS62 PCGS.** A mintage in excess of 123,000 coins was insufficient for the widespread survival of Mint State 1896-S gold eagles. Such pieces are scarce in any grade, and exceedingly rare finer than MS62. This representative shows sharp design definition and glowing honey-gold luster. Light, scattered abrasions limit the grade, but none are individually detracting. Population: 26 in 62, 7 finer (10/14). NGC ID# 267C, PCGS# 8736

1899 Ten Dollar, MS65
Conditionally Elusive

4676 **1899 MS65 PCGS.** With a mintage of more than 1.2 million coins, one would hardly think of the 1899 eagle as scarce in any grade, but at the Gem level it is just that. Thickly frosted mint bloom encompasses each side in shades of honey, yellow, and green-gold. The strike is sharp and a few minute surface ticks are all that preclude an even finer grade. Population: 41 in 65 (5 in 65+), 5 finer (10/14). NGC ID# 267J, PCGS# 8742

1899 Liberty Ten, MS65+
Heavily Frosted, Vibrant Luster

4677 **1899 MS65+ PCGS.** Frosty green-gold margins frame warmer rose-gold centers on this high-end Gem representative. The strike is crisp and only a few light luster grazes limit the technical grade. This issue is readily available in grades through MS64, but it becomes scarce at the Gem level and finer pieces are rare. Population: 41 in 65 (5 in 65+), 5 finer (10/14). NGC ID# 267J, PCGS# 8742

4678 **1899-O MS62 PCGS. Variety 3.** A semiprooflike and crisply struck apricot-gold New Orleans ten. The scattered marks are inoffensive for the designated grade. Despite a low business mintage of 37,047 pieces, at least four die varieties are known for the 1899-O. These differ chiefly in minute placement of the date and mintmark. NGC ID# 267K, PCGS# 8743

4679 **1899-S MS63 NGC.** The pleasing orange-gold surfaces of this attractive Select example show the expected number of minor contact marks for the grade. The design elements are well-detailed and both sides radiate vibrant mint luster. Census: 68 in 63 (1 in 63+), 17 finer (10/14). NGC ID# 267L, PCGS# 8744

4680 **1899-S MS63 PCGS.** The surfaces display pleasing yellow-gold coloration and exceptionally intense mint frost. The motifs are fully struck and scattered surface marks are not excessive for the MS63 designation. A conditionally scarce issue at this grade level, and rare any finer. Population: 67 in 63, 20 finer (11/14). NGC ID# 267L, PCGS# 8744

4681 **1899-S MS63 PCGS. CAC.** Radiant lemon-gold luster engulfs each side of this minimally abraded Select example. The strike is sharp and the eye appeal is excellent. This issue had a mintage of 841,000 coins, but it is conditionally scarce at the MS63 grade level. Population: 67 in 63, 20 finer (10/14). NGC ID# 267L, PCGS# 8744

4682 **1899-S MS61 Prooflike NGC.** The deeply mirrored fields of this rare prooflike example contrast noticeably with the sharply detailed design elements and the yellow-gold surfaces show the expected number of minor contact marks for the grade. Census: 6 in 61 (1 in 61 ★) Prooflike, 5 finer (10/14). PCGS# 78744

4683 **1901 MS64+ NGC.** This high-end Choice example exhibits sharply detailed design elements throughout and the apricot-gold surfaces show only minor signs of contact, with vibrant mint luster on both sides. NGC ID# 267P, PCGS# 8747

4684 **1901 MS64+ PCGS. CAC.** The well-preserved orange-gold surfaces of this high-end Choice example retain their original vibrant mint luster and show only minor signs of contact. The design elements are sharply detailed and overall eye appeal is outstanding. NGC ID# 267P, PCGS# 8747

4685 **1901-S MS64+ PCGS.** Frosty luster and yellow-gold color blend over each side. The surfaces display sharply struck design features and lightly scattered marks. From a mintage of over 2.8 million eagles, this S-mint issue is popular as a type coin. NGC ID# 267S, PCGS# 8749

4686 **1903-O MS63 NGC. Variety 1.** Sea-green margins frame peach-gold fields and devices. A lustrous and precisely struck Select New Orleans type coin with a smattering of small marks on the obverse field. NGC ID# 267W, PCGS# 8753

4687 **1904 MS63 NGC.** The 1904 Liberty eagle is very scarce in grades above the MS63 level. This attractive Select specimen is well-detailed and brightly lustrous, with lightly marked orange and rose-gold surfaces. NGC ID# 267Y, PCGS# 8755

4688 **1906-D MS64 PCGS.** An attractive Choice example from the first year of operations at the Denver Mint, this coin exhibits pinpoint definition on all design elements and the well-preserved greenish-gold surfaces are brightly lustrous. PCGS has graded 28 numerically finer examples (10/14). NGC ID# 2685, PCGS# 8760

1906-S Ten Dollar, MS63
Conditionally Rare Issue

4689 **1906-S MS63 PCGS.** Given its mintage of 457,000 pieces, the 1906-S should be prevalent in Uncirculated grades. However, it is much scarcer in Mint State than the 1891-CC, which has less than one-fourth the mintage of the '06-S. The present lustrous and boldly struck sun-gold example has a surprisingly smooth obverse, and is limited in grade solely by a small field scuff near the ER in AMERICA. Population: 32 in 63, 9 finer (10/14). NGC ID# 2687, PCGS# 8762

1907 Liberty Head Ten Dollar, Sharp MS65

4690 **1907 MS65 NGC.** The 1907 Liberty eagle is much more difficult to locate in high grade than the large mintage exceeding 1.2 million pieces would suggest. In fact, Gems take a precipitous drop from the near-Gem level to about 100 coins. This delightful MS65 exhibits sharply detailed design elements and satiny mint luster with pleasing peach-gold surfaces that show few signs of contact. Census: 80 in 65 (2 in 65+), 6 finer (10/14). NGC ID# 2688, PCGS# 8763

1907 Liberty Ten Dollar, MS65
Two-Toned Surfaces

4691 **1907 MS65 NGC.** Remarkably few high-grade 1907 tens are known, relative to the mintage of 1.2 million pieces. This Gem has an interesting appearance. The interiors are bright yellow-gold and significantly deeper greenish patina surrounds the margins, a sure indication of untampered originality. The strike is strong throughout, and there are only small abrasions scattered over each side. Census: 80 in 65 (2 in 65+), 6 finer (10/14). NGC ID# 2688, PCGS# 8763

INDIAN EAGLES

1907 No Periods Ten, MS63
Glowing Original Luster

4692 **1907 No Periods MS63 NGC. CAC.** The 1907 No Periods Indian eagle represents the final product of Charles Barber's modifications to Augustus Saint-Gaudens' designs. The motifs struck up well as far as the Mint was concerned, though the central hair strands on the obverse were not fully engraved to begin with, as all surviving examples show minor softness in this area. The present coin displays luminous honey-gold luster and sharp detail throughout the headdress feathers and the eagle's wing. Minute surface ticks on the cheek contribute to the numeric grade, but the overall eye appeal is outstanding. NGC ID# 28GF, PCGS# 8852

1907 No Periods Ten, MS63
Smooth, Luminous Surfaces

4693 **1907 No Periods MS63 PCGS. CAC.** The No Periods 1907 Indian eagle was the final product of Charles Barber's modifications to Saint-Gaudens design. The issue is relatively plentiful overall, ideal for type representation. This example displays satiny honey-gold luster and well-defined motifs. Despite the grade, no significant abrasions are present, giving this piece an unusually high degree of eye appeal for the grade. NGC ID# 28GF, PCGS# 8852

4694 **1908 Motto MS62 PCGS. CAC.** The second-year Motto Indian ten becomes conditionally scarce any finer than MS63, making this MS62 example a noteworthy choice for type purposes. The yellow-gold surfaces, imbued with traces of mint-green toning, exhibit bold satiny luster and minor marks. NGC ID# 28GJ, PCGS# 8859

4695 **1908 Motto MS63 NGC.** An attractive MS63 example of this popular type issue, with sharply detailed design elements and vibrant mint luster throughout. The pleasing orange and rose-gold surfaces are lightly marked. NGC ID# 28GJ, PCGS# 8859

4696 **1908 Motto MS63 NGC.** The pleasing orange-gold surfaces of this attractive Select example are brightly lustrous and lightly marked, with sharply detailed design elements and strong visual appeal. NGC ID# 28GJ, PCGS# 8859

1908 Motto Ten Dollar, MS64
A First-Year Type Coin

4697 **1908 Motto MS64 NGC.** The 1908 Indian ten dollar with Motto is significant for first-year type purposes as IN GOD WE TRUST was added to the left of the eagle in this year. This near-Gem displays lustrous yellow- and orange-gold surfaces. The design elements are well-impressed. A few minor scuffs and contact marks prevent Gem classification. NGC ID# 28GJ, PCGS# 8859

1908 Motto Ten, MS64
Uncommonly Well-Produced

4698 **1908 Motto MS64 NGC.** After a smaller mintage of No Motto eagles, the Philadelphia Mint completed the year with a sizeable production of With Motto coins. The mintage of 341,300 pieces was uncommonly well-produced, with bold strikes on the central motifs and attractive, satiny luster. This near-Gem example has many claims to an even higher grade, with no visible distractions when viewed under magnification and exceptional eye appeal. NGC ID# 28GJ, PCGS# 8859

4699 **1909 MS62 PCGS.** This Indian Head eagle is surprisingly elusive in Mint State for a Philadelphia date. A bold strike is the primary attribute of this example, with the eagle and Indian fully brought up and sharp. Soft luster glows beneath green-gold, slightly mattelike surfaces. An attractive and minimally marked coin for the assigned grade. NGC ID# 28GM, PCGS# 8862

4700 **1909 MS62 PCGS.** Lustrous, yellow-gold patina complements a bold strike with considerable original appeal. As typical for the issue, the surfaces are slightly mattelike and frosty, bothered only by a few minor grazes and delicate lines. NGC ID# 28GM, PCGS# 8862

4701 **1909 MS62 PCGS.** Satiny green-gold luster illuminates sharply struck design elements on this pleasing lower-grade Mint State example. No singularly significant abrasions are present, though we note some light field chatter that limits the grade. NGC ID# 28GM, PCGS# 8862

4702 **1909 MS62 PCGS.** A pleasing MS62 example of this early series issue, with sharply defined design elements and brightly lustrous orange-gold surfaces that show highlights of green and a scattering of minor contact marks on both sides. NGC ID# 28GM, PCGS# 8862

4703 **1909 MS62 PCGS.** The 1909 Indian eagle is a relatively available date in the series, making it a popular choice with type collectors. This attractive MS62 example offers sharply detailed design elements and lightly marked orange-gold surfaces with vibrant mint luster throughout. NGC ID# 28GM, PCGS# 8862

1909 Indian Eagle, MS63
Challenging P-Mint Issue

4704 **1909 MS63 PCGS.** A slightly better Philadelphia issue, the 1909 ten dollar becomes elusive as early as the MS63 grade level, and is genuinely scarce any finer. This example shows satiny lemon-gold luster, with minimal abrasions for the grade. The headdress feathers and eagle's wing are well-defined. NGC ID# 28GM, PCGS# 8862

1909 Ten Dollar, Well-Struck MS63
An Underrated Date

4705 **1909 MS63 NGC.** The 1909 ten dollar is one of the more underrated issues in the Indian Head series. The lustrous yellow- and orange-gold surfaces of this Select specimen exhibit well-struck design elements. Scattered light marks determine the grade. The 1909 is moderately difficult to obtain in MS63 and scarce in finer levels of preservation. NGC ID# 28GM, PCGS# 8862

1909-D Eagle, MS62
Above-Average Strike

4706 **1909-D MS62 NGC.** The yellow-gold surfaces of this MS62 ten dollar display traces of orange, and the design elements are better defined than typically encountered on this poorly struck issue. Scattered marks make occasional interruptions in the luster flow. The 1909-D becomes more difficult to locate in higher grades; NGC has seen fewer than 100 finer pieces (10/14). NGC ID# 28GN, PCGS# 8863

1909-D Eagle, MS62
Low-Mintage, High-Survival Issue

4707 **1909-D MS62 PCGS.** The 1909-D eagle is a low-mintage, high-survival issue, with most certified close to Mint State (and in generous numbers) despite the small production of 121,540 coins. This piece is boldly struck and lustrous on orange-gold surfaces that show a few luster grazes in the fields and distributed small marks on the device high points. NGC ID# 28GN, PCGS# 8863

1909-D Eagle, MS62
Better Denver Issue

4708 **1909-D MS62 PCGS. CAC.** The 1909-D Indian eagle had a moderately low mintage of little more than 120,000 coins, and is proportionately elusive in Mint State. This example is moderately abraded, as the grade suggests, but its desirability is heightened by the scarcity of finer pieces. Shades of green and rose-gold luster illuminate each side, complementing the sharply impressed design features. NGC ID# 28GN, PCGS# 8863

4709 **1910 MS64 PCGS.** The well-preserved orange-gold surfaces of this attractive Choice example radiate vibrant mint luster and the design elements are sharply detailed throughout. Overall eye appeal is terrific. NGC ID# 28GR, PCGS# 8865

4710 **1910-D MS64 PCGS.** Sharply detailed design elements and vibrant mint luster are the calling cards of this attractive Choice specimen. The pleasing surfaces show only minor signs of contact and eye appeal is outstanding. NGC ID# 28GS, PCGS# 8866

4711 **1910-S MS61 PCGS. Breen-7114.** The mintmark is clearly repunched. Breen described the variety as "extremely rare" but more examples have surfaced over the past 25 years. A satiny pale peach-gold Indian ten with a good strike and a minor rim ding near the tailfeathers. NGC ID# 268D, PCGS# 8867

4712 **1910-S MS61 PCGS.** The 1910-S Indian eagle is more difficult to locate in Mint State grades than its mintage of 811,000 pieces would suggest. This well-detailed MS61 example is lustrous and lightly abraded for the grade. NGC ID# 268D, PCGS# 8867

4713 **1910-S MS61 PCGS.** Despite its mintage of 811,000 pieces, the 1910-S Indian eagle is surprisingly difficult to locate in higher Mint State grades. This impressive MS61 example offers lustrous orange-gold surfaces with sharply detailed design elements and a scattering of minor contact marks on both sides. NGC ID# 268D, PCGS# 8867

4714 **1910-S MS61 PCGS.** From a mintage of 811,000 pieces, the 1910-S Indian eagle is surprisingly elusive in high grade. This attractive MS61 example offers sharply detailed design elements and lustrous surfaces that show the expected number of minor contact marks for the grade. NGC ID# 268D, PCGS# 8867

1910-S Indian Eagle, MS62
Conditionally Challenging

4715 **1910-S MS62 PCGS.** The difficulty of locating a Mint State 1910-S eagle increases significantly beyond MS62, making this grade ideal for the cost-conscious date and mintmark collector. This example is well-struck with frosty rose-gold luster. Scattered abrasions limit the grade, though none are singularly obtrusive. NGC ID# 268D, PCGS# 8867

1910-S Eagle, MS62
Melt Rarity in the Series

4716 **1910-S MS62 NGC.** The orange-gold surfaces of this better-date S-mint eagle show good eye appeal despite the scattered marks and smoke-gray field accents that connote bag shipping and storage. One mentionable dig shows in the reverse field below I in UNITED. This is a difficult issue in Mint State; most certified coins are no better than Choice AU. The high mintage figure of 811,000 coins is deceiving, as most of the issue was melted short decades after production. NGC ID# 268D, PCGS# 8867

1910-S Ten Dollar, Lustrous MS62

4717 **1910-S MS62 PCGS.** This golden-orange, lustrous, well-struck 1910-S eagle shows a typical appearance for the issue in Mint State, offering good luster, light high-point contact marks, and a few luster grazes in the fields determining the grade level. A melt rarity, the 1910-S's mintage figure is meaningless today. NGC ID# 268D, PCGS# 8867

4718 **1911 MS64 PCGS.** This near-Gem example is boldly struck with a radiant satiny sheen over smooth, unabraded surfaces. The light honey-gold toning yields to pleasing peach accents near the borders and in the center of the obverse. A premium-quality coin for the grade, and worthy of a second look. NGC ID# 28GT, PCGS# 8868

4719 **1911 MS64 NGC.** This well-produced issue of 506,000 coins is common in grades up to and including MS64, but it becomes scarce any finer. The satiny surfaces of this wheat-gold example are lustrous and carefully preserved. Trivial surface marks are limited almost entirely to the fields. NGC ID# 28GT, PCGS# 8868

4720 **1911 MS64+ NGC.** This high-end Choice Indian eagle exhibits razor-sharp definition on all design elements and well-preserved orange-gold surfaces that radiate vibrant mint luster throughout. Eye appeal is outstanding. NGC ID# 28GT, PCGS# 8868

4721 **1911-D — Improperly Cleaned — NGC Details. AU.** A mintage of only 30,100 pieces makes the 1911-D the rarest issue from its decade. A briefly circulated and partly lustrous representative that lacks any noticeable hairlines. A slight rim ding is noted near star 1. NGC ID# 28GU, PCGS# 8869

1912-S Eagle, Reddish-Orange MS61

4722 **1912-S MS61 PCGS.** The 1912-S Indian eagle is among the more elusive issues in the series, and most certified survivors fall short of Mint State, usually no better than AU58. This Mint State example displays good eye appeal on its lustrous reddish-orange surfaces, despite the scattered small- and medium-sized marks that determine the grade level. This coin would be a nice acquisition for a budget-minded collector. NGC ID# 28GX, PCGS# 8872

4723 **1914 MS63 PCGS.** This issue did not have a high mintage, at 151,000 pieces, yet examples are readily available in Uncirculated grades of MS61-63. The 1914 becomes scarce at MS64 and rare any finer. This Select example displays shimmering mint luster and bright yellow-gold surfaces. A small mark is noted on the eagle's shoulder, and a shallow scrape resides in the right reverse field. NGC ID# 28H2, PCGS# 8875

4724 **1914-D MS63 NGC.** The lustrous surfaces display appealing lime-gold and peach coloration blended over both sides. A bold impression from the dies imparts crisply defined motifs. A handful of nicks and shallow luster grazes limit the grade. NGC ID# 28H3, PCGS# 8876

4725 **1914-D MS63 PCGS.** This Denver issue is relatively available in mint condition, but most the graded Mint State coins are either in MS61 or MS62. This highly attractive example is intensely lustrous, with gleaming yellow-gold surfaces and bold strike definition. A mere handful of scattered, minuscule marks are seen, making this a high-end coin for the grade. NGC ID# 28H3, PCGS# 8876

1914-S Ten Dollar, MS61
Seemingly Underrated S-Mint Issue

4726 **1914-S MS61 NGC.** An oft-overlooked date, the 1914-S ten dollar is significantly scarcer in Mint State than its 208,000-coin mintage would imply. This piece shows bold design definition and original orange-gold luster. Light, evenly dispersed chatter accounts for the grade, though no individually noticeable abrasions are observed. NGC ID# 28H4, PCGS# 8877

1916-S Ten Dollar, MS62
Luminescent Coloration

4727 **1916-S MS62 NGC.** The collector who appreciates original coloration will find much to like about this coin. Both sides display soft olive-gold luster with fiery orange highlights in the recesses. The devices are sharply impressed and the surfaces are remarkably void of any obtrusive abrasions. As a date, the 1916-S ten dollar is challenging in any Mint State grade, but is genuinely scarce finer than the present example. NGC ID# 28H7, PCGS# 8880

4728 **1932 MS64 NGC.** One of the more readily available issues in the series overall, the 1932 Indian eagle is widely popular for type representation. This piece shows a sharp strike with vibrant lemon-gold luster. Grade-limiting abrasions are minor and evenly dispersed. NGC ID# 28HB, PCGS# 8884

4729 **1932 MS64+ NGC. CAC.** A high-end Choice specimen of the penultimate year of the denomination, this coin offers sharply detailed design elements and well-preserved orange and rose-gold surfaces that radiate vibrant mint luster. NGC ID# 28HB, PCGS# 8884

1932 Ten Dollar, MS65
Vibrantly Appealing Type Coin

4730 **1932 MS65 PCGS.** Long-heralded as a type issue due to its vast availability in the context of the series, the 1932 Indian eagle always finds a ready home when offered at auction. An added plus for the present coin is sheer eye appeal; both sides exhibit radiant, frosty luster, with fresh mint bloom on the obverse and deeper orange-gold patina on the reverse. The strike is bold and no obtrusive abrasions are present. NGC ID# 28HB, PCGS# 8884

LIBERTY DOUBLE EAGLES

1850 Double Eagle, XF45
In-Demand First-Year Type

4731 **1850 XF45 NGC.** This is the first regular year of issue in the double eagle series, and examples are frequently sought-after for type purposes. The motifs exhibit signs of light friction from circulation and a good impression overall. Numerous abrasions are scattered over the bright yellow-gold surfaces. Of those, only a small mark to the right of Liberty's hair is noteworthy. NGC ID# 268F, PCGS# 8902

4732 **1850 — Improperly Cleaned — NGC Details. AU.** The 1850 Liberty double eagle is always popular as the first year of the denomination. This attractive specimen shows just a touch of wear on the well-detailed design elements, with lightly abraded orange-gold surfaces that show a flat aspect, indicative of a light cleaning in the past. NGC ID# 268F, PCGS# 8902

4733 **1850 — Damaged — NGC Details. AU.** A short but broad scratch on the cheek, a cluster of tiny marks on the field near the nose, and a pinscratch above obverse star 4 correspond to the NGC notation. Nonetheless, an early double eagle with bold definition and traces of luster. NGC ID# 268F, PCGS# 8902

4734 **1851 XF45 PCGS.** Boldly defined overall, save for flatness on some of the obverse stars, this example is pleasing for the grade. Both sides exhibit lovely lime-green and peach toning, and noticeable semiprooflikeness in the fields. Light surface abrasions are not excessive for the grade. NGC ID# 268H, PCGS# 8904

4735 **1851 — Improperly Cleaned — NGC Details. AU.** This second-year double eagle is bright from cleaning but has relatively few bagmarks given its cursory encounter with pre-Civil War commerce. NGC ID# 268H, PCGS# 8904

1851 Double Eagle, AU53
Some Luster Remaining

4736 **1851 AU53 NGC.** Tinges of deep coppery-gold reside in the protected regions amid rich olive-gold patina. The strike is bold and only slight wear is evident over the finer details of the design. The 1851 double eagle is often chosen for type representation, due to its moderate availability in the AU grade range. NGC ID# 268H, PCGS# 8904

1854 Double Eagle, AU53
Attractive Small Date Representative

4737 **1854 Small Date AU53 NGC.** The Small Date variety constitutes the majority of coins struck in 1854, but examples are hardly common — especially in this grade. The peach-gold surfaces reveal considerable remaining luster and exhibit well-struck design elements. Darker copper-orange toning occurs within the recesses of UNITED, and marks are lightly scattered throughout. A lovely No Motto representative. NGC ID# 268P, PCGS# 8911

1854 Twenty, AU53
Small Date, Sharp Eye Appeal

4738 **1854 Small Date AU53 NGC.** A tinge of olive-gold suggests a fully original, honey-gold patina over the frosted surfaces on this sharp, Small Date twenty. Seven points of wear have taken the edge off numerous small abrasions, allowing the coin to gracefully assume the mantle of an attractive, About Uncirculated coin. This is a nice Type One example for a circulated type or date set. NGC ID# 268P, PCGS# 8911

4739 **1855-S XF45 NGC.** Medium S. A yellow-gold early San Francisco double eagle with plentiful remnants of luster for the designated grade. A cluster of thin marks are noted on the field beneath the chin. *From The Douglas Martin Collection.* NGC ID# 268X, PCGS# 8916

1855-S Double Eagle, AU55
Some Remaining Mint Luster

4740 **1855-S AU55 PCGS.** Medium S. Available in circulated grades, this San Francisco issue becomes distinctly scarce in Mint State. This still-lustrous Choice AU example offers the budget-minded collector an appealing alternative to a bagmarked Uncirculated piece. Medium honey-gold patina encompasses both sides, with only light wear over the high points of the design and minimal abrasions in the fields. NGC ID# 268X, PCGS# 8916

1856-S Double Eagle, AU53
Pleasing for the Grade

4741 **1856-S AU53 NGC.** The 1856-S is a highly popular issue in all grades, due in part to its connection with the famous *S.S. Central America* treasure. This AU representative is not pedigreed to the wreck, but is nonetheless pleasing in appearance, with original green-gold patina and remnants of rose-gold luster in the recesses. Numerous light abrasions are present. NGC ID# 2692, PCGS# 8919

1856-S Double Eagle, Choice AU
Considerable Luster Remains

4742 **1856-S AU55 NGC.** Although lightly worn, this early San Francisco double eagle retains considerable apricot-gold luster with an orange aspect that is more prominent on the obverse. The reverse is relatively clean, though a few sizable abrasions on and to the left of the bridge of Liberty's nose contribute to the grade. NGC ID# 2692, PCGS# 8919

1856-S Liberty Twenty, AU55

4743 **1856-S AU55 PCGS.** Made popular by the discovery of large quantities on the *S.S. Central America* shipwreck, the 1856-S is a favorite for type representation. This Choice AU example displays original lemon-gold patina with remnants of luster in the protected regions. Light chatter in the fields accompanies the grade. NGC ID# 2692, PCGS# 8919

1858 Twenty Dollar, AU55
Difficult Issue in Higher Grades

4744 **1858 AU55 NGC.** This reddish-gold Type One representative is one of 211,714 double eagles struck at the Philadelphia Mint in 1858. Examples are typically found in VF to XF condition, and Choice AU coins such as this are certainly scarce. A touch of strike incompleteness is evident on stars 1 and 2, and on UNITED. Small abrasions are peppered over each side. A nice example from an elusive issue. NGC ID# 2697, PCGS# 8923

1858-S Double Eagle, AU53
Remnants of Mint Luster

4745 **1858-S AU53 NGC.** Unlike the 1856-S and 1857-S issues, which survived in quantity on the *S.S. Central America* shipwreck, the 1858-S is a conditionally rare date in Mint State grades, making nice AU examples an attractive alternative for the date collector. This example shows remnants of original luster in the protected regions amid bright yellow-gold patina overall. Scattered abrasions are present, as usual at this grade level. NGC ID# 2699, PCGS# 8925

1858-S Twenty Dollar, AU55
Rich Original Patina

4746 **1858-S AU55 NGC.** Remnants of original luster highlight deep olive-gold patina, with tinges of fiery orange-gold in the recesses. Light, scattered abrasions are present, as is expected for this grade level. The 1858-S double eagle is conditionally scarce in Choice AU condition, and finer pieces are seldom seen. NGC ID# 2699, PCGS# 8925

4747 **1859-S XF45 NGC.** A surprisingly lustrous example for the grade. The straw-gold surfaces display well-defined motifs and moderate abrasions. NGC ID# 269C, PCGS# 8928

1860 Double Eagle, Lustrous AU55

4748 **1860 AU55 PCGS.** A lesser-seen Type One Philadelphia issue, seldom encountered in the finer AU grades and genuinely scarce in Mint State. This Choice AU coin displays substantial rose-gold luster in the recesses amid bright yellow-gold patina. Scattered abrasions accompany the grade, including a couple small scrapes near star 6. The coin is well-struck, with light wear over the high points. NGC ID# 269D, PCGS# 8929

1860-S Double Eagle, AU55
Impressive Luster for the Grade

4749 **1860-S AU55 NGC.** The San Francisco Mint produced over 500,000 twenty dollar gold pieces in 1860. The vast majority circulated heavily in West Coast commerce, yet this Choice AU No Motto double eagle shows signs of only minimal circulation. Partial luster emanates from the well-detailed devices. The khaki-gold surfaces show scattered abrasions throughout, but only a small nick below the first S in STATES is worthy of note. NGC ID# 269F, PCGS# 8931

4750 **1861 XF40 NGC.** An attractive 1861 double eagle in the often-seen grade of XF40, this coin retains much of its original design detail and mint luster and the bright orange-gold surfaces are lightly abraded. NGC ID# 269G, PCGS# 8932

4751 **1861 XF45 PCGS.** The vivid orange-gold surfaces of this Choice XF specimen retain much of their original mint luster and show the expected number of minor abrasions for the grade. The well-detailed design elements are lightly worn. NGC ID# 269G, PCGS# 8932

4752 **1861 AU50 ANACS.** A lightly worn specimen of this popular Type One double eagle, with vivid orange-gold surfaces that retain a few traces of original mint luster and show highlights of rose. NGC ID# 269G, PCGS# 8932

4753 **1861 AU53 NGC.** A well-detailed AU53 example of this popular Civil War issue, with bright orange and greenish-gold surfaces that show a moderate number of minor abrasions for the grade. Much original mint luster remains intact. NGC ID# 269G, PCGS# 8932

1861 Double Eagle, AU55
Choice Type Coin

4754 **1861 AU55 NGC.** Before the salvage of the S.S. *Central America* shipwreck, the 1861 was the most readily available Type One double eagle in high grades. Although now rivaled by the 1856-S and 1857-S, this date still ranks as an ideal candidate for type representation. The current example displays substantial luster in the recesses, with original orange-gold patina overall. The surfaces are unusually smooth, showing few of the heavy abrasions that typically affect coins in this grade. NGC ID# 269G, PCGS# 8932

1861-S Double Eagle, AU Details
Pleasing Coloration

4755 **1861-S — Cleaning — PCGS Genuine. AU Details.** While its Philadelphia counterpart is readily available through the lower Mint State grades, the 1861-S double eagle is somewhat more challenging, beginning at the AU level. This example was lightly cleaned long ago, but has since acquired rich orange-gold patina. Slight wear is present over the surprisingly smooth surfaces. NGC ID# 269K, PCGS# 8935

1862-S Twenty Dollar, AU53
Repunched Date

4756 **1862-S AU53 NGC. Breen-7214.** The date is repunched, evident primarily within the loops of the 8 and the 6. The 1862-S, like other double eagle issues of its era, circulated widely on the West Coast, and examples are frequently seen in lower circulated grades. This pleasing AU piece displays olive and reddish-gold surfaces with strongly defined design motifs. Predictably abraded for the grade. NGC ID# 269N, PCGS# 8938

4757 **1863-S VF35 PCGS. Breen-7217.** Small S. An attractive midgrade green-gold Civil War double eagle. Field marks are inconsequential, although unobtrusive rim dings are noted on the obverse at 3 o'clock and the reverse at 4 o'clock. NGC ID# 269R, PCGS# 8940

4758 **1863-S XF40 PCGS. Breen-7216.** Medium S. The wingtips display wear, but luster emerges from the legends, rays, and eagle. The cheek near the ear is abraded, and a reed mark is noted above the nose tip. NGC ID# 269R, PCGS# 8940

1864 Double Eagle, AU Details
Scarce No Motto Issue

4759 **1864 — Improperly Cleaned — NGC Details. AU.** The 1864 is a challenging date in all grades and becomes increasingly scarce at the About Uncirculated level. This brightly lustrous example is exceedingly well-struck with full star centers and sharp detail on the eagle's feathers. Wispy marks from the noted cleaning are not overly distracting, and abrasions are uniformly scattered over each side.

1864-S Liberty Double Eagle, AU58
Scarce This Nice

4760 **1864-S AU58 PCGS.** Shipwreck finds from the *S.S. Brother Jonathan* and the *S.S. Republic* brought hundreds of relatively high-grade examples of this San Francisco date on board with the grading services. Populations increased, yet natural-looking, amber-gold examples such as this near-Mint twenty remain the real jewels in the eyes of collectors. The small abrasions from coin-to-coin contact and minimal circulation are distributed over the surfaces, but none are overly numerous or of great concern. Exceptional luster remains. NGC ID# 269T, PCGS# 8942

4761 **1865-S XF45 PCGS.** A Choice AU example of this popular Type One double eagle, with light wear on the design elements and a prominent die crack through the letters on the lower reverse. The bright orange-gold surfaces show the expected number of minor abrasions for the grade. NGC ID# 269V, PCGS# 8944

4762 **1865-S XF45 NGC. Breen-7221.** Small S, usual for the issue, although a Medium S variety is known. A caramel-gold Civil War double eagle without any mentionable marks. Luster is evident across the legends, rays, and other design elements. NGC ID# 269V, PCGS# 8944

4763 **1867-S XF40 NGC.** Large S. The scarcer of the two mintmark sizes for the issue. A moderately marked peach-gold piece with prevalent glimpses of luster. The 1867-S ranks among the most elusive San Francisco issues in Uncirculated grades, although at the XF level it is readily collected. NGC ID# 26A2, PCGS# 8952

1867-S Twenty Dollar, AU55
Abundant Remaining Luster

4764 **1867-S AU55 NGC.** Small Squat S. A surprising amount of frosty mint luster illuminates the light rose-gold surfaces of this Choice AU representative from the San Francisco Mint. Sharply impressed overall, stars 6 through 8 are lightly struck and minimal friction occurs over Liberty's hair. Die cracks run through UNITED STA on the reverse, and the surfaces are moderately abraded. NGC ID# 26A2, PCGS# 8952

1868 Double Eagle, AU53
A Low-Mintage Issue

4765 **1868 AU53 NGC.** The 1868 double eagle saw a production figure of less than 100,000 pieces, helping to make this issue scarce in all grades. The yellow-gold surfaces of this AU53 example are imbued with hints of reddish-rose and assume slightly deeper hues on the reverse. Well-defined for the most part and revealing just the expected array of marks. NGC ID# 26A3, PCGS# 8953

4766 **1868-S AU53 NGC.** Small squat S. This San Francisco issue, like many others from the same era, was heavily circulated and remains scarce despite a high mintage of 837,500 pieces. The current example is well-struck overall, showing slight weakness on some of the obverse stars, and reveals evidence of light circulation including high-point wear and a few minor abrasions. An attractive example of this challenging Type Two double eagle issue. Housed in a prior generation holder. NGC ID# 26A4, PCGS# 8954

1870 Double Eagle, AU53
Scarce in All Grades

4767 **1870 AU53 NGC.** The 1870 double eagle is scarce in all grades and is infrequently found above MS62. The present AU53 coin displays yellow-gold surfaces imbued with traces of green and is relatively well-defined for the issue. A few scattered marks do not detract. NGC and PCGS have seen only 51 pieces at this grade level (10/14). NGC ID# 26A7, PCGS# 8957

4768 **1870-S AU53 NGC.** The pleasing yellow and orange-gold surfaces of this impressive Type Two double eagle retain much of their original mint luster and show a scattering of minor abrasions on both sides. The well-detailed design elements show just a touch of high-point wear. NGC ID# 26A9, PCGS# 8959

4769 **1870-S AU55 PCGS.** A Choice About Uncirculated coin from the technical aspects of its production, and the "dirty gold" patina suggests original surfaces. Some prooflike flash remains at the margins. Liberty is a bit soft at the high points of the hair, and small abrasions are distributed at infrequent intervals over the yellow-gold surfaces. Much luster remains. NGC ID# 26A9, PCGS# 8959

1871-S Twenty Dollar, AU58
Attractively Lustrous

4770 **1871-S AU58 NGC.** This San Francisco issue survives in rather limited numbers at the Mint State level, making more affordable AU examples somewhat appealing to the casual date collector. This near-Mint example retains substantial yellow-gold mint luster, with just slight friction over the sharply impressed motifs. Scattered abrasions accompany the grade, as can be expected at this level. NGC ID# 26AC, PCGS# 8962

4771 **1872 AU53 NGC.** The lightly abraded orange-gold surfaces of this attractive Type Two double eagle retain much of their original mint luster, and the well-detailed design elements show just a trace of actual wear. NGC ID# 26AD, PCGS# 8963

4772 **1872 AU58 PCGS. CAC.** Like most Type Two double eagles, the 1872 Liberty twenty is scarce in high grade. This well-detailed near-Mint example displays lightly abraded orange and greenish-gold surfaces with vibrant mint luster on both sides. NGC ID# 26AD, PCGS# 8963

4773 **1872-S AU55 NGC.** Small Squat S. A straw-gold Type Two twenty. Luster dominates most of the reverse. Obverse luster is evident at the periphery and throughout Liberty's hair. The scattered small marks are consistent with the grade and denomination. NGC ID# 26AF, PCGS# 8965

4774 **1873 Open 3 MS61 NGC.** The 1873 Liberty double eagle with an Open 3 in the date is more available than its Closed 3 counterpart. This attractive Mint State specimen is well-detailed and brightly lustrous, with the minimum number of minor contact marks for the grade. NGC ID# 26AH, PCGS# 8967

1873 Open 3 Twenty, MS62
Seldom Available Finer

4775 **1873 Open 3 MS62 PCGS.** The 3 in the date was widened in 1873, after it was discovered that the earlier Closed 3 logotype was too easily mistaken for an 8. Of the two varieties, the Open 3 variant is much more available for type representation. This example displays radiant honey-gold luster and well-struck motifs. Light, scattered abrasions contribute to the grade. NGC ID# 26AH, PCGS# 8967

4776 **1873-S Closed 3 AU58 PCGS.** The Closed 3 variety is more available than its Open 3 counterpart, at least in circulated grades. Mint State examples of either type are scarce, especially any finer than MS61. This example is somewhat softly struck on the obverse, but the coin displays a considerable degree of remaining mint luster and a few noticeable abrasions on each side. NGC ID# 26AL, PCGS# 8969

1873-S Closed 3 Twenty Dollar, MS61
Misplaced Date Variety

4777 **1873-S Closed 3 — Misplaced Date — MS61 NGC.** The top of an errant 8 is evident in the dentils beneath the right half of the 8. Designated as VP-001 by NGC since the variety is unlisted in *Cherrypickers'*. Swirling luster and light yellow-gold color blend over each side. The strike is bold overall with a degree of softness over the upper obverse and lower reverse. Expectedly abraded for the assigned grade. NGC has seen only 28 numerically finer examples (10/14). NGC ID# 26AL, PCGS# 8969

1874-S Double Eagle, MS61
Luminous Mint Luster

4778 **1874-S MS61 NGC.** The 1874-S double eagle is only marginally scarce at the MS61 grade level, but finer pieces are seldom available. This piece displays frosty orange-gold luster and well-defined motifs. No major abrasions are noted, though some light chatter in the fields precludes a finer numeric grade. NGC has encapsulated only 32 numerically finer examples (10/14). NGC ID# 26AR, PCGS# 8972

4779 **1875 MS61 NGC.** The 1875 Liberty double eagle is the only readily available gold issue struck at the Philadelphia Mint that year, as the other denominations were produced in very limited numbers. This well-detailed MS61 specimen offers vivid greenish-gold surfaces with vibrant satiny mint luster that blends with prooflike reflectivity in many areas. NGC ID# 26AS, PCGS# 8973

1875 Twenty, MS62
Frosty Cartwheel Luster

4780 **1875 MS62 PCGS.** This Type Two Philadelphia issue is only marginally scarce in MS62, but finer examples are significantly challenging and proportionately more expensive to acquire. The present coin shows light, scattered abrasions, as can be expected at this grade level, but retains frosty, honey-gold luster and well-struck devices. NGC ID# 26AS, PCGS# 8973

1875-CC Twenty Dollar, XF40
Original Patina, Remaining Luster

4781 **1875-CC XF40 NGC. Variety 5-A.** Remnants of original luster reside in the protected regions of this lightly circulated Carson City type coin, while the remainder of each side displays primarily olive-gold patina. No significant abrasions are present, and most major details retain pleasing definition. The 1875-CC is one of the more plentiful Carson City double eagles, ideal for the collector seeking a single representative from this mint. NGC ID# 26AT, PCGS# 8974

1875-CC Twenty, Unc Details
Notable Eye Appeal Remains

4782 **1875-CC — Improperly Cleaned — NGC Details. Unc. Variety 2-B.** Dramatic strike doubling is apparent on many of the reverse devices, especially along the periphery, and both Cs in the mintmark are filled. The obverse is lightly cleaned, producing some hairlines, intermingled with die polish striations, and a semi-reflective sheen. A reeding mark is noted just to the right of the date. Sharp mint luster and appealing, honey-gold coloration remain.

4783 **1875-S MS60 PCGS.** Vibrant mint luster shines forth from the yellow-gold surfaces, and the design elements are boldly impressed, if a trifle weak on Liberty's hair curls. A purplish alloy spot covers the denominational D on the lower reverse. A mildly scuffy obverse appearance defines that grade. NGC ID# 26AU, PCGS# 8975

4784 **1875-S MS61 NGC.** An attractive MS61 example of this popular Type Two issue, with unusually vibrant mint luster and well-detailed design elements. The light orange-gold surfaces show a scattering of minor contact marks and eye appeal is quite strong for the grade. NGC ID# 26AU, PCGS# 8975

1876-CC Twenty Dollar, XF45

4785 **1876-CC XF45 NGC. Variety 2-A.** Pale green-gold patina yields to remnants of original luster in the recesses when turned in-hand, while the devices are well-detailed for the grade, and there are no singularly detracting circulation scars. The 1876-CC is fairly plentiful in the context of Carson City double eagles, but finding an example that retains original coloration is somewhat challenging. NGC ID# 26AW, PCGS# 8977

4786 **1876-CC — Improperly Cleaned — NGC Details. AU. Variety 1-A.** The well-detailed design elements of this popular Carson City double eagle show just a trace of actual wear and the lightly abraded green and rose-gold surfaces remain brightly lustrous, despite the noted cleaning. NGC ID# 26AW, PCGS# 8977

4787 **1876-S MS61 NGC.** Well-struck and highly lustrous, with appealing light champagne-gold toning over both sides, this is an attractive example for the grade. Moderate bagmarks keep it from a finer rating. NGC ID# 26AX, PCGS# 8978

1877-CC Twenty, XF45
An Available Issue

4788 **1877-CC XF45 NGC. Variety 3-A.** The first C in the mintmark markedly lower than the second, the last 7 in the date centered over a dentil, and die lines after S in DOLLARS confirm the variety. The 1877-CC double eagle is available in circulated grades but becomes difficult in mint condition. Orange-gold surfaces display luster in the recesses and reveal the expected number of marks. The reverse shield is weak in spots. NGC ID# 26AZ, PCGS# 8983

4789 **1878-S MS61 PCGS.** The return of exported coins has made this issue relatively available in lower Uncirculated grades, including MS61. MS62 examples are scarce, and coins are rare any finer. This sharply struck piece has a bright, semiprooflike appearance, and a few scuffy marks that prevent a higher grade. NGC ID# 26B5, PCGS# 8987

4790 **1878-S MS61 NGC.** The striking impression was well-executed, with all but a couple of the obverse stars sharply defined. Rich honey-gold toning is illuminated by outstanding cartwheel luster. A somewhat scuffy appearance on the obverse limits the grade. NGC ID# 26B5, PCGS# 8987

4791 **1878-S MS61 PCGS.** The vivid green and orange-gold surfaces of this pleasing MS61 example display vibrant mint luster and the expected number of minor contact marks for the grade. The design elements are sharply rendered and some prooflike reflectivity is evident in sheltered areas. NGC ID# 26B5, PCGS# 8987

1879-S Double Eagle, MS61
Distinctly Original Luster

4792 **1879-S MS61 PCGS.** Small quantities of this issue were among the coins recovered from the Saddle Ridge Hoard, though these hardly affected the certified Mint State population, and the date remains scarce finer than MS61. This example is well-detailed on Liberty's hair and the eagle's feathers, with frosty green-gold luster over each side. Scattered abrasions limit the numeric grade, with a couple ticks near Liberty's nose being the only individually noticeable ones. NGC ID# 26B9, PCGS# 8991

1879-S Twenty Dollar, MS61
Seldom Found Finer

4793 **1879-S MS61 PCGS.** Original honey-gold luster and sharply struck design elements are the chief attributes on this lower-end Mint State example. A long, thin mark along the right edge of Liberty's cheek accounts for the grade, as the surfaces are otherwise fairly well-preserved. This early Type Three San Francisco issue is scarcely seen above this numeric level. NGC ID# 26B9, PCGS# 8991

1880 Liberty Twenty, AU58
Underappreciated in High Grades

4794 **1880 AU58 NGC.** A seemingly underrated Philadelphia issue, the 1880 double eagle had a low mintage of only 51,420 pieces, most of which experienced moderate circulation. Mint State examples are seldom seen, making high-end AU coins among the finest that are typically available. This near-Mint representative displays substantial straw-gold luster, with just a touch of friction over the high points of the design. The strike is sharp and no significant abrasions are noted. NGC has seen only 55 numerically finer representatives (10/14). NGC ID# 26BA, PCGS# 8992

1882-CC Double Eagle, AU53
Even High-Point Wear

4795 **1882-CC AU53 NGC. Variety 1-B.** This date can be located without too much trouble in circulated grades but is scarce in Mint State and virtually unobtainable above MS62. The orange-gold surfaces of this AU53 coin exhibit well-defined design elements save for some localized softness typically seen. Moderately abraded, but still fairly nice eye appeal. NGC ID# 26BF, PCGS# 8997

1882-S Double Eagle, MS62
Highly Lustrous

4796 **1882-S MS62 NGC.** This issue had a large mintage of 1.1 million coins, and it is available in Mint State grades of MS60 through the current grade of MS62. Examples grading any finer are exceedingly scarce, and NGC has seen only 16 coins at MS63, plus a single piece rated MS64. This highly lustrous example displays light mint-green and rose toning. Mild scuffiness on the obverse is grade-consistent. NGC ID# 26BG, PCGS# 8998

1882-S Twenty Dollar, MS62
Radiant Original Patina

4797 **1882-S MS62 PCGS Secure.** A small number of 1882-S double eagles was among the coins discovered in the Saddle Ridge Hoard, though the date's rarity in grades above MS62 was hardly affected. This example shows scattered, grade-consistent abrasions, but the sharp strike and frosty orange-gold luster balance the eye appeal. PCGS has encapsulated only 41 numerically finer examples (10/14). NGC ID# 26BG, PCGS# 8998

1883-CC Liberty Twenty
Choice XF Example

4798 **1883-CC XF45 NGC. Variety 2-A.** The 1883-CC double eagle is moderately available overall, but it is somewhat scarcer than its more often seen 1875-CC and 1876-CC counterparts. This example is sharply detailed for the grade, with small remnants of luster in the recesses amid pale green-gold patina. The surfaces are free of any singularly detracting abrasions, leaving this piece with a pleasing degree of eye appeal. NGC ID# 26BH, PCGS# 8999

1883-CC Double Eagle, AU50
An Available CC Issue

4799 **1883-CC AU50 NGC. Variety 2-A.** The raised die dot to the right of the middle of the 3 in the date and the second C in the mintmark positioned over the flag of the D in DOLLAR confirm the variety. The 1883-CC is one of the more available Carson City double eagles. The yellow- and greenish-gold surfaces of this AU53 specimen display luster in the recessed areas. Well-struck with just a few scattered, minute marks. NGC ID# 26BH, PCGS# 8999

1884-CC Double Eagle, Well-Defined AU50

4800 **1884-CC AU50 NGC. Variety 1-A.** The first C in the mintmark is almost midway between the Y in TWENTY and the D in DOLLARS, while the second C is over the left side of the D. The 1884-CC is among the more common Carson City double eagles. The greenish-gold surfaces of this AU example display relatively well-defined devices. A few minute marks do not disturb. NGC ID# 26BK, PCGS# 9001

1884-CC Double Eagle, AU50
Pleasing Original Patina

4801 **1884-CC AU50 NGC. Variety 1-A.** The 1884-CC twenty dollar is similar in overall rarity to the 1882-CC and 1883-CC, being one of the more readily available Carson City issues from this decade. The present example retains tinges of luster in the recesses amid original olive and bronze-gold patina on each side. The devices exhibit grade-appropriate wear, with minimal distractions. NGC ID# 26BK, PCGS# 9001

4802 **1884-S MS62 NGC.** The design elements of this attractive MS62 specimen are sharply rendered and the pleasing orange-gold surfaces are brightly lustrous, with a scattering of minor contact marks on both sides. NGC ID# 26BL, PCGS# 9002

4803 **1884-S MS62+ PCGS.** A number of Mint State 1884-S double eagles are known, but most are in MS62 and lower grades. This is a minimally abraded, Plus-graded example, with vibrant yellow-gold luster and sharp motifs. An unusually appealing example for the numeric level. NGC ID# 26BL, PCGS# 9002

4804 **1885-S MS62 PCGS Secure.** The scintillating cartwheel luster exhibited by this San Francisco mint double eagle is its most outstanding attribute. The coin's rich orange-gold coloration is pleasing, and surface marks are about as-expected for the MS62 assessment. NGC ID# 26BP, PCGS# 9005

4805 **1887-S MS61 PCGS.** An attractive Mint State example from a mintage of 283,000 pieces, this coin offers sharply defined design elements and pleasing orange-gold surfaces that radiate vibrant mint luster. NGC ID# 26BS, PCGS# 9007

1888 Double Eagle, MS61
Die Doubled Reverse, FS-801

4806 **1888 Doubled Die Reverse, FS-801, MS61 PCGS. CAC.** The reverse legends exhibit strong doubling. DOLLARS shows the widest spread between hubbings. This green-gold double eagle is lustrous and nicely struck. The fields and cheek display myriad minor abrasions. A conditionally rare variety. Population: 30 in 61, 8 finer (10/14). PCGS# 145738

4807 **1888-S MS62 PCGS.** The impressive strike definition on both sides of this Mint State example is nearly full, save for trace amounts of weakness on Liberty's crown and the eagle's talons. The light orange-gold and rose toning is illuminated by flashy cartwheel luster, and surface marks are not distracting. NGC ID# 26BU, PCGS# 9009

1888-S Twenty, MS63
Attractive, Lustrous Example

4808 **1888-S MS63 NGC.** This is a well-struck example with lustrous, lightly-marked surfaces and appealing coloration. All of the design motifs are fully defined, and the number of small abrasions — most located on the obverse — seems normal for the Select Mint State grade level. Few coins from this issue are graded any finer than MS63. NGC ID# 26BU, PCGS# 9009

4809 **1889-CC — Obverse Scratched — NGC Details. XF. Variety 1-A.** A scarcer Carson City issue. Luster is prevalent in protected areas. A vertical pinscratch on Liberty's cheek and neck explains the NGC notation, but the fields are less bagmarked than is usual for the denomination. The obverse exhibits vertical hairlines. NGC ID# 26BV, PCGS# 9011

4810 **1889-S MS62 PCGS.** Impressively sharp strike definition includes the obverse stars and Liberty's hair curls. The rich orange-gold coloration and vibrant luster are pleasing. An attractive example of this San Francisco issue that recently saw its population increase with the discovery of the Saddle Ridge Hoard. NGC ID# 26BW, PCGS# 9012

4811 **1890-CC VF35 PCGS. CAC. Variety 1-A.** A later die state with partially lapped tail feathers. Glimmers of orange-tinged luster outline design elements while the remainder of the moderately marked surfaces are olive-green. A popular Carson City issue. NGC ID# 26BY, PCGS# 9014

1890-CC Liberty Twenty, XF45
Popular Carson City Issue

4812 **1890-CC XF45 NGC. Variety 1-A.** The usual late die state example, with some of the eagle's outer tailfeathers partially effaced by die lapping. This lightly circulated Carson City type coin shows original olive-gold patina overall, with tinges of orange and honey in the protected regions. The strike is bold, and strong detail remains for the grade. NGC ID# 26BY, PCGS# 9014

1890-CC Liberty Head Twenty, XF45
Considerable Luster Remains

4813 **1890-CC XF45 NGC. Variety 1-A.** One of the highly popular Carson City double eagles, with enough surviving examples to help satisfy the seemingly endless allure of Western gold. Attractive, apricot-gold surfaces retain considerable mint luster. Abrasions are somewhat muted by wear. A small area of rub on Liberty's cheek is mentioned for accuracy but is not particularly significant at this grade level. NGC ID# 26BY, PCGS# 9014

1890-CC Twenty Dollar, AU53
Some Remaining Luster

4814 **1890-CC AU53 NGC. Variety 1-A.** The reverse die is lapped, with some of the outer tailfeathers partially effaced. Remnants of original luster reside in the protected regions on each side, highlighting warm honey-gold patina overall. Liberty's hair and the eagle's feathers remain sharply detailed despite slight high-point wear. A moderately plentiful Carson City issue, ideal for the collector seeking a single representative from this mint. NGC ID# 26BY, PCGS# 9014

1890-CC Double Eagle, AU55
Sharp, Early Die State Coin

4815 **1890-CC AU55 NGC. Variety 1-A.** This piece is from an early die state, with the eagle's tailfeathers boldly defined and slight die doubling evident on the reverse lettering, most notably on PLURIBUS. The strike is sharp, and only slight friction is seen over the high points of the devices. Original apricot-gold patina blankets the fields, complementing a subtle semiprooflike sheen. NGC ID# 26BY, PCGS# 9014

1890-CC Twenty Dollar, AU55
Exceptional Natural Appeal

4816 **1890-CC AU55 NGC. Variety 1-A.** The natural, medium-gold surfaces of this Carson City twenty are exceptionally attractive and Choice. Mint luster gleams from the margins and from around the well-detailed central motifs. Abrasions are minimal, and those present are further softened by five points of wear. A highly appealing About Uncirculated example. NGC ID# 26BY, PCGS# 9014

1890-CC Twenty Dollar, Unc Sharpness

4817 **1890-CC — Obverse Improperly Cleaned — NGC Details. Unc Details. Variety 1-A.** The eagle's right (facing) tailfeathers are partially effaced by die lapping, an often seen characteristic on this available Carson City issue. Deep apricot-gold margins surround brighter yellow-gold centers, with vibrant luster overall. A lens reveals scattered, faint hairlines on the obverse, accounting for the NGC Details grade, though the eye appeal is not inhibited. A pleasing, attractively toned Carson City double eagle. NGC ID# 26BY, PCGS# 9014

4818 **1890-S MS61 PCGS.** The design motifs are solidly struck throughout, and this Mint State example is highly lustrous. Lovely lime-gold toning is imbued with subtle peach accents near the centers. Surprisingly few surface marks make this attractive piece seem high-end for the grade. NGC ID# 26BZ, PCGS# 9015

4819 **1890-S MS62 NGC.** From a mintage of 802,750 coins, the 1890-S double eagle is a readily available issue in AU and lower Mint State grades, but examples rating any finer than MS62 are scarcer, making the current offering an attractive choice for type purposes. It is a sharply struck piece with full, shimmering mint luster and lovely light coloration. Surface marks are not excessive for the grade. NGC ID# 26BZ, PCGS# 9015

4820 **1892-CC — Scratches — NGC Details. AU. Variety 1-A.** The portrait has a scuff in the hair and patches of pinscratches on the cheek, neck, and profile. The fields appear prooflike due to a wipe. The borders exhibit orange-red toning. A low mintage Carson City issue. NGC ID# 26C6, PCGS# 9020

4821 **1897-S MS61 Prooflike NGC.** Seldom encountered with prooflike surfaces. Struck from Klondike gold, this readily available San Francisco date shows numerous frictionlike marks that interrupt the mirrored fields. The coin displays a bold strike and a flashy, medium-gold color. PCGS# 79032

4822 **1898 MS62 PCGS.** The strike definition is bold throughout, and satiny luster illuminates light mint-green toning intermingled with pale rose accents on each side. Minor marks keep it from grading finer. NGC ID# 26CK, PCGS# 9033

4823 **1899 MS64 NGC.** An attractive Choice representative of this popular turn-of-the-century type coin, with sharply detailed design elements and lustrous orange-gold surfaces that show only minor signs of contact. NGC ID# 26CM, PCGS# 9035

4824 **1901 MS64 NGC.** A plentiful date in lower grades, the 1901 double eagle becomes increasingly elusive in grades finer than MS64. This representative displays tinges of rose color amid primarily green-gold luster. The devices are well-struck on the finer elements, and a few minor abrasions on the cheek are all that preclude a Gem grade assessment. NGC ID# 26CS, PCGS# 9039

1901 Double Eagle, MS65
In a Prior Generation Holder

4825 **1901 MS65 NGC. CAC.** A hoard of 1901 double eagles entered the market in the 1990s, making the date plentiful in grades through MS64, and only marginally scarce in Gem condition. Finer pieces, however, remain prohibitively rare. This piece, housed in a prior generation holder, is tied for the finest certified at NGC (10/14), displaying bold design elements and frosty orange-gold luster. A few light marks on the cheek preclude a finer grade. NGC ID# 26CS, PCGS# 9039

4826 **1901-S MS61 Prooflike NGC.** Slightly baggy over the prooflike surfaces — moreso on the obverse than the reverse. Dazzling yellow-gold color grabs the eye, however, and the coin is brightly reflective. This well-struck San Francisco date has always been rumored to exist in quantity among different hoards both here and abroad, some found and others yet to be discovered. PCGS# 79040

4827 **1902-S MS61 Prooflike NGC.** The 1902-S Liberty double eagle is rarely seen with prooflike surfaces, but the pleasing MS61 specimen exhibits deeply reflective fields to complement the sharply detailed design elements on both sides. The attractive green and yellow-gold surfaces show the expected number of minor contact marks for the grade. Census: 3 in 61 Prooflike, 0 finer (10/14). PCGS# 79042

4828 **1903 MS64 PCGS.** This impressive Choice example exhibits sharp definition on all design elements and the smooth orange-gold surfaces show a few hints of rose. Vibrant mint luster adds to the outstanding eye appeal. NGC ID# 26CW, PCGS# 9043

4829 **1903 MS64+ NGC.** The 1903 Liberty double eagle was a well-produced issue and this high-end Choice example exhibits the sharply detailed design elements and vibrant mint luster expected of this date. Well-preserved peach-gold surfaces add to the outstanding eye appeal. NGC ID# 26CW, PCGS# 9043

4830 **1903-S MS63+ PCGS.** The PCGS Plus designation was particularly well-placed on this Select Uncirculated coin, which shows few marks or other distractions of any kind. The medium-gold surfaces display nice luster and pinkish highlights when rotated in light. The strike is bold. While many examples of this date came back from overseas hoards, either this one had a particularly gentle trip...or it never left in the first place. NGC ID# 26CX, PCGS# 9044

1903-S Twenty, MS64
Deeply Lustrous, Original Patina

4831 **1903-S MS64 PCGS.** Gem examples are rare for this heavily exported San Francisco date, making near-Gem coins such as this one the most logical selection for most collectors. Housed in a green label holder, the coin has a rich, original patina with lilac at the rims and a thick band of orange highlights around the gleaming gold portrait of Liberty. Exceptional mint luster shines beneath the frosted surfaces. Only minor, ticklike marks prevent a higher grade. PCGS shows just 13 coins in a numerically higher grade — all at MS65 (10/14). NGC ID# 26CX, PCGS# 9044

4832 **1904 MS64 PCGS.** The 1904 Liberty double eagle is readily available in Mint State grades, making it popular with type and date collectors alike. This sharply detailed Choice example displays vivid orange-gold surfaces with radiant mint luster and only minor signs of contact. NGC ID# 26CY, PCGS# 9045

4833 **1904 MS64+ PCGS.** A sharply detailed, near-Gem type coin with frosty green-gold luster. Light, scattered surface grazes limit the grade, but none a singularly obtrusive. NGC ID# 26CY, PCGS# 9045

4834 **1904 MS64+ NGC.** The 1904 Liberty double eagle is one of the most popular issues of the series with type collectors. This high-end Choice example is sharply detailed, with lustrous, lightly marked yellow and rose-gold surfaces. NGC ID# 26CY, PCGS# 9045

1904 Double Eagle
High-End Gem Type Coin

4835 **1904 MS65+ PCGS.** A radiant, frosty type coin, this Plus-designated Gem showcases uninhibited lemon-gold luster and delicately preserved surfaces. The strike is sharp and both sides are devoid of the the excessive die lapping that often affects examples of this type. The 1904 Liberty twenty dollar is available through the MS65 grade level, but finer pieces are only infrequently seen. NGC ID# 26CY, PCGS# 9045

4836 **1904 MS61 Prooflike NGC.** More 1904 double eagles exist than any other date in the series, a beacon for type collectors and a stalwart of the sight-unseen gold market. This MS61 example has prooflike surfaces and intense yellow-gold coloration in its corner, but displays a number of scuffs and bagmarks. It is a properly graded and attractive coin despite the frequent abrasions. PCGS# 79045

4837 **1904 MS62 Prooflike NGC.** Lime-green highlights visit the warm, orange-gold surfaces of this eye-stopping, prooflike double eagle. Marks are infrequent and the strike is bold, with a mellow mirrored appeal seldom encountered at this grade level. PCGS# 79045

4838 **1904 MS63 Prooflike NGC.** The most plentiful Liberty Head double eagle as a date and a superb target for type collectors and gold accumulators. This radiant, sun-gold example is strongly prooflike and displays a razor-sharp strike. Minimal abrasions exist for the Select Uncirculated level, with only wispy field chatter that doesn't detract at all from the overall mirrored appeal. PCGS# 79045

1904 Twenty Dollar, MS64 Prooflike
Challenging With Prooflike Designation

4839 **1904 MS64 Prooflike NGC.** The staggering overall availability of the 1904 double eagle precludes any degree of collecting challenge unless one seeks ultra high-grade or Prooflike representatives. NGC has encapsulated only 53 Prooflike 1904 double eagles at the Choice grade level, and numerically finer examples number just 12 (10/14). Struck from fresh dies, this piece shows boldly defined motifs amid deep yellow-gold mirrors. A few minute ticks in the fields limit the numeric grade, but hardly affect the impressive eye appeal. PCGS# 79045

1904 Double Eagle, MS64 Prooflike
Eye-Catching Sheen

4840 **1904 MS64 Prooflike NGC. CAC.** The most common Liberty Head double eagle date, this issue is nevertheless scarce with the Prooflike designation. This Choice example is fully struck and intensely lustrous, with untoned surfaces. Scattered small abrasions include a few beneath the temple area. Census: 53 in 64 (2 in 64 ★) Prooflike, 12 finer (10/14).
Ex: Central States Signature (Heritage, 5/2007), lot 4221. PCGS# 79045

4841 **1904-S MS64+ NGC.** Available in most grades, the 1904-S double eagle becomes elusive in grades finer than MS64. This Plus-graded example displays sharp detail and well-preserved, frosty golden luster. A highly appealing coin for the grade. NGC ID# 26CZ, PCGS# 9046

1905-S Twenty, MS63
Radiantly Frosty

4842 **1905-S MS63 PCGS.** Despite a mintage in excess of 1.8 million coins, the 1905-S double eagle becomes increasingly elusive in succeeding Mint State grades, and is decidedly rare at the Gem level. This sharply struck Select piece shows frosty orange-gold luster, with light, scattered abrasions that contribute to the grade. NGC ID# 26D3, PCGS# 9048

SAINT-GAUDENS DOUBLE EAGLES

4843 **1907 Arabic Numerals MS64 NGC.** An attractive Choice representative of this popular first-year type issue, with vibrant mint luster and well-detailed design elements throughout. The well-preserved yellow-gold surfaces add to the outstanding eye appeal. NGC ID# 26F5, PCGS# 9141

4844 **1907 Arabic Numerals MS64 NGC.** A frosty example with lovely, blended rose and antique-gold coloration. The coin's luster quality and eye appeal are exceptional. A handful of minor marks on each side keep it from grading higher. NGC ID# 26F5, PCGS# 9141

4845 **1907 Arabic Numerals MS64 PCGS.** This third design version of the Saint-Gaudens double eagle was accomplished and adopted in 1907, after the High Relief and Ultra High Relief versions proved difficult to strike. This is a lovely example with light honey-gold toning and mattelike surface textures. A bit softly struck but well-preserved and minimally abraded. NGC ID# 26F5, PCGS# 9141

1907 Arabic Numerals Twenty, MS65
Attractive Type Coin

4846 **1907 Arabic Numerals MS65 PCGS.** The 1907 Arabic Numerals twenty dollar issue is the first widely accessible date in the Saint-Gaudens series and an ideal issue for type purposes. This amazing Gem example displays frosty, peach-gold surfaces with strongly defined design motifs and a handful of small, well-hidden abrasions. The eye appeal is considerable. NGC ID# 26F5, PCGS# 9141

1907 Arabic Numerals Twenty, MS65
Vibrantly Lustrous Example

4847 **1907 Arabic Numerals MS65 PCGS.** Radiant orange-gold luster engulfs each side of this Gem first-year issue example. Liberty's knee is ill-defined, as always, though the strike is bold throughout. The frosty surfaces reveal only limited disruptions in the luster. This issue is available in Gem condition, but finer pieces are seldom seen. NGC ID# 26F5, PCGS# 9141

4848 **1908 No Motto MS65 NGC.** Long Rays obverse. Blended apricot-gold and lime-green toning adorns lustrous and impressively unabraded surfaces. A nicely struck and attractive representative of the two-year type. NGC ID# 26F6, PCGS# 9142

4849 **1908 No Motto MS66 NGC.** A stunning Premium Gem example of this popular two-year subtype, with well-detailed design elements and lustrous yellow and rose-gold surfaces that show no mentionable distractions. NGC ID# 26F6, PCGS# 9142

4850 **1908 No Motto MS66 NGC.** Popular with type collectors and series enthusiasts alike, the 1908 No Motto double eagle represents the last year of its short-lived subtype. This attractive Premium Gem displays well-preserved yellow and rose-gold surfaces, with well-detailed design elements and vibrant mint luster throughout. NGC ID# 26F6, PCGS# 9142

4851 **1908 No Motto, Wells Fargo Nevada MS65 PCGS. CAC.** Short Rays obverse. An orange-gold Gem with selected areas of lighter wheat toning. Lustrous and carefully preserved. Marketed in the late 1990s, the Wells Fargo No Motto holdings were sizeable and surprisingly high in quality. Certified in a green label holder. PCGS# 99142

4852 **1908 No Motto, Wells Fargo Nevada MS66 PCGS.** Short Rays obverse. Vibrant luster dominates this high grade sun-gold and olive-green double eagle. A loupe locates only incidental contact. The strike is good except on the upper leg feathers. Housed in a green label holder. PCGS# 99142

4853 **1908 No Motto, Wells Fargo Nevada MS66 NGC.** Sunburst blasts of full mint luster, magnificent color, a nice strike, and no contact marks of which to speak. A perfect type coin selection. *Ex: Palm Beach Signature (Heritage, 3/2006), lot 2158.* PCGS# 99142

1908-D No Motto Twenty, MS64+
Attractive, Satiny Luster

4854 **1908-D No Motto MS64+ PCGS.** This is a boldly struck, minimally abraded example of this No Motto Denver issue, with frosty luster in shades of rose and honey-gold. The 1908-D No Motto twenty is significantly scarcer than its Philadelphia counterpart, which survived in substantial quantities via the Wells Fargo Hoard. By contrast, the 1908-D is only available in grades through MS64, and finer pieces are scarce. NGC ID# 26F7, PCGS# 9143

1908-D Motto Double Eagle, Vibrant MS65
Rare Any Finer

4855 **1908-D Motto MS65 PCGS.** The 1908-D Motto double eagle was one of the most underrated issues of the series before a number of coins surfaced in a Central American hoard in 1983. The issue is still conditionally rare in grades above the Gem level. This impressive Gem displays well-detailed design elements and vibrant mint luster, with well-preserved yellow and rose-gold surfaces. PCGS has graded 32 numerically finer examples (10/14). NGC ID# 26F9, PCGS# 9148

1909/8 Twenty, MS62
Desirable Gold Overdate, FS-301

4856 **1909/8 MS62 PCGS. FS-301.** Perennially popular as the only 20th-century gold overdate, this lustrous example catches the eye with rich, orange-gold surfaces a bold strike. A few dark grazes in incidental marks account for the MS62 grade, but the minimal distractions are balanced by the sharp eye appeal and cartwheel luster. NGC ID# 26FC, PCGS# 9151

1909/8 Twenty Dollar, MS62
Strong Underdigit

4857 **1909/8 MS62 NGC. CAC. FS-301.** One of the aspects that makes this only overdate in the Saint-Gaudens series so collectible is the strong underdigit that is visible in all grades and die states. This piece is minimally abraded for the grade and shows even orange-gold mint luster. Only slight high-point softness is seen on each side. NGC ID# 26FC, PCGS# 9151

1909-D Double Eagle, AU58
Just a Whisper From Uncirculated

4858 **1909-D AU58 NGC.** A tiny bit of blending on the eagle's breast feathers and wingtips are the only signs of wear on this otherwise sharp and minimally marked twenty. Just 52,500 pieces of this desirable Denver date were struck. Nearly full mint luster remains over the attractive, medium-gold surfaces. Fewer marks exist than on many technically Mint State coins, making this near-Mint example at home in any Uncirculated set. NGC ID# 26FD, PCGS# 9152

4859 **1909-S MS64 NGC. CAC.** This attractive near-Gem Saint-Gaudens double eagle offers well-detailed design elements and brightly lustrous orange and rose-gold surfaces with only minor signs of contact. Visual appeal is quite strong. NGC ID# 26FE, PCGS# 9153

4860 **1910-S MS64 PCGS.** The radiant golden-orange surfaces are highly lustrous, and the design elements are boldly struck throughout. A handful of wispy field marks are noted on each side, keeping this attractive near-Gem from a finer grade. NGC ID# 26FH, PCGS# 9156

4861 **1911-D/D FS-501 MS64 PCGS.** The mintmark is strongly repunched east. An intricately struck near-Gem with orange-gold centers and olive-green margins. Marks are incidental aside from a small patch left of the torch, below the hair. Housed in a first generation holder. PCGS# 145010

1911-S Double Eagle
High-Quality Borderline Gem

4862 **1911-S MS64+ PCGS. CAC.** Given the considerable jump in values between MS64 and MS65 grades, this Plus-graded Saint-Gaudens twenty is at an ideal point in the grading scale for both type and date collectors. The coin is lustrous, frosted, and boldly struck. Rich, medium-gold color covers the lustrous surfaces. CAC endorsement confirms the appeal of this mintmarked double eagle. NGC ID# 26FL, PCGS# 9159

1911-S Double Eagle, MS65
Soft Cartwheel Luster

4863 **1911-S MS65 PCGS.** The 1911-S Saint-Gaudens double eagle is only marginally scarce in Gem condition, but finer pieces are rarely seen. This representative shows a bold strike with satiny honey-gold luster. A few faint surface grazes limit the grade, but these are hardly detectable to the unaided eye. PCGS has encapsulated just 32 numerically finer examples (10/14). NGC ID# 26FL, PCGS# 9159

1912 Double Eagle, MS64
Seldom Available Finer

4864 **1912 MS64 PCGS.** The 1912 Saint-Gaudens double eagle is collectible in grades through MS64, but finer pieces are rarely seen. This Choice example displays sharp design definition and frosty straw-gold luster. A few insignificant ticks contribute to the grade, though the eye appeal is nonetheless excellent. Only 43 coins are numerically finer at PCGS (10/14). NGC ID# 26FM, PCGS# 9160

4865 **1913 MS62 PCGS.** This example is intensely lustrous and displays deep greenish-gold and rose toning. Wispy surface marks are typical for the assigned grade. NGC ID# 26FN, PCGS# 9161

4866 **1913 MS62 NGC.** This is a bright, satiny, wheat-gold representative with satiny luster and small-to-moderate marks on each side. This issue had a relatively scant mintage of 168,700 pieces, and it becomes scarce any finer than the current MS62 grade level. NGC ID# 26FN, PCGS# 9161

4867 **1913-S MS61 NGC.** From a tiny mintage of 34,000 pieces, the 1913-S Saint-Gaudens twenty is perhaps more available than expected in Mint State grades. It seems that many coins were stored in European and South American bank vaults, and later repatriated to America. This example reveals a bold impression from the dies, and considerable mint luster, but some scuffiness on the high points reduces the grade of this Uncirculated example. NGC ID# 26FR, PCGS# 9163

1913-S Double Eagle, MS63
Only 34,000 Coins Struck

4868 **1913-S MS63 PCGS.** Despite its status as the second-lowest mintage among With Motto Saints (only the 1908-S has a lower mintage), Select Uncirculated examples of the issue are somewhat available for collectors. The present coin is brightly lustrous with yellow-gold color and above-average definition. A number of small abrasions account for the grade, although none are individually distracting. NGC ID# 26FR, PCGS# 9163

1915-S Double Eagle, MS65+
Radiant Original Luster

4869 **1915-S MS65+ PCGS. CAC.** This plentiful San Francisco issue is easily obtainable in Gem condition, but finer examples are scarce. This current Plus-graded example shows satiny orange-gold luster with subtle tinges of rose and lilac throughout. The strike is bold and there are no detracting abrasions. A small, mint-made planchet void is noted in the central reverse, well-hidden by the eagle's feathers. NGC ID# 26FW, PCGS# 9168

1920 Double Eagle, MS64
Only One Numerically Finer at PCGS

4870 **1920 MS64 PCGS.** This piece is well-struck, with satiny luster in shades of honey and mint-gold. A few light, scattered surface grazes limit the grade, but no singularly obtrusive abrasions are present. PCGS has certified only a single numerically finer representative of this conditionally elusive Philadelphia issue (10/14). NGC ID# 26FY, PCGS# 9170

1920 Twenty Dollar, MS64
Exceedingly Rare Any Finer

4871 **1920 MS64 NGC.** Undeniably original patina features deep olive-gold luster around the margins on each side, with brighter yellow-gold patina in the centers. The strike is well-executed and only a few minutes ticks preclude a finer numeric grade. The 1920 double eagle is marginally available in Choice condition, but finer pieces are rare, with only seven so-graded at NGC (10/14). NGC ID# 26FY, PCGS# 9170

1920 Double Eagle, MS64
Just One Coin Numerically Finer at PCGS

4872 **1920 MS64 PCGS. CAC.** This Philadelphia twenty is available in all grades through MS64, but all but unavailable any finer. A single MS65 coin is the sole finer grade at PCGS, and NGC reports just seven finer coins (10/14). This example received the CAC endorsement for eye appeal and quality, with lovely orange-gold patina and relatively few marks. A sharp strike supports gleaming mint luster over the natural gold surfaces. NGC ID# 26FY, PCGS# 9170

1922 Double Eagle, MS65
Gorgeous Type Coin

4873 1922 MS65 PCGS. CAC. This clean, attractive double eagle is notable for its minimal abrasions and outstanding eye appeal. Straw-gold deepens to reddish-orange at the centers. A sharp strike shows only nominal incompleteness on the torch hand and the Capitol dome. Rare any finer, PCGS has certified just eight examples in higher numeric grades (10/14). NGC ID# 26G3, PCGS# 9173

4874 1923-D MS65 NGC. Well-preserved yellow-gold surfaces and especially vibrant mint luster are the calling cards of this delightful Gem, with sharply detailed design elements and exceptional eye appeal. NGC ID# 26G6, PCGS# 9176

4875 1923-D MS66 PCGS. Rich reddish-apricot toning and bold, shimmering mint luster are evident over both sides of this visually appealing example. The design elements are well-defined, and a single contact mark in the right obverse field is the only minor distraction. NGC ID# 26G6, PCGS# 9176

4876 1923-D MS66 PCGS. The 1923-D is a high-mintage Denver issue that is favored by mintmark type collectors. This attractive Premium Gem example is well-struck with exceptionally bright, satiny mint luster and light honey-gold and peach toning. A single small abrasion is noted in the right obverse field. NGC ID# 26G6, PCGS# 9176

4877 1924 MS65+ NGC. This high-end Gem displays pleasing orange and rose-gold surfaces with no mentionable distractions. The design elements are well-detailed and vibrant mint luster radiates from both sides. NGC ID# 26G7, PCGS# 9177

4878 1924 MS66 PCGS. Shades of honey and mint-gold luster swirl over frosty surfaces on each side of this Premium Gem type coin. The strike is bold and there are no mentionable abrasions. Housed in an old green label holder. NGC ID# 26G7, PCGS# 9177

4879 1924 MS66 NGC. A spectacular Premium Gem example of this extremely popular type issue, with sharply detailed design elements and pristine reddish-gold surfaces that radiate vibrant mint luster. Eye appeal is terrific. NGC ID# 26G7, PCGS# 9177

4880 1924 MS66 NGC. The 1924 Saint-Gaudens double eagle is an available date in high grade and enjoys great popularity with type collectors. This impressive Premium Gem is well-detailed and brightly lustrous, with pristine orange-gold surfaces. NGC ID# 26G7, PCGS# 9177

4881 1924-D — Improperly Cleaned — NGC Details. Unc. Despite a mintage of more than 3,000,000 pieces, the 1924-D is regarded as rare, since a supermajority of the production never left Treasury vaults prior to the FDR gold recall. A lustrous sun-yellow example with a bagmark on the face and minor vertical hairlines on the right obverse and eagle's wingtips. NGC ID# 26G8, PCGS# 9178

1924-S Double Eagle, Unc Details
Strong Cartwheel Luster

4882 1924-S — Improperly Cleaned — NGC Details. Unc. A somewhat scarcer date overall, especially in comparison to the more plentiful Philadelphia issues of the period. The present coin is unworn with sharp design elements and minimal abrasions. NGC draws attention to some faint hairlines on each side, though these are hardly discernable and do not inhibit the frosty orange-gold mint luster that is this coin's strong suit. NGC ID# 26G9, PCGS# 9179

4883 1925 MS63 NGC. Gold CAC. Far nicer than implied by its designated grade, the present Saint-Gaudens type coin has refreshingly smooth apricot surfaces. Lustrous, nicely struck, and housed in a prior generation holder. NGC ID# 26GA, PCGS# 9180

4884 1925 MS66 PCGS. At the MS66 level the 1925 Saint-Gaudens double eagle is an available date, but the population plummets in any higher grade. This spectacular Premium Gem displays well-detailed design elements and vibrant mint luster, with pristine orange-gold surfaces. PCGS has graded seven numerically finer examples (10/14). NGC ID# 26GA, PCGS# 9180

4885 1926 MS66 NGC. The 1926 Saint-Gaudens double eagle is not too difficult to locate in MS66 condition, but the issue is a condition rarity in any finer grade. This sharply detailed Premium Gem presents pristine orange-gold surfaces with vibrant mint luster on both sides. NGC has graded eight numerically finer examples (10/14). NGC ID# 26GD, PCGS# 9183

1926 Double Eagle, MS66
Gorgeously Toned
Doubled Die Obverse

4886 1926 — Doubled Die Obverse — MS66 PCGS. Minor die doubling is evident on the obverse rays and the designer's monogram, though this is different than the tripled die obverse variety listed in the *Cherrypickers'* reference. Eye-catching yellow-gold mint bloom engulfs each side, with shades of coppery-orange, olive, and lime-green color also seen over the upper-right portion of the obverse. The devices are fully defined, and the frosty surfaces are devoid of any mentionable abrasions. PCGS has certified only four numerically finer representatives (10/14). NGC ID# 26GD, PCGS# 9183

4887 **1927 MS63 NGC. Gold CAC.** A lovely lemon-gold Saint-Gaudens type coin, lustrous and nicely struck with relatively few field grazes. Only a small percentage of CAC seals are gold, which in their opinion indicates that the coin merits a finer grade. Encased in a prior generation holder. NGC ID# 26GG, PCGS# 9186

4888 **1927 MS65+ ★ NGC. CAC.** This high-end Gem has been awarded the coveted Star designation and is certified by CAC. The design elements are sharply detailed and the well-preserved surfaces radiate vibrant mint luster. NGC ID# 26GG, PCGS# 9186

4889 **1927 MS66 NGC.** A delightful Premium Gem representative of one of the most popular type coins of the series, this piece offers sharply detailed design elements and vibrant mint luster combined with well-preserved yellow-gold surfaces. NGC ID# 26GG, PCGS# 9186

4890 **1927 MS66 NGC.** A spectacular Premium Gem representative of this popular Philadelphia issue, with sharply detailed design elements and vibrant mint luster throughout. The pleasing yellow and rose-gold surfaces show no mentionable distractions. NGC ID# 26GG, PCGS# 9186

4891 **1928 MS66 NGC.** This issue is one of the most readily available in the Saint-Gaudens double eagle series, but it is very scarce in grades any finer than MS66. This example is boldly struck, with pleasing honey-gold coloration and shimmering mint luster. The surfaces reveal exceptional preservation and just a couple of trivial marks. NGC ID# 26GK, PCGS# 9189

TERRITORIAL GOLD

4892 **1861 Clark, Gruber $2 1/2 Copper Die Trial — Polished — NGC Details. Unc. K-9, R.7.** Plain edge. A broad raised rim is partially present, receding near 7 o'clock on the obverse and 1 o'clock on the reverse. Fully struck at the centers, likely due to the thick planchet and the absence of a collar die. The surfaces are prooflike and glossy with iridescent orange, red, and green toning.

CALIFORNIA FRACTIONAL GOLD

4893 **1854 Liberty Round 25 Cents, BG-216, R.6, MS64 NGC.** A rare variety credited to Frontier, Deviercy & Co. The semiprooflike pumpkin-orange surfaces appear essentially as made. Struck from rusted and lapped dies, characteristic of BG-216. Census: 2 in 64, 0 finer (10/14). PCGS# 10401

1855 Round Liberty Quarter Dollar
Rare BG-227, MS65 Prooflike

4894 **1855 Liberty Round 25 Cents, BG-227, R.6, MS65 Prooflike NGC.** A rare round quarter dollar variety made by Antione Louis Nouizillet in 1855. Struck in solid California gold. The reverse die is shattered, a diagnostic of this variety, while the obverse stars are noticeably repunched. The obverse die is heavily polished from its previous use for BG-226A; it is later polished again before being employed for BG-228. The present, yellow-gold example displays deep mirroring in the fields and well-defined motifs. This is the only example of BG-227 certified as Prooflike by NGC, and is rivaled numerically at that service only by a single non-Prooflike MS65 coin, with none finer (10/14). PCGS# 10412

1870 Liberty Round 25 Cents, BG-808, MS67
One of the Finest-Known Examples

4895 **1870 Liberty Round 25 Cents, BG-808, R.3, MS67 PCGS.** This round quarter variety is attributed to Pierre Frontier, of Frontier & Co., who produced fractional gold coins in San Francisco to around 1873. This is a spectacular Superb Gem example with blazing mint luster and pristine yellow-gold surfaces. One of the finest-known examples of this Breen-Gillio variety. Population: 5 in 67 (1 in 67+), 0 finer (10/14). PCGS# 10669

4896 **1871 Liberty Round 25 Cents, BG-813, R.3, MS67 PCGS.** The single-finest certified at PCGS, separated from the pack by an even strike and smooth, prooflike canary gold fields. Retained laminations affect the lower reverse periphery. The dies are credited to Frontier & Co., successors of Frontier, Deviercy & Co.

4897 **1872 Liberty Round 25 Cents, BG-814, High R.5, MS64 Prooflike NGC.** A late die state with an advanced break on the wreath between 3 and 5 o'clock. Curiously, BG-814 is less rare than BG-815 and BG-816, the other two varieties that share the same 1872 obverse. Radiant and prominently mirrored with the customary incompleteness of strike on the denominator. PCGS# 710675

4898 **1872 Indian Octagonal 50 Cents, BG-939, Low R.5, MS65 Prooflike NGC.** A splendid sun-gold Gem with mirrored fields and a sharp central strike. No detractions are evident. A minor unlisted die state with lapped elements on the lowest portion of the wreath.

1878/6 Octagonal Half Dollar, MS66
BG-952, Sole Finest Certified

4899 **1878/6 Indian Octagonal 50 Cents, BG-952, High R.5, MS66 PCGS.** A rare octagonal half dollar variety made by Christopher Ferdinand Mohrig of San Francisco. An 1876 obverse die was reworked with 1878 date, and was employed for the 1878 issue. This is the only known variety of the 1878 octagonal half, and is usually seen with deep prooflike fields, as is the case with this Premium Gem. Heavy die polishing has effaced portions of the date numerals, though the date remains readable. Slight striking weakness is noted at the centers, as is usual for this variety. Struck with a 90 degree die rotation, and showing rich orange-gold color. Housed in an old green label holder, this piece is the sole finest of just 28 examples at PCGS (10/14). PCGS# 10810

4900 **1870 Liberty Round 50 Cents, BG-1010, R.3, MS67 PCGS.** A pristine butter-gold Superb Gem. The highly lustrous fields display concentric die polish lines but are devoid of contact. The dies were lapped, reducing neck curl definition and effacing the base of the denominator. Population: 2 in 67, 0 finer (10/14).

4901 **1871 Liberty Round 50 Cents, BG-1029, High R.4, MS63 Deep Prooflike NGC.** State I. A scarce round half dollar variety issued by the Levison brothers while running their business, the California Jewelry Company. The identifying initial L is seen on the obverse above the date. This full cameo example displays bright yellow-gold color and excellent preservation for the grade. Some minor striking weakness is noted on the obverse portrait, as is typical for this issue. This piece is the sole Deep Prooflike example of this variety certified by NGC, and is tied numerically with just two others as the finest overall (10/14). PCGS# 910858

4902 **1873/2 Indian Octagonal Dollar, BG-1122, High R.6, MS62 PCGS.** Issued by Christopher Ferdinand Mohrig of San Francisco. The obverse die failed early, accounting for the overall rarity of this issue. This is a late die state example, as usual, with several radial die cracks on the obverse. A small planchet lamination is also noted between stars 12 and 13. The fields are fully prooflike with bright yellow-gold patina. Slight striking weakness in the centers leaves still-pleasing detail in the wreath and bust. Struck from rotated dies. PCGS# 10933

4903 **1871 Liberty Round Dollar, BG-1204, High R.5, AU58 PCGS.** The caramel-gold fields display ample flash, but the high points of the upper wreath show slight wear. The strike is incomplete on the portrait, usual for BG-1204. Breen-Gillio lists only eight Period Two round dollar varieties. Population: 6 in 58, 16 finer (10/14). PCGS# 10949

COMMEMORATIVE SILVER

4904 **1893 Isabella Quarter MS64 Prooflike NGC.** At first glance, this coin has the look of a proof with squared rims and deeply prooflike obverse fields. The reverse is less prooflike with minor marks, especially in the left field. Copper-red and steel-blue shades cover the well-struck surfaces of this attractive, near-Gem commemorative quarter. NGC ID# 28HR, PCGS# 9220

4905 **1893 Isabella Quarter MS65 PCGS.** An impressive Gem example of the first commemorative quarter, with sharply detailed design elements and well-preserved lustrous surfaces under delicate shades of champagne-gold toning. NGC ID# 28HR, PCGS# 9220

1893 Isabella Quarter, MS66
Razor-Sharp Definition

4906 **1893 Isabella Quarter MS66 PCGS.** This commemorative quarter's namesake, Queen Isabella of Spain, is depicted on the obverse, representing the unique occurrence of a foreign monarch on American coinage. Delicately toned in shades of gunmetal-blue and violet-gray, the surfaces show razor-sharp definition and impeccable preservation. Vivid luster glistens from beneath the toning. NGC ID# 28HR, PCGS# 9220

4907 **1900 Lafayette Dollar MS63 PCGS. DuVall 1-B. Ex: Newman.** Shades of lavender-gray and walnut-brown toning blanket the surfaces of this impressive Select specimen. The design elements are sharply rendered and the surfaces are well preserved. NGC ID# 28N8, PCGS# 9222

4908 **1900 Lafayette Dollar MS63 PCGS. CAC. DuVall 2-C.** Dusky caramel-gold and silver-gray toning embraces the fields and devices. The borders display freckles of blue-green patina. Crisply struck and lustrous with nearly unmarked fields and a few minor imperfections on the Washington portrait. NGC ID# 28N8, PCGS# 9222

4909 **1900 Lafayette Dollar MS64 PCGS. DuVall 1-B.** Violet and brown-gray color covers the fields and centers, while lovely lime-green and red-orange iridescence adorns the obverse peripheries. Lustrous and fully struck, with a couple of wispy field grazes on the obverse that seem hardly worth mentioning. A very pleasing near-Gem example of this scarce early commemorative. NGC ID# 28N8, PCGS# 9222

1921 Alabama Centennial Half, MS66
Later 2x2 Variant

4910 **1921 Alabama 2x2 MS66 PCGS. CAC.** Mintage totals for the 2x2 variant of the Alabama Centennial half dollar are not concretely known, though Bowers suggests 15,000 pieces were struck in October and December 1921 (plus 14 coins for assay purposes), all of which were likely distributed. Interestingly, the 2x2 halves are relatively similar in rarity to the "plain" variant, which had a significantly higher distribution (estimated at nearly 50,000 pieces, per Bowers' research). The present example is boldly struck with frosty luster. Softly blended rainbow hues encompass much of each side, giving this piece impressive visual appeal. PCGS has certified only seven numerically finer representatives (10/14). NGC ID# 28HS, PCGS# 9225

4911 **1937 Antietam MS67 NGC.** A spectacular Superb Gem representative of this low-distribution issue, with sharply detailed design elements and subtle satiny mint luster under shades of lavender-gray toning. NGC has graded 23 numerically finer examples (11/14). NGC ID# 28HV, PCGS# 9229

4912 **1937 Antietam MS67 PCGS. CAC.** A sharply detailed Superb Gem from a low distribution of 18,028 pieces, this delightful representative offers impeccably preserve lustrous surfaces under shades of lavender-gray and greenish-gold toning. NGC ID# 28HV, PCGS# 9229

4913 **1939 Arkansas MS66 NGC.** This is an appealing Premium Gem example of the Arkansas commemorative half, with smooth, virtually flawless creamy-gray surfaces that reveal very slight champagne border accents. Conditionally scarce in this high grade, and essentially unobtainable any finer, with just three Superb Gems known to NGC and PCGS. Census: 29 in 66 (1 in 66+), 1 finer (11/14). NGC ID# 28JA, PCGS# 9249

4914 **1936 Bridgeport MS67 NGC.** A carefully preserved example of this infrequently seen commemorative issue. Both sides exhibit bright lemon-yellow toning with intermingled tinges of coppery-gold and amber-red. The design elements are boldly impressed. Census: 35 in 67 (1 in 67+, 4 in 67 ★), 1 finer (10/14). NGC ID# 28JX, PCGS# 9279

4915 **1936 Bridgeport MS67 PCGS.** The 1936 Bridgeport half dollar claims a distribution total of 25,015 pieces, and this coin is one of the finest survivors. This sharply detailed Premium Gem displays flawless surfaces with vibrant mint luster and outstanding eye appeal. Population: 76 in 67 (5 in 67+), 0 finer (10/14). NGC ID# 28JX, PCGS# 9279

4916 **1936 Bridgeport MS67 NGC.** Lovingly preserved throughout, with wispy apricot and plum coloration in the centers and richer forest-green, canary-yellow, and magenta coloration toward the margins. Seldom seen this well preserved or this attractive. Census: 35 in 67 (1 in 67+, 4 in 67 ★), 1 finer (11/14). *Ex: Long Beach Signature (9/2006), lot 2663.* NGC ID# 28JX, PCGS# 9279

4917 **1925-S California MS67 NGC.** Highly lustrous and frosty, this Superb Gem California half stands out aesthetically and technically. A full strike delivers bold detail on both the grizzly bear and the miner. The toning is light yet prismatically colorful. The issue is seldom seen finer, with NGC reporting just 14 coins with a finer numeric grade (10/14). NGC ID# 28JY, PCGS# 9281

4918 **1925-S California MS67 NGC.** This is an impressive Superb Gem example of the popular California Diamond Jubilee half dollar, struck in concert with the 75th anniversary of California's statehood. Well struck and flawlessly preserved, each side of the coin exhibits deep, intermingled toning in a multitude of hues. NGC ID# 28JY, PCGS# 9281

4919 **1925-S California MS67 NGC.** Fully struck and intensely lustrous, this breathtaking Superb Gem displays deep golden-brown and steel-blue colors near the reverse margins, while the obverse has bright crimson, lemon-gold, and steel-blue iridescence near its own borders. Other than a few wispy pinscratches, in the right obverse fields, the exquisitely preserved surfaces seem pristine. *Ex: Portland, OR Signature (3/2004), lot 6895.* NGC ID# 28JY, PCGS# 9281

4920 **1936 Cleveland MS67 PCGS. CAC.** Struck to celebrate the centennial of Cleveland, Ohio, this issue had a total mintage of 50,030 pieces, half of which were actually struck in 1937 but dated 1936. Light speckled patina on both sides, mainly near the borders, promotes the original appearance of this outstanding Superb Gem. A well-struck and impressive example. Population: 71 in 67 (7 in 67+), 1 finer (10/14). NGC ID# 28K4, PCGS# 9288

1936 Columbia Half Dollar, MS67+
Near-Finest at PCGS

4921 **1936 Columbia MS67+ PCGS. CAC.** Soft, satiny luster provides a glowing backdrop for iridescent highlights over silvery surfaces. Crescents of deep orange toning seem strategically placed above and below the figure of Justice, and similar tones enliven the solitary palmetto tree on the reverse. Just one coin is graded numerically finer at PCGS, making the Plus designation awarded to this coin especially meaningful. Population: 83 in 67 (9 in 67+), 1 finer (10/14). NGC ID# 28K5, PCGS# 9291

4922 **1892 Columbian MS66 NGC. CAC.** Strongly lustrous with a hint of frostiness. Blue and gold-orange peripheral toning gives way to silver-gray over the centers. A graze is noted on the cheekbone. NGC has certified 45 numerically finer pieces (10/14). NGC ID# 26H5, PCGS# 9296

4923 **1893 Columbian MS66 PCGS. CAC.** One of the first U.S. commemorative coins, along with its Isabella quarter counterpart, and popular as such. This example is sharply struck, with shimmering luster and lovely electric-blue and reddish toning along the obverse periphery. NGC ID# 26H6, PCGS# 9297

4924 **1935 Connecticut MS67 NGC.** This spectacular Superb Gem offers well-detailed design elements and impeccably preserved surfaces with satiny mint luster and hints of pale gold and lavender toning. Census: 89 in 67 (3 in 67+, 12 in 67 ★), 1 finer (11/14). NGC ID# 28K8, PCGS# 9299

4925 **1936 Gettysburg MS67 PCGS.** An exceptionally well-preserved example of this popular Gettysburg commemorative, this piece boasts satiny, shimmering luster and is nearly devoid of the minor ticks that typically affect the shields and portraits on this issue. Subtle amber-pink, olive-gold, and forest-green toning encompasses the margins, leaving shades of gunmetal and ice-blue toning over the centers. PCGS has seen only two numerically finer submissions (10/14). NGC ID# 28KB, PCGS# 9305

1922 No Star Grant Half Dollar, MS67
Visually and Technically Exceptional

4926 **1922 Grant No Star MS67 PCGS.** This piece represents the more plentiful No Star variant, though even this issue becomes distinctly scarce at the Superb Gem grade level. The present coin is an outstanding example, with frosty luster and sharp motifs. Luminous lavender-gray color graces the centers, yielding to deeper olive-gold in the margins with tinges of russet, violet, and forest-green seen periodically around the peripheries. A beautifully preserved coin, housed in an old green label holder. Population: 46 in 67 (2 in 67+), 0 finer (10/14). NGC ID# 28KD, PCGS# 9306

4927 **1922 Grant With Star MS63 PCGS.** A nicely struck semiprooflike representative of the low mintage variety. Light chestnut toning aids the eye appeal. The dies clashed early and were lapped, leaving myriad delicate die polish lines on the obverse field. Certified in a green label holder. NGC ID# 28KC, PCGS# 9307

1922 Grant Memorial Half, MS64
Scarcer With Star Variant

4928 **1922 Grant With Star MS64 PCGS. CAC.** This Choice Mint State example shows satiny golden-gray luster overall, with deeper olive-gold tinges in the protected regions. The strike is slightly soft on Grant's hair, though the design elements are otherwise well brought up. The With Star Grant Memorial half dollar had a scant distribution of just 4,256 coins, and is significantly scarcer than its No Star counterpart, which had a mintage in excess of 67,000 pieces. NGC ID# 28KC, PCGS# 9307

4929 **1928 Hawaiian — Cleaning — PCGS Genuine. Unc Details.** A dash of light golden color in the central obverse grants a touch of warmth to this satiny, unworn example. Other than evidence of light cleaning, the surfaces are devoid of major problems, and the strike is sharp throughout. A popular key issue in the classic commemorative series, with a distribution of only 10,000 pieces. NGC ID# 28KE, PCGS# 9309

4930 **1928 Hawaiian — Cleaning — PCGS Genuine. Unc Details.** A pearl-gray example of the rarest silver commemorative type. Patches of hairlines emerge beneath a loupe, and the high points display minor blending. NGC ID# 28KE, PCGS# 9309

4931 **1928 Hawaiian — Obverse Improperly Cleaned — NGC Details. Unc.** The obverse was ever-so-slightly cleaned and is just a bit less vibrant than the reverse. Gray patina overall with subtle underlying pastel iridescence. NGC ID# 28KE, PCGS# 9309

4932 **1928 Hawaiian MS63 NGC.** An attractive Select example of this silver commemorative key, with sharply detailed design elements and vibrant mint luster, over mostly brilliant surfaces that show only minor signs of contact. NGC ID# 28KE, PCGS# 9309

4933 **1928 Hawaiian MS64 NGC.** A lovely Choice example of this key silver commemorative, with well-detailed design elements and vibrant mint luster. The lightly marked surfaces show highlights of lavender toning and a few minor signs of contact. NGC ID# 28KE, PCGS# 9309

4934 **1928 Hawaiian MS64 PCGS.** The 1928 Hawaiian Sesquicentennial half dollar saw a distribution of 9,958 circulation strikes plus 50 sandblast proof specimens. Soft gold-tan patination gravitates to the margins of this near-Gem example, and lustrous surfaces exhibit well-struck design elements. Scattered light marks determine the grade. NGC ID# 28KE, PCGS# 9309

1928 Hawaiian Half Dollar, MS65
Key Issue in the Commemorative Series

4935 **1928 Hawaiian MS65 PCGS.** On March 7, 1928, Congress passed legislation providing for the coinage of 10,000 half dollars commemorating the sesquicentennial of Captain Cook's landing at the Hawaiian Islands. The issue has since become one of the most challenging and sought-after dates in the entire classic commemorative series. This carefully preserved Gem displays delicate golden patina at the borders, though most of the surfaces remain brilliant. Sharply struck and minimally marked, only two tiny ticks above the chieftain's hand merit mention. NGC ID# 28KE, PCGS# 9309

1928 Hawaii Half Dollar, MS65
Delicate Peripheral Toning

4936 **1928 Hawaiian MS65 NGC.** Peripheral rings of pastel rainbow colors surround light golden centers on this impressively attractive Gem example. The strike is bold and there are no abrasions of note. The Hawaii Sesquicentennial half dollar had a limited mintage of just 10,008 pieces, and has long been considered a key issue in the classic commemorative series. Few examples have been graded numerically finer than this piece. NGC ID# 28KE, PCGS# 9309

1928 Hawaii Sesquicentennial Half, MS65
Visually Exceptional Representative

4937 **1928 Hawaiian MS65 PCGS.** An immensely appealing high-grade example, this richly toned Gem is layered in violet-gray and amber shades that yield to a thin ring of pastel blue and gold at the borders. Hawaiian half dollars in any grade are sought-after by silver commemorative collectors and Hawaiiana specialists alike, with Gems of course taking on even greater significance.
Ex: Long Beach Signature (Heritage, 6/2006), lot 4473. NGC ID# 28KE, PCGS# 9309

1928 Hawaiian Sesquicentennial Half, MS65
Splendidly Toned

4938 **1928 Hawaiian MS65 PCGS. CAC.** The 1928 Hawaiian half dollar is the key to the silver commemorative series, from a low distribution of 9,958 circulation-strike pieces. This attractive Gem exhibits well-detailed design elements and lustrous surfaces that show few signs of contact under attractive shades of golden-brown and lavender toning. NGC ID# 28KE, PCGS# 9309

4939 **1935 Hudson MS65 PCGS.** Satiny and attractive, with well-defined motifs that are especially sharp on the reverse. Mottled olive and russet peripheral patina is noted on both sides. The smooth, carefully preserved surfaces are nearly flawless. NGC ID# 28KF, PCGS# 9312

4940 **1935 Hudson MS65 PCGS.** Scarce in Gem condition and attractive, the seafaring motifs are well brought up and pearlescent luster beams forth among the devices. Orange and lemon-gold accents appear at the margins to confirm the coin's originality. Housed in a green label holder. NGC ID# 28KF, PCGS# 9312

4941 **1935 Hudson MS66 NGC.** The Hudson commemorative half had a small mintage of 10,008 pieces, and a memorable, imaginative design by Chester Beach. This is a well-produced example with light speckled peripheral toning on each side and beige centers. NGC ID# 28KF, PCGS# 9312

4942 **1935 Hudson MS66 PCGS. CAC.** This is a pleasing representative of the Hudson, New York Sesquicentennial half dollar, with vibrant mint luster and blended pastel hues of sky-blue and champagne toning across each side. It is boldly struck save for some weakness on the figure of Neptune, and the impressively preserved surfaces are blemish-free. Only eleven examples are graded finer than MS66, by PCGS (10/14). NGC ID# 28KF, PCGS# 9312

4943 **1924 Huguenot MS66+ PCGS. CAC.** This high-end Premium Gem offers sharply detailed design elements and impeccably preserved lustrous surfaces, under attractive shades of golden-brown toning. Overall eye appeal is outstanding. NGC ID# 28KG, PCGS# 9314

4944 **1924 Huguenot MS67 PCGS.** Mottled golden-brown and olive toning occurs over the obverse. The reverse is mostly brilliant, save for a crescent of copper-orange color confined to the left-hand margin. Essentially pristine surfaces offer a sharp strike and no mentionable marks. Just two coins are rated numerically finer at PCGS (10/14). NGC ID# 28KG, PCGS# 9314

4945 **1924 Huguenot MS67 NGC.** George T. Morgan's design (modified by James Earl Fraser) is intricately produced on this Superb Gem example, which is for all purposes unavailable any finer. This brilliant, satin-white coin offers untoned and sharply lustrous, mark-free surfaces. NGC has seen no numerically finer pieces, and PCGS shows a mere two coins in higher grade. Census: 53 in 67 (2 in 67+, 4 in 67 ★, 1 in 67+★), 0 finer (10/14). NGC ID# 28KG, PCGS# 9314

4946 **1918 Lincoln MS67 PCGS.** This is a gorgeous Superb Gem example of the Illinois Centennial commemorative half dollar, which is frequently referred to as the "Lincoln" commemorative. The bright, satiny surfaces reveal sharply struck design motifs and attractive layers of variegated, iridescent toning. PCGS# 9320

4947 **1936 Long Island MS67 NGC.** Glowing, frosty luster draws the viewer's eye to the seemingly pristine surfaces of this immensely appealing Long Island Tercentenary half dollar. Subtle champagne and lavender-gray toning graces each side, while a small tinge of rainbow color is noticed along the lower-left obverse periphery. Census: 79 in 67 (2 in 67+, 19 in 67 ★, 3 in 67+★), 4 finer (10/14). NGC ID# 28KL, PCGS# 9322

4948 **1921 Missouri MS65 PCGS.** The bold strike renders a sharp, three-dimensional portrait of the frontiersman, and the coin shows equally well-struck legends across the sloping margins. Combined with the original and colorful iridescent toning, this "plain" Missouri half is compelling and deserving of the Gem grade. Just 38 pieces are certified numerically finer by PCGS (10/14). NGC ID# 28KS, PCGS# 9330

4949 **1921 Missouri 2x4 MS64 PCGS.** Attractive, unusual olive-gold and champagne toning adorns each side of this near-Gem Missouri 2X4 half dollar. It is lustrous, well struck, and free of any large or individually distracting surface flaws. NGC ID# 28KR, PCGS# 9331

4950 **1921 Missouri 2x4 MS65 NGC.** The popular 2x4 variant of the 1921 Missouri half dollar, with sharply detailed design elements and vibrant mint luster, under attractive shades of greenish-gold and turquoise toning. NGC ID# 28KR, PCGS# 9331

4951 **1921 Missouri 2x4 MS65 PCGS.** Deep shades of cinnamon and russet ring the obverse, while the reverse margin shows glints of amber. The high points of each side are largely free of the distracting contact evidence seen on so many examples, accounting for the Gem grade. PCGS has graded only 34 finer pieces (10/14). NGC ID# 28KR, PCGS# 9331

4952 **1921 Missouri 2x4 MS65 PCGS.** This is one of the earlier silver commemorative half dollars, produced in two varieties: this one with 2X4 incused on the obverse, and the other without. This is a stellar Gem example, with bolder-than-usual strike definition and glowing mint luster. NGC ID# 28KR, PCGS# 9331

4953 **1923-S Monroe MS65+ PCGS. CAC.** An impressive, high-quality Gem example with full strike definition and gleaming, satiny luster. Small dabs of speckled russet, gold, and olive patina adorn the immaculately preserved surfaces. NGC ID# 28KT, PCGS# 9333

1923-S Monroe Half Dollar, MS66
Delicate Multicolor Toning

4954 **1923-S Monroe MS66 PCGS.** The Monroe Doctrine Centennial half dollar is characteristically lacking in striking sharpness, and is by extension difficult to locate with pleasing eye appeal. This piece, while not razor-sharp, is better-struck than many, and exhibits beautifully intermingled rainbow toning over each side. No significant abrasions are observed on this conditionally scarce Premium Gem. Population: 77 in 66 (5 in 66+), 6 finer (10/14). NGC ID# 28KT, PCGS# 9333

1923-S Monroe Half Dollar, MS66
Conditionally Scarce Commemorative

4955 **1923-S Monroe MS66 NGC.** The San Francisco Mint struck 274,000 Monroe Doctrine Centennial half dollars in 1923 (plus 77 coins for assay purposes), but large quantities were left unsold and were later paid into circulation at face value, accounting for the rather large numbers of worn pieces known today. The Mint State population declines significantly beyond the MS64 level, and the issue becomes genuinely scarce in MS66. This example shows warm lavender-gold color over the central regions, with deeper mint-green, lemon-gold, and amber-orange toning around the peripheries. Some of the finer design elements are not fully defined, as is usual for this issue, though the surfaces display excellent preservation. Census: 57 in 66 (3 in 66+, 1 in 66 ★, 1 in 66+★), 8 finer (10/14). NGC ID# 28KT, PCGS# 9333

4956 **1936 Norfolk MS68 PCGS.** A beautiful, lustrous, and scarce example of the popular commemorative that celebrates the historical advancements of this Virginia port city, that now acts as home to the Atlantic Fleet of the United States Navy. PCGS and NGC have each certified one finer example (10/14). NGC ID# 28KV, PCGS# 9337

4957 **1926 Oregon MS67 PCGS. CAC.** A highly attractive, sharply struck example of this popular commemorative type. The coin's surfaces are nearly blemish-free, save for a single nick on the Indian's chest, and the overall eye appeal of the piece is enhanced by rich peripheral toning. Population: 90 in 67 (7 in 67+), 3 finer (10/14). NGC ID# 28KW, PCGS# 9340

4958 **1933-D Oregon MS67 PCGS.** The troublesome rims are especially well-struck on this Superb Gem Denver Oregon Trail half, which is boldly struck throughout.. Lustrous blue-steel toning gives way to wheat-gold accents at the edges for terrific appeal. Only a few scattered, tiny marks (none significant) prevent an even higher grade. Housed in a green label holder. NGC ID# 28KZ, PCGS# 9343

4959 **1934-D Oregon MS67 NGC.** The Oregon Trail Memorial, produced between 1926 and 1939, is one of the most popular of all the early silver commemoratives, possibly due to the outstanding design by James Earle Fraser and his wife, Laura Gardin Fraser. This Superb Gem is fully struck and the satiny pearl-gray surfaces display vivid, multicolored iridescence near the obverse border. Census: 25 in 67 (2 in 67+), 0 finer (11/14). NGC ID# 28L2, PCGS# 9344

4960 **1938 Oregon MS67 ★ NGC.** Shimmering, intense luster resides beneath vivid orange and forest-green toning for exceptional eye appeal from this Superb Gem Oregon half. The Star designation by NGC confirms the strong visual allure. Although the coin is boldly struck and technically superior, it will be noticed most for its dramatic, unequaled coloration. NGC ID# 28L6, PCGS# 9348

1938-D Oregon Trail Half, MS68 ★
Magnificent Original Toning

4961 **1938-D Oregon MS68 ★ NGC.** The NGC Star designation recognizes spectacular original toning in blended shades of fire-orange, rose-red, olive, and sun-gold, with the deeper colors most prominent around the margins. The rear-most upright of the wagon is not fully defined, though the strike is otherwise sharp, and the surfaces are devoid of noticeable abrasions. This issue had a mintage of only 6,000 coins (plus five pieces for assay purposes), and is genuinely scarce at this lofty grade level. Census: 61 in 68 (1 in 68+, 35 in 68 ★, 1 in 68+★), 2 finer (10/14). NGC ID# 28L7, PCGS# 9349

1938-S Oregon Trail Half Dollar, MS68 ★
Vividly Appealing Patina

4962 **1938-S Oregon MS68 ★ NGC.** Bold rose-red, fire-gold, sun-orange, and pale olive hues encompass each side of this impeccably preserved Superb Gem, with the deeper colors seen primarily around the margins. A sharp strike adds to the immense visual appeal, complementing the beautifully preserved luster. The San Francisco Mint produced only 6,000 Oregon Trail half dollars in 1938 (plus six coins for assay purposes), and these were distributed in three-coin sets alongside one each from Denver and Philadelphia. The date is readily obtainable in grades through MS67, but MS68 coins are rare, especially with the added Star designation. Census: 21 in 68 (4 in 68 ★), 0 finer (10/14). NGC ID# 28L8, PCGS# 9350

4963 **1915-S Panama-Pacific MS65 NGC.** A superbly toned Gem, with vivid shades of blue, lemon-yellow, reddish bronze, and olive-green covering both sides of the coin. Sharp mint luster shines through, with no serious marks to disturb the dramatic appeal. High-grade examples of this issue abound, but few are as strikingly attractive as this coin. NGC ID# 26H7, PCGS# 9357

4964 **1915-S Panama-Pacific MS65 NGC.** An attractive Gem specimen of this popular commemorative issue, with well-preserved lustrous surfaces that show delicate highlights of pale gold and lavender toning. The design elements are well-detailed and eye appeal is quite strong. NGC ID# 26H7, PCGS# 9357

1915-S Panama-Pacific Half, MS66
Myriad Multicolor Hues

4965 1915-S Panama-Pacific MS66 NGC. Congress authorized 200,000 commemorative half dollars to be struck in conjunction with the Panama-Pacific International Exposition, held in San Francisco in 1915, but only 60,000 were actually struck (plus 30 coins for assay purposes). Of these, more than half (32,896 pieces) were later melted as unsold, leaving a net distribution of only 27,134 examples. Most survivors are only in MS64 and lower grades, with a number of pieces grading as low as the XF to AU range from cleaning and improper handling. Premium Gems are seldom encountered.

This example displays deep multicolor toning in concentric bands on each side, revealing sharp design elements and satiny luster. As the lofty grade suggests, no significant abrasions are observed. NGC ID# 26H7, PCGS# 9357

4966 1915-S/S Panama-Pacific, FS-501, MS65 NGC. The mintmark is repunched east. Peripheral autumn-brown, powder-blue, and apple-green toning endows this lustrous and exceptionally preserved Gem. Prior to World War II, the Panama-Pacific half was regarded as the key silver commemorative type. PCGS# 145748

4967 1921 Pilgrim MS67 PCGS. A beautifully preserved example, this Superb Gem Pilgrim Tercentenary half dollar displays frosty ice-blue luster with small tinges of lemon-gold and amber toning around the peripheries. The strike is crisp throughout, completing the visual appeal. From a mintage of only 20,053 coins. Population: 35 in 67 (2 in 67+), 1 finer (10/14). NGC ID# 28LD, PCGS# 9360

4968 1936 Rhode Island MS67 PCGS. Satiny, light-gray surfaces display a speckling of russet-brown toning, with stronger amber-gold shades over the rims of this 1936 Superb Gem Rhode Island half. Very few marks of any kind appear on the modernistic motifs, which gleam with silver luster. Certified MS67 in a green label holder, with none finer at PCGS. Population: 37 in 67, 0 finer (10/14). NGC ID# 28LE, PCGS# 9363

4969 1936 Robinson MS67 PCGS. The obverse is tab-toned, with peripheral golden-brown patina interrupted at 2 and 8 o'clock. The reverse displays similar shades but adds forest-green along the right margin. Joseph T. Robinson was the Senate Majority Leader when the issue was struck, but the Arkansas politician died the following year. Population: 73 in 67 (1 in 67+), 2 finer (10/14). NGC ID# 28LJ, PCGS# 9369

4970 1926 Sesquicentennial MS65 NGC. Pale lemon-gold and subtle powder-blue hues encompass each side, complementing razor-sharp design elements. Surface abrasions are minimal, though a few faint ticks on Washington's cheek preclude a finer grade. NGC has encapsulated only 19 numerically finer representatives (10/14). NGC ID# 28LM, PCGS# 9374

4971 1926 Sesquicentennial MS65 PCGS. A deeply lustrous example, with a blanket of pale champagne toning giving way to deeper olive and russet hues around the borders. The strike is well-executed and there are no singularly obvious abrasions. Only eight coins are numerically finer at PCGS (10/14). NGC ID# 28LM, PCGS# 9374

4972 1935 Spanish Trail MS64 PCGS. Dusky tan and silver-gray toning embraces this satiny and fully struck Choice half dollar. Perusal beneath a loupe shows only infrequent minor contact. A low mintage type. Certified in a first generation holder. NGC ID# 28LN, PCGS# 9376

4973 1935 Spanish Trail MS65 PCGS. Typically well struck, with pleasing, very light toning, full satin luster, and a few tiny nicks that do virtually nothing to limit the grade or the eye appeal of this Gem. An outstanding example of this popular commemorative type, struck to mark the four hundredth anniversary of the overland trek of Cabeza de Vaca, in 1535, from what would eventually become northern Florida, to the future site of El Paso in far West Texas. Housed in a green label holder.
Ex: Central States Signature (Heritage, 5/2005),lot 8117. NGC ID# 28LN, PCGS# 9376

4974 1935 Spanish Trail MS66 NGC. A rainbow crescent of color covers HALF DOLLAR on this otherwise silver-gray Spanish Trail Premium Gem. Nice luster adds to the appeal of the stark design. The motifs are bold, with a few tiny field marks that are microscopic and non-distracting. NGC ID# 28LN, PCGS# 9376

4975 1935 Spanish Trail MS66 PCGS. The austere motif of the Spanish Trail commemorative half is, in fact, a steer — with the rather haunting visage of a longhorn steer on the obverse and an equally perplexing yucca tree on the reverse. Although not a favorite design of some numismatic experts, the coin was well-received by the public and sold out quickly. This Premium Gem example is lightly iridescent over unmarked, well-struck surfaces. Nice luster flows beneath the silver-gray patina. NGC ID# 28LN, PCGS# 9376

4976 1935 Spanish Trail MS66+ NGC. The soft, satiny luster that is characteristic of the Old Spanish Trail half dollars is especially prevalent on this high-end Premium Gem example. Milky-gray and pale sky-blue toning blankets both sides, masking any minor, grade-determining marks. The extreme left portion of the Texas outline is lacking in definition, though the strike is otherwise sharp. NGC ID# 28LN, PCGS# 9376

4977 1935 Spanish Trail MS66 PCGS. CAC. A beautiful high grade representative. Faint golden patina visits lustrous and smooth surfaces. Numismatist L.W. Hoffecker was the proponent, designer, and distributor for the low mintage type. Certified in a green label holder. NGC ID# 28LN, PCGS# 9376

4978 1925 Stone Mountain MS67 NGC. CAC. This is an outstanding example of the Stone Mountain Memorial half dollar, with well-struck motifs and shimmering mint luster that ensures the splendid eye appeal if the piece. A slight degree of peripheral toning is noted on the obverse. NGC ID# 26H8, PCGS# 9378

1936-D Texas Independence Centennial Half Dollar, MS68
One of the Finest-Known Examples

4979 1936-D Texas MS68 NGC. This popular type was struck to commemorate the independence of Texas in 1836. Just over 9,000 examples were struck, and this example is among the finest survivors. Only two MS68+ coins are rated even finer: one apiece at NGC and PCGS. This piece is fully struck and displays clean, immaculately preserved surfaces with only slight amounts of pale gold-tan toning noted, primarily on the obverse. Census: 12 in 68 (1 in 68 ★), 0 finer (10/14). NGC ID# 28LV, PCGS# 9387

4980 **1925 Vancouver MS66 PCGS.** This Premium Gem Fort Vancouver half offers a refreshing departure from the too-frequent handling marks due to the high-relief motifs and shallow rims. Amber-gold accents frame iridescent, pearl-like silver centers. Highly lustrous on both sides, housed in a green label holder. NGC ID# 28M5, PCGS# 9399

4981 **1925 Vancouver MS66 PCGS. CAC.** Attractive shades of lavender, silver-gray, and apple-green toning blanket the well-preserved surfaces of this delightful Premium Gem. The design elements are sharply detailed and vibrant mint luster shines through the toning. NGC ID# 28M5, PCGS# 9399

4982 **1925 Vancouver MS66 PCGS. CAC.** The 1925 Vancouver half dollar claims a distribution total of 14,994 pieces. This outstanding Premium Gem offers sharply detailed design elements and well-preserved lustrous surfaces under shades of lavender and greenish-gold toning. NGC ID# 28M5, PCGS# 9399

1925 Fort Vancouver Half Dollar
Evenly Toned Superb Gem

4983 **1925 Vancouver MS67 NGC.** Both the bust of Dr. John McLoughlin and the frontiersman are refreshingly free from the abrasions usually seen on this issue, thus the MS67 grade. Both sides are covered with deep reddish-russet toning with bright, sparkling underlying mint luster. Census: 51 in 67 (1 in 67+, 11 in 67 ★), 1 finer (10/14). *Ex: Central States Signature (Heritage, 5/2005), lot 8140; ANA Signature (Heritage, 7/2005), lot 7150; Long Beach Signature (Heritage, 9/2005), lot 4085; Central States Signature (Heritage, 4/2006), lot 5109.* NGC ID# 28M5, PCGS# 9399

4984 **1948-S Booker T. Washington MS67 PCGS. CAC.** The all-brilliant surfaces display a bold strike and frosty luster. This Superb Gem is almost free of post-striking faults, though a degree of planchet roughness affects Washington's jaw, as usually seen. Population: 24 in 67 (3 in 67+), 0 finer (10/14). NGC ID# 28MF, PCGS# 9414

4985 **1951 Booker T. Washington MS67 NGC. CAC.** Dappled cobalt-blue, golden-brown, and crimson toning resides on the radiantly lustrous surfaces of this sharply struck Superb Gem. The CAC sticker affirms the pleasing eye appeal. Census: 10 in 67 (1 in 67 ★), 1 finer (10/14). NGC ID# 28MN, PCGS# 9424

1951-S Washington-Carver Half, MS67
Nice Peripheral Toning

4986 **1951-S Washington-Carver MS67 PCGS. CAC.** The net distribution of this issue was a hair more than 10,000 pieces, but this piece is nonetheless one of only three Superb Gems graded at PCGS. Pale pastel rainbow iridescence appears on the right margins of each side, with pale silver-gold centers and outstanding preservation throughout. Population: 3 in 67 (1 in 67+), 0 finer (10/14). NGC ID# 28MU, PCGS# 9432

COMMEMORATIVE GOLD

4987 **1903 Louisiana Purchase, Jefferson, MS65 PCGS.** Vivid silver-blue margins surround the satiny gold centers of this two-tone Jefferson Head Louisiana Purchase gold dollar. Strong mint luster and a full strike make the coin nearly unimprovable for the Gem grade. Housed in a green label holder. NGC ID# 26HA, PCGS# 7443

4988 **1903 Louisiana Purchase, Jefferson, MS66+ PCGS. CAC.** Two varieties of the first U.S. commemorative gold coins were produced in 1903 for the Louisiana Purchase Exposition in St. Louis. Both were gold dollars: one featuring a portrait of Thomas Jefferson and the other a portrait of the recently-assassinated William McKinley. This is an intensely lustrous example with lovely peach-gold toning and well-preserved surfaces. NGC ID# 26HA, PCGS# 7443

1904 Lewis and Clark Gold Dollar
Radiantly Lustrous Gem Example

4989 **1904 Lewis and Clark MS65 PCGS.** Apricot-gold and pale mint-yellow hues intermingle across each side of this shimmering Gem. A few minute luster grazes limit the numeric grade, but the overall eye appeal is nonetheless outstanding. The strike is bold, and only a few of the usual metal flow lines are seen in the peripheral recesses. The 1904 Lewis and Clark gold dollar is more easily obtainable in high grade than its 1905 counterpart, making it ideal for the classic commemorative type collector. NGC ID# 26HC, PCGS# 7447

4990 **1915-S Panama-Pacific Gold Dollar MS65 PCGS.** Lustrous, frosted surfaces flash subtle orange and green accents. Charles Keck's design is fully rendered, with bold details and considerable eye appeal. Housed in a green label holder. NGC ID# 26HE, PCGS# 7449

4991 **1915-S Panama-Pacific Gold Dollar MS66 NGC.** Rich and unusual color is a highlight of this Panama-Pacific Premium Gem. Deep orange-gold hues are distinctive enough, but the prominent pink and blue accents put this piece over the top. NGC ID# 26HE, PCGS# 7449

4992 **1915-S Panama-Pacific Gold Dollar MS66 PCGS.** This lustrous Premium Gem is highly attractive and better-struck than usual for this popular commemorative gold dollar, notably on the obverse portrait and the reverse dolphins. Free of surface marks and toned in pleasing hues of apricot-gold and mint-green. NGC ID# 26HE, PCGS# 7449

4993 **1915-S Panama-Pacific Quarter Eagle — Improperly Cleaned — NGC Details. Unc.** This straw-gold representative exhibits full design detail but the luster is subdued. The fields display myriad die polish lines but no hairlines are evident. NGC ID# 26HK, PCGS# 7450

4994 **1916 McKinley MS65 PCGS.** McKinley gold dollars were struck in both 1916 and 1917, with 10,000 more coins distributed in 1916 than 1917. This example is partially prooflike with rich, orange-gold color. One or two microscopic obverse marks are the only visible distractions. NGC ID# 26HF, PCGS# 7454

4995 **1916 McKinley MS65 NGC.** The McKinley gold dollars were struck in order to finance a memorial to the assassinated president in his hometown. The Gem example has a frosty, elegant appearance, with lovely antique-gold and pale greenish coloration. A single tiny mark is noted on the lower obverse. NGC ID# 26HF, PCGS# 7454

4996 **1916 McKinley MS66 PCGS.** From a small distribution of under 10,000 pieces, this delightful Premium Gem displays sharply detailed design elements and vibrant mint luster throughout. The well-preserved yellow-gold surfaces add to the outstanding eye appeal. NGC ID# 26HF, PCGS# 7454

4997 **1916 McKinley MS66 PCGS. CAC.** This is an exceptional example of the first of two McKinley gold dollar issues, produced in 1916 and 1917. The striking definition is full on each side, and the luster quality of the coin is stellar. Surface preservation is also outstanding, and a pair of wispy die striations on the lower reverse, just above L in MEMORIAL, should not be mistaken for scratches. NGC ID# 26HF, PCGS# 7454

1916 McKinley Memorial Gold Dollar
Outstanding Superb Gem Example

4998 **1916 McKinley MS67 PCGS.** Conventional information suggests that of the 20,000 1916 McKinley Memorial gold dollars struck (plus 26 coins for assay purposes), only 9,977 examples were ever distributed. More likely, however, the distribution total was closer to the 15,000-coin mark, the estimate published in the *Guide Book*. This example displays soft tinges of honey and rose over luminous green-gold luster. The strike is sharp and the surfaces are seemingly pristine. Population: 86 in 67 (1 in 67+), 0 finer (10/14). NGC ID# 26HF, PCGS# 7454

4999 **1917 McKinley MS65 PCGS.** Just 5,000 coins were distributed for the 1917 McKinley gold dollar despite a mintage of 10,000 pieces. The unsold coins were melted. This deeply lustrous Gem example survived with frosted surfaces and sharp details on McKinley's hair. Lime-green and orange highlights add life to the light-gold coloration. NGC ID# 26HG, PCGS# 7455

1917 McKinley Memorial Gold Dollar
Heavily Frosted Superb Gem

5000 **1917 McKinley MS67 PCGS.** The 1917 McKinley Memorial gold dollar had an estimated distribution of only 5,000 coins, and is somewhat scarcer overall than its more frequently seen 1916 counterpart. This Superb Gem example is among the finest certified, showing frosty wheat-gold luster and well-struck devices. A couple microscopic marks in the upper-left obverse field appear to be the only grade-limiting factors on this eye-appealing representative. Population: 68 in 67 (2 in 67+), 0 finer (10/14). NGC ID# 26HG, PCGS# 7455

5001 **1922 Grant No Star MS63 PCGS.** A bright and lustrous example that is well struck aside from the tree trunk near the window. A planchet flaw (as made) affects GRANT, and is a minor mint error that is unusual for a Gold Commemorative. This glowing gold dollar has the eye appeal of an even higher grade. *Ex: Long Beach Signature (Heritage, 3/2003), lot 8753, which brought $1,380.00.* NGC ID# 26HJ, PCGS# 7458

5002 **1922 Grant No Star MS65 PCGS.** Struck to help raise funds for the Grant Memorial buildings near Cincinnati, most surviving pieces of the starless version are well-struck and attractive. This Gem example is especially well-made. Light yellow-gold color is enriched by orange highlights. The coin is brilliant and frosty with a bold details on Grant's hair and on the tree canopy above Grant's birth home in Point Pleasant, Ohio. NGC ID# 26HJ, PCGS# 7458

5003 **1922 Grant No Star MS65 PCGS.** With the identical mintage to the popular With Star variety, the No Star Grant gold dollar is equally appreciated by series collectors for its own merits. This sharply lustrous coin is certainly the equal of any Gem Grant dollar, With Star or No Star. Exceptionally smooth surfaces display bold devices and virtually unmarked fields. Orange accents enhance the vivid-gold patina. Housed in a green label holder. NGC ID# 26HJ, PCGS# 7458

1922 Grant Memorial Gold Dollar
Tack-Sharp MS66+

5004 **1922 Grant No Star MS66+ PCGS. CAC.** With a limited distribution of only 5,000 coins, the No Star Grant Memorial Gold dollar is understandably elusive in Premium Gem and finer condition. This Plus-graded example boasts razor-sharp definition and frosty lemon-gold luster. Close examination fails to reveal any discernable signs of contact, making this piece seem upper-end for the grade. NGC ID# 26HJ, PCGS# 7458

5005 **1922 Grant With Star AU55 NGC.** An attractive example of the Grant With Star gold dollar, with well-struck design motifs and mere traces of wear on Grant's hair and beard. Each side displays an overlay of bronze patina. There are no distracting marks to be seen. NGC ID# 26HH, PCGS# 7459

5006 **1922 Grant With Star MS65 PCGS. CAC.** Two distinct varieties exist for this commemorative issue, one with a star on the obverse and one without. Both types saw a total production of 5,106 pieces, including assay coins. This Gem example is sharply struck with gleaming luster and bright yellow-green toning. The surfaces are well-preserved and mark-free. Housed in a green label holder. NGC ID# 26HH, PCGS# 7459

1922 With Star Grant Gold Dollar
Two-Toned Superb Gem

5007 **1922 Grant With Star MS67 PCGS.** A unique combination of deep lemon-apricot and frosty mint-gold luster encompasses each side of this Superb Gem With Star Grant Memorial gold dollar. The relief elements are sharply brought up, and the surfaces are devoid of obtrusive abrasions. PCGS has encapsulated only a single numerically finer representative (10/14). NGC ID# 26HH, PCGS# 7459

1926 Sesquicentennial Quarter Eagle, MS65+
Luminescent Mint Luster

5008 **1926 Sesquicentennial MS65+ PCGS. CAC.** A well-struck, frosty example of this American Independence commemorative. Liberty is portrayed on the obverse with depictions of freedom (a torch) and the Declaration of Independence (a scroll); the reverse shows a reproduction of Independence Hall in Philadelphia, where the Declaration was signed in July 1776. The shallow relief of the design allows the mint luster to cartwheel freely around each side, delivering superb visual appeal. NGC ID# 26HL, PCGS# 7466

1926 Sesquicentennial Quarter Eagle, MS65+
Immensely Appealing for the Grade

5009 **1926 Sesquicentennial MS65+ PCGS. CAC.** Eye-catching frosty mint luster delivers impressive appeal on this high-end Gem example, while the strike is sharp and the surfaces are carefully preserved. The Sesquicentennial quarter eagle is the final gold issue in the classic commemorative series, and one of only two such pieces within the quarter eagle denomination. NGC ID# 26HL, PCGS# 7466

End of Session Four

SESSION FIVE

SPECIAL INTERNET BIDDING FEATURE

Online proxy bidding ends at HA.com two hours prior to the opening of the live auction. After proxy bidding closes, live bidding will take place through HERITAGE Live!®, that lets you bid live during the actual auction. (Important note: Due to software and Internet latency, bids placed through Live Internet Bidding may not register in time and those bids will not be recognized, so we advise placing your proxy bids in advance.)

COLONIALS

7001 1652 Pine Tree Shilling, Small Planchet — Damaged — PCGS Genuine. Poor/Fair Details. 63.88 grs. NGC Census: (0/98). PCGS Population (0/351).

7002 (1688) American Plantations 1/24 Part Real AU55 PCGS. PCGS Population (6/31). NGC Census: (1/4). PCGS# 49

7003 1722 Rosa Americana With Period, Twopence VF25 NGC. NGC Census: (0/1). PCGS Population (1/11). PCGS# 116

7004 1723 Rosa Americana Penny AU55 PCGS. PCGS Population (8/27). NGC Census: (6/7). PCGS# 125

7005 1723 Rosa Americana Twopence AU50 PCGS. PCGS Population (15/66). NGC Census: (0/0). PCGS# 128

7006 1723 Hibernia Farthing, DEI GRATIA MS63 Brown NGC. NGC Census: (8/8). PCGS Population (42/25). PCGS# 176

7007 1723 Hibernia Halfpenny MS64 Red and Brown PCGS. PCGS Population (22/9). NGC Census: (2/2). PCGS# 181

7008 1724 Hibernia Halfpenny AU53 PCGS. CAC. PCGS Population (4/16). NGC Census: (3/4). PCGS# 190

7009 1760 Hibernia-Voce Populi Halfpenny VF35 PCGS. PCGS Population (33/167). NGC Census: (10/60). PCGS# 262

7010 1785 Connecticut Copper, African Bust Right Fine 15 NGC. CAC. NGC Census: (2/11). PCGS Population (4/33). PCGS# 319

7011 1786 Connecticut Copper, Small Head Right, ETLIB INDE VF20 PCGS. CAC. PCGS Population (4/10). NGC Census: (0/0). PCGS# 325

7012 1788 Connecticut Copper, Mailed Bust Right — Environmental Damage — PCGS Genuine. VF Details. M.2-D, W-4405, R.1. NGC Census: (3/27). PCGS Population (6/44).

7013 1788 Connecticut Copper, Mailed Bust Right AU50 NGC. Miller 2-D. Ex: The Old New England Collection. NGC Census: (1/4). PCGS Population (4/2). PCGS# 397

7014 1788 Connecticut Copper, Mailed Bust Right AU50 PCGS. PCGS Population (4/2). NGC Census: (1/4). PCGS# 397

7015 1788 Connecticut Copper, Mailed Bust Left XF40 PCGS. PCGS Population (6/13). NGC Census: (2/9). PCGS# 403

7016 1788 Connecticut Copper, Draped Bust Left XF45 NGC. NGC Census: (3/7). PCGS Population (10/7). PCGS# 409

7017 1787 Nova Eborac Copper, Seated Left — Environmental Damage — NCS. AU Details. NGC Census: (2/4). PCGS Population (7/22).

7018 1787 New Jersey Copper, Outlined Shield VF35 NGC. NGC Census: (8/26). PCGS Population (31/115). PCGS# 503

7019 1783 Nova Constellatio Copper, Pointed Rays, Small US XF40 PCGS. PCGS Population (22/81). NGC Census: (5/29). PCGS# 801

7020 1785 Nova Constellatio Copper, Pointed Rays, Large Date XF40 PCGS. PCGS Population (43/121). NGC Census: (9/35). PCGS# 813

7021 1787 Fugio Cent, UNITED STATES, No Cinquefoils, Cross After Date, Good 4 PCGS. CAC. PCGS Population (2/56). NGC Census: (1/5). PCGS# 880

7022 1787 Fugio Cent, UNITED STATES, Cinquefoils Fine 12 PCGS. PCGS Population (12/291). NGC Census: (5/68). PCGS# 889

7023 1787 Fugio Cent, UNITED STATES, Cinquefoils Fine 15 PCGS. PCGS Population (12/279). NGC Census: (4/64). PCGS# 889

7024 (1792-94) Kentucky Token, LANCASTER Edge MS62 Brown PCGS. PCGS Population (15/61). NGC Census: (14/20). PCGS# 623

7025 (1792-94) Kentucky Token, LANCASTER Edge MS63 Brown PCGS. PCGS Population (37/24). NGC Census: (12/8). PCGS# 623

7026 1794 Franklin Press Token AU53 PCGS. PCGS Population (21/148). NGC Census: (3/75). PCGS# 630

7027 1795 Talbot Allum & Lee Cent AU58 PCGS. PCGS Population (34/131). NGC Census: (14/45). PCGS# 640

7028 1795 Talbot Allum & Lee Cent AU58 NGC. CAC. NGC Census: (14/45). PCGS Population (34/131). PCGS# 640

7029 1794 Talbot/Howe AU55 PCGS. PCGS Population (2/3). NGC Census: (0/0). PCGS# 979

7030 1783 Washington Unity States Cent AU50 PCGS. PCGS Population (45/92). NGC Census: (12/61). PCGS# 689

7031 Undated Washington Double Head Cent AU50 PCGS. CAC. PCGS Population (34/85). NGC Census: (4/45). PCGS# 692

7032 Undated Washington Double Head Cent AU53 PCGS. PCGS Population (22/63). NGC Census: (8/37). PCGS# 692

7033 **1791 Washington Large Eagle Cent XF40 PCGS.** PCGS Population (10/154). NGC Census: (3/43). PCGS# 702

7034 **1791 Washington Small Eagle Cent AU50 PCGS.** PCGS Population (17/160). NGC Census: (1/49). PCGS# 705

7035 **1795 Washington Grate Halfpenny, Large Buttons, Reeded Edge MS62 Brown PCGS.** PCGS Population (45/83). NGC Census: (12/28). PCGS# 746

7036 **1795 Washington Liberty & Security Halfpenny, Plain Edge XF40 PCGS.** PCGS Population (3/13). NGC Census: (0/2). PCGS# 752

7037 **1795 Washington North Wales Halfpenny, Plain Edge, One Star at Each Side of Harp XF40 PCGS.** PCGS Population (15/28). NGC Census: (3/7). PCGS# 770

HALF CENTS

7038 **1795 Lettered Edge, C-1, B-1, R.2, — Scratch — PCGS Genuine. VF Details.** NGC Census: (1/8). PCGS Population (0/5). Mintage: 139,690.

7039 **1795 LE Punctuated Date Good 4 PCGS.** PCGS Population (1/24). NGC Census: (0/0). PCGS# 1015

7040 **1795 Plain Edge, No Pole, Thin Planchet, C-6a, B-6a, R.2, VG8 Brown NGC.** NGC Census: (0/6). PCGS Population (2/11). PCGS# 35089

7041 **1800 XF40 PCGS.** PCGS Population (26/131). NGC Census: (0/0). Mintage: 202,908. Numismedia Wsl. Price for problem free NGC/PCGS coin in XF40: $550. NGC ID# 222B, PCGS# 1051

7042 **1804 Plain 4, No Stems, C-13, B-10, R.1, AU53 NGC.** NGC Census: (11/86). PCGS Population (0/11). Mintage: 1,055,312. PCGS# 35176

7043 **1805 No Stems, C-1, B-1, R.1, — Damage — PCGS Genuine. AU Details.** NGC Census: (0/21). PCGS Population (0/4).

7044 **1806 Large 6, Stems, C-4, B-4, R.1, AU58 Brown NGC.** NGC Census: (0/0). PCGS Population (0/0). PCGS# 35200

7045 **1809 AU58 PCGS.** PCGS Population (25/56). NGC Census: (60/97). Mintage: 1,154,572. Numismedia Wsl. Price for problem free NGC/PCGS coin in AU58: $450. NGC ID# 222P, PCGS# 1123

7046 **1811 — Smoothed — PCGS Genuine. VF Details.** NGC Census: (6/19). PCGS Population (11/74). Mintage: 63,140. Numismedia Wsl. Price for problem free NGC/PCGS coin in VF20: $2,125.

7047 **1826 MS63 Brown PCGS.** PCGS Population (35/31). NGC Census: (14/21). Mintage: 234,000. Numismedia Wsl. Price for problem free NGC/PCGS coin in MS63: $800. NGC ID# 222U, PCGS# 1144

7048 **1833 MS63 Brown PCGS. CAC.** PCGS Population (80/92). NGC Census: (0/0). Mintage: 120,000. Numismedia Wsl. Price for problem free NGC/PCGS coin in MS63: $525. NGC ID# 222Z, PCGS# 1162

7049 **1835 MS64 Brown PCGS.** PCGS Population (118/25). NGC Census: (122/53). Mintage: 398,000. Numismedia Wsl. Price for problem free NGC/PCGS coin in MS64: $600. NGC ID# 2233, PCGS# 1168

7050 **1850 C-1, B-1, R.2, MS63 Brown NGC.** NGC Census: (27/19). PCGS Population (0/2). Mintage: 39,800. PCGS# 35321

LARGE CENTS

7051 **1794 Head of 1794, S-43, B-32, R.2, Good 6 NGC.** NGC Census: (2/13). PCGS Population (0/5). PCGS# 35594

7052 **1795 Lettered Edge, S-74, B-2, Low R.4, VG10 NGC.** NGC Census: (2/3). PCGS Population (0/4). Mintage: 37,000. PCGS# 35714

7053 **1798 First Hair Style VF20 NGC.** NGC Census: (13/106). PCGS Population (21/117). Mintage: 1,841,745. Numismedia Wsl. Price for problem free NGC/PCGS coin in VF20: $865. NGC ID# 2244, PCGS# 1431

7054 **1798 Second Hair Style, S-170, B-29, R.3, — Graffiti — PCGS Genuine. VF Details.** NGC Census: (2/3). PCGS Population (0/4).

7055 **1801 S-213, B-1, R.2, Fine 15 PCGS.** PCGS Population (1/5). NGC Census: (1/2). PCGS# 36236

7056 **1802 No Stems, S-231, B-9, R.1, — Environmental Damage — PCGS Genuine. AU Details.** NGC Census: (0/0). PCGS Population (0/3).

7057 **1805 S-267, B-1, R.1, — Tooled — PCGS Genuine. XF Details.** NGC Census: (4/10). PCGS Population (1/5).

7058 **1811 S-287, B-1, R.2, Fine 15 NGC.** NGC Census: (5/40). PCGS Population (1/8). PCGS# 36496

7059 **1813 — Tooled — PCGS Genuine. XF Details.** NGC Census: (6/58). PCGS Population (17/64). Mintage: 418,000. Numismedia Wsl. Price for problem free NGC/PCGS coin in XF40: $1,550.

7060 **1816 MS61 Brown NGC.** NGC Census: (6/86). PCGS Population (3/135). Mintage: 2,820,982. Numismedia Wsl. Price for problem free NGC/PCGS coin in MS61: $500. NGC ID# 224Z, PCGS# 1591

7061 **1817 13 Stars MS61 Brown NGC.** NGC Census: (15/81). PCGS Population (4/122). Mintage: 3,948,400. Numismedia Wsl. Price for problem free NGC/PCGS coin in MS61: $550. NGC ID# 2252, PCGS# 1594

7062 **1818 AU58 PCGS. CAC.** PCGS Population (83/344). NGC Census: (43/322). Mintage: 3,167,000. Numismedia Wsl. Price for problem free NGC/PCGS coin in AU58: $325. NGC ID# 2253, PCGS# 1600

7063 **1818 MS62 Brown NGC.** NGC Census: (94/199). PCGS Population (116/202). Mintage: 3,167,000. Numismedia Wsl. Price for problem free NGC/PCGS coin in MS62: $550. NGC ID# 2253, PCGS# 1600

7064 **1818 MS63 Brown PCGS.** PCGS Population (141/61). NGC Census: (103/96). Mintage: 3,167,000. Numismedia Wsl. Price for problem free NGC/PCGS coin in MS63: $650. NGC ID# 2253, PCGS# 1600

7065 **1818 MS63 Red and Brown PCGS.** PCGS Population (137/45). NGC Census: (66/53). Mintage: 3,167,000. Numismedia Wsl. Price for problem free NGC/PCGS coin in MS63: $775. NGC ID# 2253, PCGS# 1601

7066 **1824 AU50 PCGS.** PCGS Population (10/51). NGC Census: (4/26). Mintage: 1,262,000. Numismedia Wsl. Price for problem free NGC/PCGS coin in AU50: $800. NGC ID# 225D, PCGS# 1636

7067 **1830 Large Letters AU58 PCGS. CAC.** PCGS Population (18/35). NGC Census: (11/13). Mintage: 1,711,500. Numismedia Wsl. Price for problem free NGC/PCGS coin in AU58: $475. NGC ID# 225L, PCGS# 1672

7068 **1831 Large Letters MS63 Brown NGC.** NGC Census: (18/25). PCGS Population (23/14). Mintage: 3,359,260. Numismedia Wsl. Price for problem free NGC/PCGS coin in MS63: $650. NGC ID# 225M, PCGS# 1678

7069 **1843 Mature Head, Large Letters, MS62 Brown PCGS.** PCGS Population (4/5). NGC Census: (0/0). PCGS# 1850

7070 **1846 Small Date MS63 Brown PCGS.** PCGS Population (41/43). NGC Census: (41/62). Mintage: 4,120,800. Numismedia Wsl. Price for problem free NGC/PCGS coin in MS63: $380. NGC ID# 226C, PCGS# 1865

7071 **1846 Small Date, N-6, R.1, MS65 Brown NGC.** NGC Census: (5/3). PCGS Population (1/0). Mintage: 4,120,800. PCGS# 403868

7072 **1847 MS64 Brown PCGS.** PCGS Population (52/15). NGC Census: (55/29). Mintage: 6,183,669. Numismedia Wsl. Price for problem free NGC/PCGS coin in MS64: $535. NGC ID# 226D, PCGS# 1877

7073 **1850 MS65 Red and Brown PCGS.** PCGS Population (99/2). NGC Census: (107/23). Mintage: 4,426,844. Numismedia Wsl. Price for problem free NGC/PCGS coin in MS65: $1,125. NGC ID# 226G, PCGS# 1890

7074 **1851 MS65 Brown PCGS. CAC.** PCGS Population (67/14). NGC Census: (119/50). Mintage: 9,889,707. Numismedia Wsl. Price for problem free NGC/PCGS coin in MS65: $675. NGC ID# 226H, PCGS# 1892

7075 **1852 MS63 Brown PCGS.** PCGS Population (115/296). NGC Census: (101/328). Mintage: 5,063,094. Numismedia Wsl. Price for problem free NGC/PCGS coin in MS63: $250. NGC ID# 226J, PCGS# 1898

7076 **1853 MS64 Red and Brown PCGS.** PCGS Population (225/101). NGC Census: (162/158). Mintage: 6,641,131. Numismedia Wsl. Price for problem free NGC/PCGS coin in MS64: $560. NGC ID# 226K, PCGS# 1902

7077 **1854 MS65 Brown PCGS. CAC.** PCGS Population (41/10). NGC Census: (86/23). Mintage: 4,236,156. Numismedia Wsl. Price for problem free NGC/PCGS coin in MS65: $665. NGC ID# 226L, PCGS# 1904

7078 **1855 Upright 5s MS64 Red and Brown PCGS.** PCGS Population (174/77). NGC Census: (84/121). Mintage: 1,574,829. Numismedia Wsl. Price for problem free NGC/PCGS coin in MS64: $575. NGC ID# 226M, PCGS# 1908

7079 **1855 Upright 5s MS64 Red and Brown PCGS. CAC.** PCGS Population (174/77). NGC Census: (84/121). Mintage: 1,574,829. Numismedia Wsl. Price for problem free NGC/PCGS coin in MS64: $575. NGC ID# 226M, PCGS# 1908

7080 **1855 Slanted 55, Knob Ear, N-9, R.1, AU55 PCGS. CAC.** PCGS Population (2/4). NGC Census: (8/76). PCGS# 403958

7081 **1856 Upright 5 MS65 Red and Brown NGC.** NGC Census: (85/13). PCGS Population (34/1). Mintage: 2,690,463. Numismedia Wsl. Price for problem free NGC/PCGS coin in MS65: $975. NGC ID# 226N, PCGS# 1920

FLYING EAGLE CENTS

7082 **1857 MS62 NGC.** NGC Census: (329/1719). PCGS Population (439/2029). Mintage: 17,450,000. Numismedia Wsl. Price for problem free NGC/PCGS coin in MS62: $520. NGC ID# 2276, PCGS# 2016

7083 **1857 MS63 PCGS.** PCGS Population (806/1223). NGC Census: (544/1175). Mintage: 17,450,000. Numismedia Wsl. Price for problem free NGC/PCGS coin in MS63: $860. NGC ID# 2276, PCGS# 2016

INDIAN CENTS

7084 **1859 MS63 NGC.** NGC Census: (3/8). PCGS Population (550/798). Mintage: 36,400,000. Numismedia Wsl. Price for problem free NGC/PCGS coin in MS63: $600. NGC ID# 227E, PCGS# 2052

7085 **1864 Bronze No L MS65 Red and Brown PCGS.** PCGS Population (208/25). NGC Census: (243/74). Mintage: 39,233,712. Numismedia Wsl. Price for problem free NGC/PCGS coin in MS65: $440. NGC ID# 227L, PCGS# 2077

7086 **1870 MS63 Brown NGC.** NGC Census: (45/66). PCGS Population (28/36). Mintage: 5,275,000. Numismedia Wsl. Price for problem free NGC/PCGS coin in MS63: $550. NGC ID# 227U, PCGS# 2097

7087 **1872 MS62 Brown PCGS.** PCGS Population (28/93). NGC Census: (65/103). Mintage: 4,042,000. Numismedia Wsl. Price for problem free NGC/PCGS coin in MS62: $700. NGC ID# 227W, PCGS# 2103

7088 **1873 Doubled LIBERTY, Snow-1, FS-101, — Obverse Scratched — NGC Details. XF.** NGC Census: (0/0). PCGS Population (0/6).

7089 **1874 MS65 Brown PCGS. CAC.** PCGS Population (11/0). NGC Census: (25/1). Mintage: 14,187,500. Numismedia Wsl. Price for problem free NGC/PCGS coin in MS65: $440. NGC ID# 227Z, PCGS# 2118

7090 **1874 MS65 Red and Brown PCGS.** PCGS Population (104/3). NGC Census: (110/23). Mintage: 14,187,500. Numismedia Wsl. Price for problem free NGC/PCGS coin in MS65: $650. NGC ID# 227Z, PCGS# 2119

7091 **1874 MS65 Red and Brown PCGS.** PCGS Population (104/3). NGC Census: (110/23). Mintage: 14,187,500. Numismedia Wsl. Price for problem free NGC/PCGS coin in MS65: $650. NGC ID# 227Z, PCGS# 2119

7092 **1876 MS65+ Red and Brown NGC.** NGC Census: (98/13). PCGS Population (77/2). Mintage: 7,944,000. Numismedia Wsl. Price for problem free NGC/PCGS coin in MS65: $925. NGC ID# 2283, PCGS# 2125

7093 **1877 VG10 NGC.** NGC Census: (184/1292). PCGS Population (345/2065). Mintage: 852,500. Numismedia Wsl. Price for problem free NGC/PCGS coin in VG10: $759. NGC ID# 2284, PCGS# 2127

7094 **1877 VG10 NGC.** NGC Census: (184/1292). PCGS Population (345/2065). Mintage: 852,500. Numismedia Wsl. Price for problem free NGC/PCGS coin in VG10: $759. NGC ID# 2284, PCGS# 2127

7095 **1877 Fine 15 NGC.** NGC Census: (109/1023). PCGS Population (217/1602). Mintage: 852,500. Numismedia Wsl. Price for problem free NGC/PCGS coin in Fine 15: $1,039. NGC ID# 2284, PCGS# 2127

7096 **1877 Fine 15 ANACS.** NGC Census: (109/1023). PCGS Population (217/1602). Mintage: 852,500. Numismedia Wsl. Price for problem free NGC/PCGS coin in Fine 15: $1,039. NGC ID# 2284, PCGS# 2127

7097 **1878 MS64 Red and Brown PCGS. CAC.** PCGS Population (229/91). NGC Census: (154/108). Mintage: 5,799,850. Numismedia Wsl. Price for problem free NGC/PCGS coin in MS64: $500. NGC ID# 2285, PCGS# 2131

7098 **1886 Type Two MS64 Red and Brown NGC.** NGC Census: (74/35). PCGS Population (126/26). Numismedia Wsl. Price for problem free NGC/PCGS coin in MS64: $1,000. NGC ID# 228E, PCGS# 92155

7099 **1891 MS65 Red and Brown PCGS.** PCGS Population (27/0). NGC Census: (69/5). Mintage: 47,072,352. Numismedia Wsl. Price for problem free NGC/PCGS coin in MS65: $400. NGC ID# 228K, PCGS# 2179

7100 **1897 MS65 Red NGC.** NGC Census: (28/10). PCGS Population (55/18). Mintage: 50,466,328. Numismedia Wsl. Price for problem free NGC/PCGS coin in MS65: $900. NGC ID# 228S, PCGS# 2198

7101 **1909 MS65 Red PCGS.** PCGS Population (643/166). NGC Census: (252/35). Mintage: 14,370,645. Numismedia Wsl. Price for problem free NGC/PCGS coin in MS65: $430. NGC ID# 2297, PCGS# 2237

7102 **1909 MS65 Red PCGS.** PCGS Population (643/166). NGC Census: (252/35). Mintage: 14,370,645. Numismedia Wsl. Price for problem free NGC/PCGS coin in MS65: $430. NGC ID# 2297, PCGS# 2237

7103 **1909-S XF40 PCGS.** PCGS Population (362/918). NGC Census: (182/786). Mintage: 309,000. Numismedia Wsl. Price for problem free NGC/PCGS coin in XF40: $550. NGC ID# 2298, PCGS# 2238

7104 **1909-S — Improperly Cleaned — NGC Details. AU.** NGC Census: (54/499). PCGS Population (118/542). Mintage: 309,000. Numismedia Wsl. Price for problem free NGC/PCGS coin in AU50: $640.

7105 **1909-S — Improperly Cleaned — NGC Details. AU.** NGC Census: (54/499). PCGS Population (118/542). Mintage: 309,000. Numismedia Wsl. Price for problem free NGC/PCGS coin in AU50: $640.

PROOF INDIAN CENTS

7106 **1859 — Spot Removed — PCGS Proof Genuine. Unc Details.** NGC Census: (0/170). PCGS Population (0/257). Mintage: 800. Numismedia Wsl. Price for problem free NGC/PCGS coin in PR60: $475.

7107 **1865 PR64 Red and Brown PCGS.** PCGS Population (70/29). NGC Census: (34/38). Mintage: 500. Numismedia Wsl. Price for problem free NGC/PCGS coin in PR64: $675. NGC ID# 229H, PCGS# 2283

7108 **1876 PR65 Brown NGC.** NGC Census: (9/6). PCGS Population (5/5). Mintage: 1,150. Numismedia Wsl. Price for problem free NGC/PCGS coin in PR65: $340. NGC ID# 229V, PCGS# 2315

7109 **1887 PR65 Red and Brown PCGS. CAC.** PCGS Population (54/10). NGC Census: (48/16). Mintage: 2,960. Numismedia Wsl. Price for problem free NGC/PCGS coin in PR65: $575. NGC ID# 22A9, PCGS# 2349

7110 **1889 PR66 Brown PCGS.** PCGS Population (11/2). NGC Census: (21/0). Mintage: 3,336. Numismedia Wsl. Price for problem free NGC/PCGS coin in PR66: $520. NGC ID# 2732, PCGS# 2354

7111 **1900 PR65 Red NGC.** NGC Census: (15/14). PCGS Population (28/20). Mintage: 2,262. Numismedia Wsl. Price for problem free NGC/PCGS coin in PR65: $875. NGC ID# 22AN, PCGS# 2389

LINCOLN CENTS

7112 **1909-S VDB VG8 ANACS.** NGC Census: (102/5555). PCGS Population (123/9380). Mintage: 484,000. Numismedia Wsl. Price for problem free NGC/PCGS coin in VG8: $620. NGC ID# 22B2, PCGS# 2426

7113 **1909-S VDB VF25 NGC.** NGC Census: (363/3594). PCGS Population (680/6528). Mintage: 484,000. Numismedia Wsl. Price for problem free NGC/PCGS coin in VF25: $733. NGC ID# 22B2, PCGS# 2426

7114 **1909-S VDB VF30 PCGS.** PCGS Population (769/5759). NGC Census: (357/3237). Mintage: 484,000. Numismedia Wsl. Price for problem free NGC/PCGS coin in VF30: $776. NGC ID# 22B2, PCGS# 2426

7115 **1909-S VDB — Obverse Scratched — NGC Details. AU.** NGC Census: (151/2008). PCGS Population (457/2756). Mintage: 484,000. Numismedia Wsl. Price for problem free NGC/PCGS coin in AU50: $1,000.

7116 **1909-S VDB — Polished — PCGS Genuine. AU Details.** NGC Census: (151/2003). PCGS Population (457/2748). Mintage: 484,000. Numismedia Wsl. Price for problem free NGC/PCGS coin in AU50: $1,000.

7117 **1909-S VDB — Improperly Cleaned — NGC Details. Unc.** NGC Census: (2/1092). PCGS Population (15/1176). Mintage: 484,000. Numismedia Wsl. Price for problem free NGC/PCGS coin in MS60: $1,340.

7118 **1909-S VDB — Questionable Color — PCGS Genuine. Unc Details.** NGC Census: (2/1092). PCGS Population (15/1176). Mintage: 484,000. Numismedia Wsl. Price for problem free NGC/PCGS coin in MS60: $1,340.

7119 **1909 MS66 Red NGC. CAC.** NGC Census: (173/5). PCGS Population (539/69). Mintage: 72,702,616. Numismedia Wsl. Price for problem free NGC/PCGS coin in MS66: $300. NGC ID# 22B3, PCGS# 2431

7120 **1909 MS66 Red PCGS. CAC.** PCGS Population (539/69). NGC Census: (173/5). Mintage: 72,702,616. Numismedia Wsl. Price for problem free NGC/PCGS coin in MS66: $300. NGC ID# 22B3, PCGS# 2431

7121 **1909-S MS65 Red and Brown PCGS.** PCGS Population (256/7). NGC Census: (140/15). Mintage: 1,825,000. Numismedia Wsl. Price for problem free NGC/PCGS coin in MS65: $550. NGC ID# 22B4, PCGS# 2433

7122 **1909-S MS65 Red and Brown PCGS.** PCGS Population (256/7). NGC Census: (140/15). Mintage: 1,825,000. Numismedia Wsl. Price for problem free NGC/PCGS coin in MS65: $550. NGC ID# 22B4, PCGS# 2433

7123 **1909-S MS64 Red PCGS.** PCGS Population (480/584). NGC Census: (175/238). Mintage: 1,825,000. Numismedia Wsl. Price for problem free NGC/PCGS coin in MS64: $550. NGC ID# 22B4, PCGS# 2434

7124 **1909-S MS64 Red NGC.** NGC Census: (175/238). PCGS Population (480/584). Mintage: 1,825,000. Numismedia Wsl. Price for problem free NGC/PCGS coin in MS64: $550. NGC ID# 22B4, PCGS# 2434

7125 **1909-S S Over Horizontal S MS64 Red PCGS.** PCGS Population (187/248). NGC Census: (55/85). PCGS# 92434

7126 **1910 MS66 ★ Red and Brown NGC. CAC.** NGC Census: (30/0). PCGS Population (16/1). Mintage: 146,801,216. Numismedia Wsl. Price for problem free NGC/PCGS coin in MS66: $230. NGC ID# 22B5, PCGS# 2436

7127 **1910 MS66 Red PCGS.** PCGS Population (152/26). NGC Census: (84/14). Mintage: 146,801,216. Numismedia Wsl. Price for problem free NGC/PCGS coin in MS66: $600. NGC ID# 22B5, PCGS# 2437

7128 **1911-D MS65 Red and Brown NGC. CAC.** NGC Census: (52/2). PCGS Population (31/0). Mintage: 12,672,000. Numismedia Wsl. Price for problem free NGC/PCGS coin in MS65: $565. NGC ID# 22B8, PCGS# 2445

7129 **1912-S MS64 Red NGC. CAC.** NGC Census: (43/27). PCGS Population (173/65). Mintage: 4,431,000. Numismedia Wsl. Price for problem free NGC/PCGS coin in MS64: $725. NGC ID# 22BC, PCGS# 2458

7130 **1913-D MS64 Red PCGS.** PCGS Population (185/123). NGC Census: (89/31). Mintage: 15,804,000. Numismedia Wsl. Price for problem free NGC/PCGS coin in MS64: $610. NGC ID# 22BE, PCGS# 2464

7131 **1913-S MS64 Red and Brown PCGS. CAC.** PCGS Population (190/34). NGC Census: (95/50). Mintage: 6,101,000. Numismedia Wsl. Price for problem free NGC/PCGS coin in MS64: $500. NGC ID# 22BF, PCGS# 2466

7132 **1914-D XF45 PCGS.** PCGS Population (321/643). NGC Census: (204/497). Mintage: 1,193,000. Numismedia Wsl. Price for problem free NGC/PCGS coin in XF45: $858. NGC ID# 22BH, PCGS# 2471

7133 **1914-D XF45 PCGS.** PCGS Population (321/643). NGC Census: (204/497). Mintage: 1,193,000. Numismedia Wsl. Price for problem free NGC/PCGS coin in XF45: $858. NGC ID# 22BH, PCGS# 2471

7134 **1914-D — Improperly Cleaned — NGC Details. AU.** NGC Census: (49/447). PCGS Population (133/508). Mintage: 1,193,000. Numismedia Wsl. Price for problem free NGC/PCGS coin in AU50: $1,150.

7135 **1914-D — Cleaning — PCGS Genuine. AU Details.** NGC Census: (49/447). PCGS Population (133/507). Mintage: 1,193,000. Numismedia Wsl. Price for problem free NGC/PCGS coin in AU50: $1,150.

7136 **1914-S MS64 Red and Brown NGC.** NGC Census: (47/27). PCGS Population (141/20). Mintage: 4,137,000. Numismedia Wsl. Price for problem free NGC/PCGS coin in MS64: $975. NGC ID# 22BJ, PCGS# 2475

7137 **1915-D MS64 Red PCGS. CAC.** PCGS Population (188/163). NGC Census: (44/50). Mintage: 22,050,000. Numismedia Wsl. Price for problem free NGC/PCGS coin in MS64: $400. NGC ID# 22BL, PCGS# 2482

7138 **1915-D MS65 Red PCGS.** PCGS Population (134/29). NGC Census: (43/7). Mintage: 22,050,000. Numismedia Wsl. Price for problem free NGC/PCGS coin in MS65: $1,175. NGC ID# 22BL, PCGS# 2482

7139 **1916-S MS64 Red and Brown PCGS.** PCGS Population (177/34). NGC Census: (105/56). Mintage: 22,510,000. Numismedia Wsl. Price for problem free NGC/PCGS coin in MS64: $440. NGC ID# 22BR, PCGS# 2493

7140 **1917-D MS64 Red NGC.** NGC Census: (34/19). PCGS Population (130/50). Mintage: 55,120,000. Numismedia Wsl. Price for problem free NGC/PCGS coin in MS64: $700. NGC ID# 22BT, PCGS# 2500

7141 **1917-S MS63 Red PCGS.** PCGS Population (10/76). NGC Census: (3/17). Mintage: 32,620,000. Numismedia Wsl. Price for problem free NGC/PCGS coin in MS63: $475. NGC ID# 22BU, PCGS# 2503

7142 **1918-D MS64 Red NGC.** NGC Census: (29/8). PCGS Population (114/38). Mintage: 47,830,000. Numismedia Wsl. Price for problem free NGC/PCGS coin in MS64: $765. NGC ID# 22BW, PCGS# 2509

7143 **1921-S MS64 Red and Brown PCGS. CAC.** PCGS Population (246/41). NGC Census: (102/38). Mintage: 15,274,000. Numismedia Wsl. Price for problem free NGC/PCGS coin in MS64: $525. NGC ID# 22C7, PCGS# 2535

7144 **1922 No D Strong Reverse VF25 PCGS.** PCGS Population (515/2168). NGC Census: (0/0). Numismedia Wsl. Price for problem free NGC/PCGS coin in VF25: $893. NGC ID# 22C9, PCGS# 3285

7145 **1922 No D, Strong Reverse, FS-401, Die 2, VF25 ANACS.** NGC Census: (0/0). PCGS Population (3/25). PCGS# 37676

7146 **1924-D MS64 Brown PCGS. CAC.** PCGS Population (47/13). NGC Census: (44/10). Mintage: 2,520,000. Numismedia Wsl. Price for problem free NGC/PCGS coin in MS64: $480. NGC ID# 22CD, PCGS# 2552

7147 **1924-D MS64 Red and Brown PCGS. CAC.** PCGS Population (174/31). NGC Census: (112/70). Mintage: 2,520,000. Numismedia Wsl. Price for problem free NGC/PCGS coin in MS64: $735. NGC ID# 22CD, PCGS# 2553

7148 **1924-S MS64 Red and Brown PCGS. CAC.** PCGS Population (198/23). NGC Census: (68/13). Mintage: 11,696,000. Numismedia Wsl. Price for problem free NGC/PCGS coin in MS64: $750. NGC ID# 22CE, PCGS# 2556

7149 **1925-S MS64 Red and Brown NGC.** NGC Census: (60/10). PCGS Population (147/8). Mintage: 26,380,000. Numismedia Wsl. Price for problem free NGC/PCGS coin in MS64: $775. NGC ID# 22CH, PCGS# 2565

7150 **1926-D MS65 Red and Brown NGC.** NGC Census: (24/1). PCGS Population (22/1). Mintage: 28,020,000. Numismedia Wsl. Price for problem free NGC/PCGS coin in MS65: $685. NGC ID# 22CK, PCGS# 2571

7151 **1928 MS66+ Red PCGS. CAC.** PCGS Population (379/61). NGC Census: (102/13). Mintage: 134,116,000. Numismedia Wsl. Price for problem free NGC/PCGS coin in MS66: $300. NGC ID# 22CR, PCGS# 2587

7152 **1928 MS67 Red PCGS.** PCGS Population (61/0). NGC Census: (13/0). Mintage: 134,116,000. Numismedia Wsl. Price for problem free NGC/PCGS coin in MS67: $885. NGC ID# 22CR, PCGS# 2587

7153 **1928-S MS64 Red PCGS.** PCGS Population (149/51). NGC Census: (33/7). Mintage: 17,266,000. Numismedia Wsl. Price for problem free NGC/PCGS coin in MS64: $580. NGC ID# 22CT, PCGS# 2593

7154 **1929-D MS65 Red PCGS. CAC.** PCGS Population (225/27). NGC Census: (54/3). Mintage: 41,730,000. Numismedia Wsl. Price for problem free NGC/PCGS coin in MS65: $460. NGC ID# 22CV, PCGS# 2599

7155 **1929-S MS66 Red NGC. CAC.** NGC Census: (24/3). PCGS Population (25/0). Mintage: 50,148,000. Numismedia Wsl. Price for problem free NGC/PCGS coin in MS66: $2,550. NGC ID# 22CW, PCGS# 2602

7156 **1930-S MS66 Red PCGS.** PCGS Population (165/5). NGC Census: (334/24). Mintage: 24,286,000. Numismedia Wsl. Price for problem free NGC/PCGS coin in MS66: $230. NGC ID# 22CZ, PCGS# 2611

7157 **1931-D MS65 Red NGC.** NGC Census: (48/9). PCGS Population (149/36). Mintage: 4,480,000. Numismedia Wsl. Price for problem free NGC/PCGS coin in MS65: $825. NGC ID# 22D3, PCGS# 2617

7158 **1931-S MS65 Red PCGS. CAC.** PCGS Population (771/97). NGC Census: (239/24). Mintage: 866,000. Numismedia Wsl. Price for problem free NGC/PCGS coin in MS65: $545. NGC ID# 22D4, PCGS# 2620

7159 **1933-D MS66 Red PCGS. CAC.** PCGS Population (347/24). NGC Census: (295/37). Mintage: 6,200,000. Numismedia Wsl. Price for problem free NGC/PCGS coin in MS66: $270. NGC ID# 22D8, PCGS# 2632

7160 **1934-D MS67 Red NGC.** NGC Census: (23/0). PCGS Population (28/0). Mintage: 28,446,000. Numismedia Wsl. Price for problem free NGC/PCGS coin in MS67: $1,525. NGC ID# 22DA, PCGS# 2638

7161 **1937-S MS67+ Red PCGS. CAC.** PCGS Population (186/0). NGC Census: (376/0). Mintage: 34,500,000. Numismedia Wsl. Price for problem free NGC/PCGS coin in MS67: $300. NGC ID# 22DK, PCGS# 2665

7162 **1946 MS67 Red NGC.** NGC Census: (37/0). PCGS Population (20/0). Mintage: 991,654,976. Numismedia Wsl. Price for problem free NGC/PCGS coin in MS67: $850. NGC ID# 22EK, PCGS# 2743

7163 **1949 MS67 Red NGC.** NGC Census: (38/0). PCGS Population (18/0). Mintage: 217,775,008. Numismedia Wsl. Price for problem free NGC/PCGS coin in MS67: $1,550. NGC ID# 22EV, PCGS# 2770

7164 **1949-D MS67 Red NGC.** NGC Census: (75/0). PCGS Population (41/0). Mintage: 153,132,496. Numismedia Wsl. Price for problem free NGC/PCGS coin in MS67: $580. NGC ID# 22EW, PCGS# 2773

7165 **1949-S MS67 Red NGC.** NGC Census: (507/0). PCGS Population (192/0). Mintage: 64,290,000. Numismedia Wsl. Price for problem free NGC/PCGS coin in MS67: $220. NGC ID# 22EX, PCGS# 2776

7166 **1950 MS67 Red NGC.** NGC Census: (70/0). PCGS Population (32/0). Mintage: 272,686,400. Numismedia Wsl. Price for problem free NGC/PCGS coin in MS67: $650. NGC ID# 22EY, PCGS# 2779

7167 **1951 MS67 Red NGC.** NGC Census: (30/0). PCGS Population (19/0). Mintage: 284,633,504. Numismedia Wsl. Price for problem free NGC/PCGS coin in MS67: $1,525. NGC ID# 22F3, PCGS# 2788

7168 **1951-S MS67 Red PCGS.** PCGS Population (85/0). NGC Census: (181/0). Mintage: 136,010,000. Numismedia Wsl. Price for problem free NGC/PCGS coin in MS67: $320. NGC ID# 22F5, PCGS# 2794

7169 **1952 MS67 Red NGC.** NGC Census: (71/0). PCGS Population (15/0). Mintage: 186,856,976. Numismedia Wsl. Price for problem free NGC/PCGS coin in MS67: $625. NGC ID# 22F6, PCGS# 2797

7170 **1952-D MS67 Red PCGS.** PCGS Population (77/0). NGC Census: (178/0). Mintage: 46,130,000. Numismedia Wsl. Price for problem free NGC/PCGS coin in MS67: $300. NGC ID# 22F7, PCGS# 2800

7171 **1953 MS67 Red NGC.** NGC Census: (22/0). PCGS Population (14/0). Mintage: 256,883,808. Numismedia Wsl. Price for problem free NGC/PCGS coin in MS67: $375. NGC ID# 22F9, PCGS# 2806

7172 **1957-D MS67 Red NGC.** NGC Census: (109/0). PCGS Population (71/0). Mintage: 1,051,342,016. Numismedia Wsl. Price for problem free NGC/PCGS coin in MS67: $515. NGC ID# 22FN, PCGS# 2845

7173 **1964 MS67 Red NGC.** NGC Census: (11/1). PCGS Population (2/0). Mintage: 2,652,525,824. Numismedia Wsl. Price for problem free NGC/PCGS coin in MS67: $750. NGC ID# 22G7, PCGS# 2890

7174 **1968 MS67 Red NGC.** NGC Census: (10/0). PCGS Population (16/0). Numismedia Wsl. Price for problem free NGC/PCGS coin in MS67: $300. NGC ID# 22GC, PCGS# 2905

7175 **1968-D MS67 Red NGC.** NGC Census: (15/0). PCGS Population (19/0). Numismedia Wsl. Price for problem free NGC/PCGS coin in MS67: $280. NGC ID# 22GD, PCGS# 2908

7176 **1969-D MS67 Red NGC.** NGC Census: (13/0). PCGS Population (8/0). NGC ID# 22GG, PCGS# 2917

7177 **1970-S Large Date MS67 Red NGC.** NGC Census: (24/0). PCGS Population (23/0). Mintage: 693,192,832. Numismedia Wsl. Price for problem free NGC/PCGS coin in MS67: $565. NGC ID# 22GN, PCGS# 2939

7178 **1972 Doubled Die Obverse MS65 Red PCGS.** PCGS Population (1279/562). NGC Census: (603/186). Mintage: 75,000. Numismedia Wsl. Price for problem free NGC/PCGS coin in MS65: $585. NGC ID# 22GU, PCGS# 2950

7179 **1972 Doubled Die Obverse MS65+ Red PCGS.** PCGS Population (1279/562). NGC Census: (603/186). Mintage: 75,000. Numismedia Wsl. Price for problem free NGC/PCGS coin in MS65: $585. NGC ID# 22GU, PCGS# 2950

7180 **1972 Doubled Die Obverse MS66 Red NGC.** NGC Census: (178/8). PCGS Population (537/25). Mintage: 75,000. Numismedia Wsl. Price for problem free NGC/PCGS coin in MS66: $1,025. NGC ID# 22GU, PCGS# 2950

7181 **1972 Doubled Die Obverse MS66 Red PCGS.** PCGS Population (537/25). NGC Census: (178/8). Mintage: 75,000. Numismedia Wsl. Price for problem free NGC/PCGS coin in MS66: $1,025. NGC ID# 22GU, PCGS# 2950

7182 **1972 Doubled Die Obverse MS66 Red PCGS.** PCGS Population (537/25). NGC Census: (178/8). Mintage: 75,000. Numismedia Wsl. Price for problem free NGC/PCGS coin in MS66: $1,025. NGC ID# 22GU, PCGS# 2950

7183 **1983-D MS68 Red NGC.** NGC Census: (0/0). PCGS Population (21/0). Numismedia Wsl. Price for problem free NGC/PCGS coin in MS68: $525. NGC ID# 22HX, PCGS# 3051

7184 **1985 MS68 Red NGC.** NGC Census: (33/5). PCGS Population (20/0). Numismedia Wsl. Price for problem free NGC/PCGS coin in MS68: $140. NGC ID# 22J3, PCGS# 3071

7185 **1999 Wide AM , FS-901 MS66 Red PCGS.** PCGS Population (48/2). NGC Census: (0/0). PCGS# 391432

7186 **1999-D MS69 Red PCGS.** PCGS Population (46/0). NGC Census: (1/0). Numismedia Wsl. Price for problem free NGC/PCGS coin in MS69: $360. NGC ID# 22K3, PCGS# 3157

PROOF LINCOLN CENTS

7187 **1954 PR68 Red Cameo NGC.** NGC Census: (21/0). PCGS Population (9/0). Numismedia Wsl. Price for problem free NGC/PCGS coin in PR68: $1,450. NGC ID# 22LE, PCGS# 83371

7188 **1959 PR68 Red Ultra Cameo NGC.** NGC Census: (21/0). PCGS Population (34/3). Numismedia Wsl. Price for problem free NGC/PCGS coin in PR68: $875. NGC ID# 22LK, PCGS# 93386

7189 **1960 Small Over Large Date, FS-102, PR66 Red Cameo PCGS.** PCGS Population (2/6). NGC Census: (0/0). PCGS# 38164

7190 **1962 PR69 Red Ultra Cameo NGC.** NGC Census: (39/0). PCGS Population (35/0). Numismedia Wsl. Price for problem free NGC/PCGS coin in PR69: $750. NGC ID# 22LP, PCGS# 93398

TWO CENT PIECES

7191 **1864 Large Motto MS65 Red and Brown PCGS.** PCGS Population (329/14). NGC Census: (589/100). Mintage: 19,847,500. Numismedia Wsl. Price for problem free NGC/PCGS coin in MS65: $540. NGC ID# 22N9, PCGS# 3577

7192 **1864 Large Motto MS64 Red PCGS.** PCGS Population (296/293). NGC Census: (118/161). Mintage: 19,847,500. Numismedia Wsl. Price for problem free NGC/PCGS coin in MS64: $600. NGC ID# 22N9, PCGS# 3578

7193 **1865 MS65 Red and Brown PCGS.** PCGS Population (272/26). NGC Census: (348/75). Mintage: 13,640,000. Numismedia Wsl. Price for problem free NGC/PCGS coin in MS65: $535. NGC ID# 22NA, PCGS# 3583

7194 **1865 MS65 Red and Brown PCGS. CAC.** PCGS Population (274/26). NGC Census: (348/75). Mintage: 13,640,000. Numismedia Wsl. Price for problem free NGC/PCGS coin in MS65: $535. NGC ID# 22NA, PCGS# 3583

7195 **1867 Doubled Die XF40 PCGS. CAC.** PCGS Population (9/46). NGC Census: (0/0). PCGS# 3594

7196 **1870 MS64 Red and Brown PCGS.** PCGS Population (102/32). NGC Census: (73/41). Numismedia Wsl. Price for problem free NGC/PCGS coin in MS64: $750. NGC ID# 22NE, PCGS# 3607

7197 **1871 MS64 Red and Brown PCGS.** PCGS Population (121/36). NGC Census: (63/65). Mintage: 721,250. Numismedia Wsl. Price for problem free NGC/PCGS coin in MS64: $665. NGC ID# 22NF, PCGS# 3610

7198 **1871 MS64 Red and Brown PCGS.** PCGS Population (121/36). NGC Census: (63/65). Mintage: 721,250. Numismedia Wsl. Price for problem free NGC/PCGS coin in MS64: $665. NGC ID# 22NF, PCGS# 3610

PROOF TWO CENT PIECES

7199 **1865 PR64 Red and Brown PCGS.** PCGS Population (56/46). NGC Census: (21/43). Mintage: 500. Numismedia Wsl. Price for problem free NGC/PCGS coin in PR64: $685. NGC ID# 274U, PCGS# 3628

7200 **1869 PR64 Brown PCGS. CAC.** PCGS Population (16/11). NGC Census: (18/22). Mintage: 600. Numismedia Wsl. Price for problem free NGC/PCGS coin in PR64: $500. NGC ID# 274Y, PCGS# 3639

7201 **1870 PR64 Brown NGC.** NGC Census: (18/18). PCGS Population (23/7). Mintage: 1,000. Numismedia Wsl. Price for problem free NGC/PCGS coin in PR64: $575. NGC ID# 274Z, PCGS# 3642

THREE CENT SILVER

7202 **1851 MS64 PCGS.** PCGS Population (378/323). NGC Census: (418/268). Mintage: 5,447,400. Numismedia Wsl. Price for problem free NGC/PCGS coin in MS64: $380. NGC ID# 22YX, PCGS# 3664

7203 **1851-O MS63 NGC. CAC.** NGC Census: (77/180). PCGS Population (102/164). Mintage: 720,000. Numismedia Wsl. Price for problem free NGC/PCGS coin in MS63: $650. NGC ID# 22YY, PCGS# 3665

7204 **1853 MS64 PCGS.** PCGS Population (186/184). NGC Census: (216/118). Mintage: 11,400,000. Numismedia Wsl. Price for problem free NGC/PCGS coin in MS64: $380. NGC ID# 22Z2, PCGS# 3667

7205 **1853 MS65 PCGS.** PCGS Population (121/63). NGC Census: (74/44). Mintage: 11,400,000. Numismedia Wsl. Price for problem free NGC/PCGS coin in MS65: $710. NGC ID# 22Z2, PCGS# 3667

7206 **1853 MS65 PCGS.** PCGS Population (121/63). NGC Census: (74/44). Mintage: 11,400,000. Numismedia Wsl. Price for problem free NGC/PCGS coin in MS65: $710. NGC ID# 22Z2, PCGS# 3667

7207 **1854 MS61 NGC.** NGC Census: (15/255). PCGS Population (2/262). Mintage: 671,000. Numismedia Wsl. Price for problem free NGC/PCGS coin in MS61: $390. NGC ID# 22Z3, PCGS# 3670

7208 **1855 AU50 NGC.** NGC Census: (6/98). PCGS Population (22/143). Mintage: 139,000. Numismedia Wsl. Price for problem free NGC/PCGS coin in AU50: $245. NGC ID# 22Z4, PCGS# 3671

7209 **1855 AU50 PCGS.** PCGS Population (22/143). NGC Census: (6/98). Mintage: 139,000. Numismedia Wsl. Price for problem free NGC/PCGS coin in AU50: $245. NGC ID# 22Z4, PCGS# 3671

7210 **1855 AU53 NGC.** NGC Census: (1/97). PCGS Population (5/138). Mintage: 139,000. Numismedia Wsl. Price for problem free NGC/PCGS coin in AU53: $275. NGC ID# 22Z4, PCGS# 3671

7211 **1858 MS63 NGC.** NGC Census: (97/252). PCGS Population (111/221). Mintage: 1,604,000. Numismedia Wsl. Price for problem free NGC/PCGS coin in MS63: $610. NGC ID# 22Z7, PCGS# 3674

7212 **1859 MS64 PCGS.** PCGS Population (84/53). NGC Census: (95/56). Mintage: 364,200. Numismedia Wsl. Price for problem free NGC/PCGS coin in MS64: $550. NGC ID# 22Z8, PCGS# 3677

7213 **1860 MS64 NGC.** NGC Census: (69/24). PCGS Population (77/36). Mintage: 286,000. Numismedia Wsl. Price for problem free NGC/PCGS coin in MS64: $480. NGC ID# 22Z9, PCGS# 3678

7214 **1862 MS64 NGC.** NGC Census: (297/371). PCGS Population (262/333). Mintage: 343,000. Numismedia Wsl. Price for problem free NGC/PCGS coin in MS64: $480. NGC ID# 22ZB, PCGS# 3680

7215 **1870 MS61 NGC.** NGC Census: (2/65). PCGS Population (2/46). Mintage: 3,000. Numismedia Wsl. Price for problem free NGC/PCGS coin in MS61: $850. NGC ID# 22ZL, PCGS# 3691

PROOF THREE CENT SILVER

7216 **1862 PR64 PCGS.** PCGS Population (68/29). NGC Census: (54/43). Mintage: 550. Numismedia Wsl. Price for problem free NGC/PCGS coin in PR64: $810. NGC ID# 27C9, PCGS# 3711

7217 **1869 PR64 PCGS.** PCGS Population (79/56). NGC Census: (51/64). Mintage: 600. Numismedia Wsl. Price for problem free NGC/PCGS coin in PR64: $850. NGC ID# 22ZR, PCGS# 3719

THREE CENT NICKELS

7218 **1868 MS65 NGC. CAC.** NGC Census: (58/20). PCGS Population (65/34). Mintage: 3,252,000. Numismedia Wsl. Price for problem free NGC/PCGS coin in MS65: $515. NGC ID# 2756, PCGS# 3734

7219 **1873 Open 3 MS64 PCGS. CAC.** PCGS Population (46/39). NGC Census: (31/11). PCGS# 3740

7220 **1875 MS65 NGC.** NGC Census: (45/19). PCGS Population (27/21). Mintage: 227,300. Numismedia Wsl. Price for problem free NGC/PCGS coin in MS65: $665. NGC ID# 22NS, PCGS# 3743

7221 **1879 MS64 PCGS.** PCGS Population (28/81). NGC Census: (29/70). Mintage: 38,000. Numismedia Wsl. Price for problem free NGC/PCGS coin in MS64: $500. NGC ID# 275B, PCGS# 3747

7222 **1880 MS64 PCGS.** PCGS Population (38/134). NGC Census: (33/93). Mintage: 21,000. Numismedia Wsl. Price for problem free NGC/PCGS coin in MS64: $460. NGC ID# 275C, PCGS# 3748

7223 **1881 MS65 PCGS. CAC.** PCGS Population (82/56). NGC Census: (48/15). Mintage: 1,080,575. Numismedia Wsl. Price for problem free NGC/PCGS coin in MS65: $520. NGC ID# 22NT, PCGS# 3749

7224 **1887 XF40 PCGS.** PCGS Population (13/136). NGC Census: (6/92). Mintage: 5,000. Numismedia Wsl. Price for problem free NGC/PCGS coin in XF40: $450. NGC ID# 22NU, PCGS# 3755

7225 **1887 XF40 PCGS. CAC.** PCGS Population (13/136). NGC Census: (6/92). Mintage: 5,000. Numismedia Wsl. Price for problem free NGC/PCGS coin in XF40: $450. NGC ID# 22NU, PCGS# 3755

7226 **1888 MS65 NGC.** NGC Census: (65/45). PCGS Population (70/102). Mintage: 36,500. Numismedia Wsl. Price for problem free NGC/PCGS coin in MS65: $550. NGC ID# 275H, PCGS# 3757

PROOF THREE CENT NICKELS

7227 **1867 PR65 Cameo NGC. CAC.** NGC Census: (59/64). PCGS Population (28/26). PCGS# 83763

7228 **1872 PR65 Cameo PCGS. CAC.** PCGS Population (28/9). NGC Census: (26/26). PCGS# 83768

7229 **1873 Closed 3 PR65 NGC. CAC.** NGC Census: (106/36). PCGS Population (98/19). Mintage: 1,100. Numismedia Wsl. Price for problem free NGC/PCGS coin in PR65: $620. NGC ID# 275U, PCGS# 3769

7230 **1874 PR65 PCGS.** PCGS Population (85/24). NGC Census: (92/29). Mintage: 700. Numismedia Wsl. Price for problem free NGC/PCGS coin in PR65: $560. NGC ID# 275V, PCGS# 3770

7231 **1878 PR64 PCGS.** PCGS Population (248/344). NGC Census: (134/333). Mintage: 2,350. Numismedia Wsl. Price for problem free NGC/PCGS coin in PR64: $750. NGC ID# 275Y, PCGS# 3774

7232 **1878 PR64+ PCGS.** PCGS Population (248/344). NGC Census: (134/333). Mintage: 2,350. Numismedia Wsl. Price for problem free NGC/PCGS coin in PR64: $750. NGC ID# 275Y, PCGS# 3774

7233 **1878 PR65 NGC.** NGC Census: (182/151). PCGS Population (237/108). Mintage: 2,350. Numismedia Wsl. Price for problem free NGC/PCGS coin in PR65: $810. NGC ID# 275Y, PCGS# 3774

7234 **1879 PR65 PCGS. CAC.** PCGS Population (298/231). NGC Census: (309/244). Mintage: 3,200. Numismedia Wsl. Price for problem free NGC/PCGS coin in PR65: $460. NGC ID# 275Z, PCGS# 3775

7235 **1880 PR67 NGC.** NGC Census: (50/3). PCGS Population (40/0). Mintage: 3,955. Numismedia Wsl. Price for problem free NGC/PCGS coin in PR67: $1,025. NGC ID# 2762, PCGS# 3776

7236 **1881 PR67 Cameo NGC.** NGC Census: (28/8). PCGS Population (28/3). PCGS# 83777

7237 **1884 PR66 PCGS. CAC.** PCGS Population (189/41). NGC Census: (229/33). Mintage: 3,942. Numismedia Wsl. Price for problem free NGC/PCGS coin in PR66: $650. NGC ID# 2766, PCGS# 3780

7238 **1888 PR66 Cameo PCGS.** PCGS Population (55/10). NGC Census: (55/11). PCGS# 83785

7239 **1888 PR66 Cameo NGC.** NGC Census: (56/11). PCGS Population (56/10). PCGS# 83785

SHIELD NICKELS

7240 **1866 Rays MS63 PCGS.** PCGS Population (351/622). NGC Census: (291/737). Mintage: 14,742,500. Numismedia Wsl. Price for problem free NGC/PCGS coin in MS63: $400. NGC ID# 22NX, PCGS# 3790

7241 **1867 Rays MS63 NGC.** NGC Census: (75/246). PCGS Population (121/176). Mintage: 2,019,000. Numismedia Wsl. Price for problem free NGC/PCGS coin in MS63: $520. NGC ID# 22NY, PCGS# 3791

7242 **1868 MS65 PCGS.** PCGS Population (75/28). NGC Census: (130/35). Mintage: 28,800,000. Numismedia Wsl. Price for problem free NGC/PCGS coin in MS65: $600. NGC ID# 22P2, PCGS# 3795

7243 **1868 Reverse of 1868, FS-901 MS65 PCGS.** (FS-002.94). PCGS Population (2/0). NGC Census: (0/0). PCGS# 400244

7244 **1873 Closed 3 MS63 PCGS. CAC.** PCGS Population (12/61). NGC Census: (0/0). PCGS# 3801

7245 **1873 Closed 3 MS64 NGC.** NGC Census: (0/0). PCGS Population (31/30). PCGS# 3801

7246 **1874 MS64+ PCGS.** PCGS Population (64/41). NGC Census: (50/26). Mintage: 3,538,000. Numismedia Wsl. Price for problem free NGC/PCGS coin in MS64: $420. NGC ID# 22P9, PCGS# 3803

7247 **1876 MS65 NGC.** NGC Census: (35/6). PCGS Population (46/13). Mintage: 2,530,000. Numismedia Wsl. Price for problem free NGC/PCGS coin in MS65: $1,100. NGC ID# 22PB, PCGS# 3805

7248 **1882 MS65 PCGS.** PCGS Population (183/78). NGC Census: (165/53). Mintage: 11,476,000. Numismedia Wsl. Price for problem free NGC/PCGS coin in MS65: $500. NGC ID# 22PC, PCGS# 3812

7249 **1882 MS66 PCGS.** PCGS Population (72/6). NGC Census: (49/4). Mintage: 11,476,000. Numismedia Wsl. Price for problem free NGC/PCGS coin in MS66: $950. NGC ID# 22PC, PCGS# 3812

7250 **1882 MS66 NGC.** NGC Census: (49/4). PCGS Population (72/6). Mintage: 11,476,000. Numismedia Wsl. Price for problem free NGC/PCGS coin in MS66: $950. NGC ID# 22PC, PCGS# 3812

7251 **1883 MS66 NGC. CAC.** NGC Census: (85/15). PCGS Population (111/12). Mintage: 1,456,919. Numismedia Wsl. Price for problem free NGC/PCGS coin in MS66: $875. NGC ID# 22PE, PCGS# 3813

PROOF SHIELD NICKELS

7252 **1867 No Rays PR64 PCGS.** PCGS Population (101/42). NGC Census: (103/68). Mintage: 600. Numismedia Wsl. Price for problem free NGC/PCGS coin in PR64: $875. NGC ID# 22PF, PCGS# 3821

7253 **1872 PR65 NGC.** NGC Census: (111/56). PCGS Population (106/56). Mintage: 950. Numismedia Wsl. Price for problem free NGC/PCGS coin in PR65: $585. NGC ID# 276N, PCGS# 3826

7254 **1873 Closed 3 PR65 NGC. CAC.** NGC Census: (107/41). PCGS Population (93/26). Mintage: 1,100. Numismedia Wsl. Price for problem free NGC/PCGS coin in PR65: $550. NGC ID# 276P, PCGS# 3827

7255 **1879/8 PR66 PCGS.** PCGS Population (110/33). NGC Census: (0/0). Mintage: 3,200. Numismedia Wsl. Price for problem free NGC/PCGS coin in PR66: $950. NGC ID# 22PG, PCGS# 3834

7256 **1879 PR66 NGC.** NGC Census: (119/13). PCGS Population (75/15). Mintage: 3,200. Numismedia Wsl. Price for problem free NGC/PCGS coin in PR66: $770. NGC ID# 22PG, PCGS# 3833

7257 **1880 PR66 Cameo NGC.** NGC Census: (49/17). PCGS Population (74/20). PCGS# 83835

7258 **1881 PR65 PCGS.** PCGS Population (278/166). NGC Census: (230/199). Mintage: 3,575. Numismedia Wsl. Price for problem free NGC/PCGS coin in PR65: $540. NGC ID# 276X, PCGS# 3836

7259 **1883 PR65 PCGS.** PCGS Population (414/231). NGC Census: (363/275). Mintage: 5,419. Numismedia Wsl. Price for problem free NGC/PCGS coin in PR65: $520. NGC ID# 276Z, PCGS# 3838

7260 **1883 PR66 NGC. CAC.** NGC Census: (229/46). PCGS Population (196/32). Mintage: 5,419. Numismedia Wsl. Price for problem free NGC/PCGS coin in PR66: $660. NGC ID# 276Z, PCGS# 3838

LIBERTY NICKELS

7261 **1883 No Cents MS66 PCGS. CAC.** PCGS Population (387/21). NGC Census: (479/64). Mintage: 5,479,519. Numismedia Wsl. Price for problem free NGC/PCGS coin in MS66: $320. NGC ID# 2772, PCGS# 3841

7262 **1885 Fine 12 PCGS.** PCGS Population (60/679). NGC Census: (25/362). Mintage: 1,476,490. Numismedia Wsl. Price for problem free NGC/PCGS coin in Fine 12: $650. NGC ID# 2773, PCGS# 3846

7263 **1885 VF20 PCGS.** PCGS Population (34/610). NGC Census: (14/339). Mintage: 1,476,490. Numismedia Wsl. Price for problem free NGC/PCGS coin in VF20: $850. NGC ID# 2773, PCGS# 3846

7264 **1888 MS65 PCGS.** PCGS Population (69/17). NGC Census: (48/11). Mintage: 10,720,483. Numismedia Wsl. Price for problem free NGC/PCGS coin in MS65: $975. NGC ID# 2774, PCGS# 3849

7265 **1903 MS66 NGC. CAC.** NGC Census: (56/3). PCGS Population (93/2). Mintage: 28,006,724. Numismedia Wsl. Price for problem free NGC/PCGS coin in MS66: $785. NGC ID# 277E, PCGS# 3864

7266 **1904 MS66 NGC.** NGC Census: (68/2). PCGS Population (80/0). Mintage: 21,404,984. Numismedia Wsl. Price for problem free NGC/PCGS coin in MS66: $810. NGC ID# 277F, PCGS# 3865

7267 **1907 MS65+ PCGS.** PCGS Population (84/29). NGC Census: (79/11). Mintage: 39,214,800. Numismedia Wsl. Price for problem free NGC/PCGS coin in MS65: $575. NGC ID# 277J, PCGS# 3868

7268 **1911 MS65+ PCGS. CAC.** PCGS Population (227/43). NGC Census: (162/26). Mintage: 39,559,372. Numismedia Wsl. Price for problem free NGC/PCGS coin in MS65: $400. NGC ID# 277M, PCGS# 3872

PROOF LIBERTY NICKELS

7269 **1887 PR65 PCGS.** PCGS Population (143/55). NGC Census: (181/48). Mintage: 2,960. Numismedia Wsl. Price for problem free NGC/PCGS coin in PR65: $500. NGC ID# 277V, PCGS# 3885

7270 **1888 PR66 NGC.** NGC Census: (88/13). PCGS Population (93/5). Mintage: 4,582. Numismedia Wsl. Price for problem free NGC/PCGS coin in PR66: $715. NGC ID# 277W, PCGS# 3886

7271 **1890 PR66 NGC.** NGC Census: (14/1). PCGS Population (9/0). Mintage: 2,740. Numismedia Wsl. Price for problem free NGC/PCGS coin in PR66: $800. NGC ID# 277Y, PCGS# 3888

7272 **1892 PR66+ PCGS.** PCGS Population (26/0). NGC Census: (46/5). Mintage: 2,745. Numismedia Wsl. Price for problem free NGC/PCGS coin in PR66: $775. NGC ID# 2782, PCGS# 3890

7273 **1898 PR66 NGC.** NGC Census: (47/8). PCGS Population (26/1). Mintage: 1,795. Numismedia Wsl. Price for problem free NGC/PCGS coin in PR66: $840. NGC ID# 2788, PCGS# 3896

7274 **1900 PR65 PCGS. CAC.** PCGS Population (146/98). NGC Census: (143/101). Mintage: 2,262. Numismedia Wsl. Price for problem free NGC/PCGS coin in PR65: $500. NGC ID# 278A, PCGS# 3898

7275 **1902 PR66 NGC.** NGC Census: (90/16). PCGS Population (70/13). Mintage: 2,018. Numismedia Wsl. Price for problem free NGC/PCGS coin in PR66: $665. NGC ID# 278C, PCGS# 3900

7276 **1903 PR66 NGC.** NGC Census: (98/32). PCGS Population (66/18). Mintage: 1,790. Numismedia Wsl. Price for problem free NGC/PCGS coin in PR66: $700. NGC ID# 278D, PCGS# 3901

BUFFALO NICKELS

7277 **1913 Type One MS67 PCGS.** PCGS Population (484/14). NGC Census: (275/8). Mintage: 30,993,520. Numismedia Wsl. Price for problem free NGC/PCGS coin in MS67: $800. NGC ID# 22PW, PCGS# 3915

7278 **1913-D Type One MS66+ PCGS.** PCGS Population (350/57). NGC Census: (176/16). Mintage: 5,337,000. Numismedia Wsl. Price for problem free NGC/PCGS coin in MS66: $535. NGC ID# 22PX, PCGS# 3916

7279 **1913 Type Two MS66 PCGS.** PCGS Population (199/20). NGC Census: (82/6). Mintage: 29,858,700. Numismedia Wsl. Price for problem free NGC/PCGS coin in MS66: $860. NGC ID# 22PZ, PCGS# 3921

7280 **1914 MS65 PCGS.** PCGS Population (333/180). NGC Census: (196/63). Mintage: 20,665,738. Numismedia Wsl. Price for problem free NGC/PCGS coin in MS65: $400. NGC ID# 22R4, PCGS# 3924

7281 **1914-D MS64 PCGS.** PCGS Population (353/221). NGC Census: (244/88). Mintage: 3,912,000. Numismedia Wsl. Price for problem free NGC/PCGS coin in MS64: $600. NGC ID# 22R5, PCGS# 3925

7282 **1914-D MS64 PCGS. CAC.** PCGS Population (353/221). NGC Census: (244/88). Mintage: 3,912,000. Numismedia Wsl. Price for problem free NGC/PCGS coin in MS64: $600. NGC ID# 22R5, PCGS# 3925

7283 **1914-S MS64 PCGS.** PCGS Population (440/154). NGC Census: (388/76). Mintage: 3,470,000. Numismedia Wsl. Price for problem free NGC/PCGS coin in MS64: $550. NGC ID# 22R6, PCGS# 3926

7284 **1915 MS66 PCGS.** PCGS Population (241/40). NGC Census: (76/8). Mintage: 20,987,270. Numismedia Wsl. Price for problem free NGC/PCGS coin in MS66: $500. NGC ID# 22R7, PCGS# 3927

7285 **1915-D MS64 PCGS.** PCGS Population (232/176). NGC Census: (185/78). Mintage: 7,569,000. Numismedia Wsl. Price for problem free NGC/PCGS coin in MS64: $460. NGC ID# 22R8, PCGS# 3928

7286 **1918 MS64 PCGS.** PCGS Population (390/249). NGC Census: (228/76). Mintage: 32,086,314. Numismedia Wsl. Price for problem free NGC/PCGS coin in MS64: $460. NGC ID# 22RG, PCGS# 3937

7287 **1918/7-D Good 6 NGC.** NGC Census: (117/537). PCGS Population (203/855). Mintage: 8,362,000. Numismedia Wsl. Price for problem free NGC/PCGS coin in Good 6: $989. NGC ID# 22RJ, PCGS# 3939

7288 **1918-D MS62 NGC.** NGC Census: (72/230). PCGS Population (61/476). Mintage: 8,362,000. Numismedia Wsl. Price for problem free NGC/PCGS coin in MS62: $625. NGC ID# 22RH, PCGS# 3938

7289 **1919 MS65 NGC.** NGC Census: (189/45). PCGS Population (410/163). Mintage: 60,868,000. Numismedia Wsl. Price for problem free NGC/PCGS coin in MS65: $400. NGC ID# 22RL, PCGS# 3941

7290 **1919 MS65 PCGS.** PCGS Population (409/161). NGC Census: (190/47). Mintage: 60,868,000. Numismedia Wsl. Price for problem free NGC/PCGS coin in MS65: $400. NGC ID# 22RL, PCGS# 3941

7291 **1919-D AU58 PCGS. CAC.** PCGS Population (64/449). NGC Census: (78/276). Mintage: 8,006,000. Numismedia Wsl. Price for problem free NGC/PCGS coin in AU58: $455. NGC ID# 22RM, PCGS# 3942

7292 **1920-D AU53 PCGS.** PCGS Population (20/541). NGC Census: (9/484). Mintage: 9,418,000. Numismedia Wsl. Price for problem free NGC/PCGS coin in AU53: $285. NGC ID# 22RR, PCGS# 3945

7293 **1920-D MS61 PCGS.** PCGS Population (6/446). NGC Census: (18/393). Mintage: 9,418,000. Numismedia Wsl. Price for problem free NGC/PCGS coin in MS61: $525. NGC ID# 22RR, PCGS# 3945

7294 **1920-S AU58 PCGS.** PCGS Population (99/448). NGC Census: (77/409). Mintage: 9,689,000. Numismedia Wsl. Price for problem free NGC/PCGS coin in AU58: $385. NGC ID# 22RS, PCGS# 3946

7295 **1921 MS65+ PCGS. CAC.** PCGS Population (262/187). NGC Census: (134/68). Mintage: 10,663,000. Numismedia Wsl. Price for problem free NGC/PCGS coin in MS65: $685. NGC ID# 22RT, PCGS# 3947

7296 **1923-S MS63 PCGS.** PCGS Population (249/445). NGC Census: (185/348). Mintage: 6,142,000. Numismedia Wsl. Price for problem free NGC/PCGS coin in MS63: $775. NGC ID# 22RW, PCGS# 3950

7297 **1925 MS65 PCGS.** PCGS Population (506/263). NGC Census: (211/130). Mintage: 35,565,100. Numismedia Wsl. Price for problem free NGC/PCGS coin in MS65: $320. NGC ID# 22S2, PCGS# 3954

7298 **1925 MS66 PCGS.** PCGS Population (254/12). NGC Census: (125/5). Mintage: 35,565,100. Numismedia Wsl. Price for problem free NGC/PCGS coin in MS66: $575. NGC ID# 22S2, PCGS# 3954

7299 **1926 MS66 PCGS.** PCGS Population (394/35). NGC Census: (162/16). Mintage: 44,693,000. Numismedia Wsl. Price for problem free NGC/PCGS coin in MS66: $400. NGC ID# 22S5, PCGS# 3957

7300 **1926 MS66 NGC.** NGC Census: (161/16). PCGS Population (395/35). Mintage: 44,693,000. Numismedia Wsl. Price for problem free NGC/PCGS coin in MS66: $400. NGC ID# 22S5, PCGS# 3957

7301 **1927 MS66 PCGS.** PCGS Population (303/6). NGC Census: (89/10). Mintage: 37,981,000. Numismedia Wsl. Price for problem free NGC/PCGS coin in MS66: $460. NGC ID# 22S8, PCGS# 3960

7302 **1927 MS66 PCGS.** PCGS Population (303/6). NGC Census: (89/10). Mintage: 37,981,000. Numismedia Wsl. Price for problem free NGC/PCGS coin in MS66: $460. NGC ID# 22S8, PCGS# 3960

7303 **1927 MS66 PCGS. CAC.** PCGS Population (304/6). NGC Census: (89/10). Mintage: 37,981,000. Numismedia Wsl. Price for problem free NGC/PCGS coin in MS66: $460. NGC ID# 22S8, PCGS# 3960

7304 **1927-D MS64 ★ NGC.** NGC Census: (274/35). PCGS Population (440/64). Mintage: 5,730,000. Numismedia Wsl. Price for problem free NGC/PCGS coin in MS64: $735. NGC ID# 22S9, PCGS# 3961

7305 **1928 MS66 PCGS.** PCGS Population (216/15). NGC Census: (49/6). Mintage: 23,411,000. Numismedia Wsl. Price for problem free NGC/PCGS coin in MS66: $460. NGC ID# 22SB, PCGS# 3963

7306 **1928 MS66 PCGS. CAC.** PCGS Population (216/15). NGC Census: (49/6). Mintage: 23,411,000. Numismedia Wsl. Price for problem free NGC/PCGS coin in MS66: $460. NGC ID# 22SB, PCGS# 3963

7307 **1928-S MS64 NGC.** NGC Census: (256/54). PCGS Population (362/79). Mintage: 6,936,000. Numismedia Wsl. Price for problem free NGC/PCGS coin in MS64: $800. NGC ID# 22SD, PCGS# 3965

7308 **1929 MS66 NGC.** NGC Census: (49/1). PCGS Population (186/6). Mintage: 36,446,000. Numismedia Wsl. Price for problem free NGC/PCGS coin in MS66: $675. NGC ID# 22SE, PCGS# 3966

7309 **1929-D MS65 PCGS.** PCGS Population (177/52). NGC Census: (57/14). Mintage: 8,370,000. Numismedia Wsl. Price for problem free NGC/PCGS coin in MS65: $875. NGC ID# 22SF, PCGS# 3967

7310 **1929-S MS66 PCGS.** PCGS Population (195/8). NGC Census: (46/4). Mintage: 7,754,000. Numismedia Wsl. Price for problem free NGC/PCGS coin in MS66: $585. NGC ID# 22SG, PCGS# 3968

7311 **1929-S MS66 PCGS.** PCGS Population (194/8). NGC Census: (46/4). Mintage: 7,754,000. Numismedia Wsl. Price for problem free NGC/PCGS coin in MS66: $585. NGC ID# 22SG, PCGS# 3968

7312 **1930 MS66 PCGS.** PCGS Population (403/29). NGC Census: (90/6). Mintage: 22,849,000. Numismedia Wsl. Price for problem free NGC/PCGS coin in MS66: $320. NGC ID# 22SH, PCGS# 3969

7313 **1931-S MS66 PCGS.** PCGS Population (453/4). NGC Census: (69/3). Mintage: 1,200,000. Numismedia Wsl. Price for problem free NGC/PCGS coin in MS66: $545. NGC ID# 22SK, PCGS# 3971

7314 **1931-S MS66 PCGS.** PCGS Population (453/4). NGC Census: (69/3). Mintage: 1,200,000. Numismedia Wsl. Price for problem free NGC/PCGS coin in MS66: $545. NGC ID# 22SK, PCGS# 3971

7315 **1934 MS66 NGC.** NGC Census: (80/6). PCGS Population (191/24). Mintage: 20,213,004. Numismedia Wsl. Price for problem free NGC/PCGS coin in MS66: $440. NGC ID# 22SL, PCGS# 3972

7316 **1934-D MS65 PCGS.** PCGS Population (370/61). NGC Census: (106/16). Mintage: 7,480,000. Numismedia Wsl. Price for problem free NGC/PCGS coin in MS65: $440. NGC ID# 22SM, PCGS# 3973

7317 **1937 MS67 PCGS.** PCGS Population (340/7). NGC Census: (391/5). Mintage: 79,485,768. Numismedia Wsl. Price for problem free NGC/PCGS coin in MS67: $320. NGC ID# 22SV, PCGS# 3980

7318 **1937 MS67+ NGC. CAC.** NGC Census: (396/5). PCGS Population (340/7). Mintage: 79,485,768. Numismedia Wsl. Price for problem free NGC/PCGS coin in MS67: $320. NGC ID# 22SV, PCGS# 3980

7319 **1937-D MS67 ★ NGC.** NGC Census: (107/2). PCGS Population (91/1). Mintage: 17,826,000. Numismedia Wsl. Price for problem free NGC/PCGS coin in MS67: $460. NGC ID# 22SW, PCGS# 3981

7320 **1937-D Three-Legged VF25 NGC.** NGC Census: (257/5444). PCGS Population (349/6048). Mintage: 17,826,000. Numismedia Wsl. Price for problem free NGC/PCGS coin in VF25: $620. NGC ID# 22SX, PCGS# 3982

7321 **1937-D Three-Legged AU55 NGC. CAC.** NGC Census: (730/2977). PCGS Population (927/1779). Mintage: 17,826,000. Numismedia Wsl. Price for problem free NGC/PCGS coin in AU55: $965. NGC ID# 22SX, PCGS# 3982

7322 **1937-D Three-Legged, FS-901, XF40 NGC.** (FS-020.2). NGC Census: (0/0). PCGS Population (8/34). Mintage: 17,826,000. PCGS# 38475

7323 **(15)1938-D MS66 NGC.** NGC Census: (20605/2101). PCGS Population (28903/1655). Mintage: 7,020,000. Numismedia Wsl. Price for problem free NGC/PCGS coin in MS66: $50. (Total: 15 coins)

7324 **(15)1938-D MS66 NGC.** NGC Census: (20605/2101). PCGS Population (28903/1655). Mintage: 7,020,000. Numismedia Wsl. Price for problem free NGC/PCGS coin in MS66: $50. (Total: 15 coins)

JEFFERSON NICKELS

7325 **1940-S MS67 Six Full Steps NGC.** NGC Census: (5/0). PCGS Population (0/0). PCGS# 74009

7326 **1945-P MS67 PCGS.** PCGS Population (41/0). NGC Census: (337/2). Mintage: 119,408,096. Numismedia Wsl. Price for problem free NGC/PCGS coin in MS67: $325. NGC ID# 22TX, PCGS# 4025

7327 **1945-S MS67+ PCGS.** PCGS Population (132/1). NGC Census: (1690/2). Mintage: 58,939,000. Numismedia Wsl. Price for problem free NGC/PCGS coin in MS67: $60. NGC ID# 22TZ, PCGS# 4027

7328 **1945-S MS68 NGC.** NGC Census: (2/0). PCGS Population (1/0). Mintage: 58,939,000. Numismedia Wsl. Price for problem free NGC/PCGS coin in MS68: $1,625. NGC ID# 22TZ, PCGS# 4027

7329 **1945-S MS66 Full Steps PCGS.** PCGS Population (98/5). NGC Census: (18/6). Numismedia Wsl. Price for problem free NGC/PCGS coin in MS66: $675. NGC ID# 22TZ, PCGS# 84027

7330 **1948 MS67 NGC.** NGC Census: (13/0). PCGS Population (1/0). Mintage: 89,348,000. NGC ID# 22U8, PCGS# 4034

7331 **1948-D MS66 Six Full Steps NGC.** NGC Census: (4/1). PCGS Population (0/0). PCGS# 74035

7332 **1949-D/S MS66 PCGS. CAC.** PCGS Population (58/2). NGC Census: (13/0). Mintage: 36,498,000. Numismedia Wsl. Price for problem free NGC/PCGS coin in MS66: $650. NGC ID# 22UC, PCGS# 4039

SMS JEFFERSON NICKEL

7333 **1965 SMS MS68 Cameo NGC.** NGC Census: (12/0). PCGS Population (5/0). PCGS# 84197

PROOF JEFFERSON NICKELS

7334 **1951 Doubled Die Obverse, FS-101 PR69 Cameo NGC.** (FS-032.5). This DDO has a Registry Point Value of 7594. NGC Census: (0/0). PCGS Population (0/0). PCGS# 38544

7335 **1953 Doubled Die Obverse , FS-101 PR68 ★ NGC.** This DDO has Registry Point Value of 4503. NGC Census: (0/0). PCGS Population (1/0). Mintage: 128,800. PCGS# 38546

7336 **1953 Doubled Die Obverse, FS-101, PR69 NGC.** The Registry Points for this DDO variety are 7061. NGC Census: (0/0). PCGS Population (0/0). Mintage: 128,800. PCGS# 38546

7337 **1957 PR69 Cameo NGC.** NGC Census: (21/0). PCGS Population (0/0). Numismedia Wsl. Price for problem free NGC/PCGS coin in PR69: $650. NGC ID# 22YH, PCGS# 84189

7338 **1957 Quadrupled Die Obverse, FS-101, PR67 NGC.** NGC Census: (0/0). PCGS Population (6/0). Mintage: 1,247,952. PCGS# 38555

7339 **1958 PR69 Cameo NGC.** NGC Census: (34/0). PCGS Population (1/0). Numismedia Wsl. Price for problem free NGC/PCGS coin in PR69: $300. NGC ID# 27A8, PCGS# 84190

7340 **1960 PR68 Ultra Cameo NGC.** NGC Census: (22/6). PCGS Population (59/6). Numismedia Wsl. Price for problem free NGC/PCGS coin in PR68: $340. NGC ID# 22YJ, PCGS# 94192

7341 **1962 PR69 Ultra Cameo NGC.** NGC Census: (25/0). PCGS Population (56/0). Numismedia Wsl. Price for problem free NGC/PCGS coin in PR69: $500. NGC ID# 27AA, PCGS# 94194

7342 **1963 PR69 Ultra Cameo NGC.** NGC Census: (50/0). PCGS Population (75/1). Numismedia Wsl. Price for problem free NGC/PCGS coin in PR69: $340. NGC ID# 27AB, PCGS# 94195

EARLY HALF DIME

7343 **1800 V-1, LM-1, R.3, — Bent — PCGS Genuine. VF Details.** NGC Census: (0/10). PCGS Population (0/1). Mintage: 40,000.

BUST HALF DIMES

7344 **1833 MS63 PCGS.** PCGS Population (100/132). NGC Census: (89/175). Mintage: 1,370,000. Numismedia Wsl. Price for problem free NGC/PCGS coin in MS63: $825. NGC ID# 232F, PCGS# 4280

7345 **1835 Small Date, Large 5C, — Artificially Toned — NGC Details. Unc.** NGC Census: (0/0). PCGS Population (1/25).

SEATED HALF DIMES

7346 **1837 No Stars, Small Date (Flat Top 1) AU58 PCGS.** PCGS Population (37/127). NGC Census: (0/0). Numismedia Wsl. Price for problem free NGC/PCGS coin in AU58: $475. NGC ID# 232M, PCGS# 4312

7347 **1845 MS64 PCGS. CAC.** PCGS Population (46/43). NGC Census: (47/41). Mintage: 1,564,000. Numismedia Wsl. Price for problem free NGC/PCGS coin in MS64: $500. NGC ID# 2337, PCGS# 4335

7348 **1852 MS65 NGC.** NGC Census: (32/15). PCGS Population (18/13). Mintage: 1,000,500. Numismedia Wsl. Price for problem free NGC/PCGS coin in MS65: $1,025. NGC ID# 233K, PCGS# 4349

7349 **1853-O No Arrows VF20 NGC.** NGC Census: (3/21). PCGS Population (5/34). Mintage: 160,000. Numismedia Wsl. Price for problem free NGC/PCGS coin in VF20: $925. NGC ID# 233N, PCGS# 4352

7350 **1858 MS66 PCGS.** PCGS Population (62/13). NGC Census: (58/26). Mintage: 3,500,000. Numismedia Wsl. Price for problem free NGC/PCGS coin in MS66: $1,100. NGC ID# 233U, PCGS# 4367

PROOF SEATED HALF DIME

7351 **1859 PR62+ PCGS.** PCGS Population (30/175). NGC Census: (22/181). Mintage: 800. Numismedia Wsl. Price for problem free NGC/PCGS coin in PR62: $580. NGC ID# 235P, PCGS# 4438

EARLY DIMES

7352 **1796 JR-2, R.4, Fair 2 PCGS.** PCGS Population (1/1). NGC Census: (0/5). Mintage: 22,135. PCGS# 38743

7353 **1805 4 Berries VG8 PCGS.** PCGS Population (20/325). NGC Census: (2/30). Mintage: 120,780. Numismedia Wsl. Price for problem free NGC/PCGS coin in VG8: $800. NGC ID# 236S, PCGS# 4477

7354 **1807 JR-1, R.2, — Damage — PCGS Genuine. XF Details.** NGC Census: (8/183). PCGS Population (0/5). Mintage: 165,000.

BUST DIMES

7355 **1831 AU55 NGC.** NGC Census: (23/213). PCGS Population (30/176). Mintage: 771,350. Numismedia Wsl. Price for problem free NGC/PCGS coin in AU55: $450. NGC ID# 237B, PCGS# 4520

7356 **1835 JR-4, R.2, AU58 PCGS.** PCGS Population (1/2). NGC Census: (0/2). Mintage: 1,410,000. PCGS# 38882

SEATED DIMES

7357 **1837 No Stars, Large Date — Filed Rims — PCGS Genuine. AU Details.** NGC Census: (14/335). PCGS Population (34/238). Mintage: 682,500. Numismedia Wsl. Price for problem free NGC/PCGS coin in AU50: $575.

7358 **1837 No Stars, Large Date AU53 PCGS.** PCGS Population (19/219). NGC Census: (9/326). Mintage: 682,500. Numismedia Wsl. Price for problem free NGC/PCGS coin in AU53: $600. NGC ID# 237R, PCGS# 4561

7359 **1839-O No Drapery AU55 PCGS.** PCGS Population (9/39). NGC Census: (7/50). Mintage: 1,323,000. Numismedia Wsl. Price for problem free NGC/PCGS coin in AU55: $350. NGC ID# 237Y, PCGS# 4572

7360 1846 Fine 12 PCGS. PCGS Population (17/93). NGC Census: (0/39). Mintage: 31,300. Numismedia Wsl. Price for problem free NGC/PCGS coin in Fine 12: $425. NGC ID# 238D, PCGS# 4588

7361 1856-S — Cleaning — PCGS Genuine. VF Details. NGC Census: (0/21). PCGS Population (5/43). Mintage: 70,000. Numismedia Wsl. Price for problem free NGC/PCGS coin in VF20: $750.

7362 1865-S VF20 PCGS. PCGS Population (9/50). NGC Census: (0/22). Mintage: 175,000. Numismedia Wsl. Price for problem free NGC/PCGS coin in VF20: $400. NGC ID# 239R, PCGS# 4642

7363 1867-S XF45 NGC. NGC Census: (3/15). PCGS Population (3/21). Mintage: 140,000. Numismedia Wsl. Price for problem free NGC/PCGS coin in XF45: $480. NGC ID# 239V, PCGS# 4646

7364 1876-CC MS62 PCGS. PCGS Population (36/194). NGC Census: (31/196). Mintage: 8,270,000. Numismedia Wsl. Price for problem free NGC/PCGS coin in MS62: $425. NGC ID# 23AJ, PCGS# 4680

7365 1877-CC MS64 PCGS. PCGS Population (86/94). NGC Census: (86/130). Mintage: 7,700,000. Numismedia Wsl. Price for problem free NGC/PCGS coin in MS64: $725. NGC ID# 23AM, PCGS# 4683

7366 1879 MS64 PCGS. PCGS Population (55/133). NGC Census: (30/96). Mintage: 14,000. Numismedia Wsl. Price for problem free NGC/PCGS coin in MS64: $625. NGC ID# 23AS, PCGS# 4687

7367 1880 AU58 PCGS. PCGS Population (3/137). NGC Census: (4/121). Mintage: 36,000. Numismedia Wsl. Price for problem free NGC/PCGS coin in AU58: $400. NGC ID# 23AT, PCGS# 4688

7368 1881 MS63 PCGS. PCGS Population (22/33). NGC Census: (6/44). Mintage: 24,000. Numismedia Wsl. Price for problem free NGC/PCGS coin in MS63: $600. NGC ID# 23AU, PCGS# 4689

7369 1890 MS65 NGC. NGC Census: (90/73). PCGS Population (59/53). Mintage: 9,910,951. Numismedia Wsl. Price for problem free NGC/PCGS coin in MS65: $650. NGC ID# 23BB, PCGS# 4704

7370 1890 MS66 NGC. NGC Census: (62/10). PCGS Population (51/4). Mintage: 9,910,951. Numismedia Wsl. Price for problem free NGC/PCGS coin in MS66: $925. NGC ID# 23BB, PCGS# 4704

7371 1891 MS64 PCGS. PCGS Population (221/185). NGC Census: (287/204). Mintage: 15,310,600. Numismedia Wsl. Price for problem free NGC/PCGS coin in MS64: $340. NGC ID# 23BD, PCGS# 4706

PROOF SEATED DIMES

7372 1873 Arrows PR61 PCGS. PCGS Population (6/127). NGC Census: (3/87). Mintage: 800. Numismedia Wsl. Price for problem free NGC/PCGS coin in PR61: $535. NGC ID# 23DH, PCGS# 4769

7373 1879 PR62 NGC. NGC Census: (29/202). PCGS Population (69/206). Mintage: 1,100. Numismedia Wsl. Price for problem free NGC/PCGS coin in PR62: $425. NGC ID# 23D4, PCGS# 4776

7374 1891 PR63 Cameo PCGS. PCGS Population (7/40). NGC Census: (2/38). PCGS# 84788

BARBER DIMES

7375 1892 MS65 PCGS. CAC. PCGS Population (139/104). NGC Census: (135/88). Mintage: 12,121,245. Numismedia Wsl. Price for problem free NGC/PCGS coin in MS65: $510. NGC ID# 23DK, PCGS# 4796

7376 1892-S MS62 PCGS. PCGS Population (14/71). NGC Census: (22/64). Mintage: 990,710. Numismedia Wsl. Price for problem free NGC/PCGS coin in MS62: $475. NGC ID# 23DM, PCGS# 4798

7377 1896-O — Cleaning — PCGS Genuine. AU Details. NGC Census: (2/32). PCGS Population (5/52). Mintage: 610,000. Numismedia Wsl. Price for problem free NGC/PCGS coin in AU50: $615.

7378 1901-S — Cleaning — PCGS Genuine. AU Details. NGC Census: (1/51). PCGS Population (4/68). Mintage: 593,022. Numismedia Wsl. Price for problem free NGC/PCGS coin in AU50: $580.

7379 1907 MS65+ PCGS. PCGS Population (47/19). NGC Census: (46/45). Mintage: 22,220,576. Numismedia Wsl. Price for problem free NGC/PCGS coin in MS65: $500. NGC ID# 23F3, PCGS# 4842

7380 1916 MS64 PCGS. PCGS Population (340/151). NGC Census: (313/186). Mintage: 18,490,000. Numismedia Wsl. Price for problem free NGC/PCGS coin in MS64: $280. NGC ID# 23FY, PCGS# 4870

PROOF BARBER DIMES

7381 1904 PR64 PCGS. CAC. PCGS Population (93/71). NGC Census: (60/76). Mintage: 670. Numismedia Wsl. Price for problem free NGC/PCGS coin in PR64: $710. NGC ID# 23GH, PCGS# 4888

7382 1907 PR64 NGC. NGC Census: (55/77). PCGS Population (47/65). Mintage: 575. Numismedia Wsl. Price for problem free NGC/PCGS coin in PR64: $735. NGC ID# 23GM, PCGS# 4891

MERCURY DIMES

7383 1916-D AG3 PCGS. PCGS Population (2165/3763). NGC Census: (0/1499). Mintage: 264,000. Numismedia Wsl. Price for problem free NGC/PCGS coin in AG3: $409. NGC ID# 23GY, PCGS# 4906

7384 1916-D — Reverse Scratched — NGC Details. Good. NGC Census: (462/1039). PCGS Population (1288/2480). Mintage: 264,000. Numismedia Wsl. Price for problem free NGC/PCGS coin in Good 4: $670.

7385 1916-D Good 4 PCGS. PCGS Population (1288/2480). NGC Census: (462/1039). Mintage: 264,000. Numismedia Wsl. Price for problem free NGC/PCGS coin in Good 4: $670. NGC ID# 23GY, PCGS# 4906

7386 1916-D Good 6 NGC. NGC Census: (200/839). PCGS Population (640/1840). Mintage: 264,000. Numismedia Wsl. Price for problem free NGC/PCGS coin in Good 6: $856. NGC ID# 23GY, PCGS# 4906

7387 **1916-D — Bent — NGC Details. VG.** NGC Census: (218/621). PCGS Population (395/1445). Mintage: 264,000. Numismedia Wsl. Price for problem free NGC/PCGS coin in VG8: $1,200.

7388 **1916-D — Obverse Damage — NGC Details. VG.** NGC Census: (217/621). PCGS Population (395/1445). Mintage: 264,000. Numismedia Wsl. Price for problem free NGC/PCGS coin in VG8: $1,200.

7389 **1916-S MS65 Full Bands PCGS.** Ex: Col. Green-Newman. PCGS Population (142/100). NGC Census: (76/30). Mintage: 10,450,000. Numismedia Wsl. Price for problem free NGC/PCGS coin in MS65: $575. NGC ID# 23GZ, PCGS# 4909

7390 **1916-S MS66 Full Bands NGC.** NGC Census: (25/5). PCGS Population (80/20). Mintage: 10,450,000. Numismedia Wsl. Price for problem free NGC/PCGS coin in MS66: $1,100. NGC ID# 23GZ, PCGS# 4909

7391 **1917 MS66 Full Bands PCGS.** PCGS Population (93/21). NGC Census: (40/8). Mintage: 55,230,000. Numismedia Wsl. Price for problem free NGC/PCGS coin in MS66: $825. NGC ID# 23H2, PCGS# 4911

7392 **1917-D MS64 Full Bands NGC. CAC.** NGC Census: (67/18). PCGS Population (109/52). Mintage: 9,402,000. Numismedia Wsl. Price for problem free NGC/PCGS coin in MS64: $785. NGC ID# 23H3, PCGS# 4913

7393 **1917-S MS64 Full Bands PCGS.** PCGS Population (183/189). NGC Census: (75/45). Mintage: 27,330,000. Numismedia Wsl. Price for problem free NGC/PCGS coin in MS64: $340. NGC ID# 23H4, PCGS# 4915

7394 **1918-D MS65 PCGS.** PCGS Population (75/11). NGC Census: (44/14). Mintage: 22,674,800. Numismedia Wsl. Price for problem free NGC/PCGS coin in MS65: $550. NGC ID# 23H6, PCGS# 4918

7395 **1921 AU55 PCGS.** PCGS Population (38/46). NGC Census: (18/41). Mintage: 1,230,000. Numismedia Wsl. Price for problem free NGC/PCGS coin in AU55: $785. NGC ID# 23HE, PCGS# 4934

7396 **1921-D XF40 PCGS.** PCGS Population (57/296). NGC Census: (42/205). Mintage: 1,080,000. Numismedia Wsl. Price for problem free NGC/PCGS coin in XF40: $520. NGC ID# 23HF, PCGS# 4936

7397 **1921-D — Cleaning — PCGS Genuine. Unc Details.** NGC Census: (0/103). PCGS Population (3/114). Mintage: 1,080,000. Numismedia Wsl. Price for problem free NGC/PCGS coin in MS60: $1,200.

7398 **1924 MS66 Full Bands PCGS.** PCGS Population (93/29). NGC Census: (64/16). Mintage: 24,010,000. Numismedia Wsl. Price for problem free NGC/PCGS coin in MS66: $750. NGC ID# 23HJ, PCGS# 4943

7399 **1924-D MS64 Full Bands PCGS.** PCGS Population (166/125). NGC Census: (122/79). Mintage: 6,810,000. Numismedia Wsl. Price for problem free NGC/PCGS coin in MS64: $525. NGC ID# 23HK, PCGS# 4945

7400 **1925 MS65 Full Bands NGC.** NGC Census: (45/19). PCGS Population (94/76). Mintage: 25,610,000. Numismedia Wsl. Price for problem free NGC/PCGS coin in MS65: $635. NGC ID# 23HM, PCGS# 4949

7401 **1925-D MS62 PCGS.** PCGS Population (12/36). NGC Census: (18/35). Mintage: 5,117,000. Numismedia Wsl. Price for problem free NGC/PCGS coin in MS62: $450. NGC ID# 23HN, PCGS# 4950

7402 **1928 MS66+ Full Bands PCGS. CAC.** PCGS Population (124/32). NGC Census: (32/5). Mintage: 19,480,000. Numismedia Wsl. Price for problem free NGC/PCGS coin in MS66: $380. NGC ID# 23HX, PCGS# 4967

7403 **1931-D MS66 Full Bands PCGS.** PCGS Population (173/53). NGC Census: (55/13). Mintage: 1,260,000. Numismedia Wsl. Price for problem free NGC/PCGS coin in MS66: $625. NGC ID# 23J8, PCGS# 4985

7404 **1931-D MS66 Full Bands PCGS. CAC.** PCGS Population (173/53). NGC Census: (55/13). Mintage: 1,260,000. Numismedia Wsl. Price for problem free NGC/PCGS coin in MS66: $625. NGC ID# 23J8, PCGS# 4985

7405 **1931-S MS64 Full Bands PCGS.** PCGS Population (60/102). NGC Census: (14/20). Mintage: 1,800,000. Numismedia Wsl. Price for problem free NGC/PCGS coin in MS64: $635. NGC ID# 23J9, PCGS# 4987

7406 **1934 MS67+ Full Bands PCGS. CAC.** PCGS Population (186/21). NGC Census: (61/8). Mintage: 24,080,000. Numismedia Wsl. Price for problem free NGC/PCGS coin in MS67: $380. NGC ID# 23JA, PCGS# 4989

7407 **1935-S MS66 Full Bands PCGS.** PCGS Population (150/95). NGC Census: (72/27). Mintage: 15,840,000. Numismedia Wsl. Price for problem free NGC/PCGS coin in MS66: $380. NGC ID# 23JE, PCGS# 4997

7408 **1936-S MS67 Full Bands PCGS.** PCGS Population (174/3). NGC Census: (51/1). Mintage: 9,210,000. Numismedia Wsl. Price for problem free NGC/PCGS coin in MS67: $440. NGC ID# 23JH, PCGS# 5003

7409 **1941 MS67+ Full Bands PCGS. CAC.** PCGS Population (291/9). NGC Census: (287/5). Mintage: 175,106,560. Numismedia Wsl. Price for problem free NGC/PCGS coin in MS67: $185. NGC ID# 23JX, PCGS# 5029

7410 **1942/1 VF30 PCGS.** PCGS Population (277/1459). NGC Census: (185/1098). Mintage: 205,432,336. Numismedia Wsl. Price for problem free NGC/PCGS coin in VF30: $455. NGC ID# 23K4, PCGS# 5036

7411 **1942/1 — Cleaning — PCGS Genuine. AU Details.** NGC Census: (80/465). PCGS Population (132/407). Mintage: 205,432,336. Numismedia Wsl. Price for problem free NGC/PCGS coin in AU50: $790.

7412 **1942/1 — Improperly Cleaned — NGC Details. AU.** NGC Census: (80/466). PCGS Population (133/411). Mintage: 205,432,336. Numismedia Wsl. Price for problem free NGC/PCGS coin in AU50: $790.

7413 **1942 MS67 Full Bands PCGS. CAC.** PCGS Population (173/7). NGC Census: (222/1). Mintage: 205,432,336. Numismedia Wsl. Price for problem free NGC/PCGS coin in MS67: $300. NGC ID# 23K3, PCGS# 5035

7414 **1942-S MS67 Full Bands PCGS. CAC.** PCGS Population (183/4). NGC Census: (81/2). Mintage: 49,300,000. Numismedia Wsl. Price for problem free NGC/PCGS coin in MS67: $340. NGC ID# 23K7, PCGS# 5043

7415 **1944 MS66 Full Bands PCGS. Gold CAC.** PCGS Population (443/107). NGC Census: (195/60). Mintage: 231,410,000. Numismedia Wsl. Price for problem free NGC/PCGS coin in MS66: $135. NGC ID# 23KB, PCGS# 5051

PROOF MERCURY DIME

7416 **1941 PR67 PCGS.** PCGS Population (312/20). NGC Census: (388/47). Mintage: 16,557. Numismedia Wsl. Price for problem free NGC/PCGS coin in PR67: $285. NGC ID# 27DM, PCGS# 5076

ROOSEVELT DIMES

7417 **1946-D MS67+ Full Bands PCGS.** PCGS Population (84/2). NGC Census: (137/2). Mintage: 61,043,500. Numismedia Wsl. Price for problem free NGC/PCGS coin in MS67: $120. NGC ID# 23KK, PCGS# 85083

7418 **1946-S MS67+ Full Bands PCGS.** PCGS Population (143/9). NGC Census: (208/3). Mintage: 27,900,000. Numismedia Wsl. Price for problem free NGC/PCGS coin in MS67: $135. NGC ID# 23KL, PCGS# 85084

7419 **1948-D MS68 Full Bands NGC.** NGC Census: (4/0). PCGS Population (3/0). Mintage: 52,841,000. Numismedia Wsl. Price for problem free NGC/PCGS coin in MS68: $2,185. NGC ID# 23KS, PCGS# 85089

7420 **1948-S MS67+ Full Bands PCGS.** PCGS Population (4/1). NGC Census: (8/0). Mintage: 35,520,000. Numismedia Wsl. Price for problem free NGC/PCGS coin in MS67: $140. NGC ID# 23KT, PCGS# 85090

7421 **1949-D MS67+ Full Bands PCGS.** PCGS Population (103/8). NGC Census: (61/1). Mintage: 26,034,000. Numismedia Wsl. Price for problem free NGC/PCGS coin in MS67: $135. NGC ID# 23KV, PCGS# 85092

7422 **1949-S MS67 Full Bands NGC.** NGC Census: (17/0). PCGS Population (13/0). Mintage: 13,510,000. Numismedia Wsl. Price for problem free NGC/PCGS coin in MS67: $1,050. NGC ID# 23KW, PCGS# 85093

7423 **1952-S MS67 ★ Full Bands NGC.** NGC Census: (52/1). PCGS Population (43/4). Mintage: 44,419,500. Numismedia Wsl. Price for problem free NGC/PCGS coin in MS67: $190. NGC ID# 23L7, PCGS# 85102

7424 **1955 MS67 Full Bands NGC.** NGC Census: (14/0). PCGS Population (6/0). Mintage: 12,400,000. Numismedia Wsl. Price for problem free NGC/PCGS coin in MS67: $1,350. NGC ID# 23LE, PCGS# 85109

7425 **1956 MS67 Full Bands NGC.** NGC Census: (25/0). PCGS Population (14/1). Mintage: 108,640,000. Numismedia Wsl. Price for problem free NGC/PCGS coin in MS67: $800. NGC ID# 23LH, PCGS# 85112

7426 **1957 MS67 Full Bands NGC.** NGC Census: (7/0). PCGS Population (7/0). Mintage: 160,100,000. Numismedia Wsl. Price for problem free NGC/PCGS coin in MS67: $1,875. NGC ID# 23LK, PCGS# 85114

7427 **1960-D MS67 ★ Full Bands NGC.** NGC Census: (35/0). PCGS Population (22/0). Mintage: 200,160,400. Numismedia Wsl. Price for problem free NGC/PCGS coin in MS67: $525. NGC ID# 23LT, PCGS# 85121

7428 **1963 MS67 Full Bands NGC.** NGC Census: (8/0). PCGS Population (3/0). Mintage: 123,600,000. Numismedia Wsl. Price for problem free NGC/PCGS coin in MS67: $700. NGC ID# 23LY, PCGS# 85126

7429 **1964 MS67+ ★ Full Bands NGC.** NGC Census: (29/0). PCGS Population (22/0). Mintage: 929,299,968. Numismedia Wsl. Price for problem free NGC/PCGS coin in MS67: $240. NGC ID# 23M2, PCGS# 85128

7430 **1964-D Doubled Die Reverse MS65 PCGS.** PCGS Population (6/1). NGC Census: (0/0). PCGS# 95129

7431 **1965 MS68 Full Bands NGC.** NGC Census: (3/0). PCGS Population (1/0). Numismedia Wsl. Price for problem free NGC/PCGS coin in MS68: $2,075. NGC ID# 23M4, PCGS# 85130

7432 **1966 MS68 Full Bands NGC.** NGC Census: (3/0). PCGS Population (1/0). Numismedia Wsl. Price for problem free NGC/PCGS coin in MS68: $2,000. NGC ID# 23M5, PCGS# 85131

7433 **1967 MS68 Full Bands NGC.** NGC Census: (7/0). PCGS Population (2/0). NGC ID# 23M6, PCGS# 85132

7434 **1968-D MS68 Full Bands NGC.** NGC Census: (9/0). PCGS Population (7/0). Mintage: 480,748,288. NGC ID# 23M8, PCGS# 85134

7435 **1969-D MS68 Full Bands NGC.** NGC Census: (1/0). PCGS Population (0/0). Mintage: 563,323,840. NGC ID# 23MA, PCGS# 85136

7436 **1970 MS66 Full Bands NGC.** NGC Census: (2/1). PCGS Population (1/0). Mintage: 345,569,984. NGC ID# 23MB, PCGS# 85137

7437 **1972 MS67 Full Bands NGC.** NGC Census: (2/0). PCGS Population (1/0). Mintage: 431,540,000. NGC ID# 23MF, PCGS# 85141

7438 **1973 MS67 Full Bands NGC.** NGC Census: (1/0). PCGS Population (3/0). Mintage: 315,670,016. NGC ID# 23MH, PCGS# 85143

7439 **1974-D MS67 Full Bands NGC.** NGC Census: (5/0). PCGS Population (2/0). Mintage: 571,083,008. NGC ID# 23ML, PCGS# 85146

7440 **1975 MS67 Full Bands NGC.** NGC Census: (1/0). PCGS Population (3/0). Mintage: 585,673,920. NGC ID# 23MM, PCGS# 85147

7441 **1977-D MS67 Full Bands NGC.** NGC Census: (4/0). PCGS Population (4/0). Mintage: 376,607,232. NGC ID# 23MT, PCGS# 85152

7442 **1979-D MS67 Full Bands NGC.** NGC Census: (2/0). PCGS Population (1/0). Mintage: 390,921,184. NGC ID# 23MX, PCGS# 85156

7443 **1983-P MS67 Full Bands NGC.** NGC Census: (0/0). PCGS Population (0/0). Mintage: 647,025,024. NGC ID# 23N8, PCGS# 85164

7444 **1983-D MS67 Full Bands NGC.** NGC Census: (0/0). PCGS Population (1/0). Mintage: 730,129,216. NGC ID# 23N9, PCGS# 85165

7445 **1984-D MS68 Full Bands NGC.** NGC Census: (1/0). PCGS Population (1/0). Mintage: 704,803,968. NGC ID# 23NB, PCGS# 85167

7446 **1985-P MS69 Full Bands NGC.** NGC Census: (1/0). PCGS Population (0/0). Mintage: 705,200,960. NGC ID# 23NC, PCGS# 85168

7447 **1988-P MS68 Full Bands PCGS.** PCGS Population (2/0). NGC Census: (7/0). Mintage: 1,030,550,016. NGC ID# 23NJ, PCGS# 85174

7448 **1989-D MS69 Full Bands NGC.** NGC Census: (1/0). PCGS Population (0/0). Mintage: 896,535,616. NGC ID# 23NM, PCGS# 85177

7449 **1990-P MS68 Prooflike NGC.** NGC Census: (9/0). PCGS Population (6/0). Mintage: 1,034,339,968. NGC ID# 23NN, PCGS# 5178

7450 **1990-D MS69 NGC.** NGC Census: (1/0). PCGS Population (0/0). Mintage: 839,995,840. NGC ID# 23NP, PCGS# 5179

7451 **1992-P MS69 Full Bands NGC.** NGC Census: (1/0). PCGS Population (0/0). Mintage: 593,500,032. NGC ID# 23NT, PCGS# 85182

7452 **1992-D MS68 Full Bands NGC.** NGC Census: (4/0). PCGS Population (0/0). Mintage: 616,273,920. NGC ID# 23NU, PCGS# 85183

7453 **1993-P MS68 Full Bands NGC.** NGC Census: (4/0). PCGS Population (0/0). Mintage: 766,179,968. NGC ID# 23NV, PCGS# 85184

7454 **1993-D MS67 Full Bands NGC.** NGC Census: (4/0). PCGS Population (4/0). Mintage: 750,110,144. NGC ID# 23NW, PCGS# 85185

7455 **1995-P MS68 Full Bands NGC.** NGC Census: (5/0). PCGS Population (1/0). Mintage: 1,125,500,032. NGC ID# 23NZ, PCGS# 85188

7456 **1997-P MS68 Full Bands NGC.** NGC Census: (6/0). PCGS Population (2/0). Mintage: 991,640,000. NGC ID# 23P6, PCGS# 85193

7457 **1999-D MS68 Prooflike Full Bands NGC.** NGC Census: (5/0). PCGS Population (94/3). NGC ID# 23PB, PCGS# 85198

7458 **2006-D MS68 Full Bands NGC.** NGC Census: (1/1). PCGS Population (0/0). NGC ID# 27DY, PCGS# 85214

7459 **2008-D MS68 Full Bands NGC.** NGC Census: (2/0). PCGS Population (1/0). PCGS# 394930

7460 **2009-D MS69 Full Bands NGC.** NGC Census: (0/0). PCGS Population (0/0). NGC ID# 27EC, PCGS# 407268

PROOF ROOSEVELT DIMES

7461 **1956 PR69 Ultra Cameo NGC.** NGC Census: (15/0). PCGS Population (1/0). Numismedia Wsl. Price for problem free NGC/PCGS coin in PR69: $1,150. NGC ID# 27ER, PCGS# 95231

7462 **1957 PR69 Ultra Cameo NGC.** NGC Census: (20/0). PCGS Population (4/0). Numismedia Wsl. Price for problem free NGC/PCGS coin in PR69: $880. NGC ID# 27ES, PCGS# 95232

7463 **1958 PR69 Ultra Cameo NGC.** NGC Census: (11/0). PCGS Population (2/0). Numismedia Wsl. Price for problem free NGC/PCGS coin in PR69: $1,350. NGC ID# 27ET, PCGS# 95233

7464 **1960 Doubled Die Obverse, FS-103, PR68 Deep Cameo PCGS.** PCGS Population (0/0). NGC Census: (0/0). PCGS# 510052

7465 **1963 Doubled Die Reverse , FS-801 PR68 Deep Cameo PCGS.** (FS-017). PCGS Population (5/0). NGC Census: (0/0). PCGS# 146353

7466 **1963 Doubled Die Reverse , FS-803 PR69 NGC.** (FS-018). NGC Census: (0/0). PCGS Population (1/0). Mintage: 3,075,645. PCGS# 145364

TWENTY CENT PIECES

7467 **1875-CC VF30 PCGS.** PCGS Population (73/810). NGC Census: (37/541). Mintage: 133,290. Numismedia Wsl. Price for problem free NGC/PCGS coin in VF30: $668. NGC ID# 23R6, PCGS# 5297

7468 **1875-CC XF45 NGC.** NGC Census: (42/451). PCGS Population (74/590). Mintage: 133,290. Numismedia Wsl. Price for problem free NGC/PCGS coin in XF45: $900. NGC ID# 23R6, PCGS# 5297

7469 **1875-CC XF45 PCGS. CAC.** PCGS Population (74/590). NGC Census: (42/451). Mintage: 133,290. Numismedia Wsl. Price for problem free NGC/PCGS coin in XF45: $900. NGC ID# 23R6, PCGS# 5297

7470 **1875-CC — Cleaning — PCGS Genuine. AU Details.** NGC Census: (22/430). PCGS Population (59/528). Mintage: 133,290. Numismedia Wsl. Price for problem free NGC/PCGS coin in AU50: $975.

7471 **1875-S AU55 PCGS.** PCGS Population (250/1793). NGC Census: (172/1744). Mintage: 1,155,000. Numismedia Wsl. Price for problem free NGC/PCGS coin in AU55: $400. NGC ID# 23R7, PCGS# 5298

7472 **1875-S MS61 NGC.** NGC Census: (150/1278). PCGS Population (78/1381). Mintage: 1,155,000. Numismedia Wsl. Price for problem free NGC/PCGS coin in MS61: $625. NGC ID# 23R7, PCGS# 5298

7473 **1876 — Improperly Cleaned — NGC Details. Unc.** NGC Census: (4/276). PCGS Population (12/256). Mintage: 14,600. Numismedia Wsl. Price for problem free NGC/PCGS coin in MS60: $765.

EARLY QUARTER

7474 **1804 Poor 1 PCGS.** PCGS Population (1/252). NGC Census: (0/87). Mintage: 6,738. Numismedia Wsl. Price for problem free NGC/PCGS coin in Poor 1: $444. NGC ID# 23RB, PCGS# 5312

BUST QUARTERS

7475 **1818 VF35 PCGS.** PCGS Population (32/282). NGC Census: (15/256). Mintage: 361,174. Numismedia Wsl. Price for problem free NGC/PCGS coin in VF35: $983. NGC ID# 23RH, PCGS# 5322

7476 **1824/2 B-1, R.3, Good 4 PCGS.** PCGS Population (0/5). NGC Census: (7/64). Mintage: 168,000. PCGS# 38972

7477 **1825/4/(2) B-3, R.3, — Scratch — PCGS Genuine. XF Details.** NGC Census: (0/1). PCGS Population (4/8).

7478 1834 AU55 NGC. NGC Census: (37/210). PCGS Population (51/178). Mintage: 286,000. Numismedia Wsl. Price for problem free NGC/PCGS coin in AU55: $775. NGC ID# 23RZ, PCGS# 5353

7479 1835 B-2, R.2, — Cleaning — PCGS Genuine. AU Details. NGC Census: (0/5). PCGS Population (0/0). Mintage: 1,952,000.

7480 1837 AU53 NGC. NGC Census: (10/133). PCGS Population (7/108). Mintage: 252,400. Numismedia Wsl. Price for problem free NGC/PCGS coin in AU53: $625. NGC ID# 23S4, PCGS# 5356

7481 1837 AU55 NGC. NGC Census: (18/115). PCGS Population (16/92). Mintage: 252,400. Numismedia Wsl. Price for problem free NGC/PCGS coin in AU55: $750. NGC ID# 23S4, PCGS# 5356

SEATED QUARTERS

7482 1851 — Improperly Cleaned — NGC Details. AU. NGC Census: (1/23). PCGS Population (2/34). Mintage: 160,000. Numismedia Wsl. Price for problem free NGC/PCGS coin in AU50: $450.

7483 1851-O — Environmental Damage — NGC Details. Fine. NGC Census: (2/22). PCGS Population (8/44). Mintage: 88,000. Numismedia Wsl. Price for problem free NGC/PCGS coin in Fine 12: $600.

7484 1854 Arrows MS62 NGC. NGC Census: (58/145). PCGS Population (46/139). Mintage: 12,380,000. Numismedia Wsl. Price for problem free NGC/PCGS coin in MS62: $650. NGC ID# 23U6, PCGS# 5432

7485 1858 MS64 PCGS. PCGS Population (80/46). NGC Census: (82/46). Mintage: 7,368,000. Numismedia Wsl. Price for problem free NGC/PCGS coin in MS64: $925. NGC ID# 23TH, PCGS# 5445

7486 1858-S — Improperly Cleaned — NGC Details. VF. NGC Census: (0/29). PCGS Population (4/46). Mintage: 121,000. Numismedia Wsl. Price for problem free NGC/PCGS coin in VF20: $1,125.

7487 1859-S — Repaired — PCGS Genuine. VF Details. NGC Census: (0/14). PCGS Population (6/37). Mintage: 80,000. Numismedia Wsl. Price for problem free NGC/PCGS coin in VF20: $1,125.

7488 1860 MS63 NGC. NGC Census: (14/18). PCGS Population (10/29). Mintage: 805,400. Numismedia Wsl. Price for problem free NGC/PCGS coin in MS63: $835. NGC ID# 23TP, PCGS# 5451

7489 1875-S MS62 PCGS. CAC. PCGS Population (5/47). NGC Census: (14/39). Mintage: 680,000. Numismedia Wsl. Price for problem free NGC/PCGS coin in MS62: $725. NGC ID# 23UZ, PCGS# 5500

7490 1877-CC AU55 PCGS. PCGS Population (30/412). NGC Census: (21/365). Mintage: 4,192,000. Numismedia Wsl. Price for problem free NGC/PCGS coin in AU55: $315. NGC ID# 23V6, PCGS# 5505

PROOF SEATED QUARTERS

7491 1870 PR63 CameoNGC. Ex: Jules Reiver Collection. NGC Census: (8/23). PCGS Population (7/30). PCGS# 85569

7492 1875 — Artificially Toned — NGC Details. Proof. NGC Census: (1/121). PCGS Population (6/127). Mintage: 700. Numismedia Wsl. Price for problem free NGC/PCGS coin in PR60: $325.

7493 1882 PR62 Cameo PCGS. PCGS Population (2/65). NGC Census: (1/43). PCGS# 85583

BARBER QUARTERS

7494 1900-S MS62 PCGS. PCGS Population (8/58). NGC Census: (9/28). Mintage: 1,858,585. Numismedia Wsl. Price for problem free NGC/PCGS coin in MS62: $500. NGC ID# 23YM, PCGS# 5627

7495 1902-S MS62 PCGS. PCGS Population (8/58). NGC Census: (11/43). Mintage: 1,524,612. Numismedia Wsl. Price for problem free NGC/PCGS coin in MS62: $515. NGC ID# 23YU, PCGS# 5633

7496 1907-D MS64 NGC. NGC Census: (27/9). PCGS Population (34/14). Mintage: 2,484,000. Numismedia Wsl. Price for problem free NGC/PCGS coin in MS64: $875. NGC ID# 23Z9, PCGS# 5646

7497 1907-O MS64 PCGS. PCGS Population (48/35). NGC Census: (38/27). Mintage: 4,560,000. Numismedia Wsl. Price for problem free NGC/PCGS coin in MS64: $685. NGC ID# 23ZA, PCGS# 5647

7498 1908-D MS66 PCGS. PCGS Population (14/1). NGC Census: (3/4). Mintage: 5,788,000. Numismedia Wsl. Price for problem free NGC/PCGS coin in MS66: $2,275. NGC ID# 23ZD, PCGS# 5650

7499 1909-O — Reverse Graffiti — NGC Details. AU. NGC Census: (1/44). PCGS Population (3/54). Mintage: 712,000. Numismedia Wsl. Price for problem free NGC/PCGS coin in AU50: $1,350.

7500 1911-D AU50 PCGS. PCGS Population (8/83). NGC Census: (0/65). Mintage: 933,600. Numismedia Wsl. Price for problem free NGC/PCGS coin in AU50: $425. NGC ID# 23ZP, PCGS# 5660

7501 1913-D MS64 PCGS. PCGS Population (38/45). NGC Census: (37/27). Mintage: 1,450,800. Numismedia Wsl. Price for problem free NGC/PCGS coin in MS64: $520. NGC ID# 23ZV, PCGS# 5665

7502 1916-D MS65 PCGS. CAC. PCGS Population (343/168). NGC Census: (175/66). Mintage: 6,540,800. Numismedia Wsl. Price for problem free NGC/PCGS coin in MS65: $925. NGC ID# 2426, PCGS# 5674

7503 1916-D MS65 PCGS. CAC. PCGS Population (343/168). NGC Census: (175/66). Mintage: 6,540,800. Numismedia Wsl. Price for problem free NGC/PCGS coin in MS65: $925. NGC ID# 2426, PCGS# 5674

7504 1916-D MS65+ NGC. CAC. NGC Census: (175/66). PCGS Population (343/168). Mintage: 6,540,800. Numismedia Wsl. Price for problem free NGC/PCGS coin in MS65: $925. NGC ID# 2426, PCGS# 5674

7505 1916-D MS65+ PCGS. CAC. PCGS Population (343/168). NGC Census: (175/66). Mintage: 6,540,800. Numismedia Wsl. Price for problem free NGC/PCGS coin in MS65: $925. NGC ID# 2426, PCGS# 5674

7506 1916-D MS65+ PCGS. CAC. PCGS Population (343/168). NGC Census: (175/66). Mintage: 6,540,800. Numismedia Wsl. Price for problem free NGC/PCGS coin in MS65: $925. NGC ID# 2426, PCGS# 5674

7507 1916-D MS65+ PCGS. CAC. PCGS Population (343/168). NGC Census: (175/66). Mintage: 6,540,800. Numismedia Wsl. Price for problem free NGC/PCGS coin in MS65: $925. NGC ID# 2426, PCGS# 5674

PROOF BARBER QUARTERS

7508 **1897 PR64 NGC.** NGC Census: (56/86). PCGS Population (55/62). Mintage: 731. Numismedia Wsl. Price for problem free NGC/PCGS coin in PR64: $1,000. NGC ID# 242C, PCGS# 5683

7509 **1906 PR63 PCGS.** PCGS Population (52/132). NGC Census: (19/161). Mintage: 675. Numismedia Wsl. Price for problem free NGC/PCGS coin in PR63: $725. NGC ID# 242M, PCGS# 5692

7510 **1913 PR64+ NGC.** NGC Census: (55/96). PCGS Population (45/70). Mintage: 613. Numismedia Wsl. Price for problem free NGC/PCGS coin in PR64: $1,000. NGC ID# 242V, PCGS# 5699

STANDING LIBERTY QUARTERS

7511 **1917 Type One MS64 Full Head PCGS.** PCGS Population (1803/1541). NGC Census: (1306/1122). Mintage: 8,740,000. Numismedia Wsl. Price for problem free NGC/PCGS coin in MS64: $420. NGC ID# 242Z, PCGS# 5707

7512 **1917-S Type One MS62 Full Head PCGS. CAC.** PCGS Population (91/658). NGC Census: (109/464). Mintage: 1,952,000. Numismedia Wsl. Price for problem free NGC/PCGS coin in MS62: $475. NGC ID# 2433, PCGS# 5711

7513 **1918 MS64+ Full Head PCGS.** PCGS Population (142/126). NGC Census: (114/80). Mintage: 14,240,000. Numismedia Wsl. Price for problem free NGC/PCGS coin in MS64: $625. NGC ID# 2437, PCGS# 5721

7514 **1918-D MS64 PCGS.** PCGS Population (160/73). NGC Census: (85/62). Mintage: 7,380,000. Numismedia Wsl. Price for problem free NGC/PCGS coin in MS64: $585. NGC ID# 2438, PCGS# 5722

7515 **1918-S MS64 PCGS.** PCGS Population (200/83). NGC Census: (144/85). Mintage: 11,072,000. Numismedia Wsl. Price for problem free NGC/PCGS coin in MS64: $560. NGC ID# 2439, PCGS# 5724

7516 **1920 MS66 PCGS.** PCGS Population (59/15). NGC Census: (69/17). Mintage: 27,860,000. Numismedia Wsl. Price for problem free NGC/PCGS coin in MS66: $750. NGC ID# 243E, PCGS# 5734

7517 **1920-S MS64 PCGS.** PCGS Population (141/63). NGC Census: (96/60). Mintage: 6,380,000. Numismedia Wsl. Price for problem free NGC/PCGS coin in MS64: $1,175. NGC ID# 243G, PCGS# 5738

7518 **1925 MS65 Full Head NGC.** NGC Census: (87/49). PCGS Population (148/70). Mintage: 12,280,000. Numismedia Wsl. Price for problem free NGC/PCGS coin in MS65: $825. NGC ID# 243P, PCGS# 5753

7519 **1927-D MS66 NGC.** NGC Census: (33/4). PCGS Population (31/1). Mintage: 976,000. Numismedia Wsl. Price for problem free NGC/PCGS coin in MS66: $925. NGC ID# 243V, PCGS# 5762

7520 **1928 MS66 Full Head NGC.** NGC Census: (15/11). PCGS Population (41/6). Mintage: 6,336,000. Numismedia Wsl. Price for problem free NGC/PCGS coin in MS66: $2,150. NGC ID# 243X, PCGS# 5767

7521 **1928-D MS66 PCGS. CAC.** PCGS Population (82/4). NGC Census: (110/10). Mintage: 1,627,600. Numismedia Wsl. Price for problem free NGC/PCGS coin in MS66: $575. NGC ID# 243Y, PCGS# 5768

7522 **1929 MS65 Full Head PCGS. CAC.** PCGS Population (314/114). NGC Census: (144/65). Mintage: 11,140,000. Numismedia Wsl. Price for problem free NGC/PCGS coin in MS65: $665. NGC ID# 2442, PCGS# 5773

7523 **1929-S MS66 PCGS. CAC.** PCGS Population (118/10). NGC Census: (119/22). Mintage: 1,764,000. Numismedia Wsl. Price for problem free NGC/PCGS coin in MS66: $590. NGC ID# 2444, PCGS# 5776

7524 **1929-S MS65 Full Head PCGS.** PCGS Population (165/132). NGC Census: (130/113). Mintage: 1,764,000. Numismedia Wsl. Price for problem free NGC/PCGS coin in MS65: $700. NGC ID# 2444, PCGS# 5777

7525 **1930 MS66 NGC.** NGC Census: (31/5). PCGS Population (64/5). Mintage: 5,632,000. Numismedia Wsl. Price for problem free NGC/PCGS coin in MS66: $580. NGC ID# 2445, PCGS# 5778

WASHINGTON QUARTERS

7526 **1932 MS66 PCGS.** PCGS Population (204/3). NGC Census: (95/2). Mintage: 5,404,000. Numismedia Wsl. Price for problem free NGC/PCGS coin in MS66: $725. NGC ID# 2447, PCGS# 5790

7527 **1932 MS66 PCGS. CAC.** PCGS Population (204/3). NGC Census: (95/2). Mintage: 5,404,000. Numismedia Wsl. Price for problem free NGC/PCGS coin in MS66: $725. NGC ID# 2447, PCGS# 5790

7528 **1932-D MS62 NGC.** NGC Census: (366/542). PCGS Population (473/1355). Mintage: 436,800. Numismedia Wsl. Price for problem free NGC/PCGS coin in MS62: $1,125. NGC ID# 2448, PCGS# 5791

7529 **1932-S MS62 NGC.** NGC Census: (503/1179). PCGS Population (573/2177). Mintage: 408,000. Numismedia Wsl. Price for problem free NGC/PCGS coin in MS62: $480. NGC ID# 2449, PCGS# 5792

7530 **1932-S MS64 PCGS.** PCGS Population (1042/134). NGC Census: (630/71). Mintage: 408,000. Numismedia Wsl. Price for problem free NGC/PCGS coin in MS64: $945. NGC ID# 2449, PCGS# 5792

7531 **1932-S MS64 PCGS.** PCGS Population (1044/134). NGC Census: (631/71). Mintage: 408,000. Numismedia Wsl. Price for problem free NGC/PCGS coin in MS64: $945. NGC ID# 2449, PCGS# 5792

7532 **1935 MS67 PCGS. CAC.** PCGS Population (109/1). NGC Census: (118/0). Mintage: 32,484,000. Numismedia Wsl. Price for problem free NGC/PCGS coin in MS67: $440. NGC ID# 244D, PCGS# 5797

7533 **1935-S MS66 NGC.** NGC Census: (121/36). PCGS Population (255/30). Mintage: 5,660,000. Numismedia Wsl. Price for problem free NGC/PCGS coin in MS66: $420. NGC ID# 244F, PCGS# 5799

7534 **1936-D MS64+ PCGS.** PCGS Population (672/433). NGC Census: (312/215). Mintage: 5,374,000. Numismedia Wsl. Price for problem free NGC/PCGS coin in MS64: $710. NGC ID# 244H, PCGS# 5801

7535 **1936-S MS66 PCGS.** PCGS Population (279/31). NGC Census: (154/8). Mintage: 3,828,000. Numismedia Wsl. Price for problem free NGC/PCGS coin in MS66: $360. NGC ID# 244J, PCGS# 5802

7536 **1937 MS67 PCGS.** PCGS Population (75/0). NGC Census: (67/0). Mintage: 19,701,542. Numismedia Wsl. Price for problem free NGC/PCGS coin in MS67: $700. NGC ID# 244K, PCGS# 5803

7537 **1937-S MS66 PCGS. CAC.** PCGS Population (188/31). NGC Census: (149/27). Mintage: 1,652,000. Numismedia Wsl. Price for problem free NGC/PCGS coin in MS66: $525. NGC ID# 244M, PCGS# 5805

7538 **1938 MS67 PCGS.** PCGS Population (49/0). NGC Census: (59/1). Mintage: 9,480,045. Numismedia Wsl. Price for problem free NGC/PCGS coin in MS67: $950. NGC ID# 244N, PCGS# 5806

7539 **1938 MS67 PCGS.** PCGS Population (49/0). NGC Census: (59/1). Mintage: 9,480,045. Numismedia Wsl. Price for problem free NGC/PCGS coin in MS67: $950. NGC ID# 244N, PCGS# 5806

7540 **1938-S MS67 PCGS.** PCGS Population (53/0). NGC Census: (44/1). Mintage: 2,832,000. Numismedia Wsl. Price for problem free NGC/PCGS coin in MS67: $900. NGC ID# 244P, PCGS# 5807

7541 **1939-S MS67 PCGS.** PCGS Population (70/0). NGC Census: (36/0). Mintage: 2,628,000. Numismedia Wsl. Price for problem free NGC/PCGS coin in MS67: $1,225. NGC ID# 244T, PCGS# 5810

7542 **1941-S MS67 PCGS.** PCGS Population (57/0). NGC Census: (81/0). Mintage: 16,080,000. Numismedia Wsl. Price for problem free NGC/PCGS coin in MS67: $765. NGC ID# 244Z, PCGS# 5816

7543 **1942-S MS67 NGC.** NGC Census: (63/0). PCGS Population (44/1). Mintage: 19,384,000. Numismedia Wsl. Price for problem free NGC/PCGS coin in MS67: $735. NGC ID# 2454, PCGS# 5819

7544 **1946-D MS67 PCGS.** PCGS Population (39/0). NGC Census: (259/1). Mintage: 9,072,800. Numismedia Wsl. Price for problem free NGC/PCGS coin in MS67: $350. NGC ID# 245F, PCGS# 5831

7545 **1947 MS67 PCGS. CAC.** PCGS Population (71/0). NGC Census: (201/0). Mintage: 22,556,000. Numismedia Wsl. Price for problem free NGC/PCGS coin in MS67: $300. NGC ID# 245H, PCGS# 5833

7546 **1947-D MS67 PCGS. CAC.** PCGS Population (131/1). NGC Census: (526/1). Mintage: 15,338,400. Numismedia Wsl. Price for problem free NGC/PCGS coin in MS67: $200. NGC ID# 245J, PCGS# 5834

7547 **1949 MS67 NGC. CAC.** NGC Census: (117/2). PCGS Population (58/2). Mintage: 9,312,000. Numismedia Wsl. Price for problem free NGC/PCGS coin in MS67: $440. NGC ID# 245P, PCGS# 5839

7548 **1952-S MS67+ PCGS. CAC.** PCGS Population (176/4). NGC Census: (352/7). Mintage: 13,707,800. Numismedia Wsl. Price for problem free NGC/PCGS coin in MS67: $195. NGC ID# 2463, PCGS# 5851

7549 **1959 MS67 NGC.** NGC Census: (67/0). PCGS Population (9/0). Mintage: 24,300,000. Numismedia Wsl. Price for problem free NGC/PCGS coin in MS67: $480. NGC ID# 246H, PCGS# 5866

7550 **1961 MS67 NGC.** NGC Census: (29/0). PCGS Population (5/0). Mintage: 37,000,000. Numismedia Wsl. Price for problem free NGC/PCGS coin in MS67: $1,550. NGC ID# 246M, PCGS# 5870

PROOF WASHINGTON QUARTERS

7551 **1936 PR64 PCGS.** PCGS Population (494/423). NGC Census: (338/433). Mintage: 3,837. Numismedia Wsl. Price for problem free NGC/PCGS coin in PR64: $775. NGC ID# 27HN, PCGS# 5975

7552 **1938 PR67 NGC.** NGC Census: (91/9). PCGS Population (82/3). Mintage: 8,045. Numismedia Wsl. Price for problem free NGC/PCGS coin in PR67: $700. NGC ID# 27HR, PCGS# 5977

7553 **1951 PR67 Cameo NGC.** NGC Census: (91/25). PCGS Population (57/6). Numismedia Wsl. Price for problem free NGC/PCGS coin in PR67: $650. NGC ID# 27HX, PCGS# 85983

EARLY HALF DOLLARS

7554 **1795 2 Leaves, A Over E in STATES, O-113a, R.4, — Damage — PCGS Genuine. VG Details.** NGC Census: (0/0). PCGS Population (2/11).

7555 **1795 2 Leaves, O-125, High R.4, — Cleaning — PCGS Genuine. Good Details.** NGC Census: (1/9). PCGS Population (0/2).

7556 **1805 VF30 NGC.** NGC Census: (25/141). PCGS Population (65/218). Mintage: 211,722. Numismedia Wsl. Price for problem free NGC/PCGS coin in VF30: $1,130. NGC ID# 24EG, PCGS# 6069

7557 **1805 O-111, R.2, VG8 PCGS.** PCGS Population (1/9). NGC Census: (0/32). PCGS# 39285

7558 **1806/5 Large Stars, O-102, High R.3, VF20 PCGS.** PCGS Population (1/5). NGC Census: (2/10). PCGS# 39298

7559 **1806 Knob 6, Small Stars, O-105, R.2, — Tooled — PCGS Genuine. XF Details.** NGC Census: (0/0). PCGS Population (1/0).

7560 **1806 Pointed 6, No Stem, O-109, R.1, VG10 PCGS.** PCGS Population (2/25). NGC Census: (5/78). PCGS# 39310

7561 **1807 Draped Bust, O-107a, High R.4, Fine 12 PCGS.** PCGS Population (1/0). NGC Census: (1/2). PCGS# 39347

BUST HALF DOLLARS

7562 **1808 XF45 PCGS.** PCGS Population (66/269). NGC Census: (39/184). Mintage: 1,368,600. Numismedia Wsl. Price for problem free NGC/PCGS coin in XF45: $546. NGC ID# 24EP, PCGS# 6090

7563 **1809 Normal Edge, O-115, R.2, AU53 PCGS.** PCGS Population (2/0). NGC Census: (0/1). PCGS# 39402

7564 **1812 Large 8, O-103, R.1, XF45 PCGS.** PCGS Population (5/14). NGC Census: (7/35). Mintage: 1,628,059. PCGS# 39446

7565 **1817 AU50 PCGS.** PCGS Population (63/215). NGC Census: (20/184). Mintage: 1,215,567. Numismedia Wsl. Price for problem free NGC/PCGS coin in AU50: $565. NGC ID# 24F6, PCGS# 6109

7566 **1821 AU55 PCGS.** PCGS Population (102/176). NGC Census: (53/153). Mintage: 1,305,797. Numismedia Wsl. Price for problem free NGC/PCGS coin in AU55: $825. NGC ID# 24FF, PCGS# 6128

7567 **1825 O-114, R.1, AU55 PCGS.** PCGS Population (4/2). NGC Census: (7/12). Mintage: 2,900,000. PCGS# 39661

7568 1827 Square Base 2, O-114, R.3, AU58 NGC. NGC Census: (2/8). PCGS Population (1/1). Mintage: 5,493,400. PCGS# 39709

7569 1828 Square Base 2, Small 8s, Large Letters AU58 NGC. NGC Census: (1/2). PCGS Population (78/88). PCGS# 6151

7570 1830 Small 0 AU58 PCGS. PCGS Population (234/311). NGC Census: (303/396). Mintage: 4,764,800. Numismedia Wsl. Price for problem free NGC/PCGS coin in AU58: $675. NGC ID# 24FU, PCGS# 6156

7571 1830 Small 0 AU58 PCGS. PCGS Population (234/311). NGC Census: (303/396). Mintage: 4,764,800. Numismedia Wsl. Price for problem free NGC/PCGS coin in AU58: $675. NGC ID# 24FU, PCGS# 6156

7572 1831 AU58 PCGS. PCGS Population (246/479). NGC Census: (265/413). Mintage: 5,873,660. Numismedia Wsl. Price for problem free NGC/PCGS coin in AU58: $640. NGC ID# 24FV, PCGS# 6159

7573 1832 Small Letters AU58 NGC. NGC Census: (340/395). PCGS Population (329/349). Mintage: 4,797,000. Numismedia Wsl. Price for problem free NGC/PCGS coin in AU58: $650. NGC ID# 24FW, PCGS# 6160

7574 1834 Large Date, Large Letters, AU58 PCGS. PCGS Population (133/268). NGC Census: (483/655). Mintage: 6,412,004. Numismedia Wsl. Price for problem free NGC/PCGS coin in AU58: $600. NGC ID# 24FY, PCGS# 6164

7575 1836 Lettered Edge AU55 PCGS. PCGS Population (180/438). NGC Census: (131/496). Mintage: 6,545,000. Numismedia Wsl. Price for problem free NGC/PCGS coin in AU55: $450. NGC ID# 24G2, PCGS# 6169

REEDED EDGE HALF DOLLARS

7576 1836 Reeded Edge — Damage — PCGS Genuine. Good Details. NGC Census: (3/200). PCGS Population (0/323). Mintage: 1,200. Numismedia Wsl. Price for problem free NGC/PCGS coin in Good 4: $745.

7577 1838 AU58 NGC. NGC Census: (221/306). PCGS Population (124/235). Mintage: 3,546,000. Numismedia Wsl. Price for problem free NGC/PCGS coin in AU58: $765. NGC ID# 24G5, PCGS# 6177

7578 1839 Large Letters AU58 PCGS. PCGS Population (49/115). NGC Census: (85/114). Mintage: 1,392,976. Numismedia Wsl. Price for problem free NGC/PCGS coin in AU58: $800. NGC ID# 24G6, PCGS# 6179

SEATED HALF DOLLARS

7579 1839 Drapery MS62 PCGS. PCGS Population (11/30). NGC Census: (11/33). Mintage: 1,872,400. Numismedia Wsl. Price for problem free NGC/PCGS coin in MS62: $1,325. NGC ID# 24GL, PCGS# 6232

7580 1843 AU58 PCGS. PCGS Population (14/54). NGC Census: (31/62). Mintage: 3,844,000. Numismedia Wsl. Price for problem free NGC/PCGS coin in AU58: $450. NGC ID# 24GX, PCGS# 6243

7581 1843 MS62 NGC. NGC Census: (19/29). PCGS Population (13/30). Mintage: 3,844,000. Numismedia Wsl. Price for problem free NGC/PCGS coin in MS62: $700. NGC ID# 24GX, PCGS# 6243

7582 1846-O Medium Date AU58 PCGS. PCGS Population (9/16). NGC Census: (12/23). Mintage: 2,304,000. Numismedia Wsl. Price for problem free NGC/PCGS coin in AU58: $475. NGC ID# 27SW, PCGS# 6255

7583 1851-O AU58 PCGS. PCGS Population (8/30). NGC Census: (6/23). Mintage: 402,000. Numismedia Wsl. Price for problem free NGC/PCGS coin in AU58: $800. NGC ID# 24HK, PCGS# 6267

7584 1854-O Arrows AU58 PCGS. CAC. Ex: Newman Collection. PCGS Population (68/210). NGC Census: (102/213). Mintage: 5,240,000. Numismedia Wsl. Price for problem free NGC/PCGS coin in AU58: $460. NGC ID# 24JM, PCGS# 6280

7585 1854-O Arrows MS62 NGC. NGC Census: (44/118). PCGS Population (52/146). Mintage: 5,240,000. Numismedia Wsl. Price for problem free NGC/PCGS coin in MS62: $965. NGC ID# 24JM, PCGS# 6280

7586 1855-O Arrows MS62 NGC. NGC Census: (31/95). PCGS Population (38/153). Mintage: 3,688,000. Numismedia Wsl. Price for problem free NGC/PCGS coin in MS62: $975. NGC ID# 24JP, PCGS# 6283

7587 1858-O SS Republic — Shipwreck Effect — NGC. Wooden display box, book and COA included. Mintage: 7,294,000.

7588 1860 MS62 NGC. NGC Census: (9/19). PCGS Population (10/39). Mintage: 302,700. Numismedia Wsl. Price for problem free NGC/PCGS coin in MS62: $775. NGC ID# 24J3, PCGS# 6299

7589 1860-O WB-7, SS Republic, High O — Shipwreck Effect — NGC. Wooden display box, book and COA included. Mintage: 1,290,000.

7590 1861 MS62 PCGS. CAC. PCGS Population (50/165). NGC Census: (35/149). Mintage: 2,888,400. Numismedia Wsl. Price for problem free NGC/PCGS coin in MS62: $700. NGC ID# 24J7, PCGS# 6302

7591 1861-O W-15, SS Republic, Confederate States Issue — Shipwreck Effect (B) — NGC. Unc. NGC Census: (0/108). PCGS Population (4/128). Mintage: 2,532,633. Numismedia Wsl. Price for problem free NGC/PCGS coin in MS60: $515.

7592 1861-O W-07, SS Republic, Louisiana Issue — Shipwreck Effect (B) — NGC. Unc. Picture frame style wooden display box and COA included. Mintage: 2,532,633.

7593 1863-S AU55 PCGS. PCGS Population (20/74). NGC Census: (12/69). Mintage: 916,000. Numismedia Wsl. Price for problem free NGC/PCGS coin in AU55: $385. NGC ID# 24JC, PCGS# 6310

7594 1866 Motto MS62 PCGS. PCGS Population (8/34). NGC Census: (12/29). Mintage: 744,900. Numismedia Wsl. Price for problem free NGC/PCGS coin in MS62: $675. NGC ID# 24JS, PCGS# 6319

7595 1875-S MS63 PCGS. PCGS Population (62/151). NGC Census: (35/98). Mintage: 3,200,000. Numismedia Wsl. Price for problem free NGC/PCGS coin in MS63: $765. NGC ID# 24KF, PCGS# 6351

7596 1876 MS63 PCGS. PCGS Population (70/74). NGC Census: (50/50). Mintage: 8,419,150. Numismedia Wsl. Price for problem free NGC/PCGS coin in MS63: $785. NGC ID# 24KG, PCGS# 6352

7597 1876 MS63 Prooflike NGC. NGC Census: (50/50). PCGS Population (70/74). Mintage: 8,419,150. Numismedia Wsl. Price for problem free NGC/PCGS coin in MS63: $785. NGC ID# 24KG, PCGS# 6352

7598 **1877 MS63 PCGS.** PCGS Population (37/88). NGC Census: (37/87). Mintage: 8,304,510. Numismedia Wsl. Price for problem free NGC/PCGS coin in MS63: $765. NGC ID# 24KK, PCGS# 6355

7599 **1877-S MS62 NGC.** NGC Census: (45/187). PCGS Population (66/207). Mintage: 5,356,000. Numismedia Wsl. Price for problem free NGC/PCGS coin in MS62: $600. NGC ID# 24KM, PCGS# 6357

7600 **1878 MS63 PCGS.** PCGS Population (18/34). NGC Census: (8/21). Mintage: 1,378,400. Numismedia Wsl. Price for problem free NGC/PCGS coin in MS63: $885. NGC ID# 24KN, PCGS# 6358

7601 **1878 MS63 PCGS.** PCGS Population (18/34). NGC Census: (8/21). Mintage: 1,378,400. Numismedia Wsl. Price for problem free NGC/PCGS coin in MS63: $885. NGC ID# 24KN, PCGS# 6358

PROOF SEATED HALF DOLLARS

7602 **1885 — Stained — NGC Details. Proof.** NGC Census: (2/228). PCGS Population (13/262). Mintage: 930. Numismedia Wsl. Price for problem free NGC/PCGS coin in PR60: $535.

7603 **1891 PR64 PCGS.** PCGS Population (51/33). NGC Census: (52/65). Mintage: 600. Numismedia Wsl. Price for problem free NGC/PCGS coin in PR64: $1,550. NGC ID# 27UT, PCGS# 6452

BARBER HALF DOLLARS

7604 **1892 MS62 NGC.** NGC Census: (150/504). PCGS Population (171/568). Mintage: 934,000. Numismedia Wsl. Price for problem free NGC/PCGS coin in MS62: $565. NGC ID# 24LF, PCGS# 6461

7605 **1892-O VG10 PCGS.** PCGS Population (24/354). NGC Census: (8/245). Mintage: 390,000. Numismedia Wsl. Price for problem free NGC/PCGS coin in VG10: $385. NGC ID# 24LG, PCGS# 6462

7606 **1892-O AU53 NGC.** NGC Census: (10/193). PCGS Population (19/217). Mintage: 390,000. Numismedia Wsl. Price for problem free NGC/PCGS coin in AU53: $715. NGC ID# 24LG, PCGS# 6462

7607 **1893-S Fine 12 PCGS.** PCGS Population (16/172). NGC Census: (4/85). Mintage: 740,000. Numismedia Wsl. Price for problem free NGC/PCGS coin in Fine 12: $275. NGC ID# 24LM, PCGS# 6467

7608 **1894 AU58 PCGS.** PCGS Population (20/125). NGC Census: (19/122). Mintage: 1,148,972. Numismedia Wsl. Price for problem free NGC/PCGS coin in AU58: $450. NGC ID# 24LN, PCGS# 6468

7609 **1897 — Cleaning — PCGS Genuine. Unc Details.** NGC Census: (0/131). PCGS Population (1/140). Mintage: 2,480,731. Numismedia Wsl. Price for problem free NGC/PCGS coin in MS60: $475.

7610 **1897 MS62 PCGS.** PCGS Population (26/111). NGC Census: (18/101). Mintage: 2,480,731. Numismedia Wsl. Price for problem free NGC/PCGS coin in MS62: $575. NGC ID# 24LY, PCGS# 6477

7611 **1897-O Fine 15 PCGS.** PCGS Population (27/133). NGC Census: (4/66). Mintage: 632,000. Numismedia Wsl. Price for problem free NGC/PCGS coin in Fine 15: $513. NGC ID# 24LZ, PCGS# 6478

7612 **1897-S — Cleaning — PCGS Genuine. VF Details.** NGC Census: (2/92). PCGS Population (11/169). Mintage: 933,900. Numismedia Wsl. Price for problem free NGC/PCGS coin in VF20: $540.

7613 **1900 AU58 PCGS.** PCGS Population (38/218). NGC Census: (40/196). Mintage: 4,762,912. Numismedia Wsl. Price for problem free NGC/PCGS coin in AU58: $400. NGC ID# 24M9, PCGS# 6486

7614 **1901 AU58 PCGS. CAC.** PCGS Population (58/174). NGC Census: (51/139). Mintage: 4,268,813. Numismedia Wsl. Price for problem free NGC/PCGS coin in AU58: $400. NGC ID# 24MC, PCGS# 6489

7615 **1902-O XF45 PCGS. CAC.** PCGS Population (21/87). NGC Census: (6/80). Mintage: 2,526,000. Numismedia Wsl. Price for problem free NGC/PCGS coin in XF45: $310. NGC ID# 24MG, PCGS# 6493

7616 **1903-O XF45 PCGS.** PCGS Population (15/147). NGC Census: (7/122). Mintage: 2,100,000. Numismedia Wsl. Price for problem free NGC/PCGS coin in XF45: $293. NGC ID# 24MK, PCGS# 6496

7617 **1905-O — Environmental Damage — PCGS Genuine. Unc Details.** NGC Census: (2/82). PCGS Population (0/99). Mintage: 505,000. Numismedia Wsl. Price for problem free NGC/PCGS coin in MS60: $685.

7618 **1906 MS62 NGC.** NGC Census: (48/122). PCGS Population (57/171). Mintage: 2,638,675. Numismedia Wsl. Price for problem free NGC/PCGS coin in MS62: $550. NGC ID# 24MU, PCGS# 6504

7619 **1911 MS61 NGC.** NGC Census: (15/177). PCGS Population (8/287). Mintage: 1,406,543. Numismedia Wsl. Price for problem free NGC/PCGS coin in MS61: $500. NGC ID# 24ND, PCGS# 6521

7620 **1911 MS63 PCGS.** PCGS Population (72/160). NGC Census: (44/86). Mintage: 1,406,543. Numismedia Wsl. Price for problem free NGC/PCGS coin in MS63: $835. NGC ID# 24ND, PCGS# 6521

7621 **1915 — Improperly Cleaned — NGC Details. AU.** NGC Census: (2/64). PCGS Population (6/109). Mintage: 138,000. Numismedia Wsl. Price for problem free NGC/PCGS coin in AU50: $675.

7622 **1915-S MS62 PCGS.** PCGS Population (51/220). NGC Census: (71/186). Mintage: 1,604,000. Numismedia Wsl. Price for problem free NGC/PCGS coin in MS62: $575. NGC ID# 24NT, PCGS# 6534

PROOF BARBER HALF DOLLARS

7623 **1900 PR62 NGC.** NGC Census: (22/170). PCGS Population (48/174). Mintage: 912. Numismedia Wsl. Price for problem free NGC/PCGS coin in PR62: $690. NGC ID# 24P4, PCGS# 6547

7624 **1910 PR62 PCGS.** PCGS Population (28/151). NGC Census: (11/197). Mintage: 551. Numismedia Wsl. Price for problem free NGC/PCGS coin in PR62: $750. NGC ID# 24PE, PCGS# 6557

7625 **1911 — Artificially Toned — NGC Details. Proof.** NGC Census: (2/186). PCGS Population (5/191). Mintage: 543. Numismedia Wsl. Price for problem free NGC/PCGS coin in PR60: $455.

WALKING LIBERTY HALF DOLLARS

7626 **1916-D MS64 PCGS.** PCGS Population (511/284). NGC Census: (353/217). Mintage: 1,014,400. Numismedia Wsl. Price for problem free NGC/PCGS coin in MS64: $985. NGC ID# 24PM, PCGS# 6567

7627 **1916-S — Cleaning — PCGS Genuine. AU Details.** NGC Census: (5/485). PCGS Population (19/795). Mintage: 508,000. Numismedia Wsl. Price for problem free NGC/PCGS coin in AU50: $710.

7628 **1917 MS65 PCGS.** PCGS Population (327/92). NGC Census: (223/42). Mintage: 12,292,000. Numismedia Wsl. Price for problem free NGC/PCGS coin in MS65: $925. NGC ID# 24PP, PCGS# 6569

7629 **1917 MS65 PCGS.** PCGS Population (327/92). NGC Census: (223/42). Mintage: 12,292,000. Numismedia Wsl. Price for problem free NGC/PCGS coin in MS65: $925. NGC ID# 24PP, PCGS# 6569

7630 **1917-D Reverse — Cleaning — PCGS Genuine. AU Details.** NGC Census: (14/433). PCGS Population (23/623). Mintage: 1,940,000. Numismedia Wsl. Price for problem free NGC/PCGS coin in AU50: $480.

7631 **1917-D Reverse AU58 PCGS. CAC.** PCGS Population (125/395). NGC Census: (93/290). Mintage: 1,940,000. Numismedia Wsl. Price for problem free NGC/PCGS coin in AU58: $850. NGC ID# 24PS, PCGS# 6571

7632 **1918-D — Cleaning — PCGS Genuine. AU Details.** NGC Census: (11/609). PCGS Population (33/746). Mintage: 3,853,040. Numismedia Wsl. Price for problem free NGC/PCGS coin in AU50: $440.

7633 **1919 AU50 NGC. CAC.** NGC Census: (8/316). PCGS Population (13/427). Mintage: 962,000. Numismedia Wsl. Price for problem free NGC/PCGS coin in AU50: $740. NGC ID# 24PY, PCGS# 6577

7634 **1920-S — Cleaning — PCGS Genuine. AU Details.** NGC Census: (12/349). PCGS Population (24/421). Mintage: 4,624,000. Numismedia Wsl. Price for problem free NGC/PCGS coin in AU50: $440.

7635 **1921-D — Rim Damage — PCGS Genuine. Fine Details.** NGC Census: (98/361). PCGS Population (137/563). Mintage: 208,000. Numismedia Wsl. Price for problem free NGC/PCGS coin in Fine 12: $450.

7636 **1921-S VF20 NGC.** NGC Census: (88/308). PCGS Population (114/417). Mintage: 548,000. Numismedia Wsl. Price for problem free NGC/PCGS coin in VF20: $800. NGC ID# 24R8, PCGS# 6585

7637 **1936-D MS65 NGC.** NGC Census: (516/225). PCGS Population (1068/400). Mintage: 4,252,400. Numismedia Wsl. Price for problem free NGC/PCGS coin in MS65: $380. NGC ID# 24RN, PCGS# 6599

7638 **1936-S MS65 NGC. CAC.** NGC Census: (453/160). PCGS Population (728/252). Mintage: 3,884,000. Numismedia Wsl. Price for problem free NGC/PCGS coin in MS65: $625. NGC ID# 24RP, PCGS# 6600

7639 **1937 MS66+ PCGS. CAC.** PCGS Population (641/136). NGC Census: (346/84). Mintage: 9,527,728. Numismedia Wsl. Price for problem free NGC/PCGS coin in MS66: $230. NGC ID# 24RR, PCGS# 6601

7640 **1937 MS67 PCGS.** PCGS Population (131/5). NGC Census: (82/2). Mintage: 9,527,728. Numismedia Wsl. Price for problem free NGC/PCGS coin in MS67: $1,075. NGC ID# 24RR, PCGS# 6601

7641 **1937-D MS66 NGC.** NGC Census: (147/35). PCGS Population (321/49). Mintage: 1,676,000. Numismedia Wsl. Price for problem free NGC/PCGS coin in MS66: $860. NGC ID# 24RS, PCGS# 6602

7642 **1938-D MS64 PCGS.** PCGS Population (806/1276). NGC Census: (408/522). Mintage: 491,600. Numismedia Wsl. Price for problem free NGC/PCGS coin in MS64: $725. NGC ID# 24RV, PCGS# 6605

7643 **1939 MS67 NGC.** NGC Census: (260/19). PCGS Population (271/21). Mintage: 6,820,808. Numismedia Wsl. Price for problem free NGC/PCGS coin in MS67: $675. NGC ID# 24RW, PCGS# 6606

7644 **1939 MS67 PCGS. CAC.** PCGS Population (272/21). NGC Census: (260/19). Mintage: 6,820,808. Numismedia Wsl. Price for problem free NGC/PCGS coin in MS67: $675. NGC ID# 24RW, PCGS# 6606

7645 **1939-S MS66+ PCGS. CAC.** PCGS Population (936/157). NGC Census: (543/119). Mintage: 2,552,000. Numismedia Wsl. Price for problem free NGC/PCGS coin in MS66: $400. NGC ID# 24RY, PCGS# 6608

7646 **1940 MS67 NGC. CAC.** NGC Census: (215/14). PCGS Population (245/24). Mintage: 9,167,279. Numismedia Wsl. Price for problem free NGC/PCGS coin in MS67: $665. NGC ID# 24RZ, PCGS# 6609

7647 **1941 MS67 PCGS.** PCGS Population (575/18). NGC Census: (591/22). Mintage: 24,207,412. Numismedia Wsl. Price for problem free NGC/PCGS coin in MS67: $510. NGC ID# 24S3, PCGS# 6611

7648 **1942-D MS67 NGC. CAC.** NGC Census: (134/6). PCGS Population (151/4). Mintage: 10,973,800. Numismedia Wsl. Price for problem free NGC/PCGS coin in MS67: $685. NGC ID# 24S7, PCGS# 6615

7649 **1943-S MS66 PCGS. CAC.** PCGS Population (685/35). NGC Census: (298/24). Mintage: 13,450,000. Numismedia Wsl. Price for problem free NGC/PCGS coin in MS66: $460. NGC ID# 24SB, PCGS# 6620

7650 **1945-D MS67 PCGS.** PCGS Population (174/0). NGC Census: (215/1). Mintage: 9,966,800. Numismedia Wsl. Price for problem free NGC/PCGS coin in MS67: $725. NGC ID# 24SG, PCGS# 6625

PROOF WALKING LIBERTY HALF DOLLARS

7651 **1937 PR65 PCGS.** PCGS Population (612/721). NGC Census: (379/649). Mintage: 5,728. Numismedia Wsl. Price for problem free NGC/PCGS coin in PR65: $740. NGC ID# 27V5, PCGS# 6637

7652 **1937 PR66 NGC.** NGC Census: (398/251). PCGS Population (470/249). Mintage: 5,728. Numismedia Wsl. Price for problem free NGC/PCGS coin in PR66: $890. NGC ID# 27V5, PCGS# 6637

7653 **1939 PR66 NGC.** NGC Census: (633/423). PCGS Population (676/386). Mintage: 8,808. Numismedia Wsl. Price for problem free NGC/PCGS coin in PR66: $640. NGC ID# 27V7, PCGS# 6639

7654 **1939 PR66 PCGS.** PCGS Population (676/385). NGC Census: (633/425). Mintage: 8,808. Numismedia Wsl. Price for problem free NGC/PCGS coin in PR66: $640. NGC ID# 27V7, PCGS# 6639

7655 **1941 PR65 PCGS.** PCGS Population (1437/1301). NGC Census: (894/1446). Mintage: 15,412. Numismedia Wsl. Price for problem free NGC/PCGS coin in PR65: $500. NGC ID# 24SP, PCGS# 6641

7656 **1942 PR66 NGC.** NGC Census: (1331/1014). PCGS Population (1643/820). Mintage: 21,120. Numismedia Wsl. Price for problem free NGC/PCGS coin in PR66: $520. NGC ID# 27V9, PCGS# 6642

7657 **1942 PR66 PCGS.** PCGS Population (1643/820). NGC Census: (1331/1014). Mintage: 21,120. Numismedia Wsl. Price for problem free NGC/PCGS coin in PR66: $520. NGC ID# 27V9, PCGS# 6642

7658 **1942 PR67 PCGS.** PCGS Population (774/46). NGC Census: (846/168). Mintage: 21,120. Numismedia Wsl. Price for problem free NGC/PCGS coin in PR67: $710. NGC ID# 27V9, PCGS# 6642

FRANKLIN HALF DOLLARS

7659 **1948 MS66 Full Bell Lines PCGS. CAC.** PCGS Population (377/4). NGC Census: (125/6). Numismedia Wsl. Price for problem free NGC/PCGS coin in MS66: $340. NGC ID# 24SR, PCGS# 86651

7660 **1949-S MS66 Full Bell Lines PCGS. CAC.** PCGS Population (164/5). NGC Census: (38/1). Numismedia Wsl. Price for problem free NGC/PCGS coin in MS66: $600. NGC ID# 24SV, PCGS# 86655

7661 **1951 MS66 Full Bell Lines PCGS. CAC.** PCGS Population (130/3). NGC Census: (20/2). Numismedia Wsl. Price for problem free NGC/PCGS coin in MS66: $675. NGC ID# 24SY, PCGS# 86658

7662 **1951 MS66 Full Bell Lines NGC. CAC.** NGC Census: (20/2). PCGS Population (130/3). Numismedia Wsl. Price for problem free NGC/PCGS coin in MS66: $675. NGC ID# 24SY, PCGS# 86658

7663 **1951 MS66 Full Bell Lines PCGS. CAC.** PCGS Population (129/3). NGC Census: (20/2). Numismedia Wsl. Price for problem free NGC/PCGS coin in MS66: $675. NGC ID# 24SY, PCGS# 86658

7664 **1952 MS66 Full Bell Lines PCGS.** PCGS Population (303/14). NGC Census: (105/2). Numismedia Wsl. Price for problem free NGC/PCGS coin in MS66: $250. NGC ID# 24T3, PCGS# 86661

7665 **1952-D MS66 Full Bell Lines PCGS.** PCGS Population (88/2). NGC Census: (20/0). Numismedia Wsl. Price for problem free NGC/PCGS coin in MS66: $800. NGC ID# 24T4, PCGS# 86662

7666 **1952-D MS66 Full Bell Lines PCGS. CAC.** PCGS Population (87/2). NGC Census: (20/0). Numismedia Wsl. Price for problem free NGC/PCGS coin in MS66: $800. NGC ID# 24T4, PCGS# 86662

7667 **1958-D MS66+ Full Bell Lines PCGS.** PCGS Population (777/50). NGC Census: (270/16). Numismedia Wsl. Price for problem free NGC/PCGS coin in MS66: $150. NGC ID# 24TH, PCGS# 86675

7668 **1958-D MS66+ Full Bell Lines PCGS.** PCGS Population (777/50). NGC Census: (270/16). Numismedia Wsl. Price for problem free NGC/PCGS coin in MS66: $150. NGC ID# 24TH, PCGS# 86675

7669 **1958-D MS67 Full Bell Lines PCGS.** PCGS Population (51/0). NGC Census: (16/0). Numismedia Wsl. Price for problem free NGC/PCGS coin in MS67: $1,425. NGC ID# 24TH, PCGS# 86675

PROOF FRANKLIN HALF DOLLARS

7670 **1955 PR68 Cameo NGC.** NGC Census: (0/0). PCGS Population (81/0). Numismedia Wsl. Price for problem free NGC/PCGS coin in PR68: $450. NGC ID# 27VF, PCGS# 86696

7671 **1956 Type Two PR69 ★ Cameo NGC.** NGC Census: (183/0). PCGS Population (31/0). Numismedia Wsl. Price for problem free NGC/PCGS coin in PR69: $625. NGC ID# 24TW, PCGS# 86697

7672 **1963 PR68 Deep Cameo PCGS. CAC.** PCGS Population (242/17). NGC Census: (182/8). Numismedia Wsl. Price for problem free NGC/PCGS coin in PR68: $550. NGC ID# 27VL, PCGS# 96704

KENNEDY HALF DOLLAR

7673 **1972-D No FG, FS-901 MS64 PCGS.** PCGS Population (1/0). NGC Census: (0/0). PCGS# 147888

EARLY DOLLARS

7674 **1798 Large Eagle, Pointed 9 Fair 2 PCGS.** PCGS Population (3/1813). NGC Census: (1/1199). Mintage: 327,536. Numismedia Wsl. Price for problem free NGC/PCGS coin in Fair 2: $308. NGC ID# 24X6, PCGS# 6873

7675 **1798 Large Eagle, Pointed 9 Good 4 PCGS.** PCGS Population (14/1780). NGC Census: (8/1191). Mintage: 327,536. Numismedia Wsl. Price for problem free NGC/PCGS coin in Good 4: $850. NGC ID# 24X6, PCGS# 6873

7676 **1799 Irregular Date, 13 Stars Reverse, B-15, BB-152, R.3, — Graffiti — PCGS Genuine. VF Details.** NGC Census: (0/0). PCGS Population (0/12).

7677 **1799 7x6 Stars — Questionable Color — PCGS Genuine. VG Details.** NGC Census: (48/1638). PCGS Population (72/2766). Mintage: 423,515. Numismedia Wsl. Price for problem free NGC/PCGS coin in VG8: $1,025.

7678 **1799 7x6 Stars — Repaired — PCGS Genuine. VF Details.** NGC Census: (95/1353). PCGS Population (257/2055). Mintage: 423,515. Numismedia Wsl. Price for problem free NGC/PCGS coin in VF20: $2,075.

7679 **1799 7x6 Stars, B-22, BB-168, R.4, — Cleaned, Scratched, Repaired — ANACS. Fine 15 Details.** NGC Census: (0/0). PCGS Population (1/7).

7680 **1800 — Damage — PCGS Genuine. VF Details.** NGC Census: (43/614). PCGS Population (85/814). Mintage: 220,920. Numismedia Wsl. Price for problem free NGC/PCGS coin in VF20: $2,100.

7681 **1801 — Cleaning — PCGS Genuine. Fine Details.** NGC Census: (13/200). PCGS Population (33/425). Mintage: 54,454. Numismedia Wsl. Price for problem free NGC/PCGS coin in Fine 12: $1,625.

SEATED DOLLARS

7682 **1842 XF40 PCGS.** PCGS Population (87/465). NGC Census: (41/439). Mintage: 184,618. Numismedia Wsl. Price for problem free NGC/PCGS coin in XF40: $575. NGC ID# 24YC, PCGS# 6928

7683 **1842 XF40 PCGS.** PCGS Population (86/464). NGC Census: (40/438). Mintage: 184,618. Numismedia Wsl. Price for problem free NGC/PCGS coin in XF40: $575. NGC ID# 24YC, PCGS# 6928

7684 **1842 AU55 NGC.** NGC Census: (92/156). PCGS Population (75/120). Mintage: 184,618. Numismedia Wsl. Price for problem free NGC/PCGS coin in AU55: $1,150. NGC ID# 24YC, PCGS# 6928

7685 **1843 AU53 NGC.** NGC Census: (38/202). PCGS Population (41/150). Mintage: 165,100. Numismedia Wsl. Price for problem free NGC/PCGS coin in AU53: $865. NGC ID# 24YD, PCGS# 6929

7686 **1845 XF45 PCGS.** PCGS Population (56/117). NGC Census: (27/116). Mintage: 24,500. Numismedia Wsl. Price for problem free NGC/PCGS coin in XF45: $1,031. NGC ID# 24YF, PCGS# 6931

7687 **1846 AU53 PCGS.** PCGS Population (50/190). NGC Census: (42/246). Mintage: 110,600. Numismedia Wsl. Price for problem free NGC/PCGS coin in AU53: $950. NGC ID# 24YG, PCGS# 6932

7688 **1847 XF45 NGC.** NGC Census: (65/339). PCGS Population (121/344). Mintage: 140,750. Numismedia Wsl. Price for problem free NGC/PCGS coin in XF45: $670. NGC ID# 24YJ, PCGS# 6934

7689 **1847 XF45 NGC.** NGC Census: (65/339). PCGS Population (121/344). Mintage: 140,750. Numismedia Wsl. Price for problem free NGC/PCGS coin in XF45: $670. NGC ID# 24YJ, PCGS# 6934

7690 **1847 AU53 NGC.** NGC Census: (42/256). PCGS Population (58/198). Mintage: 140,750. Numismedia Wsl. Price for problem free NGC/PCGS coin in AU53: $900. NGC ID# 24YJ, PCGS# 6934

7691 **1849 XF40 NGC.** NGC Census: (10/252). PCGS Population (38/295). Mintage: 62,600. Numismedia Wsl. Price for problem free NGC/PCGS coin in XF40: $610. NGC ID# 24YL, PCGS# 6936

7692 **1860-O XF45 NGC.** NGC Census: (50/696). PCGS Population (91/1022). Mintage: 515,000. Numismedia Wsl. Price for problem free NGC/PCGS coin in XF45: $552. NGC ID# 24Z3, PCGS# 6950

7693 **1867 AU53 PCGS.** PCGS Population (10/72). NGC Census: (5/36). Mintage: 46,900. Numismedia Wsl. Price for problem free NGC/PCGS coin in AU53: $1,150. NGC ID# 24ZA, PCGS# 6960

TRADE DOLLARS

7694 **1873-CC VF35 PCGS. CAC.** PCGS Population (11/200). NGC Census: (2/113). Mintage: 124,500. Numismedia Wsl. Price for problem free NGC/PCGS coin in VF35: $931. NGC ID# 252X, PCGS# 7032

7695 **1873-CC — Improperly Cleaned — NGC Details. AU.** NGC Census: (2/100). PCGS Population (20/116). Mintage: 124,500. Numismedia Wsl. Price for problem free NGC/PCGS coin in AU50: $2,125.

7696 **1875-CC — Repaired, Scratched, Cleaned — ANACS. AU50 Details.** NGC Census: (7/244). PCGS Population (34/317). Mintage: 1,573,700. Numismedia Wsl. Price for problem free NGC/PCGS coin in AU50: $700.

7697 **1875-CC — Scratched — ANACS. AU50 Details.** NGC Census: (7/244). PCGS Population (34/317). Mintage: 1,573,700. Numismedia Wsl. Price for problem free NGC/PCGS coin in AU50: $700.

7698 **1875-S — Chopmarked — NGC Details. Unc.** NGC Census: (0/0). PCGS Population (2/84).

7699 **1876 — Cleaned — PCGS Genuine. Unc Details.** NGC Census: (9/315). PCGS Population (7/356). Mintage: 455,000. Numismedia Wsl. Price for problem free NGC/PCGS coin in MS60: $850.

7700 **1877-S MS60 NGC.** NGC Census: (41/693). PCGS Population (51/762). Mintage: 9,519,000. Numismedia Wsl. Price for problem free NGC/PCGS coin in MS60: $825. NGC ID# 253E, PCGS# 7046

7701 **1878-S — Improperly Cleaned — NGC Details. Unc.** NGC Census: (20/402). PCGS Population (19/443). Mintage: 4,162,000. Numismedia Wsl. Price for problem free NGC/PCGS coin in MS60: $850.

PROOF TRADE DOLLAR

7702 **1873 PR62 NGC.** NGC Census: (31/88). PCGS Population (52/86). Mintage: 865. Numismedia Wsl. Price for problem free NGC/PCGS coin in PR62: $2,125. NGC ID# 27YJ, PCGS# 7053

MORGAN DOLLARS

7703 **1878 8TF MS64 PCGS.** PCGS Population (2567/576). NGC Census: (1970/393). Mintage: 699,300. Numismedia Wsl. Price for problem free NGC/PCGS coin in MS64: $440. NGC ID# 253H, PCGS# 7072

7704 **1878 8TF MS64+ PCGS. CAC.** PCGS Population (2567/576). NGC Census: (1970/393). Mintage: 699,300. Numismedia Wsl. Price for problem free NGC/PCGS coin in MS64: $440. NGC ID# 253H, PCGS# 7072

7705 **1878 8TF MS63 Deep Mirror Prooflike PCGS.** PCGS Population (57/37). NGC Census: (6/1). Numismedia Wsl. Price for problem free NGC/PCGS coin in MS63: $725. NGC ID# 253H, PCGS# 97073

7706 **1878 7/8TF Strong MS64 NGC.** NGC Census: (1042/103). PCGS Population (1494/295). Mintage: 544,000. Numismedia Wsl. Price for problem free NGC/PCGS coin in MS64: $460. NGC ID# 2TXZ, PCGS# 7078

7707 **1878 7/8TF Strong MS64+ PCGS.** PCGS Population (1494/295). NGC Census: (1042/103). Mintage: 544,000. Numismedia Wsl. Price for problem free NGC/PCGS coin in MS64: $460. NGC ID# 2TXZ, PCGS# 7078

7708 **1878 7TF Reverse of 1878 MS65 NGC.** NGC Census: (490/26). PCGS Population (534/33). Mintage: 4,900,000. Numismedia Wsl. Price for problem free NGC/PCGS coin in MS65: $935. NGC ID# 253K, PCGS# 7074

7709 **1878 7TF Reverse of 1878 MS64 Prooflike PCGS.** PCGS Population (182/38). NGC Census: (241/32). Numismedia Wsl. Price for problem free NGC/PCGS coin in MS64: $440. NGC ID# 253K, PCGS# 7075

7710 1878 7TF Reverse of 1879 MS64 NGC. NGC Census: (1132/197). PCGS Population (1299/391). Mintage: 4,300,000. Numismedia Wsl. Price for problem free NGC/PCGS coin in MS64: $460. NGC ID# 253L, PCGS# 7076

7711 1878-CC MS62 PCGS. PCGS Population (4014/16904). NGC Census: (2955/11246). Mintage: 2,212,000. Numismedia Wsl. Price for problem free NGC/PCGS coin in MS62: $310. NGC ID# 253M, PCGS# 7080

7712 1878-CC MS63 NGC. NGC Census: (5264/5982). PCGS Population (8491/8413). Mintage: 2,212,000. Numismedia Wsl. Price for problem free NGC/PCGS coin in MS63: $425. NGC ID# 253M, PCGS# 7080

7713 1878-CC MS63 PCGS. PCGS Population (8491/8413). NGC Census: (5264/5982). Mintage: 2,212,000. Numismedia Wsl. Price for problem free NGC/PCGS coin in MS63: $425. NGC ID# 253M, PCGS# 7080

7714 1878-CC MS64+ PCGS. CAC. PCGS Population (6388/2025). NGC Census: (4500/1482). Mintage: 2,212,000. Numismedia Wsl. Price for problem free NGC/PCGS coin in MS64: $535. NGC ID# 253M, PCGS# 7080

7715 1878-CC Lines in Wing, VAM-11, Top 100 MS64 PCGS. PCGS Population (38/18). NGC Census: (32/16). PCGS# 133843

7716 1878-CC MS64 Prooflike PCGS. PCGS Population (458/127). NGC Census: (321/97). Numismedia Wsl. Price for problem free NGC/PCGS coin in MS64: $865. NGC ID# 253M, PCGS# 7081

7717 1878-CC MS64 Prooflike PCGS. PCGS Population (458/127). NGC Census: (321/97). Numismedia Wsl. Price for problem free NGC/PCGS coin in MS64: $865. NGC ID# 253M, PCGS# 7081

7718 (20)1878-S MS63 NGC. NGC Census: (13874/19462). PCGS Population (14471/18496). Mintage: 9,774,000. Numismedia Wsl. Price for problem free NGC/PCGS coin in MS63: $85. (Total: 20 coins)

7719 1878-S MS66 NGC. NGC Census: (496/29). PCGS Population (641/28). Mintage: 9,774,000. Numismedia Wsl. Price for problem free NGC/PCGS coin in MS66: $725. NGC ID# 253R, PCGS# 7082

7720 1878-S MS66 NGC. CAC. NGC Census: (496/29). PCGS Population (641/28). Mintage: 9,774,000. Numismedia Wsl. Price for problem free NGC/PCGS coin in MS66: $725. NGC ID# 253R, PCGS# 7082

7721 1879 MS65 PCGS. PCGS Population (1027/149). NGC Census: (679/98). Mintage: 14,807,100. Numismedia Wsl. Price for problem free NGC/PCGS coin in MS65: $760. NGC ID# 253S, PCGS# 7084

7722 1879 MS65 PCGS. PCGS Population (1034/151). NGC Census: (678/98). Mintage: 14,807,100. Numismedia Wsl. Price for problem free NGC/PCGS coin in MS65: $760. NGC ID# 253S, PCGS# 7084

7723 1879-CC — Cleaning — PCGS Genuine. AU Details. NGC Census: (63/1334). PCGS Population (83/2482). Mintage: 756,000. Numismedia Wsl. Price for problem free NGC/PCGS coin in AU50: $1,725.

7724 1879-CC Capped Die VF35 PCGS. PCGS Population (115/1924). NGC Census: (0/0). Numismedia Wsl. Price for problem free NGC/PCGS coin in VF35: $504. NGC ID# 253T, PCGS# 7088

7725 1879-CC Capped Die — Cleaning — PCGS Genuine. AU Details. NGC Census: (0/0). PCGS Population (58/1587). Numismedia Wsl. Price for problem free NGC/PCGS coin in AU50: $1,600.

7726 1879-CC Capped Die, VAM-3, — Improperly Cleaned — NGC Details. XF. Top 100. NGC Census: (86/1289). PCGS Population (1/26).

7727 1879-O MS63 Prooflike PCGS. PCGS Population (94/39). NGC Census: (93/45). Numismedia Wsl. Price for problem free NGC/PCGS coin in MS63: $360. NGC ID# 253V, PCGS# 7091

7728 1879-S Reverse of 1878, Top 100 MS62 NGC. NGC Census: (385/731). PCGS Population (833/1398). Numismedia Wsl. Price for problem free NGC/PCGS coin in MS62: $350. NGC ID# 253W, PCGS# 7094

7729 1879-S Reverse of 1878, Top 100 MS62 NGC. NGC Census: (385/731). PCGS Population (833/1398). Numismedia Wsl. Price for problem free NGC/PCGS coin in MS62: $350. NGC ID# 253W, PCGS# 7094

7730 1879-S Reverse of 1878 MS63 PCGS. PCGS Population (803/595). NGC Census: (445/286). Numismedia Wsl. Price for problem free NGC/PCGS coin in MS63: $510. NGC ID# 253W, PCGS# 7094

7731 (20)1879-S MS64 NGC. NGC Census: (38221/31093). PCGS Population (37263/31915). Mintage: 9,110,000. Numismedia Wsl. Price for problem free NGC/PCGS coin in MS64: $71. (Total: 20 coins)

7732 1879-S MS65 NGC. NGC Census: (21954/9158). PCGS Population (23556/8376). Mintage: 9,110,000. Numismedia Wsl. Price for problem free NGC/PCGS coin in MS65: $160. NGC ID# 253X, PCGS# 7092

7733 1879-S MS66 PCGS. CAC. PCGS Population (6919/1445). NGC Census: (7034/2125). Mintage: 9,110,000. Numismedia Wsl. Price for problem free NGC/PCGS coin in MS66: $280. NGC ID# 253X, PCGS# 7092

7734 1879-S MS66 PCGS. CAC. PCGS Population (6919/1445). NGC Census: (7034/2125). Mintage: 9,110,000. Numismedia Wsl. Price for problem free NGC/PCGS coin in MS66: $280. NGC ID# 253X, PCGS# 7092

7735 1879-S MS67 NGC. NGC Census: (1971/154). PCGS Population (1351/94). Mintage: 9,110,000. Numismedia Wsl. Price for problem free NGC/PCGS coin in MS67: $650. NGC ID# 253X, PCGS# 7092

7736 1879-S MS67 PCGS. PCGS Population (1351/94). NGC Census: (1971/154). Mintage: 9,110,000. Numismedia Wsl. Price for problem free NGC/PCGS coin in MS67: $650. NGC ID# 253X, PCGS# 7092

7737 1879-S MS67+ NGC. NGC Census: (1966/154). PCGS Population (1355/95). Mintage: 9,110,000. Numismedia Wsl. Price for problem free NGC/PCGS coin in MS67: $650. NGC ID# 253X, PCGS# 7092

7738 1879-S MS65 Deep Mirror Prooflike NGC. NGC Census: (107/32). PCGS Population (150/56). Numismedia Wsl. Price for problem free NGC/PCGS coin in MS65: $1,050. NGC ID# 253X, PCGS# 97093

7739 **1880 MS65 PCGS.** PCGS Population (1038/137). NGC Census: (713/42). Mintage: 12,601,355. Numismedia Wsl. Price for problem free NGC/PCGS coin in MS65: $690. NGC ID# 253Y, PCGS# 7096

7740 **1880 MS65 NGC.** NGC Census: (713/42). PCGS Population (1039/137). Mintage: 12,601,355. Numismedia Wsl. Price for problem free NGC/PCGS coin in MS65: $690. NGC ID# 253Y, PCGS# 7096

7741 **1880/79-CC Reverse of 1878 MS61 PCGS.** PCGS Population (71/2823). NGC Census: (0/0). Mintage: 591,000. Numismedia Wsl. Price for problem free NGC/PCGS coin in MS61: $485. NGC ID# 253Z, PCGS# 7108

7742 **1880-CC MS62 PCGS.** PCGS Population (1140/11064). NGC Census: (913/7037). Mintage: 591,000. Numismedia Wsl. Price for problem free NGC/PCGS coin in MS62: $500. NGC ID# 2542, PCGS# 7100

7743 **1880-CC MS65 PCGS.** PCGS Population (2367/773). NGC Census: (1208/557). Mintage: 591,000. Numismedia Wsl. Price for problem free NGC/PCGS coin in MS65: $1,075. NGC ID# 2542, PCGS# 7100

7744 **1880-CC MS65 PCGS.** PCGS Population (2367/773). NGC Census: (1208/557). Mintage: 591,000. Numismedia Wsl. Price for problem free NGC/PCGS coin in MS65: $1,075. NGC ID# 2542, PCGS# 7100

7745 **1880-CC MS65 PCGS.** PCGS Population (2367/773). NGC Census: (1208/557). Mintage: 591,000. Numismedia Wsl. Price for problem free NGC/PCGS coin in MS65: $1,075. NGC ID# 2542, PCGS# 7100

7746 **(20)1880-S MS64 NGC.** NGC Census: (54239/47156). PCGS Population (55563/45899). Mintage: 8,900,000. Numismedia Wsl. Price for problem free NGC/PCGS coin in MS64: $71. (Total: 20 coins)

7747 **(10)1880-S MS65 NGC.** NGC Census: (32494/14662). PCGS Population (33918/11981). Mintage: 8,900,000. Numismedia Wsl. Price for problem free NGC/PCGS coin in MS65: $160. (Total: 10 coins)

7748 **1880-S MS67 PCGS.** PCGS Population (1942/194). NGC Census: (3151/264). Mintage: 8,900,000. Numismedia Wsl. Price for problem free NGC/PCGS coin in MS67: $650. NGC ID# 2544, PCGS# 7118

7749 **1880-S MS67 PCGS.** PCGS Population (1942/194). NGC Census: (3151/264). Mintage: 8,900,000. Numismedia Wsl. Price for problem free NGC/PCGS coin in MS67: $650. NGC ID# 2544, PCGS# 7118

7750 **1880-S MS67 PCGS.** PCGS Population (1942/194). NGC Census: (3151/264). Mintage: 8,900,000. Numismedia Wsl. Price for problem free NGC/PCGS coin in MS67: $650. NGC ID# 2544, PCGS# 7118

7751 **1880-S MS67 PCGS.** PCGS Population (1943/196). NGC Census: (3147/262). Mintage: 8,900,000. Numismedia Wsl. Price for problem free NGC/PCGS coin in MS67: $650. NGC ID# 2544, PCGS# 7118

7752 **1880-S MS67 PCGS. CAC.** PCGS Population (1943/196). NGC Census: (3147/262). Mintage: 8,900,000. Numismedia Wsl. Price for problem free NGC/PCGS coin in MS67: $650. NGC ID# 2544, PCGS# 7118

7753 **1880-S MS65 Deep Mirror Prooflike PCGS.** PCGS Population (619/212). NGC Census: (432/123). Numismedia Wsl. Price for problem free NGC/PCGS coin in MS65: $685. NGC ID# 2544, PCGS# 97119

7754 **1881-CC — Environmental Damage — PCGS Genuine. Unc Details.** NGC Census: (16/9715). PCGS Population (29/19144). Mintage: 296,000. Numismedia Wsl. Price for problem free NGC/PCGS coin in MS60: $440.

7755 **1881-CC MS62 PCGS.** PCGS Population (1224/17737). NGC Census: (780/8816). Mintage: 296,000. Numismedia Wsl. Price for problem free NGC/PCGS coin in MS62: $490. NGC ID# 2547, PCGS# 7126

7756 **1881-CC MS64+ PCGS.** PCGS Population (7326/5975). NGC Census: (3502/3016). Mintage: 296,000. Numismedia Wsl. Price for problem free NGC/PCGS coin in MS64: $550. NGC ID# 2547, PCGS# 7126

7757 **1881-CC MS64+ PCGS.** PCGS Population (7333/5983). NGC Census: (3508/3018). Mintage: 296,000. Numismedia Wsl. Price for problem free NGC/PCGS coin in MS64: $550. NGC ID# 2547, PCGS# 7126

7758 **1881-CC MS65 NGC.** NGC Census: (2069/947). PCGS Population (4393/1582). Mintage: 296,000. Numismedia Wsl. Price for problem free NGC/PCGS coin in MS65: $835. NGC ID# 2547, PCGS# 7126

7759 **4 Piece Rainbow Toned Morgan Dollar Set. This set includes: 1881-S $1 MS64 NGC and (3)1883-O $1 MS64 NGC.** (Total: 4 coins)

7760 **(20)1881-S MS64 NGC.** NGC Census: (95087/72000). PCGS Population (95004/63649). Mintage: 12,760,000. Numismedia Wsl. Price for problem free NGC/PCGS coin in MS64: $71. (Total: 20 coins)

7761 **(10)1881-S MS65 NGC.** NGC Census: (51361/20639). PCGS Population (49202/14447). Mintage: 12,760,000. Numismedia Wsl. Price for problem free NGC/PCGS coin in MS65: $160. (Total: 10 coins)

7762 **1881-S MS67 NGC.** NGC Census: (4070/211). PCGS Population (1799/112). Mintage: 12,760,000. Numismedia Wsl. Price for problem free NGC/PCGS coin in MS67: $650. NGC ID# 2549, PCGS# 7130

7763 **1881-S MS67 PCGS.** PCGS Population (1799/112). NGC Census: (4070/211). Mintage: 12,760,000. Numismedia Wsl. Price for problem free NGC/PCGS coin in MS67: $650. NGC ID# 2549, PCGS# 7130

7764 **1881-S MS67 PCGS.** PCGS Population (1799/112). NGC Census: (4070/211). Mintage: 12,760,000. Numismedia Wsl. Price for problem free NGC/PCGS coin in MS67: $650. NGC ID# 2549, PCGS# 7130

7765 **1881-S MS67 PCGS. CAC.** PCGS Population (1812/112). NGC Census: (4062/211). Mintage: 12,760,000. Numismedia Wsl. Price for problem free NGC/PCGS coin in MS67: $650. NGC ID# 2549, PCGS# 7130

7766 **1881-S MS67 PCGS. CAC.** PCGS Population (1799/112). NGC Census: (4070/211). Mintage: 12,760,000. Numismedia Wsl. Price for problem free NGC/PCGS coin in MS67: $650. NGC ID# 2549, PCGS# 7130

7767 **1881-S MS67 PCGS. CAC.** PCGS Population (1799/112). NGC Census: (4070/211). Mintage: 12,760,000. Numismedia Wsl. Price for problem free NGC/PCGS coin in MS67: $650. NGC ID# 2549, PCGS# 7130

7768 **1881-S MS65 Deep Mirror Prooflike NGC.** NGC Census: (314/103). PCGS Population (231/80). Numismedia Wsl. Price for problem free NGC/PCGS coin in MS65: $700. NGC ID# 2549, PCGS# 97131

7769 **1882 MS65 NGC.** NGC Census: (1197/243). PCGS Population (1359/257). Mintage: 11,101,100. Numismedia Wsl. Price for problem free NGC/PCGS coin in MS65: $480. NGC ID# 254A, PCGS# 7132

7770 **1882-CC MS65+ PCGS. CAC.** PCGS Population (4968/1288). NGC Census: (2682/750). Mintage: 1,133,000. Numismedia Wsl. Price for problem free NGC/PCGS coin in MS65: $435. NGC ID# 254B, PCGS# 7134

7771 **1882-CC MS66 NGC.** NGC Census: (697/53). PCGS Population (1223/68). Mintage: 1,133,000. Numismedia Wsl. Price for problem free NGC/PCGS coin in MS66: $1,050. NGC ID# 254B, PCGS# 7134

7772 **1882-CC MS66 PCGS.** PCGS Population (1224/68). NGC Census: (696/53). Mintage: 1,133,000. Numismedia Wsl. Price for problem free NGC/PCGS coin in MS66: $1,050. NGC ID# 254B, PCGS# 7134

7773 **1882-CC MS65 Prooflike PCGS.** PCGS Population (356/87). NGC Census: (200/40). Numismedia Wsl. Price for problem free NGC/PCGS coin in MS65: $540. NGC ID# 254B, PCGS# 7135

7774 **1882-CC MS63 Deep Mirror Prooflike NGC.** NGC Census: (262/423). PCGS Population (594/1226). Numismedia Wsl. Price for problem free NGC/PCGS coin in MS63: $440. NGC ID# 254B, PCGS# 97135

7775 **1882-CC MS64 Deep Mirror Prooflike NGC.** NGC Census: (321/102). PCGS Population (804/422). Numismedia Wsl. Price for problem free NGC/PCGS coin in MS64: $600. NGC ID# 254B, PCGS# 97135

7776 **1882-O MS65 PCGS.** PCGS Population (806/35). NGC Census: (486/13). Mintage: 6,090,000. Numismedia Wsl. Price for problem free NGC/PCGS coin in MS65: $1,075. NGC ID# 254C, PCGS# 7136

7777 **1882-O/S MS63 NGC.** NGC Census: (330/227). PCGS Population (349/229). Mintage: 1,039. Numismedia Wsl. Price for problem free NGC/PCGS coin in MS63: $735. NGC ID# 254D, PCGS# 7138

7778 **(20)1882-S MS64 NGC.** NGC Census: (29684/26433). PCGS Population (30314/22695). Mintage: 9,250,000. Numismedia Wsl. Price for problem free NGC/PCGS coin in MS64: $71. (Total: 20 coins)

7779 **(10)1882-S MS65 NGC.** NGC Census: (18308/8125). PCGS Population (17302/5393). Mintage: 9,250,000. Numismedia Wsl. Price for problem free NGC/PCGS coin in MS65: $160. (Total: 10 coins)

7780 **1882-S MS64 Prooflike PCGS.** PCGS Population (916/524). NGC Census: (1008/795). Numismedia Wsl. Price for problem free NGC/PCGS coin in MS64: $140. NGC ID# 254F, PCGS# 7141

7781 **1883 MS66 PCGS.** PCGS Population (897/103). NGC Census: (794/125). Mintage: 12,291,039. Numismedia Wsl. Price for problem free NGC/PCGS coin in MS66: $480. NGC ID# 254G, PCGS# 7142

7782 **1883-CC MS64 NGC. CAC.** NGC Census: (7183/5255). PCGS Population (15026/9855). Mintage: 1,204,000. Numismedia Wsl. Price for problem free NGC/PCGS coin in MS64: $230. NGC ID# 254H, PCGS# 7144

7783 **1883-CC MS65 NGC.** NGC Census: (4149/1127). PCGS Population (7730/2122). Mintage: 1,204,000. Numismedia Wsl. Price for problem free NGC/PCGS coin in MS65: $420. NGC ID# 254H, PCGS# 7144

7784 **1883-CC MS66 PCGS.** PCGS Population (1942/183). NGC Census: (1011/117). Mintage: 1,204,000. Numismedia Wsl. Price for problem free NGC/PCGS coin in MS66: $800. NGC ID# 254H, PCGS# 7144

7785 **1883-CC MS66 PCGS.** PCGS Population (1937/183). NGC Census: (1009/117). Mintage: 1,204,000. Numismedia Wsl. Price for problem free NGC/PCGS coin in MS66: $800. NGC ID# 254H, PCGS# 7144

7786 **1883-CC MS66 ★ NGC.** NGC Census: (1009/117). PCGS Population (1937/183). Mintage: 1,204,000. Numismedia Wsl. Price for problem free NGC/PCGS coin in MS66: $800. NGC ID# 254H, PCGS# 7144

7787 **1883-CC MS66 PCGS. CAC.** PCGS Population (1942/183). NGC Census: (1011/117). Mintage: 1,204,000. Numismedia Wsl. Price for problem free NGC/PCGS coin in MS66: $800. NGC ID# 254H, PCGS# 7144

7788 **1883-CC MS66 PCGS. CAC.** PCGS Population (1942/183). NGC Census: (1011/117). Mintage: 1,204,000. Numismedia Wsl. Price for problem free NGC/PCGS coin in MS66: $800. NGC ID# 254H, PCGS# 7144

7789 **1883-CC MS66 PCGS. CAC.** PCGS Population (1937/183). NGC Census: (1009/117). Mintage: 1,204,000. Numismedia Wsl. Price for problem free NGC/PCGS coin in MS66: $800. NGC ID# 254H, PCGS# 7144

7790 **1883-CC MS65+ Prooflike NGC.** NGC Census: (320/76). PCGS Population (604/141). Numismedia Wsl. Price for problem free NGC/PCGS coin in MS65: $480. NGC ID# 254H, PCGS# 7145

7791 **2 Piece Toned Morgan Dollar Set. This set includes: 1882-S MS64 PCGS and an 1883-O MS64 PCGS. CAC.** (Total: 2 coins)

7792 **1883-O MS65 PCGS.** PCGS Population (7612/786). NGC Census: (9910/1010). Mintage: 8,725,000. Numismedia Wsl. Price for problem free NGC/PCGS coin in MS65: $160. NGC ID# 254J, PCGS# 7146

7793 **1883-O MS66 PCGS.** PCGS Population (742/44). NGC Census: (975/35). Mintage: 8,725,000. Numismedia Wsl. Price for problem free NGC/PCGS coin in MS66: $300. NGC ID# 254J, PCGS# 7146

7794 **1883-O MS66+ PCGS.** PCGS Population (742/44). NGC Census: (975/35). Mintage: 8,725,000. Numismedia Wsl. Price for problem free NGC/PCGS coin in MS66: $300. NGC ID# 254J, PCGS# 7146

7795 **1884 MS66 PCGS.** PCGS Population (446/40). NGC Census: (246/35). Mintage: 14,070,875. Numismedia Wsl. Price for problem free NGC/PCGS coin in MS66: $775. NGC ID# 254L, PCGS# 7150

7796 **1884 MS66 PCGS. CAC.** PCGS Population (446/40). NGC Census: (246/35). Mintage: 14,070,875. Numismedia Wsl. Price for problem free NGC/PCGS coin in MS66: $775. NGC ID# 254L, PCGS# 7150

7797 **1884-CC MS66 PCGS.** PCGS Population (1578/92). NGC Census: (915/109). Mintage: 1,136,000. Numismedia Wsl. Price for problem free NGC/PCGS coin in MS66: $750. NGC ID# 254M, PCGS# 7152

7798 **1884-CC MS66 PCGS. CAC.** PCGS Population (1584/93). NGC Census: (917/109). Mintage: 1,136,000. Numismedia Wsl. Price for problem free NGC/PCGS coin in MS66: $750. NGC ID# 254M, PCGS# 7152

7799 **(20)1884-O MS64 NGC.** NGC Census: (81764/20280). PCGS Population (67194/15067). Mintage: 9,730,000. Numismedia Wsl. Price for problem free NGC/PCGS coin in MS64: $71. (Total: 20 coins)

7800 **(10)1884-O MS65 NGC.** NGC Census: (18260/2020). PCGS Population (13645/1422). Mintage: 9,730,000. Numismedia Wsl. Price for problem free NGC/PCGS coin in MS65: $160. (Total: 10 coins)

7801 **1884-O MS66 PCGS. CAC.** PCGS Population (1321/100). NGC Census: (1895/110). Mintage: 9,730,000. Numismedia Wsl. Price for problem free NGC/PCGS coin in MS66: $280. NGC ID# 254N, PCGS# 7154

7802 **1884-O MS64 Deep Mirror Prooflike NGC.** NGC Census: (550/121). PCGS Population (716/291). Numismedia Wsl. Price for problem free NGC/PCGS coin in MS64: $400. NGC ID# 254N, PCGS# 97155

7803 **1884-O MS64+ Deep Mirror Prooflike PCGS. CAC.** PCGS Population (716/291). NGC Census: (550/121). Numismedia Wsl. Price for problem free NGC/PCGS coin in MS64: $400. NGC ID# 254N, PCGS# 97155

7804 **1884-S AU55 NGC.** NGC Census: (1651/2140). PCGS Population (1636/1272). Mintage: 3,200,000. Numismedia Wsl. Price for problem free NGC/PCGS coin in AU55: $475. NGC ID# 254P, PCGS# 7156

7805 **1884-S AU55 NGC.** NGC Census: (1651/2140). PCGS Population (1636/1272). Mintage: 3,200,000. Numismedia Wsl. Price for problem free NGC/PCGS coin in AU55: $475. NGC ID# 254P, PCGS# 7156

7806 **1885 MS64 PCGS. CAC.** PCGS Population (25481/9749). NGC Census: (31121/12024). Mintage: 17,787,768. Numismedia Wsl. Price for problem free NGC/PCGS coin in MS64: $71. NGC ID# 254R, PCGS# 7158

7807 **1885 MS66 PCGS.** PCGS Population (1366/122). NGC Census: (1718/212). Mintage: 17,787,768. Numismedia Wsl. Price for problem free NGC/PCGS coin in MS66: $360. NGC ID# 254R, PCGS# 7158

7808 **1885 MS65 Deep Mirror Prooflike PCGS.** PCGS Population (313/78). NGC Census: (197/54). Numismedia Wsl. Price for problem free NGC/PCGS coin in MS65: $865. NGC ID# 254R, PCGS# 97159

7809 **1885 MS65 Deep Mirror Prooflike PCGS.** PCGS Population (313/78). NGC Census: (197/54). Numismedia Wsl. Price for problem free NGC/PCGS coin in MS65: $865. NGC ID# 254R, PCGS# 97159

7810 **1885 MS65 Deep Mirror Prooflike PCGS. CAC.** PCGS Population (313/78). NGC Census: (197/54). Numismedia Wsl. Price for problem free NGC/PCGS coin in MS65: $865. NGC ID# 254R, PCGS# 97159

7811 **1885-CC AG3 NGC.** NGC Census: (0/9739). PCGS Population (17/19399). Mintage: 228,000. Numismedia Wsl. Price for problem free NGC/PCGS coin in AG3: $183. NGC ID# 254S, PCGS# 7160

7812 **1885-CC — Cleaning — PCGS Genuine. Unc Details.** NGC Census: (20/9622). PCGS Population (46/19161). Mintage: 228,000. Numismedia Wsl. Price for problem free NGC/PCGS coin in MS60: $580.

7813 **1885-CC MS61 NGC.** NGC Census: (177/9455). PCGS Population (256/18917). Mintage: 228,000. Numismedia Wsl. Price for problem free NGC/PCGS coin in MS61: $625. NGC ID# 254S, PCGS# 7160

7814 **1885-CC MS62 PCGS.** PCGS Population (1564/17341). NGC Census: (922/8524). Mintage: 228,000. Numismedia Wsl. Price for problem free NGC/PCGS coin in MS62: $650. NGC ID# 254S, PCGS# 7160

7815 **1885-CC MS62 PCGS.** PCGS Population (1564/17353). NGC Census: (923/8532). Mintage: 228,000. Numismedia Wsl. Price for problem free NGC/PCGS coin in MS62: $650. NGC ID# 254S, PCGS# 7160

7816 **1885-CC MS64 PCGS.** PCGS Population (7318/5061). NGC Census: (3406/2614). Mintage: 228,000. Numismedia Wsl. Price for problem free NGC/PCGS coin in MS64: $765. NGC ID# 254S, PCGS# 7160

7817 **1885-CC MS64 PCGS.** PCGS Population (7320/5066). NGC Census: (3407/2617). Mintage: 228,000. Numismedia Wsl. Price for problem free NGC/PCGS coin in MS64: $765. NGC ID# 254S, PCGS# 7160

7818 **1885-CC MS64 PCGS.** PCGS Population (7320/5066). NGC Census: (3407/2617). Mintage: 228,000. Numismedia Wsl. Price for problem free NGC/PCGS coin in MS64: $765. NGC ID# 254S, PCGS# 7160

7819 **1885-CC MS64 PCGS.** PCGS Population (7320/5066). NGC Census: (3407/2617). Mintage: 228,000. Numismedia Wsl. Price for problem free NGC/PCGS coin in MS64: $765. NGC ID# 254S, PCGS# 7160

7820 **1885-CC MS64 PCGS.** PCGS Population (7320/5066). NGC Census: (3407/2617). Mintage: 228,000. Numismedia Wsl. Price for problem free NGC/PCGS coin in MS64: $765. NGC ID# 254S, PCGS# 7160

7821 **1885-CC MS65 PCGS.** PCGS Population (3962/1099). NGC Census: (1776/838). Mintage: 228,000. Numismedia Wsl. Price for problem free NGC/PCGS coin in MS65: $975. NGC ID# 254S, PCGS# 7160

7822 **1885-CC MS65 PCGS.** PCGS Population (3967/1099). NGC Census: (1778/839). Mintage: 228,000. Numismedia Wsl. Price for problem free NGC/PCGS coin in MS65: $975. NGC ID# 254S, PCGS# 7160

7823 **1885-CC MS62 Prooflike NGC.** NGC Census: (94/523). PCGS Population (157/969). Numismedia Wsl. Price for problem free NGC/PCGS coin in MS62: $675. NGC ID# 254S, PCGS# 7161

7824 **1885-CC MS63 Deep Mirror Prooflike NGC.** NGC Census: (145/262). PCGS Population (398/687). Numismedia Wsl. Price for problem free NGC/PCGS coin in MS63: $885. NGC ID# 254S, PCGS# 97161

7825 **(20)1885-O MS64 NGC.** NGC Census: (84271/32004). PCGS Population (67719/21012). Mintage: 9,185,000. Numismedia Wsl. Price for problem free NGC/PCGS coin in MS64: $71. (Total: 20 coins)

7826 **1885-O MS66+ PCGS. CAC.** PCGS Population (2371/245). NGC Census: (4394/551). Mintage: 9,185,000. Numismedia Wsl. Price for problem free NGC/PCGS coin in MS66: $280. NGC ID# 254T, PCGS# 7162

7827 **1885-O MS66+ PCGS. CAC.** PCGS Population (2368/243). NGC Census: (4414/551). Mintage: 9,185,000. Numismedia Wsl. Price for problem free NGC/PCGS coin in MS66: $280. NGC ID# 254T, PCGS# 7162

7828 **1885-S MS63 NGC.** NGC Census: (1624/1670). PCGS Population (2938/2848). Mintage: 1,497,000. Numismedia Wsl. Price for problem free NGC/PCGS coin in MS63: $300. NGC ID# 254U, PCGS# 7164

7829 **1885-S MS64 ★ NGC.** NGC Census: (1389/281). PCGS Population (2320/528). Mintage: 1,497,000. Numismedia Wsl. Price for problem free NGC/PCGS coin in MS64: $610. NGC ID# 254U, PCGS# 7164

7830 **(20)1886 MS64 NGC.** NGC Census: (52553/26838). PCGS Population (42197/17934). Mintage: 19,963,886. Numismedia Wsl. Price for problem free NGC/PCGS coin in MS64: $71. (Total: 20 coins)

7831 **1886 MS66+ NGC. CAC.** NGC Census: (4933/914). PCGS Population (2649/344). Mintage: 19,963,886. Numismedia Wsl. Price for problem free NGC/PCGS coin in MS66: $300. NGC ID# 254V, PCGS# 7166

7832 **1886 Line in 6, VAM-1A, Top 100 MS66+ PCGS.** PCGS Population (15/1). NGC Census: (32/3). PCGS# 133902

7833 **1886-O MS61 NGC.** NGC Census: (507/892). PCGS Population (393/1529). Mintage: 10,710,000. Numismedia Wsl. Price for problem free NGC/PCGS coin in MS61: $950. NGC ID# 254W, PCGS# 7168

7834 **1886-S MS61 NGC.** NGC Census: (336/2587). PCGS Population (294/4577). Mintage: 750,000. Numismedia Wsl. Price for problem free NGC/PCGS coin in MS61: $350. NGC ID# 254X, PCGS# 7170

7835 **1886-S MS61 NGC.** NGC Census: (336/2587). PCGS Population (294/4577). Mintage: 750,000. Numismedia Wsl. Price for problem free NGC/PCGS coin in MS61: $350. NGC ID# 254X, PCGS# 7170

7836 **1886-S MS62 NGC.** NGC Census: (742/1845). PCGS Population (1191/3386). Mintage: 750,000. Numismedia Wsl. Price for problem free NGC/PCGS coin in MS62: $390. NGC ID# 254X, PCGS# 7170

7837 **1886-S MS63 NGC.** NGC Census: (995/850). PCGS Population (1794/1592). Mintage: 750,000. Numismedia Wsl. Price for problem free NGC/PCGS coin in MS63: $465. NGC ID# 254X, PCGS# 7170

7838 **1886-S MS64 PCGS.** PCGS Population (1246/346). NGC Census: (719/131). Mintage: 750,000. Numismedia Wsl. Price for problem free NGC/PCGS coin in MS64: $775. NGC ID# 254X, PCGS# 7170

7839 **(20)1887 MS64 NGC.** NGC Census: (78732/29876). PCGS Population (57886/16998). Mintage: 20,290,710. Numismedia Wsl. Price for problem free NGC/PCGS coin in MS64: $71. (Total: 20 coins)

7840 **1887 MS66+ PCGS. CAC.** PCGS Population (1458/113). NGC Census: (3692/326). Mintage: 20,290,710. Numismedia Wsl. Price for problem free NGC/PCGS coin in MS66: $320. NGC ID# 254Y, PCGS# 7172

7841 **1887-O MS64+ PCGS. CAC.** PCGS Population (2539/327). NGC Census: (1824/96). Mintage: 11,550,000. Numismedia Wsl. Price for problem free NGC/PCGS coin in MS64: $375. NGC ID# 2552, PCGS# 7176

7842 **1887-S MS64 PCGS.** PCGS Population (1799/378). NGC Census: (929/168). Mintage: 1,771,000. Numismedia Wsl. Price for problem free NGC/PCGS coin in MS64: $600. NGC ID# 2554, PCGS# 7180

7843 **(13)1888-O MS63 NGC.** NGC Census: (8154/10840). PCGS Population (8331/9520). Mintage: 12,150,000. Numismedia Wsl. Price for problem free NGC/PCGS coin in MS63: $65. (Total: 13 coins)

7844 **1888-O MS63+ NGC.** NGC Census: (8154/10840). PCGS Population (8331/9520). Mintage: 12,150,000. Numismedia Wsl. Price for problem free NGC/PCGS coin in MS63: $65. NGC ID# 2556, PCGS# 7184

7845 **(20)1888-O MS64 NGC.** NGC Census: (9462/1378). PCGS Population (7388/2132). Mintage: 12,150,000. Numismedia Wsl. Price for problem free NGC/PCGS coin in MS64: $92. (Total: 20 coins)

7846 **1888-O Clashed E, VAM-1A, Top 100 MS64 PCGS.** PCGS Population (30/2). NGC Census: (36/0). PCGS# 133917

7847 **1888-O Doubled Die Obverse, Hot Lips AU50 PCGS.** PCGS Population (63/112). NGC Census: (0/0). PCGS# 7308

7848 **1888-O Doubled Die Obverse, Hot Lips AU50 PCGS.** PCGS Population (63/112). NGC Census: (0/0). PCGS# 7308

7849 **1888-S MS62 NGC.** NGC Census: (837/2017). PCGS Population (1235/3977). Mintage: 657,000. Numismedia Wsl. Price for problem free NGC/PCGS coin in MS62: $395. NGC ID# 2557, PCGS# 7186

7850 **1888-S MS62 PCGS.** PCGS Population (1235/3977). NGC Census: (837/2017). Mintage: 657,000. Numismedia Wsl. Price for problem free NGC/PCGS coin in MS62: $395. NGC ID# 2557, PCGS# 7186

7851 **1888-S MS63 NGC.** NGC Census: (1016/1001). PCGS Population (2169/1808). Mintage: 657,000. Numismedia Wsl. Price for problem free NGC/PCGS coin in MS63: $440. NGC ID# 2557, PCGS# 7186

7852 **1888-S MS64 PCGS.** PCGS Population (1468/347). NGC Census: (887/114). Mintage: 657,000. Numismedia Wsl. Price for problem free NGC/PCGS coin in MS64: $875. NGC ID# 2557, PCGS# 7186

7853 **(20)1889 MS64 NGC.** NGC Census: (15061/2265). PCGS Population (10663/2130). Mintage: 21,726,812. Numismedia Wsl. Price for problem free NGC/PCGS coin in MS64: $77. (Total: 20 coins)

7854 1889 MS66 PCGS. PCGS Population (252/4). NGC Census: (220/1). Mintage: 21,726,812. Numismedia Wsl. Price for problem free NGC/PCGS coin in MS66: $1,150. NGC ID# 2558, PCGS# 7188

7855 1889-CC Poor 1 NGC. CAC. NGC Census: (2/4030). PCGS Population (1/6343). Mintage: 350,000. Numismedia Wsl. Price for problem free NGC/PCGS coin in Poor 1: $77. NGC ID# 2559, PCGS# 7190

7856 1889-CC Fine 12 ANACS. NGC Census: (296/3023). PCGS Population (443/4709). Mintage: 350,000. Numismedia Wsl. Price for problem free NGC/PCGS coin in Fine 12: $775. NGC ID# 2559, PCGS# 7190

7857 1889-CC — Improperly Cleaned — NGC Details. VF. NGC Census: (273/2504). PCGS Population (427/3782). Mintage: 350,000. Numismedia Wsl. Price for problem free NGC/PCGS coin in VF20: $1,100.

7858 1889-CC VF20 NGC. NGC Census: (273/2502). PCGS Population (427/3769). Mintage: 350,000. Numismedia Wsl. Price for problem free NGC/PCGS coin in VF20: $1,100. NGC ID# 2559, PCGS# 7190

7859 1889-CC — Filed Rims — PCGS Genuine. XF Details. NGC Census: (285/1595). PCGS Population (556/1848). Mintage: 350,000. Numismedia Wsl. Price for problem free NGC/PCGS coin in XF40: $2,775.

7860 1889-CC — Smoothed — PCGS Genuine. XF Details. NGC Census: (285/1595). PCGS Population (561/1849). Mintage: 350,000. Numismedia Wsl. Price for problem free NGC/PCGS coin in XF40: $2,775.

7861 1889-O MS63 NGC. NGC Census: (1412/1058). PCGS Population (2121/1788). Mintage: 11,875,000. Numismedia Wsl. Price for problem free NGC/PCGS coin in MS63: $340. NGC ID# 255A, PCGS# 7192

7862 1889-O MS63 NGC. NGC Census: (1412/1058). PCGS Population (2121/1788). Mintage: 11,875,000. Numismedia Wsl. Price for problem free NGC/PCGS coin in MS63: $340. NGC ID# 255A, PCGS# 7192

7863 1889-S MS63 NGC. NGC Census: (1478/1598). PCGS Population (2656/2832). Mintage: 700,000. Numismedia Wsl. Price for problem free NGC/PCGS coin in MS63: $325. NGC ID# 255B, PCGS# 7194

7864 1889-S MS64 NGC. NGC Census: (1318/280). PCGS Population (2134/698). Mintage: 700,000. Numismedia Wsl. Price for problem free NGC/PCGS coin in MS64: $575. NGC ID# 255B, PCGS# 7194

7865 1890-CC Tail Bar, VAM-4, Top 100 — Improperly Cleaned — NGC Details. AU. NGC Census: (14/275). PCGS Population (1/32).

7866 1890-CC MS62 PCGS. PCGS Population (2338/5868). NGC Census: (1322/2588). Mintage: 2,309,041. Numismedia Wsl. Price for problem free NGC/PCGS coin in MS62: $585. NGC ID# 255D, PCGS# 7198

7867 1890-CC MS63 NGC. NGC Census: (1477/1111). PCGS Population (3428/2440). Mintage: 2,309,041. Numismedia Wsl. Price for problem free NGC/PCGS coin in MS63: $750. NGC ID# 255D, PCGS# 7198

7868 1890-CC MS63 PCGS. PCGS Population (3428/2440). NGC Census: (1477/1111). Mintage: 2,309,041. Numismedia Wsl. Price for problem free NGC/PCGS coin in MS63: $750. NGC ID# 255D, PCGS# 7198

7869 1890-CC MS63 PCGS. PCGS Population (3431/2446). NGC Census: (1479/1110). Mintage: 2,309,041. Numismedia Wsl. Price for problem free NGC/PCGS coin in MS63: $750. NGC ID# 255D, PCGS# 7198

7870 1890-CC MS63 PCGS. PCGS Population (3431/2446). NGC Census: (1479/1110). Mintage: 2,309,041. Numismedia Wsl. Price for problem free NGC/PCGS coin in MS63: $750. NGC ID# 255D, PCGS# 7198

7871 1890-CC MS63 PCGS. PCGS Population (3431/2446). NGC Census: (1479/1110). Mintage: 2,309,041. Numismedia Wsl. Price for problem free NGC/PCGS coin in MS63: $750. NGC ID# 255D, PCGS# 7198

7872 1890-CC AU58 Prooflike NGC. NGC Census: (0/0). PCGS Population (0/443). Numismedia Wsl. Price for problem free NGC/PCGS coin in AU58: $300. NGC ID# 255D, PCGS# 7199

7873 1891 MS64 PCGS. CAC. PCGS Population (1860/147). NGC Census: (1179/130). Mintage: 8,694,206. Numismedia Wsl. Price for problem free NGC/PCGS coin in MS64: $875. NGC ID# 255G, PCGS# 7204

7874 1891 MS64+ NGC. CAC. NGC Census: (1179/130). PCGS Population (1862/147). Mintage: 8,694,206. Numismedia Wsl. Price for problem free NGC/PCGS coin in MS64: $875. NGC ID# 255G, PCGS# 7204

7875 1891-CC MS62 PCGS. PCGS Population (3095/8863). NGC Census: (1092/2930). Mintage: 1,618,000. Numismedia Wsl. Price for problem free NGC/PCGS coin in MS62: $500. NGC ID# 255H, PCGS# 7206

7876 1891-CC MS62 PCGS. PCGS Population (3101/8883). NGC Census: (1098/2942). Mintage: 1,618,000. Numismedia Wsl. Price for problem free NGC/PCGS coin in MS62: $500. NGC ID# 255H, PCGS# 7206

7877 1891-CC MS63 PCGS. PCGS Population (4986/3897). NGC Census: (1603/1339). Mintage: 1,618,000. Numismedia Wsl. Price for problem free NGC/PCGS coin in MS63: $680. NGC ID# 255H, PCGS# 7206

7878 1891-CC MS64 PCGS. PCGS Population (3283/614). NGC Census: (1182/157). Mintage: 1,618,000. Numismedia Wsl. Price for problem free NGC/PCGS coin in MS64: $1,175. NGC ID# 255H, PCGS# 7206

7879 1891-CC MS64 PCGS. PCGS Population (3283/614). NGC Census: (1182/157). Mintage: 1,618,000. Numismedia Wsl. Price for problem free NGC/PCGS coin in MS64: $1,175. NGC ID# 255H, PCGS# 7206

7880 1891-CC Spitting Eagle, VAM-3, Top 100 MS62 NGC. NGC Census: (1053/1457). PCGS Population (68/178). PCGS# 133937

7881 **1892 MS64 PCGS.** PCGS Population (1454/287). NGC Census: (823/101). Mintage: 1,037,245. Numismedia Wsl. Price for problem free NGC/PCGS coin in MS64: $1,125. NGC ID# 255L, PCGS# 7212

7882 **1892-CC AU55 PCGS.** PCGS Population (223/6811). NGC Census: (195/4154). Mintage: 1,352,000. Numismedia Wsl. Price for problem free NGC/PCGS coin in AU55: $725. NGC ID# 255M, PCGS# 7214

7883 **1892-CC — Obverse Improperly Cleaned — NGC Details. Unc.** NGC Census: (96/3805). PCGS Population (135/6388). Mintage: 1,352,000. Numismedia Wsl. Price for problem free NGC/PCGS coin in MS60: $1,200.

7884 **1892-CC — Cleaning — PCGS Genuine. Unc Details.** NGC Census: (97/3807). PCGS Population (135/6410). Mintage: 1,352,000. Numismedia Wsl. Price for problem free NGC/PCGS coin in MS60: $1,200.

7885 **1892-O MS63 NGC.** NGC Census: (1601/1569). PCGS Population (2571/2212). Mintage: 2,744,000. Numismedia Wsl. Price for problem free NGC/PCGS coin in MS63: $380. NGC ID# 255N, PCGS# 7216

7886 **1892-O MS64 NGC.** NGC Census: (1486/83). PCGS Population (2024/188). Mintage: 2,744,000. Numismedia Wsl. Price for problem free NGC/PCGS coin in MS64: $1,075. NGC ID# 255N, PCGS# 7216

7887 **1892-O MS64 PCGS.** PCGS Population (2024/188). NGC Census: (1486/83). Mintage: 2,744,000. Numismedia Wsl. Price for problem free NGC/PCGS coin in MS64: $1,075. NGC ID# 255N, PCGS# 7216

7888 **1892-O MS64 PCGS.** PCGS Population (2030/189). NGC Census: (1484/82). Mintage: 2,744,000. Numismedia Wsl. Price for problem free NGC/PCGS coin in MS64: $1,075. NGC ID# 255N, PCGS# 7216

7889 **1893-CC VF25 NGC.** NGC Census: (180/2541). PCGS Population (217/4748). Mintage: 677,000. Numismedia Wsl. Price for problem free NGC/PCGS coin in VF25: $647. NGC ID# 255S, PCGS# 7222

7890 **1893-CC VF30 NGC.** NGC Census: (178/2363). PCGS Population (261/4487). Mintage: 677,000. Numismedia Wsl. Price for problem free NGC/PCGS coin in VF30: $837. NGC ID# 255S, PCGS# 7222

7891 **1893-CC — Smoothed — PCGS Genuine. XF Details.** NGC Census: (181/2079). PCGS Population (292/3929). Mintage: 677,000. Numismedia Wsl. Price for problem free NGC/PCGS coin in XF40: $1,275.

7892 **1893-O VF35 NGC.** NGC Census: (85/2040). PCGS Population (166/2677). Mintage: 300,000. Numismedia Wsl. Price for problem free NGC/PCGS coin in VF35: $385. NGC ID# 255T, PCGS# 7224

7893 **1893-O XF45 NGC.** NGC Census: (258/1636). PCGS Population (362/2070). Mintage: 300,000. Numismedia Wsl. Price for problem free NGC/PCGS coin in XF45: $545. NGC ID# 255T, PCGS# 7224

7894 **1893-O — Improperly Cleaned — NGC Details. AU.** NGC Census: (138/1498). PCGS Population (236/1834). Mintage: 300,000. Numismedia Wsl. Price for problem free NGC/PCGS coin in AU50: $675.

7895 **1893-O AU55 NGC.** NGC Census: (296/978). PCGS Population (365/1242). Mintage: 300,000. Numismedia Wsl. Price for problem free NGC/PCGS coin in AU55: $975. NGC ID# 255T, PCGS# 7224

7896 **1894 — Improperly Cleaned — NGC Details. VF.** NGC Census: (51/2922). PCGS Population (76/4107). Mintage: 110,972. Numismedia Wsl. Price for problem free NGC/PCGS coin in VF20: $1,050.

7897 **1894 VF20 PCGS.** PCGS Population (76/4121). NGC Census: (51/2923). Mintage: 110,972. Numismedia Wsl. Price for problem free NGC/PCGS coin in VF20: $1,050. NGC ID# 255V, PCGS# 7228

7898 **1894 — Damaged — PCGS Genuine. XF Details.** NGC Census: (187/2436). PCGS Population (335/3243). Mintage: 110,972. Numismedia Wsl. Price for problem free NGC/PCGS coin in XF40: $1,225.

7899 **1894 — Improperly Cleaned — NGC Details. XF.** NGC Census: (187/2436). PCGS Population (334/3231). Mintage: 110,972. Numismedia Wsl. Price for problem free NGC/PCGS coin in XF40: $1,225.

7900 **1894 — Altered Surfaces — PCGS Genuine. AU Details.** NGC Census: (148/1970). PCGS Population (304/2427). Mintage: 110,972. Numismedia Wsl. Price for problem free NGC/PCGS coin in AU50: $1,400.

7901 **1894-O AU58 NGC.** NGC Census: (817/1001). PCGS Population (564/1254). Mintage: 1,723,000. Numismedia Wsl. Price for problem free NGC/PCGS coin in AU58: $350. NGC ID# 255W, PCGS# 7230

7902 **1894-O AU58 PCGS.** PCGS Population (564/1254). NGC Census: (817/1001). Mintage: 1,723,000. Numismedia Wsl. Price for problem free NGC/PCGS coin in AU58: $350. NGC ID# 255W, PCGS# 7230

7903 **1894-S AU50 NGC.** NGC Census: (73/2494). PCGS Population (136/3915). Mintage: 1,260,000. Numismedia Wsl. Price for problem free NGC/PCGS coin in AU50: $330. NGC ID# 255X, PCGS# 7232

7904 **1894-S AU53 NGC.** NGC Census: (122/2372). PCGS Population (155/3760). Mintage: 1,260,000. Numismedia Wsl. Price for problem free NGC/PCGS coin in AU53: $360. NGC ID# 255X, PCGS# 7232

7905 **1894-S AU53 NGC.** NGC Census: (122/2372). PCGS Population (155/3760). Mintage: 1,260,000. Numismedia Wsl. Price for problem free NGC/PCGS coin in AU53: $360. NGC ID# 255X, PCGS# 7232

7906 **1895-O VF20 PCGS.** PCGS Population (236/4435). NGC Census: (120/4081). Mintage: 450,000. Numismedia Wsl. Price for problem free NGC/PCGS coin in VF20: $320. NGC ID# 255Y, PCGS# 7236

7907 **1895-O XF45 PCGS.** PCGS Population (975/2046). NGC Census: (826/2327). Mintage: 450,000. Numismedia Wsl. Price for problem free NGC/PCGS coin in XF45: $643. NGC ID# 255Y, PCGS# 7236

7908 **1895-S VG8 PCGS.** PCGS Population (185/3346). NGC Census: (129/1964). Mintage: 400,000. Numismedia Wsl. Price for problem free NGC/PCGS coin in VG8: $360. NGC ID# 255Z, PCGS# 7238

7909 **1895-S VF20 PCGS.** PCGS Population (152/2598). NGC Census: (63/1537). Mintage: 400,000. Numismedia Wsl. Price for problem free NGC/PCGS coin in VF20: $660. NGC ID# 255Z, PCGS# 7238

7910 **1895-S VF20 PCGS.** PCGS Population (152/2598). NGC Census: (63/1537). Mintage: 400,000. Numismedia Wsl. Price for problem free NGC/PCGS coin in VF20: $660. NGC ID# 255Z, PCGS# 7238

7911 **1895-S — Cleaning — PCGS Genuine. XF Details.** NGC Census: (96/1192). PCGS Population (196/1917). Mintage: 400,000. Numismedia Wsl. Price for problem free NGC/PCGS coin in XF40: $1,050.

7912 **1895-S — Cleaning — PCGS Genuine. XF Details.** NGC Census: (96/1193). PCGS Population (196/1927). Mintage: 400,000. Numismedia Wsl. Price for problem free NGC/PCGS coin in XF40: $1,050.

7913 **1896 MS66 NGC.** NGC Census: (822/59). PCGS Population (1571/177). Mintage: 9,976,762. Numismedia Wsl. Price for problem free NGC/PCGS coin in MS66: $480. NGC ID# 2562, PCGS# 7240

7914 **1896 MS66+ PCGS.** PCGS Population (1571/177). NGC Census: (822/59). Mintage: 9,976,762. Numismedia Wsl. Price for problem free NGC/PCGS coin in MS66: $480. NGC ID# 2562, PCGS# 7240

7915 **1896 MS66+ PCGS.** PCGS Population (1571/177). NGC Census: (822/59). Mintage: 9,976,762. Numismedia Wsl. Price for problem free NGC/PCGS coin in MS66: $480. NGC ID# 2562, PCGS# 7240

7916 **1896 MS66+ PCGS.** PCGS Population (1571/177). NGC Census: (822/59). Mintage: 9,976,762. Numismedia Wsl. Price for problem free NGC/PCGS coin in MS66: $480. NGC ID# 2562, PCGS# 7240

7917 **1896 MS66+ PCGS.** PCGS Population (1571/177). NGC Census: (822/59). Mintage: 9,976,762. Numismedia Wsl. Price for problem free NGC/PCGS coin in MS66: $480. NGC ID# 2562, PCGS# 7240

7918 **1896 MS66+ PCGS.** PCGS Population (1571/177). NGC Census: (822/59). Mintage: 9,976,762. Numismedia Wsl. Price for problem free NGC/PCGS coin in MS66: $480. NGC ID# 2562, PCGS# 7240

7919 **1896 MS66 PCGS. CAC.** PCGS Population (1565/177). NGC Census: (826/59). Mintage: 9,976,762. Numismedia Wsl. Price for problem free NGC/PCGS coin in MS66: $480. NGC ID# 2562, PCGS# 7240

7920 **1896 MS66+ PCGS. CAC.** PCGS Population (1571/177). NGC Census: (822/59). Mintage: 9,976,762. Numismedia Wsl. Price for problem free NGC/PCGS coin in MS66: $480. NGC ID# 2562, PCGS# 7240

7921 **1896 MS66+ PCGS. CAC.** PCGS Population (1571/177). NGC Census: (822/59). Mintage: 9,976,762. Numismedia Wsl. Price for problem free NGC/PCGS coin in MS66: $480. NGC ID# 2562, PCGS# 7240

7922 **1896-O AU58 NGC.** NGC Census: (1537/1318). PCGS Population (1122/1344). Mintage: 4,900,000. Numismedia Wsl. Price for problem free NGC/PCGS coin in AU58: $330. NGC ID# 2563, PCGS# 7242

7923 **1896-O AU58 PCGS.** PCGS Population (1122/1344). NGC Census: (1537/1318). Mintage: 4,900,000. Numismedia Wsl. Price for problem free NGC/PCGS coin in AU58: $330. NGC ID# 2563, PCGS# 7242

7924 **1896-S AU50 NGC.** NGC Census: (65/943). PCGS Population (82/1749). Mintage: 5,000,000. Numismedia Wsl. Price for problem free NGC/PCGS coin in AU50: $665. NGC ID# 2564, PCGS# 7244

7925 **1896-S AU55 NGC.** NGC Census: (83/772). PCGS Population (66/1616). Mintage: 5,000,000. Numismedia Wsl. Price for problem free NGC/PCGS coin in AU55: $815. NGC ID# 2564, PCGS# 7244

7926 **1897 MS65 Prooflike PCGS.** PCGS Population (52/13). NGC Census: (33/6). Numismedia Wsl. Price for problem free NGC/PCGS coin in MS65: $625. NGC ID# 2565, PCGS# 7247

7927 **1897 MS65 Prooflike PCGS.** PCGS Population (52/13). NGC Census: (33/6). Numismedia Wsl. Price for problem free NGC/PCGS coin in MS65: $625. NGC ID# 2565, PCGS# 7247

7928 **1897-S MS65 NGC.** NGC Census: (709/126). PCGS Population (1124/294). Mintage: 5,825,000. Numismedia Wsl. Price for problem free NGC/PCGS coin in MS65: $540. NGC ID# 2567, PCGS# 7250

7929 **1898 MS66 PCGS. CAC.** PCGS Population (663/80). NGC Census: (499/17). Mintage: 5,884,735. Numismedia Wsl. Price for problem free NGC/PCGS coin in MS66: $625. NGC ID# 2568, PCGS# 7252

7930 **(20)1898-O MS64 NGC.** NGC Census: (32826/14855). PCGS Population (28668/13800). Mintage: 4,440,000. Numismedia Wsl. Price for problem free NGC/PCGS coin in MS64: $78. (Total: 20 coins)

7931 **1898-O MS66 PCGS. CAC.** PCGS Population (1940/199). NGC Census: (1948/177). Mintage: 4,440,000. Numismedia Wsl. Price for problem free NGC/PCGS coin in MS66: $360. NGC ID# 2569, PCGS# 7254

7932 **1898-O MS66+ PCGS. CAC.** PCGS Population (1940/199). NGC Census: (1948/177). Mintage: 4,440,000. Numismedia Wsl. Price for problem free NGC/PCGS coin in MS66: $360. NGC ID# 2569, PCGS# 7254

7933 **1898-O MS66 Prooflike NGC.** NGC Census: (22/3). PCGS Population (50/2). Numismedia Wsl. Price for problem free NGC/PCGS coin in MS66: $800. NGC ID# 2569, PCGS# 7255

7934 **1898-S MS62 NGC.** NGC Census: (415/1338). PCGS Population (603/2792). Mintage: 4,102,000. Numismedia Wsl. Price for problem free NGC/PCGS coin in MS62: $350. NGC ID# 256A, PCGS# 7256

7935 **1898-S MS62 NGC.** NGC Census: (415/1338). PCGS Population (603/2792). Mintage: 4,102,000. Numismedia Wsl. Price for problem free NGC/PCGS coin in MS62: $350. NGC ID# 256A, PCGS# 7256

7936 **1898-S MS63 NGC.** NGC Census: (595/743). PCGS Population (1147/1645). Mintage: 4,102,000. Numismedia Wsl. Price for problem free NGC/PCGS coin in MS63: $410. NGC ID# 256A, PCGS# 7256

7937 **1898-S MS64 PCGS.** PCGS Population (1149/496). NGC Census: (620/123). Mintage: 4,102,000. Numismedia Wsl. Price for problem free NGC/PCGS coin in MS64: $585. NGC ID# 256A, PCGS# 7256

7938 **1898-S MS64 PCGS.** PCGS Population (1152/497). NGC Census: (620/123). Mintage: 4,102,000. Numismedia Wsl. Price for problem free NGC/PCGS coin in MS64: $585. NGC ID# 256A, PCGS# 7256

7939 **1899 MS63 NGC.** NGC Census: (2790/3604). PCGS Population (3776/5243). Mintage: 330,846. Numismedia Wsl. Price for problem free NGC/PCGS coin in MS63: $275. NGC ID# 256B, PCGS# 7258

7940 **1899 MS64 PCGS.** PCGS Population (3841/1402). NGC Census: (2924/680). Mintage: 330,846. Numismedia Wsl. Price for problem free NGC/PCGS coin in MS64: $350. NGC ID# 256B, PCGS# 7258

7941 **(20)1899-O MS64 NGC.** NGC Census: (24618/8958). PCGS Population (22522/9009). Mintage: 12,290,000. Numismedia Wsl. Price for problem free NGC/PCGS coin in MS64: $76. (Total: 20 coins)

7942 **1899-S MS63 PCGS.** PCGS Population (1168/1758). NGC Census: (616/862). Mintage: 2,562,000. Numismedia Wsl. Price for problem free NGC/PCGS coin in MS63: $445. NGC ID# 256D, PCGS# 7262

7943 **1899-S MS64 PCGS.** PCGS Population (1230/528). NGC Census: (672/190). Mintage: 2,562,000. Numismedia Wsl. Price for problem free NGC/PCGS coin in MS64: $775. NGC ID# 256D, PCGS# 7262

7944 **(20)1900-O MS64 NGC.** NGC Census: (19241/7812). PCGS Population (17225/7142). Mintage: 12,590,000. Numismedia Wsl. Price for problem free NGC/PCGS coin in MS64: $77. (Total: 20 coins)

7945 **1900-O MS66 PCGS. CAC.** PCGS Population (977/55). NGC Census: (982/74). Mintage: 12,590,000. Numismedia Wsl. Price for problem free NGC/PCGS coin in MS66: $380. NGC ID# 256F, PCGS# 7266

7946 **1900-O MS65 Prooflike PCGS. CAC.** PCGS Population (81/25). NGC Census: (94/15). Numismedia Wsl. Price for problem free NGC/PCGS coin in MS65: $420. NGC ID# 256F, PCGS# 7267

7947 **1900-O/CC Top 100 MS62 NGC. CAC.** NGC Census: (395/1719). PCGS Population (619/4254). Numismedia Wsl. Price for problem free NGC/PCGS coin in MS62: $420. NGC ID# 256G, PCGS# 7268

7948 **1900-O/CC MS64 PCGS.** PCGS Population (1843/818). NGC Census: (787/188). Numismedia Wsl. Price for problem free NGC/PCGS coin in MS64: $865. NGC ID# 256G, PCGS# 7268

7949 **1900-O/CC VAM-8A, Top 100 MS64 PCGS. CAC.** PCGS Population (13/7). NGC Census: (13/2). PCGS# 133961

7950 **1900-S MS62 NGC.** NGC Census: (497/2018). PCGS Population (625/3872). Mintage: 3,540,000. Numismedia Wsl. Price for problem free NGC/PCGS coin in MS62: $300. NGC ID# 256H, PCGS# 7270

7951 **1900-S MS63 NGC.** NGC Census: (895/1123). PCGS Population (1557/2315). Mintage: 3,540,000. Numismedia Wsl. Price for problem free NGC/PCGS coin in MS63: $375. NGC ID# 256H, PCGS# 7270

7952 **1900-S MS64 PCGS.** PCGS Population (1666/649). NGC Census: (899/224). Mintage: 3,540,000. Numismedia Wsl. Price for problem free NGC/PCGS coin in MS64: $575. NGC ID# 256H, PCGS# 7270

7953 **1900-S MS64+ PCGS.** PCGS Population (1666/649). NGC Census: (899/224). Mintage: 3,540,000. Numismedia Wsl. Price for problem free NGC/PCGS coin in MS64: $575. NGC ID# 256H, PCGS# 7270

7954 **1901 AU55 NGC.** NGC Census: (874/2070). PCGS Population (1013/1580). Mintage: 6,962,813. Numismedia Wsl. Price for problem free NGC/PCGS coin in AU55: $360. NGC ID# 256J, PCGS# 7272

7955 **1901 AU55 PCGS.** PCGS Population (1013/1580). NGC Census: (874/2070). Mintage: 6,962,813. Numismedia Wsl. Price for problem free NGC/PCGS coin in AU55: $360. NGC ID# 256J, PCGS# 7272

7956 **1901 AU55 PCGS.** PCGS Population (1013/1580). NGC Census: (874/2070). Mintage: 6,962,813. Numismedia Wsl. Price for problem free NGC/PCGS coin in AU55: $360. NGC ID# 256J, PCGS# 7272

7957 **1901 AU58 NGC.** NGC Census: (1373/699). PCGS Population (933/649). Mintage: 6,962,813. Numismedia Wsl. Price for problem free NGC/PCGS coin in AU58: $900. NGC ID# 256J, PCGS# 7272

7958 **1901 — Questionable Color — PCGS Genuine. Unc Details.** NGC Census: (86/613). PCGS Population (53/596). Mintage: 6,962,813. Numismedia Wsl. Price for problem free NGC/PCGS coin in MS60: $2,025.

7959 **1901-O Super CD, Late Die State, VAM-1A, AU55 ANACS.** NGC Census: (20/34655). PCGS Population (35/27711). Mintage: 13,320,000. Numismedia Wsl. Price for problem free NGC/PCGS coin in AU55: $35. NGC ID# 256K, PCGS# 7274

7960 **1902-O MS66 PCGS. CAC.** PCGS Population (565/15). NGC Census: (575/23). Mintage: 8,636,000. Numismedia Wsl. Price for problem free NGC/PCGS coin in MS66: $460. NGC ID# 256N, PCGS# 7280

7961 **1902-O MS66+ PCGS. CAC.** PCGS Population (571/15). NGC Census: (570/23). Mintage: 8,636,000. Numismedia Wsl. Price for problem free NGC/PCGS coin in MS66: $460. NGC ID# 256N, PCGS# 7280

7962 **1902-S MS64 PCGS.** PCGS Population (1425/343). NGC Census: (833/114). Mintage: 1,530,000. Numismedia Wsl. Price for problem free NGC/PCGS coin in MS64: $810. NGC ID# 256P, PCGS# 7282

7963 **1902-S MS64 PCGS.** PCGS Population (1425/343). NGC Census: (833/114). Mintage: 1,530,000. Numismedia Wsl. Price for problem free NGC/PCGS coin in MS64: $810. NGC ID# 256P, PCGS# 7282

7964 **1903-O MS64 PCGS.** PCGS Population (4234/2829). NGC Census: (2668/1721). Mintage: 4,450,000. Numismedia Wsl. Price for problem free NGC/PCGS coin in MS64: $420. NGC ID# 256S, PCGS# 7286

7965 **1903-O MS65 PCGS.** PCGS Population (2141/692). NGC Census: (1331/388). Mintage: 4,450,000. Numismedia Wsl. Price for problem free NGC/PCGS coin in MS65: $560. NGC ID# 256S, PCGS# 7286

7966 **1903-O MS65 PCGS.** PCGS Population (2141/692). NGC Census: (1331/388). Mintage: 4,450,000. Numismedia Wsl. Price for problem free NGC/PCGS coin in MS65: $560. NGC ID# 256S, PCGS# 7286

7967 **1903-O MS66 PCGS.** PCGS Population (621/71). NGC Census: (346/42). Mintage: 4,450,000. Numismedia Wsl. Price for problem free NGC/PCGS coin in MS66: $785. NGC ID# 256S, PCGS# 7286

7968 **1903-S XF40 NGC.** NGC Census: (211/908). PCGS Population (370/1273). Mintage: 1,241,000. Numismedia Wsl. Price for problem free NGC/PCGS coin in XF40: $350. NGC ID# 256T, PCGS# 7288

7969 **1904 MS64 NGC.** NGC Census: (965/103). PCGS Population (1326/255). Mintage: 2,788,650. Numismedia Wsl. Price for problem free NGC/PCGS coin in MS64: $565. NGC ID# 256U, PCGS# 7290

7970 **(20)1904-O MS64 NGC.** NGC Census: (62389/18022). PCGS Population (49092/11891). Mintage: 3,720,000. Numismedia Wsl. Price for problem free NGC/PCGS coin in MS64: $71. (Total: 20 coins)

7971 **1904-O MS66 PCGS. CAC.** PCGS Population (884/39). NGC Census: (1409/95). Mintage: 3,720,000. Numismedia Wsl. Price for problem free NGC/PCGS coin in MS66: $300. NGC ID# 256V, PCGS# 7292

7972 **1904-O MS66 Prooflike NGC. CAC.** NGC Census: (47/3). PCGS Population (66/0). Numismedia Wsl. Price for problem free NGC/PCGS coin in MS66: $675. NGC ID# 256V, PCGS# 7293

7973 **1904-O MS65 Deep Mirror Prooflike PCGS.** PCGS Population (108/20). NGC Census: (85/8). Numismedia Wsl. Price for problem free NGC/PCGS coin in MS65: $925. NGC ID# 256V, PCGS# 97293

7974 **1904-S AU50 NGC.** NGC Census: (117/922). PCGS Population (132/1610). Mintage: 2,304,000. Numismedia Wsl. Price for problem free NGC/PCGS coin in AU50: $475. NGC ID# 256W, PCGS# 7294

7975 **1904-S AU53 PCGS.** PCGS Population (104/1515). NGC Census: (94/825). Mintage: 2,304,000. Numismedia Wsl. Price for problem free NGC/PCGS coin in AU53: $515. NGC ID# 256W, PCGS# 7294

7976 **1904-S AU55 PCGS. CAC.** PCGS Population (117/1398). NGC Census: (101/724). Mintage: 2,304,000. Numismedia Wsl. Price for problem free NGC/PCGS coin in AU55: $700. NGC ID# 256W, PCGS# 7294

7977 **1904-S AU58 NGC.** NGC Census: (90/637). PCGS Population (78/1312). Mintage: 2,304,000. Numismedia Wsl. Price for problem free NGC/PCGS coin in AU58: $925. NGC ID# 256W, PCGS# 7294

7978 **(20)1921 MS64 NGC.** NGC Census: (39597/8862). PCGS Population (27728/4929). Mintage: 44,690,000. Numismedia Wsl. Price for problem free NGC/PCGS coin in MS64: $58. (Total: 20 coins)

7979 **1921 MS66 PCGS. CAC.** PCGS Population (420/8). NGC Census: (573/7). Mintage: 44,690,000. Numismedia Wsl. Price for problem free NGC/PCGS coin in MS66: $775. NGC ID# 256X, PCGS# 7296

7980 **1921-D MS66 PCGS.** PCGS Population (298/7). NGC Census: (265/6). Mintage: 20,345,000. Numismedia Wsl. Price for problem free NGC/PCGS coin in MS66: $975. NGC ID# 256Y, PCGS# 7298

7981 **1921-S MS65 NGC.** Ex: Great Falls Collection. NGC Census: (749/54). PCGS Population (889/63). Mintage: 21,695,000. Numismedia Wsl. Price for problem free NGC/PCGS coin in MS65: $1,000. NGC ID# 256Z, PCGS# 7300

7982 **1921-S MS65 PCGS.** PCGS Population (889/63). NGC Census: (749/54). Mintage: 21,695,000. Numismedia Wsl. Price for problem free NGC/PCGS coin in MS65: $1,000. NGC ID# 256Z, PCGS# 7300

PROOF MORGAN DOLLAR

7983 **1891 — Damaged — NGC Details. Proof AU.** NGC Census: (1/152). PCGS Population (1/169). Mintage: 650.

PEACE DOLLARS

7984 **1921 MS63 NGC.** NGC Census: (2985/4787). PCGS Population (3878/5409). Mintage: 1,006,473. Numismedia Wsl. Price for problem free NGC/PCGS coin in MS63: $395. NGC ID# 2U4E, PCGS# 7356

7985 **1921 MS64 NGC.** NGC Census: (3502/1285). PCGS Population (3948/1461). Mintage: 1,006,473. Numismedia Wsl. Price for problem free NGC/PCGS coin in MS64: $750. NGC ID# 2U4E, PCGS# 7356

7986 **1921 MS64 PCGS.** PCGS Population (3958/1461). NGC Census: (3489/1285). Mintage: 1,006,473. Numismedia Wsl. Price for problem free NGC/PCGS coin in MS64: $750. NGC ID# 2U4E, PCGS# 7356

7987 **1921 MS64 PCGS.** PCGS Population (3958/1461). NGC Census: (3489/1285). Mintage: 1,006,473. Numismedia Wsl. Price for problem free NGC/PCGS coin in MS64: $750. NGC ID# 2U4E, PCGS# 7356

7988 **1921 MS64 PCGS. CAC.** PCGS Population (3959/1461). NGC Census: (3498/1286). Mintage: 1,006,473. Numismedia Wsl. Price for problem free NGC/PCGS coin in MS64: $750. NGC ID# 2U4E, PCGS# 7356

7989 **(20)1922 MS64 NGC.** NGC Census: (82502/16437). PCGS Population (45506/7323). Mintage: 51,737,000. Numismedia Wsl. Price for problem free NGC/PCGS coin in MS64: $60. (Total: 20 coins)

7990 **1922 MS66 PCGS.** PCGS Population (778/25). NGC Census: (1442/34). Mintage: 51,737,000. Numismedia Wsl. Price for problem free NGC/PCGS coin in MS66: $480. NGC ID# 257C, PCGS# 7357

7991 **1922 MS66 PCGS. CAC.** PCGS Population (778/25). NGC Census: (1442/34). Mintage: 51,737,000. Numismedia Wsl. Price for problem free NGC/PCGS coin in MS66: $480. NGC ID# 257C, PCGS# 7357

7992 **1922-S MS64+ PCGS.** PCGS Population (1974/328). NGC Census: (1804/299). Mintage: 17,475,000. Numismedia Wsl. Price for problem free NGC/PCGS coin in MS64: $270. NGC ID# 257E, PCGS# 7359

7993 **1923 MS66 PCGS.** PCGS Population (2045/54). NGC Census: (3064/97). Mintage: 30,800,000. Numismedia Wsl. Price for problem free NGC/PCGS coin in MS66: $480. NGC ID# 257F, PCGS# 7360

7994 **1923 MS66 PCGS. CAC.** PCGS Population (2044/54). NGC Census: (3089/97). Mintage: 30,800,000. Numismedia Wsl. Price for problem free NGC/PCGS coin in MS66: $480. NGC ID# 257F, PCGS# 7360

7995 **1923 MS66 NGC. CAC.** NGC Census: (3089/97). PCGS Population (2044/54). Mintage: 30,800,000. Numismedia Wsl. Price for problem free NGC/PCGS coin in MS66: $480. NGC ID# 257F, PCGS# 7360

7996 **1923 MS66 PCGS. CAC.** PCGS Population (2044/54). NGC Census: (3089/97). Mintage: 30,800,000. Numismedia Wsl. Price for problem free NGC/PCGS coin in MS66: $480. NGC ID# 257F, PCGS# 7360

7997 **1923 MS66 PCGS. CAC.** PCGS Population (2045/54). NGC Census: (3064/97). Mintage: 30,800,000. Numismedia Wsl. Price for problem free NGC/PCGS coin in MS66: $480. NGC ID# 257F, PCGS# 7360

7998 **1923 MS66 PCGS. CAC.** PCGS Population (2045/54). NGC Census: (3064/97). Mintage: 30,800,000. Numismedia Wsl. Price for problem free NGC/PCGS coin in MS66: $480. NGC ID# 257F, PCGS# 7360

7999 **1923 Extra Hair, VAM-1B, Top 50 MS65 PCGS.** PCGS Population (7/0). NGC Census: (0/0). PCGS# 133753

8000 **1923-D MS64 NGC.** NGC Census: (1024/270). PCGS Population (1430/526). Mintage: 6,811,000. Numismedia Wsl. Price for problem free NGC/PCGS coin in MS64: $340. NGC ID# 257G, PCGS# 7361

8001 **1923-D MS65 NGC.** NGC Census: (245/25). PCGS Population (437/89). Mintage: 6,811,000. Numismedia Wsl. Price for problem free NGC/PCGS coin in MS65: $1,150. NGC ID# 257G, PCGS# 7361

8002 **1923-S MS64 PCGS.** PCGS Population (1956/130). NGC Census: (1833/81). Mintage: 19,020,000. Numismedia Wsl. Price for problem free NGC/PCGS coin in MS64: $400. NGC ID# 257H, PCGS# 7362

8003 **1923-S MS64+ PCGS. CAC.** PCGS Population (1952/130). NGC Census: (1831/81). Mintage: 19,020,000. Numismedia Wsl. Price for problem free NGC/PCGS coin in MS64: $400. NGC ID# 257H, PCGS# 7362

8004 **1923-S MS64+ PCGS. CAC.** PCGS Population (1956/130). NGC Census: (1833/81). Mintage: 19,020,000. Numismedia Wsl. Price for problem free NGC/PCGS coin in MS64: $400. NGC ID# 257H, PCGS# 7362

8005 **1924 MS66 PCGS. CAC.** PCGS Population (646/29). NGC Census: (1394/84). Mintage: 11,811,000. Numismedia Wsl. Price for problem free NGC/PCGS coin in MS66: $525. NGC ID# 257J, PCGS# 7363

8006 **1924 MS66 PCGS. CAC.** PCGS Population (646/29). NGC Census: (1394/84). Mintage: 11,811,000. Numismedia Wsl. Price for problem free NGC/PCGS coin in MS66: $525. NGC ID# 257J, PCGS# 7363

8007 **1924-S MS63 NGC.** NGC Census: (813/977). PCGS Population (1495/1346). Mintage: 1,728,000. Numismedia Wsl. Price for problem free NGC/PCGS coin in MS63: $460. NGC ID# 257K, PCGS# 7364

8008 **(20)1925 MS64 NGC.** NGC Census: (22228/12285). PCGS Population (18315/9246). Mintage: 10,198,000. Numismedia Wsl. Price for problem free NGC/PCGS coin in MS64: $60. (Total: 20 coins)

8009 **1925 MS66 PCGS. CAC.** PCGS Population (1742/93). NGC Census: (1769/74). Mintage: 10,198,000. Numismedia Wsl. Price for problem free NGC/PCGS coin in MS66: $500. NGC ID# 257L, PCGS# 7365

8010 **1925 MS66 PCGS. CAC.** PCGS Population (1736/94). NGC Census: (1741/74). Mintage: 10,198,000. Numismedia Wsl. Price for problem free NGC/PCGS coin in MS66: $500. NGC ID# 257L, PCGS# 7365

8011 **1925 MS66+ NGC. CAC.** NGC Census: (1769/74). PCGS Population (1742/93). Mintage: 10,198,000. Numismedia Wsl. Price for problem free NGC/PCGS coin in MS66: $500. NGC ID# 257L, PCGS# 7365

8012 **1925 MS66+ PCGS. CAC.** PCGS Population (1736/94). NGC Census: (1741/74). Mintage: 10,198,000. Numismedia Wsl. Price for problem free NGC/PCGS coin in MS66: $500. NGC ID# 257L, PCGS# 7365

8013 **1925 MS66+ PCGS. CAC.** PCGS Population (1742/93). NGC Census: (1769/74). Mintage: 10,198,000. Numismedia Wsl. Price for problem free NGC/PCGS coin in MS66: $500. NGC ID# 257L, PCGS# 7365

8014 **1925 MS66+ PCGS. CAC.** PCGS Population (1742/93). NGC Census: (1769/74). Mintage: 10,198,000. Numismedia Wsl. Price for problem free NGC/PCGS coin in MS66: $500. NGC ID# 257L, PCGS# 7365

8015 **1925-S MS64 NGC.** NGC Census: (1683/64). PCGS Population (1869/39). Mintage: 1,610,000. Numismedia Wsl. Price for problem free NGC/PCGS coin in MS64: $950. NGC ID# 257M, PCGS# 7366

8016 **1926 MS65 NGC. CAC.** NGC Census: (729/51). PCGS Population (1285/192). Mintage: 1,939,000. Numismedia Wsl. Price for problem free NGC/PCGS coin in MS65: $480. NGC ID# 257N, PCGS# 7367

8017 **1926 MS65 PCGS. CAC.** PCGS Population (1290/193). NGC Census: (729/51). Mintage: 1,939,000. Numismedia Wsl. Price for problem free NGC/PCGS coin in MS65: $480. NGC ID# 257N, PCGS# 7367

8018 **1926 MS65 NGC. CAC.** NGC Census: (729/51). PCGS Population (1290/193). Mintage: 1,939,000. Numismedia Wsl. Price for problem free NGC/PCGS coin in MS65: $480. NGC ID# 257N, PCGS# 7367

8019 **1926 MS65 PCGS. CAC.** PCGS Population (1290/193). NGC Census: (729/51). Mintage: 1,939,000. Numismedia Wsl. Price for problem free NGC/PCGS coin in MS65: $480. NGC ID# 257N, PCGS# 7367

8020 **1926-D MS64 PCGS.** PCGS Population (1632/937). NGC Census: (1019/593). Mintage: 2,348,700. Numismedia Wsl. Price for problem free NGC/PCGS coin in MS64: $360. NGC ID# 257P, PCGS# 7368

8021 **1926-D MS65+ NGC. CAC.** NGC Census: (481/112). PCGS Population (726/211). Mintage: 2,348,700. Numismedia Wsl. Price for problem free NGC/PCGS coin in MS65: $925. NGC ID# 257P, PCGS# 7368

8022 **1926-S MS65 PCGS.** PCGS Population (653/74). NGC Census: (400/33). Mintage: 6,980,000. Numismedia Wsl. Price for problem free NGC/PCGS coin in MS65: $850. NGC ID# 257R, PCGS# 7369

8023 **1927 VAM-2, Doubled Motto, Top 50 MS63 NGC.** NGC Census: (0/0). PCGS Population (12/20). PCGS# 133776

8024 **1927 VAM-2, Doubled Motto, Top 50 MS64 ANACS.** NGC Census: (0/0). PCGS Population (16/4). PCGS# 133776

8025 **1927-D MS64 NGC.** NGC Census: (785/79). PCGS Population (1254/167). Mintage: 1,268,900. Numismedia Wsl. Price for problem free NGC/PCGS coin in MS64: $900. NGC ID# 257T, PCGS# 7371

8026 **1928 AU58 NGC.** NGC Census: (1012/4822). PCGS Population (1142/6513). Mintage: 360,649. Numismedia Wsl. Price for problem free NGC/PCGS coin in AU58: $365. NGC ID# 257V, PCGS# 7373

8027 **1928 MS62 NGC.** NGC Census: (1488/2594). PCGS Population (1645/4505). Mintage: 360,649. Numismedia Wsl. Price for problem free NGC/PCGS coin in MS62: $530. NGC ID# 257V, PCGS# 7373

8028 **1928 MS63 PCGS.** PCGS Population (2348/2159). NGC Census: (1494/1097). Mintage: 360,649. Numismedia Wsl. Price for problem free NGC/PCGS coin in MS63: $800. NGC ID# 257V, PCGS# 7373

8029 **1928-S MS64 PCGS.** PCGS Population (1857/55). NGC Census: (1271/39). Mintage: 1,632,000. Numismedia Wsl. Price for problem free NGC/PCGS coin in MS64: $1,175. NGC ID# 257W, PCGS# 7374

8030 **1934 MS65 ANACS.** NGC Census: (374/41). PCGS Population (663/161). Mintage: 954,057. Numismedia Wsl. Price for problem free NGC/PCGS coin in MS65: $675. NGC ID# 257X, PCGS# 7375

8031 **1934-S AU55 PCGS.** PCGS Population (381/2451). NGC Census: (333/1645). Mintage: 1,011,000. Numismedia Wsl. Price for problem free NGC/PCGS coin in AU55: $550. NGC ID# 257Z, PCGS# 7377

EISENHOWER DOLLAR

8032 **1972-S Silver MS68+ PCGS. CAC.** PCGS Population (1590/18). NGC Census: (403/4). Mintage: 2,193,056. Numismedia Wsl. Price for problem free NGC/PCGS coin in MS68: $155. NGC ID# 2589, PCGS# 7411

SACAGAWEA DOLLAR

8033 **2000-P Goodacre Presentation 68 PCGS.** PCGS Population (751/31). NGC Census: (0/0). Numismedia Wsl. Price for problem free NGC/PCGS coin in 68: $62. NGC ID# 259K, PCGS# 99584

GOLD DOLLARS

8034 **1849 Open Wreath AU58 NGC.** NGC Census: (205/1279). PCGS Population (104/871). Mintage: 687,500. Numismedia Wsl. Price for problem free NGC/PCGS coin in AU58: $260. NGC ID# 25B9, PCGS# 7502

8035 **1849 Open Wreath MS62 NGC.** NGC Census: (403/562). PCGS Population (249/491). Mintage: 687,500. Numismedia Wsl. Price for problem free NGC/PCGS coin in MS62: $445. NGC ID# 25B9, PCGS# 7502

8036 **1854 Type One MS62 PCGS.** PCGS Population (547/567). NGC Census: (1307/930). Mintage: 855,502. Numismedia Wsl. Price for problem free NGC/PCGS coin in MS62: $445. NGC ID# 25BY, PCGS# 7525

8037 **1854 Type Two AU58 PCGS.** PCGS Population (538/1219). NGC Census: (2308/1628). Mintage: 783,943. Numismedia Wsl. Price for problem free NGC/PCGS coin in AU58: $640. NGC ID# 25C3, PCGS# 7531

8038 **1855 AU58 NGC.** NGC Census: (1975/1595). PCGS Population (467/1247). Mintage: 758,269. Numismedia Wsl. Price for problem free NGC/PCGS coin in AU58: $660. NGC ID# 25C4, PCGS# 7532

8039 **1855 AU58 NGC.** NGC Census: (1975/1595). PCGS Population (467/1247). Mintage: 758,269. Numismedia Wsl. Price for problem free NGC/PCGS coin in AU58: $660. NGC ID# 25C4, PCGS# 7532

8040 **1855 — Obverse Planchet Flaw — NGC Details. Unc.** NGC Census: (63/1531). PCGS Population (34/1214). Mintage: 758,269. Numismedia Wsl. Price for problem free NGC/PCGS coin in MS60: $1,475.

8041 **1860-S AU55 NGC.** NGC Census: (28/93). PCGS Population (36/45). Mintage: 13,000. Numismedia Wsl. Price for problem free NGC/PCGS coin in AU55: $875. NGC ID# 25CT, PCGS# 7557

8042 **1862 MS62 NGC.** NGC Census: (957/954). PCGS Population (570/923). Mintage: 1,361,390. Numismedia Wsl. Price for problem free NGC/PCGS coin in MS62: $470. NGC ID# 25CW, PCGS# 7560

8043 **1873 Closed 3 AU55 PCGS.** PCGS Population (9/64). NGC Census: (8/102). Mintage: 1,825. Numismedia Wsl. Price for problem free NGC/PCGS coin in AU55: $900. NGC ID# 25DA, PCGS# 7574

8044 **1874 MS64 PCGS.** PCGS Population (504/239). NGC Census: (522/241). Mintage: 198,820. Numismedia Wsl. Price for problem free NGC/PCGS coin in MS64: $710. NGC ID# 25DC, PCGS# 7575

8045 **1888 MS63 PCGS.** PCGS Population (194/542). NGC Census: (114/420). Mintage: 15,501. Numismedia Wsl. Price for problem free NGC/PCGS coin in MS63: $620. NGC ID# 25DT, PCGS# 7589

CLASSIC QUARTER EAGLE

8046 **1836 Script 8 — Harshly Cleaned — NGC Details. AU.** NGC Census: (109/869). PCGS Population (67/272). Mintage: 547,986. Numismedia Wsl. Price for problem free NGC/PCGS coin in AU50: $1,000.

LIBERTY QUARTER EAGLES

8047 **1851 MS62 NGC.** NGC Census: (167/120). PCGS Population (70/94). Mintage: 1,372,748. Numismedia Wsl. Price for problem free NGC/PCGS coin in MS62: $575. NGC ID# 25HL, PCGS# 7759

8048 **1855 AU55 PCGS.** PCGS Population (45/141). NGC Census: (30/334). Mintage: 235,480. Numismedia Wsl. Price for problem free NGC/PCGS coin in AU55: $320. NGC ID# 25J4, PCGS# 7774

8049 **1859 New Reverse, Type Two, AU58 NGC.** NGC Census: (48/39). PCGS Population (9/31). Mintage: 39,444. Numismedia Wsl. Price for problem free NGC/PCGS coin in AU58: $585. NGC ID# 25JK, PCGS# 7788

8050 **1869 AU55 NGC.** NGC Census: (27/83). PCGS Population (21/37). Mintage: 4,300. Numismedia Wsl. Price for problem free NGC/PCGS coin in AU55: $850. NGC ID# 25KD, PCGS# 7809

8051 **1870 AU55 NGC.** NGC Census: (20/52). PCGS Population (11/22). Mintage: 4,555. Numismedia Wsl. Price for problem free NGC/PCGS coin in AU55: $925. NGC ID# 25KF, PCGS# 7811

8052 **1872-S AU53 NGC.** NGC Census: (16/89). PCGS Population (10/36). Mintage: 18,000. Numismedia Wsl. Price for problem free NGC/PCGS coin in AU53: $675. NGC ID# 25KL, PCGS# 7816

8053 **1873-S AU53 PCGS.** PCGS Population (9/43). NGC Census: (17/115). Mintage: 27,000. Numismedia Wsl. Price for problem free NGC/PCGS coin in AU53: $660. NGC ID# 25KP, PCGS# 7820

8054 **1878-S MS62 NGC.** NGC Census: (121/67). PCGS Population (71/52). Mintage: 178,000. Numismedia Wsl. Price for problem free NGC/PCGS coin in MS62: $445. NGC ID# 25KZ, PCGS# 7829

8055 **1896 MS62 NGC.** NGC Census: (207/329). PCGS Population (151/366). Mintage: 19,000. Numismedia Wsl. Price for problem free NGC/PCGS coin in MS62: $510. NGC ID# 25LL, PCGS# 7848

8056 **1896 MS63 PCGS.** PCGS Population (143/223). NGC Census: (129/199). Mintage: 19,000. Numismedia Wsl. Price for problem free NGC/PCGS coin in MS63: $540. NGC ID# 25LL, PCGS# 7848

8057 **1898 MS64 PCGS.** PCGS Population (152/121). NGC Census: (152/157). Mintage: 24,000. Numismedia Wsl. Price for problem free NGC/PCGS coin in MS64: $775. NGC ID# 25LN, PCGS# 7850

8058 **1902 MS64+ PCGS.** PCGS Population (732/517). NGC Census: (706/545). Mintage: 133,500. Numismedia Wsl. Price for problem free NGC/PCGS coin in MS64: $650. NGC ID# 25LT, PCGS# 7854

INDIAN QUARTER EAGLES

8059 **1908 MS62 PCGS.** PCGS Population (1292/3337). NGC Census: (2793/3259). Mintage: 564,800. Numismedia Wsl. Price for problem free NGC/PCGS coin in MS62: $520. NGC ID# 288Y, PCGS# 7939

8060 **1908 MS62 PCGS.** PCGS Population (1292/3337). NGC Census: (2793/3259). Mintage: 564,800. Numismedia Wsl. Price for problem free NGC/PCGS coin in MS62: $520. NGC ID# 288Y, PCGS# 7939

8061 **1909 MS62 PCGS.** PCGS Population (966/1701). NGC Census: (2278/2101). Mintage: 441,700. Numismedia Wsl. Price for problem free NGC/PCGS coin in MS62: $550. NGC ID# 288Z, PCGS# 7940

8062 **1909 MS62 PCGS.** PCGS Population (966/1701). NGC Census: (2278/2101). Mintage: 441,700. Numismedia Wsl. Price for problem free NGC/PCGS coin in MS62: $550. NGC ID# 288Z, PCGS# 7940

8063 **1910 MS62 PCGS.** PCGS Population (1026/1205). NGC Census: (2894/2413). Mintage: 492,000. Numismedia Wsl. Price for problem free NGC/PCGS coin in MS62: $535. NGC ID# 2892, PCGS# 7941

8064 **1911 MS63 NGC.** NGC Census: (1871/1420). PCGS Population (1198/804). Mintage: 704,000. Numismedia Wsl. Price for problem free NGC/PCGS coin in MS63: $800. NGC ID# 2893, PCGS# 7942

8065 **1911 MS63 PCGS. CAC.** PCGS Population (1198/805). NGC Census: (1871/1422). Mintage: 704,000. Numismedia Wsl. Price for problem free NGC/PCGS coin in MS63: $800. NGC ID# 2893, PCGS# 7942

8066 **1912 MS62 NGC.** NGC Census: (2631/1852). PCGS Population (1093/1362). Mintage: 616,000. Numismedia Wsl. Price for problem free NGC/PCGS coin in MS62: $550. NGC ID# 2896, PCGS# 7944

8067 **1912 MS62 PCGS.** PCGS Population (1093/1365). NGC Census: (2630/1850). Mintage: 616,000. Numismedia Wsl. Price for problem free NGC/PCGS coin in MS62: $550. NGC ID# 2896, PCGS# 7944

8068 **1913 MS63 NGC.** NGC Census: (1701/1176). PCGS Population (1180/932). Mintage: 722,000. Numismedia Wsl. Price for problem free NGC/PCGS coin in MS63: $800. NGC ID# 2897, PCGS# 7945

8069 **1913 MS63 NGC.** NGC Census: (1701/1176). PCGS Population (1180/932). Mintage: 722,000. Numismedia Wsl. Price for problem free NGC/PCGS coin in MS63: $800. NGC ID# 2897, PCGS# 7945

8070 **1914 MS61 NGC.** NGC Census: (1939/3771). PCGS Population (367/1984). Mintage: 240,000. Numismedia Wsl. Price for problem free NGC/PCGS coin in MS61: $725. NGC ID# 2898, PCGS# 7946

8071 **1914-D MS62 NGC.** NGC Census: (3530/2909). PCGS Population (1669/1852). Mintage: 448,000. Numismedia Wsl. Price for problem free NGC/PCGS coin in MS62: $600. NGC ID# 2899, PCGS# 7947

8072 **1914-D MS62 NGC.** NGC Census: (3524/2912). PCGS Population (1671/1852). Mintage: 448,000. Numismedia Wsl. Price for problem free NGC/PCGS coin in MS62: $600. NGC ID# 2899, PCGS# 7947

8073 **1914-D MS62 PCGS.** PCGS Population (1671/1852). NGC Census: (3524/2912). Mintage: 448,000. Numismedia Wsl. Price for problem free NGC/PCGS coin in MS62: $600. NGC ID# 2899, PCGS# 7947

8074 **1914-D MS62 PCGS.** PCGS Population (1671/1852). NGC Census: (3524/2912). Mintage: 448,000. Numismedia Wsl. Price for problem free NGC/PCGS coin in MS62: $600. NGC ID# 2899, PCGS# 7947

8075 **1914-D MS62 NGC.** NGC Census: (3524/2912). PCGS Population (1671/1852). Mintage: 448,000. Numismedia Wsl. Price for problem free NGC/PCGS coin in MS62: $600. NGC ID# 2899, PCGS# 7947

8076 **1915 MS63 NGC.** NGC Census: (1727/1493). PCGS Population (1124/950). Mintage: 606,000. Numismedia Wsl. Price for problem free NGC/PCGS coin in MS63: $825. NGC ID# 289A, PCGS# 7948

8077 **1925-D MS64+ NGC. CAC.** NGC Census: (3633/984). PCGS Population (2266/582). Mintage: 578,000. Numismedia Wsl. Price for problem free NGC/PCGS coin in MS64: $700. NGC ID# 289B, PCGS# 7949

8078 **1926 MS64 NGC.** NGC Census: (3441/586). PCGS Population (2587/721). Mintage: 446,000. Numismedia Wsl. Price for problem free NGC/PCGS coin in MS64: $700. NGC ID# 289C, PCGS# 7950

8079 **1926 MS64 PCGS.** PCGS Population (2587/721). NGC Census: (3441/586). Mintage: 446,000. Numismedia Wsl. Price for problem free NGC/PCGS coin in MS64: $700. NGC ID# 289C, PCGS# 7950

8080 **1926 MS64+ PCGS.** PCGS Population (2591/720). NGC Census: (3443/586). Mintage: 446,000. Numismedia Wsl. Price for problem free NGC/PCGS coin in MS64: $700. NGC ID# 289C, PCGS# 7950

8081 **1927 MS64 PCGS.** PCGS Population (1936/451). NGC Census: (2603/430). Mintage: 388,000. Numismedia Wsl. Price for problem free NGC/PCGS coin in MS64: $700. NGC ID# 289D, PCGS# 7951

8082 **1927 MS64 NGC. CAC.** NGC Census: (2603/430). PCGS Population (1936/451). Mintage: 388,000. Numismedia Wsl. Price for problem free NGC/PCGS coin in MS64: $700. NGC ID# 289D, PCGS# 7951

8083 **1928 MS64 NGC.** NGC Census: (2659/451). PCGS Population (1518/313). Mintage: 416,000. Numismedia Wsl. Price for problem free NGC/PCGS coin in MS64: $700. NGC ID# 289E, PCGS# 7952

8084 **1928 MS64 PCGS.** PCGS Population (1518/313). NGC Census: (2659/451). Mintage: 416,000. Numismedia Wsl. Price for problem free NGC/PCGS coin in MS64: $700. NGC ID# 289E, PCGS# 7952

8085 **1928 MS64 NGC. CAC.** NGC Census: (2664/451). PCGS Population (1520/315). Mintage: 416,000. Numismedia Wsl. Price for problem free NGC/PCGS coin in MS64: $700. NGC ID# 289E, PCGS# 7952

8086 **1929 MS64 NGC.** NGC Census: (2807/238). PCGS Population (1660/139). Mintage: 532,000. Numismedia Wsl. Price for problem free NGC/PCGS coin in MS64: $825. NGC ID# 289F, PCGS# 7953

8087 **1929 MS64 NGC.** NGC Census: (2807/239). PCGS Population (1650/140). Mintage: 532,000. Numismedia Wsl. Price for problem free NGC/PCGS coin in MS64: $825. NGC ID# 289F, PCGS# 7953

8088 **1929 MS64+ NGC. CAC.** NGC Census: (2807/238). PCGS Population (1660/139). Mintage: 532,000. Numismedia Wsl. Price for problem free NGC/PCGS coin in MS64: $825. NGC ID# 289F, PCGS# 7953

THREE DOLLAR GOLD PIECES

8089 **1855 — Obverse Scratched — NGC Details. AU.** NGC Census: (78/941). PCGS Population (132/540). Mintage: 50,555. Numismedia Wsl. Price for problem free NGC/PCGS coin in AU50: $1,175.

8090 **1856 XF45 PCGS.** PCGS Population (43/490). NGC Census: (58/653). Mintage: 26,010. Numismedia Wsl. Price for problem free NGC/PCGS coin in XF45: $1,011. NGC ID# 25M8, PCGS# 7974

8091 **1874 XF40 PCGS.** PCGS Population (50/2148). NGC Census: (38/2695). Mintage: 41,800. Numismedia Wsl. Price for problem free NGC/PCGS coin in XF40: $900. NGC ID# 25MX, PCGS# 7998

8092 **1878 — Reverse Scratched — NGC Details. AU.** NGC Census: (69/5019). PCGS Population (205/5250). Mintage: 82,304. Numismedia Wsl. Price for problem free NGC/PCGS coin in AU50: $1,025.

CLASSIC HALF EAGLE

8093 **1836 XF45 PCGS.** PCGS Population (166/387). NGC Census: (169/776). Mintage: 553,147. Numismedia Wsl. Price for problem free NGC/PCGS coin in XF45: $840. NGC ID# 25RY, PCGS# 8174

LIBERTY HALF EAGLES

8094 **1844 XF45 NGC.** NGC Census: (45/238). PCGS Population (42/106). Mintage: 340,330. Numismedia Wsl. Price for problem free NGC/PCGS coin in XF45: $454. NGC ID# 25T7, PCGS# 8219

8095 **1847/7 AU55 NGC.** NGC Census: (30/86). PCGS Population (2/1). PCGS# 8232

8096 **1847 Misplaced Date, FS-302, AU50 PCGS.** (FS-004). PCGS Population (1/3). NGC Census: (0/0). Mintage: 915,981. PCGS# 145698

8097 **1851 AU58 PCGS.** PCGS Population (18/39). NGC Census: (99/59). Mintage: 377,505. Numismedia Wsl. Price for problem free NGC/PCGS coin in AU58: $850. NGC ID# 25U5, PCGS# 8246

8098 **1855 AU55 NGC.** NGC Census: (58/80). PCGS Population (16/39). Mintage: 117,098. Numismedia Wsl. Price for problem free NGC/PCGS coin in AU55: $540. NGC ID# 25UP, PCGS# 8261

8099 **1855-D Large D — Holed — PCGS Genuine. XF Details.** NGC Census: (11/69). PCGS Population (20/59). Mintage: 22,432. Numismedia Wsl. Price for problem free NGC/PCGS coin in XF40: $1,850.

8100 **1856 AU58 NGC. CAC.** NGC Census: (105/40). PCGS Population (31/30). Mintage: 197,990. Numismedia Wsl. Price for problem free NGC/PCGS coin in AU58: $765. NGC ID# 25UV, PCGS# 8266

8101 **1861 XF45 ANACS.** NGC Census: (85/1371). PCGS Population (63/684). Mintage: 688,150. Numismedia Wsl. Price for problem free NGC/PCGS coin in XF45: $484. NGC ID# 25VK, PCGS# 8288

8102 **1861-S — Improperly Cleaned, Obverse Rim Damaged — NCS. VF Details.** NGC Census: (1/33). PCGS Population (2/28). Mintage: 18,000. Numismedia Wsl. Price for problem free NGC/PCGS coin in VF20: $1,050.

8103 **1878-S AU53 NGC.** NGC Census: (33/371). PCGS Population (15/141). Mintage: 144,700. Numismedia Wsl. Price for problem free NGC/PCGS coin in AU53: $365. NGC ID# 25X6, PCGS# 8347

8104 **1883-CC — Corroded, Cleaned — ANACS. AU50 Details.** NGC Census: (8/68). PCGS Population (11/51). Mintage: 12,958. Numismedia Wsl. Price for problem free NGC/PCGS coin in AU50: $3,150.

8105 **1884 MS62 NGC.** NGC Census: (70/27). PCGS Population (40/24). Mintage: 191,078. Numismedia Wsl. Price for problem free NGC/PCGS coin in MS62: $775. NGC ID# 25XN, PCGS# 8364

8106 **1884 MS62 NGC.** NGC Census: (70/27). PCGS Population (40/24). Mintage: 191,078. Numismedia Wsl. Price for problem free NGC/PCGS coin in MS62: $775. NGC ID# 25XN, PCGS# 8364

8107 **1884-S MS61 NGC.** NGC Census: (116/169). PCGS Population (42/153). Mintage: 177,000. Numismedia Wsl. Price for problem free NGC/PCGS coin in MS61: $470. NGC ID# 25XR, PCGS# 8366

8108 **1885-S MS63 PCGS.** PCGS Population (694/437). NGC Census: (852/594). Mintage: 1,211,500. Numismedia Wsl. Price for problem free NGC/PCGS coin in MS63: $700. NGC ID# 25XT, PCGS# 8368

8109 1885-S MS64 PCGS. PCGS Population (380/57). NGC Census: (476/118). Mintage: 1,211,500. Numismedia Wsl. Price for problem free NGC/PCGS coin in MS64: $1,125. NGC ID# 25XT, PCGS# 8368

8110 1886 MS62 NGC. NGC Census: (140/72). PCGS Population (92/64). Mintage: 388,300. Numismedia Wsl. Price for problem free NGC/PCGS coin in MS62: $500. NGC ID# 25XU, PCGS# 8369

8111 1892-CC — Cleaned — ANACS. VF Details, Net Fine 12. NGC Census: (2/721). PCGS Population (4/466). Mintage: 82,968. Numismedia Wsl. Price for problem free NGC/PCGS coin in Fine 12: $520.

8112 1894-S AU58 NGC. NGC Census: (51/25). PCGS Population (11/13). Mintage: 55,900. Numismedia Wsl. Price for problem free NGC/PCGS coin in AU58: $750. NGC ID# 25YG, PCGS# 8389

8113 1895 MS64 NGC. NGC Census: (466/83). PCGS Population (150/20). Mintage: 1,345,936. Numismedia Wsl. Price for problem free NGC/PCGS coin in MS64: $1,050. NGC ID# 25YH, PCGS# 8390

8114 1895 MS64 NGC. NGC Census: (466/83). PCGS Population (150/20). Mintage: 1,345,936. Numismedia Wsl. Price for problem free NGC/PCGS coin in MS64: $1,050. NGC ID# 25YH, PCGS# 8390

8115 1895 MS64 NGC. NGC Census: (466/83). PCGS Population (150/20). Mintage: 1,345,936. Numismedia Wsl. Price for problem free NGC/PCGS coin in MS64: $1,050. NGC ID# 25YH, PCGS# 8390

8116 1895 MS64 NGC. NGC Census: (466/83). PCGS Population (150/20). Mintage: 1,345,936. Numismedia Wsl. Price for problem free NGC/PCGS coin in MS64: $1,050. NGC ID# 25YH, PCGS# 8390

8117 1903-S MS62 NGC. NGC Census: (1193/1861). PCGS Population (876/1835). Mintage: 1,855,000. Numismedia Wsl. Price for problem free NGC/PCGS coin in MS62: $500. NGC ID# 25Z3, PCGS# 8408

8118 1906 MS64 PCGS. CAC. PCGS Population (186/96). NGC Census: (196/77). Mintage: 348,700. Numismedia Wsl. Price for problem free NGC/PCGS coin in MS64: $700. NGC ID# 25Z9, PCGS# 8413

8119 1906-D MS64 PCGS. PCGS Population (281/59). NGC Census: (351/70). Mintage: 320,000. Numismedia Wsl. Price for problem free NGC/PCGS coin in MS64: $700. NGC ID# 25ZA, PCGS# 8414

8120 1907 MS62 NGC. NGC Census: (3446/3184). PCGS Population (1911/2515). Mintage: 626,192. Numismedia Wsl. Price for problem free NGC/PCGS coin in MS62: $500. NGC ID# 25ZC, PCGS# 8416

8121 1908 MS64 NGC. NGC Census: (990/326). PCGS Population (900/243). Mintage: 421,874. Numismedia Wsl. Price for problem free NGC/PCGS coin in MS64: $700. NGC ID# 25ZE, PCGS# 8418

8122 1908 MS64 NGC. CAC. NGC Census: (990/326). PCGS Population (901/243). Mintage: 421,874. Numismedia Wsl. Price for problem free NGC/PCGS coin in MS64: $700. NGC ID# 25ZE, PCGS# 8418

INDIAN HALF EAGLES

8123 1908 — Reverse Planchet Flaw — NGC Details. Unc. NGC Census: (174/6258). PCGS Population (97/4580). Mintage: 577,800. Numismedia Wsl. Price for problem free NGC/PCGS coin in MS60: $540.

8124 1908 MS62 PCGS. CAC. PCGS Population (1832/2165). NGC Census: (2672/1993). Mintage: 577,800. Numismedia Wsl. Price for problem free NGC/PCGS coin in MS62: $650. NGC ID# 28DE, PCGS# 8510

8125 1908 MS63 NGC. NGC Census: (1050/940). PCGS Population (1160/1004). Mintage: 577,800. Numismedia Wsl. Price for problem free NGC/PCGS coin in MS63: $1,400. NGC ID# 28DE, PCGS# 8510

8126 1908-D MS62 PCGS. PCGS Population (933/1656). NGC Census: (826/1446). Mintage: 148,000. Numismedia Wsl. Price for problem free NGC/PCGS coin in MS62: $950. NGC ID# 28DF, PCGS# 8511

8127 1908-D MS62 NGC. NGC Census: (825/1443). PCGS Population (934/1660). Mintage: 148,000. Numismedia Wsl. Price for problem free NGC/PCGS coin in MS62: $950. NGC ID# 28DF, PCGS# 8511

8128 1909 MS62 NGC. NGC Census: (2309/1327). PCGS Population (1468/1364). Mintage: 627,138. Numismedia Wsl. Price for problem free NGC/PCGS coin in MS62: $675. NGC ID# 28DH, PCGS# 8513

8129 1909 MS62 PCGS. PCGS Population (1468/1364). NGC Census: (2309/1327). Mintage: 627,138. Numismedia Wsl. Price for problem free NGC/PCGS coin in MS62: $675. NGC ID# 28DH, PCGS# 8513

8130 1909-D MS63 NGC. NGC Census: (8024/2697). PCGS Population (9818/2916). Mintage: 3,423,560. Numismedia Wsl. Price for problem free NGC/PCGS coin in MS63: $1,075. NGC ID# 28DJ, PCGS# 8514

8131 1910 MS62 NGC. NGC Census: (2120/1342). PCGS Population (1445/871). Mintage: 604,250. Numismedia Wsl. Price for problem free NGC/PCGS coin in MS62: $665. NGC ID# 28DK, PCGS# 8517

8132 1910 MS62 NGC. NGC Census: (2120/1342). PCGS Population (1445/871). Mintage: 604,250. Numismedia Wsl. Price for problem free NGC/PCGS coin in MS62: $665. NGC ID# 28DK, PCGS# 8517

8133 1910-S AU58 NGC. NGC Census: (609/417). PCGS Population (205/239). Mintage: 770,200. Numismedia Wsl. Price for problem free NGC/PCGS coin in AU58: $775. NGC ID# 28DM, PCGS# 8519

8134 1911-D — Improperly Cleaned — NGC Details. AU. NGC Census: (75/1205). PCGS Population (100/465). Mintage: 72,500. Numismedia Wsl. Price for problem free NGC/PCGS coin in AU50: $1,025.

8135 1912 MS62+ NGC. CAC. NGC Census: (3747/1505). PCGS Population (2710/1861). Mintage: 790,000. Numismedia Wsl. Price for problem free NGC/PCGS coin in MS62: $650. NGC ID# 28DS, PCGS# 8523

8136 1915 MS62 PCGS. PCGS Population (1350/1365). NGC Census: (1815/1225). Mintage: 588,075. Numismedia Wsl. Price for problem free NGC/PCGS coin in MS62: $700. NGC ID# 28DX, PCGS# 8530

8137 1915 MS62+ PCGS. PCGS Population (1350/1367). NGC Census: (1815/1225). Mintage: 588,075. Numismedia Wsl. Price for problem free NGC/PCGS coin in MS62: $700. NGC ID# 28DX, PCGS# 8530

8138 1915 MS63+ NGC. NGC Census: (648/578). PCGS Population (842/532). Mintage: 588,075. Numismedia Wsl. Price for problem free NGC/PCGS coin in MS63: $1,475. NGC ID# 28DX, PCGS# 8530

LIBERTY EAGLES

8139 1847-O — Rim Filed, Rotated Dies — ANACS. VF30 Details. NGC Census: (11/722). PCGS Population (10/456). Mintage: 571,500. Numismedia Wsl. Price for problem free NGC/PCGS coin in VF30: $900.

8140 1850 Large Date XF40 NGC. NGC Census: (42/311). PCGS Population (33/145). Mintage: 291,451. Numismedia Wsl. Price for problem free NGC/PCGS coin in XF40: $850. NGC ID# 2637, PCGS# 8603

8141 1866-S No Motto — Obverse Repaired — NCS. VG Details. NGC Census: (0/34). PCGS Population (1/32). Mintage: 8,500. Numismedia Wsl. Price for problem free NGC/PCGS coin in VG8: $1,225.

8142 1872-S — Repaired — NGC Details. XF. NGC Census: (7/116). PCGS Population (21/58). Mintage: 17,300. Numismedia Wsl. Price for problem free NGC/PCGS coin in XF40: $1,050.

8143 1877-S — Improperly Cleaned — NGC Details. VF. NGC Census: (5/154). PCGS Population (2/113). Mintage: 17,000. Numismedia Wsl. Price for problem free NGC/PCGS coin in VF20: $975.

8144 1878-S — Graffiti — ANACS. VF30 Details. NGC Census: (5/201). PCGS Population (8/134). Mintage: 26,100. Numismedia Wsl. Price for problem free NGC/PCGS coin in VF30: $1,017.

8145 1879 Breen-6993 XF40 ANACS. NGC Census: (2/918). PCGS Population (7/546). Mintage: 384,770. Numismedia Wsl. Price for problem free NGC/PCGS coin in XF40: $660. NGC ID# 265M, PCGS# 8683

8146 1879 AU58 NGC. NGC Census: (294/496). PCGS Population (120/199). Mintage: 384,770. Numismedia Wsl. Price for problem free NGC/PCGS coin in AU58: $710. NGC ID# 265M, PCGS# 8683

8147 1879 MS61 NGC. NGC Census: (244/146). PCGS Population (66/103). Mintage: 384,770. Numismedia Wsl. Price for problem free NGC/PCGS coin in MS61: $925. NGC ID# 265M, PCGS# 8683

8148 1879-S AU58 NGC. NGC Census: (202/118). PCGS Population (58/66). Mintage: 224,000. Numismedia Wsl. Price for problem free NGC/PCGS coin in AU58: $710. NGC ID# 265R, PCGS# 8686

8149 1881-CC — Rim Damaged — PCGS Genuine. VF Details. NGC Census: (1/330). PCGS Population (2/266). Mintage: 24,015. Numismedia Wsl. Price for problem free NGC/PCGS coin in VF20: $975.

8150 1881-CC — Tooled — NGC Details. XF. NGC Census: (19/305). PCGS Population (40/200). Mintage: 24,015. Numismedia Wsl. Price for problem free NGC/PCGS coin in XF40: $1,025.

8151 1883-CC — Cleaned — ANACS. XF40 Details. NGC Census: (18/122). PCGS Population (19/109). Mintage: 12,000. Numismedia Wsl. Price for problem free NGC/PCGS coin in XF40: $1,450.

8152 1884-CC — Reverse Damage — NGC Details. VG. NGC Census: (0/172). PCGS Population (0/142). Mintage: 9,925. Numismedia Wsl. Price for problem free NGC/PCGS coin in VG8: $950.

8153 1885-S MS62 NGC. NGC Census: (232/56). PCGS Population (254/104). Mintage: 228,000. Numismedia Wsl. Price for problem free NGC/PCGS coin in MS62: $865. NGC ID# 266E, PCGS# 8707

8154 1887-S MS62 PCGS. PCGS Population (317/98). NGC Census: (556/82). Mintage: 817,000. Numismedia Wsl. Price for problem free NGC/PCGS coin in MS62: $830. NGC ID# 266J, PCGS# 8711

8155 1888 MS61 NGC. NGC Census: (135/63). PCGS Population (46/55). Mintage: 132,996. Numismedia Wsl. Price for problem free NGC/PCGS coin in MS61: $1,025. NGC ID# 266K, PCGS# 8712

8156 1888-O AU55 NGC. NGC Census: (20/570). PCGS Population (49/402). Mintage: 21,335. Numismedia Wsl. Price for problem free NGC/PCGS coin in AU55: $850. NGC ID# 266L, PCGS# 8713

8157 1888-S MS62 NGC. NGC Census: (538/84). PCGS Population (485/152). Mintage: 648,700. Numismedia Wsl. Price for problem free NGC/PCGS coin in MS62: $1,050. NGC ID# 266M, PCGS# 8714

8158 1888-S MS62+ PCGS. PCGS Population (485/152). NGC Census: (538/84). Mintage: 648,700. Numismedia Wsl. Price for problem free NGC/PCGS coin in MS62: $1,050. NGC ID# 266M, PCGS# 8714

8159 1891 MS62 NGC. NGC Census: (217/49). PCGS Population (149/55). Mintage: 91,868. Numismedia Wsl. Price for problem free NGC/PCGS coin in MS62: $1,090. NGC ID# 266T, PCGS# 8719

8160 1892 AU55 Prooflike NGC. NGC Census: (0/0). PCGS Population (0/0). Mintage: 797,400. PCGS# 78721

8161 1892-CC — Polished — NCS. XF Details. NGC Census: (24/443). PCGS Population (43/339). Mintage: 40,000. Numismedia Wsl. Price for problem free NGC/PCGS coin in XF40: $1,150.

8162 1894-O AU55 PCGS. PCGS Population (91/255). NGC Census: (139/574). Mintage: 107,500. Numismedia Wsl. Price for problem free NGC/PCGS coin in AU55: $785. NGC ID# 2676, PCGS# 8730

8163 1896-S AU58 PCGS. PCGS Population (38/56). NGC Census: (127/68). Mintage: 123,750. Numismedia Wsl. Price for problem free NGC/PCGS coin in AU58: $1,100. NGC ID# 267C, PCGS# 8736

8164 1897 MS62 NGC. NGC Census: (3727/1509). PCGS Population (2099/803). Mintage: 1,000,159. Numismedia Wsl. Price for problem free NGC/PCGS coin in MS62: $830. NGC ID# 267D, PCGS# 8737

8165 **1898 MS63 PCGS.** PCGS Population (228/76). NGC Census: (359/153). Mintage: 812,197. Numismedia Wsl. Price for problem free NGC/PCGS coin in MS63: $1,000. NGC ID# 267G, PCGS# 8740

8166 **1899 MS63 NGC.** NGC Census: (5793/1522). PCGS Population (2113/401). Mintage: 1,262,305. Numismedia Wsl. Price for problem free NGC/PCGS coin in MS63: $1,000. NGC ID# 267J, PCGS# 8742

8167 **1899-O AU55 NGC.** NGC Census: (16/207). PCGS Population (27/185). Mintage: 37,047. Numismedia Wsl. Price for problem free NGC/PCGS coin in AU55: $800. NGC ID# 267K, PCGS# 8743

8168 **1900 MS63 NGC.** NGC Census: (1619/420). PCGS Population (898/222). Mintage: 293,960. Numismedia Wsl. Price for problem free NGC/PCGS coin in MS63: $1,000. NGC ID# 267M, PCGS# 8745

8169 **1907 MS62 NGC.** NGC Census: (10098/7125). PCGS Population (7160/4318). Mintage: 1,203,973. Numismedia Wsl. Price for problem free NGC/PCGS coin in MS62: $830. NGC ID# 2688, PCGS# 8763

INDIAN EAGLES

8170 **1908 Motto MS62 NGC.** NGC Census: (1519/748). PCGS Population (1585/1141). Mintage: 341,300. Numismedia Wsl. Price for problem free NGC/PCGS coin in MS62: $1,100. NGC ID# 28GJ, PCGS# 8859

8171 **1908 Motto MS62 NGC.** NGC Census: (1519/748). PCGS Population (1585/1141). Mintage: 341,300. Numismedia Wsl. Price for problem free NGC/PCGS coin in MS62: $1,100. NGC ID# 28GJ, PCGS# 8859

8172 **1908 Motto MS62 PCGS.** PCGS Population (1585/1141). NGC Census: (1519/748). Mintage: 341,300. Numismedia Wsl. Price for problem free NGC/PCGS coin in MS62: $1,100. NGC ID# 28GJ, PCGS# 8859

8173 **1908-D Motto AU58 NGC.** NGC Census: (228/462). PCGS Population (187/522). Mintage: 836,500. Numismedia Wsl. Price for problem free NGC/PCGS coin in AU58: $1,000. NGC ID# 28GK, PCGS# 8860

8174 **1909-D AU58 NGC.** NGC Census: (303/626). PCGS Population (268/786). Mintage: 121,540. Numismedia Wsl. Price for problem free NGC/PCGS coin in AU58: $1,150. NGC ID# 28GN, PCGS# 8863

8175 **1909-S AU53 PCGS.** PCGS Population (62/688). NGC Census: (44/691). Mintage: 292,350. Numismedia Wsl. Price for problem free NGC/PCGS coin in AU53: $900. NGC ID# 28GP, PCGS# 8864

8176 **1910-D MS63 NGC.** NGC Census: (2119/1058). PCGS Population (2283/781). Mintage: 2,356,640. Numismedia Wsl. Price for problem free NGC/PCGS coin in MS63: $1,175. NGC ID# 28GS, PCGS# 8866

8177 **1910-S AU58 ANACS.** NGC Census: (703/616). PCGS Population (536/812). Mintage: 811,000. Numismedia Wsl. Price for problem free NGC/PCGS coin in AU58: $1,075. NGC ID# 268D, PCGS# 8867

8178 **1911 AU58 PCGS.** PCGS Population (1202/6374). NGC Census: (1136/8782). Mintage: 505,595. Numismedia Wsl. Price for problem free NGC/PCGS coin in AU58: $740. NGC ID# 28GT, PCGS# 8868

8179 **1912 MS61 NGC.** NGC Census: (1781/3975). PCGS Population (892/3566). Mintage: 405,083. Numismedia Wsl. Price for problem free NGC/PCGS coin in MS61: $925. NGC ID# 28GW, PCGS# 8871

8180 **1913 MS62+ NGC.** NGC Census: (2014/1169). PCGS Population (1908/1146). Mintage: 442,071. Numismedia Wsl. Price for problem free NGC/PCGS coin in MS62: $1,000. NGC ID# 28GY, PCGS# 8873

8181 **1914 AU53 PCGS.** PCGS Population (31/2119). NGC Census: (15/2227). Mintage: 151,050. Numismedia Wsl. Price for problem free NGC/PCGS coin in AU53: $720. NGC ID# 28H2, PCGS# 8875

8182 **1914-D MS61 NGC.** NGC Census: (820/1213). PCGS Population (379/1483). Mintage: 343,500. Numismedia Wsl. Price for problem free NGC/PCGS coin in MS61: $975. NGC ID# 28H3, PCGS# 8876

8183 **1926 MS62 PCGS.** PCGS Population (12748/15048). NGC Census: (14620/20034). Mintage: 1,014,000. Numismedia Wsl. Price for problem free NGC/PCGS coin in MS62: $900. NGC ID# 28H9, PCGS# 8882

8184 **1926 MS63 NGC.** NGC Census: (14959/5075). PCGS Population (11272/3776). Mintage: 1,014,000. Numismedia Wsl. Price for problem free NGC/PCGS coin in MS63: $1,000. NGC ID# 28H9, PCGS# 8882

8185 **1926 MS63 NGC.** NGC Census: (14959/5075). PCGS Population (11272/3776). Mintage: 1,014,000. Numismedia Wsl. Price for problem free NGC/PCGS coin in MS63: $1,000. NGC ID# 28H9, PCGS# 8882

8186 **1932 MS62 PCGS.** PCGS Population (13649/29626). NGC Census: (15783/39120). Mintage: 4,463,000. Numismedia Wsl. Price for problem free NGC/PCGS coin in MS62: $900. NGC ID# 28HB, PCGS# 8884

8187 **1932 MS63 PCGS.** PCGS Population (19083/10543). NGC Census: (24741/14379). Mintage: 4,463,000. Numismedia Wsl. Price for problem free NGC/PCGS coin in MS63: $1,000. NGC ID# 28HB, PCGS# 8884

LIBERTY DOUBLE EAGLES

8188 **1854 Small Date — Improperly Cleaned — NGC Details. XF.** NGC Census: (33/610). PCGS Population (94/389). Mintage: 757,899. Numismedia Wsl. Price for problem free NGC/PCGS coin in XF40: $2,225.

8189 **1855-S — Bent — PCGS Genuine. AU Details.** NGC Census: (97/513). PCGS Population (89/202). Mintage: 879,675. Numismedia Wsl. Price for problem free NGC/PCGS coin in AU50: $2,425.

8190 **1857-S — Improperly Cleaned — NGC Details. XF.** NGC Census: (60/988). PCGS Population (51/526). Mintage: 970,500. Numismedia Wsl. Price for problem free NGC/PCGS coin in XF40: $2,300.

8191 **1860 — Polished — NGC Details. AU.** NGC Census: (87/553). PCGS Population (95/283). Mintage: 577,670. Numismedia Wsl. Price for problem free NGC/PCGS coin in AU50: $2,450.

8192 1860-S — Obverse Scratched — NGC Details. AU. NGC Census: (82/387). PCGS Population (76/150). Mintage: 544,950. Numismedia Wsl. Price for problem free NGC/PCGS coin in AU50: $2,625.

8193 1861 — Cleaned, Scratched — ANACS. XF40 Details. NGC Census: (90/2668). PCGS Population (86/1413). Mintage: 2,976,453. Numismedia Wsl. Price for problem free NGC/PCGS coin in XF40: $2,150.

8194 1862-S VF20 NGC. NGC Census: (1/834). PCGS Population (0/532). Mintage: 854,173. Numismedia Wsl. Price for problem free NGC/PCGS coin in VF20: $2,050. NGC ID# 269N, PCGS# 8938

8195 1871-S — Improperly Cleaned — NGC Details. AU. NGC Census: (157/1123). PCGS Population (86/345). Mintage: 928,000. Numismedia Wsl. Price for problem free NGC/PCGS coin in AU50: $1,575.

8196 1872-S AU50 NGC. NGC Census: (122/1092). PCGS Population (119/360). Mintage: 780,000. Numismedia Wsl. Price for problem free NGC/PCGS coin in AU50: $1,440. NGC ID# 26AF, PCGS# 8965

8197 1873 Open 3 AU55 NGC. NGC Census: (525/5989). PCGS Population (516/3737). Numismedia Wsl. Price for problem free NGC/PCGS coin in AU55: $1,470. NGC ID# 26AH, PCGS# 8967

8198 1873 Open 3 AU58 NGC. NGC Census: (2235/3757). PCGS Population (739/2996). Numismedia Wsl. Price for problem free NGC/PCGS coin in AU58: $1,650. NGC ID# 26AH, PCGS# 8967

8199 1873 Open 3 AU58 NGC. NGC Census: (2234/3755). PCGS Population (741/2996). Numismedia Wsl. Price for problem free NGC/PCGS coin in AU58: $1,650. NGC ID# 26AH, PCGS# 8967

8200 1873 Open 3 MS60 NGC. NGC Census: (939/2818). PCGS Population (680/2316). Numismedia Wsl. Price for problem free NGC/PCGS coin in MS60: $1,850. NGC ID# 26AH, PCGS# 8967

8201 1873 Open 3 MS60 NGC. NGC Census: (939/2818). PCGS Population (680/2316). Numismedia Wsl. Price for problem free NGC/PCGS coin in MS60: $1,850. NGC ID# 26AH, PCGS# 8967

8202 1873 Open 3 MS61 NGC. NGC Census: (1990/826). PCGS Population (1219/1096). Numismedia Wsl. Price for problem free NGC/PCGS coin in MS61: $2,125. NGC ID# 26AH, PCGS# 8967

8203 1873-S Closed 3 AU50 NGC. NGC Census: (129/1465). PCGS Population (97/630). Mintage: 1,040,600. Numismedia Wsl. Price for problem free NGC/PCGS coin in AU50: $1,625. NGC ID# 26AL, PCGS# 8969

8204 1873-S Closed 3 AU53 PCGS. PCGS Population (91/526). NGC Census: (171/1292). Mintage: 1,040,600. Numismedia Wsl. Price for problem free NGC/PCGS coin in AU53: $1,675. NGC ID# 26AL, PCGS# 8969

8205 1873-S Closed 3 AU53 PCGS. PCGS Population (91/526). NGC Census: (171/1292). Mintage: 1,040,600. Numismedia Wsl. Price for problem free NGC/PCGS coin in AU53: $1,675. NGC ID# 26AL, PCGS# 8969

8206 1873-S Closed 3 AU58 NGC. NGC Census: (682/301). PCGS Population (159/209). Mintage: 1,040,600. Numismedia Wsl. Price for problem free NGC/PCGS coin in AU58: $2,075. NGC ID# 26AL, PCGS# 8969

8207 1873-S Open 3 AU53 NGC. NGC Census: (71/525). PCGS Population (38/198). Numismedia Wsl. Price for problem free NGC/PCGS coin in AU53: $1,450. NGC ID# 26AM, PCGS# 8979

8208 1874-CC — Polished — NGC Details. AU. NGC Census: (151/631). PCGS Population (136/265). Mintage: 115,085. Numismedia Wsl. Price for problem free NGC/PCGS coin in AU50: $3,475.

8209 1875-CC — Harshly Cleaned — NGC Details. XF. NGC Census: (99/1542). PCGS Population (140/1228). Mintage: 111,151. Numismedia Wsl. Price for problem free NGC/PCGS coin in XF40: $2,550.

8210 1875-CC — Harshly Cleaned — NGC Details. AU. NGC Census: (104/1195). PCGS Population (153/816). Mintage: 111,151. Numismedia Wsl. Price for problem free NGC/PCGS coin in AU50: $3,425.

8211 1875-S AU55 NGC. NGC Census: (462/2497). PCGS Population (368/1135). Mintage: 1,230,000. Numismedia Wsl. Price for problem free NGC/PCGS coin in AU55: $1,470. NGC ID# 26AU, PCGS# 8975

8212 1875-S AU58 NGC. NGC Census: (1503/994). PCGS Population (495/640). Mintage: 1,230,000. Numismedia Wsl. Price for problem free NGC/PCGS coin in AU58: $1,530. NGC ID# 26AU, PCGS# 8975

8213 1876 AU58 NGC. NGC Census: (923/803). PCGS Population (365/658). Mintage: 583,905. Numismedia Wsl. Price for problem free NGC/PCGS coin in AU58: $1,530. NGC ID# 26AV, PCGS# 8976

8214 1877-S MS61 NGC. CAC. NGC Census: (727/184). PCGS Population (482/300). Mintage: 1,735,000. Numismedia Wsl. Price for problem free NGC/PCGS coin in MS61: $2,250. NGC ID# 26B2, PCGS# 8984

8215 1882-S MS61 PCGS. PCGS Population (349/409). NGC Census: (423/207). Mintage: 1,125,000. Numismedia Wsl. Price for problem free NGC/PCGS coin in MS61: $2,150. NGC ID# 26BG, PCGS# 8998

8216 1882-S MS61 PCGS. PCGS Population (349/409). NGC Census: (423/207). Mintage: 1,125,000. Numismedia Wsl. Price for problem free NGC/PCGS coin in MS61: $2,150. NGC ID# 26BG, PCGS# 8998

8217 1883-CC — Harshly Cleaned — NGC Details. AU. NGC Census: (121/849). PCGS Population (135/418). Mintage: 59,962. Numismedia Wsl. Price for problem free NGC/PCGS coin in AU50: $3,425.

8218 1883-S MS61 NGC. NGC Census: (733/530). PCGS Population (506/962). Mintage: 1,189,000. Numismedia Wsl. Price for problem free NGC/PCGS coin in MS61: $1,775. NGC ID# 26BJ, PCGS# 9000

8219 1884-S MS61 NGC. NGC Census: (1005/811). PCGS Population (580/1274). Mintage: 916,000. Numismedia Wsl. Price for problem free NGC/PCGS coin in MS61: $1,875. NGC ID# 26BL, PCGS# 9002

8220 1885-S MS61 NGC. NGC Census: (858/836). PCGS Population (514/1307). Mintage: 683,500. Numismedia Wsl. Price for problem free NGC/PCGS coin in MS61: $1,800. NGC ID# 26BP, PCGS# 9005

8221 **1885-S MS61 PCGS.** PCGS Population (514/1307). NGC Census: (858/836). Mintage: 683,500. Numismedia Wsl. Price for problem free NGC/PCGS coin in MS61: $1,800. NGC ID# 26BP, PCGS# 9005

8222 **1888 Doubled Die Reverse FS-801 MS60 PCGS.** PCGS Population (3/38). NGC Census: (0/0). PCGS# 145738

8223 **1889-S MS61 NGC.** NGC Census: (0/0). PCGS Population (375/1205). Mintage: 774,700. Numismedia Wsl. Price for problem free NGC/PCGS coin in MS61: $1,550. NGC ID# 26BW, PCGS# 9012

8224 **1890-CC — Improperly Cleaned — NGC Details. AU.** NGC Census: (179/1582). PCGS Population (203/801). Mintage: 91,209. Numismedia Wsl. Price for problem free NGC/PCGS coin in AU50: $3,375.

8225 **1890-S AU58 PCGS.** PCGS Population (231/1103). NGC Census: (333/1237). Mintage: 802,750. Numismedia Wsl. Price for problem free NGC/PCGS coin in AU58: $1,405. NGC ID# 26BZ, PCGS# 9015

8226 **1891-S MS62 PCGS.** PCGS Population (1835/901). NGC Census: (1904/547). Mintage: 1,288,125. Numismedia Wsl. Price for problem free NGC/PCGS coin in MS62: $1,800. NGC ID# 26C4, PCGS# 9018

8227 **1891-S MS62 NGC.** NGC Census: (1904/545). PCGS Population (1845/903). Mintage: 1,288,125. Numismedia Wsl. Price for problem free NGC/PCGS coin in MS62: $1,800. NGC ID# 26C4, PCGS# 9018

8228 **1891-S MS62 NGC.** NGC Census: (1904/545). PCGS Population (1845/903). Mintage: 1,288,125. Numismedia Wsl. Price for problem free NGC/PCGS coin in MS62: $1,800. NGC ID# 26C4, PCGS# 9018

8229 **1891-S MS62 NGC.** NGC Census: (1904/547). PCGS Population (1835/901). Mintage: 1,288,125. Numismedia Wsl. Price for problem free NGC/PCGS coin in MS62: $1,800. NGC ID# 26C4, PCGS# 9018

8230 **1894-S MS62 PCGS.** PCGS Population (1545/890). NGC Census: (1849/653). Mintage: 1,048,550. Numismedia Wsl. Price for problem free NGC/PCGS coin in MS62: $1,480. NGC ID# 26CC, PCGS# 9026

8231 **1895 MS62 NGC.** NGC Census: (9116/3937). PCGS Population (6324/2047). Mintage: 1,114,656. Numismedia Wsl. Price for problem free NGC/PCGS coin in MS62: $1,480. NGC ID# 26CD, PCGS# 9027

8232 **1895 MS63 NGC.** NGC Census: (3406/531). PCGS Population (1786/261). Mintage: 1,114,656. Numismedia Wsl. Price for problem free NGC/PCGS coin in MS63: $1,900. NGC ID# 26CD, PCGS# 9027

8233 **1896 Repunched Date, FS-301, MS62 PCGS.** PCGS Population (18/14). NGC Census: (0/0). PCGS# 145739

8234 **1896 Repunched Date, FS-301, MS62 PCGS.** PCGS Population (18/14). NGC Census: (0/0). PCGS# 145739

8235 **1896-S MS62 PCGS.** PCGS Population (2539/1182). NGC Census: (3244/907). Mintage: 1,403,925. Numismedia Wsl. Price for problem free NGC/PCGS coin in MS62: $1,625. NGC ID# 26CG, PCGS# 9030

8236 **1896-S MS62+ PCGS.** PCGS Population (2533/1175). NGC Census: (3243/908). Mintage: 1,403,925. Numismedia Wsl. Price for problem free NGC/PCGS coin in MS62: $1,625. NGC ID# 26CG, PCGS# 9030

8237 **1896-S MS62+ PCGS.** PCGS Population (2533/1175). NGC Census: (3243/908). Mintage: 1,403,925. Numismedia Wsl. Price for problem free NGC/PCGS coin in MS62: $1,625. NGC ID# 26CG, PCGS# 9030

8238 **1897-S MS63 NGC.** NGC Census: (1896/334). PCGS Population (1769/459). Mintage: 1,470,250. Numismedia Wsl. Price for problem free NGC/PCGS coin in MS63: $2,000. NGC ID# 26CJ, PCGS# 9032

8239 **1898-S MS62 PCGS.** PCGS Population (6617/4494). NGC Census: (8631/4933). Mintage: 2,575,175. Numismedia Wsl. Price for problem free NGC/PCGS coin in MS62: $1,480. NGC ID# 26CL, PCGS# 9034

8240 **1898-S MS63 PCGS.** PCGS Population (3162/1332). NGC Census: (3786/1147). Mintage: 2,575,175. Numismedia Wsl. Price for problem free NGC/PCGS coin in MS63: $2,075. NGC ID# 26CL, PCGS# 9034

8241 **1899-S MS63 PCGS.** PCGS Population (1218/256). NGC Census: (1287/295). Mintage: 2,010,300. Numismedia Wsl. Price for problem free NGC/PCGS coin in MS63: $2,225. NGC ID# 26CN, PCGS# 9036

8242 **1900 MS63 PCGS.** PCGS Population (11036/4388). NGC Census: (16789/4928). Mintage: 1,874,584. Numismedia Wsl. Price for problem free NGC/PCGS coin in MS63: $1,650. NGC ID# 26CP, PCGS# 9037

8243 **1900 MS64 PCGS.** PCGS Population (4265/123). NGC Census: (4696/232). Mintage: 1,874,584. Numismedia Wsl. Price for problem free NGC/PCGS coin in MS64: $1,850. NGC ID# 26CP, PCGS# 9037

8244 **1901 MS63 NGC.** NGC Census: (1655/1682). PCGS Population (1711/1779). Mintage: 111,400. Numismedia Wsl. Price for problem free NGC/PCGS coin in MS63: $1,580. NGC ID# 26CS, PCGS# 9039

8245 **1901 MS63 NGC.** NGC Census: (1655/1682). PCGS Population (1711/1779). Mintage: 111,400. Numismedia Wsl. Price for problem free NGC/PCGS coin in MS63: $1,580. NGC ID# 26CS, PCGS# 9039

8246 **1903-S MS63 NGC.** NGC Census: (1364/286). PCGS Population (1425/381). Mintage: 954,000. Numismedia Wsl. Price for problem free NGC/PCGS coin in MS63: $2,125. NGC ID# 26CX, PCGS# 9044

8247 **1903-S MS63 NGC.** NGC Census: (1364/286). PCGS Population (1425/381). Mintage: 954,000. Numismedia Wsl. Price for problem free NGC/PCGS coin in MS63: $2,125. NGC ID# 26CX, PCGS# 9044

8248 **1904 MS61 NGC.** NGC Census: (25925/189129). PCGS Population (15850/148258). Mintage: 6,256,797. Numismedia Wsl. Price for problem free NGC/PCGS coin in MS61: $1,460. NGC ID# 26CY, PCGS# 9045

8249 **1904 MS63 PCGS.** PCGS Population (55329/36045). NGC Census: (75675/41705). Mintage: 6,256,797. Numismedia Wsl. Price for problem free NGC/PCGS coin in MS63: $1,580. NGC ID# 26CY, PCGS# 9045

8250 **1904 — Minor Struck Thru Obverse — MS63 PCGS.** PCGS Population (55329/36045). NGC Census: (75675/41705). Mintage: 6,256,797. Numismedia Wsl. Price for problem free NGC/PCGS coin in MS63: $1,580.

8251 1904 MS63 NGC. NGC Census: (75666/41642). PCGS Population (55454/36157). Mintage: 6,256,797. Numismedia Wsl. Price for problem free NGC/PCGS coin in MS63: $1,580. NGC ID# 26CY, PCGS# 9045

8252 1904 MS63 NGC. NGC Census: (75666/41642). PCGS Population (55454/36157). Mintage: 6,256,797. Numismedia Wsl. Price for problem free NGC/PCGS coin in MS63: $1,580. NGC ID# 26CY, PCGS# 9045

8253 1904-S MS63 NGC. NGC Census: (8259/3472). PCGS Population (6200/3339). Mintage: 5,134,175. Numismedia Wsl. Price for problem free NGC/PCGS coin in MS63: $2,050. NGC ID# 26CZ, PCGS# 9046

SAINT-GAUDENS DOUBLE EAGLES

8254 1907 Arabic Numerals MS63 NGC. NGC Census: (2732/2909). PCGS Population (3782/6955). Mintage: 361,667. Numismedia Wsl. Price for problem free NGC/PCGS coin in MS63: $1,725. NGC ID# 26F5, PCGS# 9141

8255 1907 Arabic Numerals MS63 NGC. NGC Census: (2732/2909). PCGS Population (3782/6955). Mintage: 361,667. Numismedia Wsl. Price for problem free NGC/PCGS coin in MS63: $1,725. NGC ID# 26F5, PCGS# 9141

8256 1908 No Motto MS62 PCGS. PCGS Population (18174/88760). NGC Census: (28310/93727). Mintage: 4,271,551. Numismedia Wsl. Price for problem free NGC/PCGS coin in MS62: $1,480. NGC ID# 26F6, PCGS# 9142

8257 1908 No Motto MS63 NGC. NGC Census: (46250/47472). PCGS Population (33571/55451). Mintage: 4,271,551. Numismedia Wsl. Price for problem free NGC/PCGS coin in MS63: $1,530. NGC ID# 26F6, PCGS# 9142

8258 1908 No Motto MS63 NGC. NGC Census: (46250/47472). PCGS Population (33571/55451). Mintage: 4,271,551. Numismedia Wsl. Price for problem free NGC/PCGS coin in MS63: $1,530. NGC ID# 26F6, PCGS# 9142

8259 1908 No Motto MS64 NGC. NGC Census: (33547/13939). PCGS Population (34432/20816). Mintage: 4,271,551. Numismedia Wsl. Price for problem free NGC/PCGS coin in MS64: $1,585. NGC ID# 26F6, PCGS# 9142

8260 1909/8 — Rim Filed — PCGS Genuine. Unc Details. NGC Census: (77/867). PCGS Population (71/1284). Numismedia Wsl. Price for problem free NGC/PCGS coin in MS60: $2,050.

8261 1911 MS62 PCGS. PCGS Population (693/1274). NGC Census: (952/998). Mintage: 197,200. Numismedia Wsl. Price for problem free NGC/PCGS coin in MS62: $1,700. NGC ID# 26FJ, PCGS# 9157

8262 1911-D MS64 PCGS. CAC. PCGS Population (3523/2373). NGC Census: (3516/2442). Mintage: 846,500. Numismedia Wsl. Price for problem free NGC/PCGS coin in MS64: $1,800. NGC ID# 26FK, PCGS# 9158

8263 1914-D MS63 NGC. NGC Census: (2015/2515). PCGS Population (1906/3326). Mintage: 453,000. Numismedia Wsl. Price for problem free NGC/PCGS coin in MS63: $1,650. NGC ID# 26FT, PCGS# 9165

8264 1914-S MS64 NGC. NGC Census: (5906/1507). PCGS Population (5382/2096). Mintage: 1,498,000. Numismedia Wsl. Price for problem free NGC/PCGS coin in MS64: $1,725. NGC ID# 26FU, PCGS# 9166

8265 1920 MS63 NGC. NGC Census: (1465/424). PCGS Population (2016/872). Mintage: 228,250. Numismedia Wsl. Price for problem free NGC/PCGS coin in MS63: $1,925. NGC ID# 26FY, PCGS# 9170

8266 1920 MS63 NGC. NGC Census: (1466/424). PCGS Population (2013/874). Mintage: 228,250. Numismedia Wsl. Price for problem free NGC/PCGS coin in MS63: $1,925. NGC ID# 26FY, PCGS# 9170

8267 1920 MS63+ PCGS. PCGS Population (2007/869). NGC Census: (1464/425). Mintage: 228,250. Numismedia Wsl. Price for problem free NGC/PCGS coin in MS63: $1,925. NGC ID# 26FY, PCGS# 9170

8268 1923 MS62 PCGS. PCGS Population (6994/13318). NGC Census: (12292/13824). Mintage: 566,000. Numismedia Wsl. Price for problem free NGC/PCGS coin in MS62: $1,480. NGC ID# 26G5, PCGS# 9175

8269 1923 MS63 PCGS. PCGS Population (9080/4238). NGC Census: (11086/2738). Mintage: 566,000. Numismedia Wsl. Price for problem free NGC/PCGS coin in MS63: $1,650. NGC ID# 26G5, PCGS# 9175

8270 1923 MS63 PCGS. PCGS Population (9045/4213). NGC Census: (11081/2734). Mintage: 566,000. Numismedia Wsl. Price for problem free NGC/PCGS coin in MS63: $1,650. NGC ID# 26G5, PCGS# 9175

8271 1924 MS63 NGC. NGC Census: (104022/142482). PCGS Population (81200/133776). Mintage: 4,323,500. Numismedia Wsl. Price for problem free NGC/PCGS coin in MS63: $1,530. NGC ID# 26G7, PCGS# 9177

8272 1924 MS63 NGC. NGC Census: (104022/142482). PCGS Population (81200/133776). Mintage: 4,323,500. Numismedia Wsl. Price for problem free NGC/PCGS coin in MS63: $1,530. NGC ID# 26G7, PCGS# 9177

8273 1924 MS63 PCGS. PCGS Population (81338/134405). NGC Census: (104039/142460). Mintage: 4,323,500. Numismedia Wsl. Price for problem free NGC/PCGS coin in MS63: $1,530. NGC ID# 26G7, PCGS# 9177

8274 1924 MS64 PCGS. PCGS Population (84386/50019). NGC Census: (103910/38550). Mintage: 4,323,500. Numismedia Wsl. Price for problem free NGC/PCGS coin in MS64: $1,585. NGC ID# 26G7, PCGS# 9177

8275 1925 MS63 NGC. NGC Census: (18049/20910). PCGS Population (14599/20228). Mintage: 2,831,750. Numismedia Wsl. Price for problem free NGC/PCGS coin in MS63: $1,530. NGC ID# 26GA, PCGS# 9180

8276 1926 MS64 NGC. NGC Census: (9258/3900). PCGS Population (7410/4873). Mintage: 816,750. Numismedia Wsl. Price for problem free NGC/PCGS coin in MS64: $1,585. NGC ID# 26GD, PCGS# 9183

8277 1927 MS64 NGC. NGC Census: (52057/21949). PCGS Population (45401/31519). Mintage: 2,946,750. Numismedia Wsl. Price for problem free NGC/PCGS coin in MS64: $1,585. NGC ID# 26GG, PCGS# 9186

COMMEMORATIVE SILVER

8278 1893 Isabella Quarter MS62 NGC. NGC Census: (507/2458). PCGS Population (828/3052). Mintage: 24,214. Numismedia Wsl. Price for problem free NGC/PCGS coin in MS62: $440. NGC ID# 28HR, PCGS# 9220

8279 1893 Isabella Quarter MS64 PCGS. CAC. PCGS Population (1189/692). NGC Census: (1045/645). Mintage: 24,214. Numismedia Wsl. Price for problem free NGC/PCGS coin in MS64: $725. NGC ID# 28HR, PCGS# 9220

8280 1900 Lafayette Dollar — Cleaned — ANACS. AU55 Details. NGC Census: (53/2371). PCGS Population (173/3031). Mintage: 36,026. Numismedia Wsl. Price for problem free NGC/PCGS coin in AU55: $480.

8281 1900 Lafayette Dollar — Tooled — PCGS Genuine. Unc Details. NGC Census: (22/2164). PCGS Population (61/2651). Mintage: 36,026. Numismedia Wsl. Price for problem free NGC/PCGS coin in MS60: $750.

8282 1900 Lafayette Dollar MS62 PCGS. PCGS Population (461/2087). NGC Census: (435/1544). Mintage: 36,026. Numismedia Wsl. Price for problem free NGC/PCGS coin in MS62: $900. NGC ID# 28N8, PCGS# 9222

8283 1921 Alabama MS65 PCGS. PCGS Population (457/106). NGC Census: (372/82). Mintage: 59,038. Numismedia Wsl. Price for problem free NGC/PCGS coin in MS65: $1,050. NGC ID# 28HT, PCGS# 9224

8284 1921 Alabama 2x2 MS65 NGC. NGC Census: (363/78). PCGS Population (438/109). Mintage: 6,006. Numismedia Wsl. Price for problem free NGC/PCGS coin in MS65: $1,150. NGC ID# 28HS, PCGS# 9225

8285 1936 Albany MS66 PCGS. PCGS Population (826/145). NGC Census: (525/139). Mintage: 17,671. Numismedia Wsl. Price for problem free NGC/PCGS coin in MS66: $460. NGC ID# 28HU, PCGS# 9227

8286 1937 Antietam MS65 PCGS. PCGS Population (1562/1564). NGC Census: (996/919). Mintage: 18,028. Numismedia Wsl. Price for problem free NGC/PCGS coin in MS65: $740. NGC ID# 28HV, PCGS# 9229

8287 1937 Antietam MS65 PCGS. CAC. PCGS Population (1562/1564). NGC Census: (996/919). Mintage: 18,028. Numismedia Wsl. Price for problem free NGC/PCGS coin in MS65: $740. NGC ID# 28HV, PCGS# 9229

8288 1937 Antietam MS66 PCGS. PCGS Population (1261/303). NGC Census: (733/186). Mintage: 18,028. Numismedia Wsl. Price for problem free NGC/PCGS coin in MS66: $825. NGC ID# 28HV, PCGS# 9229

8289 1937 Antietam MS66 PCGS. PCGS Population (1261/303). NGC Census: (733/186). Mintage: 18,028. Numismedia Wsl. Price for problem free NGC/PCGS coin in MS66: $825. NGC ID# 28HV, PCGS# 9229

8290 1937 Antietam MS66 PCGS. CAC. PCGS Population (1261/303). NGC Census: (733/186). Mintage: 18,028. Numismedia Wsl. Price for problem free NGC/PCGS coin in MS66: $825. NGC ID# 28HV, PCGS# 9229

8291 1937 Arkansas PDS Set PCGS. This set includes: **1937 MS64, 1937-D MS65 and 1937-S MS64.** PCGS Population (0/0). NGC Census: (0/0). (Total: 3 coins)

8292 1937 Arkansas PDS Set MS66 PCGS. PCGS Population (0/0). NGC Census: (0/0). (Total: 3 coins)

8293 1938 Arkansas MS65 PCGS. PCGS Population (211/105). NGC Census: (153/52). Mintage: 3,156. Numismedia Wsl. Price for problem free NGC/PCGS coin in MS65: $365. NGC ID# 28J7, PCGS# 9245

8294 1938-D Arkansas MS65 PCGS. PCGS Population (216/154). NGC Census: (175/51). Mintage: 3,155. Numismedia Wsl. Price for problem free NGC/PCGS coin in MS65: $360. NGC ID# 28J8, PCGS# 9246

8295 1938-S Arkansas MS65 PCGS. PCGS Population (187/82). NGC Census: (137/42). Mintage: 3,156. Numismedia Wsl. Price for problem free NGC/PCGS coin in MS65: $320. NGC ID# 28J9, PCGS# 9247

8296 1939-D Arkansas MS66 PCGS. PCGS Population (101/8). NGC Census: (32/8). Mintage: 2,104. Numismedia Wsl. Price for problem free NGC/PCGS coin in MS66: $1,325. NGC ID# 28JB, PCGS# 9250

8297 1935 Boone MS67 PCGS. CAC. PCGS Population (54/0). NGC Census: (24/2). Mintage: 10,000. Numismedia Wsl. Price for problem free NGC/PCGS coin in MS67: $1,225. NGC ID# 28JF, PCGS# 9258

8298 1935/34 Boone MS66 PCGS. CAC. PCGS Population (247/53). NGC Census: (257/44). Mintage: 10,008. Numismedia Wsl. Price for problem free NGC/PCGS coin in MS66: $340. NGC ID# 28JJ, PCGS# 9262

8299 1935/34-S Boone MS66 PCGS. PCGS Population (104/17). NGC Census: (86/22). Mintage: 2,004. Numismedia Wsl. Price for problem free NGC/PCGS coin in MS66: $1,150. NGC ID# 28JL, PCGS# 9264

8300 1936 Boone PDS Set MS65 NGC. NGC Census: (0/0). PCGS Population (0/0). (Total: 3 coins)

8301 1937 Boone MS67 PCGS. CAC. PCGS Population (94/3). NGC Census: (53/0). Mintage: 9,810. Numismedia Wsl. Price for problem free NGC/PCGS coin in MS67: $900. NGC ID# 28JR, PCGS# 9270

8302 1937-D Boone MS66 PCGS. PCGS Population (154/52). NGC Census: (116/28). Mintage: 2,506. Numismedia Wsl. Price for problem free NGC/PCGS coin in MS66: $400. NGC ID# 28JS, PCGS# 9271

8303 1937-S Boone MS66 PCGS. PCGS Population (143/40). NGC Census: (151/34). Mintage: 2,506. Numismedia Wsl. Price for problem free NGC/PCGS coin in MS66: $565. NGC ID# 28JT, PCGS# 9272

8304 **1937-S Boone MS66 PCGS.** PCGS Population (143/40). NGC Census: (151/34). Mintage: 2,506. Numismedia Wsl. Price for problem free NGC/PCGS coin in MS66: $565. NGC ID# 28JT, PCGS# 9272

8305 **1938-S Boone MS66 PCGS.** PCGS Population (140/37). NGC Census: (105/31). Mintage: 2,100. Numismedia Wsl. Price for problem free NGC/PCGS coin in MS66: $725. NGC ID# 28JW, PCGS# 9276

8306 **1938 Boone PDS Set NGC.** The set includes: **1938 MS66, 1938-D MS65 and 1938-S MS66.** NGC Census: (0/0). PCGS Population (0/0). (Total: 3 coins)

8307 **1925-S California MS66 PCGS.** PCGS Population (359/105). NGC Census: (424/151). Mintage: 86,394. Numismedia Wsl. Price for problem free NGC/PCGS coin in MS66: $935. NGC ID# 28JY, PCGS# 9281

8308 **1925-S California MS66 NGC.** NGC Census: (424/151). PCGS Population (359/107). Mintage: 86,394. Numismedia Wsl. Price for problem free NGC/PCGS coin in MS66: $935. NGC ID# 28JY, PCGS# 9281

8309 **Four Uncertified Uncirculated Columbia Half Dollars.** The lot includes: **1936, 1936-D, and (2) 1936-S.** Housed in a four-slot black cardboard holder. *Ex: Public Sale #222 (R.M. Smythe, 7/2002), lot 6561.* (Total: 4 coins)

8310 **1936-D Columbia MS67 NGC.** NGC Census: (229/19). PCGS Population (176/19). Mintage: 8,009. Numismedia Wsl. Price for problem free NGC/PCGS coin in MS67: $775. NGC ID# 28K6, PCGS# 9292

8311 **1893 Columbian MS65 NGC.** NGC Census: (640/170). PCGS Population (542/218). Mintage: 1,550,405. Numismedia Wsl. Price for problem free NGC/PCGS coin in MS65: $320. NGC ID# 26H6, PCGS# 9297

8312 **1893 Columbian MS66 PCGS.** PCGS Population (203/15). NGC Census: (143/27). Mintage: 1,550,405. Numismedia Wsl. Price for problem free NGC/PCGS coin in MS66: $885. NGC ID# 26H6, PCGS# 9297

8313 **1893 Columbian MS66 PCGS.** PCGS Population (203/15). NGC Census: (143/27). Mintage: 1,550,405. Numismedia Wsl. Price for problem free NGC/PCGS coin in MS66: $885. NGC ID# 26H6, PCGS# 9297

8314 **1893 Columbian MS66 PCGS. CAC.** PCGS Population (203/15). NGC Census: (143/27). Mintage: 1,550,405. Numismedia Wsl. Price for problem free NGC/PCGS coin in MS66: $885. NGC ID# 26H6, PCGS# 9297

8315 **1935 Connecticut MS65 PCGS.** PCGS Population (1236/582). NGC Census: (1251/543). Mintage: 25,018. Numismedia Wsl. Price for problem free NGC/PCGS coin in MS65: $340. NGC ID# 28K8, PCGS# 9299

8316 **1935 Connecticut MS66 NGC.** NGC Census: (469/74). PCGS Population (517/65). Mintage: 25,018. Numismedia Wsl. Price for problem free NGC/PCGS coin in MS66: $700. NGC ID# 28K8, PCGS# 9299

8317 **1935 Connecticut MS66 PCGS.** PCGS Population (522/65). NGC Census: (469/74). Mintage: 25,018. Numismedia Wsl. Price for problem free NGC/PCGS coin in MS66: $700. NGC ID# 28K8, PCGS# 9299

8318 **1936 Delaware MS66 PCGS.** PCGS Population (675/103). NGC Census: (474/92). Mintage: 20,993. Numismedia Wsl. Price for problem free NGC/PCGS coin in MS66: $440. NGC ID# 28K9, PCGS# 9301

8319 **1936 Delaware MS66 PCGS. CAC.** PCGS Population (676/103). NGC Census: (474/92). Mintage: 20,993. Numismedia Wsl. Price for problem free NGC/PCGS coin in MS66: $440. NGC ID# 28K9, PCGS# 9301

8320 **1936 Elgin MS67 PCGS.** PCGS Population (182/4). NGC Census: (129/2). Mintage: 20,015. Numismedia Wsl. Price for problem free NGC/PCGS coin in MS67: $1,125. NGC ID# 28KA, PCGS# 9303

8321 **1936 Gettysburg — Cleaning — PCGS Genuine. Unc Details.** NGC Census: (0/3249). PCGS Population (3/5328). Mintage: 26,928. Numismedia Wsl. Price for problem free NGC/PCGS coin in MS60: $355.

8322 **1936 Gettysburg MS64 NGC.** NGC Census: (1244/1668). PCGS Population (2063/2402). Mintage: 26,928. Numismedia Wsl. Price for problem free NGC/PCGS coin in MS64: $460. NGC ID# 28KB, PCGS# 9305

8323 **1936 Gettysburg MS65 NGC.** NGC Census: (1277/392). PCGS Population (1632/774). Mintage: 26,928. Numismedia Wsl. Price for problem free NGC/PCGS coin in MS65: $700. NGC ID# 28KB, PCGS# 9305

8324 **1936 Gettysburg MS66 PCGS.** PCGS Population (677/97). NGC Census: (330/62). Mintage: 26,928. Numismedia Wsl. Price for problem free NGC/PCGS coin in MS66: $875. NGC ID# 28KB, PCGS# 9305

8325 **1936 Gettysburg MS66 PCGS.** PCGS Population (677/97). NGC Census: (330/62). Mintage: 26,928. Numismedia Wsl. Price for problem free NGC/PCGS coin in MS66: $875. NGC ID# 28KB, PCGS# 9305

8326 **1922 Grant No Star MS65 NGC.** NGC Census: (688/228). PCGS Population (754/300). Mintage: 67,405. Numismedia Wsl. Price for problem free NGC/PCGS coin in MS65: $500. NGC ID# 28KD, PCGS# 9306

8327 **1922 Grant No Star MS65 PCGS. CAC.** PCGS Population (754/300). NGC Census: (686/227). Mintage: 67,405. Numismedia Wsl. Price for problem free NGC/PCGS coin in MS65: $500. NGC ID# 28KD, PCGS# 9306

8328 **1922 Grant No Star MS65+ PCGS. CAC.** PCGS Population (754/300). NGC Census: (686/227). Mintage: 67,405. Numismedia Wsl. Price for problem free NGC/PCGS coin in MS65: $500. NGC ID# 28KD, PCGS# 9306

8329 **1935 Hudson — Cleaning — PCGS Genuine. Unc Details.** NGC Census: (1/1895). PCGS Population (12/2983). Mintage: 10,008. Numismedia Wsl. Price for problem free NGC/PCGS coin in MS60: $685.

8330 **1935 Hudson MS63 PCGS.** PCGS Population (660/2132). NGC Census: (298/1501). Mintage: 10,008. Numismedia Wsl. Price for problem free NGC/PCGS coin in MS63: $775. NGC ID# 28KF, PCGS# 9312

8331 **1935 Hudson MS64 PCGS.** PCGS Population (1219/913). NGC Census: (821/680). Mintage: 10,008. Numismedia Wsl. Price for problem free NGC/PCGS coin in MS64: $1,025. NGC ID# 28KF, PCGS# 9312

8332 **1935 Hudson MS65 NGC.** NGC Census: (501/179). PCGS Population (687/226). Mintage: 10,008. Numismedia Wsl. Price for problem free NGC/PCGS coin in MS65: $1,125. NGC ID# 28KF, PCGS# 9312

8333 1925 Lexington MS66 NGC. NGC Census: (206/14). PCGS Population (351/19). Mintage: 162,013. Numismedia Wsl. Price for problem free NGC/PCGS coin in MS66: $1,075. NGC ID# 28KK, PCGS# 9318

8334 1925 Lexington MS66 PCGS. PCGS Population (351/19). NGC Census: (206/14). Mintage: 162,013. Numismedia Wsl. Price for problem free NGC/PCGS coin in MS66: $1,075. NGC ID# 28KK, PCGS# 9318

8335 1925 Lexington MS66 PCGS. PCGS Population (352/19). NGC Census: (206/14). Mintage: 162,013. Numismedia Wsl. Price for problem free NGC/PCGS coin in MS66: $1,075. NGC ID# 28KK, PCGS# 9318

8336 1925 Lexington MS66 PCGS. CAC. PCGS Population (354/19). NGC Census: (206/14). Mintage: 162,013. Numismedia Wsl. Price for problem free NGC/PCGS coin in MS66: $1,075. NGC ID# 28KK, PCGS# 9318

8337 1925 Lexington MS66 PCGS. CAC. PCGS Population (354/19). NGC Census: (206/14). Mintage: 162,013. Numismedia Wsl. Price for problem free NGC/PCGS coin in MS66: $1,075. NGC ID# 28KK, PCGS# 9318

8338 1936 Long Island MS66 NGC. NGC Census: (343/59). PCGS Population (455/55). Mintage: 81,826. Numismedia Wsl. Price for problem free NGC/PCGS coin in MS66: $650. NGC ID# 28KL, PCGS# 9322

8339 1920 Maine MS66 NGC. NGC Census: (292/30). PCGS Population (404/33). Mintage: 50,028. Numismedia Wsl. Price for problem free NGC/PCGS coin in MS66: $600. NGC ID# 28KN, PCGS# 9326

8340 1920 Maine MS66 PCGS. CAC. PCGS Population (406/33). NGC Census: (292/30). Mintage: 50,028. Numismedia Wsl. Price for problem free NGC/PCGS coin in MS66: $600. NGC ID# 28KN, PCGS# 9326

8341 1921 Missouri MS62 PCGS. PCGS Population (228/1628). NGC Census: (152/1695). Mintage: 10,428. Numismedia Wsl. Price for problem free NGC/PCGS coin in MS62: $625. NGC ID# 28KS, PCGS# 9330

8342 1921 Missouri MS63 PCGS. PCGS Population (515/1114). NGC Census: (359/1336). Mintage: 10,428. Numismedia Wsl. Price for problem free NGC/PCGS coin in MS63: $725. NGC ID# 28KS, PCGS# 9330

8343 1921 Missouri MS64 PCGS. PCGS Population (813/301). NGC Census: (992/344). Mintage: 10,428. Numismedia Wsl. Price for problem free NGC/PCGS coin in MS64: $925. NGC ID# 28KS, PCGS# 9330

8344 1921 Missouri MS64 NGC. NGC Census: (992/344). PCGS Population (813/301). Mintage: 10,428. Numismedia Wsl. Price for problem free NGC/PCGS coin in MS64: $925. NGC ID# 28KS, PCGS# 9330

8345 1921 Missouri 2x4 MS64 NGC. NGC Census: (871/320). PCGS Population (747/335). Mintage: 5,000. Numismedia Wsl. Price for problem free NGC/PCGS coin in MS64: $1,050. NGC ID# 28KR, PCGS# 9331

8346 1938 New Rochelle MS65 PCGS. PCGS Population (1547/1109). NGC Census: (1005/642). Mintage: 15,266. Numismedia Wsl. Price for problem free NGC/PCGS coin in MS65: $365. NGC ID# 28KU, PCGS# 9335

8347 1938 New Rochelle MS66 PCGS. PCGS Population (929/181). NGC Census: (541/100). Mintage: 15,266. Numismedia Wsl. Price for problem free NGC/PCGS coin in MS66: $525. NGC ID# 28KU, PCGS# 9335

8348 1938 New Rochelle MS66 NGC. CAC. NGC Census: (541/100). PCGS Population (929/183). Mintage: 15,266. Numismedia Wsl. Price for problem free NGC/PCGS coin in MS66: $525. NGC ID# 28KU, PCGS# 9335

8349 1938 New Rochelle MS67 NGC. NGC Census: (85/15). PCGS Population (179/4). Mintage: 15,266. Numismedia Wsl. Price for problem free NGC/PCGS coin in MS67: $1,200. NGC ID# 28KU, PCGS# 9335

8350 1938 New Rochelle MS67 PCGS. CAC. PCGS Population (176/4). NGC Census: (85/15). Mintage: 15,266. Numismedia Wsl. Price for problem free NGC/PCGS coin in MS67: $1,200. NGC ID# 28KU, PCGS# 9335

8351 1936 Norfolk MS66 PCGS. PCGS Population (1672/1246). NGC Census: (1094/735). Mintage: 16,936. Numismedia Wsl. Price for problem free NGC/PCGS coin in MS66: $410. NGC ID# 28KV, PCGS# 9337

8352 1936 Norfolk MS67+ PCGS. CAC. PCGS Population (1071/176). NGC Census: (653/81). Mintage: 16,936. Numismedia Wsl. Price for problem free NGC/PCGS coin in MS67: $535. NGC ID# 28KV, PCGS# 9337

8353 1926 Oregon MS67 PCGS Secure. Ex: Bruce Scher. PCGS Population (83/2). NGC Census: (66/1). Mintage: 47,955. Numismedia Wsl. Price for problem free NGC/PCGS coin in MS67: $1,225. NGC ID# 28KW, PCGS# 9340

8354 1926-S Oregon MS67 NGC. NGC Census: (176/11). PCGS Population (153/6). Mintage: 83,055. Numismedia Wsl. Price for problem free NGC/PCGS coin in MS67: $1,125. NGC ID# 28KX, PCGS# 9341

8355 1926-S Oregon MS67 NGC. NGC Census: (176/11). PCGS Population (153/6). Mintage: 83,055. Numismedia Wsl. Price for problem free NGC/PCGS coin in MS67: $1,125. NGC ID# 28KX, PCGS# 9341

8356 1928 Oregon MS67 PCGS. PCGS Population (83/3). NGC Census: (93/3). Mintage: 6,028. Numismedia Wsl. Price for problem free NGC/PCGS coin in MS67: $1,250. NGC ID# 28KY, PCGS# 9342

8357 1933-D Oregon MS66 PCGS. PCGS Population (405/99). NGC Census: (259/43). Mintage: 5,008. Numismedia Wsl. Price for problem free NGC/PCGS coin in MS66: $460. NGC ID# 28KZ, PCGS# 9343

8358 1936 Oregon MS66 PCGS. PCGS Population (569/186). NGC Census: (545/151). Mintage: 10,006. Numismedia Wsl. Price for problem free NGC/PCGS coin in MS66: $320. NGC ID# 28L3, PCGS# 9345

8359 1936-S Oregon MS67 NGC. NGC Census: (150/12). PCGS Population (153/3). Mintage: 5,006. Numismedia Wsl. Price for problem free NGC/PCGS coin in MS67: $800. NGC ID# 28L4, PCGS# 9346

8360 1937-D Oregon MS66 PCGS. PCGS Population (1171/676). NGC Census: (913/610). Mintage: 12,008. Numismedia Wsl. Price for problem free NGC/PCGS coin in MS66: $275. NGC ID# 28L5, PCGS# 9347

8361 1938-D Oregon MS66 NGC. NGC Census: (574/270). PCGS Population (668/266). Mintage: 6,005. Numismedia Wsl. Price for problem free NGC/PCGS coin in MS66: $360. NGC ID# 28L7, PCGS# 9349

8362 1939 Oregon MS66 NGC. NGC Census: (302/108). PCGS Population (284/97). Mintage: 3,004. Numismedia Wsl. Price for problem free NGC/PCGS coin in MS66: $635. NGC ID# 28L9, PCGS# 9352

8363 1939-D Oregon MS65 PCGS. PCGS Population (364/534). NGC Census: (210/468). Mintage: 3,004. Numismedia Wsl. Price for problem free NGC/PCGS coin in MS65: $500. NGC ID# 28LA, PCGS# 9353

8364 1939-S Oregon MS65 PCGS. PCGS Population (392/382). NGC Census: (245/406). Mintage: 3,005. Numismedia Wsl. Price for problem free NGC/PCGS coin in MS65: $520. NGC ID# 28LB, PCGS# 9354

8365 1939-S Oregon MS66 PCGS. PCGS Population (277/106). NGC Census: (299/107). Mintage: 3,005. Numismedia Wsl. Price for problem free NGC/PCGS coin in MS66: $600. NGC ID# 28LB, PCGS# 9354

8366 1915-S Panama-Pacific MS63 PCGS. Original "Souvenir Coin" envelope included. PCGS Population (678/1791). NGC Census: (436/1806). Mintage: 27,134. Numismedia Wsl. Price for problem free NGC/PCGS coin in MS63: $610. NGC ID# 26H7, PCGS# 9357

8367 1915-S Panama-Pacific MS64 PCGS. PCGS Population (940/864). NGC Census: (1004/801). Mintage: 27,134. Numismedia Wsl. Price for problem free NGC/PCGS coin in MS64: $925. NGC ID# 26H7, PCGS# 9357

8368 1915-S Panama-Pacific MS64 NGC. NGC Census: (1004/801). PCGS Population (940/864). Mintage: 27,134. Numismedia Wsl. Price for problem free NGC/PCGS coin in MS64: $925. NGC ID# 26H7, PCGS# 9357

8369 1936 Rhode Island MS67 NGC. NGC Census: (30/0). PCGS Population (37/0). Mintage: 20,013. Numismedia Wsl. Price for problem free NGC/PCGS coin in MS67: $1,575. NGC ID# 28LE, PCGS# 9363

8370 1937 Roanoke MS67 PCGS. CAC. PCGS Population (317/14). NGC Census: (240/17). Mintage: 29,030. Numismedia Wsl. Price for problem free NGC/PCGS coin in MS67: $785. NGC ID# 28LH, PCGS# 9367

8371 1935-S San Diego MS67 PCGS. CAC. PCGS Population (145/5). NGC Census: (84/4). Mintage: 70,132. Numismedia Wsl. Price for problem free NGC/PCGS coin in MS67: $1,075. NGC ID# 28LK, PCGS# 9371

8372 1935 Spanish Trail — Cleaning — PCGS Genuine. Unc Details. NGC Census: (0/1772). PCGS Population (1/3441). Mintage: 10,008. Numismedia Wsl. Price for problem free NGC/PCGS coin in MS60: $1,025.

8373 1925 Stone Mountain MS66 PCGS. PCGS Population (806/193). NGC Census: (676/144). Mintage: 1,314,709. Numismedia Wsl. Price for problem free NGC/PCGS coin in MS66: $300. NGC ID# 26H8, PCGS# 9378

8374 1925 Stone Mountain MS67 NGC. NGC Census: (133/11). PCGS Population (188/5). Mintage: 1,314,709. Numismedia Wsl. Price for problem free NGC/PCGS coin in MS67: $1,050. NGC ID# 26H8, PCGS# 9378

8375 1935 Texas PDS Set MS66 NGC. NGC Census: (0/0). PCGS Population (0/0). (Total: 3 coins)

8376 1936-D Texas MS67 PCGS. CAC. PCGS Population (341/13). NGC Census: (277/11). Mintage: 9,039. Numismedia Wsl. Price for problem free NGC/PCGS coin in MS67: $550. NGC ID# 28LV, PCGS# 9387

8377 1937-D Texas MS67 PCGS. CAC. PCGS Population (145/2). NGC Census: (96/4). Mintage: 6,605. Numismedia Wsl. Price for problem free NGC/PCGS coin in MS67: $585. NGC ID# 28LY, PCGS# 9391

8378 1937-S Texas MS67 PCGS. CAC. PCGS Population (101/0). NGC Census: (96/5). Mintage: 6,637. Numismedia Wsl. Price for problem free NGC/PCGS coin in MS67: $775. NGC ID# 28LZ, PCGS# 9392

8379 1937 Texas PDS Set MS66 NGC. NGC Census: (0/0). PCGS Population (0/0). (Total: 3 coins)

8380 1938 Texas MS66+ PCGS. CAC. PCGS Population (211/51). NGC Census: (233/47). Mintage: 3,780. Numismedia Wsl. Price for problem free NGC/PCGS coin in MS66: $525. NGC ID# 28M2, PCGS# 9394

8381 1938-S Texas MS66 PCGS. PCGS Population (306/75). NGC Census: (279/92). Mintage: 3,814. Numismedia Wsl. Price for problem free NGC/PCGS coin in MS66: $500. NGC ID# 28M4, PCGS# 9396

8382 1925 Vancouver MS65 NGC. CAC. NGC Census: (578/298). PCGS Population (699/378). Mintage: 14,994. Numismedia Wsl. Price for problem free NGC/PCGS coin in MS65: $850. NGC ID# 28M5, PCGS# 9399

8383 1927 Vermont MS65 NGC. NGC Census: (771/232). PCGS Population (958/404). Mintage: 28,142. Numismedia Wsl. Price for problem free NGC/PCGS coin in MS65: $550. NGC ID# 28M6, PCGS# 9401

8384 1927 Vermont MS66 PCGS. PCGS Population (373/31). NGC Census: (213/19). Mintage: 28,142. Numismedia Wsl. Price for problem free NGC/PCGS coin in MS66: $925. NGC ID# 28M6, PCGS# 9401

8385 1927 Vermont MS66 PCGS. CAC. PCGS Population (377/31). NGC Census: (213/19). Mintage: 28,142. Numismedia Wsl. Price for problem free NGC/PCGS coin in MS66: $925. NGC ID# 28M6, PCGS# 9401

8386 1946 Booker T. Washington MS67 NGC. NGC Census: (64/0). PCGS Population (73/1). Mintage: 1,000,546. Numismedia Wsl. Price for problem free NGC/PCGS coin in MS67: $1,100. NGC ID# 28M7, PCGS# 9404

8387 1946-S Booker T. Washington MS67 NGC. CAC. NGC Census: (79/2). PCGS Population (84/2). Mintage: 500,279. Numismedia Wsl. Price for problem free NGC/PCGS coin in MS67: $950. NGC ID# 28M9, PCGS# 9406

8388 1947 Booker T. Washington PDS Set MS66 NGC. NGC Census: (0/28). PCGS Population (0/0). (Total: 3 coins)

8389 **1949-S Booker T. Washington MS67 PCGS. CAC.** PCGS Population (48/0). NGC Census: (59/0). Mintage: 6,004. Numismedia Wsl. Price for problem free NGC/PCGS coin in MS67: $950. NGC ID# 28MJ, PCGS# 9418

8390 **1951-D Booker T. Washington MS67 NGC. CAC.** NGC Census: (39/0). PCGS Population (24/0). Mintage: 7,004. Numismedia Wsl. Price for problem free NGC/PCGS coin in MS67: $1,075. NGC ID# 28MP, PCGS# 9425

8391 **1951-S Booker T. Washington MS67 PCGS. CAC.** PCGS Population (45/0). NGC Census: (61/0). Mintage: 7,004. Numismedia Wsl. Price for problem free NGC/PCGS coin in MS67: $1,025. NGC ID# 28MR, PCGS# 9426

8392 **1951 Washington-Carver MS66 PCGS. CAC.** PCGS Population (68/3). NGC Census: (29/3). Mintage: 110,018. Numismedia Wsl. Price for problem free NGC/PCGS coin in MS66: $975. NGC ID# 28MS, PCGS# 9430

8393 **1952 Washington-Carver MS66+ PCGS. CAC.** PCGS Population (280/15). NGC Census: (287/16). Mintage: 2,006,292. Numismedia Wsl. Price for problem free NGC/PCGS coin in MS66: $200. NGC ID# 28MV, PCGS# 9434

8394 **1954 Washington-Carver MS66 NGC.** NGC Census: (63/4). PCGS Population (94/2). Mintage: 12,006. Numismedia Wsl. Price for problem free NGC/PCGS coin in MS66: $440. NGC ID# 28N3, PCGS# 9442

8395 **1936 Wisconsin MS67 PCGS.** PCGS Population (479/27). NGC Census: (406/28). Mintage: 25,015. Numismedia Wsl. Price for problem free NGC/PCGS coin in MS67: $735. NGC ID# 28N6, PCGS# 9447

8396 **1936 Wisconsin MS67 PCGS. CAC.** PCGS Population (485/27). NGC Census: (406/27). Mintage: 25,015. Numismedia Wsl. Price for problem free NGC/PCGS coin in MS67: $735. NGC ID# 28N6, PCGS# 9447

8397 **1936 York MS67 PCGS.** PCGS Population (571/25). NGC Census: (378/28). Mintage: 25,015. Numismedia Wsl. Price for problem free NGC/PCGS coin in MS67: $420. NGC ID# 28N7, PCGS# 9449

COMMEMORATIVE GOLD

8398 **1903 Louisiana Purchase, Jefferson, MS62 NGC.** NGC Census: (192/1821). PCGS Population (233/2839). Mintage: 17,500. Numismedia Wsl. Price for problem free NGC/PCGS coin in MS62: $570. NGC ID# 26HA, PCGS# 7443

8399 **1903 Louisiana Purchase, McKinley, MS64 PCGS.** PCGS Population (884/1122). NGC Census: (513/893). Mintage: 17,500. Numismedia Wsl. Price for problem free NGC/PCGS coin in MS64: $735. NGC ID# 26HB, PCGS# 7444

8400 **1903 Louisiana Purchase, McKinley, MS64 NGC.** NGC Census: (513/893). PCGS Population (884/1122). Mintage: 17,500. Numismedia Wsl. Price for problem free NGC/PCGS coin in MS64: $735. NGC ID# 26HB, PCGS# 7444

8401 **1904 Lewis and Clark AU55 NGC.** NGC Census: (15/1188). PCGS Population (39/1883). Mintage: 10,025. Numismedia Wsl. Price for problem free NGC/PCGS coin in AU55: $700. NGC ID# 26HC, PCGS# 7447

8402 **1915-S Panama-Pacific Gold Dollar MS63 PCGS.** PCGS Population (1001/3685). NGC Census: (504/2477). Mintage: 15,000. Numismedia Wsl. Price for problem free NGC/PCGS coin in MS63: $585. NGC ID# 26HE, PCGS# 7449

8403 **1915-S Panama-Pacific Gold Dollar MS64+ PCGS.** PCGS Population (1666/2019). NGC Census: (1057/1420). Mintage: 15,000. Numismedia Wsl. Price for problem free NGC/PCGS coin in MS64: $700. NGC ID# 26HE, PCGS# 7449

8404 **1916 McKinley MS64 NGC. CAC.** NGC Census: (770/886). PCGS Population (1371/1662). Mintage: 9,977. Numismedia Wsl. Price for problem free NGC/PCGS coin in MS64: $600. NGC ID# 26HF, PCGS# 7454

8405 **1922 Grant With Star — Improperly Cleaned — NGC Details. Unc.** NGC Census: (1/1271). PCGS Population (7/2265). Mintage: 5,016. Numismedia Wsl. Price for problem free NGC/PCGS coin in MS60: $1,325.

8406 **1926 Sesquicentennial MS63 PCGS.** PCGS Population (2367/6351). NGC Census: (1436/4135). Mintage: 46,019. Numismedia Wsl. Price for problem free NGC/PCGS coin in MS63: $550. NGC ID# 26HL, PCGS# 7466

8407 **1926 Sesquicentennial MS64 PCGS.** PCGS Population (4250/2099). NGC Census: (2824/1308). Mintage: 46,019. Numismedia Wsl. Price for problem free NGC/PCGS coin in MS64: $825. NGC ID# 26HL, PCGS# 7466

8408 **1926 Sesquicentennial MS64 NGC.** NGC Census: (2824/1311). PCGS Population (4246/2105). Mintage: 46,019. Numismedia Wsl. Price for problem free NGC/PCGS coin in MS64: $825. NGC ID# 26HL, PCGS# 7466

8409 **1926 Sesquicentennial MS64 PCGS.** PCGS Population (4246/2105). NGC Census: (2824/1311). Mintage: 46,019. Numismedia Wsl. Price for problem free NGC/PCGS coin in MS64: $825. NGC ID# 26HL, PCGS# 7466

8410 **1926 Sesquicentennial MS64 NGC. CAC.** NGC Census: (2824/1308). PCGS Population (4250/2099). Mintage: 46,019. Numismedia Wsl. Price for problem free NGC/PCGS coin in MS64: $825. NGC ID# 26HL, PCGS# 7466

8411 **1926 Sesquicentennial MS64 PCGS. CAC.** PCGS Population (4246/2105). NGC Census: (2824/1311). Mintage: 46,019. Numismedia Wsl. Price for problem free NGC/PCGS coin in MS64: $825. NGC ID# 26HL, PCGS# 7466

8412 **1926 Sesquicentennial MS64 PCGS. CAC.** PCGS Population (4250/2099). NGC Census: (2824/1308). Mintage: 46,019. Numismedia Wsl. Price for problem free NGC/PCGS coin in MS64: $825. NGC ID# 26HL, PCGS# 7466

8413 **1926 Sesquicentennial MS64+ NGC. CAC.** NGC Census: (2824/1311). PCGS Population (4246/2105). Mintage: 46,019. Numismedia Wsl. Price for problem free NGC/PCGS coin in MS64: $825. NGC ID# 26HL, PCGS# 7466

MODERN ISSUES

8414 **1986-W Statue of Liberty Gold Five Dollar MS70 NGC.** NGC Census: (2045). PCGS Population (317). Mintage: 95,248. Numismedia Wsl. Price for problem free NGC/PCGS coin in MS70: $360. NGC ID# 28PM, PCGS# 9622

8415 1993-W Bill of Rights Gold Five Dollar PR70 Ultra Cameo NGC. NGC Census: (1209). PCGS Population (248). Mintage: 78,651. Numismedia Wsl. Price for problem free NGC/PCGS coin in PR70: $380. NGC ID# 28S6, PCGS# 9673

8416 1995-W Olympic/Torch Runner Gold Five Dollar MS69 NGC. NGC Census: (277/700). PCGS Population (1503/234). Numismedia Wsl. Price for problem free NGC/PCGS coin in MS69: $340. NGC ID# 28TH, PCGS# 9732

8417 1995-W Olympic/Stadium Gold Five Dollar MS69 PCGS. PCGS Population (1781/185). NGC Census: (397/539). Numismedia Wsl. Price for problem free NGC/PCGS coin in MS69: $975. NGC ID# 28TK, PCGS# 9734

8418 1996-W Olympic/Flag Bearer Gold Five Dollar MS69 PCGS. PCGS Population (1491/131). NGC Census: (320/371). Numismedia Wsl. Price for problem free NGC/PCGS coin in MS69: $965. NGC ID# 28U2, PCGS# 9736

8419 1996-W Olympic/Cauldron Gold Five Dollar MS69 NGC. NGC Census: (459/318). PCGS Population (1551/73). Numismedia Wsl. Price for problem free NGC/PCGS coin in MS69: $950. NGC ID# 28U4, PCGS# 9738

8420 1997-W Franklin D. Roosevelt Gold Five Dollar MS69 NGC. NGC Census: (382/453). PCGS Population (1586/226). Mintage: 11,894. Numismedia Wsl. Price for problem free NGC/PCGS coin in MS69: $625. NGC ID# 28UJ, PCGS# 9748

8421 2000-W Library of Congress Bimetallic Ten Dollar PR69 Deep Cameo PCGS. PCGS Population (4064/488). NGC Census: (2408/557). Numismedia Wsl. Price for problem free NGC/PCGS coin in PR69: $1,000. NGC ID# 28V6, PCGS# 99784

8422 2000-W Library of Congress Bimetallic Ten Dollar PR69 Ultra Cameo NGC. NGC Census: (2408/557). PCGS Population (4067/488). Numismedia Wsl. Price for problem free NGC/PCGS coin in PR69: $1,000. NGC ID# 28V6, PCGS# 99784

8423 2000-W Library of Congress Bimetallic Ten Dollar PR69 Deep Cameo PCGS. PCGS Population (4067/488). NGC Census: (2408/557). Numismedia Wsl. Price for problem free NGC/PCGS coin in PR69: $1,000. NGC ID# 28V6, PCGS# 99784

8424 2003-W First Flight Gold Ten Dollar MS70 NGC. NGC Census: (1425). PCGS Population (467). Numismedia Wsl. Price for problem free NGC/PCGS coin in MS70: $850. NGC ID# 28VS, PCGS# 21003

8425 2007-W Jamestown Gold Five Dollar MS70 PCGS. PCGS Population (748). NGC Census: (2423). Numismedia Wsl. Price for problem free NGC/PCGS coin in MS70: $380. NGC ID# 28WE, PCGS# 147441

8426 2008-W Bald Eagle Gold Five Dollar PR70 Ultra Cameo NGC. NGC Census: (1379). PCGS Population (469). Numismedia Wsl. Price for problem free NGC/PCGS coin in PR70: $420. NGC ID# 28WP, PCGS# 394420

8427 2014-W Baseball Hall Of Fame Gold Five Dollar, Early Releases PR70 Ultra Cameo NGC. NGC Census: (1609). PCGS Population (687). PCGS# 525860

MODERN BULLION COINS

8428 1986 Tenth-Ounce Gold Eagle MS70 PCGS. PCGS Population (26). NGC Census: (551). Mintage: 912,609. Numismedia Wsl. Price for problem free NGC/PCGS coin in MS70: $575. NGC ID# 26KV, PCGS# 9803

8429 1986-W One-Ounce Gold Eagle PR70 Deep Cameo PCGS. PCGS Population (363). NGC Census: (1332). Numismedia Wsl. Price for problem free NGC/PCGS coin in PR70: $1,950. NGC ID# 28YV, PCGS# 9807

8430 1987-P Half-Ounce Gold Eagle PR70 Deep Cameo PCGS; 1987-W One-Ounce Gold Eagle PR70 Deep Cameo PCGS. (Total: 2 coins)

8431 1987-P Half-Ounce Gold Eagle PR70 Ultra Cameo NGC. NGC Census: (628). PCGS Population (212). Mintage: 143,398. Numismedia Wsl. Price for problem free NGC/PCGS coin in PR70: $1,075. NGC ID# 28Y9, PCGS# 9813

8432 1987-W One-Ounce Gold Eagle PR69 Deep Cameo PCGS. PCGS Population (6133/470). NGC Census: (2993/1259). Mintage: 147,498. Numismedia Wsl. Price for problem free NGC/PCGS coin in PR69: $1,500. NGC ID# 28YW, PCGS# 9815

8433 1987-W One-Ounce Gold Eagle PR70 Deep Cameo PCGS. PCGS Population (470). NGC Census: (1259). Mintage: 147,498. Numismedia Wsl. Price for problem free NGC/PCGS coin in PR70: $1,825. NGC ID# 28YW, PCGS# 9815

8434 1988-P Quarter-Ounce Gold Eagle PR70 Deep Cameo PCGS. PCGS Population (464). NGC Census: (1141). Numismedia Wsl. Price for problem free NGC/PCGS coin in PR70: $610. NGC ID# 28XM, PCGS# 9821

8435 1988-P Quarter-Ounce Gold Eagle PR70 Ultra Cameo NGC. NGC Census: (1141). PCGS Population (464). Numismedia Wsl. Price for problem free NGC/PCGS coin in PR70: $610. NGC ID# 28XM, PCGS# 9821

8436 1988-P Half-Ounce Gold Eagle PR70 Ultra Cameo NGC. NGC Census: (689). PCGS Population (228). Numismedia Wsl. Price for problem free NGC/PCGS coin in PR70: $1,100. NGC ID# 28YA, PCGS# 9823

8437 1988-W One-Ounce Gold Eagle PR70 Ultra Cameo NGC. NGC Census: (1142). PCGS Population (429). Numismedia Wsl. Price for problem free NGC/PCGS coin in PR70: $1,850. NGC ID# 28YX, PCGS# 9825

8438 1989-P Quarter-Ounce Gold Eagle PR70 Deep Cameo PCGS. PCGS Population (233). NGC Census: (732). Mintage: 54,170. Numismedia Wsl. Price for problem free NGC/PCGS coin in PR70: $540. NGC ID# 28XN, PCGS# 9831

8439 1989-P Quarter-Ounce Gold Eagle PR70 Ultra Cameo NGC. NGC Census: (732). PCGS Population (233). Mintage: 54,170. Numismedia Wsl. Price for problem free NGC/PCGS coin in PR70: $540. NGC ID# 28XN, PCGS# 9831

8440 1989-W One-Ounce Gold Eagle PR70 Deep Cameo PCGS. PCGS Population (408). NGC Census: (902). Mintage: 54,570. Numismedia Wsl. Price for problem free NGC/PCGS coin in PR70: $1,875. NGC ID# 28YY, PCGS# 9835

8441 1989-W One-Ounce Gold Eagle PR70 Ultra Cameo NGC. NGC Census: (902). PCGS Population (408). Mintage: 54,570. Numismedia Wsl. Price for problem free NGC/PCGS coin in PR70: $1,875. NGC ID# 28YY, PCGS# 9835

8442 1990-W One-Ounce Gold Eagle PR70 Deep Cameo PCGS. PCGS Population (279). NGC Census: (811). Numismedia Wsl. Price for problem free NGC/PCGS coin in PR70: $1,875. NGC ID# 28YZ, PCGS# 9845

8443 1990-W One-Ounce Gold Eagle PR70 Ultra Cameo NGC. NGC Census: (811). PCGS Population (279). Numismedia Wsl. Price for problem free NGC/PCGS coin in PR70: $1,875. NGC ID# 28YZ, PCGS# 9845

8444 1991 Half-Ounce Gold Eagle MS69 NGC. NGC Census: (3512/68). PCGS Population (959/13). Mintage: 24,100. Numismedia Wsl. Price for problem free NGC/PCGS coin in MS69: $3,125. NGC ID# 26NC, PCGS# 9852

8445 1992-P Gold Eagle Proof Set PR70 Deep Cameo PCGS. This set includes the Tenth-Ounce, Quarter-Ounce, Half-Ounce and One-Ounce Eagles. (Total: 4 coins)

8446 1992-P Half-Ounce Gold Eagle PR70 Ultra Cameo NGC. NGC Census: (474). PCGS Population (160). Numismedia Wsl. Price for problem free NGC/PCGS coin in PR70: $1,100. NGC ID# 28YE, PCGS# 9863

8447 1993-P Quarter-Ounce Gold Eagle PR70 Ultra Cameo NGC. NGC Census: (320). PCGS Population (148). Mintage: 46,464. Numismedia Wsl. Price for problem free NGC/PCGS coin in PR70: $800. NGC ID# 28XT, PCGS# 9871

8448 1994-W Gold Eagle Proof Set PR70 Deep Cameo PCGS. This set includes the Tenth-Ounce, Quarter-Ounce, Half-Ounce and One-Ounce Eagles. (Total: 4 coins)

8449 1994-W Half-Ounce Gold Eagle PR70 Deep Cameo PCGS. PCGS Population (193). NGC Census: (594). Numismedia Wsl. Price for problem free NGC/PCGS coin in PR70: $1,000. NGC ID# 28YG, PCGS# 9883

8450 1994-W Half-Ounce Gold Eagle PR70 Ultra Cameo NGC. NGC Census: (594). PCGS Population (193). Numismedia Wsl. Price for problem free NGC/PCGS coin in PR70: $1,000. NGC ID# 28YG, PCGS# 9883

8451 1994-W Half-Ounce Gold Eagle, Saint Gaudens Signature PR70 Deep Cameo PCGS. PCGS Population (1). NGC Census: (0). PCGS# 100098

8452 1995-W Gold Eagle Proof Set PR70 Deep Cameo PCGS. This set includes the Tenth-Ounce, Quarter-Ounce, Half-Ounce and One-Ounce Eagles. (Total: 4 coins)

8453 1995-W Gold Eagle Proof Set, PR70 Deep Cameo PCGS. This set includes: Tenth-Ounce, Quarter-Ounce, Half-Ounce and One-Ounce Eagles. (Total: 4 coins)

8454 1995-W Half-Ounce Gold Eagle PR70 Deep Cameo PCGS. PCGS Population (294). NGC Census: (1045). Numismedia Wsl. Price for problem free NGC/PCGS coin in PR70: $860. NGC ID# 28YH, PCGS# 9893

8455 1995-W Half-Ounce Gold Eagle PR70 Ultra Cameo NGC. NGC Census: (1045). PCGS Population (294). Numismedia Wsl. Price for problem free NGC/PCGS coin in PR70: $860. NGC ID# 28YH, PCGS# 9893

8456 1995-W One-Ounce Gold Eagle PR70 Ultra Cameo NGC. NGC Census: (16). PCGS Population (227). Numismedia Wsl. Price for problem free NGC/PCGS coin in PR70: $1,875. NGC ID# 28Z7, PCGS# 9895

8457 1996-W Gold Eagle Proof Set PR70 Deep Cameo PCGS. This set includes the Tenth-Ounce, Quarter-Ounce, Half-Ounce and One-Ounce Eagles. (Total: 4 coins)

8458 1996-W Half-Ounce Gold Eagle PR70 Ultra Cameo NGC. NGC Census: (649). PCGS Population (255). Numismedia Wsl. Price for problem free NGC/PCGS coin in PR70: $870. NGC ID# 28YJ, PCGS# 9907

8459 1996-W One-Ounce Gold Eagle PR70 Ultra Cameo NGC. NGC Census: (534). PCGS Population (181). Numismedia Wsl. Price for problem free NGC/PCGS coin in PR70: $2,175. NGC ID# 28Z8, PCGS# 9909

8460 1997-W Gold Eagle Proof Set PR70 Deep Cameo PCGS. This set includes the Tenth-Ounce, Quarter-Ounce, Half-Ounce and One-Ounce Eagles. (Total: 4 coins)

8461 1997-W Half-Ounce Gold Eagle PR70 Ultra Cameo NGC. NGC Census: (522). PCGS Population (154). Numismedia Wsl. Price for problem free NGC/PCGS coin in PR70: $940. NGC ID# 28YK, PCGS# 9919

8462 1997-W One-Ounce Gold Eagle PR70 Deep Cameo PCGS. PCGS Population (188). NGC Census: (570). Numismedia Wsl. Price for problem free NGC/PCGS coin in PR70: $1,975. NGC ID# 28Z9, PCGS# 9928

8463 1997-W One-Ounce Gold Eagle PR70 Ultra Cameo NGC. NGC Census: (570). PCGS Population (188). Numismedia Wsl. Price for problem free NGC/PCGS coin in PR70: $1,975. NGC ID# 28Z9, PCGS# 9928

8464 1997-W Quarter-Ounce Platinum Eagle PR70 Deep Cameo PCGS. PCGS Population (135). NGC Census: (534). Mintage: 18,726. Numismedia Wsl. Price for problem free NGC/PCGS coin in PR70: $460. NGC ID# 2934, PCGS# 9753

8465 1997-W Quarter-Ounce Platinum Eagle PR70 Deep Cameo PCGS. PCGS Population (135). NGC Census: (534). Mintage: 18,726. Numismedia Wsl. Price for problem free NGC/PCGS coin in PR70: $460. NGC ID# 2934, PCGS# 9753

8466 1998-W Half-Ounce Gold Eagle PR70 Deep Cameo PCGS. PCGS Population (127). NGC Census: (1328). Numismedia Wsl. Price for problem free NGC/PCGS coin in PR70: $950. NGC ID# 28YL, PCGS# 9936

8467 1998-W Half-Ounce Gold Eagle PR70 Ultra Cameo NGC. NGC Census: (1328). PCGS Population (127). Numismedia Wsl. Price for problem free NGC/PCGS coin in PR70: $950. NGC ID# 28YL, PCGS# 9936

8468 1998-W One-Ounce Gold Eagle PR70 Ultra Cameo NGC. NGC Census: (445). PCGS Population (117). Numismedia Wsl. Price for problem free NGC/PCGS coin in PR70: $2,450. NGC ID# 28ZA, PCGS# 9938

8469 1998-W Quarter-Ounce Platinum Eagle PR70 Deep Cameo PCGS. PCGS Population (135). NGC Census: (492). Mintage: 14,203. Numismedia Wsl. Price for problem free NGC/PCGS coin in PR70: $415. NGC ID# 2935, PCGS# 99766

8470 1998-W Quarter-Ounce Platinum Eagle PR70 Deep Cameo PCGS. PCGS Population (137). NGC Census: (492). Mintage: 14,203. Numismedia Wsl. Price for problem free NGC/PCGS coin in PR70: $415. NGC ID# 2935, PCGS# 99766

8471 1998-W Half-Ounce Platinum Eagle PR70 Deep Cameo PCGS. PCGS Population (474). NGC Census: (481). Mintage: 13,919. Numismedia Wsl. Price for problem free NGC/PCGS coin in PR70: $1,047. NGC ID# 293D, PCGS# 99767

8472 1998-W Half-Ounce Platinum Eagle PR70 Deep Cameo PCGS. PCGS Population (478). NGC Census: (481). Mintage: 13,919. Numismedia Wsl. Price for problem free NGC/PCGS coin in PR70: $1,047. NGC ID# 293D, PCGS# 99767

8473 1999-W Quarter-Ounce Gold Eagle PR70 Deep Cameo PCGS. PCGS Population (142). NGC Census: (785). Numismedia Wsl. Price for problem free NGC/PCGS coin in PR70: $628. NGC ID# 28XZ, PCGS# 9942

8474 1999-W Quarter-Ounce Gold Eagle PR70 Ultra Cameo NGC. NGC Census: (785). PCGS Population (142). Numismedia Wsl. Price for problem free NGC/PCGS coin in PR70: $628. NGC ID# 28XZ, PCGS# 9942

8475 1999-W Half-Ounce Gold Eagle PR70 Ultra Cameo NGC. NGC Census: (991). PCGS Population (136). Numismedia Wsl. Price for problem free NGC/PCGS coin in PR70: $1,200. NGC ID# 28YM, PCGS# 9944

8476 1999-W One-Ounce Gold Eagle PR70 Ultra Cameo NGC. NGC Census: (455). PCGS Population (115). Numismedia Wsl. Price for problem free NGC/PCGS coin in PR70: $2,150. NGC ID# 28ZB, PCGS# 9946

8477 1999-W Half-Ounce Platinum Eagle PR70 Deep Cameo PCGS. PCGS Population (241). NGC Census: (563). Mintage: 11,098. Numismedia Wsl. Price for problem free NGC/PCGS coin in PR70: $1,047. NGC ID# 293E, PCGS# 99775

8478 1999-W Half-Ounce Platinum Eagle PR70 Deep Cameo PCGS. PCGS Population (242). NGC Census: (563). Mintage: 11,098. Numismedia Wsl. Price for problem free NGC/PCGS coin in PR70: $1,047. NGC ID# 293E, PCGS# 99775

8479 2000-W Gold Eagle Proof Set PR70 Deep Cameo PCGS. This set includes the Tenth-Ounce, Quarter-Ounce, Half-Ounce and One-Ounce Eagles. (Total: 4 coins)

8480 **2000-W Half-Ounce Gold Eagle PR70 Ultra Cameo NGC.** NGC Census: (623). PCGS Population (169). Numismedia Wsl. Price for problem free NGC/PCGS coin in PR70: $850. NGC ID# 28YP, PCGS# 99952

8481 **2000-W One-Ounce Gold Eagle PR70 Deep Cameo PCGS.** PCGS Population (155). NGC Census: (593). Numismedia Wsl. Price for problem free NGC/PCGS coin in PR70: $2,125. NGC ID# 28ZC, PCGS# 99953

8482 **2000-W One-Ounce Gold Eagle PR70 Ultra Cameo NGC.** NGC Census: (593). PCGS Population (155). Numismedia Wsl. Price for problem free NGC/PCGS coin in PR70: $2,125. NGC ID# 28ZC, PCGS# 99953

8483 **2000-W Half-Ounce Platinum Eagle PR70 Deep Cameo PCGS.** PCGS Population (289). NGC Census: (561). Numismedia Wsl. Price for problem free NGC/PCGS coin in PR70: $1,047. NGC ID# 293F, PCGS# 99781

8484 **2000-W Half-Ounce Platinum Eagle PR70 Deep Cameo PCGS.** PCGS Population (293). NGC Census: (561). Numismedia Wsl. Price for problem free NGC/PCGS coin in PR70: $1,047. NGC ID# 293F, PCGS# 99781

8485 **2001-W Tenth-Ounce Gold Eagle PR70 Deep Cameo PCGS.** PCGS Population (127). NGC Census: (802). Numismedia Wsl. Price for problem free NGC/PCGS coin in PR70: $314. NGC ID# 28XH, PCGS# 99955

8486 **2001-W Quarter-Ounce Gold Eagle PR70 Ultra Cameo NGC.** NGC Census: (687). PCGS Population (182). Numismedia Wsl. Price for problem free NGC/PCGS coin in PR70: $628. NGC ID# 28Y3, PCGS# 99956

8487 **2001-W Half-Ounce Gold Eagle PR70 Deep Cameo PCGS.** PCGS Population (237). NGC Census: (726). Numismedia Wsl. Price for problem free NGC/PCGS coin in PR70: $920. NGC ID# 28YR, PCGS# 99957

8488 **2001-W One-Ounce Gold Eagle PR70 Deep Cameo PCGS.** PCGS Population (114). NGC Census: (558). Numismedia Wsl. Price for problem free NGC/PCGS coin in PR70: $2,275. NGC ID# 28ZD, PCGS# 99958

8489 **2001-W Quarter-Ounce Platinum Eagle PR70 Deep Cameo PCGS.** PCGS Population (164). NGC Census: (453). Numismedia Wsl. Price for problem free NGC/PCGS coin in PR70: $480. NGC ID# 2938, PCGS# 99787

8490 **2002-W Gold Eagle Proof Set, PR70 Ultra Cameo NGC. This set includes: Tenth-Ounce, Quarter-Ounce, Half-Ounce and One-Ounce Eagles.** (Total: 4 coins)

8491 **2002-W Half-Ounce Gold Eagle PR70 Deep Cameo PCGS.** Ex: U.S. Mint Director Signature Series, Philip Diehl, 35th U.S. Mint Director. PCGS Population (354). NGC Census: (775). Numismedia Wsl. Price for problem free NGC/PCGS coin in PR70: $850. NGC ID# 28YS, PCGS# 99962

8492 **2002-W Half-Ounce Gold Eagle PR70 Ultra Cameo NGC.** NGC Census: (775). PCGS Population (354). Numismedia Wsl. Price for problem free NGC/PCGS coin in PR70: $850. NGC ID# 28YS, PCGS# 99962

8493 **2002-W Half-Ounce Gold Eagle, Augustus Saint-Gaudens Signature, PR70 Deep Cameo PCGS.** PCGS Population (5). NGC Census: (0). PCGS# 100008

8494 **2002-W One-Ounce Gold Eagle PR69 Ultra Cameo NGC.** NGC Census: (714/685). PCGS Population (1240/229). Numismedia Wsl. Price for problem free NGC/PCGS coin in PR69: $1,500. NGC ID# 28ZE, PCGS# 99963

8495 **2002-W One-Ounce Gold Eagle PR70 Ultra Cameo NGC.** NGC Census: (685). PCGS Population (229). Numismedia Wsl. Price for problem free NGC/PCGS coin in PR70: $1,875. NGC ID# 28ZE, PCGS# 99963

8496 **2002-W Half-Ounce Platinum Eagle PR70 Deep Cameo PCGS.** PCGS Population (215). NGC Census: (477). Numismedia Wsl. Price for problem free NGC/PCGS coin in PR70: $1,047. NGC ID# 293H, PCGS# 99796

8497 **2002-W Half-Ounce Platinum Eagle PR70 Deep Cameo PCGS.** PCGS Population (218). NGC Census: (478). Numismedia Wsl. Price for problem free NGC/PCGS coin in PR70: $1,047. NGC ID# 293H, PCGS# 99796

8498 **2003-W Half-Ounce Gold Eagle PR70 Deep Cameo PCGS.** PCGS Population (410). NGC Census: (938). Numismedia Wsl. Price for problem free NGC/PCGS coin in PR70: $850. NGC ID# 26NR, PCGS# 99967

8499 **2003-W Half-Ounce Gold Eagle PR70 Deep Cameo PCGS.** PCGS Population (410). NGC Census: (938). Numismedia Wsl. Price for problem free NGC/PCGS coin in PR70: $850. NGC ID# 26NR, PCGS# 99967

8500 **2003-W Half-Ounce Gold Eagle PR70 Ultra Cameo NGC.** NGC Census: (938). PCGS Population (410). Numismedia Wsl. Price for problem free NGC/PCGS coin in PR70: $850. NGC ID# 26NR, PCGS# 99967

8501 **2003-W Half-Ounce Gold Eagle PR70 Ultra Cameo NGC.** NGC Census: (938). PCGS Population (410). Numismedia Wsl. Price for problem free NGC/PCGS coin in PR70: $850. NGC ID# 26NR, PCGS# 99967

8502 **2003-W Half-Ounce Gold Eagle, Augustus Saint Gaudens Signature PR70 Deep Cameo PCGS.** PCGS Population (2). NGC Census: (0). PCGS# 100009

8503 **2003-W One-Ounce Gold Eagle PR70 Deep Cameo PCGS.** PCGS Population (311). NGC Census: (821). Numismedia Wsl. Price for problem free NGC/PCGS coin in PR70: $1,875. NGC ID# 26PU, PCGS# 99968

8504 **2003-W One-Ounce Gold Eagle PR70 Deep Cameo PCGS.** PCGS Population (311). NGC Census: (821). Numismedia Wsl. Price for problem free NGC/PCGS coin in PR70: $1,875. NGC ID# 26PU, PCGS# 99968

8505 **2004-W Gold Eagle Proof Set PR70 Deep Cameo PCGS. This set includes the Tenth-Ounce, Quarter-Ounce, Half-Ounce and One-Ounce Eagles.** (Total: 4 coins)

8506 **2004-W One-Ounce Gold Eagle, Saint-Gaudens Signature, PR70 Deep Cameo PCGS.** PCGS Population (2). NGC Census: (0). PCGS# 100112

8507 **2005 Silver Eagle, First Strike MS70 PCGS.** PCGS Population (438). NGC Census: (0). PCGS# 89975

8508 **2005-W Tenth-Ounce Gold Eagle, Saint-Gaudens Signature, PR70 Deep Cameo PCGS.** PCGS Population (3). NGC Census: (0). PCGS# 100184

8509 **2005-W Gold Eagle Proof Set With Saint Gaudens Signature PR70 Deep Cameo PCGS. This set includes the Tenth-Ounce, Quarter-Ounce, Half-Ounce and One-Ounce Eagles.** (Total: 4 coins)

8510 2005-W Half-Ounce Gold Eagle **PR70 Deep Cameo PCGS.** Ex: U.S. Mint Director Signature Series. Philip Diehl, 35th U.S. Mint Director. PCGS Population (290). NGC Census: (1193). Numismedia Wsl. Price for problem free NGC/PCGS coin in PR70: $875. NGC ID# 28YU, PCGS# 99978

8511 2005-W Half-Ounce Gold Eagle **PR70 Deep Cameo PCGS.** PCGS Population (290). NGC Census: (1193). Numismedia Wsl. Price for problem free NGC/PCGS coin in PR70: $875. NGC ID# 28YU, PCGS# 99978

8512 2005-W Half-Ounce Gold Eagle PR70 **Ultra Cameo NGC.** NGC Census: (1193). PCGS Population (290). Numismedia Wsl. Price for problem free NGC/PCGS coin in PR70: $875. NGC ID# 28YU, PCGS# 99978

8513 2005-W One-Ounce Gold Eagle **PR70 Deep Cameo PCGS.** PCGS Population (279). NGC Census: (1137). Numismedia Wsl. Price for problem free NGC/PCGS coin in PR70: $1,725. NGC ID# 28ZG, PCGS# 99979

8514 2005-W One-Ounce Gold Eagle PR70 **Ultra Cameo NGC.** NGC Census: (1137). PCGS Population (279). Numismedia Wsl. Price for problem free NGC/PCGS coin in PR70: $1,725. NGC ID# 28ZG, PCGS# 99979

8515 2005-W Quarter-Ounce Platinum Eagle **PR70 Deep Cameo PCGS.** PCGS Population (154). NGC Census: (568). Numismedia Wsl. Price for problem free NGC/PCGS coin in PR70: $500. NGC ID# 293B, PCGS# 921109

8516 2005-W Half-Ounce Platinum Eagle **PR70 Deep Cameo PCGS.** PCGS Population (141). NGC Census: (490). Numismedia Wsl. Price for problem free NGC/PCGS coin in PR70: $1,047. NGC ID# 293K, PCGS# 921110

8517 2005-W Half-Ounce Platinum Eagle **PR70 Ultra Cameo NGC.** NGC Census: (490). PCGS Population (141). Numismedia Wsl. Price for problem free NGC/PCGS coin in PR70: $1,047. NGC ID# 293K, PCGS# 921110

8518 2006-W One-Ounce Silver, 20th **Anniversary, First Strike MS70 PCGS.** PCGS Population (287). NGC Census: (0). PCGS# 89991

8519 2006-P Silver Eagle, Reverse Proof, 20th Anniversary **PR70 First Strike PCGS.** PCGS Population (576). NGC Census: (0). PCGS# 899977

8520 2006-W Gold Eagle Proof Set, PR70 **Ultra Cameo NGC.** This set includes: Tenth-Ounce, Quarter-Ounce, Half-Ounce and One-Ounce Eagles. (Total: 4 coins)

8521 2006-W Quarter-Ounce Gold Eagle, Saint-Gaudens Signature, **PR70 Deep Cameo PCGS.** PCGS Population (1). NGC Census: (0). PCGS# 100196

8522 2006-W Half-Ounce Gold Eagle **PR70 Deep Cameo PCGS.** Ex: U.S. Mint Director Signature Series. Philip Diehl, 35th U.S. Mint Director. PCGS Population (451). NGC Census: (0). Numismedia Wsl. Price for problem free NGC/PCGS coin in PR70: $885. NGC ID# 26NW, PCGS# 99987

8523 2006-W Half-Ounce Gold Eagle, Saint-Gaudens Signature, **PR70 Deep Cameo PCGS.** PCGS Population (1). NGC Census: (0). PCGS# 100197

8524 2006-W One-Ounce Gold Eagle **PR70 Deep Cameo PCGS.** PCGS Population (0). NGC Census: (2049). Numismedia Wsl. Price for problem free NGC/PCGS coin in PR70: $1,700. NGC ID# 26Y4, PCGS# 99988

8525 2006-W One-Ounce Gold Buffalo **PR70 Deep Cameo PCGS.** .9999 Fine. PCGS Population (4445). NGC Census: (15719). Numismedia Wsl. Price for problem free NGC/PCGS coin in PR70: $1,450. NGC ID# 26RM, PCGS# 9990

8526 2006-W Half-Ounce Platinum Eagle **PR70 Deep Cameo PCGS.** PCGS Population (200). NGC Census: (641). PCGS# 921118

8527 2007-W Gold Eagle Proof Set, PR70 **Deep Cameo PCGS.** This set includes: Tenth-Ounce, Quarter-Ounce, Half-Ounce and One-Ounce Eagles. (Total: 4 coins)

8528 2007-W Gold Eagle Proof Set With Saint Gaudens Signature **PR70 Deep Cameo PCGS.** This set includes the Tenth-Ounce, Quarter-Ounce, Half-Ounce and One-Ounce Eagles. (Total: 4 coins)

8529 2007-W Half-Ounce Gold Eagle **PR70 Deep Cameo PCGS.** Ex: U.S. Mint Director Signature Series. Philip Diehl, 35th U.S. Mint Director. PCGS Population (296). NGC Census: (0). Numismedia Wsl. Price for problem free NGC/PCGS coin in PR70: $880. NGC ID# 26NZ, PCGS# 148080

8530 2007-W Half-Ounce Gold Eagle PR70 **Deep Cameo PCGS.** PCGS Population (296). NGC Census: (0). Numismedia Wsl. Price for problem free NGC/PCGS coin in PR70: $880. NGC ID# 26NZ, PCGS# 148080

8531 2007-W One-Ounce Gold Buffalo **PR70 Deep Cameo PCGS.** .9999 Fine. PCGS Population (753). NGC Census: (3318). Numismedia Wsl. Price for problem free NGC/PCGS coin in PR70: $1,450. NGC ID# 26RP, PCGS# 149583

8532 2007-W One-Ounce Gold Eagle **PR70 Deep Cameo PCGS.** PCGS Population (257). NGC Census: (0). Numismedia Wsl. Price for problem free NGC/PCGS coin in PR70: $1,775. NGC ID# 26R4, PCGS# 148082

8533 2007-W Half-Ounce Platinum Eagle **PR70 Deep Cameo PCGS.** PCGS Population (523). NGC Census: (865). Numismedia Wsl. Price for problem free NGC/PCGS coin in PR70: $1,047. NGC ID# 26TU, PCGS# 149577

8534 2007-W Half-Ounce Platinum Eagle, 10th Anniversary **PR69 Deep Cameo PCGS.** PCGS Population (267/109). NGC Census: (554/2127). PCGS# 393053

8535 2007-W Half-Ounce Platinum Eagle, Reverse Proof, 10th Anniversary **PR69 PCGS.** PCGS Population (512/646). NGC Census: (0/0). Numismedia Wsl. Price for problem free NGC/PCGS coin in PR69: $1,047. NGC ID# 293L, PCGS# 393055

8536 2008-W Silver Eagle, Reverse of 2007 **MS70 NGC.** NGC Census: (4441). PCGS Population (313). Numismedia Wsl. Price for problem free NGC/PCGS coin in MS70: $725. NGC ID# 26KM, PCGS# 396411

8537 2008-W Silver Eagle, Reverse of 2007, First Strike **MS70 PCGS.** PCGS Population (202). NGC Census: (0). PCGS# 396437

8538 **2008-W Gold Eagle Proof Set PR70 Deep Cameo PCGS.** This set includes the Tenth-Ounce, Quarter-Ounce, Half-Ounce and One-Ounce Eagles. (Total: 4 coins)

8539 **2008-W Gold Eagle Proof Set, PR70 Deep Cameo PCGS.** This set includes: Tenth-Ounce, Quarter-Ounce, Half-Ounce and One-Ounce Eagles. (Total: 4 coins)

8540 **2008-W Tenth-Ounce Gold Buffalo, First Year Of Issue MS70 NGC.** .9999 Fine. NGC Census: (2387). PCGS Population (620). Numismedia Wsl. Price for problem free NGC/PCGS coin in MS70: $510. PCGS# 399926

8541 **2008-W Tenth-Ounce Gold Buffalo, Fraser Signature, MS70 PCGS.** .9999 Fine. PCGS Population (9). NGC Census: (0). PCGS# 91013

8542 **2008-W Tenth-Ounce Gold Buffalo, James Earle Fraser Signature, MS70 PCGS.** .9999 Fine. PCGS Population (9). NGC Census: (0). PCGS# 91013

8543 **2008-W Tenth-Ounce Gold Buffalo, First Year of Issue PR70 Ultra Cameo NGC.** .9999 Fine. NGC Census: (1836). PCGS Population (451). Numismedia Wsl. Price for problem free NGC/PCGS coin in PR70: $640. PCGS# 399932

8544 **2008-W Quarter-Ounce Gold Eagle, Saint Gaudens Signature PR70 Deep Cameo PCGS.** PCGS Population (1). NGC Census: (0). PCGS# 100230

8545 **2008-W Quarter-Ounce Gold Buffalo, Fraser Signature, MS70 PCGS.** .9999 Fine. PCGS Population (9). NGC Census: (0). PCGS# 91014

8546 **2008-W Quarter-Ounce Gold Buffalo, James Earle Fraser Signature, MS70 PCGS.** .9999 Fine. PCGS Population (9). NGC Census: (0). PCGS# 91014

8547 **2008-W Half-Ounce Gold Eagle PR70 Deep Cameo PCGS.** Ex: U.S. Mint Director Signature Series. Philip Diehl, 35th U.S. Mint Director. PCGS Population (418). NGC Census: (0). Numismedia Wsl. Price for problem free NGC/PCGS coin in PR70: $950. PCGS# 393074

8548 **2008-W Half-Ounce Gold Eagle PR70 Deep Cameo PCGS.** PCGS Population (418). NGC Census: (0). Numismedia Wsl. Price for problem free NGC/PCGS coin in PR70: $950. PCGS# 393074

8549 **2008-W Half-Ounce Gold Eagle, Saint-Gaudens Signature, PR70 Deep Cameo PCGS.** PCGS Population (3). NGC Census: (0). PCGS# 100231

8550 **2008-W Half-Ounce Gold Eagle, Saint-Gaudens Signature, PR70 Deep Cameo PCGS.** PCGS Population (3). NGC Census: (0). PCGS# 100231

8551 **2008-W Half-Ounce Gold Buffalo, Fraser Signature, MS70 PCGS.** .9999 Fine. PCGS Population (5). NGC Census: (0). PCGS# 91015

8552 **2008-W Half-Ounce Gold Buffalo, James Earle Fraser Signature, MS70 PCGS.** .9999 Fine. PCGS Population (5). NGC Census: (0). PCGS# 91015

8553 **2008 Quarter-Ounce Platinum Eagle MS70 NGC.** NGC Census: (0). PCGS Population (274). Numismedia Wsl. Price for problem free NGC/PCGS coin in MS70: $475. PCGS# 393106

8554 **2009 One-Ounce Gold Ultra High Relief Twenty Dollar MS70 PCGS.** PCGS Population (6498). NGC Census: (8064). Numismedia Wsl. Price for problem free NGC/PCGS coin in MS70: $2,425. NGC ID# 26S4, PCGS# 407404

8555 **2009-W One-Ounce Gold Buffalo PR70 Deep Cameo PCGS.** .9999 Fine. PCGS Population (1365). NGC Census: (2000). Numismedia Wsl. Price for problem free NGC/PCGS coin in PR70: $1,500. NGC ID# 26RU, PCGS# 414463

8556 **2010-W Gold Eagle Proof Set PR70 Deep Cameo PCGS.** This set includes the Tenth-Ounce, Quarter-Ounce, Half-Ounce and One-Ounce Eagles. (Total: 4 coins)

8557 **2010-W Quarter-Ounce Gold Eagle, Saint-Gaudens Signature, PR70 Deep Cameo PCGS.** PCGS Population (3). NGC Census: (0). PCGS# 100259

8558 **2010-W Half-Ounce Gold Eagle PR70 Deep Cameo PCGS.** PCGS Population (884). NGC Census: (0). Numismedia Wsl. Price for problem free NGC/PCGS coin in PR70: $860. NGC ID# 26P7, PCGS# 502743

8559 **2010-W Half-Ounce Gold Eagle PR70 Deep Cameo PCGS.** PCGS Population (884). NGC Census: (0). Numismedia Wsl. Price for problem free NGC/PCGS coin in PR70: $860. NGC ID# 26P7, PCGS# 502743

8560 **2010-W Half-Ounce Gold Eagle PR70 Deep Cameo PCGS.** Ex: U.S. Mint Director Signature Series, Philip Diehl, 35th U.S. Mint Director. PCGS Population (884). NGC Census: (0). Numismedia Wsl. Price for problem free NGC/PCGS coin in PR70: $860. NGC ID# 26P7, PCGS# 502743

8561 **2010-W One-Ounce Gold Eagle PR70 Deep Cameo PCGS.** PCGS Population (911). NGC Census: (347). Numismedia Wsl. Price for problem free NGC/PCGS coin in PR70: $1,700. NGC ID# 26RA, PCGS# 415544

8562 **2010-W One-Ounce Gold Eagle PR70 Deep Cameo PCGS.** PCGS Population (911). NGC Census: (347). Numismedia Wsl. Price for problem free NGC/PCGS coin in PR70: $1,700. NGC ID# 26RA, PCGS# 415544

8563 **2010-W One-Ounce Gold Eagle, Saint-Gaudens Signature, PR70 Deep Cameo PCGS.** PCGS Population (2). NGC Census: (0). PCGS# 100257

8564 **2010-W One-Ounce Gold Buffalo PR70 Deep Cameo PCGS.** .9999 Fine. PCGS Population (1020). NGC Census: (1527). Numismedia Wsl. Price for problem free NGC/PCGS coin in PR70: $1,500. PCGS# 418865

8565 **2010-W One-Ounce Platinum Eagle PR70 Deep Cameo PCGS.** PCGS Population (232). NGC Census: (335). Numismedia Wsl. Price for problem free NGC/PCGS coin in PR70: $1,775. NGC ID# 26UL, PCGS# 415546

8566 **2011 Silver Eagle, 25th Anniversary, Early Releases Set NGC Black.** This set includes: 2011 MS70, 2011-S MS70, 2011-W MS70, 2011-P Reverse Proof PR70 and a 2011-W PR70 Ultra Cameo. (Total: 5 coins)

8567 **2011-W Gold Eagle Proof Set With Saint Gaudens Signature PR70 Deep Cameo PCGS.** This set includes the Tenth-Ounce, Quarter-Ounce, Half-Ounce and One-Ounce Eagles. (Total: 4 coins)

8568 **2011-W Quarter-Ounce Gold Eagle, Saint-Gaudens Signature, PR70 Deep Cameo PCGS.** PCGS Population (2). NGC Census: (0). PCGS# 100266

8569 **2011-W One-Ounce Gold Eagle, Saint-Gaudens Signature, PR70 Deep Cameo PCGS.** PCGS Population (2). NGC Census: (0). PCGS# 100270

8570 2011-W One-Ounce Platinum Eagle PR70 Deep Cameo PCGS. PCGS Population (259). NGC Census: (410). Numismedia Wsl. Price for problem free NGC/PCGS coin in PR70: $1,750. NGC ID# 26UM, PCGS# 507770

8571 2012-W Quarter-Ounce Gold Eagle, Saint-Gaudens Signature, PR70 Deep Cameo PCGS. PCGS Population (1). NGC Census: (0). PCGS# 100286

8572 2012-W Half-Ounce Gold Eagle, Saint-Gaudens Signature, PR70 Deep Cameo PCGS. PCGS Population (2). NGC Census: (0). PCGS# 100287

8573 2012-W One-Ounce Gold Buffalo PR70 Deep Cameo PCGS. .9999 Fine. PCGS Population (243). NGC Census: (644). PCGS# 511523

8574 2012-W One-Ounce Platinum Eagle PR70 Deep Cameo PCGS. PCGS Population (219). NGC Census: (376). Numismedia Wsl. Price for problem free NGC/PCGS coin in PR70: $1,775. NGC ID# 2U2H, PCGS# 515152

8575 2013-W One-Ounce Gold American Eagle PR70 Deep Cameo PCGS. PCGS Population (460). NGC Census: (0). PCGS# 518214

8576 2013-W One-Ounce Gold Buffalo, Reverse Proof, 100th Anniversary PR70 PCGS. .9999 Fine. PCGS Population (856). NGC Census: (1930). PCGS# 520050

8577 2013-W One-Ounce Gold Buffalo, Reverse Proof PR70 NGC. .9999 Fine. NGC Census: (1930). PCGS Population (856). PCGS# 520050

8578 2013-W One-Ounce Gold Buffalo, Reverse Proof PR70 NGC. .9999 Fine. NGC Census: (1930). PCGS Population (856). PCGS# 520050

8579 "1876" (2005) One-Ounce Gold George T. Morgan $100 Union, Gem Proof Ultra Cameo NGC. Accompanied by a presentation box and certificate from the New York Mint.

8580 1853 Liberty Octagonal 1 Dollar, BG-514, High R.5, — Obverse Damage — NGC Details. Unc. NGC Census: (0/3). PCGS Population (1/27).

CALIFORNIA FRACTIONAL GOLD

8581 1853 Liberty Octagonal 1 Dollar, BG-530, R.2, MS61 NGC. NGC Census: (22/38). PCGS Population (27/58). PCGS# 10507

8582 1871 Liberty Octagonal 25 Cents, BG-714, R.3, MS64 Prooflike NGC. NGC Census: (2/1). PCGS Population (0/0). PCGS# 710541

8583 1874 Indian Octagonal 25 Cents, BG-795, R.3, MS65 Prooflike NGC. NGC Census: (10/4). PCGS Population (0/0). PCGS# 710622

8584 1881 Indian Round 25 Cents, BG-887, R.3, MS64 Prooflike NGC. NGC Census: (5/17). PCGS Population (0/2). PCGS# 710748

8585 1864 Liberty Round 50 Cents, BG-1015, R.7, AU55 PCGS. PCGS Population (1/5). NGC Census: (0/0). PCGS# 10844

COINS OF HAWAII

8586 1883 Hawaii Half Dollar AU55 PCGS. PCGS Population (64/284). NGC Census: (58/228). Mintage: 700,000. PCGS# 10991

8587 1883 Hawaii Dollar XF45 PCGS. PCGS Population (170/264). NGC Census: (65/211). Mintage: 500,000. PCGS# 10995

8588 1883 Hawaii Dollar — Improperly Cleaned — NGC Details. AU. NGC Census: (30/181). PCGS Population (64/200). Mintage: 500,000.

8589 1883 Hawaii Dollar — Cleaned — ANACS. AU50 Details. NGC Census: (29/180). PCGS Population (64/200). Mintage: 500,000.

PATTERNS

8590 1859 Indian Cent, Judd-228, Pollock-272, R.1, — Spot Removed — PCGS Genuine. Unc Details. NGC Census: (0/112). PCGS Population (2/271).

8591 1869 Three Cent Nickel, Judd-676, Pollock-753, 755, R.4, — Cleaned — PCGS Genuine. AU Details. NGC Census: (1/21). PCGS Population (3/42).

ERRORS

8592 Punched Copper Cent Planchet Strip. A rectangular section, 150 mm x 60 mm of "webbing." The interior has 20 complete cent-sized punches, and the margins have 8 partial punches.

8593 1872 Indian Cent — Obverse Struck Thru — AU53 Brown NGC.

8594 1998 Lincoln Cent — Over Struck on a 1998-P 10C, Double Denomination — MS67 NGC.

8595 1936 Buffalo Nickel — Struck 5% Off-Center — MS63 PCGS.

8596 Unpunched Clad Dime Planchet Strip. 29 mm x 127 mm.

8597 197X-D Washington Quarter — Struck on a Cent Planchet — MS63 PCGS.

8598 1972-D Washington Quarter — Double Struck On A 5C Planchet (5.0 g) — MS64 NGC.

8599 1999 Statehood Quarter — Multi Struck Fragment — MS63 ANACS.

8600 1921-S Walking Liberty Half Dollar — Obverse Planchet Lamination — VF25 PCGS.

8601 1942 Walking Liberty Half Dollar — Double Struck in Collar, Close Overlap — XF45 PCGS.

8602 1881-CC Morgan Dollar — Reverse Struck Thru — MS63 NGC.

8603 1883-O Morgan Dollar — Broadstruck — MS62 NGC.

8604 1895-S Morgan Dollar — Struck-Thru Obverse — VF20 PCGS.

8605 1921-S Morgan Dollar — Uncentered Broadstrike — AU55 PCGS.

8606 1923 Peace Dollar — Planchet Crack @ 2:00 — MS65 NGC.

8607 1976-D Type One Eisenhower Dollar — Double Struck, Second Strike 95% Off Center — MS64 NGC.

8608 1999-P Susan B. Anthony Dollar — Struck 25% Off Center — MS64 PCGS.

8609 1999-P Susan B. Anthony Dollar — Broadstruck Out of Collar — MS65 PCGS.

8610 1851 Gold Dollar — Rotated Dies — AU58 NGC.

8611 1861 Gold Dollar — Medallic Alignment — MS61 NGC.

8612 1877 Gold Dollar — Reverse Struck Thru — MS61 NGC.

8613 1911 Indian Quarter Eagle — Broadstruck Out of Collar — AU58 PCGS.

8614 **1998 One-Ounce Gold Eagle — Struck Thru Reverse, Coin #1/5 — MS68 PCGS.** PCGS Population (213/1899). NGC Census: (42/1498). Numismedia Wsl. Price for problem free NGC/PCGS coin in MS68: $1,325.

U.S. MINT MEDAL

8615 **(1849) Major General Winfield Scott SP62 PCGS.** Julian-MI-27. Bronzed copper.

SO-CALLED DOLLARS

8616 **1909 Alaska-Yukon-Pacific Exposition, W.H. Seward, Chief Seattle, MS62 NGC.** HK-363A.

8617 **(1962) Continental Dollar Bashlow Restrike, Silver, MS65 Prooflike NGC.** HK-852A, R.4. 'S' on Reverse.

8618 **1933 Century of Progress, Colorado, MS62 NGC.** HK-867.

MISCELLANEOUS MEDALS AND TOKENS

8619 **"1852" (2009) Humbert Fifty Dollar Facsimile, Pewter Die Trial, Gem Proof NGC.** One of 49 pieces struck.

GSA DOLLARS

8620 **1878-CC GSA Hoard MS63 NGC.** NGC Census: (1119/831). PCGS Population (25/3). Mintage: 2,212,000. PCGS# 518845

8621 **1881-CC GSA Hoard MS64+ NGC.** NGC Census: (3136/1913). PCGS Population (52/28). Mintage: 296,000.

8622 **1881-CC GSA Hoard MS64+ NGC.** NGC Census: (3136/1913). PCGS Population (52/28). Mintage: 296,000.

8623 **1881-CC GSA HOARD MS63 Prooflike NGC.** NGC Census: (0/0). PCGS Population (0/0). PCGS# 518863

8624 **1883-CC GSA Hoard MS66 NGC.** Box included. NGC Census: (682/26). PCGS Population (11/0). Mintage: 1,204,000. PCGS# 518869

8625 **1885-CC GSA Hoard MS63 NGC.** NGC Census: (2382/4641). PCGS Population (52/76). Mintage: 228,000.

PROOF SETS

8626 **1938 Proof Set NGC.** The set includes: 1C PR65 Red and Brown, 5C PR64, 10C PR66, 25C PR66 and 50C PR65. (Total: 5 coins)

8627 **1939 Proof Set NGC.** The set includes: 1C PR64 Red and Brown, 5C Reverse of 1938 PR66, 10C PR66, 25C PR67 and 50C PR66. (Total: 5 coins)

8628 **1940 Proof Set NGC.** The set includes: 1C PR62 Red and Brown, 5C Reverse of 1940 PR65, 10C PR66, 25C PR64 and 50C — Obverse Scratched — Proof Details. (Total: 5 coins)

End of Auction

HERITAGE AUCTIONS HA.com **BID SHEET**

3500 Maple Avenue | Dallas, Texas 75219-3941
Direct Client Service Line – Toll Free: 866-835-3243 | Fax: 214-409-1425

U.S. Coins Auction #1212

Bid Live & Online at HA.com/1212

ALL INFORMATION MUST BE COMPLETED AND FORM SIGNED

CLIENT# (IF KNOWN)   BIDDER#

❏ Mr. ❏ Mrs. ❏ Ms. ❏ Dr.
NAME

ADDRESS

CITY   **STATE**   **ZIP CODE**   **COUNTRY**

EMAIL

(COUNTRY CODE)   **DAY PHONE**   (COUNTRY CODE)   **NIGHT PHONE**

(COUNTRY CODE)   **CELL**   (COUNTRY CODE)   **FAX**

❏ **IF NECESSARY, PLEASE INCREASE MY BIDS BY** ❏1 ❏2 ❏3 **INCREMENT(S)**
Lots will be purchased as much below top bids as possible.

❏ **I WANT TO LIMIT MY BIDDING TO A TOTAL OF $** _____
at the hammer amount for all lots listed on this bid sheet. I am aware that by utilizing the Budget Bidding feature, all bids on this sheet will be affected. If I intend to have regular bidding on other lots I will need to use a separate bid sheet.

Do you want to receive an email, text message, or fax confirming receipt of your bids?
❏ Email   ❏ Cell Phone Text   ❏ Fax

Payment by check may result in your property not being released until purchase funds clear our bank. Checks must be drawn on a U.S. bank. All bids are subject to the applicable Buyer's Premium. See HA.com for details.

I have read and agree to all of the Terms and Conditions of Auction: inclusive of paying interest at the lesser of 1.5% per month (18% per annum) or the maximum contract interest rate under applicable state law from the date of auction.

REFERENCES: New bidders who are unknown to us must furnish satisfactory industry references or a valid credit card in advance of the auction date.

(Signature required) *Please make a copy of this bid sheet for your records.*

❏ I HAVE PREVIOUSLY BOUGHT FROM HERITAGE AUCTIONS

❏ I HAVE A RESALE PERMIT – *please contact 877-HERITAGE (437-4824)*

Non-Internet bids (including but not limited to, podium, fax, phone and mail bids) may be submitted at any time and are treated similar to floor bids. These types of bids must be on-increment or at a half increment (called a cut bid). Any podium, fax, phone or mail bids that do not conform to a full or half increment will be rounded up or down to the nearest full or half increment and will be considered your high bid.

Current Bid	Bid Increment
< – $10	$1
$10 – $29	$2
$30 – $49	$3
$50 – $99	$5
$100 – $199	$10
$200 – $299	$20
$300 – $499	$25
$500 – $999	$50
$1,000 – $1,999	$100
$2,000 – $2,999	$200
$3,000 – $4,999	$250
$5,000 – $9,999	$500
$10,000 – $19,999	$1,000
$20,000 – $29,999	$2,000
$30,000 – $49,999	$2,500
$50,000 – $99,999	$5,000
$100,000 – $199,999	$10,000
$200,000 – $299,999	$20,000
$300,000 – $499,999	$25,000
$500,000 – $999,999	$50,000
$1,000,000 – $4,999,999	$100,000
$5,000,000 – $9,999,999	$250,000
>$10,000,000	$500,000

Bid in whole dollar amounts only.   Please print your bids.

LOT NO.	AMOUNT	LOT NO.	AMOUNT	LOT NO.	AMOUNT

Last Name: _____

Bid in whole dollar amounts only.   **Please print your bids.**

LOT NO.	AMOUNT	LOT NO.	AMOUNT	LOT NO.	AMOUNT

Please make a copy of this bid sheet for your records.

7 Easy Ways to Bid

1 Internet
Simply go to www.HA.com, find the auction you are looking for and click "View Lots" or type your desired Lot # into the "Search" field. Every lot is listed with full descriptions and images. Enter your bid and click "Place Bid." Internet bids will be accepted until 10:00 PM CT the day before the live auction session takes place.

2 eMail
You can also email your bids to us at Bid@HA.com. List lot numbers and bids, and include your name, address, phone, and customer # (if known) as well as a statement of your acceptance of the Terms and Conditions of Sale. Email bids will be accepted up to 24 hours before the live auction.

3 Postal Mail
Simply complete the Bid Sheet on the reverse side of this page with your bids on the lots you want, sign it and mail it in. If yours is the high bid on any lot, we act as your representative at the auction and buy the lot as cheaply as competition permits.

4 In Person
Come to the auction and view the lots in person and bid live on the floor.

5 FAX
Follow the instructions for completing your mail bid, but this time FAX it to (214) 409-1425. FAX bids will be accepted until 12:00 PM CT the day prior to the auction date.

6 Live By Phone
Call 877-HERITAGE (437-4824) Ext. 1150 and ask for phone bidding assistance at least 24 hours prior to the auction.

7 Live using HERITAGE Live!
Auctions designated as "Heritage Live Enabled" have continuous bidding from the time the auction is posted on our site through the live event. When normal Internet bidding ends, visit HA.com/Live and continue to place Live Proxy bids. When the item hits the auction block, you can continue to bid live against the floor and other live bidders.

Because of the many avenues by which bids may be submitted, there is the real possibility of a tie for the high bid. In the event of a tie, Internet bidders, within their credit limit, will win by default.

Terms and Conditions of Auction

Auctioneer and Auction:

1. This Auction is presented by Heritage Auctions, a d/b/a/ of Heritage Auctioneers & Galleries, Inc., or Heritage Auctions, Inc., or Heritage Numismatic Auctions, Inc., or Heritage Vintage Sports Auctions, Inc., or Currency Auctions of America, Inc., as identified with the applicable licensing information on the title page of the catalog or on the HA.com Internet site (the "Auctioneer"). The Auction is conducted under these Terms and Conditions of Auction and applicable state and local law. Announcements and corrections from the podium and those made through the Terms and Conditions of Auctions appearing on the Internet at HA.com supersede those in the printed catalog.

Buyer's Premium:

2. All bids are subject to a Buyer's Premium which is in addition to the placed successful bid:

- Fifteen percent (15%) on Domain Names & Intellectual Property Auction lots;
- Seventeen and one-half percent (17.5%) on Currency, US Coin, and World & Ancient Coin Auction lots, except for Gallery Auction lots as noted below;
- Nineteen and one-half percent (19.5%) on Comic, Movie Poster, Sports Collectibles, and Gallery Auction (sealed bid auctions of mostly bulk numismatic material) lots;
- Twenty-two percent (22%) on Wine Auction lots;
- For lots in all other categories not listed above, the Buyer's Premium per lot is twenty-five percent (25%) on the first $100,000 (minimum $14), plus twenty percent (20%) of any amount between $100,000 and $1,000,000, plus twelve percent (12%) of any amount over $1,000,000.

Auction Venues:

3. The following Auctions are conducted solely on the Internet: Heritage Weekly Internet Auctions (Coin, Currency, Comics, Rare Books, Jewelry & Watches, Guitars & Musical Instruments, and Vintage Movie Posters); Heritage Monthly Internet Auctions (Sports, World Coins and Rare Wine). Signature® Auctions and Grand Format Auctions accept bids from the Internet, telephone, fax, or mail first, followed by a floor bidding session; HeritageLive! and real- time telephone bidding are available to registered clients during these auctions.

Bidders:

4. Any person participating or registering for the Auction agrees to be bound by and accepts these Terms and Conditions of Auction ("Bidder(s)").
5. All Bidders must meet Auctioneer's qualifications to bid. Any Bidder who is not a client in good standing of the Auctioneer may be disqualified at Auctioneer's sole option and will not be awarded lots. Such determination may be made by Auctioneer in its sole and unlimited discretion, at any time prior to, during, or even after the close of the Auction. Auctioneer reserves the right to exclude any person from the auction.
6. If an entity places a bid, then the person executing the bid on behalf of the entity agrees to personally guarantee payment for any successful bid.

Credit:

7. In order to place bids, Bidders who have not established credit with the Auctioneer must either furnish satisfactory credit information (including two collectibles-related business references) or supply valid credit card information along with a social security number, well in advance of the Auction. Bids placed through our Interactive Internet program will only be accepted from pre-registered Bidders. Bidders who are not members of HA.com or affiliates should preregister at least 48 hours before the start of the first session (exclusive of holidays or weekends) to allow adequate time to contact references. Credit will be granted at the discretion of Auctioneer. Additionally Bidders who have not previously established credit or who wish to bid in excess of their established credit history may be required to provide their social security number or the last four digits thereof so a credit check may be performed prior to Auctioneer's acceptance of a bid. Check writing privileges and immediate delivery of merchandise may also be determined by pre-approval of credit based on a combination of criteria: HA.com history, related industry references, bank verification, a credit bureau report and/or a personal guarantee for a corporate or partnership entity in advance of the auction venue.

Bidding Options:

8. Bids in Signature® Auctions or Grand Format Auctions may be placed as set forth in the printed catalog section entitled "Choose your bidding method." For auctions held solely on the Internet, see the alternatives on HA.com. Review at http://www.ha.com/c/ref/web-tips.zx#biddingTutorial.
9. Presentment of Bids: Non-Internet bids (including but not limited to podium, fax, phone and mail bids) are treated similar to floor bids in that they must be on-increment or at a half increment (called a cut bid). Any podium, fax, phone, or mail bids that do not conform to a full or half increment will be rounded up or down to the nearest full or half increment and this revised amount will be considered your high bid.
10. Auctioneer's Execution of Certain Bids. Auctioneer cannot be responsible for your errors in bidding, so carefully check that every bid is entered correctly. When identical mail or FAX bids are submitted, preference is given to the first received. To ensure the greatest accuracy, your written bids should be entered on the standard printed bid sheet and be received at Auctioneer's place of business at least two business days before the Auction start. Auctioneer is not responsible for executing mail bids or FAX bids received on or after the day the first lot is sold, nor Internet bids submitted after the published closing time; nor is Auctioneer responsible for proper execution of bids submitted by telephone, mail, FAX, e-mail, Internet, or in person once the Auction begins. Bids placed electronically via the internet may not be withdrawn until your written request is received and acknowledged by Auctioneer (FAX: 214-409-1425); such requests must state the reason, and may constitute grounds for withdrawal of bidding privileges. Lots won by mail Bidders will not be delivered at the Auction unless prearranged.
11. Caveat as to Bid Increments. Bid increments (over the current bid level) determine the lowest amount you may bid on a particular lot. Bids greater than one increment over the current bid can be any whole dollar amount. It is possible under several circumstances for winning bids to be between increments, sometimes only $1 above the previous increment. Please see: "How can I lose by less than an increment?" on our website. Bids will be accepted in whole dollar amounts only. No "buy" or "unlimited" bids will be accepted.

The following chart governs current bidding increments (see HA.com/c/ref/web-tips.zx#guidelines-increments).

Current Bid	Bid Increment	Current Bid	Bid Increment
< - $10	$1	$10,000 - $19,999	$1,000
$10 - $29	$2	$20,000 - $29,999	$2,000
$30 - $49	$3	$30,000 - $49,999	$2,500
$50 - $99	$5	$50,000 - $99,999	$5,000
$100 - $199	$10	$100,000 - $199,999	$10,000
$200 - $299	$20	$200,000 - $299,999	$20,000
$300 - $499	$25	$300,000 - $499,999	$25,000
$500 - $999	$50	$500,000 - $999,999	$50,000
$1,000 - $1,999	$100	$1,000,000 - $4,999,999	$100,000
$2,000 - $2,999	$200	$5,000,000- $9,999,999	$250,000
$3,000 - $4,999	$250	>$10,000,000	$500,000
$5,000 - $9,999	$500		

12. If Auctioneer calls for a full increment, a bidder may request Auctioneer to accept a bid at half of the increment ("Cut Bid") only once per lot. After offering a Cut Bid, bidders may continue to participate only at full increments. Off-increment bids may be accepted by the Auctioneer at Signature® Auctions and Grand Format Auctions. If the Auctioneer solicits bids other than the expected increment, these bids will not be considered Cut Bids.

Conducting the Auction:

13. Notice of the consignor's liberty to place bids on his lots in the Auction is hereby made in accordance with Article 2 of the Texas Business and Commercial Code. A "Minimum Bid" is an amount below which the lot will not sell. THE CONSIGNOR OF PROPERTY MAY PLACE WRITTEN "Minimum Bids" ON HIS LOTS IN ADVANCE OF THE AUCTION; ON SUCH LOTS, IF THE HAMMER PRICE DOES NOT MEET THE "Minimum Bid", THE CONSIGNOR MAY PAY A REDUCED COMMISSION ON THOSE LOTS. "Minimum Bids" are generally posted online several days prior to the Auction closing. For any successful bid placed by a consignor on his Property on the Auction floor, or by any means during the live session, or after the "Minimum Bid" for an Auction have been posted, we will require the consignor to pay full Buyer's Premium and Seller's Commissions on such lot.
14. The highest qualified Bidder recognized by the Auctioneer shall be the Buyer. In the event of a tie bid, the earliest bid received or recognized wins. In the event of any dispute between any Bidders at an Auction, Auctioneer may at his sole discretion reoffer the lot. Auctioneer's decision and declaration of the winning Bidder shall be final and binding upon all Bidders. Bids properly offered, whether by floor Bidder or other means of bidding, may on occasion be missed or go unrecognized; in such cases, the Auctioneer may declare the recognized bid accepted as the winning bid, regardless of whether a competing bid may have been higher. Auctioneer reserves the right after the hammer fall to accept bids and reopen bidding for bids placed through the Internet or otherwise.
15. Auctioneer reserves the right to refuse to honor any bid or to limit the amount of any bid, in its sole discretion. A bid is considered not made in "Good Faith" when made by an insolvent or irresponsible person, a person under the age of eighteen, or is not supported by satisfactory credit, collectibles references, or otherwise. Regardless of the disclosure of his identity, any bid by a consignor or his agent on a lot consigned by him is deemed to be made in "Good Faith." Any person apparently appearing on the OFAC list is not eligible to bid.
16. Nominal Bids. The Auctioneer in its sole discretion may reject nominal bids, small opening bids, or very nominal advances. If a lot bearing estimates fails to open for 40–60% of the low estimate, the Auctioneer may pass the item or may place a protective bid on behalf of the consignor.
17. Lots bearing bidding estimates shall open at Auctioneer's discretion (approximately 50%-60% of the low estimate). In the event that no bid meets or exceeds that opening amount, the lot shall pass as unsold.
18. All items are to be purchased per lot as numerically indicated and no lots will be broken. Auctioneer reserves the right to withdraw, prior to the close, any lots from the Auction.
19. Auctioneer reserves the right to rescind the sale in the event of nonpayment, breach of a warranty, disputed ownership, auctioneer's clerical error or omission in exercising bids and reserves, or for any other reason and in Auctioneer's sole discretion. In cases of nonpayment, Auctioneer's election to void a sale does not relieve the Bidder from their obligation to pay Auctioneer its fees (seller's and buyer's premium) and any other damages or expenses pertaining to the lot.
20. Auctioneer occasionally experiences Internet and/or Server service outages, and Auctioneer periodically schedules system downtime for maintenance and other purposes, during which Bidders cannot participate or place bids. If such outages occur, we may at our discretion extend bidding for the Auction. Bidders unable to place their Bids through the Internet are directed to contact Client Services at 877-HERITAGE (437-4824).
21. The Auctioneer, its affiliates, or their employees consign items to be sold in the Auction, and may bid on those lots or any other lots. Auctioneer or affiliates expressly reserve the right to modify any such bids at any time prior to the hammer based upon data made known to the Auctioneer or its affiliates. The Auctioneer may extend advances, guarantees, or loans to certain consignors.
22. The Auctioneer has the right to sell certain unsold items after the close of the Auction. Such lots shall be considered sold during the Auction and all these Terms and Conditions shall apply to such sales including but not limited to the Buyer's Premium, return rights, and disclaimers.

Payment:

23. All sales are strictly for cash in United States dollars (including U.S. currency, bank wire, cashier checks, travelers checks, eChecks, and bank money orders, and are subject to all reporting requirements). All deliveries are subject to good funds; funds being received in Auctioneer's account before delivery of the Purchases; and all payments are subject to a clearing period. Auctioneer reserves the right to determine if a check constitutes "good funds": checks drawn on a U.S. bank are subject to a ten business day hold, and thirty days when drawn on an international bank. Clients with pre-arranged credit status may receive immediate credit for payments via eCheck, personal, or corporate checks. All others will be subject to a hold of 5 days, or more, for the funds to clear prior to releasing merchandise. (Ref. T&C item 7 Credit for additional information.) Payments can be made 24-48 hours post auction from the My Orders page of the HA.com website.
24. Payment is due upon closing of the Auction session, or upon presentment of an invoice. Auctioneer reserves the right to void an invoice if payment in full is not received within 7 days after the close of the Auction. In cases of nonpayment, Auctioneer's election to void a sale does not relieve the Bidder from their obligation to pay Auctioneer its fees (seller's and buyer's premium) on the lot and any other damages pertaining to the lot or Auctioneer, at its option, may charge a twenty (20%) restock fee on the amount of the purchase and offset the restock fee against any monies paid to the Auctioneer or against any of the purchaser's properties held by the Auctioneer.
25. Lots delivered to you, or your representative in the States of Texas, California, New York, or other states where the Auction may be held, are subject to all applicable state and local taxes, unless appropriate permits are on file with Auctioneer. (Note: Coins are only subject to sales tax in California on invoices under $1,500, and there is no sales tax on coins in Texas.) Bidder agrees to pay Auctioneer the actual amount of tax due in the event that sales tax is not properly collected due to: 1) an expired, inaccurate, or inappropriate tax certificate or declaration, 2) an incorrect interpretation of the applicable statute, 3) or any other reason. The appropriate form or certificate must be on file at and verified by Auctioneer five days prior to Auction, or tax must be paid; only if such form or certificate is received by Auctioneer within 4 days after the Auction can a refund of tax paid be made. Lots from different Auctions may not be aggregated for sales tax purposes.
26. In the event that a Bidder's payment is dishonored upon presentment(s), Bidder shall pay the maximum statutory processing fee set by applicable state law. If you attempt to pay via eCheck and your financial institution denies this transfer from your bank account, or the payment cannot be completed using the selected funding source, you agree to complete payment using your credit card on file.
27. If any Auction invoice submitted by Auctioneer is not paid in full when due, the unpaid balance will bear interest at the highest rate permitted by law from the date of invoice until paid. Any invoice not paid when due will bear a three percent (3%) late fee on the invoice amount. If the Auctioneer refers any invoice to an attorney for collection, the buyer agrees to pay attorney's fees, court costs, and other collection costs incurred by Auctioneer. If Auctioneer assigns collection to its in-house legal staff, such attorney's time expended on the matter shall be compensated at a rate comparable to the hourly rate of independent attorneys.
28. In the event a successful Bidder fails to pay any amounts due, Auctioneer reserves the right to sell the lot(s) securing the invoice to any underbidders in the Auction that the lot(s) appeared, or at subsequent private or public sale, or relist the lot(s) in a future auction conducted by Auctioneer. A defaulting Bidder agrees to pay for the reasonable costs of resale (including a 15% seller's commission, if consigned to an auction conducted by Auctioneer). The defaulting Bidder is liable to pay any difference between his total original invoice for the lot(s), plus any applicable interest, and the net proceeds for the lot(s) if sold at private sale or the subsequent hammer price of the lot(s) less the 15% seller's commissions, if sold at an Auctioneer's auction.
29. Auctioneer reserves the right to require payment in full in good funds before delivery of the merchandise.

Terms and Conditions of Auction

30. Auctioneer shall have a lien against the merchandise purchased by the buyer to secure payment of the Auction invoice. Auctioneer is further granted a lien and the right to retain possession of any other property of the buyer then held by the Auctioneer or its affiliates to secure payment of any Auction invoice or any other amounts due the Auctioneer or affiliates from the buyer. With respect to these lien rights, Auctioneer shall have all the rights of a secured creditor under Article 9 of the Texas Uniform Commercial Code, including but not limited to the right of sale (including a 15% seller's commission, if consigned to an auction conducted by Auctioneer). In addition, with respect to payment of the Auction invoice(s), the buyer waives any and all rights of offset he might otherwise have against the Auctioneer and the consignor of the merchandise included on the invoice. If a Bidder owes Auctioneer or its affiliates on any account, Auctioneer and its affiliates shall have the right to offset such unpaid account by any credit balance due Bidder, and it may secure by possessory lien any unpaid amount by any of the Bidder's property in their possession..
31. Title shall not pass to the successful Bidder until all invoices are paid in full. It is the responsibility of the buyer to provide adequate insurance coverage for the items once they have been delivered to a common carrier or third-party shipper.

Delivery; Shipping; and Handling Charges:

32. Buyer is liable for shipping, handling, registration, and renewal fees, if any. Please refer to Auctioneer's website www.HA.com/common/shipping.php for the latest charges or call Auctioneer. Auctioneer is unable to combine purchases from other auctions or affiliates into one package for shipping purposes. Lots won will be shipped in a commercially reasonable time after payment in good funds for the merchandise and the shipping fees is received or credit extended, except when third-party shipment occurs. Buyer agrees that Service and Handling charges related to shipping items which are not pre-paid may be charged to the credit card on file with Auctioneer.
33. Successful international Bidders shall provide written shipping instructions, including specified customs declarations, to the Auctioneer for any lots to be delivered outside of the United States. NOTE: Declaration value shall be the item'(s) hammer price together with its buyer's premium and Auctioneer shall use the correct harmonized code for the lot. Domestic Buyers on lots designated for third-party shipment must designate the common carrier, accept risk of loss, and prepay shipping costs.
34. All shipping charges will be borne by the successful Bidder. On all domestic shipments, any risk of loss during shipment will be borne by Heritage until the shipping carrier's confirmation of delivery to the address of record in Auctioneer's file (carrier's confirmation is conclusive to prove delivery to Bidder; if the client has a Signature release on file with the carrier, the package is considered delivered without Signature) or delivery by Heritage to Bidder's selected third-party shipper. On all foreign shipments, any risk of loss during shipment will be borne by the Bidder following Auctioneer's delivery to the Bidder's designated common carrier or third-party shipper.
35. Due to the nature of some items sold, it shall be the responsibility for the successful Bidder to arrange pick-up and shipping through third-parties; as to such items Auctioneer shall have no liability. Failure to pick-up or arrange shipping in a timely fashion (within ten days) shall subject Lots to storage and moving charges, including a $100 administration fee plus $10 daily storage for larger items and $5.00 daily for smaller items (storage fee per item) after 35 days. In the event the Lot is not removed within ninety days, the Lot may be offered for sale to recover any past due storage or moving fees, including a 10% Seller's Commission.

36A. The laws of various countries regulate the import or export of certain plant and animal properties, including (but not limited to) items made of (or including) ivory, whalebone, turtle shell, coral, crocodile, or other wildlife. Transport of such lots may require special licenses for export, import, or both. Bidder is responsible for: 1) obtaining all information on such restricted items for both export and import; 2) obtaining all such licenses and/or permits. Delay or failure to obtain any such license or permit does not relieve the buyer of timely compliance with standard payment terms. For further information, please contact Ron Brackemyre at 800- 872-6467 ext. 1312.

36B. California State law prohibits the importation of any product containing Python skin into the State of California, thus no lot containing Python skin will be shipped to or invoiced to a person or company in California.

36C. Auctioneer shall not be liable for any loss caused by or resulting from:

a. Seizure or destruction under quarantine or Customs regulation, or confiscation by order of any Government or public authority, or risks of contraband or illegal transportation of trade, or

b. Breakage of statuary, marble, glassware, bric-a-brac, porcelains, jewelry, and similar fragile articles

37. Any request for shipping verification for undelivered packages must be made within 30 days of shipment by Auctioneer.

Cataloging, Warranties and Disclaimers:

38. NO WARRANTY, WHETHER EXPRESSED OR IMPLIED, IS MADE WITH RESPECT TO ANY DESCRIPTION CONTAINED IN THIS AUCTION OR ANY SECOND OPINE. Any description of the items or second opine contained in this Auction is for the sole purpose of identifying the items for those Bidders who do not have the opportunity to view the lots prior to bidding, and no description of items has been made part of the basis of the bargain or has created any express warranty that the goods would conform to any description made by Auctioneer. Color variations can be expected in any electronic or printed imaging, and are not grounds for the return of any lot. NOTE: Auctioneer, in specified auction venues, for example, Fine Art, may have express written warranties and you are referred to those specific terms and conditions. .
39. Auctioneer is selling only such right or title to the items being sold as Auctioneer may have by virtue of consignment agreements on the date of auction and disclaims any warranty of title to the Property. Auctioneer disclaims any warranty of merchantability or fitness for any particular purposes. All images, descriptions, sales data, and archival records are the exclusive property of Auctioneer, and may be used by Auctioneer for advertising, promotion, archival records, and any other uses deemed appropriate.
40. Translations of foreign language documents may be provided as a convenience to interested parties. Auctioneer makes no representation as to the accuracy of those translations and will not be held responsible for errors in bidding arising from inaccuracies in translation.
41. Auctioneer disclaims all liability for damages, consequential or otherwise, arising out of or in connection with the sale of any Property by Auctioneer to Bidder. No third party may rely on any benefit of these Terms and Conditions and any rights, if any, established hereunder are personal to the Bidder and may not be assigned. Any statement made by the Auctioneer is an opinion and does not constitute a warranty or representation. No employee of Auctioneer may alter these Terms and Conditions, and, unless signed by a principal of Auctioneer, any such alteration is null and void.
42. Auctioneer shall not be liable for breakage of glass or damage to frames (patent or latent); such defects, in any event, shall not be a basis for any claim for return or reduction in purchase price.

Release:

43. In consideration of participation in the Auction and the placing of a bid, Bidder expressly releases Auctioneer, its officers, directors and employees, its affiliates, and its outside experts that provide second opines, from any and all claims, cause of action, chose of action, whether at law or equity or any arbitration or mediation rights existing under the rules of any professional society or affiliation based upon the assigned description, or a derivative theory, breach of warranty express or implied, representation or other matter set forth within these Terms and Conditions of Auction or otherwise. In the event of a claim, Bidder agrees that such rights and privileges conferred therein are strictly construed as specifically declared herein; e.g., authenticity, typographical error, etc. and are the exclusive remedy. Bidder, by non-compliance to these express terms of a granted remedy, shall waive any claim against Auctioneer.
44. Notice: Some Property sold by Auctioneer are inherently dangerous e.g. firearms, cannons, and small items that may be swallowed or ingested or may have latent defects all of which may cause harm to a person. Purchaser accepts all risk of loss or damage from its purchase of these items and Auctioneer disclaims any liability whether under contract or tort for damages and losses, direct or inconsequential, and expressly disclaims any warranty as to safety or usage of any lot sold.

Dispute Resolution and Arbitration Provision:

45. By placing a bid or otherwise participating in the auction, Bidder accepts these Terms and Conditions of Auction, and specifically agrees to the dispute resolution provided herein. Consumer disputes shall be resolved through court litigation which has an exclusive Dallas, Texas venue clause and jury waiver. Non-consumer dispute shall be determined in binding arbitration which arbitration replaces the right to go to court, including the right to a jury trial.
46. Auctioneer in no event shall be responsible for consequential damages, incidental damages, compensatory damages, or any other damages arising or claimed to be arising from the auction of any lot. In the event that Auctioneer cannot deliver the lot or subsequently it is established that the lot lacks title, or other transfer or condition issue is claimed, in such cases the sole remedy shall be limited to rescission of sale and refund of the amount paid by Bidder; in no case shall Auctioneer's maximum liability exceed the high bid on that lot, which bid shall be deemed for all purposes the value of the lot. After one year has elapsed, Auctioneer's maximum liability shall be limited to any commissions and fees Auctioneer earned on that lot.
47. In the event of an attribution error, Auctioneer may at its sole discretion, correct the error on the Internet, or, if discovered at a later date, to refund the buyer's purchase price without further obligation.
48. Exclusive Dispute Resolution Process: All claims, disputes, or controversies in connection with, relating to and /or arising out of your Participation in the Auction or purchase of any lot, any interpretation of the Terms and Conditions of Sale or any amendments thereto, any description of any lot or condition report, any damage to any lot, any alleged verbal modification of any term of sale or condition report or description and/or any purported settlement whether asserted in contract, tort, under Federal or State statute or regulation or any claim made by you of a lot or your Participation in the auction involving the auction or a specific lot involving a warranty or representation of a consignor or other person or entity including Auctioneer { which claim you consent to be made a party} (collectively, "Claim") shall be exclusively heard by, and the claimant (or respondent as the case may be) and Heritage each consent to the Claim being presented in a confidential binding arbitration before a single arbitrator administrated by and conducted under the rules of, the American Arbitration Association. The locale for all such arbitrations shall be Dallas, Texas. The arbitrator's award may be enforced in any court of competent jurisdiction. If a Claim involves a consumer, exclusive subject matter jurisdiction for the Claim is in the State District Courts of Dallas County, Texas and the consumer consents to subject matter and in personam jurisdiction; further CONSUMER EXPRESSLY WAIVES ANY RIGHT TO TRIAL BY JURY. A consumer may elect arbitration as specified above. Any claim involving the purchase or sale of numismatic or related items may be submitted through binding PNG arbitration. Any Claim must be brought within two (2) years of the alleged breach, default or misrepresentation or the Claim is waived. Exemplary or punitive damages are not permitted and are waived. A Claim is not subject to class certification. Nothing herein shall be construed to extend the time of return or conditions and restrictions for return. This Agreement and any Claim shall be determined and construed under Texas law. The prevailing party (a party that is awarded substantial and material relief on its damage claim based on damages sought vs. awarded or the successful defense of a Claim based on damages sought vs. awarded) may be awarded its reasonable attorneys' fees and costs.
49. No claims of any kind can be considered after the settlements have been made with the consignors. Any dispute after the settlement date is strictly between the Bidder and consignor without involvement or responsibility of the Auctioneer.
50. In consideration of their participation in or application for the Auction, a person or entity (whether the successful Bidder, a Bidder, a purchaser and/or other Auction participant or registrant) agrees that all disputes in any way relating to, arising under, connected with, or incidental to these Terms and Conditions and purchases, or default in payment thereof, shall be arbitrated pursuant to the arbitration provision. In the event that any matter including actions to compel arbitration, construe the agreement, actions in aid or arbitration or otherwise needs to be litigated, such litigation shall be exclusively in the Courts of the State of Texas, in Dallas County, Texas, and if necessary the corresponding appellate courts. For such actions, the successful Bidder, purchaser, or Auction participant also expressly submits himself to the personal jurisdiction of the State of Texas.
51. These Terms & Conditions provide specific remedies for occurrences in the auction and delivery process. Where such remedies are afforded, they shall be interpreted strictly. Bidder agrees that any claim shall utilize such remedies; Bidder making a claim in excess of those remedies provided in these Terms and Conditions agrees that in no case whatsoever shall Auctioneer's maximum liability exceed the high bid on that lot, which bid shall be deemed for all purposes the value of the lot.

Miscellaneous:

52. Agreements between Bidders and consignors to effectuate a non-sale of an item at Auction, inhibit bidding on a consigned item to enter into a private sale agreement for said item, or to utilize the Auctioneer's Auction to obtain sales for non-selling consigned items subsequent to the Auction, are strictly prohibited. If a subsequent sale of a previously consigned item occurs in violation of this provision, Auctioneer reserves the right to charge Bidder the applicable Buyer's Premium and consignor a Seller's Commission as determined for each auction venue and by the terms of the seller's agreement.
53. Acceptance of these Terms and Conditions qualifies Bidder as a client who has consented to be contacted by Heritage in the future. In conformity with "do-not-call" regulations promulgated by the Federal or State regulatory agencies, participation by the Bidder is affirmative consent to being contacted at the phone number shown in his application and this consent shall remain in effect until it is revoked in writing. Heritage may from time to time contact Bidder concerning sale, purchase, and auction opportunities available through Heritage and its affiliates and subsidiaries.
54. Rules of Construction: Auctioneer presents properties in a number of collectible fields, and as such, specific venues have promulgated supplemental Terms and Conditions. Nothing herein shall be construed to waive the general Terms and Conditions of Auction by these additional rules and shall be construed to give force and effect to the rules in their entirety.

State Notices:

Notice as to an Auction in California. Auctioneer has in compliance with Title 2.95 of the California Civil Code as amended October 11, 1993 Sec. 1812.600, posted with the California Secretary of State its bonds for it and its employees, and the auction is being conducted in compliance with Sec. 2338 of the Commercial Code and Sec. 535 of the Penal Code.

Notice as to an Auction in New York City. These Terms and Conditions of Sale are designed to conform to the applicable sections of the New York City Department of Consumer Affairs Rules and Regulations as Amended. This sale is a Public Auction Sale conducted by Heritage Auctioneers & Galleries, Inc. # 41513036. The New York City licensed auctioneers are: Sam Foose, #095260; Kathleen Guzman, #0762165; Nicholas Dawes, #1304724; Ed Beardsley, #1183220; Scott Peterson, #1306933; Andrea Voss, #1320558, who will conduct the Sale on behalf of itself and Heritage Numismatic Auctions, Inc. (for Coins) and Currency Auctions of America, Inc. (for currency). All lots are subject to: the consignor's rights to bid thereon in accord with these Terms and Conditions of Sale, consignor's option to receive advances on their consignments, and Auctioneer, in its sole discretion, may offer limited extended financing to registered bidders, in accord with Auctioneer's internal credit standards. A registered bidder may inquire whether a lot is subject to an advance or a reserve. Auctioneer has made advances to various consignors in this sale. On lots bearing an estimate, the term refers to a value range placed on an item by the Auctioneer in its sole opinion but the final price is determined by the bidders.

Notice as to an Auction in Texas. In compliance with TDLR rule 67.100(c)(1), notice is hereby provided that this auction is covered by a Recovery Fund administered by the Texas Department of Licensing and Regulation, P.O. Box 12157, Austin, Texas 78711 (512) 463-6599. Any complaints may be directed to the same address.

Notice as to an Auction in Ohio: Auction firm and Auctioneer are licensed by the Dept. of Agriculture, and either the licensee is bonded in favor of the state or an aggrieved person may initiate a claim against the auction recovery fund created in Section 4707.25 of the Revised Code as a result of the licensee's actions, whichever is applicable.

Rev.10-3-2014

Terms and Conditions of Auction

Additional Terms & Conditions:
COINS & CURRENCY

COINS and CURRENCY TERM A: Signature₅ Auctions are not on approval. No certified material may be returned because of possible differences of opinion with respect to the grade offered by any third-party organization, dealer, or service. No guarantee of grade is offered for uncertified Property sold and subsequently submitted to a third-party grading service. There are absolutely no exceptions to this policy. Under extremely limited circumstances, (e.g. gross cataloging error) a purchaser, who did not bid from the floor, may request Auctioneer to evaluate voiding a sale: such request must be made in writing detailing the alleged gross error; submission of the lot to the Auctioneer must be pre-approved by the Auctioneer; and bidder must notify Ron Brackemyre (1-800-872-6467 Ext. 1312) in writing of such request within three (3) days of the non-floor bidder's receipt of the lot. Any lot that is to be evaluated must be in our offices within 30 days after Auction. Grading or method of manufacture do not qualify for this evaluation process nor do such complaints constitute a basis to challenge the authenticity of a lot. AFTER THAT 30-DAY PERIOD, NO LOTS MAY BE RETURNED FOR REASONS OTHER THAN AUTHENTICITY. Lots returned must be housed intact in their original holder. No lots purchased by floor Bidders may be returned (including those Bidders acting as agents for others) except for authenticity. Late remittance for purchases may be considered just cause to revoke all return privileges.

COINS and CURRENCY TERM B: Auctions conducted solely on the Internet THREE (3) DAY RETURN POLICY: Certified Coin and Uncertified and Certified Currency lots paid for within seven days of the Auction closing are sold with a three (3) day return privilege unless otherwise noted in the description as "Sold As Is, No Return Lot". You may return lots under the following conditions: Within three days of receipt of the lot, you must first notify Client Service by phone (877-HERITAGE (437-4824)) or e-mail (Bid@HA.com), and immediately ship the lot(s) fully insured to the attention of Returns, Heritage, 3500 Maple Avenue, 17th Floor, Dallas TX 75219-3941. Lots must be housed intact in their original holder and condition. You are responsible for the insured, safe delivery of any lots. A non-negotiable return fee of 5% of the purchase price ($10 per lot minimum) will be deducted from the refund for each returned lot or billed directly. Postage and handling fees are not refunded. After the three-day period (from receipt), no items may be returned for any reason. Late remittance for purchases revokes these Return privileges.

COINS and CURRENCY TERM C: Bidders who have inspected the lots prior to any Auction, or attended the Auction, or bid through an Agent, will not be granted any return privileges, except for reasons of authenticity.

COINS and CURRENCY TERM D: Coins sold referencing a third-party grading service are sold "as is" without any express or implied warranty, except for a guarantee by Auctioneer that they are genuine. Certain warranties may be available from the grading services and the Bidder is referred to them for further details: Numismatic Guaranty Corporation (NGC), P.O. Box 4776, Sarasota, FL 34230, http://www.ngccoin.com/services/writtenguarantee.asp; Professional Coin Grading Service (PCGS), PO Box 9458, Newport Beach, CA 92658, http://www.pcgs.com/guarantee.html; ANACS, 6555 S. Kenton St. Ste. 303, Englewood, CO 80111; and Independent Coin Grading Co. (ICG), 7901 East Belleview Ave., Suite 50, Englewood, CO 80111.

COINS and CURRENCY TERM E: Notes sold referencing a third-party grading service are sold "as is" without any express or implied warranty, except for guarantee by Auctioneer that they are genuine. Grading, condition or other attributes of any lot may have a material effect on its value, and the opinion of others, including third-party grading services such as PCGS Currency, PMG, and CGA may differ with that of Auctioneer. Auctioneer shall not be bound by any prior or subsequent opinion, determination, or certification by any grading service. Bidder specifically waives any claim to right of return of any item because of the opinion, determination, or certification, or lack thereof, by any grading service. Certain warranties may be available from the grading services and the Bidder is referred to them for further details: Paper Money Guaranty (PMG), PO Box 4711, Sarasota FL 34230; PCGS Currency, PO Box 9458, Newport Beach, CA 92658; Currency Grading & Authentication (CGA), PO Box 418, Three Bridges, NJ 08887. Third party graded notes are not returnable for any reason whatsoever.

COINS and CURRENCY TERM F: Since we cannot examine encapsulated coins or notes, they are sold "as is" without our grading opinion, and may not be returned for any reason. Auctioneer shall not be liable for any patent or latent defect or controversy pertaining to or arising from any encapsulated collectible. In any such instance, purchaser's remedy, if any, shall be solely against the service certifying the collectible.

COINS and CURRENCY TERM G: Due to changing grading standards over time, differing interpretations, and to possible mishandling of items by subsequent owners, Auctioneer reserves the right to grade items differently than shown on certificates from any grading service that accompany the items. Auctioneer also reserves the right to grade items differently than the grades shown in the prior catalog should such items be reconsigned to any future auction.

COINS and CURRENCY TERM H: Although consensus grading is employed by most grading services, it should be noted as aforesaid that grading is not an exact science. In fact, it is entirely possible that if a lot is broken out of a plastic holder and resubmitted to another grading service or even to the same service, the lot could come back with a different grade assigned.

COINS and CURRENCY TERM I: Certification does not guarantee protection against the normal risks associated with potentially volatile markets. The degree of liquidity for certified coins and collectibles will vary according to general market conditions and the particular lot involved. For some lots there may be no active market at all at certain points in time.

COINS and CURRENCY TERM J: All non-certified coins and currency are guaranteed genuine, but are not guaranteed as to grade, since grading is a matter of opinion, an art and not a science, and therefore the opinion rendered by the Auctioneer or any third party grading service may not agree with the opinion of others (including trained experts), and the same expert may not grade the same item with the same grade at two different times. Auctioneer has graded the non-certified numismatic items, in the Auctioneer's opinion, to their current interpretation of the American Numismatic Association's standards as of the date the catalog was prepared. There is no guarantee or warranty implied or expressed that the grading standards utilized by the Auctioneer will meet the standards of any grading service at any time in the future.

COINS and CURRENCY TERM K: Storage of purchased coins and currency: Purchasers are advised that certain types of plastic may react with a coin's metal or transfer plasticizer to notes and may cause damage. Caution should be used to avoid storage in materials that are not inert.

COINS and CURRENCY TERM L: NOTE: Purchasers of rare coins or currency through Heritage have available the option of arbitration by the Professional Numismatists Guild (PNG); if an election is not made within ten (10) days of an unresolved dispute, Auctioneer may elect either PNG or A.A.A. Arbitration.

COINS and CURRENCY TERM M: For more information regarding Canadian lots attributed to the Charlton reference guides, please contact: Charlton International, PO Box 820, Station Willowdale B, North York, Ontario M2K 2R1 Canada.

COINS and CURRENCY TERM N: Some of the lots offered herein have been assigned to 1031 Services, Inc. for the purpose of consignor's tax deferred exchange.

COINS and CURRENCY TERM O: Financing. Auctioneer offers various extended payment options to qualified pre-approved persons and companies. The options include Extended Payment Programs (EPP) Flexible Payment Program (FPP) and Dealer Terms. Each program has its specific terms and conditions and such terms and conditions are strictly enforced. Each program has to be executed by the purchaser. Auctioneer reserves the right to alter or deny credit and in such case these auction terms shall control.

For wiring instructions call the Credit department at 877-HERITAGE (437-4824) or e-mail: CreditDept@HA.com

---

New York State Auctions Only

Notice as to an Auction in New York City. These Terms and Conditions of Sale are designed to conform to the applicable sections of the New York City Department of Consumer Affairs Rules and Regulations as Amended. This sale is a Public Auction Sale conducted by Heritage Auctioneers & Galleries, Inc. #1364738. The New York City licensed auctioneers are: Samuel Foose 0952360; Robert Korver 1096338; Kathleen Guzman 0762165; Michael J. Sadler 1304630; Scott Peterson 1306933; Andrea Voss 1320558; Nicholas Dawes 1304724; Ed Beardsley 1183220; Bob Merrill 1473403; Paul Minshull 2001161; Fiona Elias 2001163; Brian Nalley 2001162; Jennifer Marsh 2009623; Alissa Ford 2009565, who will conduct the Sale on behalf of itself and Heritage Auctioneers & Galleries, Inc. All lots are subject to: the consignor's rights to bid thereon in accord with these Terms and Conditions of Sale, consignor's option to receive advances on their consignments, and Auctioneer, in its sole discretion, may offer limited extended financing to registered bidders, in accord with Auctioneer's internal credit standards. A registered bidder may inquire whether a lot is subject to an advance or a reserve. Auctioneer has made advances to various consignors in this sale. On lots bearing an estimate, the term refers to a value range placed on an item by the Auctioneer in its sole opinion but the final price is determined by the bidders. Rev 10-6-2014

Rev. 8-14-2014

HERITAGE LUXURY REAL ESTATE

SPECIALISTS IN AUCTIONING UNIQUE PROPERTIES

Catskills Estate
Bethel, NY

Sold For: $3,400,000

Isle of Palms Oceanfront Estate
Charleston, SC

Sold For: $3,217,500

Royal Oaks Country Club Estate
Houston, TX

Sold For: $1,980,000

For a free evaluation of your luxury property, please call 855-261-0573, or visit HA.com/SellHome

Inquiries: 877-HERITAGE (437-4824)
Nate Schar | ext. 1457 | NateS@HA.com
Amelia Barber | ext. 1603 | AmeliaB@HA.com

HERITAGE
LUXURY REAL ESTATE AUCTIONS

34521

LUXURY BOUTIQUE
AVAILABLE FOR IMMEDIATE PURCHASE

HA.COM/BOUTIQUE

Hermès 30cm Braise Shiny Nilo Crocodile Birkin Bag with Palladium Hardware
Heritage Auctions' Luxury Boutique allows you to shop and purchase outright some of the rarest and most sought-after luxury accessories from Hermès, Chanel, Louis Vuitton and more. No bidding necessary. Luxury Accessories available at a wide range of price points.

Shop at HA.com/Boutique.

Inquiries: 877-HERITAGE (437-4824)

Luxury@HA.com

THE WORLD'S THIRD LARGEST AUCTION HOUSE

31259

WATCHES & FINE TIMEPIECES AUCTION

Rolex Rare Ref. 6538
"James Bond" Big Crown
Submariner, circa 1956
Sold For: $45,313

Patek Philippe Ref.
1463 Very Fine, Rare &
Important 18k Yellow Gold
Gentlemen's Chronograph,
circa 1949
Sold For: $98,500

Patek Philippe Ref. 5004P Extremely Rare
And Important Platinum Wristwatch With
Split-Seconds Chronograph, Registers,
Perpetual Calendar, Moon Phases, Leap Year
And 24 Hour Indication
Sold For: $242,500

Always Accepting Consignments in each of our 38 Categories.

Immediate Cash Advances Available up to $50 Million.

Inquiries: 877-HERITAGE (437-4824)

Jim Wolf | ext. 1659 | JWolf@HA.com

Michael Fossner | ext. 1208 | MichaelF@HA.com

THE WORLD'S LARGEST COLLECTIBLES AUCTIONEER

32869

THE WORLD'S FINEST JEWELRY & HANDBAGS
BY AUCTION AND PRIVATE SALE

Contact Us to Sell Your Pieces Outright or at Auction

Hermès Extraordinary Collection 18cm Diamond Blue Jean
Porosus Crocodile Constance with 18K White Gold Hardware
Sold for: $50,000

J.E. Caldwell Art Deco Natural Fancy Blue Diamond,
Diamond, Platinum Ring
Sold for: $1,650,500

Van Cleef & Arpels Sapphire, Diamond, Platinum Bracelet
Sold for: $140,500

Hermès 35cm Shiny Blue Electric Porosus Crocodile Birkin
Sold for: $61,250

Always Accepting Quality Consignments in 38 Categories.
Immediate Cash Advances up to $50 Million.

Inquiries: 877-HERITAGE (437-4824)

Luxury Accessories
Max Brownawell | ext. 3576 | MaxB@HA.com

Fine Jewelry
Jill Burgum | ext. 1697 | JillB@HA.com

THE WORLD'S THIRD LARGEST AUCTION HOUSE

HERITAGE HA.com
AUCTIONS

30326

SPORTS COLLECTIBLES AUCTIONS

1927-1928 Lou Gehrig Game Worn New
York Yankees Road Jersey.
Realized: $717,000

1965 Mickey Mantle Original Painting by
LeRoy Neiman.
Realized: $131,450

1970 Lew Alcindor Game
Worn Milwaukee Bucks Jersey.
Realized: $95,600

1909-11 T206 Ty Cobb Bat Off Shoulder
PSA NM-MT 8.
Realized: $26,290

1949 Mickey Mantle Signed (Endorsed)
New York Yankees Signing Bonus Check.
Realized: $286,800

1910 T206 Eddie Plank
SGC 40 VG 3.
Realized: $65,725

Inquiries: 877-HERITAGE (437-4824)

CHRIS IVY | Director, Sports Auctions | CIvy@HA.com | ext. 1319
DEREK GRADY | VP, Sports Auctions | DerekG@HA.com | ext. 1975
ROB ROSEN | VP, Private Sales & Consignments | RRosen@HA.com | ext. 1767
MARK JORDAN | Consignment Director | MarkJ@HA.com ext. 1187
MIKE GUTIERREZ | Consignment Director | MikeG@HA.com | ext. 1183

SEEKING CONSIGNMENTS
DELIVERING RESULTS

THE WORLD'S LARGEST COLLECTIBLES AUCTIONEER
HERITAGE HA.com
A U C T I O N S

30301

MyRecommendations
ONLINE SUGGESTION TOOL

The last piece of the puzzle? Heritage has it.

Our new online tool, **MyRecommendations** looks at your collecting history and preferences, and notifies you when a potentially desired item becomes available – even items you have never bid on before.

MyRecommendations constantly combs Heritage's upcoming auctions and in-house inventory, and updates your personalized list as auctions open and close. It's a convenient new way to stay aware of the latest opportunities to expand and improve your collection.

Find that special piece with **MyRecommendations** visit Heritage's US Coin pages now at HA.com/Coin.

Inquiries: 800.USCOINS (872.6467)

THE WORLD'S LARGEST NUMISMATIC AUCTIONEER

33830

20ᵀᴴ & 21ˢᵀ CENTURY DESIGN
JANUARY 29, 2015 | DALLAS | LIVE & ONLINE

Always Accepting Quality Consignments.

SAM MALOOF
Rocker (No. 43), 1989
Walnut, ebony
45-1/2 x 26-1/4 x 44-3/4 inches
Estimate: $30,000-$40,000

DAVID HOCKNEY
Cat, circa 1955
Glazed earthenware
13-1/2 x 15 x 5 inches
Estimate: $20,000-$30,000

Inquiries: 877-HERITAGE (437-4824)

Brandon Kennedy | Ext. 1965 | BrandonK@HA.com

View All Lots and Bid Online
at HA.com/5205

THE WORLD'S THIRD LARGEST AUCTION HOUSE
HERITAGE HA.com
AUCTIONS

34446

FINE ART AUCTIONS

UPCOMING ART AUCTIONS | CONSIGN NOW

FINE & DECORATIVE ARTS | NATURE & SCIENCE | PHOTOGRAPHS
ILLUSTRATION ART | TEXAS ART | FINE SILVER & OBJECTS OF VERTU
MODERN & CONTEMPORARY ART | ETHNOGRAPHIC ART
TIFFANY, LALIQUE, & ART GLASS | AMERICAN ART | EUROPEAN ART
20TH AND 21ST CENTURY DESIGN

Always Accepting Quality Consignments in 38 Categories.

SAM FRANCIS
Bright Saddle (detail), 1985
Acrylic on canvas
36 x 42 in.
Sold for $275,000, May 2014

Inquiries: 877-HERITAGE (437-4824)

THE WORLD'S THIRD LARGEST AUCTION HOUSE

34976

U.S. COINS® PLATINUM NIGHT® & SIGNATURE® AUCTION

JANUARY 7-13, 2015 | ORLANDO | LIVE & ONLINE

SELECTIONS FROM
THE DONALD G. PARTRICK COLLECTION, PART I
TO BE OFFERED IN OUR UPCOMING
OFFICIAL AUCTIONS AT FUN 2015

1792 Judd-9 Silver Disme, AU50 NGC
Finest Known
Only Three Known
Ex: Judd Collection

1792 Judd-1a Silver Center Cent
MS62 RB NGC
Unique Sans Silver Example

1792 Judd-11 Copper Disme, MS64 RB NGC
Finest Known
Only Three Known Plain Edge Pieces
Ex: Garrett Collection

1792 Judd-12 Wright Quarter Dollar
MS63 BN NGC
Finest Known
Only Two Known in Copper
Ex: Judd Collection

1861 Original Confederate Half Dollar
PR30 NGC
Ex: Jefferson Davis Estate

(1739) Higley WHEELE GOES ROUND
Copper, VF30 NGC
Unique Higley Design
Ex: Garrett Collection

1776 Newman 3-D Continental Dollar, Silver, MS62 NGC
Ex: Boyd Collection

1792 Judd-4 Birch Cent, MS65★ RB NGC
Substantial Mint Color
Finest Known
Ex: Garrett Collection

Consignment deadline
November 25

Inquiries: 800.USCOINS (872.6467)

THE WORLD'S LARGEST NUMISMATIC AUCTIONEER

HERITAGE HA.com
A U C T I O N S

35012

LONG BEACH EXPO

COIN, CURRENCY, STAMP & SPORTS COLLECTIBLE SHOW

Jan 29
Jan 30
Jan 31

More Commerce · More Convenience · More Collectibles

The Largest Collectibles Show on the West Coast

BUY— Purchase coins from hundreds of top dealers in the country.

SELL — Put your inventory in front of thousands of collectors.

CERTIFY— Have your coins certified by third-party authentication services.

APPRAISE — Free appraisals by industry experts in all numismatic fields.

CONSIGN — Meet and consign your coins with Heritage Auctions.

Dealers — Reserve your Booth Today! Or if you can't man a booth, get in early with an Early Bird Dealer Badge. Call **888-743-9316** or email **Info@LongBeachExpo.com.**

2015 Expo Dates
Jan. 29-31 • June 4-6 • Sept. 17-19

Official Auctioneer

THE WORLD'S LARGEST NUMISMATIC AUCTIONEER

HERITAGE HA.com
AUCTIONS

LongBeachExpo.com • 888-743-9316

©2014 Long Beach Expo • A Division of Collectors Universe, Inc. • NASDAQ: CLCT

430101

Department Specialists

Comics & Comic Art
HA.com/Comics

Ed Jaster, Ext. 1288 • EdJ@HA.com **
Lon Allen, Ext. 1261 • LonA@HA.com
Barry Sandoval, Ext. 1377 • BarryS@HA.com
Todd Hignite, Ext. 1790 • ToddH@HA.com

Animation Art
Jim Lentz, Ext. 1991 • JimL@HA.com

Entertainment & Music Memorabilia
HA.com/Entertainment

Margaret Barrett, Ext. 1912 • MargaretB@HA.com **
Garry Shrum, Ext. 1585 • GarryS@HA.com
Dean Harmeyer, Ext. 1956 • DeanH@HA.com
John Hickey, Ext. 1264 • JohnH@HA.com

Vintage Guitars & Musical Instruments
HA.com/Guitar

Mike Gutierrez, Ext. 1183 • MikeG@HA.com
Isaiah Evans, Ext. 1201 • IsaiahE@HA.com

Fine Art

American Indian Art
HA.com/AmericanIndian
Delia Sullivan, Ext. 1343 • DeliaS@HA.com

American & European Art
HA.com/FineArt
Brian Roughton, Ext. 1210 • BrianR@HA.com
Ed Jaster, Ext. 1288 • EdJ@HA.com **
Aviva Lehmann, Ext. 1519 • AvivaL@HA.com *
Ariana Hartsock, Ext. 1283 • ArianaH@HA.com
Alissa Ford, Ext. 1926 • AlissaF@HA.com ***
Marianne Berardi, Ph.D., Ext. 1506 • MarianneB@HA.com

Decorative Arts & 20th Century Design
HA.com/Decorative
Karen Rigdon, Ext. 1723 • KarenR@HA.com
Carolyn Mani, Ext. 1677 • CarolynM@HA.com **
Brandon Kennedy, Ext. 1965 • BrandonK@HA.com

Illustration Art
HA.com/Illustration
Ed Jaster, Ext. 1288 • EdJ@HA.com **
Todd Hignite, Ext. 1790 • ToddH@HA.com

Lalique & Art Glass
HA.com/Design
Nicholas Dawes, Ext. 1605 • NickD@HA.com *

Modern & Contemporary Art
HA.com/Modern
Frank Hettig, Ext. 1157 • FrankH@HA.com
Brandon Kennedy, Ext. 1965 • BrandonK@HA.com
Holly Sherratt Ext. 1505 • HollyS@HA.com ***

Photographs
HA.com/Photographs
Ed Jaster, Ext. 1288 • EdJ@HA.com **
Rachel Peart, Ext. 1625 • RPeart@HA.com *

Silver & Vertu
HA.com/Silver
Karen Rigdon, Ext. 1723 • KarenR@HA.com

Texas Art
HA.com/TexasArt
Atlee Phillips, Ext. 1786 • AtleeP@HA.com

Handbags & Luxury Accessories
HA.com/Luxury

Diane D'Amato, Ext. 1901 • DianeD@HA.com *
Kathleen Guzman, Ext. 1672 • Kathleen@HA.com *
Max Brownawell, Ext. 1693 • MaxB@HA.com *
Barbara Conn, Ext. 1336 • BarbaraC@HA.com

Historical

Americana & Political
HA.com/Historical
Tom Slater, Ext. 1441 • TomS@HA.com
Don Ackerman, Ext. 1736 • DonA@HA.com
Michael Riley, Ext. 1467 • MichaelR@HA.com
John Hickey, Ext. 1264 • JohnH@HA.com

Arms & Armor
HA.com/Arms
David Carde, Ext. 1881 • DavidC@HA.com
Cliff Chappell, Ext. 1887 • CliffordC@HA.com ***
Jason Watson, Ext. 1630 • JasonW@HA.com

Automobilia
HA.com/Automobilia
Karl Chiao, Ext. 1958 • KarlC@HA.com

Civil War & Militaria
HA.com/CivilWar
David Carde, Ext. 1881 • DavidC@HA.com

Historical Manuscripts
HA.com/Manuscripts
Sandra Palomino, Ext. 1107 • SandraP@HA.com *
Bryan Booher, Ext. 1845 • BBooher@HA.com
David Boozer, Ext. 1711 • DavidB@HA.com

Rare Books
HA.com/Books
James Gannon, Ext. 1609 • JamesG@HA.com

Space Exploration
HA.com/Space
Michael Riley, Ext. 1467 • MichaelR@HA.com
John Hickey, Ext. 1264 • JohnH@HA.com

Texana
HA.com/Texana
Sandra Palomino, Ext. 1107 • SandraP@HA.com *
Bryan Booher, Ext. 1845 • BBooher@HA.com
David Boozer, Ext. 1711 • DavidB@HA.com

Domain Names & Intellectual Property
HA.com/IP
Aron Meystedt, Ext. 1362 • AronM@HA.com

Jewelry
HA.com/Jewelry

Jill Burgum, Ext. 1697 • JillB@HA.com
Peggy Gottlieb, Ext. 1847 • PGottlieb@HA.com **
Karen Sampieri, Ext. 1542 • KarenS@HA.com *

Luxury Real Estate
HA.com/LuxuryRealEstate

Amelia Barber, Ext. 1603 • AmeliaB@HA.com
Nate Schar, Ext. 1457 • NateS@HA.com

Movie Posters
HA.com/MoviePosters
Grey Smith, Ext. 1367 • GreySm@HA.com
Bruce Carteron, Ext. 1551 • BruceC@HA.com

Nature & Science
HA.com/NatureAndScience
Jim Walker, Ext. 1869 • JimW@HA.com
Mary Fong/Walker, Ext. 1870 • MaryW@HA.com
Craig Kissick, Ext. 1995 • CraigK@HA.com

Numismatics

Coins – United States
HA.com/Coins

David Mayfield, Ext. 1277 • David@HA.com
Win Callender, Ext. 1415 • WinC@HA.com
Chris Dykstra, Ext. 1380 • ChrisD@HA.com
Mark Feld, Ext. 1321 • MFeld@HA.com
Sam Foose, Ext. 1227 • Sam@HA.com
Jim Jelinski, Ext. 1257 • JimJ@HA.com
Bob Marino, Ext. 1374 • BobMarino@HA.com
Brian Mayfield, Ext. 1668 • BMayfield@HA.com
Harry Metrano, Ext. 1809 • HarryM@HA.com **
Sarah Miller, Ext. 1597 • SarahM@HA.com *
Al Pinkall, Ext. 1835 • AlP@HA.com
Will Robins, Ext. 1604 • WillR@HA.com
Mike Sadler, Ext. 1332 • MikeS@HA.com
LeeAnn Sparkman, Ext. 1326 • LeeAnnS@HA.com
Beau Streicher, Ext. 1645 • BeauS@HA.com

Rare Currency
HA.com/Currency

Allen Mincho, Ext. 1327 • Allen@HA.com
Len Glazer, Ext. 1390 • Len@HA.com
Dustin Johnston, Ext. 1302 • Dustin@HA.com
Michael Moczalla, Ext. 1481 • MichaelM@HA.com
Jason Friedman, Ext. 1582 • JasonF@HA.com
Carl Becker, Ext. 1748 • CarlB@HA.com

World & Ancient Coins
HA.com/WorldCoins

Cristiano Bierrenbach, Ext. 1661 • CrisB@HA.com
Warren Tucker, Ext. 1287 • WTucker@HA.com
David Michaels, Ext. 1606 • DMichaels@HA.com **
Matt Orsini, Ext. 1523 • MattO@HA.com
Michael Peplinski, Ext. 1959 • MPeplinski@HA.com
Sam Spiegel, Ext. 1524 • SamS@HA.com

Sports Collectibles
HA.com/Sports

Chris Ivy, Ext. 1319 • CIvy@HA.com
Mark Anderson, Ext. 1638 • MAnderson@HA.com
Calvin Arnold, Ext. 1341 • CalvinA@HA.com **
Peter Calderon, Ext. 1789 • PeterC@HA.com
Tony Giese, Ext. 1997 • TonyG@HA.com
Derek Grady, Ext. 1975 • DerekG@HA.com
Mike Gutierrez, Ext. 1183 • MikeG@HA.com
Lee Iskowitz, Ext. 1601 • LeeI@HA.com *
Mark Jordan, Ext. 1187 • MarkJ@HA.com
Chris Nerat, Ext. 1615 • ChrisN@HA.com
Rob Rosen, Ext. 1767 • RRosen@HA.com
Jonathan Scheier, Ext. 1314 • JonathanS@HA.com

Timepieces
HA.com/Timepieces
Jim Wolf, Ext. 1659 • JWolf@HA.com
Michael Fossner, Ext. 1208 • MichaelF@HA.com *

Wine
HA.com/Wine

Frank Martell, Ext. 1753 • FrankM@HA.com **
Amanda Crawford, Ext 1821 • AmandaC@HA.com **

Services

Appraisal Services
HA.com/Appraisals
Meredith Meuwly, Ext. 1631• MeredithM@HA.com

Careers
HA.com/Careers

Charity Auctions
Kristen Schultz, Ext. 1775 • KristenS@HA.com

Corporate & Institutional Collections/Ventures
Meredith Meuwly, Ext. 1631 • MeredithM@HA.com

Credit Department
Marti Korver, Ext. 1248 • Marti@HA.com

Media & Public Relations
Noah Fleisher, Ext. 1143 • NoahF@HA.com

Museum Services
Meredith Meuwly, Ext. 1631 • MeredithM@HA.com

Special Collections
Nicholas Dawes, Ext. 1605 • NickD@HA.com *

Trusts & Estates
HA.com/Estates

Mark Prendergast, Ext. 1632 • MPrendergast@HA.com
Karl Chiao, Ext. 1958 • KarlC@HA.com
Carolyn Mani, Ext. 1677 • CarolynM@HA.com **
Michelle Castro, Ext. 1824 • MichelleC@HA.com
Elyse Luray, Ext. 1369 • ElyseL@HA.com *

Locations

Dallas (World Headquarters)
214.528.3500 • 877-HERITAGE (437-4824)
3500 Maple Ave. • Dallas, TX 75219

Dallas (Fine & Decorative Arts – Design District Annex)
214.528.3500 • 877-HERITAGE (437-4824)
1518 Slocum St. • Dallas, TX 75207

New York
212.486.3500
445 Park Avenue • New York, NY 10022

Beverly Hills
310.492.8600
9478 W. Olympic Blvd.
Beverly Hills, CA 90212

San Francisco
877-HERITAGE (437-4824)
478 Jackson Street
San Francisco, CA 94111

DALLAS | NEW YORK | SAN FRANCISCO | BEVERLY HILLS | HOUSTON | PARIS | GENEVA

Corporate Officers

R. Steven Ivy, CEO & Co-Chairman
James L. Halperin, Co-Chairman
Gregory J. Rohan, President *
Paul Minshull, Chief Operating Officer
Todd Imhof, Executive Vice President
Kathleen Guzman, Managing Director-New York

* Primary office location: New York
** Primary office location: Beverly Hills
*** Primary office location: San Francisco

9-2014

Upcoming Auctions

U.S. Rare Coin Auctions	Location	Auction Dates	Consignment Deadline
U.S. Rare Coins (Houston Money Show)	Houston	December 4-8, 2014	Closed
U.S. Rare Coins (FUN)	Orlando	January 7-12, 2015	November 24, 2014
U.S. Rare Coins (Long Beach Expo)	Long Beach	January 28 - February 2, 2015	December 15, 2014

World & Ancient Coin Auctions	Location	Auction Dates	Consignment Deadline
World Coins (NYINC)	New York	January 4-5, 2015	Closed
World Coins (CICF)	Chicago	April 8-13, 2015	February 16, 2015

Rare Currency Auctions	Location	Auction Dates	Consignment Deadline
Rare World Paper Money (FUN)	Orlando	January 7-8, 12-13, 2015	November 17, 2014
Currency (FUN)	Orlando	January 7-10 & 13, 2015	November 17, 2014
Rare World Paper Money	Chicago	April 22-27, 2015	March 2, 2015
Currency	Chicago	April 22-27, 2015	March 2, 2015

Fine & Decorative Arts Auctions	Location	Auction Dates	Consignment Deadline
American Indian Art	Dallas	November 14, 2014	Closed
American Art	New York	November 17, 2014	Closed
Tiffany, Lalique & Art Glass	Dallas	November 21, 2014	Closed
European Art	Dallas	December 10, 2014	Closed
20th & 21st Century Design	Dallas	January 29, 2015	November 21, 2014
Decorative Art, Estates & Fine Art	Dallas	February 21-22, 2015	December 15, 2014
Photographs	Dallas	April 1, 2015	January 23, 2015
Fine Silver & Objects of Vertu	Dallas	April 29, 2015	February 25, 2015
American Art	Dallas	May 2, 2015	February 23, 2015
Illustration Art	Beverly Hills	May 6 & 7, 2015	February 27, 2015
American Indian Art	Dallas	May 15-16, 2015	February 23, 2015
Texas Art	Dallas	May 16, 2015	March 9, 2015
European Art	Dallas	May 18, 2015	March 11, 2015
Modern & Contemporary Art	Dallas	May 30, 2015	March 23, 2015

Jewelry, Timepieces & Luxury Accessories Auctions	Location	Auction Dates	Consignment Deadline
Timepieces	New York	November 20, 2014	Closed
Fine Jewelry + Luxury Accessories	Dallas	December 8-10, 2014	Closed
Luxury Accessories	New York	February 9, 2015	December 9, 2014
Fine Jewelry + Luxury Accessories	Dallas	April 20-22, 2015	February 17, 2015
Timepieces	New York	May 21, 2015	March 20, 2015

Vintage Poster Auctions	Location	Auction Dates	Consignment Deadline
Vintage Posters	Dallas	November 22-23, 2014	Closed
Vintage Posters	Dallas	March 28, 2015	February 3, 2015

Comics Auctions	Location	Auction Dates	Consignment Deadline
Comics & Original Comic Art	Beverly Hills	November 20-21, 2014	Closed
Animation Art	Dallas	January 14, 2015	December 1, 2014
Comics & Original Comic Art	Dallas	February 19-20, 2015	January 6, 2015

Entertainment & Music Memorabilia Auctions	Location	Auction Dates	Consignment Deadline
Entertainment & Music Memorabilia	Dallas	December 6, 2014	Closed
Vintage Guitars & Musical Instruments	Beverly Hills	February 28, 2015	January 7, 2015
Entertainment & Music Memorabilia	Dallas	April 4, 2015	February 11, 2015

Historical Grand Format Auctions	Location	Auction Dates	Consignment Deadline
Space Exploration	Dallas	November 12, 2014	Closed
Civil War + Arms & Armor	Dallas	December 12-14, 2014	Closed
Americana & Political (The Donald P. Dow Collection)	Dallas	January 24, 2015	December 3, 2014
Rare Books	Beverly Hills	February 3, 2015	December 12, 2014
Texana	Dallas	March 14, 2015	January 21, 2015
Historical Manuscripts + Rare Books	New York	April 8-9, 2015	February 16, 2015

Sports Collectibles Auctions	Location	Auction Dates	Consignment Deadline
Sports Platinum Night Auction	New York	February 21-22, 2015	December 31, 2014
Sports Catalog Auction	Dallas	May 14-16, 2015	March 23, 2015

Nature & Science Auctions	Location	Auction Dates	Consignment Deadline
Nature & Science	Dallas	June 7, 2015	April 13, 2015

Fine & Rare Wine	Location	Auction Dates	Consignment Deadline
Fine & Rare Wine	Beverly Hills	December 5-6, 2014	Closed

Luxury Real Estate	Location	Auction Dates	Consignment Deadline
Luxury Real Estate	TBD	Spring	March 1, 2015

Domain Names	Location	Auction Dates	Consignment Deadline
Domain Names	Dallas	Winter 2015	December 1, 2014

34329
11-3-14

HA.com/Consign • Consignment Hotline 877-HERITAGE (437-4824) • All dates and auctions subject to change after press time. Go to HA.com for updates.

HERITAGE INTERNET-ONLY AUCTIONS AT 10PM CT:

Comics – Sundays
Movie Posters - Sundays
Sports - Sundays
U.S. Coins - Sundays & Tuesdays
Currency – Tuesdays
Luxury Accessories - Tuesdays

Timepiece & Jewelry – Tuesdays
Modern Coins - Thursdays
Rare Books & Autographs – Thursdays
World Coins - Thursdays
Wine - 2nd Thursdays

Auctioneers: Andrea Voss: TX 16406; FL AU4034; IL 441001787; CA Bond LSM0602700; NYC 1320558; OH 2014000076; Samuel Foose: TX 11727; CA Bond LSM0602702; FL AU3244; IL 441001482; OH 2006000048; PA AU005443; TN 6093; NYC 0952360; NC 8373; MA 03015; Robert Korver: TX 13754; CA Bond LSM0602699; FL AU2916; IL 441001421; NC 8363; OH 2006000049; TN 6439; NYC 1096338; Denver 1021446; MA 03014; GA AUNR003023; Teia Baber: TX 16624; CA Bond LSM0606714; Ed Beardsley: NYC 1183220; IL 441001991; CA Bond LSM0626564; TX 16632; Steve Dance, participating auctioneer: Baltimore Auctioneer license AU000018; H. Stephens Dance, Milton J. Dance Co., Inc., Anne Arundel Auctioneer License A000275; Nicholas Dawes: NYC 1304724; Chris Dykstra: TX 16601; FL AU4069; IL 441001788; PA AU005733; CA Bond RSB2005738; TN 6463; Fiona Elias: TX 17126; IL 441001988; FL AU4469; CA Bond LSM0479796; NYC 2001163; GA AU004089; Alissa Ford: CA Bond RSB2005920; IL 441001561; NYC 2009623; Bob Merrill: TX 13408; FL AU4043; IL 441001683; CA Bond LSM0602705; NYC LSM0602226; Paul Minshull: CA Bond LSM0605473; IL 441002067; TX 16591; NYC 2001161; GA AU4086; FL AU4563; Brian Nalley: TX 17134; CA Bond LSM0602698; GA AU004082; IL 441002055; NYC 2001162; FL AU4604; Stephanie O'Barr: TX 17116; Scott Peterson: TX 13256; NYC 1306933; IL 441001659; CA Bond RSB2006812; Mark Prendergast: TX 17118; Mike Provenzale: TX 17157; IL 441002022; OH 2014000077; NYC 2004271; Michael J. Sadler: TX 16129; FL AU3795; IL 441001478; NYC 1304630; CA Bond RSB2006814; MA 03021; OH 2014000075; Shawn Schiller: TX 17111; IL 441001993; Wayne Shoemaker: TX 16600; Jacob Walker: TX 16413; FL AU4031; IL 441001677; CA Bond RSB2006811; PA AU005711; Nathan Schar: TX 17365; Amelia Barber: TX 17364; Hayley Brigham: CA Bond LSM0606157; Sarah Davies: TX 17505; Anthony Singleton: TX 17507